India Studies in Business and Economics

The Indian economy is considered to be one of the fastest growing economies of the world with India amongst the most important G-20 economies. Ever since the Indian economy made its presence felt on the global platform, the research community is now even more interested in studying and analyzing what India has to offer. This series aims to bring forth the latest studies and research about India from the areas of economics, business, and management science. The titles featured in this series will present rigorous empirical research, often accompanied by policy recommendations, evoke and evaluate various aspects of the economy and the business and management landscape in India, with a special focus on India's relationship with the world in terms of business and trade.

More information about this series at http://www.springer.com/series/11234

Utpal Kumar De · Manoranjan Pal
Premananda Bharati
Editors

Issues on Health and Healthcare in India

Focus on the North Eastern Region

Springer

Editors
Utpal Kumar De
Department of Economics
North-Eastern Hill University
Shillong, Meghalaya
India

Premananda Bharati
Biological Anthropology Unit
Indian Statistical Institute
Kolkata, West Bengal
India

Manoranjan Pal
Economic Research Unit
Indian Statistical Institute
Kolkata, West Bengal
India

ISSN 2198-0012 ISSN 2198-0020 (electronic)
India Studies in Business and Economics
ISBN 978-981-10-6103-5 ISBN 978-981-10-6104-2 (eBook)
https://doi.org/10.1007/978-981-10-6104-2

Library of Congress Control Number: 2017949498

Printed on acid-free paper

This Springer imprint is published by Springer Nature
The registered company is Springer Nature Singapore Pte Ltd.
The registered company address is: 152 Beach Road, #21-01/04 Gateway East, Singapore 189721, Singapore

Foreword

Here is a book that serves as a goldmine of data on health and health-related issues among very diverse and marginalized sections and societies. This book deals on "Issues on Health and Healthcare in India: Focus on the North-Eastern Region". Conceptually planning the issues related to health and healthcare in India, the editors of the present volume, Profs. Utpal Kumar De, Manoranjan Pal and Premananda Bharati, who are highly respected in their own professions, have done a commendable job by compiling and editing papers on diverse but important aspects of health. Inviting papers from distinguished scientists who have made a significant mark in research on these issues must have been a Herculean task for the editors. United Nations deadline for achieving the Millennium Development Goals (MDGs) is already over and has met with moderate success only. New initiative with reframed set of goals emphasizing on saving the environment and saving the planet popularly known as Sustainable Development Goals (SDGs) has just begun. On 25 September 2015, almost all countries adopted a set of 17 goals to end poverty, protect the planet, and ensure prosperity for all. Started on 1 January 2016, these goals are promised to be fulfilled by 2030. Readers will find this volume with linkages to the United Nations SDGs and full of important findings obtained through original empirical data on health. Most of the contributors focused their analysis in North-Eastern regions of India. I am also amazed to see some of the foreign contributions in the volume.

Keeping consistency among the topics of the papers, the present volume has been divided into three parts, each one with similar type of themes. Part I deals with the Determinants of Status of Health. The papers in this part deal with the problems of nutrition deficient anaemia, low birth weight, teenage pregnancy, child immunization, mothers' composite health index, psychological well-being, nutritional status, health seeking behaviour and chronic energy deficiency.

Methods and Modelling forms Part II of the book. The papers in this section of the book have dealt in detail on the prevalence of Malaria and HbE, health and educational deprivation, budget allocation and expenditure for health and family welfare in India, effects of socio-economic classes on infant mortality, India's fertility trend and rural–urban gaps and differentials, prevalence of child undernutrition, health expenditures in India, inequality in child mortality and out-of-pocket (OOP) payments for healthcare in Bangladesh

Part III refers to the existing health Facilities and Prevalence of Morbidity. Research in this section focuses on reviewing the policies related to essential medicines, meteorological conditions and occurrence of malaria in Meghalaya, health-related physical fitness among children of municipal and international schools, confrontation between an environment and an individual, management in the public health government hospital services organizations, factors affecting morbidity and utilization of healthcare services, chronic diseases among the elderly, drinking water availability and nutritional status of children of North-East India.

Hopefully it will find its readership among researchers and students of anthropology, sociology, economics, healthcare professionals, social workers, medical doctors and paramedical staff, health planners and administrators. Such a venture should come handy for the concerned governments whose task is to meet the health related SDGs set by the United Nations.

Editor-in-Chief, Human Biology Review (www. HumanBiolohyJournal.com)

Dr. S.P. Singh
Professor (Retired), Former Dean, Faculty of Life Sciences
and Head of Human Biology
Punjabi University, Patiala, India

Preface

UN Millennium Development Goals (MDGs) identified eight major goals for addressing development perspectives in the new millennium. These goals were targeted to be achieved by the end of 2015. Apart from reducing poverty, inequality, promoting gender equality and empowering women, ensuring environmental sustainability; reducing child mortality, improving maternal health and halting the spread of HIV/AIDS are also very important goals under health and healthcare which are important components of human development.

Despite progress in several dimensions, hunger, malnutrition and starvation deaths are common in many parts of the world, particularly in a number of countries in Asia and Sub-Saharan Africa. Health still remains a critical issue and without proper health human resource development remain incomplete, which is crucial for the overall progress of any country. Proportion of underweight children in India has come down from 43% in 1998–1999 to only 40% in 2005–2006. This proportion, for the children below 3 years, was expected to reach about 33% by 2015. In this respect, discrimination between men and women is also prevalent in India. Moreover, there is also substantial spatial variation in the achievement of nutritional intake. Some states have prevalence of underweight children above the national average. These states are namely Madhya Pradesh (57.9%), Bihar (54.9%), Jharkhand (54.6%), Chhattisgarh (47.8%), Meghalaya (42.9%), UP (41.6%) and even economically vibrant Gujarat (41.1%). Thus, despite several efforts undertaken, it remains a challenge to achieve the target. The trend shows that Maternal Mortality Rate (MMR) would have come down to 140 per lakh population, which was above 31 points of the targeted figure of 2015. Also, in terms of infant mortality rate, India may be behind the target by 27 points in 2015. Several cases of malaria, incidences of malnutrition and work-related hazards have been observed all over the country and that is also prevalent in North-Eastern region of India.

Nutritional intake, which is directly related to the economic status and socio-economic relationship matters for the human development and performance of the workers in various sectors and that in turn affect nutritional intake through income. In many societies, nutritional intake of women and girl children is comparatively poorer than that of men or boys. Also, it reflects an aspect of deprivation of women in the society.

From the above discussion, it is clear that we could not achieve the MDGs in all targets and there are also significant spatial variations in healthcare, nutritional intake, healthcare infrastructure, etc. Thus it is high time, we review our achievements and lapses incurred in comparison with the targets of the MDGs.

Shillong, India Utpal Kumar De
Kolkata, India Manoranjan Pal
Kolkata, India Premananda Bharati

Contents

Editors and Contributors

About the Editors

Utpal Kumar De is currently a Professor of Economics and Head of the Department of Economics at the North-Eastern Hill University, Shillong, India. Professor De has been engaged in teaching at the postgraduate level since 1994. His research interests include agricultural economics and rural development, issues concerning environmental and natural resources, climate change adaptation, and empowerment of women. Prof. De has visited Europe and Asia in connection with research and delivered keynote and invited lectures at a number of conferences. Besides presenting over 60 research papers at various international and national conferences, he has published seven volumes, completed a number of research projects and published over 75 research articles in reputed national and international journals. He is listed in the Who's Who in the World 2013 Pearl Anniversary Edition, inclusion in which is limited to those individuals who have demonstrated outstanding achievements in their own fields of endeavour and who have, thereby, contributed significantly to the betterment of contemporary society.

Manoranjan Pal is currently a Professor at the Economic Research Unit (ERU) of the Indian Statistical Institute (ISI), Kolkata. At the institute, besides teaching graduate and postgraduate courses, he is also engaged in carrying out projects of the Government of India and other organizations, while also guiding doctoral students. He was the Head of the ERU and Professor-In-Charge of the ISI's Social Sciences Division (SSD). He worked as Member Secretary, Board of Directors, International Statistical Education Centre (ISEC), Kolkata, for more than 10 years starting from February 1999. Prof. Pal has held the post of a Visiting Professor at many international institutions. He has published more than 100 papers in reputed national and international journals and books. His research interests include the measurement of poverty, inequality and segregation, applied econometrics, and health and nutrition. Professor Pal's name is included in the World 2013 Pearl Anniversary Edition in Marquis Who's Who, inclusion in which is limited to those individuals who have demonstrated outstanding achievements in their own fields of endeavour.

Premananda Bharati is currently a Visiting Professor at the Biological Anthropology Unit of the Indian Statistical Institute (ISI), Kolkata. He was Professor and Head of the same unit before his retirement in 2016, after having served at the institute for more than 30 years. His fields of interest include human biology, physical anthropology, growth, nutrition, poverty, gender issues and demography. He has taught at the Center of Statistics, Human Sciences Research Council (HSRC), Pretoria, South Africa. Prof. Bharati was named the International Man of the Year (1993/94) by the

International Biographical Centre, Cambridge, England; and Man of the Year 1994 by the American Biographical Institute, North Carolina, USA. He is a fellow of the Human Biology Association, Michigan, USA. In addition to teaching, he has published more than 100 research papers in journals of national and international repute and completed a number of research projects. He has visited America, Europe and Asia extensively in connection with short-term courses and has delivered invited lectures and presented papers at various international and national seminars and conferences.

Contributors

Imteyaz Ahmad Tata Institute of Social Sciences, Mumbai, India

Gurudas Bandyopadhyay Regional College of Management, Bengaluru, India; Department of HSS, IIT Kharagpur, Kharagpur, India

Rajshree Bedamatta Department of Humanities and Social Sciences, Indian Institute of Technology (IIT), Guwahati, Assam, India

Manjusha Bhakay Food Science and Nutrition, S.M.R.K.B.K.A.K. Mahila Mahavidyalaya, Nasik, India

Premananda Bharati Biological Anthropology Unit, Indian Statistical Institute, Kolkata, West Bengal, India

Susmita Bharati Sociological Research Unit, Indian Statistical Institute, Kolkata, India

Subhasis Bhattacharya Department of Economics, Sidho-Kanho-Birsha University, Purulia, India

Rimee Bhuyan Department of Economics, Gauhati University, Guwahati, Assam, India

Tapan Kumar Chakrabarty Department of Statistics, North-Eastern Hill University, Shillong, Meghalaya, India

Poulomi Chowdhury International Institute for Population Sciences, Mumbai, India

Ramesh Chandra Das Katwa College, Purba Bardhaman, West Bengal, India

Utpal Das Katwa College, Purba Bardhaman, West Bengal, India

Soumyendra Kishore Datta University of Burdwan, Burdwan, West Bengal, India

Partha De Population Studies Unit, Indian Statistical Institute, Kolkata, India

Utpal Kumar De Department of Economics, North-Eastern Hill University, Shillong, Meghalaya, India

Mallika Deb Department of Statistics, North-Eastern Hill University, Shillong, Meghalaya, India

Avijit Debnath Department of Economics, Assam University Silchar, Silchar, India

Nirmala Devi Department of Humanities and Social Sciences, Indian Institute of Technology (IIT), Guwahati, Assam, India

Pranti Dutta Department of Humanities and Social Sciences, IIT Guwahati, Guwahati, Assam, India

Mausam Kumar Garg International Institute for Population Sciences, Mumbai, India

Amrita Ghatak Gujarat Institute of Development Research, Gota, Ahmedabad, Gujarat, India

Maumita Ghosh Department of Economics, Southfield College, Darjeeling, West Bengal, India

Gayatri Goswami Department of Economics, Gauhati University, Guwahati, Assam, India

Md. Golam Hossain Department of Statistics, Health Research Group, University of Rajshahi, Rajshahi, Bangladesh

Md. Ripter Hossain Department of Statistics, Health Research Group, University of Rajshahi, Rajshahi, Bangladesh

Md. Nurul Islam Department of Statistics, Health Research Group, University of Rajshahi, Rajshahi, Bangladesh

Sanjeeva Kumar Jha Department of Statistics, North-Eastern Hill University, Shillong, India

Nizara Kalita Department of Economics, Gauhati University, Guwahati, Assam, India

Kamruzzaman Department of Statistics, University of Rajshahi, Rajshahi, Bangladesh

Parnasudha Karmodak Economics Department, Burdwan University, Burdwan, India

Laishram Ladusingh Department of Mathematical Demography and Statistics, International Institute for Population Sciences, Mumbai, India

N. Lalitha Gujarat Institute of Development Research, Gota, Ahmedabad, Gujarat, India

Rashidul Alam Mahumud Health Economics and Financing Research, Health Systems and Population Studies Division, International Centre for Diarrhoeal Disease Research, Bangladesh (icddr,b), Dhaka, Bangladesh

Shrabanti Maity Assam University, Silchar, Assam, India

Strong P. Marbaniang International Institute for Population Sciences (IIPS), Mumbai, India

B.K. Misra RDAP, North-Eastern Hill University, Tura Campus, India

Manoranjan Pal Economic Research Unit, Indian Statistical Institute, Kolkata, India

Anita Rath Tata Institute of Social Sciences, Mumbai, India

Kamal Ray Katwa College, Purba Bardhaman, West Bengal, India

Dipankar Roy Department of Economics, Assam University Silchar, Silchar, India

Papiya Roy Biological Anthropology Unit, Indian Statistical Institute, Kolkata, India

R. Sarada RDAP, North-Eastern Hill University, Tura Campus, India

Abdur Razzaque Sarker Health Economics and Financing Research, Health Systems and Population Studies Division, International Centre for Diarrhoeal Disease Research, Bangladesh (icddr,b), Dhaka, Bangladesh

Atanu Sengupta Economics Department, Burdwan University, Burdwan, India

Nurnabi Sheikh Department of Statistics, Health Research Group, University of Rajshahi, Rajshahi, Bangladesh

Krishna Singh Department of Economics, University of Gour Banga, Malda, West Bengal, India

Ningthoukhongjam Vikimchandra Singh Department of Statistics, North-Eastern Hill University, Shillong, India

Madhuparna Srivastava Economic Research Unit, Indian Statistical Institute, Kolkata, India

Marufa Sultana Health Economics and Financing Research, Health Systems and Population Studies Division, International Centre for Diarrhoeal Disease Research, Bangladesh (icddr,b), Dhaka, Bangladesh

Sabiha Vali Home Science (Retired), RSTM Nagpur University, Nagpur, India

T. Vasulu BAU, Indian Statistical Institute, Kolkata, India

Abdul Wadood Medical Centre, University of Rajshahi, Rajshahi, Bangladesh

Abbreviations

AAMR	Age-Adjusted Mortality Rate
AARR	Average Annual Rate of Reduction
ABER	Annual Blood Examination Rate
ACF	Autocorrelation Function
ANC	Antenatal Care
ANM	Auxiliary Nurse Midwifer
AOR	Adjusted Odds Ratios
AP	Andhra Prades
API	Annual Parasite Index
ARI	Acute Respiratory Infection
ASHA	Accredited Social Health Activist
BBS	Bangladesh Bureau of Statistics
BDHS	Bangladesh Demographic and Health Survey
BIC	Bayesian Information Criteria
BMI	Body Mass Index
BPHC	Block Primary Health Centre
CAGR	Compound Annual Growth Rate
CBR	Crude Birth Rate
CC	Concentration Curves
CD	Communicable Diseases
CDR	Crude Death Rate
CDSCO	Central Drugs Standard Control
CEA	Clinical Establishment Act
CED	Chronic Energy Deficiency
CHC	Community Health Centres
CI	Concentration Index
CI	Confidence Interval
CIHI	Child Ill Health Index

CMR	Child Mortality Rate
CPA	Change-Point Analysis
DGHS	Director General of Health Services
DHS	Demographic and Health Survey
DLHS	District-Level Household and Facility Survey
DMPR	District Malaria Prevalence Rate
DPCO	Drug Price Control Order
EA	Enumeration Areas
EAG	Empowered Action Group
ECOWAS	Economic Community of West African States
FAOC	First Axis Ordering Consistency
FERA	Foreign Exchange Regulation Act
FFM	Five Factor Model
FRU	First Referral Unit
GDP	Gross Domestic Product
GFATM	Global Fund Against Aids Tuberculosis and Malaria
GSK	GlaxoSmithKline
GzLMM	Generalized Linear Mixed Model
HAZ	Height-for-Age H/A
Hb	Haemoglobin
HDI	Human Development Index
HI	Health Index
HKI	Helen Keller International
HP	Himachal Pradesh
ICC	Intra-class Correlation Coefficient
ICD	International Classification of Diseases
IFA	Iron and Folic Acid
IIPS	International Institute for Population Sciences
IMR	Infant Mortality Rate
IPHN	Institute of Public Health Nutrition
IRDA	Insurance Regulatory and Development Authority
IRS	Indoor Residual Spray
IS	International School
J&K	Jammu and Kashmir
LBW	Low birth weight
LE	Life Expectancy
LISA	Local Indicators of Spatial Association
LMIC	Low–Middle Income Countries
MBP	Market Based Pricing
MCA	Multiple Correspondence Analysis
MCH	Maternal and Child Health
MCHI	Mother Composite Health Index

MCI	Maternal Care Index
MDG	Millennium Development Goal
MGRS	Multicentre Growth Reference Study
MH	Mental Health
MIR	Malaria Incidence Rate
MMR	Maternal Mortality Rate
MoHFW	Ministry of Health & Family Welfare
MP	Madhya Pradesh
MRA	Multiple Regression Analysis
MS	Municipal School
MTP	Medical Termination of Pregnancy
NCAER	National Council of Applied Economic Research
NCD	Non-Communicable Diseases
NCHS	National Centre for Health Statistics
NES	North-Eastern States
NFHS	National Family Health Survey
NHI	Negative Health Index
NLEM	National List of Essential Medicines
NMR	Neo-Natal Mortality
NRHM	National Rural Health Mission
NSS	National Service Scheme
NSSO	National Sample Survey Office
NTI	Negative Translation Invariance
NVBDCP	National Vector Borne Disease Control Programme
OBC	Other Backward Class
OC	Organizational Culture
OLS	Ordinary Least Square
OOP	Out-of-Pocket
OOPP	Out-of-Pocket Payment
PACF	Partial Autocorrelation Function
PCA	Principal Componcnt Analysis
PCNSDP	Per Capita Net State Domestic Product
PHC	Primary Health Centre
PPC	Positive Psychological Capital
PWB	Psychological Wellbeing
QWL	Quality of Work Life
SES	Socio-Economic Status
SNP	Single Nucleotide Polymorphisms
SRS	Sample Registration System
SSA	Sub-Saharan Africa
ST	Schedule Tribe
STG	Standard Treatment Guidelines

TFR	Total Fertility Rate
TMR	Truncated Mortality Rate
TN	Tamil Nadu
TP	Teenage Pregnancy
TT	Tetanus Toxoid
UMR	Under 5 Mortality Rate
UNDG	United Nations Development Group
UNESCAP	United Nations Economic and Social Commission for Asia and the Pacific
UP	Uttar Pradesh
UT	Union Territories
VBD	Vector-Borne Diseases
VIF	Variance Inflation Factor
WAZ	Weight-for-Age W/A
WB	West Bengal
WHO	World Health Organization
WHtR	Waist to Height Ratio
WHZ	Weight-for-Height W/H
WI	Wealth Index
WLR	Women Literacy Rate

Chapter 1
Introduction

Utpal Kumar De, Manoranjan Pal and Premananda Bharati

The book covers a wide range of issues related to health and healthcare at the international and national level, its regional complexities, socioeconomic factors behind observed healthcare pattern and morbidity. Sophisticated statistical techniques have been utilized for the analysis of health and healthcare dynamics, regional disparities, etc. A large number of studies also addressed the issues in northeast India.

Besides introducing some new questions on health and healthcare development, cross-country analyses, convergence of healthcare across Indian states and mortality, morbidity in northeast India have been included. Also, special techniques like two-level logistic regression, analysis of mental health, probabilistic and predictive analysis of nutritional deficit, generalized linear mixed model have been used to analyze mortality and morbidity and factors affecting out-of-pocket expenses on healthcare.

The book, therefore, covers a wide range of issues related to various socioeconomic factors like education, incidence of poverty, inequality, etc., in connection with health and healthcare services in India in general and northeast India in particular. We hope that the readers of the volume will be highly benefitted and be

U.K. De (✉)
Department of Economics, North-Eastern Hill University,
Shillong, Meghalaya, India
e-mail: utpalkde@gmail.com

M. Pal
Economic Research Unit, Indian Statistical Institute, Kolkata, West Bengal, India
e-mail: Manoranjan.pal@gmail.com

P. Bharati
Biological Anthropology Unit, Indian Statistical Institute,
Kolkata, West Bengal, India
e-mail: pbharati@gmail.com

U.K. De et al. (eds.), *Issues on Health and Healthcare in India*, India Studies in Business and Economics, https://doi.org/10.1007/978-981-10-6104-2_1

in health facilities that force the consumers to seek healthcare beyond their own states and (b) reducing the health induced economic vulnerabilities among consumers in the northeastern region of India.

Chapter 9 examines the magnitude of the difference of Chronic Energy Deficiency (CED) between poor and nonpoor women and its variation across the states of northeast India, and it further analyses the probable reasons for such variation. The study finds that there is a large disparity between the occurrence of poor and nonpoor conditions as well as undernutrition in different states of northeast India. Here attainment of higher education, service holding, safe drinking, and toilet facility are found to have a positive impact on undernutrition.

1.2 Part II: Methods and Modeling

Chapter 10 emphasizes on the prevalence of Malaria and HbE which are endemic in some regions of northeast India. Of the total burden of malaria and its mortality in northeastern states of India contribute 10% of malaria incidence, and 20% of deaths. Similarly, the frequency of HbE varies from less than 10% to more than 50% in different populations in the region. It is known that the genes like HbE and G6PD are involved in the protection against malarial infection that might explain the differential prevalence of malaria in the region. Based on the field studies in Meghalaya the study investigates into the health and administrative implications that are of vital importance for the control of malaria and HbE. It is emphasized that for health planning, knowledge about the genetic basis or causes are important as well.

SK Datta and Krishna Singh, in Chap. 11, uses a recursive simultaneous equation framework to explain the variation of health deprivation of children as well as educational deprivation across the major Indian states, on the basis of some identified explanatory variables. The empirical analysis of health deprivation index reveals that factors like poverty, female literacy rate, low body mass index of mother and full antenatal care have significant association with the level of deprivation. The dropout rate of children is considered as reflective of their education deprivation. Household characteristics of the deprived children indicate that female literacy, poverty, availability of electricity, the gender of household head and children health status significantly influence the extent of their educational deprivation. This calls for urgent implementation of different Government schemes for promoting better health and education of children of identified poor and deprived families.

Chapter 12 examines budget allocation and expenditure, the utilization and per capita investment, etc., for health and family welfare in India as a whole and for states separately. The authors also propose to analyze the comparative status of northeastern states (Arunachal Pradesh, Assam, Manipur, Meghalaya, Mizoram, Nagaland, and Tripura) vis a vis rest of the states in respect of the above variables.

Rimee Bhuyan, Nizara Kalita and Gayatri Goswami attempt to examine the performance of health indicators in Assam over the years. In order to investigate whether there is any structural change in pre-launch and post-launch of NRHM, Bai and Perron test has been used for the period 1995–2013. The study also examines the relative influence of state public expenditure on the performance index of health indicators of Assam with the help of linear regression model. The study reveals that performance of health indicators of Assam has been showing a positive trend over time and there are three break points in the performance index namely 2002, 2005, and 2009. It has found that there is a positive and significant impact of increasing public expenditure on the performance index of health indicators of Assam.

The burden of infant mortality on socioeconomic classes by measuring the effects of socioeconomic classes on infant mortality is assessed in Chap. 13. The socioeconomic classes as provided by the district level household and facility survey (DLHS-3) conducted by International Institute of Population Sciences (IIPS), Mumbai in collaboration with Ministry of Health and Family Welfare (MoHFW), Government of India, and district level infant mortality data for the seven northeast Indian states as reported by MoHFW, are used for the analysis. The data exhibit a high degree of intra-state correlation as well as a high degree of inter-district spatial correlation. A generalized linear mixed model approach capitalizing on the intra-state correlation is adopted for the analysis. Further, spatial analysis of data has been performed using Conditional Autoregressive (CAR) model.

Chapter 14 aims at probing India's fertility trend from the perspectives of rural–urban gaps and differentials and to answer the following questions. (i) Is the nation's fertility transition is typical of its rural part or has it proceeded at a different pace of decline? (ii) To what extent the transition characteristics, e.g., pace and timing are different in rural and urban parts of the nation? Do we identify distinct rural–urban trajectories? (iii) Do these differentials play a significant role in taking the nation from third to the fourth stage of demographic transition? The authors used the method of change point analysis to identify the significant change points associated with the TFR series of rural, urban and the entire country as a whole during 1971–2013. Finally, using a class of ARIMA models forecasts are obtained and the implications of the results are discussed.

Using a distribution of nutritional outcomes, Chap. 15 examines the prevalence of child undernutrition and its extent in India. Distribution of Z-scores is found to follow a general class of skew normal distribution, in which the reference population is a member and compares two and more members in this family. The degree of nutritional deficit is then quantified in terms of the population parameters. The findings of this study are indicative of the existence of comprehensive gaps in the perceived level of undernutrition prevalence for selected Indian states.

Health expenditures across the major states of India has been investigated in Chap. 16. Health expenditure in India has become an important policy variable so far as the concept of social sector development is concerned. The distributional aspect of such expenditure is one of the important sides of the overall development of a country or state using the data of Reserve Bank of India.

Impact of literacy and other factors like societies outlook on healthcare and deprivation is analyzed by constructing a suitable health index in Chap. 17. The authors provide a theoretical axiomatic structure for constructing the index. Then the index has been applied to the state level data for northeast India across two time points to understand the relative dynamics of the constructed index.

In the study on inequality in child mortality in the northeastern states of India, Partha De concentrates on how do these disparities differ from state to state within the northeastern states of India? As a measure of inequality and to compare the disparities among different states of northeast India, concentration curves and indices are constructed from infant and under-5 mortality data classified under different quintiles of wealth index from the National Family Health Survey (NFHS-3) data. The result shows that the states may be classified into different groups according to the level of inequality in infant and under-5 mortalities. The states of Tripura, Manipur, and Meghalaya have shown higher inequality levels compared to remaining selected states, where as the group of states are Sikkim and Arunachal Pradesh where inequality in child mortality among different socioeconomic groups are least.

Chapter 19 intends to examine the factors that are mostly influencing out-of-pocket (OOP) payments for healthcare in Bangladesh. A multiple regression model is used for the estimation of impacts of determinants on OOP payments. They mainly used economic, demographic, social, financial safety, and health-related variables in our analysis. The findings from the multivariate analysis show that the variables reflecting socioeconomic status of Bangladeshi households are important determinants of incidence of OOPP expenditure. The result shows that household characteristics like unsafe water, unhygienic toilet and household belonging to the urban community are significantly associated with OOP payments. The other significant factors are household income, age, sex, informal healthcare.

1.3 Part III: Facilities and Prevalence of Morbidity

Imteyaz Ahmad and Anita Rath in Chap. 20 review the policies related to essential medicines in Aurangabad district of Bihar and assess the availability and accessibility to essential medicines and healthcare in primary health centers. Scarcity and low-quality medicine and healthcare treatment are highlighted in the area.

The association between meteorological conditions and occurrence of malaria in Meghalaya is examined in Chap. 21. It also tries to understand the district-wise prevalence of Malaria cases in Meghalaya. The results from the data portray that average temperature has a significant positive association (coeff 0.2, $p < 0.01$), whereas the rainfall indicates a significantly negative association with the incidence rate of malarial cases in Meghalaya. However, there is a relatively small effects that rainfall contributes to the rise in malarial cases (coeff 0.0006, $p < 0.01$). This study shows that weather conditions like temperature play a major role which leads to the rise in the malaria cases in the state of Meghalaya, but the rainfall shows a very small negative effect in increasing the malaria cases. The study also shows that there is significant regional variation in the prevalence of malaria cases in Meghalaya.

Manjusha Bhakay and Sabiha Vali, in Chap. 22, compare the health related physical fitness among children aged 7–9 years attending municipal schools and international schools in Nasik city. Children from municipal schools reflects lower mean height, weight, and BMI. Whereas, the Municipal school children has larger mean muscular strength and endurance (21.52 sit ups). Many of the children from the international school have completed the one-mile run test but those from municipal school have completed the test in lesser time (10.66 min). Municipal school children are more flexible (13.37 in.). They also have a lower waist-to-height ratio (0.40) as compared to the international school children (0.46). Physical activity is considered a key factor for healthy physical and mental development of children. The municipal school children being more physically active have better physical fitness and hence are at a lesser risk of developing lifestyle related disorders.

Natália Talita Araújo Nascimento et al. in their study examine the causal relationship between the confrontation between an environment and an individual; which is defended by Contingency Theory of Management in the public health government (hospital) services organizations. The study is done through the qualitative analysis, by questionnaires from stake holders in the location of investigations and by support from the focus group. The results of individual behavior are described after an investigation in the context of the processes of the service delivery. The participation of social actors in the interaction with the public body in order to infer in the quality of service delivery is analyzed. Following the scientific recommendations, the citizen participation in the projects can improve this process. This research activity contributes as an academic tool for improvement of the service delivery quality offered by public institutions. The findings and suggestions developed from the analysis of data obtained from employees delivering services and the service users would be used to diagnose the necessities and opportunities aiming the elaboration of government policies for the process of community development.

In the next chapter (Chap. 24), Nirmala Devi and Rajshree Bedamatta examine the extent of morbidity, factors affecting morbidity, as well as the extent of utilization of healthcare services in one of the villages of Nagaon district of Assam. The study is based on a household survey conducted in 2014 in Bamunipathar village of Nagaon district. The morbidity prevalence rate is found higher among males as compared to females. However, cases of untreated morbidity are higher among females. Regression analysis shows that morbidity increases with increase in age of an individual. Low levels of literacy and nonavailability of toilet facilities pose as risk factors to morbid conditions. Households having access to safe drinking water shows a negative causal relationship with morbidity.

Chapter 25 sheds light on the pattern and trend of chronic diseases among the elderly over time. Trends in prevalence of diseases under these three broad classifications by sex, age groups, and residence are estimated and analyzed.

A decomposition method has been used, to check the significant difference in the gender gaps in the prevalence of morbidity. Non-communicable and other diseases and disabilities are found to have increased over time regardless of background characteristics of individuals, whereas it is the reverse case for communicable diseases and the prevalence of diseases are higher among elderly females than the males. The gender differentials in the prevalence of diseases are found to be statistically significant. The concluding message of the study is that morbidities among the elderly are expected to escalate in future.

Chapter 26 intends to focus on the association of drinking water with the nutritional status of children (0–5 years) of northeast India. Results show that undernutrition level is the highest in Tripura and Assam as compared to the other northeastern states. The authors have also checked the relation between nutritional status and other socio-demographic variables. Statistically significant association is found between drinking water and nutritional status. The study also discusses the possibilities of integrating human rights-based approaches, in relevant national MDG-based policies to combat the problem.

Part I
Determinants of Status of Health

Chapter 2
Two-Level Logistic Regression Analysis of Factors Influencing Anemia Among Nonpregnant Married Women of Reproductive Age in Bangladesh

Md. Golam Hossain, Kamruzzaman and Abdul Wadood

2.1 Introduction

Anemia is a global health problem for women (Benoist et al. 2008). Numerous morbidities including miscarriage (Szerafin and Jakó 2010), preterm delivery (Scholl et al. 1992), abruption placenta (Arnold et al. 2009), and low birth weight (Rasmussen 2001) are associated with anemia of women during their reproductive age. The high risk of maternal and prenatal mortality is also related to anemia (Lee et al. 2006; Mulayim et al. 2008). In addition, anemic individuals are more likely to get infectious diseases (Ndyomugyenyi et al. 2008), and they loss their ability to do properly physical labor (Scholz et al. 1997). Study on rate of anemia among nonpregnant married women is mainly significant for rising countries, where health and medically related improvement are being actively applied.

In Bangladesh, USDHEW (1966) has reported the prevalence of anemia among of women and children since early 1960s as part of national nutrition surveys using small population samples. Helen Keller International (HKI) conducted anemia surveys in Bangladesh first in 1997–1998 and again in 2001 with collaboration of the Institute of Public Health Nutrition (IPHN), but these were restricted to inhabitants in rural environment (HKI/IPHN 2002). Three among the eight goals of Millennium Development Goals (MDGs) are related to health, and the Bangladesh government is working towards achieving these goals (NIPORT 2013).

In developing countries like Bangladesh, married women are often responsible for maintaining the family, and many are also contributing toward the workforce and productivity of the nation. Their outstanding role in the nation, it is important to

Md.G. Hossain (✉) · Kamruzzaman
Department of Statistics, University of Rajshahi, Rajshahi 6205, Bangladesh
e-mail: hossain95@yahoo.com

A. Wadood
Medical Centre, University of Rajshahi, Rajshahi 6205, Bangladesh

U.K. De et al. (eds.), *Issues on Health and Healthcare in India*, India Studies in Business and Economics, https://doi.org/10.1007/978-981-10-6104-2_2

examine the association between the anemia among nonpregnant married women and important variables such as residence, education level, toilet facilities at home, religion, contraceptive, breastfeeding, economical condition, age group, body mass index (BMI), and parity, in order to make sure remedial measures can be undertaken.

The aim of this study is to examine the association between various socioeconomic, demographic, and nutritional factors and anemia of Bangladeshi nonpregnant married women in reproductive age.

2.2 Materials and Methods

A total number of 5293 sample used in the present study, they were nonpregnant married Bangladeshi women in age range between 15–49 years. This study is a cross-sectional study and the secondary data was taken from Bangladesh Demographic and Health Survey (BDHS)-2011. Socio-demographic, anthropometric, health and lifestyle information were collected from 17,842 ever-married Bangladeshi by BDHS-2011, and they surveyed from July 8, 2011 to December 27, 2011 from overall Bangladesh. The average age of subject was 30.78 $\pm$ 9.27 years at the measurement time. Bangladesh Bureau of Statistics (BBS) (Khan and Shaw 2011) created enumeration areas (EAs) for the 2011 Population and Housing Census as a sampling frame, and those EAs were used by BDHS-2011 for selecting house hold from Bangladesh. They utilized two-stage stratified cluster sampling for collecting data from Bangladeshi nonpregnant married women. All the information about the survey design, sampling technique, survey instruments, measuring system, ethical approval, subject consent, and quality control have been described in NIPORT (2013). Process of blood testing and the definition of anemia have been described elsewhere (NIPORT 2013). Pregnant women were excluded in this study. Informal statistical technique was used to detect the outliers from the data set (Dunn and Clark 1974). After removing results from women who were currently pregnant, outliers, and cases with incomplete information, finally 5293 samples were used in the present study. According hemoglobin level (HGL), the sample was classified into two groups (i) Anemic (HGL $<$ 12.0 g/dl) and (ii) Non-anemic (HGL $\geq$ 12.0 g/dl). Again, anemic women were subdivided into three subgroups according to hemoglobin level, (i) Mild (HGL lies between 10.0 and 11.9 g/dl), (ii) Moderate (HGL lies between 7.0 and 9.9 g/dl), and (iii) Severe (HGL $<$ 7.0 g/dl) (CDC 1998).

Since BDHS-2011 collected data from Bangladeshi women using two-stage clustered sampling and the sample came from several levels of the hierarchy, so there was a cluster effect of the data set. In the data set, the single-level statistical model is not appropriate (Khan and Shaw 2011). In this study, intra-class correlation coefficient,

$\text{ICC} = \frac{\text{Variation of constant}}{\text{Variation of constant} + \text{variation of residual}}$ was used to determine whether or not multilevel is even necessary for our data, the value of ICC ranges from 0–1. If ICC is greater than 0, only when multilevel regression model is needed for the analysis (Park and Lake 2005). Two-level multiple logistic regression model was utilized to remove the cluster effect for investigating the association between anemia and socioeconomic, demographic, and nutritional factors among married women. The category of anemia level was used as dependent variable. Multilevel logistic regression model is a powerful statistical tool to remove the cluster effect for finding association between dependent (category) and independent variables at different levels of the hierarchy data. Sometimes in multiple logistic model, there is multicollinearity problem that is the explanatory variables are dependent of each other. We need to remove the multicollinearity problem otherwise we cannot get accurate results. The magnitude of the standard error (SE) was used in the present study to detect the multicollinearity problem. If the magnitude of the SE lies between 0.001 and 0.5, there is no evidence of multicollinearity (Chan 2004). Chi-square test was utilized in this study for selecting independent factors for multilevel logistic regression model. The p-values less than 0.05 were used to accept the result. All Statistical analyses were approved using STATA (version 11) and SPSS software (version IBM 19).

2.3 Results and Discussion

Bangladeshi nonpregnant married women in reproductive age were investigated their anemia level and factors associated with anemia. It was noted that the prevalence of anemia among nonpregnant married women was 41.29%, among them in urban 37.18% and in rural 43.51%. The prevalence of mild, moderate, and severe anemia among anemic women were 35.5% (urban 31.9% and rural 37.5%), 5.6% (urban 5.2% and rural 5.9%), and 0.2% (urban 0.1% and rural 0.2%) respectively (Table 2.1).

In this study, we evaluated the cause of socioeconomic, demographic, and nutritional factors on anemia of Bangladeshi nonpregnant married women. The study allowed us to provide a more comprehensive analysis of the target population, because the sample population was derived from various geographical regions of the country. Previous studies reported prevalence and factors associated of anemia for women from rural population (Merrill et al. 2011), among university students in

Table 2.1 Prevalence of anemia among Bangladeshi nonpregnant married women

		Total frequency (%)	Urban	Rural
Anemia	No	3108 (58.71)	1167 (62.82)	1941 (56.51)
	Yes	2185 (41.29)	690 (37.18)	1495 (43.51)
Categories of anemia	Severe	8 (0.20)	2 (0.10)	6 (0.20)
	Moderate	298 (5.60)	96 (5.20)	202 (5.90)
	Mild	1880 (35.50)	592 (31.90)	1288 (37.50)

Source Data extracted from BDHS-2011

a particular region (Shill et al. 2014), infants (Rawat et al. 2014), students of a particular medical college (Bari et al. 2013), etc. BDHS-2011 collected data from different level using cluster sampling, in this study those cluster effects were minimized using by multilevel logistic regression analysis.

The present study showed high prevalence (41.29%) of anemia among nonpregnant Bangladeshi married nonpregnant women, and was this worse among those from the rural area (43.5% in rural area compared to 37.2% in urban area). A previous study reported that the prevalence of anemia among Bangladeshi rural women was 73%, and this result was higher than what we found (41.29%) even if we only considered women from the rural area (43.5%). In 2003, BBS reported that the prevalence of anemia among Bangladeshi urban women was 34% (BBS 2003), and this was relatively similar to our findings (37.2% among urban population). The prevalence (41.29%) of anemia among nonpregnant Bangladeshi women in reproductive age was higher than that of many countries like Iran, 14.5% (Sadeghian et al. 2013), Europe [Serbia, 27.7% (Rakic 2013), Belgium, 7.7% (Massot and Vanderpas 2003)], Japan, 15.7% (Takimoto et al. 2003), South America [Brazil, 32.7% (Coimbra et al. 2013), Mexico, 15.5% (Shamah-Levy et al. 2009)], Kazakhstan, 39% (Smagulova et al. 2013), Turkey, 32.8% (Pala and Dundar 2008), China, 15.1% (Liao 2004), also in Global, 29% (Stevens et al. 2013), and rather similar to countries in west and central Africa, 40% (Ayoya et al. 2012). However, the prevalence was less than that of India, 56% (Balarajan et al. 2013) and Tanzania, 49% (Massawe et al. 2002).

We used chi-square (χ^2) test to investigate the association between anemia status and some selected factors. χ^2-test demonstrated that the association between anemia and residence, education level, currently breastfeeding, currently amenorrheic, contraceptive, toilet facility, religion, economic condition (wealth index), BMI, age group and parity were statistically significant ($p < 0.01$). On the other hand, current working status, source of drinking water, and age at their first marriage did not show significant association between anemia ($p > 0.05$) (Table 2.2).

In multilevel regression model, the above significantly associated factors were considered as independent variables. The intra-class correlation coefficient (ICC) of this model was 0.069, multilevel model was appropriate for this study. Multilevel logistic regression model showed that women who were living in rural area (AOR = 0.0.86, 95% CI: 0.74–1.00; $p < 0.05$), living in poor family (AOR = 0.79, 95% CI: 0.66–0.93; $p < 0.01$), being uneducated (AOR = 0.69, 95% CI: 0.48–0.88; $p < 0.01$), non-Muslims (AOR = 1.52, 95% CI: 1.25–1.83; $p < 0.01$), currently not using contraceptive (AOR = 0.89, 95% CI: 0.78–0.99; $p < 0.05$), currently breastfeeding (AOR = 1.34, 95% CI: 1.13–1.59; $p < 0.01$), currently amenorrheic (AOR = 1.65, 95% CI: 1.23–2.21; $p < 0.01$), underweight (AOR = 0.73, 95% CI: 0.63–0.84; $p < 0.01$), and those from 30–49-year age group (AOR = 1.48, 95% CI: 1.26–1.73; $p < 0.01$) (Table 2.3).

There are two important factors poverty and lack of education which are related to having anemia among married women in Bangladesh. Household wealth index is another risk factor for anemia, and women living in poor families are more likely to be anemic than women living in rich family. Education is also risk factor that

Table 2.2 Association between anemia and socioeconomic, demographic, and nutritional factors

Variables	Group (*N*)	Anemic (%)	χ^2-value	*p*-value
Residence	Urban (1855)	37.18	20.14	0.001
	Rural (3438)	43.51		
Education level	No (1401)	45.91	32.95	0.001
	Primary (1621)	43.01		
	Secondary (1872)	38.11		
	Higher (399)	33.21		
Breastfeeding	No (3936)	39.71	16.30	0.002
	Yes (1359)	45.90		
Currently amenorrhea	No (5005)	40.42	28.13	0.008
	Yes (288)	56.23		
Contraceptive	No (2025)	44.18	10.63	0.007
	Yes (3266)	39.60		
Currently working	No (4550)	40.91	1.92	0.1681
	Yes (745)	43.65		
Drinking water source	Non-improved (458)	41.01	0.02	0.9091
	Improved (4835)	41.29		
Toilet facility	Unhygienic (2465)	43.30	7.88	0.006
	Hygienic (2828)	39.51		
Religion	Muslim (4667)	40.20	19.34	0.001
	Non-Muslim (626)	49.42		
Wealth index	Poor (1891)	47.50	57.37	0.006
	Middle (1017)	42.11		
	Rich (2385)	36.01		
Body mass index	Underweight (1301)	50.51	94.33	0.005
	Normal weight (3036)	40.80		
	Overweight (788)	31.01		
	Obese (168)	27.42		
Age group	15–29 years (2411)	38.60	13.59	0.001
	30–49 years (2882)	43.61		
Age at first marriage	Less than 18 years (4138)	41.93	2.54	0.1131
	18 years and above (1155)	39.30		
Number of ever born children	No (423)	37.71	27.56	0.001
	1–2 (2410)	38.40		
	3–6 (2220)	44.12		
	7 and more (240)	51.01		

Source Data extracted from BDHS-2011

influences anemia especially among married women. Particularly among women, education level is directly related with positive socioeconomic reimbursement, but more 27% women in Bangladesh is uneducated (NIPORT 2013). To increase the literacy rate among women, several steps towards including taking on the national

Table 2.3 Impact of socio-demographic factors and BMI on anemia of married women in reproductive age

Variable	Coefficients	*p*-value	Adjusted odds ratio (AOR)	95% CI of AOR	
				Lower	Upper
Residence, urban versus rural	−0.036	$p < 0.05$	0.86	0.74	1.01
Education level					
Primary versus no	−0.024	0.179	0.91	0.77	1.05
Secondary versus no	−0.058	$p < 0.01$	0.78	0.64	0.92
Higher versus no	−0.098	$p < 0.01$	0.69	0.48	0.88
Type of toilet at home, Unhygienic versus hygienic	−0.024	0.099	0.91	0.80	1.02
Religion, Non-Muslim versus muslim	0.935	$p < 0.01$	1.52	1.25	1.83
Currently contraceptive, Yes versus no	−0.294	$p < 0.05$	0.89	0.78	0.99
Currently breastfeeding, Yes versus no	0.066	$p < 0.01$	1.34	1.13	1.59
Currently amenorrhea, Yes versus no	0.113	$p < 0.01$	1.65	1.23	2.21
Wealth index,					
Middle versus poor	−0.034	0.086	0.88	0.73	1.03
Rich versus poor	−0.056	$p < 0.01$	0.79	0.66	0.93
Age group, (30–49) years versus (15–29) years	0.084	$p < 0.01$	1.48	1.26	1.73
Body mass index,					
Normal versus under weight	−0.077	$p < 0.01$	0.73	0.63	0.84
Over versus under weight	−0.159	$p < 0.01$	0.42	0.37	0.61
Obese versus under weight	−0.189	$p < 0.01$	0.41	0.27	0.58
Number of ever born children,					
1–2 versus no	−0.023	0.426	0.93	0.71	1.15
3–6 versus no	0.002	0.980	0.99	0.76	1.29
7 and more versus no	0.029	0.508	1.13	0.77	1.63
Constant	0.484	$p < 0.01$			

Source Data extracted from BDHS-2011

education policy has been enhanced by the Government of Bangladesh (NIPORT 2013), openly stipulated that education in primary and secondary school level would be free of cost. The government of Bangladesh also provides subsidies for the poor girl students to increase education level among especially Bangladeshi women. Elimination of poverty and increasing the level of education among women can able to reduce the prevalence of anemia in Bangladesh. The information about the prevalence of anemia among Bangladeshi married women that has been got from this study would be used by the health authorities of Bangladesh Government as indicators to assess the effectiveness of these programs, and they can also provide a reference for future assessment. Nutritional status (BMI) is important predictors of anemia. This study demonstrated women who were using oral contraceptive method had lower chance to get anemia than women who were using intra-uterine device, this result also supported to the finding of Massawe et al. (2002) and Heck et al. (2008) studies. Our study also showed that lactating women had more risk to be anemic than their counterpart, the same result was found by Pei et al. (2013). It was noted that amenorrheic women had also more risk to get anemia compared to non-amenorrheic women. Amenorrhea is a multifactorial condition that can be due to undiagnosed pregnancy, prolonged lactation and poor general health. We also noted that underweight women were more likely to have anemia than normal weight women, overweight and obese women. Dangour et al. (2001) reported that the positive association between level of serum hemoglobin and body mass index (BMI).

2.4 Conclusions

In this study, we found that prevalence of anemia among married women in Bangladesh was 41.29%. Uneducated women living in rural environment have significantly higher rates of anemia. Unhygienic toilet, non-Muslim, currently not using contraceptive method, currently breastfeeding, amenorrheic, older (30–49-years old) and underweight were also important factors of anemia. In addition to identifying modifiable risk factors of anemia among women, results from this study provide useful baseline information for reference on ongoing socioeconomic development by the Bangladesh Government.

Acknowledgements The authors would like to thank the Bangladesh Demographic and Health Survey (BDHS) for providing nationally representative data collected in 2011.

References

Arnold, D. L., Williams, M. A., Miller, R. S., Qiu, C., & Sorensen, T. K. (2009). Iron deficiency anemia, cigarette smoking and risk of abruptio placentae. *Journal of Obstetrics and Gynaecology Research, 35*(3), 446–452.

Ayoya, M. A., Bendech, M. A., Zagré, N. M., & Tchibindat, F. (2012). Maternal anaemia in West and Central Africa: Time for urgent action. *Public Health Nutrition, 15*(5), 916–927.

Balarajan, Y. S., Fawzi, W. W., & Subramanian, S. V. (2013). Changing patterns of social inequalities in anaemia among women in India: Cross-sectional study using nationally representative data. *BMJ Open, 19; 3*(3). doi:10.1136/bmjopen-2012-002233.

Bangladesh Bureau of Statistics (BBS). (2003). *Statistics division, ministry of planning* (p. 56). Population & Housing Census: Preliminary Results.

Bari, M. A., Sutradhar, S. R., Sarker, C. N., Ahmed, S., Miah, A. H., Alam, M. K., et al. (2013). Assessment of anaemia in patients with rheumatoid arthritis. *Mymensingh Medical Journal, 22*(2), 248–254.

Benoist, B. D., McLean, E., Egli, I., & Cogswell, M. (Eds.). (2008). *Worldwide prevalence of anemia 1993–2005: WHO global database on anemia* (p. 1). Geneva, Switzerland: World Health Organization.

CDC: Recommendations to prevent and control iron deficiency in the United States. (1998). Centers for disease control prevention. *MMWR Recommendations and Reports, 47*(RR-3), 1–29.

Chan, Y. H. (2004). Biostatistics 202: Logistic regression analysis. *Singapore Medical Journal, 45* (4), 149–153.

Coimbra, C. E., Jr., Santos, R. V., Welch, J. R., Cardoso, A. M., de Souza, M. C., Garnelo, L., et al. (2013). The first national survey of indigenous people's health and nutrition in Brazil: Rationale, methodology, and overview of results. *BMC Public Health, 13,* 52. doi:10.1186/1471-2458-13-52.

Dangour, A. D., Hill, H. L., & Ismail, S. J. (2001). Haemoglobin status of adult non-pregnant Kazakh women living in Kzyl-Orda region, Kazakhstan. *European Journal of Clinical Nutrition, 55*(12), 1068–1075.

Dunn, O. J., & Clark, V. A. (1974). *Applied statistics: Analysis of variance and regression* (p. 33). Toronto: Wiley.

Heck, J. E., Chen, Y., Grann, V. R., Slavkovich, V., Parvez, F., & Ahsan, H. (2008). Arsenic exposure and anemia in Bangladesh: A population-based study. *Journal of Occupational and Environmental Medicine, 50*(1), 80–87.

HKI/IPHN. (2002). Anemia is a severe public health problem in pre-school children and pregnant women in rural Bangladesh. *NSP Bulletin Number 10,* 1–4.

Khan, M. H. R., & Shaw, J. E. H. (2011). Multilevel logistic regression analysis applied to binary contraceptive prevalence data. *Journal of Data Science, 9,* 93–110.

Lee, H. S., Kim, M. S., Kim, M. H., Kim, Y. J., & Kim, W. Y. (2006). Iron status and its association with pregnancy outcome in Korean pregnant women. *European Journal of Clinical Nutrition, 60*(9), 1130–1135.

Liao, Q. K. (2004). Prevalence of iron deficiency in pregnant and premenopausal women in China: A nationwide epidemiological survey. *Zhonghua Xue Ye Xue Za Zhi, 25*(11), 653–657.

Massawe, S. N., Urassa, E. N., Nyström, L., & Lindmark, G. (2002). Anaemia in women of reproductive age in Dar-es-Salaam, Tanzania. *East African Medical Journal, 2002, 79*(9), 461–466.

Massot, C., & Vanderpas, J. (2003). A survey of iron deficiency anemia during pregnancy in Belgium: Analysis of routine hospital laboratory data in Mons. *Acta Clinica Belgica, 58*(3), 169–177.

Merrill, R. D., Shamim, A. A., Ali, H., Jahan, N., Labrique, A. B., Schulze, K., et al. (2011). Iron status of women is associated with the iron concentration of potable groundwater in rural Bangladesh. *Journal of Nutrition, 141*(5), 944–949.

Mulayim, B., Celik, N. Y., & Yanik, F. F. (2008). Helicobacter pylori infection detected by 14C-urea breath test is associated with iron deficiency anemia in pregnant women. *Journal of Obstetrics and Gynaecology Research, 34*(6), 980–985.

Ndyomugyenyi, R., Kabatereine, N., Olsen, A., & Magnussen, P. (2008). Malaria and hookworm infections in relation to hemoglobin and serum ferritin levels in pregnancy in Masindi district, western Uganda. *Transactions of the Royal Society of Tropical Medicine and Hygiene, 102*(2), 130–136.

NIPORT. (2013). Bangladesh Demographic and Health Survey, 2011. National Institute of Population Research and Training, Dhaka; Mitra & Associates and ORC Macro, Bangladesh and Calverton, MD, USA, 1–8.

Pala, K., & Dundar, N. (2008). Prevalence & risk factors of anaemia among women of reproductive age in Bursa, Turkey. *Indian Journal of Medical Research, 128*(3), 282–286.

Park, S., & Lake, E. T. (2005). Multilevel modeling of a clustered continuous outcome: Nurses' work hours and burnout. *Nursing Research, 54*(6), 406–413.

Pei, L., Ren, L., Wang, D., & Yan, H. (2013). Assessment of maternal anemia in rural Western China between 2001 and 2005: A two-level logistic regression approach. *BMC Public Health, 13,* 366. doi:10.1186/1471-2458-13-366.

Rakic, L., Djokic, D., Drakulovic, M., Pejic, A., Radojicic, Z., & Marinkovic, M. (2013). Risk factors associated with anemia among Serbian non-pregnant women 20–49 years old. *A cross-sectional study. Hippokratia, 17*(1), 47–54.

Rasmussen, K. (2001). Is there a causal relationship between iron deficiency or iron-deficiency anemia and weight at birth, length of gestation and perinatal mortality? *Journal of Nutrition, 131* (2S-2), 590–601S.

Rawat, R., Saha, K. K., Kennedy, A., Rohner, F., Ruel, M., & Menon, P. (2014). Anaemia in infancy in rural Bangladesh: Contribution of iron deficiency, infections and poor feeding practices. *British Journal of Nutrition, 111*(1), 172–181.

Sadeghian, M., Fatourechi, A., Lesanpezeshki, M., & Ahmadnezhad, E. (2013). Prevalence of anemia and correlated factors in the reproductive age women in rural areas of Tabas. *Journal of Family and Reproductive Health, 7*(3), 139–144.

Scholl, T. O., Hediger, M. L., Fischer, R. L., & Shearer, J. W. (1992). Anemia vs iron deficiency: Increased risk of preterm delivery in a prospective study. *The American Journal of Clinical Nutrition, 55*(5), 985–988.

Scholz, B. D., Gross, R., Schultink, W., & Sastroamidjojo, S. (1997). Anaemia is associated with reduced productivity of women workers even in less-physically-strenuous tasks. *British Journal of Nutrition, 77*(1), 47–57.

Shamah-Levy, T., Villalpando-Hernández, S., García-Guerra, A., Mundo-Rosas, V., Mejía-Rodríguez, F., & Domínguez-Islas, C. P. (2009). Anemia in Mexican women: Results of two national probabilistic surveys. *Salud Pública de México, 51*(4), S515–S522.

Shill, K. B., Karmakar, P., Kibria, M. G., Das, A., Rahman, M. A., Hossain, M. S., et al. (2014). Prevalence of iron-deficiency anaemia among university students in Noakhali region, Bangladesh. *Journal of Health, Population and Nutrition, 32*(1), 103–110.

Smagulova, I. E., Sharmanov, T Sh, & Balgimekov, Sh A. (2013). The prevalence of anemia among children and women of reproductive age in Kazakhstan and basis of its prevention. *Voprosy Pitaniia, 82*(5), 58–63.

Stevens, G. A., Finucane, M. M., De-Regil, L. M., Paciorek, C. J., Flaxman, S. R., Branca, F., et al. (2013). Global, regional, and national trends in haemoglobin concentration and prevalence of total and severe anaemia in children and pregnant and non-pregnant women for 1995–2011: A systematic analysis of population-representative data. *Lancet Global Health, 1*(1), 16–25.

Szerafin, L., & Jakó, J. (2010). Anemia in pregnancy: Characteristics in Szabolcs- Szatmár-Bereg County, Hungary. *Orvosi Hetilap, 151*(33), 1347–1352.

Takimoto, H., Yoshiike, N., Katagiri, A., Ishida, H., & Abe, S. (2003). Nutritional status of pregnant and lactating women in Japan: A comparison with non-pregnant/non-lactating controls in the National Nutrition Survey. *Journal of Obstetrics and Gynaecology Research, 9* (2), 96–103.

USDHEW. (1966). The Nutrition Survey of East Pakistan. US Department of Health, Education and Welfare and Department of Biochemistry, Dhaka University, Dhaka, 50–60.

Chapter 3
Prevalence and Associated Determinants of Low Birth Weight in Developing Countries: A Multi-country Analysis from Nationwide Population-Based Survey

Rashidul Alam Mahumud, Abdur Razzaque Sarker, Marufa Sultana, Md. Nurul Islam, Md. Ripter Hossain and Md. Golam Hossain

3.1 Introduction

Low birth weight (LBW) is a public health concern and one of the risk factors for child morbidity and mortality in many developing countries (Assefa et al. 2012). The World Health Organization (WHO) estimates that globally, the prevalence of LBW is 15.5 and 96.5% of these LBW babies are born in developing countries (Bramer 1988; Sachdew 2001). LBW of an infant has been defined as a birth weight of less than 2500 grams regardless of gestational age and considered to have a higher than average risk of early childhood death (Dey et al. 1983; CSA 2006). Previous studies showed that LBW infants are more likely to die than normal weight of infants (Suggested 1981; Park 2007). The birth weight of an infant is a significant factor that relate to higher probabilities of infection, susceptibility of childhood illness, chance of child survival, long-term physical, mental deficiencies, problems related to behavior, learning, and psychosocial improvement during childhood (Assefa et al. 2012; Metgud et al. 2012). In perinatal period, LBW infant is critical to surviving and about half of all deaths are directly or indirectly linked with this aspect (Chase 1960). Moreover, children who survive LBW have a higher incidence of disease. There is also evidence that LBW or its determinant factors are associated with early and late morbidity conditions such as heart disease (Eriksson et al.1999; Leon et al. 1998), diabetes (Leger et al. 1997), hypertension (Forrester et al. 1996), behavioral disorders (Schothorst et al. 1996), impaired cognitive

R.A. Mahumud (✉) · A.R. Sarker · M. Sultana
Health Economics and Financing Research, Health Systems and Population Studies Division, International Centre for Diarrhoeal Disease Research, Bangladesh (icddr,b), 68, Shaheed Tajuddin Ahmed Sarani, Dhaka 1212, Bangladesh
e-mail: rashidul.alam@icddrb.org

Md.N. Islam · Md.R. Hossain · Md.G. Hossain
Department of Statistics, Health Research Group, University of Rajshahi, Rajshahi 6205, Bangladesh

U.K. De et al. (eds.), *Issues on Health and Healthcare in India*, India Studies in Business and Economics, https://doi.org/10.1007/978-981-10-6104-2_3

function (Richards et al. 2001; Sorensen et al. 1997), psychological disorders (Olsen et al. 1998) and usually have long-term financial burden related to households (GBC 2006). Furthermore, with the demographic change of increased life expectancy at birth in developing countries, children born with LBW may create increased burden of diseases (Leon et al. 1998; Barker et al. 2001). Thus, LBW is considered as a universal threat for developing countries which create a barrier to child development (McCormick et al. 1985). Previous studies have recognized a number of determinants of LBW and preventing them can help in reducing early childhood morbidity and mortality resulting from LBW (McCormick et al. 1985; Kramer et al. 1987; Deshpande et al. 2011). Among the determinants, genetic, constitutional, obstetric, nutritional, maternal morbidities in antenatal period, toxic exposures, and antenatal care are broadly classified (Kramer et al. 1987). Other factors including smoking, maternal age, birth spacing, antenatal care, anemia, genital infections, maternal ill health, and stress have also been reported (Deshpande et al. 2011). In order to build knowledge on determinants of LBW in developing countries taking data from the latest Demographic and Health Surveys (DHS). The knowledge gained from the study can be applied in developing countries to develop future community-based intervention programs and help to reduce childhood morbidity and mortality.

3.2 Materials and Methods

3.2.1 Study Design

This is a population-based study that utilized a combined dataset of 2010–2013 from Demographic and Health Survey (DHS) in 10 selected developing countries; Armenia (2010), Cambodia (2010), Colombia (2010), Indonesia (2012), Jordan (2012), Nepal (2011), Pakistan (2012–2013), Tanzania (2010), Uganda (2011), and Zimbabwe (2010–2011). This study emphasizes the numerical type of birth weight data from latest DHS survey.

3.2.2 Data Collection and Sampling Technique

The DHS is a national-level household-based survey that utilized a stratified, two-stage cluster design: the first stage involved selecting samples from a master sampling frame constructed from enumeration; the second stage involved the systematic sampling of the households listed from each cluster, to ensure adequate numbers of completed individual interviews were obtained. The survey collected data through questionnaire-based face-to-face interviews, for which women of reproductive age (15–49 years) were interviewed based on the MEASURE DHS program model. The detailed information on the sampling techniques and data collection method has been published elsewhere (DHS 2012).

3.2.3 *Variables*

Reasonable socio-demographic variables were selected based on a review of the relevant DHS literature (Hazarika 2011; West et al. 2008; Titaley et al. 2008). Individual-level factors (maternal age, age of mother at childbirth, education, occupation, frequency of ANC visits, intake of iron during pregnancy, predelivery BMI, anemia level) and household-level factors (wealth status) were extracted from the DHS database (Titaley et al. 2008). Like earlier study, wealth status was regrouped into poor (lower 40%), middle (middle 40%), and rich (upper 20%) (Agho et al. 2011; Khanal et al. 2013). Maternal education level was recategorized as no education, primary, and secondary or higher. Residential location (rural vs urban) was used for the geographical variations within the country. On contrary, birth weight data was classified into two groups '0' means Non-LBW ($\geq$2.5 kg) and '1' means LBW (<2.5 kg) in entire analysis. Women with a history of previous chronic conditions or those with twin or multiple pregnancies and missing responses were excluded from the analysis.

3.2.4 *Statistical Analysis*

In the descriptive analyses, the characteristic of the study population for selected countries were expressed in terms of the percentages (%) with 95% confidence Interval (CI). For independent variables, the category found to be at lower risk in the odds of the having a LBW baby in analysis was selected as the reference group and score as '0' for constructing odds ratio. A multivariate logistic regression model was applied to estimate the adjusted odds ratios (AORs) as a measure of the associations between LBW and related possible risk factors after considering potential confounders. We used the sampling weight of the DHS like previous study (Rutstein 2012) and all statistical analyses were done by using STATA version-13.

3.3 Results

3.3.1 *Population Characteristics*

A total of 61,162 live births weights were measured from the study countries. The overall prevalence of LBW was 15.9% (95% CI: 15.6–16.2%) and average birth

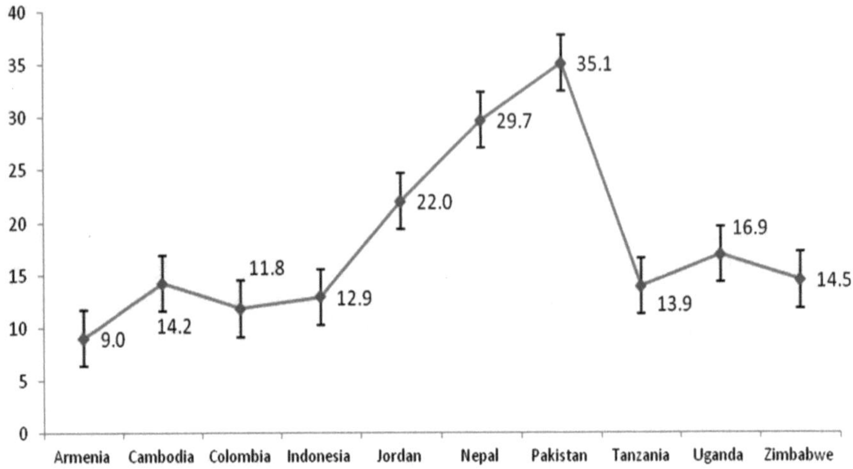

Fig. 3.1 Prevalence of low birth weight in developing countries

weight was 2179 grams (Fig. 3.1). Prevalence of LBW was highest in Pakistan (35.1%, 95% CI: 32.9–37.3%) followed by Nepal (29.7%; 95% CI: 27.7–31.7%), compared to other countries and the average LBW were 1988 and 2255 grams respectively (Table 3.1). The numeric type of birth weight data was found to be normally distributed in all countries (Fig. 3.2).

The majority of the mothers (74%) were aged between 20 and 34 years and more than half of mother's did not have any formal education, in which a higher proportion was found in Pakistan (57.2%) and Nepal (46.5%) respectively (Table 3.2). Overall 52%, were nonworking mothers and the highest amount was observed in Jordan (85.7%) followed by Pakistan (74.2%). Most of the mothers (93.8%) had taken iron pills during pregnancy period. More than 62% of mothers had reported acceptable level of maternal anemia. A greater percentage of mothers (70%) attended at least four ANC visits in all countries and lived in rural communities except Armenia, Colombia, and Jordan. Considering the wealth status, about half of the mothers (50%) were from the lower 40% (Table 3.2).

3.3.2 Association Between LBW and Determinants Using Bivariate Analysis

The bivariate analysis showed a significant association between the LBW and the maternal age, education, first birth interval, iron pills, wealth status, antenatal visits, working status, and maternity BMI due to pregnancy in all of the countries (Table 3.3).

Table 3.1 Distribution of birth weight in selected 10 developing countries

Countries and years	Overall birth weight				Low birth weight			
	No. of birth (*N*)		Average weight (grams)		No. of birth		Average weight (g)	
	Unweighted	Weighted	Unweighted	Weighted	Unweighted	Weighted	Unweighted	Weighted
Armenia (2010)	1447	1426.1	3139.1	3131.1	130.0	126.5	2159.0	2199.5
Cambodia (2010)	5781	5929.1	3155.1	3135.9	821.0	886.1	2263.0	2250.8
Colombia (2010)	12,634	12,029.4	3213.2	3170.4	1492.0	1591.6	2176.6	2162.0
Indonesia (2012)	15,124	15,134.7	3164.9	3148.9	1958.0	1953.5	2234.6	2221.0
Jordan (2012)	10,248	9733.9	3079.6	3090.4	2257.0	2033.6	2124.2	2131.2
Nepal (2011)	1959	1955.3	3012.5	3058.0	582.0	548.8	2257.7	2254.9
Pakistan (2012–2013)	1802	1458.5	2978.1	2981.0	632.0	543.6	1965.4	1987.8
Tanzania (2010)	4145	4324.7	3210.5	3219.2	575.0	579.5	2239.4	2251.2
Uganda (2011)	4142	4078.2	3378.0	3413.5	699.0	677.2	2175.4	2166.7
Zimbabwe (2010–2011)	3880	3861.9	3135.4	3126.5	564.0	579.8	2207.3	2191.5
Total	61,162	59,931.8	3165.4	3156.6	9710.0	9520.0	2179.7	2179.3

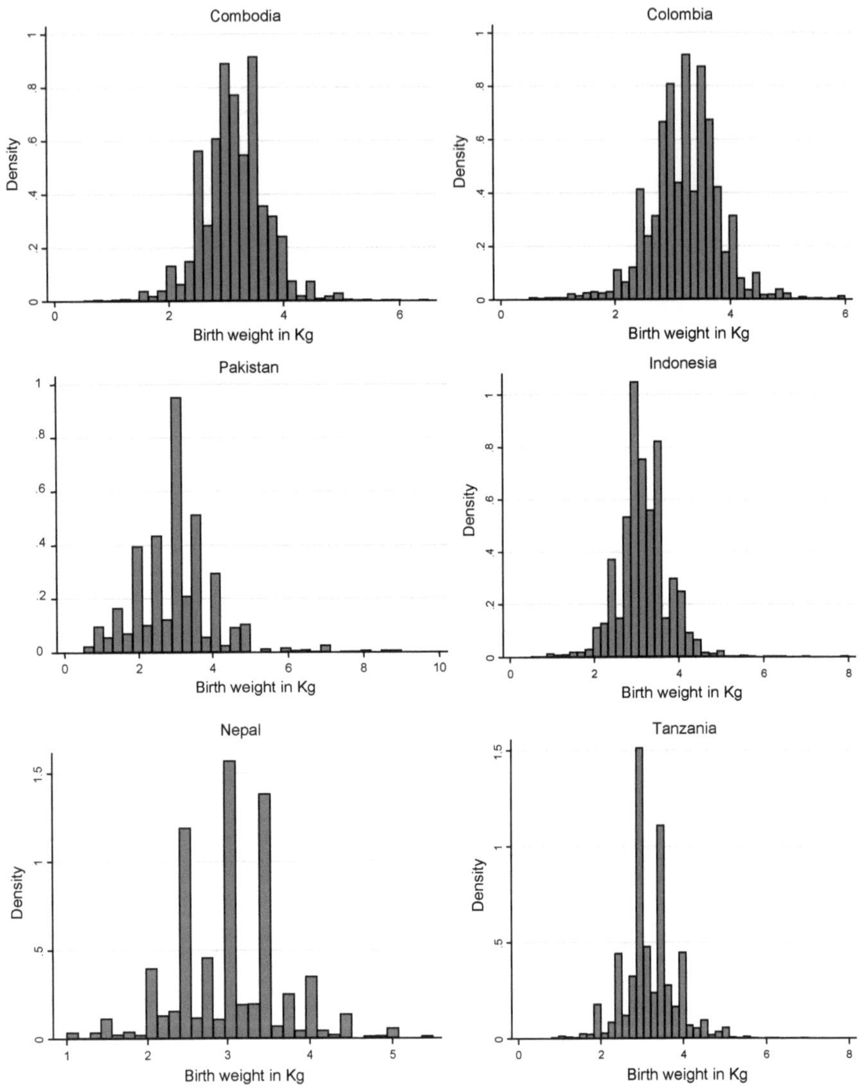

Fig. 3.2 Countries distribution of birth weight in developing countries

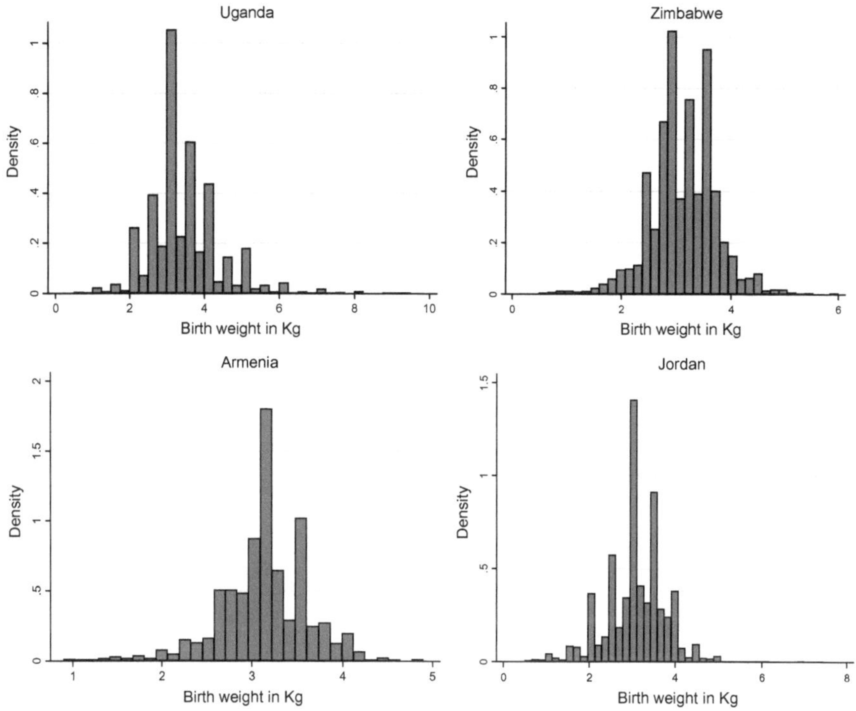

Fig. 3.2 (continued)

3.3.3 Factors Influencing LBW Babies in Developing Countries

Mothers aged 35–49 years were significantly more likely to deliver LBW babies compared to teenage (≤ 19 years) mothers ($P < 0.05$) in most of the selected countries (Table 3.3). Illiterate (no formal education) mothers had delivered more LBW babies compared with higher educated mothers in Armenia (OR = 1.43, 95% CI: 1.03–2.23, $p < 0.05$), Indonesia (OR = 2.53, 95% CI: 1.44–4.42, $p < 0.01$), Jordan (OR = 1.26, 95% CI: 0.59–2.70; $p < 0.01$), Nepal (OR = 1.19, 95% CI: 1.07–1.52; $p < 0.01$), Pakistan (OR = 2.61, 95% CI: 1.03–6.59; $p < 0.01$), and Uganda (OR = 2.06, 95% CI: 1.55–7.63; $p < 0.05$).

It was observed that LBW was associated with working mothers in Pakistan (OR = 0.31, 95% CI: 0.13–0.74, $p < 0.01$) and Nepal (OR = 1.66, 95% CI: 0.98–2.81; $p < 0.05$). Later conception (over 48 months) had strongly significant role in LBW in Armenia (OR = 2.76, 95% CI: 1.61–4.11; $p < 0.01$), Cambodia (OR = 1.91, 95% CI: 0.99–3.70, $p < 0.05$), Colombia (OR = 1.41, 95% CI: 1.07–1.86, $p < 0.05$), Jordan (OR = 2.16, 95% CI: 1.41–3.33; $p < 0.01$), Tanzania (OR = 2.42, 95% CI: 1.09–5.37; $p < 0.05$), and Uganda (OR = 2.24, 95%

Table 3.2 Background characteristics of population

Variables	Countries										
	Armenia	Cambodia	Colombia	Indonesia	Jordan	Nepal	Pakistan	Tanzania	Uganda	Zimbabwe	All countries
	% (95% CI)	% (95% CI)	% (95% CI)	% (95% CI)	% (95% CI)	% (95% CI)	% (95% CI)	% (95% CI)	% (95% CI)	% (95% CI)	% (95% CI)
Maternal age (years)											
≤19	2.2 (1.5–3.3)	2.6 (2.3–3.1)	10.5 (9.9–11.1)	3.0 (2.6–3.3)	1.8 (1.4–2.3)	7.1 (6.2–8.0)	2.2 (1.9–2.6)	5.3 (4.7–5.9)	5.8 (5.2–6.4)	7.2 (6.4–8.0)	5.1 (5.0–5.2)
20–34	89.0 (86.8–91.0)	76.5 (75.3–77.6)	72.4 (71.5–73.2)	71.4 (70.5–72.4)	69.5 (68.0–71.0)	81.3 (80.0–82.5)	78.0 (77.0–79.0)	70.2 (69.0–71.4)	72.4 (71.2–73.5)	76.9 (75.6–78.1)	73.5 (73.2–73.7)
35–49	8.8 (7.0–10.9)	20.9 (19.7–22.1)	17.2 (16.5–18.0)	25.6 (24.7–26.6)	28.7 (27.2–30.2)	11.7 (10.7–12.7)	19.8 (18.8–20.7)	24.6 (23.5–25.7)	21.8 (20.8–22.9)	16.0 (14.9–17.1)	21.4 (21.2–21.7)
Maternal education											
No education	16.6 (16.2–16.9)	17.0 (16.7–17.2)	3.0 (2.7–3.2)	3.2 (3.0–3.5)	3.0 (2.7–3.3)	46.5 (45.1–47.8)	57.2 (56.3–58.1)	25.4 (24.4–26.3)	18.1 (17.3–19.00	1.8 (1.4–2.1)	50.9 (50.6–51.2)
Primary	32.2 (32.8–33.6)	32.1 (31.8–32.4)	30.4 (29.7–31.1)	30.7 (30.1–31.4)	7.0 (6.5–7.5)	20.0 (18.9–21.1)	14.4 (13.7–15.0)	63.1 (62.1–64.2)	59.4 (58.3–60.5)	32.8 (31.6–32.1)	17.0 (16.7–17.2)
Secondary or higher	50.2 (49.8–50.7)	50.9 (50.6–51.2)	66.7 (66.0–67.4)	66.0 (65.4–66.7)	90.0 (89.4–90.5)	33.5 (32.3–34.8)	28.5 (27.7–29.3)	11.5 (10.8–12.2)	22.4 (21.5–23.4)	65.4 (64.1–66.7)	32.1 (31.8–32.4)
Maternal occupation											
Not working	84.9 (82.6–87.0)	33.5 (32.2–34.8)	54.4 (53.5–55.4)	52.3 (51.2–53.3)	85.7 (84.6–86.8)	45.1 (43.4–46.7)	74.2 (73.1–75.4)	13.2 (12.3–14.1)	25.0 (23.9–26.1)	65.2 (63.8–66.6)	52.9 (52.6–53.2)
Working	15.1 (13.0–17.4)	66.5 (65.2–67.8)	45.6 (44.6–46.5)	47.8 (46.7–48.8)	14.3 (13.2–15.4)	54.9 (53.3–56.6)	25.8 (24.6–27.0)	86.8 (85.9–87.7)	75.0 (73.9–76.1)	34.8 (33.5–36.2)	47.1 (46.8–47.4)
Marriage to first birth interval (months)											
First birth	54.6 (51.3–57.8)	35.6 (34.3–36.9)	44.6 (43.5–45.8)	46.9 (45.8–47.9)	49.5 (47.8–51.1)	24.4 (23.0–25.9)	32.6 (31.4–33.8)	43.5 (42.1–45.0)	48.6 (47.1–50.0)	58.3 (56.7–59.9)	43.2 (42.9–43.5)
<24	32.0 (29.2–35.0)	35.7 (34.3–37.0)	24.9 (24.0–25.9)	31.4(30.4–32.4)	31.7 (30.2–33.3)	32.3 (30.8–33.9)	28.7 (27.6–29.9)	36.2 (34.8–37.7)	29.6 (28.3–30.9)	26.7 (25.3–28.1)	31.0 (30.7–31.3)
24–47	11.2 (9.2–13.5)	22.2 (21.1–23.4)	20.6 (19.7–21.6)	15.9 (15.1–16.75)	14.2 (13.1–15.4)	28.9 (27.5–30.5)	25.3 (24.2–26.4)	16.2 (15.1–17.3)	16.2 (15.1–17.3)	11.0 (10.0–12.0)	18.4 (18.1–18.6)
48+	2.3 (1.5–3.3)	6.5 (5.9–7.2)	9.8 (9.1–10.5)	5.8 (5.3–6.4)	4.6 (4.0–5.4)	14.3 (13.2–15.5)	13.4 (12.6–14.3)	4.0 (3.5–4.6)	5.7 (5.1–6.4)	4.1 (3.5–4.7)	7.4 (7.2–7.6)

(continued)

Table 3.2 (continued)

Variables	Countries										
	Armenia	Cambodia	Colombia	Indonesia	Jordan	Nepal	Pakistan	Tanzania	Uganda	Zimbabwe	All countries
	% (95% CI)	% (95% CI)	% (95% CI)	% (95% CI)	% (95% CI)	% (95% CI)	% (95% CI)	% (95% CI)	% (95% CI)	% (95% CI)	% (95% CI)
Age at first cohabitation											
≤ 12	0.40 (0.16–0.97)	0.53 (0.38–0.75)	1.5 (1.3–1.8)	1.1 (0.9–1.4)	0.02 (0.01–0.05)	1.7 (1.4–2.2)	1.1 (0.8–1.3)	1.1 (0.9–1.4)	4.2 (3.7–4.8)	1.2 (0.9–1.7)	1.5 (1.4–1.6)
13–17	13.8 (11.8–16.1)	28.3 (27.1–29.5)	36.5 (35.5–37.5)	23.2 (22.3–24.1)	18.1 (16.9–19.4)	57.2 (55.6–58.8)	39.6 (38.4–40.8)	46.2 (44.9–47.6)	51.2 (49.8–52.5)	38.1 (36.6–39.5)	35.3 (35.0–35.6)
18+	85.8 (83.5–87.8)	71.2 (69.9–72.4)	62.0 (61.0–62.9)	75.7 (74.8–76.6)	81.9 (80.6–83.1)	41.1 (39.5–42.7)	59.4 (58.2–60.6)	52.7 (51.3–54.0)	44.6 (43.3–45.9)	60.7 (59.2–62.1)	63.2 (62.9–63.5)
Taken Iron pills during pregnancy											
No	93.8 (91.6–95.5)	98.4 (98.0–98.7)	NA	86.8 (86.0–87.6)	96.1 (95.3–96.7)	97.7 (97.2–98.1)	92.9 (92.2–93.5)	98.7 (98.3–99.0)	93.2 (92.5–93.8)	NA	93.8 (93.6–94.0)
Yes	6.2 (4.6–8.4)	1.6 (1.32–2.02)		13.2 (12.4–13.9)	3.9 (3.3–4.7)	2.3 (1.9–2.8)	7.2 (6.5–7.8)	1.3 (1.0–1.7)	6.8 (6.2–7.5)		6.2 (6.0–6.4)
Variables	Countries										
	Armenia	Cambodia	Colombia	Indonesia	Jordan	Nepal	Pakistan	Tanzania	Uganda	Zimbabwe	All countries
	% (95% CI)	% (95% CI)	% (95% CI)	% (95% CI)	% (95% CI)	% (95% CI)	% (95% CI)	% (95% CI)	% (95% CI)	% (95% CI)	% (95% CI)
Maternal anemia											
No	NA	44.9 (43.0–46.8)	NA	NA	38.7 (36.7–40.7)	37.9 (35.6–40.3)	NA	40.6 (39.3–42.0)	25.1 (23.2–27.2)	27.7 (26.4–29.1)	37.7 (37.2–38.3)
Yes		55.1 (53.2–57.0)			61.3 (59.3–63.3)	62.1 (59.7–64.4)		59.4 (58.1–60.7)	74.9 (72.8–76.8)	72.3 (70.9–73.6)	62.3 (61.7–62.8)
Number of ANC visits											
No ANC	0.95 (0.46–1.95)	10.4 (9.5–11.3)	3.1 (2.7–3.4)	3.1 (2.8–3.5)	0.9 (0.6–1.4)	15.2 (13.9–16.5)	24.4 (23.1–25.8)	1.8 (1.4–2.4)	4.3 (3.7–5.1)	10.1 (9.1–11.2)	8.0 (7.8–8.2)
1	0.24 (0.07–0.88)	4.8 (4.2–5.5)	0.9 (0.8–1.1)	1.6 (1.3–1.8)	0.6 (0.4–1.0)	6.1 (5.3–7.1)	13.3(12.3–14.5)	3.6 (3.0–4.2)	4.1 (3.5–4.8)	2.6 (2.1–3.2)	3.5 (3.3–3.6)
2	1.03 (0.51–2.08)	8.2 (7.4–9.0)	2.1 (1.8–2.4)	2.1 (1.9–2.4)	1.3 (0.9–1.9)	12.3 (11.0–13.6)	13.3 (12.3–14.4)	14.6 (13.5–15.8)	11.9(10.8–13.0)	6.1 (5.3–6.9)	6.3 (6.1–6.5)

(continued)

Table 3.2 (continued)

Variables	Countries										
	Armenia	Cambodia	Colombia	Indonesia	Jordan	Nepal	Pakistan	Tanzania	Uganda	Zimbabwe	All countries
	% (95% CI)	% (95% CI)	% (95% CI)	% (95% CI)	% (95% CI)	% (95% CI)	% (95% CI)	% (95% CI)	% (95% CI)	% (95% CI)	% (95% CI)
3	3.00 (2.04–4.41)	17.0 (15.9–18.2)	4.2 (3.8–4.6)	4.8 (4.4–5.2)	2.7 (2.1–3.4)	16.4 (15.0–17.8)	12.3 (11.3–13.4)	36.9 (35.4–38.5)	31.3 (29.8–32.9)	15.5 (14.4–16.7)	12.5 (12.2–12.7)
4+	94.8 (93.0–96.1)	59.6 (58.2–61.1)	89.8 (89.1–90.4)	88.4 (87.8–89.1)	94.5 (93.5–95.4)	50.1 (48.2–52.0)	36.6 (35.1–38.1)	43.0 (41.4–44.7)	48.5 (46.8–50.1)	65.7 (64.1–67.3)	69.8 (69.5–70.1)
Maternity BMI											
Thin BMI	NA	17.5 (16.1–19.0)	NA	NA	2.1 (1.5–2.8)	19.5 (17.6–21.5)	14.6 (13.1–16.3)	9.0 (8.3–9.8)	9.7 (8.5–11.0)	4.9 (5.3–6.6)	7.6 (7.4–7.8)
Normal		73.2 (71.5–74.9)			32.8 (30.8–34.7)	71.0 (68.7–73.1)	54.2 (52.1–56.3)	73.2 (72.0–74.4)	73.9 (71.9–75.8)	64.7 (63.3–66.1)	57.2 (56.8–57.6)
Over weight		9.3 (8.3–10.5)			65.2 (63.2–67.1)	9.5 (8.2–11.0)	31.2 (29.3–33.1)	17.8 (16.8–18.9)	16.5 (14.9–18.2)	29.4 (28.1–30.8)	35.2 (34.8–35.6)
Wealth status											
Poor (lower 40%)	40.8 (37.7–43.9)	48.1 (46.8–49.5)	48.2 (47.3–49.2)	41.2 (40.2–42.2)	45.5 (43.9–47.1)	47.7 (46.1–49.3)	45.1 (43.8–46.3)	44.7 (43.4–46.1)	43.8 (42.5–45.1)	43.9 (42.5–45.3)	50.5 (50.1–50.8)
Middle (middle 40%)	40.5 (37.3–43.7)	35.5 (34.2–36.8)	39.8 (38.8–40.8)	39.8 (38.8–40.9)	40.8 (39.2–42.4)	38.4 (36.8–40.1)	39.2 (38.0–40.4)	41.1 (39.8–42.4)	37.7 (36.4–38.9)	40.4 (39.0–41.9)	35.5 (35.2–35.8)
Rich (upper 20%)	18.7 (16.0–21.8)	16.4 (15.5–17.4)	12.0 (11.3–12.7)	19.0 (18.1–19.9)	13.8 (12.4–15.3)	13.9 (12.8–15.0)	15.7 (14.9–16.6)	14.2 (13.2–15.1)	18.5 (17.5–19.6)	15.7 (14.7–16.8)	14.1 (13.9–14.3)
Place of residence											
Urban	58.4 (55.23–61.5)	15.6 (14.8–16.5)	72.0 (71.1–72.8)	49.6 (48.5–50.7)	81.46 (80.5–82.4)	9.3 (8.7–10.0)	29.1 (28.1–30.2)	20.3 (19.2–21.5)	14.2 (13.4–15.1)	29.8 (28.4–31.2)	42.0 (41.6–42.4)
Rural	41.6 (38.5–44.77)	84.4 (83.5–85.2)	28.0 (27.2–28.9)	50.4 (49.3–51.5)	18.5 (17.7–19.5)	90.7 (90.0–91.3)	70.9 (69.8–72.0)	79.7 (78.6–80.8)	85.8 (84.9–86.6)	70.2 (68.8–71.6)	58.0 (57.6–58.5)

Table 3.3 Logistic regression output of determinants of low birth weights (LBW) in 10 developing countries

Variables	Countries									
	Armenia		Cambodia		Colombia		Indonesia		Jordan	
	Unadjusted	Adjusted	Unadjusted	Adjusted	Unadjusted	Adjusted	Unadjusted	Adjusted	Unadjusted	Adjusted
	OR (95% CI)	OR (95% CI)	OR (95% CI)	OR (95% CI)	OR (95% CI)	OR (95% CI)	OR (95% CI)	OR (95% CI)	OR (95% CI)	OR (95% CI)
Maternal age (years)										
≤ 19 (Ref)	1.00	1.00	1.00	1.00	1.00	1.00	1.00	1.00	1.00	1.00
20–34	0.42 (0.17, 1.04)	0.31(0.09–1.10)	0.96 (0.63, 1.49)	2.03 (0.52, 8.02)	0.81* (0.68, 0.96)	0.78(0.58, 1.06)	0.64*** (0.50, 0.82)	0.80(0.54, 1.19)	0.89 (0.61, 1.32)	0.52(0.29, 0.94)
35–49	0.60*(0.21, 1.72)	0.16*(0.03–0.83)	1.13 (0.72, 1.78)	3.70** (1.89, 15.31)	0.81*** (0.66, 0.99)	0.85*** (0.59, 0.98)	0.64*** (0.49, 0.82)	0.86*(0.57, 1.29)	0.78* (0.53, 1.16)	0.41*** (0.22, 0.76)
Maternal education										
No education	2.64*** (1.16, 4.79)	1.43**(1.03, 2.23)	1.61*** (1.28, 2.04)	0.92 (0.47, 1.78)	1.34(0.8,2.26)	1.27 (0.57, 2.86)	1.63** (1.1,2.43)	2.53*** (1.44,4.42)	1.81*** (1.41,2.32)	1.26** (0.59,2.7)
Primary	1.91*** (1.56,3.11)	1.63 (0.57,4.61)	1.40*** (1.17,1.66)	2.14** (1.72, 2.81)	1.04 (0.91,1.18)	0.94(0.74, 1.19)	1.69*** (1.52,1.86)	1.41** (1.19,1.68)	1.55*** (1.3,1.83)	1.39* (0.94,2.06)
Secondary or higher (Ref)	1.00	1.00	1.00	1.00	1.00	1.00	1.00	1.00	1.00	1.00
Currently working										
Nonworking (Ref)	1.00	1.00	1.00	1.00	1.00	1.00	1.00	1.00	1.00	1.00
Working	0.86 (0.52,1.43)	1.05 (0.50,2.20)	1.01 (0.86 1.18)	1.16 (0 79, 1.70)	1.01(0.9,1.12)	1.01 (0.85, 1.2)	0.89 (0.81,0.98)	0.99 (0.86,1.15)	0.75** (0.66,0.86)	0.95 (0.72,1.27)
Age at first cohabitation										
≤ 12 (Ref)	1.00	1.00	1.00	1.00	1.00	1.00	1.00	1.00	1.00	1.00
13–17	0.61 (0.49,0.75)	0.74 (0.32,1.71)	3.25 (1.37,7.71)	0.40 (0.04, 3.85)	1.31 (0.35,2.03)	0.91 (0.46, 1.83)	1.8(1.2,2.72)	0.75 (0.4,1.39)	3.62 (0.73,17.94)	1.11 (0.86,1.44)
18+	1.36 (0.84,2.19)	1.16 (0.79, 1.70)	1 01 (0.85,1.2)	0.46 (0.05, 4.41)	1.13(1,1.27)	0.94 (0.46, 1.89)	1.27 (1.14,1.42)	0.76 (0.41,1.41)	1.12 (0.99,1.26)	0.75 (0.4,1.39)

(continued)

Table 3.3 (continued)

Variables	Countries									
	Armenia		Cambodia		Colombia		Indonesia		Jordan	
	Unadjusted	Adjusted	Unadjusted	Adjusted	Unadjusted	Adjusted	Unadjusted	Adjusted	Unadjusted	Adjusted
	OR (95% CI)	OR (95% CI)	OR (95% CI)	OR (95% CI)	OR (95% CI)	OR (95% CI)	OR (95% CI)	OR (95% CI)	OR (95% CI)	OR (95% CI)
Marriage to first birth interval (months)										
First birth (Ref)	1.00	1.00	1.00	1.00	1.00	1.00	1.00	1.00	1.00	1.00
<24	0.42(0.18,1)	0.50 (0.26, 0.98)	0.98 (0.71,1.35)	1.34 (0.87, 2.05)	0.86 (0.69,1.07)	1.09 (0.88,1.35)	0.84 (0.68,1.04)	0.83 (0.7,0.98)	0.60 (0.49,0.73)	1.19 (0.95,1.48)
24–47	0.30** (0.12,0.73)	1.35 (0.62, 2.96)	0.86 (0.62,1.19)	1.21 (0.74, 1.99)	0.82 (0.65,1.03)	1.13(0.9,1.42)	0.87* (0.7,1.09)	0.95 (0.77,1.17)	0.61 (0.49,0.75)	1.13 (0.84,1.51)
48+	0.23*** (0.08,0.66)	2.76*** (1.61, 4.11)	1.21* (0.98,1.69)	1.91**(0.99, 3.70)	0.83* (0.65,0.95)	1.41** (1.07,1.86)	0.94* (0.74,1.2)	0.99* (0.73,1.36)	0.71** (0.57,0.9)	2.16*** (1.41,3.33)
Taken Iron pills during pregnancy										
No	0.52* (0.26,0.85)	1.82**(1.27, 4.29)	1.64** (1.58,1.87)	2.51*(1.85, 7.45)	1.07* (1.00,1.24)	0.86* (0.62,1.19)	0.81** (0.62,1.02)	1.24** (1.01,1.52)	1.12** (0.57,2.19)	4.44*** (3.21,6.13)
Yes (ref)	1.00	1.00	1.00	1.00	1.00	1.00	1.00	1.00	1.00	1.00
Maternal anemia										
No (ref)	1.00	1.00	1.00	1.00	1.00	1.00	1.00	1.00	1.00	1.00
Yes	NA	NA	1.25 (1.01,1.54)	1.32 (0.92, 1.88)	NA	NA	NA	NA	0.96 (0.85,1.08)	0.9 (0.74,1.11)
Number of ANC visits										
No ANC	2.87 (0.6,13.72)	0.86 (0.05, 13.86)	1.60*** (1.14,2.25)	1.25** (1.08, 2.73)	1.84*** (1.33,2.55)	2.79*** (1.69,4.6)	1.94*** (1.39,2.72)	2.02*** (1.23,3.3)	1.61** (0.86,3.02)	1.67** (0.66,4.27)
1	5.74(0.51,8.9)	1.87 (0.01, 263.52)	1.52** (1.01,2.29)	1.05 (0.41, 2.74)	1.62** (0.98,2.69)	2.34** (1.03,5.32)	1.87*** (1.26,2.76)	2.04*** (1.22,3.41)	2.17** (1.07,4.43)	3.62*** (1.61,8.12)
2	1.64(0.2,3.48)	3.59(0.70, 18.43)	1.16 (0.83,1.61)	0.39 (0.15, 0.99)	2.29 (1.67,3.13)	3.43** (2.2,5.35)	1.81** (1.34,2.45)	1.21 (0.72,2.03)	1.5* (0.93,2.41)	0.66 (0.23,1.9)
3	1.35 (0.47,3.89)	0.08(0.00, 10.73)	1.16 (0.93,1.45)	0.94 (0.59, 1.49)	2.06 (1.63,2.59)	1.94 (1.33, 2.82)	1.74 (1.42,2.13)	1.43** (1.04,1.95)	1.11 (0.78,1.57)	0.85 (0.43,1.68)

(continued)

Table 3.3 (continued)

Variables	Countries									
	Armenia		Cambodia		Colombia		Indonesia		Jordan	
	Unadjusted	Adjusted	Unadjusted	Adjusted	Unadjusted	Adjusted	Unadjusted	Adjusted	Unadjusted	Adjusted
	OR (95% CI)	OR (95% CI)	OR (95% CI)	OR (95% CI)	OR (95% CI)	OR (95% CI)	OR (95% CI)	OR (95% CI)	OR (95% CI)	OR (95% CI)
4+ (Ref)	1.00	1.00	1.00	1.00	1.00	1.00	1.00	1.00	1.00	1.00
Maternity BMI										
Thin BMI	NA	NA	0.64** (0.50,0.84)	2.94*** (1.38, 5.27)	NA	NA	NA	NA	0.66** (0.44,0.97)	2.22*** (1.26,3.9)
Normal	NA	NA	0.34 (0.21,0.53)	1.56 (0.77, 3.14)	NA	NA	NA	NA	0.53 (0.36,0.78)	1.27** (1.03,1.56)
Over weight (Ref)	1.00	1.00		1.00	1.00	1.00	1.00	1.00	1.00	1.00
Wealth status										
Poor (lower 40%)	1.14** (0.67,1.91)	2.02*(0.82, 5.01)	2.14*** (1.74,2.62)	1.56**(1.27, 3.16)	1.07 (0.88,1.31)	0.92 (0.68,1.26)	1.98*** (1.71,2.3)	1.33** (1.04,1.69)	2.15*** (1.74,2.66)	0.7** (0.52,0.95)
Middle (middle 40%)	0.71 (0.41,1.22)	1.12(0.54, 2.33)	1.71** (1.39,2.1)	1.24 (0.64, 2.40)	1.03 (0.84,1.27)	0.99 (0.77,1.28)	1.37** (1.17,1.61)	1.2(0.96,1.5)	1.44** (1.16,1.79)	0.85 (0.63,1.13)
Rich (upper 20%) (Ref)	1.00	1.00	1.00	1.00	1.00	1.00	1.00	1.00	1.00	1.00
Place of residence										
Urban (Ref)	1.00	1.00	1.00	1.00	1.00	1.00	1.00	1.00	1.00	1.00
Rural	0.97 (0.66,1.42)	0.61 (0.29, 1.26)	1.56*** (1.32,1.85)	1.45** (1.35, 2.80)	1.03 (0.92,1.16)	1.01 (0.78,1.31)	1.44*** (1.31,1.59)	1.18** (1,1.38)	1.04 (0.94,1.15)	1.16 (0.9,1.49)

Variables	Countries											
	Nepal		Pakistan		Tanzania		Uganda		Zimbabwe		All Countries	
	Unadjusted	Adjusted	Unadjusted	Adjusted	Unadjusted	Adjusted	Unadjusted	Adjusted	Unadjusted	Adjusted	Unadjusted	Adjusted
	OR (95% CI)	OR (95% CI)	OR (95% CI)	OR (95% CI)	OR (95% CI)	OR (95% CI)	OR (95% CI)	OR (95% CI)	OR (95% CI)	OR (95% CI)	OR (95% CI)	OR (95% CI)
Maternal age (years)												
≤ 19 (Ref)	1.00	1.00	1.00	1.00	1.00	1.00	1.00	1.00	1.00	1.00	1.00	1.00

(continued)

Table 3.3 (continued)

Variables	Countries											
	Nepal		Pakistan		Tanzania		Uganda		Zimbabwe		All Countries	
	Unadjusted	Adjusted	Unadjusted	Adjusted	Unadjusted	Adjusted	Unadjusted	Adjusted	Unadjusted	Adjusted	Unadjusted	Adjusted
	OR (95% CI)	OR (95% CI)	OR (95% CI)	OR (95% CI)	OR (95% CI)	OR (95% CI)	OR (95% CI)	OR (95% CI)	OR (95% CI)	OR (95% CI)	OR (95% CI)	OR (95% CI)
20–34	0.74 (0.53,1.02)	0.47 (0.21,1.03)	1.03 (0.52, 2.04)	9.74 (0.2,8.35)	0.86 (0.59,1.25)	0.6 (0.26,1.37)	0.85 (0.63,1.16)	2.18 (0.24,19.47)	0.68 (0.49, 0.94)	0.50 (0.29,0.84)	0.88** (0.80,0.97)	0.71 (0.5,1.01)
35–49	0.70* (0.42,1.18)	0.75** (0.23,0.89)	0.69* (0.34,0.92)	7.71** (1.15, 14.05)	0.71* (0.47,0.86)	0.40** (0.16,1.01)	0.73* (0.52, 1.04)	1.39** (1.14,13.89)	0.82* (0.56,0.99)	0.60** (0.32,1.15)	0.84*** (0.76,0.93)	1.66** (1.45,1.96)
Maternal education												
No education	1.30** (1.02,1.65)	1.19*** (1.07,1.52)	1.98*** (1.53,2.57)	2.61*** (1.03,6.59)	0.98 (0.72,1.34)	0.64 (0.28,1.45)	0.95** (0.7,1.28)	2.06** (0.55,7.63)	0.96 (0.33,2.78)	0.83 (0.13,5.51)	1.62*** (1.49,1.77)	1.54*** (1.19,1.74)
Primary	1.53*** (1.19,1.96)	1.14 (0.6,2.2)	1.87*** (1.4,2.51)	2.75*** (1.25,6.05)	1.01 (0.79,1.29)	0.61* (0.33,1.11)	0.98 (0.82,1.18)	0.56 (0.22,1.46)	1.11 (0.91,1.36)	1.06 (0.71,1.58)	1.13*** (1.08,1.18)	1.66* (1.24,1.80)
Secondary or higher (Ref)	1.00	1.00		1.00		1.00		1.00	1.00	1.00	1.00	1.00
Currently working												
No (Ref)	1.00	1.00	1.00	1.00	1.00	1.00	1.00	1.00	1.00	1.00	1.00	1.00
Yes	0.96 (0.79,1.16)	1.66** (0.98,2.81)	1.00* (0.75,1.32)	0.31*** (0.13,0.74)	0.79* (0.64,0.98)	0.73 (0.46,1.18)	0.87 (0.73,1.04)	0.96 (0.45,2.05)	0.82** (0.68,1.00)	1.15 (0.83,1.59)	0.79*** (0.76,0.83)	0.79*** (0.67,0.93)
Age at first cohabitation												
≤ 12 (Ref)	1.00	1.00	1.00	1.00	1.00	1.00	1.00	1.00	1.00	1.00	1.00	1.00
13–17	1.85 (0.9,3.8)	0.24 (0.03,2.14)	0.76 (0.2,2.86)	0.57* (0.28,0.93)	0.61 (0.18,1.99)	7.95 (0.07,8.68)	0.59 (0.36,0.97)	10.32 (0.16,659.02)	0.98 (0.34,2.83)	0.61 (0.18,1.99)	1.10 (0.89,1.36)	1.97 (0.56,6.91)
18+	1.3 (1.07,1.58)	0.35 (0.04,3.14)	1.5 (1.19,1.9)	0.24 (0.03,2.14)	1.04 (0.86,1.25)	11.82 (0.11,12.94)	1.02 (0.87,1.21)	12.66(0.19, 18.48)	0.95 (0.78,1.16)	0.81 (0.56,1.18)	1.09 (1.04,1.15)	2.2 (0.63,7.74)
Marriage to first birth interval (months)												
First birth (Ref)	1.00	1.00	1.00	1.00	1.00	1.00	1.00	1.00	1.00	1.00	1.00	1.00

(continued)

Table 3.3 (continued)

Variables	Countries											
	Nepal		Pakistan		Tanzania		Uganda		Zimbabwe		All Countries	
	Unadjusted	Adjusted	Unadjusted	Adjusted	Unadjusted	Adjusted	Unadjusted	Adjusted	Unadjusted	Adjusted	Unadjusted	Adjusted
	OR (95% CI)	OR (95% CI)	OR (95% CI)	OR (95% CI)	OR (95% CI)	OR (95% CI)	OR (95% CI)	OR (95% CI)	OR (95% CI)	OR (95% CI)	OR (95% CI)	OR (95% CI)
<24	0.82 (0.58,1.15)	0.92 (0.49,1.7)	0.83 (0.56,1.22)	0.85 (0.44,1.66)	0.51 (0.34,0.77)	0.98 (0.61,1.55)	1.56 (0.95,2.56)	1.78 (0.78,4.11)	0.94 (0.56,1.58)	1.26 (0.87,1.82)	0.78 (0.71,0.85)	1.15 (0.97,1.35)
24–47	0.73* (0.52,0.98)	1.07 (0.54,2.1)	0.96 (0.65,1.42)	1.48 (0.71,3.11)	0.57 (0.38,0.86)	1.34 (0.77,2.33)	1.38 (0.83,2.29)	2.88 (1.17,7.10)	0.9 (0.52,1.55)	1.4 (0.83,2.36)	0.79** (0.72,0.87)	1.21 (0.99,1.48)
48+	0.77** (0.55,1.08)	0.84 (0.31,2.29)	1.19 (0.79,1.8)	0.83 (0.29,2.34)	0.53** (0.34,0.84)	2.42*** (1.09,5.37)	1.41** (1.33,2.41)	2.24*** (1.15, 3.52)	0.96 (0.53,1.74)	1.45 (0.63,3.32)	0.88*** (0.8,0.98)	1.88*** (1.4,2.53)
Taken Iron pills during pregnancy												
No	0.99 (0.7,1.41)	0.23* (0,13.47)	0.66** (0.33,0.91)	4.18*** (1.84,9.5)	0.66 (0.33,1.31)	0.52 (0.07,3.86)	1.31* (0.95,1.81)	0.97 (0.3,3.18)	1.56 (0.95,2.56)	0.98 (0.61,1.55)	1.13** (1.02,1.25)	3.12*** (2.38,4.10)
Yes (ref)	1.00	1.00	1.00	1.00	1.00	1.00	1.00	1.00	1.00	1.00	1.00	1.00
Maternal anemia												
No (ref)	1.00	1.00	1.00	1.00	1.00	1.00	1.00	1.00	1.00	1.00	1.00	1.00
Yes	1.26 (0.93,1.7)	2.01 (1.22,3.33)	NA	NA	1.34 (1.12,1.6)	1.23 (0.82,1.83)	1.06 (0.75,1.49)	1.26 (0.54,2.92)	0.94 (0.76,1.16)	0.76 (0.52,1.11)	1.08 (1,1.16)	1.03 (0.89,1.20)
Number of ANC visits												
No ANC	0.92 (0.44,1.9)	1.52 (0.39,5.94)	1.58** (1.29,3.65)	0.11** (0.01,0.65)	1.21** (1.07,5.44)	2.09 (0.21,20.99)	2.05*** (1.16,3.63)	3.15*** (3.83,7.08)	1.88*** (1.23,2.87)	4.94*** (2.96,8.24)	1.61*** (1.38,1.87)	1.75** (1.08,2.82)
1	1.45 (0.71,2.96)	1.00(0.56, 2.13)	1.57 (0.81,3.04)	2.32 (0.55,9.79)	1.67** (0.99,2 99)	3.6*** (1.45,8.94)	1.98** (1.06,3.68)	2.34 (0.29,19.1)	1.65** (0.89,3.06)	3.17*** (1.39,7.22)	1.69*** (1.42,2.01)	1.78** (1.12,2.84)
2	1.05 (0.66,1.67)	1.66 (0.57,4.83)	1.52 (0.94,2.46)	0.68 (0.2,2.32)	1.15 (0.8,1.64)	1.18 (0.59,2.38)	1.33 (0.93,1.91)	2.08 (0.59,7.41)	1.62** (1.1,2.39)	2.11*** (1.19,3.76)	1.47** (1.3,1.65)	0.75 (0.50,1.11)
3	1 (0.72,1.39)	1.05 (0.47,2.35)	2.64 (1.78,3.9)	2.75** (1.17,6.46)	1.04 (0.82,1.32)	1.55** (1,2.41)	1.06 (0.83,1.35)	1.11 (0.51,2.41)	1.07 (0.8,1.43)	0.99 (0.62,1.6)	1.25 (1.15,1.36)	0.96 (0.76,1.21)
4+ (Ref)	1.00	1.00	1.00	1.00	1.00	1.00		1.00		1.00		1.00

(continued)

Table 3.3 (continued)

Variables	Countries											
	Nepal		Pakistan		Tanzania		Uganda		Zimbabwe		All Countries	
	Unadjusted	Adjusted	Unadjusted	Adjusted	Unadjusted	Adjusted	Unadjusted	Adjusted	Unadjusted	Adjusted	Unadjusted	Adjusted
	OR (95% CI)	OR (95% CI)	OR (95% CI)	OR (95% CI)	OR (95% CI)	OR (95% CI)	OR (95% CI)	OR (95% CI)	OR (95% CI)	OR (95% CI)	OR (95% CI)	OR (95% CI)
Maternity BMI												
Thin BMI	0.62** (0.42,0.9)	1.99** (1.8,4.93)	0.27*** (0.14,0.52)	1.47** (1.12,4.14)	0.70** (0.52,0.95)	1.21* (0.56,2.59)	1.18* (0.72,1.94)	1.87** (1.16,4.78)	1.08** (0.99,1.41)	0.91 (0.43,1.93)	0.69*** (0.62,0.78)	1.59*** (1.21,2.09)
Normal	0.4 (0.24,0.68)	1.36 (0.64,2.9)	0.29 (0.15,0.56)	0.68 (0.38,1.23)	0.57 (0.4,0.79)	1.02 (0.62,1.69)	0.75 (0.42,1.33)	2.04 (0.75,5.53)	0.66 (0.44,0.98)	0.97 (0.68,1.38)	0.61 (0.55,0.69)	1.11 (0.94,1.31)
Over weight (Ref)	1.00	1.00	1.00	1.00	1.00	1.00	1.00	1.00	1.00	1.00	1.00	1.00
Wealth status												
Poor (lower 40%)	1.45*** (1.12,1.89)	1.32* (1.05,2.31)	1.91*** (1.43,2.55)	3.45** (1.95,12.45)	0.89 (0.7,1.12)	1.34* (0.63,2.84)	1.06* (0.87,1.3)	1.65** (1.07,2.58)	1.24** (1.16,1.59)	1.22** (1.09,2.16)	1.29*** (1.21,1.37)	1.15** (0.99,1.41)
Middle (middle 40%)	1.39*** (1.1,1.75)	0.78 (0.41,1.48)	1.45*** (1.17,1.8)	0.85 (0.44,1.67)	0.93 (0.75,1.15)	0.83 (0.45,1.54)	1.13 (0.93,1.39)	1.09 (0.33,3.6)	1.19* (1.06,1.4)	1.18 (0.76,1.84)	1.09** (1.02,1.16)	1.07 (0.88,1.3)
Rich (upper 20%) (Ref)	1.00	1.00	1.00	1.00	1.00	1.00	1.00	1.00	1.00	1.00	1.00	1.00
Place of residence												
Urban (Ref)	1.00	1.00	1.00	1.00	1.00	1.00	1.00	1.00	1.00	1.00	1.00	1.00
Rural	0.93 (0.76,1.13)	1.11 (0.55,2.24)	1.62*** (1.31,1.99)	0.67** (0.47,0.98)	0.84* (0.7,1.00)	0.53** (0.3,0.95)	1.02 (0.86,1.21)	0.66 (0.23,1.95)	1.00 (0.84,1.21)	0.83 (0.56,1.25)	1.11*** (1.06,1.15)	0.81** (0.68,0.97)

$*p < 0.05$; $**p < 0.01$; $***p < 0.001$

CI: 1.15–3.52, $p < 0.01$). In all of these countries, ANC visits significantly influenced reducing LBW and those who did not receive any ANC visit were at high risk to deliver LBW babies (OR = 1.75, 95% CI: 1.08–2.82, $p < 0.05$). Furthermore, low BMI of mothers had also significant role with LBW babies in all of the countries (OR = 1.59, 95% CI: 1.21–2.09, $p < 0.01$). Overall, mothers who lived in rural communities were also more likely to deliver LBW babies (OR = 0.81, 95% CI: 0.68–0.97, $p < 0.05$). Similarly, wealth status also significantly influences delivering LBW and it was found that those who had lower wealth status were more likely to deliver LBW babies than the richest (OR = 1.15, 95% CI: 1.09–1.41, $p < 0.05$).

3.4 Discussion

This study intended to identify the determinants of LBW in selected developing countries. Our study found that different socioeconomics, demographics factors, predelivery care, and later conception had influence on LBW infants. The study also showed that maternal age significantly influences delivery of LBW babies. Some of the previous studies found that mother's age was an important factor in determining LBW infants (Assefa et al. 2012; Isiugo-abanihe et al. 2011; Nahar et al. 1998; Nobile et al. 2007). The likelihood of having infants with LBW was significantly associated with maternal education. This relationship is in line with observations from previous studies conducted in developing countries which showed that maternal literacy tend to be protecting from having a LBW infant (Khatun et al. 2009; Sebayang et al. 2012; Muthayya et al. 2009). This study also found that working mothers were more likely to deliver LBW babies compared to nonworking mothers. Hardworking (agricultural laborers, hard work in industries, and so on) mothers might be generally affected by the maternal- and pregnancy-related problems that created a higher risk of LBW. A previous community-based study did not show any significant association between later conception and delivery of LBW babies (Khatun et al. 2009), but our study observed that there was a significant relationship between them which might be reflected the overall countrywide characteristics. Maternal BMI played an important role on birth weight of the baby and it was found that low BMI mothers were 1.5 times more likely to deliver LBW babies. This finding is in accordance with prior studies conducted in developing countries showing that infants of underweight mothers had significant association to deliver LBW babies (Khatun et al. 2009; Euser et al. 2005; Yazdanpanahi et al. 2008; Kayode et al. 2014; Ronnenberg et al. 2003). Conversely, our study found that, low socioeconomic status was one of the predictors of LBW which confirms with previous studies that most poor women in developing countries give birth to LBW baby (Olsén et al. 2008; Sebayang et al. 2012). Pregnant women who did not attend ANC or minimum number of ANC service attended had significantly delivered LBW babies compared to mothers who received standard antenatal care. This finding is consistent with previous studies developing countries found that no or few number of ANC services had influence on delivery of LBW babies (Kramer 1987; Nahar et al. 1998; Khatun et al. 2009) which varies with different socioeconomic status of population (Isiugo-abanihe et al. 2011; Nahar et al. 1998; Khatun et al. 2009; Kayode et al. 2014). The study has some limitations. Women's reported motivations of reducing LBW which are probably influenced by social, cultural and economic factors are likely to be country and region specific, and to change over time. This study did not examine for possible cross-level interaction effect, thus we suggest that subsequent study should explore this area.

3.5 Conclusions

This study has demonstrated that determinants have independent effects on the prevalence of LBW infants in developing countries regardless of individual-level characteristics of the mothers. Community-based intervention programs that improve the overall maternal health of mother, behavior change communication; infrastructural development of rural communities may reduce the prevalence of LBW which can help to reduce childhood morbidity and mortality in developing countries.

Acknowledgements The International Centre for Diarrheal Disease Research of Bangladesh (icddr'b) is thankful to the Governments of Australia, Bangladesh, Canada, Sweden, and the UK for providing core/unrestricted support.

References

Agho, K. E., Dibley, M. J., Odiase, J. I., & Ogbonmwan, S. M. (2011). Determinants of exclusive breastfeeding in Nigeria. *BMC Pregnancy Childbirth, 11,* 2–16.

Assefa, N., Berhane, Y., & Worku, A. (2012). Wealth status, mid upper arm circumference (MUAC) and ante natal care (ANC) are determinants for low birth weight in Kersa, Ethiopia. *PLoS One, 7,* e40090.

Brämer, G. R. (1988). International statistical classification of diseases and related health Problems, Tenth revision. *World Health Statistics Quarterly, 41,* 32–36.

Barker, D. J. P., Uutela, A., Osmond, C., & Eriksson, J. G. (2001). Size at birth and resilience to effects of poor living conditions in adult life: Longitudinal study. *BMJ, 323*(7324), 1273–1276.

Central Statistical Agency (CSA) [Ethiopia] and ICF. (2005). Ethiopia Demographic and Health Survey 2005: Key Indicators Report. Addis Ababa, Ethiopia, and Rockville, Maryland, USA. CSA and ICF.

[Internet]. Health San Francisco. (2006). *Central Statistical Agency and ORC Macro*; p. 446. Available http://www.measuredhs.com/pubs/pdf/FR179/FR179[23June2011].pdf.

Chase, H. C. (1960). *Infant mortality and weight at birth*, 59, 23–56. Retrieved from http://www.ncbi.nlm.nih.gov/pmc/articles/PMC1226678/pdf/amjphnation00051-0052.pdf.

Dey, A. C., Ahmed, F. U., Mannan, A., Saha, L., Barua, C., & Mahmood, C. B. (1983). Small for gestational age babies: Morbidity and immediate outcome in a tertiary care hospital—A prospective study, Bangladesh. *Journal of Child Health, 38*(3), 1–7.

Deshpande, J. D., Phalke, D. B., Bangal, V. B., Peeyuusha, D., & Bhatt, S. (2011). Maternal risk factors for low birth weight neonates: A hospital based case-control study in rural area of western Maharashtra, India. *National Journal of Community Medicine, 2,* 394–398.

Eriksson, J. G., Forsén, T., Tuomilehto, J., Winter, P. D., Osmond, C., & Barker, D. J. P. (1999). Catch-up growth in childhood and death from coronary heart disease : Longitudinal study. *BMJ, 318*(7181), 427–431.

Euser, A. M., Finken, M. J. J., Keijzer-veen, M. G., Hille, E. T. M., Wit, J. M., & Dekker, F. W. (2005). Associations between prenatal and infancy weight gain and BMI, fat mass, and fat distribution in young adulthood : A prospective cohort study in males and females born very preterm. *American Journal* of *Clinical Nutrition,* 1–3, 480–487.

Forrester, T. E., Wilks, R. J., Bennett, F. I., Simeon, D., Osmond, C., Allen, M., et al. (1996). Fetal growth and cardiovascular risk factors in Jamaican school children. *BMJ, 312,* 156–160.

Giving Birth in Canada (GBC): The cost. (2006). *Canadian Institute for Health Information.* Available from https://secure.cihi.ca/free_products/Costs_Report_06_Eng.pdf.

Hazarika, I. (2011). Factors that determine the use of skilled care during delivery in India: Implications for achievement of MDG-5 targets. *Maternal and Child Health Journal, 15,* 1381–1388.

Isiugo-abanihe, U. C. (2011). Maternal and environmental factors influencing infant birth weight in Ibadan, Nigeria. *African Population Studies, 25,* 45–62.

Kayode, G., Amoakoh-Coleman, M., Agyepong, I. A., Ansah, E., Grobbee, D. E., & Klipstein-Grobusch, K. (2014). Contextual risk factors for low birth weight: A multilevel analysis. *PLoS ONE, 9,* e109333.

Khanal, V., Adhikari, M., Sauer, K., & Zhao, Y. (2013). Factors associated with the introduction of prelacteal feeds in Nepal: Findings from the Nepal Demographic and Health Survey 2011. *International Breastfeeding Journal, 8,* 9–15.

Khatun, S., & Rahman, M. (2009). Socio-economic determinants of low birth weight in Bangladesh: A multivariate approach. *Bangladesh Medical Research Council Bulletin, 34,* 81–86.

Kramer, M. S. (1987). Determinants of low birth weight: Methodological assessment and meta-analysis. *Bulletin of the World Health Organization, 65,* 663–737.

Leon, D. A., Lithell, H. O., Vågerö, D., Koupilová, I., Mohsen, R., Berglund, L., Lithell, U., & Mckeigue, P. M. (1998). Reduced fetal growth rate and increased risk of death from ischaemic heart disease : Cohort study of 15 000 Swedish men and women born 1915–29. *BMJ, 317* (7153), 241–245.

Leger, J., Levy-Marchal, C., Bloch, J., Pinet, A., Chevenne, D., Porquet, D., et al. (1997). Reduced final height and indications for insulin resistance in 20 year olds born small for gestational age: Regional cohort study. *BMJ, 315,* 341–347.

McCormick, M. C. (1985). The contribution of low birth weight to infant mortality and childhood morbidity. *The New England Journal of Medicine, 312,* 82–90.

MEASURE DHS. (2012). *DHS model questionnaires. Calverton: ICF International.* Available from http://www.measuredhs.com/What-We-Do/Questionnaires.cfm. Accessed 21 Jan 2015.

Metgud, C. S., Naik, V., & Mallapur, M. D. (2012). Factors affecting birth weight of a newborn—A community based study in rural Karnataka, India. *PLoS One, 7,* e40040.

Muthayya, S. (2009). Maternal nutrition & low birth weight—What is really important? *Indian Journal of Medical Research, 130*(5), 600–608.

Nahar, N., Afroza, S., & Hossain, M. (1998). Incidence of low birth weight in three selected communities of Bangladesh. *Bangladesh Medical Research Council Bulletin, 24,* 49–54.

Nobile, C. G., Raffaele, G., Altomare, C., & Pavia, M. (2007). Influence of maternal and social factors as predictors of low birth weight in Italy. *BMC Public Health, 7,* 192–199.

Olsén, P., Vainionpää, L., Pääkkö, E., Korkman, M., Pyhtinen, J., & Järvelin, M. R. (1998). Psychological findings in preterm children related to neurologic status and magnetic resonance imaging. *Pediatrics, 102,* 329–336.

Park, K. (2007). *Park's text book of preventive and social medicine,* 426–428. Retrieved from http://www.amazon.in/Park-Textbook-Preventive-Social-Medicine/dp/9382219056.

Richards, M., Hardy, R., Kuh, D., & Wadsworth, M. E. (2001). Birth weight and cognitive function in the British 1946 birth cohort: Longitudinal population based study. *BMJ, 322*, 199–203.

Ronnenberg, A. G., Wang, X., Xing, H., Chen, C., Chen, D., Guang, W., et al. (2003). Community and international nutrition low preconception body mass index is associated with birth outcome in a prospective cohort of chinese women. *Journal of Nutrition, 133*(11), 3449–3455.

Rutstein, S. G. (2012). *Guide to DHS Statistics. In Book Guide to DHS Statistics*. Calverton: Elsevier.

Rutstein, S. O., Rojas, G. (2006). *Guide to DHS Statistics*. Demographic and Health Surveys ORC Macro Calverton: Maryland.

Sachdev, H. P. S. (2001). Low birth weight in South Asia. *International Journal of Diabetes, 21*, 13–31.

Saugstad, L. F. (1981). Weight of all births and infant mortality. *The Journal of pidemiology and Community Health, 35*, 185–191.

Schothorst, P. F., & Engeland, V. H. (1996). Long-term behavioral sequelae of prematurity. *Journal of the American Academy of Child and Adolescent Psychiatry, 35*, 175–183.

Sebayang, S. K., Dibley, M. J., Kelly, P. J., Shankar, A. V., & Shankar, A. H. (2012). Determinants of low birthweight, small-for-gestational-age and preterm birth in Lombok, Indonesia: Analyses of the birthweight cohort of the SUMMIT trial. *Tropical Medicine* and *International Health, 17*, 938–950.

Sorensen, H. T., Sabroe, S., Olsen, J., Rothman, K. J., Gillman, M. W., & Fischer, P. (1997). Birth weight and cognitive function in young adult life: Historical cohort study. *British Medical Journal, 197*, 401–403.

Titaley, C. R., Dibley, M. J., Agho, K., Roberts, C. L., & Hall, J. (2008). Determinants of neonatal mortality in Indonesia. *BMC Public Health, 8*, 232.

West, B. T., & Arbor, A. (2008). Statistical and methodological issues in the analysis of complex sample survey data : Practical guidance for Trauma researchers. *Journal of Traumatic Stress, 21*, 440–447.

Yazdanpanahi, Z., Forouhari, S., & Parsanezhad, M. E. (2008). Prepregnancy body mass index and gestational weight gain and their association with some pregnancy outcomes. *Iranian Red Crescent Medical Journal, 10*, 326–331.

Chapter 4
On the Determinants of Child Health in India: Does Teenage Pregnancy Matter?

Dipankar Roy and Avijit Debnath

4.1 Introduction

Children are vital to the nation's present and its future. In recent years, there has been an increased focus on issues that affect children and on improving their health. In determining the factors associated with child health, along with other determinants, age of mother at the time of pregnancy is also considered as a crucial one. Pregnancy is an overwhelming experience at any age but in case of a teenager it can lead to developmental crisis (Rodriquez & Moore, 1995). Generally teenagers, enjoying their parenthood have not had enough maturity to identify their role (Hanna, 2001) and their cognitive immaturity makes them more inclined to put their needs ahead of the developmental needs of their child. In recent years teenage pregnancy has become a concerning issue in every economy irrespective of its level of development or under development. A number of economic, societal and personal factors actually contribute to this. The figures of the incidence of teenage pregnancy vary across countries and worldwide the incidence of teenage pregnancy rate range from 143 per 1000 in some sub-Saharan African countries to 2.9 per 1000 in South Korea. Like that of women in their 20s and 30s, teenage pregnants also face many of the same obstetrics issues and thus additional medical concerns are required. Research has shown that the risk of low birth weight is connected to the biological age itself. Incidence of teenage pregnancy is thus associated with higher rates of adverse health consequences like morbidity and mortality of both teen pregnant and newly born babies, and thus has important implications for human resources and development prospects of a country. In spite of these

D. Roy (✉) · A. Debnath
Department of Economics, Assam University Silchar, Silchar, India
e-mail: roydp.34@gmail.com

A. Debnath
e-mail: debnath_avi@yahoo.com

U.K. De et al. (eds.), *Issues on Health and Healthcare in India*, India Studies in Business and Economics, https://doi.org/10.1007/978-981-10-6104-2_4

recognitions, very rare studies have been conducted in India, where early marriage custom is still being practiced. And in this context, the present study is an attempt to investigate spatial variations in the incidence of teenage pregnancy, and to assess if incidence of teenage pregnancy really matters for child health in India.

4.1.1 Incidence of Teenage Pregnancy in India: An Overview

Teenage births carry a higher risk of complicated pregnancies, low birth weight, premature births and need for neonatal intensive care (Skinner & Hickey, 2003). The incidence of teenage pregnancy is quite acute in developed countries. However, it is also experienced in less developed or developing countries. Because of its potential adverse impact on child health, a crucial determinant of future human resources, it is quite pertinent to look into the status of teenage pregnancy for a developing country like India. Teenage pregnancy may vary across regions and states because of differences in socioeconomic, institutional, and cultural factors. Table 4.1 summarizes variations in the incidence of teenage pregnancy across the states/UTs of India. It has been found that on an average 16 percentages of the teenagers have begun child bearing in India. The incidence of teenage pregnancy varies from states to states, having lowest incidence of 3.1% in Himachal Pradesh to the highest percentage of 27.5% in Jharkhand. However some of the better off states/UTs in this aspect are Maharashtra (3.6%), Jammu and Kashmir (4.2%), Delhi (5 %), and Punjab (5.5%). On the other hand, the states/UTs experiencing higher incidence of teenage pregnancy than the national average include Jharkhand (27.5%), West Bengal (25.3%), Bihar (25%), Tripura (18.5%) Andhra Pradesh (18.1%), and Karnataka (17%) etc.

Some socioeconomic factors like place of residence, level education, adolescence's religion, caste, economic status etc. can also influence the incidence of teenage pregnancy. Table 4.2 summarizes variations in the incidence of teenage pregnancy by socioeconomic characteristics. The incidence of teenage pregnancy is found to be more than twice in rural areas (19%) as compare to urban areas (9%). The level of teenage pregnancy and motherhood is 9 times higher among women with no education than women with 12 or more years of education. With no education the percentage of teenage pregnancy has been found to be 32.6%. Now if we concentrate on the religion section, the level of teenage pregnancy is higher in Muslim women 17% followed by Hindu (16%), Buddhists/Neo-Buddhists (11%), Christians (8%), Sikhs (6%), and Jains (13%). Turned to caste, the proportion of women age 15–19 that have begun childbearing is higher among women from scheduled castes (20%) and scheduled tribes (21%) than women from other backward classes (16%) and women who do not belong to any of these communities (12%). And last but not the least, the incidence of teenage pregnancy has been

Table 4.1 Incidence of teenage pregnancy across states, 2005–2006

	Region/State/Nation	Teenage pregnancy (%)		Region/State/Nation	Teenage pregnancy (%)
	India	16		India	16
	Delhi	5	Central	Chhattisgarh	14.6
North	Haryana	12.1		Madhya Pradesh	13.6
	Himachal Pradesh	3.1		Uttar Pradesh	14.3
	Jammu & Kashmir	4.2	East	Bihar	25
	Punjab	5.5		Jharkhand	27.5
	Rajasthan	16		Orissa	14.4
	Uttaranchal	6.2			
Northeast	Arunachal Pradesh	15.4		West Bengal	25.3
	Assam	16.4	West	Goa	12.7
	Manipur	7.3		Gujarat	13.8
	Meghalaya	8.3		Maharashtra	3.6
	Mizoram	10.1	South	Andhra Pradesh	18.1
	Nagaland	7.5		Karnataka	17
	Sikkim	12		Kerala	5.8
	Tripura	18.5		Tamil Nadu	7.7

Note Teenage pregnancy is defined as the percentage of women aged 15–19 who have had a live birth or currently pregnant with their first child
Source Compiled by author using data from National Family Health Survey 3 (NFHS 3) 2005–06

found to be five times as high for women in households with the lowest wealth index than for women in households with the highest wealth index.

4.1.2 Status of Child Health in India

Child health includes number of indicators like Under 5 Mortality Rate (UMR), Infant Mortality Rate (IMR), Child Mortality Rate (CMR), Weight of the children at birth, Size of the children at birth, Acute Respiratory Infection (ARI) so it becomes very difficult to analyze the child health status in different states in general. Thus, to have a clear idea about child health status in India we have calculated a composite Child Ill Health Index (CIHI) using Principal Component Analysis (PCA).

The value of the index can be positive or negative, however for the use of comparison this index has been standardize to a score of 0–1.[1]

Standardize Index of *i*th state,

[1]Similar approach has been used by Antony & Rao, (2007).

Table 4.2 Teenage pregnancy in India by socioeconomic characteristics

Characteristics		Teenage pregnancy (in %)
Residence	Rural	19.1
	Urban	8.7
Education	No education	32.6
	<5 years	21.2
	5–7 years complete	19.6
	8–9 years complete	8.5
	10–11 years complete	6.1
	12 or more years complete	3.6
Religion	Hindu	16.3
	Muslim	17
	Christian	7.8
	Sikh	5.7
	Buddhist/Neo-Buddhist	10.6
	Jain	13.1
	Others	15.6
Caste	Schedule caste	19.8
	Schedule tribe	21.1
	Other backward caste	16.0
	Other	11.9
	Don't know	17.6
Wealth Index	Lowest	25.3
	Second	21.9
	Middle	16.3
	Fourth	11.7
	Highest	5.1

Source Compiled by author using data from National Family Health Survey 3 (NFHS 3) 2005–06

$$\mathrm{SI} = \frac{\text{Actual Index} - \text{Minimum Index}}{\text{Maximum Index} - \text{Minimum Index}}$$

Table 4.3 summarizes this composite child ill health index for different states/UTs in India.

The national average for CIHI in India has been found to be 0.491. However, the value varies significantly from a lowest value of 0.000 in Kerala to a highest value of 1.000 in Arunachal Pradesh. Along with Kerala, Himachal Pradesh (0.103), Goa (0.105), Tamil Nadu (0.137), Jammu and Kashmir (0.155) and Delhi (0.158) were among the states/UTs with lower CIHI. States like Nagaland (0.997), Meghalaya (0.941), Orissa (0.938), Jharkhand (0.889), and Mizoram (0.728) were at the other end. This resembles that the child health in the former states is much better than that of their counter parts.

Table 4.3 State wise child ill health index for India, 2005–06

	Region/State/Nation	CIHI		Region/State/Nation	CIHI
	India	0.491		India	0.491
	Delhi	0.158	Central	Chhattisgarh	0.720
North	Haryana	0.263		Madhya Pradesh	0.881
	Himachal	0.103		Uttar Pradesh	0.838
	Jammu & Kashmir	0.155	East	Bihar	0.789
	Punjab	0.276		Jharkhand	0.889
	Rajasthan	0.667		Orissa	0.938
	Uttaranchal	0.469			
Northeast	Arunachal Pradesh	1.000		West Bengal	0.347
	Assam	0.675	West	Goa	0.105
	Manipur	0.438		Gujarat	0.352
	Meghalaya	0.941		Maharashtra	0.271
	Mizoram	0.728	South	Andhra Pradesh	0.318
	Nagaland	0.997		Karnataka	0.380
	Sikkim	0.240		Kerala	0.000
	Tripura	0.164		Tamil Nadu	0.137

Source The figures are estimated by the author from the original data in [NFS 3]
Note Higher value of child ill health index for a state indicates poor child health in that state

4.1.3 Inter-state Variations in Women Educational Attainment in India

Educational attainment plays an important role in every aspect of our life. And it also plays a key role in decision-making sense. And it is quite obvious that with a better level general literacy there will be better level of health literacy, which is again plays a vital role in health relating outcomes. However, the percentage of women educational attainment differs from state to state. Table 4.4 demonstrates the variation in women literacy[2] across states in India.

It can be observed from Table 4.4 that the national average of women literacy rate is 12%. However few states mark a remarkable figure pointing toward better attainment of the same. Delhi (37.2%), Goa (28.1%), Kerala (25.7%) are the states with better attainment of women education, whereas states like Bihar (4.9%), Tripura (6.7%), Chhattisgarh (7.7%) are the states where the level of women educational attainment is even below the national average.

[2]Women literacy is defined as the percentage of women with 12 or more years of schooling.

Table 4.4 State wise woman literacy rate across India, 2005–06

	Region/State/Nation	Women literacy (%)		Region/State/Nation	Women literacy (%)
	India	12.0		India	12.0
	Delhi	37.2	Central	Chhattisgarh	7.7
North	Haryana	14.3		Madhya Pradesh	8.8
	Himachal	21.4		Uttar Pradesh	10.7
	Jammu & Kashmir	14.2	East	Bihar	4.9
	Punjab	19.1		Jharkhand	7.8
	Rajasthan	7.3		Orissa	8.0
	Uttaranchal	22.0			
Northeast	Arunachal Pradesh	9.6		West Bengal	8.6
	Assam	10.2	West	Goa	28.1
	Manipur	20.9		Gujarat	13.2
	Meghalaya	13.4		Maharashtra	16.4
	Mizoram	14.3	South	Andhra Pradesh	8.8
	Nagaland	10.9		Karnataka	13.5
	Sikkim	12.5		Kerala	25.7
	Tripura	6.7		Tamil Nadu	19.2

Source Compiled by author using data from National Family Health Survey 3 (NFHS 3) 2005–06

4.2 Teenage Pregnancy and Child Health: Theoretical Framework

Teenage births carry a higher risk of complicated pregnancies, babies are more likely to be born prematurely and 50% more likely to be low-birth weight babies (less than five and a half pounds) when compared to the children of mothers whose age was 20 or 21 when they had their first child (Moore, Morrison, & Greene, 1997). Additionally, It has been found that infants born to young adolescent mothers are more prone to exhibit inferior cognitive development and lower educational attainment; they are more likely to demonstrate childhood behavioral problems and adolescent antisocial behavior; and are at an increased risk of suffering from poor nutrition, abuse, neglect and abandonment (Hillis et al., 2004). According to parents' reports of their children's health status, 60% of children born to non-teen mothers were rated in "excellent" health, compared to 38% for children born to the youngest adolescent mothers (Wolfe & Perozek, 1997). It has been noticed that Infant Mortality within this group is 60% higher than for babies of older women. Some of the scholars mentioned that children born to teenagers are at increased risk of growing up in poverty, to misuse alcohol and drugs, to become involved in crime and to become teenage parents themselves (Williams & Davidson, 2004). Studies show that children of adolescent mothers are more likely to drop out of high school when compared to the children of mothers age 20–21. Only 77% of children born to adolescent mothers complete high school by early adulthood compared to 89% of the comparison group (Haveman, Wolfe, & Peterson, 1997). Moreover, there has been ongoing debates on whether these psychological and health disadvantages arise from pre-existing socio economic environments or whether it is the result of the teenage mother that exacerbates these inequalities (Quinlivan, 2005). Hillis et al., (2004) and Woodward et al., (2001) on the basis of the intergenerational cycle of social disadvantage, unemployment, and poor social functioning suggested that family pathology may contribute to the etiology of teenage pregnancy. For instance, exposure to family violence, early parental divorce or separation, poor relationship with parents are all widely recognized as antecedents to teenage pregnancy (Quinlivan et al., 2005).

And all the above mentioned studies create the necessity to examine the fact of teenage pregnancy and child health in Indian context.

4.3 Methods and Data description

The quality of research findings is directly dependent on the accountability of the research methodology followed. Therefore, it is important to describe the way in which the research has been planned, structured, and executed.

Since there are different dimensions of child health, so it is necessary to construct a composite index. And for this purpose we have used principal component analysis (PCA). Although there are different techniques of constructing composite index, we have chosen PCA for the reason that different dimensions of child health may not be equally important. We thought PCA will help us to construct the index assigning appropriate weight to different dimensions objectively.

The method of PCA is a special case of the more general method of factor analysis. The method of Principal, Components has wide applications in the social sciences. In econometrics it has been suggested that this method is appropriate in two cases: firstly, when the number of explanatory variables which should on a prior grounds, be included in a function, is very large relative to the size of sample. Second, the method of principal components has been suggested as a solution to the problem of multicollinearity. This method is also useful in the field of index number in order to assess the reliability of such indexes.

Data used in this study are collected from secondary sources. Data on teenage pregnancy, child health, and maternal care has been collected from National Family Health Survey 3 (NFHS 3) of Government of India.

As found from the available theoretical and empirical literature, young women, who became pregnant and mothers experiences relatively high level of pregnancy complications. Teenage pregnancy has also adverse impact on child health. This section tries to examine whether teenage pregnancy has any adverse impact on child health in India or not in a multiple regression framework. And to do this following model has been used.

$$\begin{aligned}\mathrm{CIHI}_i = \beta_0 + \beta_1 \mathrm{TP}_i + \beta_2 \mathrm{VACFUL}_i + \beta_3 \mathrm{MCI}_i + \beta_4 \mathrm{D1}_i + \beta_5 D_{2i} + \beta_6 D_{3i} \\ + \beta_7 D_{4i} + \beta_8 D_{5i} + U_i\end{aligned} \tag{4.1}$$

where CIHI_i = Child ill health index for the ith state; TP_i = Teenage pregnancy for the ith state. The other variables used in the model act as control variables:

$VACFUL_i$ = Full vaccination given for the *i*th state; MCI_i = Maternal Care Index for the *i*th state,[3] WLR_i = Women Literacy Rate for the *i*th state, D_1, D_2, D_3, D_4, and D_5 are dummy variables used to capture region specific characteristics[4] and U_i = Disturbance term. β_s are the parameters to be estimated.

Since the main focus of the study is to find out if teenage pregnancy affects child health, hence teenage pregnancy (TP) naturally arises as the independent variable.

Extent of vaccination coverage plays an important role in determining child heath. Higher the extent of coverage better will be the child health for obvious reasons. This, thus, signifies the inclusion of full vaccination coverage in the model.

Maternal care during pregnancy plays an important role for child health. Generally, a proper care of would be mother during pregnancy makes a newly born baby healthy. Thus, the inclusion of the variable is justified.

Literacy can influence child health in many ways. This is because a literate mother possesses better knowledge of childbearing than an illiterate one and thus having a probability of better child health. So, inclusion this variable is important and justified.

To capture the probable impact of regional specific characteristics on child health regional dummies have been included in the model. Keep in view six regions under the present study; five regional dummies have been included taking Northern region as the reference category.

4.4 Empirical Analysis and Discussions

We have estimated three different equations by adding or subtracting one or more o f the explanatory variables while keeping the dependent variable (child Ill health Index) un-changed. Table 4.5 summarizes estimated results.

Before we analyze the results, it is important to note that the null hypothesis that teenage pregnancy adversely affects child health is accepted in the first equation at the conventional level of significance. The adjusted R^2 ranges from 0.79 to 0.81, which means that 79 to 81 per cent variations in the dependent variable are being explained by the explanatory variables. The F statistic is found to be significant at 1 per cent level of significance which implies a reasonably good fit of the model. Moreover, J–B statistic is found to be statistically insignificant thus the null hypothesis that the error terms are normally distributed cannot be rejected which in turn implies that the model estimation is meaningful.

[3]Maternal care index has been constructed by using the following methodology. First a dimension index has been constricted for each indicator by using following formula. DI = (Actual value − Minimum value)/(Maximum value − Minimum value). Then maternal care index has been obtained by taking average of the three dimension index.

[4]$D_1 = 1$ for Central region, 0 otherwise, $D_2 = 1$ for Eastern region, 0 otherwise, $D_3 = 1$ for Northeastern region, 0 otherwise, $D_4 = 1$ for Western region, 0 otherwise, $D_5 = 1$ for Southern region, 0 otherwise.

Table 4.5 Impact of Teenage Pregnancy on Child Health; Dependent Variable: Child Ill Health Index

Variable	Model 1	Model 2	Model 3
C	66.57 (7.17)***	74.42 (6.76)***	84.11 (17.29)***
TP	0.66(2.50)**	0.38(1.20)	–
VACFUL	−0.23(−1.83)*	−0.21(−1.74)*	−0.23(−2.14)*
MCI	−30.47(−3.63)***	−26.39(−3.70)***	−25.59(−3.70)***
WLR	–	−0.48(−1.15)	−0.71(−1.89)*
Central	10.87(2.95)***	9.72(3.00)***	8.44(−3.10)***
NER	−11.09(−3.39)***	−11.66(-3.78)***	−12.98(−4.00)***
Adj. R^2	0.79	0.81	0.80
F	22.32***	20.34***	23.27***
J–B	0.24 (0.88)	0.22 (0.90)	2.24 (0.32)

Source Computed by author using data from National Family Health Survey 3 (NFHS 3) 2005–06
Note *, **, *** imply significant at 10, 5 and 1% respectively

Turning to analytical part, column 1 presents the base specification in which we have TP as the sole regressor. Column (2) and (3) presents alternative specification that examines the association between teenage pregnancy (TP) and women literacy rate (WLR) while controlling other factors. We can see that in the first equation TP proved significant indicating that there is significant association between TP and child health. This result immediately accepts the null hypothesis that TP adversely affects child health. Another important aspect of child health, vaccination coverage, as expected assumes negative sign and it is statistically significant in Eqs. (2) and (3). This indicates that full vaccination has a positive association with child health. Similarly maternal care index (MCI) also proved significant with negative sign, implying that maternal care has also a positive association with child health.

$$\begin{aligned}\mathrm{CIHI}_i = \beta_0 + \beta_1 \mathrm{TP}_i + \beta_2 \mathrm{VACFUL}_i + \beta_3 \mathrm{MCI}_i + \beta_4 \mathrm{WLR}_i + \beta_5 D_{1i} + \beta_6 D_{2i} \\ + \beta_7 D_{3i} + \beta_8 D_{4i} + \beta_9 D_{5i} + U_i\end{aligned} \quad (4.2)$$

$$\begin{aligned}\mathrm{CIHI}_i = \beta_0 + \beta_1 \mathrm{VACFUL}_i + \beta_2 \mathrm{MCI}_i + \beta_3 \mathrm{WLR}_i + \beta_4 D_{1i} + \beta_5 D_{2i} \\ + \beta_6 D_{3i} + \beta_7 D_{4i} + \beta_8 D_{5i} + U_i\end{aligned} \quad (4.3)$$

But WLR has not been included in the Model (1) this is because there is a probability of presence of collinearity between TP and WLR. To justify this we have run the second model, Model (2), including both TP and WLR and as expected both are found to be statistically insignificant. This clearly indicates the presence of collinearity. And it is quite justifiable, because having a longer association with educational institutions the probability of getting pregnant at teenage becomes lesser. Now for further clarification we have run another model, model 3, in which TP has been excluded and in this case WLR has been found to be statistically insignificant with negative sign implying negative association with the index or in other words positive association with child health. That is higher literacy rate results in better child health. Now coming to regional disparities captured by dummy variables D_1 is found to be positive and significant which implies that child health in Central region is poorer than that of Northern region and D_3 is proved to be statistically significant with negative sign which implies that children of Northeastern (NE) region are healthier than their counter parts. However, one may argue that based on CIHI child health should have to be poorer in NE region. But, here one thing has to be remembered that in the model estimation other control variables have been included. That is other thing remaining constant child health is better in NE region.

4.5 Conclusion

In this paper, we have tried to identify the determinants of child health in India mainly emphasizing on teenage pregnancy. Our analysis shows that teenage pregnancy is a very crucial factor that leads to poor child health. Thus government should focus on some constructive ways to control teenage pregnancy to have better child health. We have, however, identified some factors which were found to have significant association with child health. Vaccination coverage as captured by VACFUL has a significant positive impact on child health, and factors like maternal care index, women literacy rate also found to have positive association with child health. Thus, the obvious policy suggestion that appears is that government should take initiative to provide better maternal care facilities in terms of establishing health centers in each and every corner of the country, providing free maternal care facilities and vaccination facilities to the newly born babies. Apart from this, there should be strict legal action against marriage of women below 18 years of age.

And keeping in view the role of literacy among women government should concentrate on providing incentive to women to keep them busy in education so that the probability of getting pregnant at teen ages becomes lesser. Like that of providing bicycle to girls in primary classes, incentives should also be given in higher classes to make the education system attractive. Along with this government should also provide some other incentive packages like transportation facility, security facility in general and particularly in rural areas too for women.

Appendix 1

Definition of variables and data sources

Variable name	Definition
Child Ill health index (CIHI)	Composite child health index of child mortality rate, weight at the time of birth (less than 2.5 kg), size at the time of birth (very small), children under 5 with acute respiratory infection
Teenage pregnancy (TP)	Here teenagers refer to women in the age group of 15–19 as data on pregnant women of age below 15 were not available
Maternal care index (MCI)	Composite index of Percentage who received all recommended antenatal care refers to first check-up within the first trimester of pregnancy, who received two or more tetanus toxoid injections, and took iron and folic acid tablets or syrup for three or more months
Full vaccination coverage (VACFUL)	Percentage of children age 12–23 months who received specific vaccines at any time before the survey (according to a vaccination card or the mother's report), and percentage with a vaccination card seen by the interviewer, by state, India, 2005–06
Women literacy rate (WLR)	Percentage of respondents completed 12 or more years of education

Note (a) Child Ill health index has been calculated by author using data from National Family Health Survey 3; (b) National Family Health Survey 3 for the other variables

Appendix 2

Mean values and standard deviations of variables

Variable	Mean	Standard Deviation
Child Ill health index (CIHI)	0.491	0.322
Teenage pregnancy (TP)	12.45	6.57
Maternal care index (MCI)	0.36	0.25
Women literacy rate (WLR)	14.31	7.41

References

Antony, G. M., & Rao, K. V. (2007). A composite index to explain variations in poverty, health, nutritional status and standard of living: Use of multivariate statistical methods. *Public Health, 121*(8), 578–587.

Hanna, B. (2001). Negotiating motherhood: The struggles of teenage mothers. *Journal of Advanced Nursing, 34*(4), 456–464.

Haveman, R. H., Wolfe, B. L., & Peterson, E. (1997). Children of early childbearers as young adults (Vol. 757). Institute for Research on Poverty, University of Wisconsin-Madison.

Hillis, S. D., Anda, R. F., Dube, S. R., Felitti, V. J., Marchbanks, P. A., & Marks, J. S. (2004). The association between adverse childhood experiences and adolescent pregnancy, long-term psychosocial consequences, and fetal death. *Pediatrics, 113*(2), 320–327.

Moore, K. A., Morrison, D. R., & Greene, A. D. (1997). Effects on the children born to adolescent mothers. In *Kids having kids: Economic costs and social consequences of teen pregnancy.* Washington, DC: The Urban Institute. To order visit: http://www.urban.org/publications/106764.html.

Quinlivan, J. A. (2005). Teenagers who plan parenthood. *Sexual health, 1*(4), 201–208.

Rodriquez, C., & Moore, N. B. (1995). Perceptions of pregnant/parenting teens: Reframing issues for an integrated approach to pregnancy problems. *Adolescence, 30*(119), 685.

Skinner, S. R., & Hickey, M. (2003). Current priorities for adolescent sexual and reproductive health in Australia. *The Medical Journal of Australia, 179*(3), 158–161.

Williams, H., & Davidson, S. (2004). Improving adolescent sexual and reproductive health. *A view from Australia: Learning from world's best practice, Sex Health, 1,* 95–100.

Wolfe, B. L., & Perozek, M. (1997). Teen children's health and health care use. Institute for Research on Poverty, University of Wisconsin-Madison

Woodward, L., Fergusson, D. M., & Horwood, L. J. (2001). Risk factors and life processes associated with teenage pregnancy: Results of a prospective study from birth to 20 Years. *Journal of Marriage and Family, 63,* 1170–1184.

Chapter 5
Determinants of Psychological Well-being and Its Impact on Mental Health

Gurudas Bandyopadhyay

5.1 Introduction

Researchers now are more inclined to measure life satisfaction as a measure of well-being. There has been a paradigm shift from emphasizing on negative aspects like disorder and dysfunction to focusing on well-being and positive mental health. This shift has been especially prominent in current psychological research (Ryff and Singer 1998: Seligman 2002). This positive perspective is also supported by World Health Organization (WHO), where positive mental health is considered as a state of well-being, where individuals can realize their abilities, can cope with life stressors and work productively to make a positive contribution (WHO 2001). Several humanistic psychologists have developed theories and practices pertaining to human happiness, well-being and flourishing. Work on basic life tendencies and fulfilment, conceptualization of personality change and expressing a higher level of PWB have significantly contributed to the development of PWB construct, which is largely exhibited through one's health, happiness and prosperity (Ryff 1995). Positive psychologists like Seligman (1998) have found empirical support for the humanistic theories of flourishing. Positive psychology is stated as the scientific study of what makes life worth living (Seligman and Csikszentmihalyi 2000; Seligman et al. 2005). In addition, positive psychology has moved ahead, where research is being carried out on positive experiences like happiness and engagement, positive traits like character strength and virtues, positive relations like friendship and larger institutions like family, local community (Peterson 2006). Ryff (1989) proposed six dimensions of psychological well-being, and Ryff and

G. Bandyopadhyay (✉)
Regional College of Management, Bengaluru, India
e-mail: gurudas.iitkgp@gmail.com

G. Bandyopadhyay
Department of HSS, IIT Kharagpur, Kharagpur, India

U.K. De et al. (eds.), *Issues on Health and Healthcare in India*, India Studies in Business and Economics, https://doi.org/10.1007/978-981-10-6104-2_5

Keyes (1995) indicated that person with higher levels of PWB are mentally strong and can better utilize their capabilities. Thus, the recognition that well-being of employees is more important, calls for its exploration on how the well-being can be enhanced in Indian social cultural context where the construct of well-being may be understood differently. It is argued that the drivers of well-being would also be different depending on our context as Indians believe in collectivism and may be driven spirituality when it comes to well-being (Sinha 1982; Sinha et al. 2001). Collectivism and individualism are viewed as cultural syndromes that extensively differentiate cultures in terms of values, norms, beliefs in India, which is geographically well spreaded and comprising over 1.2 billion people. A comprehensive understanding of the dynamics of psychological well-being will help in enhancing mental health and improving better engagement and social involvement.

Thus, there is a need to pay attention to the psychological well-being of employees as it is crucial and it influences behaviour, decision making and interactions with colleagues; and also spilling over to the family and social life (Warr 1990). The success of an organization and its fallout depends largely on employee engagement and their performance, which in turn is dependent on the employee's psychological well-being (Kahn 1990). This study has focused on positive aspects of well-being. It proposes to examine the factors affecting psychological well-being, and its consequences on mental health and thereby employee engagement. Available research documents covering similar and separate concepts were reviewed, and evidence of the benefits that psychological well-being confers on mental health were established. Thus, it is realized that the integration of psychological well-being with individual and organizational factors can provide a clear understanding on how to improve it to ensure better mental health and so employee engagement level.

5.2 Theoretical Framework and Significance of the Study

The basic source of well-being is of two types—first, well-being is produced as a consequence of intrinsic benefits derived from the activities engaged in by an individual, and people derive utilities from the existence of various stocks of the societies and satisfaction with these goods. Thus, the conceptualization of PWB has emerged from the research interests of two groups of social scientists—economists who were concerned with material well-being where well-being depends upon the availability of goods and pleasure. Second, sociologists, social psychologists who relate well-being with social indicators like the quality of life. This perspective views economic concern with material goods and service flow as too narrow. They suggest that wealth alone cannot bring life satisfaction, and there is a need for a subjective assessment of well-being through empirical investigation using subjective measures. Another theory which emphasizes the importance of social context in PWB is self-determination theory (Ryan and Deci 2000), which influences PWB through the need satisfaction related to competence, relatedness and autonomy, and social environment allows the satisfaction of these needs by promoting optimum outcome for personal development and quality of experiences. More recently, two major theories of PWB represent approaches to understand mental health and satisfaction: (1) Theory of emotional well-being, which suggests that PWB is related to life satisfaction and lack of psychological distress and (2) The theory of positive functioning where PWB refers to aspects of human development and existential life challenges. In this context, life satisfaction is the key indicator of well-being, and is considered as a cognitive component and complement happiness (affective dimension of positive functioning). Thus, I have used the theoretical framework suggested by Ryff and Keyes (1995) which suggest that positive affect and life satisfaction are important for well-being. The significance and importance of the study emphasize on following aspects:

(1) The study of psychological well-being is important and relevant in today's business context, which is very chaotic and uncertain. The understanding of PWB, and its social, behavioural factors results in enhanced well-being, prevention of psychological dysfunction leading to better mental health, engagement and involvement.
(2) The study aims to identify and measure the range of variables affecting the well-being of the employees, which includes an understanding of the construct of PWB, and their determinants and outcome variables in Indian social cultural context.
(3) The study assumes a significant relationship between determinants of PWB and outcome variables like mental health and engagement in organizational context. It would have significant implications as how to enhance the well-being of employees and their engagement level.

The study is important in terms of its implications for employees at work place as it would help in identifying the level of PWB to develop proper intervention strategies for its enhancement, as increased PWB would result in better mental health, more engagement at work for better performance. It would also make employees motivated, happy and satisfied, which help in improved productivity. When employee flourishing is ascertained in this way, it helps to reduce some mental and behavioural problems instead of focusing on treatment and control of mental disorders. The findings of this study would have practical utility for managers and researchers have given the effects of continued reforms taking place in the work place, and how it influences employee well-being. An organization can develop their policies based on research evidence to address the employee-related issue of mental health, how to increase their engagement level and make them socially active and engaged. This study can also provide information that could be instrumental in enhancing individual performance through improved well-being. The focus on PWB can provide a basis to understand its impact on the workplace and add to the existing knowledge base, and also check its effects on employee physical and mental health which affects their organizational engagement positively.

5.3 The Literature Review

The literature review has identified several factors affecting PWB. A number of factors were identified in the literature related to PWB, which include individual and organizational factors. In addition, several demographic characteristics were reported to check its relationship with PWB. In view of the large number of factors affecting PWB, only a select number of these variables were grouped under individual and organizational factors. Variables were selected, which were supposed to be relevant, important and critical, and contribute to enhance employee PWB. The strength of association of PWB with mental health and organizational engagement is explored. A brief overview of the literature related to these concepts and variables are discussed below.

5.3.1 *The Concept of Well-Being*

Well-being (WB) is argued to be a contented state of being happy, healthy and prosperous. It is a concept which includes both physical and psychological well-being (Warr 1990). Within a business or organization, employee WB is directly related to the climate and culture of the company as set forth, and monitored by the executives, managers, and human resource staff. This in turn has a direct relationship to the triple bottom line, i.e. economic growth, social and environmental development to ensure all-round growth with sustainable development. It is argued that WB shows influenced by three main parts, viz. Individual (physical and psychological health), organizational (workplace culture, environment, income and benefits) and social (relationship and conflicts). Harter et al. (2003) observed that workplace WB and performance are complementary. WB at work is not merely managing a safe and conducive work environment with the aim of no injury and no occupational illness to employees, but it actively assists employees to maximize their physical and mental health to ensure personal growth, engagement and contribution to organizations, fulfil the purpose of life, and have a network of relationships. Five domains of WB are generally practiced, e.g. physical, emotional, values, organizational practices and personal development.

Ryan and Deci (2001) suggested that WB is a complex construct that concerns optimal experience and functioning. WB is concerned beyond money and connected to fitness, nutrition, diet and good health; work life balance; intrinsic happiness; social, cultural and spiritual development; satisfaction and motivation. Organizations having a desire to have healthier workplaces should focus on employees and not to neglect supervisor's attitude, as supervisors can affect employees WB. WB may be perceived as subjective well-being (SWB), which is an important ingredient of a good life (Diener et al. 1998), and help people to live fulfilling lives as evaluated by themselves (Biswas and Diener 2001). It lays emphasis on subjective experiences of the individuals and life satisfaction (Sousa and Lyubomirsky 2001). Spiritual well-being is a more abstract state than social or physical well-being, but it is a most intangible state, and also the most evident when it is lacking. Workplace spirituality is stated as the recognition that employees have an inner life which nourishes, and is nourished by meaningful work taking place in the community (Ashmos and Duchon 2000). Spirituality gives oneness with other co-workers, family and friends in the organization as well as in the society (Petchsawang and Duchon 2009; Rego and Cunha 2008). Swami Vivekananda taught that pleasure is not the goal of a person, but the wisdom (Jnana) is the goal of all life. Pleasure comes to an end. The highest wisdom must be the spiritual knowledge and with this real knowledge, will come bliss. It is also taught from Katha Upanishad that both perfection and enjoyment approach a person. The wise chooses the perfection in preference to enjoyment (Ashrama 2005). Care for employee WB from all such angles is the feed to improve their all-round personal development and engagement level in the organization, treating it as a basic necessity for the satisfactory condition of existence and sustenance, characterised by health, happiness and prosperity.

Health is a prerequisite for happiness and the relationship between physical health (PH), mental health (MH) and happiness appears to be remarkably strong. Pleasant emotions can foster health and longevity. Taking care of your PH is a first step towards developing mental and emotional health, e.g. exercise not only strengthens one's heart and lungs, but also releases endorphins, powerful chemicals that energize and lift mood. There is a strong relationship between PWB and physical health as observed by many researchers (Roysamb et al. 2003). Happy and healthy people live longer and enjoy life on the fulfilment of purpose (Ryff et al. 2004). Maslow (1943, 1970) noted that the behaviour of the healthy person is less determined by anxiety, fear, insecurity, guilt and shame, and more by truth, logic, self-actualisation and satisfaction, justice, reality and fairness. The daily activities and choices affect people physically and emotionally like getting enough rest; learning about nutrition and practicing it and exercise to relieve stress and lift the mood. One should try to maintain a balance between daily responsibilities and the things one can enjoy with the right sense like games and sports, social engagements.

World Health Organization (WHO 2001) defined health as "a complete state of physical, mental and social well-being and not merely the absence of disease or infirmity". Social well-being involves interaction with others, including friends, family, educators and other members of the society. The relationship amongst people helps stimulate physical and mental faculties and improve overall well-being. Health must not be equated only with the absence of illness rather than the presence of wellness (Ryff and Singer 1996). Organization-centred view of Luthans (2002) and the employee centred view of Wright and Staw (1999) can be integrated into the business value model of employee well-being and health. Approach to Integral Health Management (Zwetsloot and Pot 2004) indicates favourable outcomes, both for the employee as well as for the organization (Bakker and Schaufeli 2008) through the development of employee WB. DeNeve and Cooper (1998) found a relationship between personality and several dimensions of subjective well-being. Positive emotions facilitated by meaningful actions, encourage individual contributions and fulfilment, promote a chance to prosper continually (Harter et al. 2003). In contrast, emotional deficiency can lead to uncertainty, lack of initiative, low morale and poor work performance (Jonker and Scholtz 2004).

Happiness is considered as a measure of individual and social progress in the recent world happiness report (Helliwell et al. 2013), which indicates how people rate both their emotions and their lives as a whole. It is a feeling of well-being one experiences with emotions in immediate situations, and also sense of life satisfaction based on the recent past (Lyubomorsky 2013; Meyers and Diener 1995). In happy moods, behaviour changes significantly, affects positive psychological capital and produce high-performance levels on the jobs. Researchers emphasized that happiness is something for which we strive and work hard (Argyle 1999; Freedman 1978). Happiness is determined not by an individual's material condition like financial richness, poverty, health and illness, but by individual's prosperity in various forms of wealth including character strength and virtues as well as moral character. Happiness with spiritual understanding is extremely valuable in one's life, and gives enormous positive outcomes at the individual and social level. A strong cyclic relationship exists amongst happiness, WB and socially desirable outcomes. These approaches provide complementary insights to enrich one's ability to assess whether life is getting better (Tella and MacCulloch 2006; Pavot and Diener 1993). True happiness depends on the fulfilment of the purpose of life, work life balance and personal and organizational culture. Temporary happiness based on substance abuse and other compulsive problems destroy lives of millions of individuals and their families, while occupational satisfaction and warm family and social relations count more towards continued happiness. Happy people tend to function better in life and are more productive and satisfied (Diener 2000; Ryan and Deci 2001). Positive illusions have also been observed to be related to happiness. People who have high self-esteem and self-confidence are more likely to be happier than people who lack these perceptions (Freedman 1978). Happy people have higher opinions of themselves as compared to those who are relatively distressed (Taylor and Brown 1988), show self serving causal attributions (Kuiper 1978); extended beliefs in environmental mastery (Abramson and Alloy 1981); and are more likely to be unrealistically optimistic (Alloy and Ahrens 1987), which improve their overall WB.

Belle et al. (2000) pointed out that the experience of happiness is not limited to the wealthy, nor do riches ensure happiness. Yet wealth, poverty and economic inequality have profound implications for the well-being of the individuals. For the relatively poor, money can buy happiness, but for the relatively well off, more money does not typically mean more happiness, although it is established in the literature that unemployed individuals show significantly low score on SWB (Clark 2001; Shamir 1986), and this affects their PWB. Happiness, however, in general is more important than money (Diener and Seligman 2004). Happy people show better physical and mental health outcomes and behaviour (Lyubomirsky et al. 2005). Studies have shown the linkage between happiness (Graham et al. 2004), welfare and prosperity (Sen 2008), life satisfaction (Aspinwall and Taylor 1993) and PWB (Mroczek and Spiro 2005).

Prosperity is another indicator of employee PWB. The state of being prosperous indicates all-round prosperity not only for monetary and materialistic gains, but also the development of individual personality and qualities, character strength, family relations, social relationships by making more friends, promotions, developed in spiritual strength and fulfilment of life's purpose. Prosperity is the state of flourishing, acquiring good fortune and successful social status and the development in the emotional and spiritual field. Workplace spirituality is noted as the recognition that employees have an inner life, which is nourished by meaningful work in the organization and the society (Ashmos and Duchon 2000). It is also found by Mishra (2001) that effort orientation rather than concern for outcome leads to greater intrinsic satisfaction and prosperity.

The economic notions of prosperity often compete or interact negatively with health, happiness or spiritual notions of prosperity. In Buddhism, prosperity is viewed with an emphasis on spirituality. This perspective can be at odds with capitalistic notions of prosperity, due to their association with greed. The data from social surveys show that an increase in income does not result in a lasting increase in happiness. PWB is observed to be associated with prosperity, through the development of health, happiness, openness, love and freedom. The condition of being prosperous is judged by success, good fortune and fulfilment of the purpose of life, which are also leading indicators of PWB. Researchers argue that part of adult life satisfaction can be accounted for by satisfaction with work (Spector 1997), and accordingly prosperity is estimated by the satisfaction level. Employee survey shows that the majority of employees desire greater meaning and personal development of their work and feel prospering when they realize their work as fulfilling individual and organizational objectives and socially meaningful.

5.3.2 Psychological Well-Being

Psychological well-being (PWB) is generally stated as one's evaluative reaction to life, either in terms of life satisfaction or emotional reaction. While traditionally PWB has been defined by negative outcomes like depression, anxiety, mental disorders; over time, the term has taken a positive side (Keyes and Megyar-Moe 2003). Major dimensions of PWB include empowerment, self-initiation, purpose in life, self-acceptance, autonomy, environmental mastery. These skills can be learnt to promote PWB by cultivating supporting relationships, learning different coping strategies and develop meaning and purpose in the recovery process (Jacobson and Greenley 2001). Diminished PWB has been associated with difficulties in coping with major transitions in life (Ryff 1995; Edwards 1992; Diener et al. 2003); an increase in distress symptoms (Rafanelli et al. 2000); negative self-evaluations and impaired productivity (Lindfors and Lundberg 2002). Enhanced PWB has shown to predict successful identity formation (Vleioras and Bosma 2005) and improve coping with trauma (Ryff and Singer 1998). It also predicts improvement in physical health (Lindfors and Lundberg 2002; Ryff et al. 2004) and enhancing one's ability to bounce back after hardships (Ryff et al. 1998). It is a vital factor guiding employee behaviour, which in turn is closely related to employee satisfaction, engagement and performance standard. This study proposes to examine the impact of PWB on certain employee behaviour, which considerably accounts for productivity, organizational growth and development of social capital. The PWB includes emotional aspects like happiness (Diener and Seligman 2002) as well as purposeful aspects (Ryff and Keyes 1995). Accordingly, the core dimensions of PWB include self-acceptance which accounts for positive attitude towards self and evaluation of one's past life; positive relations with others showing trusting relationship and concern for welfare of others; autonomy with the sense of self determination and regulation of behaviour from within; environmental mastery, i.e. capacity to manage effectively one's life and the surrounding environment making use of available opportunities; and purpose in life, which emphasizes the belief that one's life is purposeful and meaningful and a sense of continued personal growth being open to new experiences having the feeling of self-development (Ryff and Singer 1996). Ryff (1989) describes these factors as contributing to people's experience of WB, over the PWB structure proposed by Bradburn (1969). Psychological well-being is the affective and purposive psychological state that people experience in the workplace, Robertson and Cooper (2010) integrates it with the individual, organizational and social outcomes. Individual outcomes through satisfaction and increased presence and productivity, organizational outcomes through high employee engagement and customer satisfaction and social outcomes are envisaged through more social involvement, better relationships and coping behaviours.

Employee PWB is argued to be associated with good health, happiness, peace and prosperity (HHPP). Hedonic approach focuses on happiness and explains well-being in terms of pleasure attainment. Eudaimonic approach focuses on self-realization and illustrates well-being in terms of the degree to which a person is fully functioning (Ryan and Deci 2001) and focuses on prosperity. Most of the earlier researches on well-being were concerned with the hedonic view of well-being (Diener 1984). Diener et al. (2010) identified life satisfaction as one of the aspects of PWB. Hedonic view states that WB is a function of attaining valued, expected outcomes (Ryan and Deci 2001). Based on the eudaimonic perspective, contemporary researchers have argued that PWB is a multidimensional construct (Abbey and Andrews 1985; Bradburn 1969; Carmeli et al. 2009; Huppert 2009; Marks et al. 2002; Ryff 2014; Ryff and Singer 2006; Strauser and Lustig 2008; Wissing and Temane 2008; Wright and Cropanzano 2000). Social science researchers have also assessed PWB on the basis of three important measures such as self-esteem, self-acceptance and life satisfaction. But very few literature are available on important predictors of psychological well-being from different perspectives. Ryff (1989) asserts that PWB is the state at which an individual can function psychologically well realizing their true potential. Psychologically healthy individuals have warm and trusting relationships, feel they are growing as a person, have a purpose in life, feel they can shape the environment around them to suit their needs and feel enabled to direct their actions to attain the objectives (Ryff and Keyes 1995). Since PWB is more than the absence of illness and connected to fulfilment of purpose, it needs to be further explored in its own right. Avey et al. (2010) concluded in their research that future research is required to understand the predictors of PWB, which, including Psycap, may be the most appropriate technique to enhance employee PWB to meet specific personal and organizational challenges. This study aims cater to such needs of clarifying predictors of PWB and accordingly hypothesis H_2 is formulated to test how individual factors positively affect PWB.

PWB is a subjective term that appears differently to different people, based on their perceptions. It generally means contentment, satisfaction with all elements in life, self-actualization, peace, prosperity and happiness. It is very difficult to provide a definitive list of traits, which mirrors PWB. It takes care of employee health, emotions, happiness and life satisfaction on past performance, present engagement and future opportunities. Factors that affect PWB are feeling of accomplishment, using one's abilities to the fullest extent, adequate recognition of works by superiors and peers, promotional opportunities and good remuneration. Indicators of PWB are job satisfaction, life satisfaction, career satisfaction and life stress. Researchers have found meaningful relationship between PWB and performance in the workplace (Cropanzano and Wright 1999; Wright and Cropanzano 2000; Wright and Staw 1999). It is illustrated by Seligman and Csikszentmihalyi (2000) that psychology is not just the study of weakness and damage; it is also the study of personality strength and virtue. Many personal attributes, organizational systems and social situations are intricately related to PWB, which affects individual health, organizational engagement and social capital base. It is a challenge for the organizations to improve employee PWB, which in turn will benefit them increasingly in the long run. Organizations are constantly searching an integral approach that benefits organizations while employees and societies also remain benefitted, and it would be interesting to find out how PWB manifests in developing economies like India. This has incited interest for the formulation of hypothesis H_5 and to test the same.

In this flat world (Friedman 2005), competition is a part of life, for existence and survival, and requires higher than average performance (Luthans et al. 2006). Organizations not only require to develop the human resource and to keep them constantly engaged for the benefit of themselves, but also take care of their PWB to keep them happy, healthy and prosperous. Donald et al. (2005) found that employee productivity can be predicted by PWB. PWB comes up from the experience of the individual. Some researchers have pointed out the role of personality and social support in PWB (Nahawat and Rathore 1996). Based on the effect of personality characteristics on PWB, this study is focussed on finding out the specific relationship of two factors, viz. Agreeableness and conscientiousness on PWB and accordingly hypothesis H_2 is formulated.

There are multiple aspects of PWB (Eudaimonic and Hedonic), and higher levels of purposeful life engagement (Eudaimonic Well-Being) are associated with PWB, leading to work and personal life outcomes. There is considerable research on the positive relationship between PWB and performance at work (Diener and Seligman 2002), mental health (Warr 1990) and physical health (Roysamb et al. 2003), which are found at times to co-vary with happiness and positivity levels. Employees feel a higher level of PWB, if they have a high degree of satisfaction with themselves, the organization and the society involved; if their mood is good (positive effect), and if only occasionally they feel unpleasant emotions (Fierro 2006). The perception of PWB can be considered as the cognitive component of life satisfaction as it involves an assessment of how people lead their life (Diener and Suh 2001). Basically, PWB refers to well-being of the individual that takes care of creativeness (like emotions and intelligence); coping capability (stress management and beliefs); social relationship (friendship, love); physical necessities (nutrition, exercise) and essential requirements (spirituality, culture). Higher PWB does not require an employee to feel good all the time but being able to manage painful situations for long-term gains and continual flourishing (Huppert 2009). Effect of social status, income, ageing and marital tensions on WB are studied by researchers (Deaton 2008). Age and gender differences in perception of PWB are also studied by researchers (Ryff and Keyes 1995). But such research on the effect of demographic variables on employee PWB in Indian context is much less observed. Keeping in view such gap in information, hypothesis H_1 is formulated for study in-depth and it is tested.

A substantial body of research is available on the effect of workplace factors and how they interact with personal factors (Abbey and Andrews 1985) to affect employee psychological health, and shows a clear association between workplace conditions and well-being. PWB appears to be concerned with psychological functioning and experiences and entails the perception of engagement with the existential challenges of life, e.g. pursuing meaningful goals, growing as a person and establishing quality ties with others (Keyes 2007). PWB is more than the achievement of happiness, an appropriate balance of positive and negative effect and overall life satisfaction and develops from a person's striving for perfection and the realization of their true potential (Ryff 1995). PWB is the by-product of a life that is well-lived (Ryff and Singer 1998). The components of PWB may be highlighted as effective component, that is the frequency of experiencing pleasurable feelings and the extent to which the positive effects outweighs the negative effects; social component, which represents meaningful interpersonal relationship (Ryff and Singer 1998); cognitive component, which encompasses self-acceptance, optimism, resilience, motivation (Wissing and Temane 2008); spiritual component, which seek deeper quests in life and carefully conceived life's purpose, which is also conceived as connectedness to a higher being.

The concept of PWB has thus come up with both pleasure and purpose and a workable view of PWB, therefore, needs to encompass both the degree to which employee's positive experience at work, and the extent to which they experience meaning and purpose in roles and responsibilities. Integration of the six core dimensions of PWB broadens the view of PWB beyond the hedonic constructs of happiness and satisfaction. It is a multidimensional human process that involves an individual setting and pursuing personal goals, maximizing one's potential, helping organizations to fulfil objectives, developing meaningful social relationships, successfully managing environmental demands and opportunities, exercising self-direction and developing positive self-regard (Ryff and Singer 1996). It was found by Wright and Staw (1999) that employees can have the opportunity to learn ways to enhance their PWB through training based interventions, which organizations must take care.

5.3.3 Determinants of Psychological Well-Being

The determinants of PWB are categorised here at two different levels, which incorporates very relevant and important factors related to the individual (conscientiousness, optimism and resilience) and organizational (organizational culture). A brief description of these factors is given below.

5.3.3.1 Individual Factors

Major determinants of PWB at the individual level were identified as personality traits like conscientiousness, and optimism and resilience. Personality appears to be related to most of the psychological contract dimensions and it affects mind set, behaviour and work performance (Bozionelos 2004). Nahawat and Rathore (1996) have pointed out the role of personality and social support for PWB. The important characteristics of personality factor which concerns PWB include self-image, social, personality, leadership, competency and mastery, intelligence, high aspiration level, optimism, being worry free, religious and more realistic than idealistic. Optimism and resilience, the two important aspects of positive psychological capital (PPC) are the significant contributors to performance, which can considerably change the status of employee's PWB. Positive Psychology traits act as buffers against mental illness and depression and directly affect PWB.

Conscientiousness

Conscientiousness is a trait of being careful, the quality of acting according to one's conscience. It includes elements such as self-discipline, personal confidence and the need for achievement. Conscientious people are generally hard working and reliable. They value duty, competence and achievement (Costa and McCrae 1990). Conscientiousness focuses on how people approach their work, show a sense of obligation to their work, have high intention for better job performance, career success, motivation and higher job satisfaction (Barrick and Mount 1996; Jawahar and Carr 2007). Researchers have shown that conscientiousness contributes to the sense of purpose. Those high in conscientiousness are generally more motivated and strenuous, efficient and reliable in task performance, while those low in conscientiousness tend to be disorganized, careless, inefficient and unreliable (Costa and McCrae 1992). Conscientiousness is believed to alter mood due to its direct effect on dedication to duty, performance and achievement (Costa and McCrae 1990). Empirical evidence suggests that conscientiousness is an indicator of actual performance tendencies, since a person low in conscientiousness tend to have poorer personal health habits, lower perceptions of ability, worse job performance and proficiency (Barrick and Mount 1996), poorer academic performance (Digman 1990), less restraint from dishonest activities, poorer leadership abilities, and are less compliant with home work assignment during treatment (Miller 1986).

The sense of duty and consequent obligation impacts degree of well-being felt by individuals (Marzuki 2013). Positive emotions and sense of purpose are normally measured to check the degree of PWB felt by an individual. Individual low on conscientiousness is not motivated to perform a task, less organized and more disorganized at home and office. Conscientiousness improves performance at the work place and appears to be the specific personality trait that correlates with performance across all ranks and files. In contemporary psychology, the five factor model (FFM) (Costa and McCrae 1992), and global Factors of personality, conscientiousness is exemplified by being disciplined, organized and achievement oriented; a tendency to show self-discipline, act dutifully, be efficient, focussed and organized, aim for achievement, planned rather than showing spontaneous behaviour. It is also linked to job performance (Luthans 2002) and job satisfaction (Schimmack et al. 2004). Conscientiousness is expected to enhance the possibility of constructive encounters at work resulting in better performance and high PWB among employees. Thoughtfulness and goal-oriented behaviour make them more careful for details. It increases positive experiences at the organizational and social levels, which help people to improve their PWB. Thus, the literature review indicates its positive link with employee PWB and it is taken for study and hypothesis is formulated to test it with empirical data.

Optimism

Optimism is defined as the attributions one makes and the explanatory style one uses in response to events (Seligman 1998). It indicates the conviction that the future holds desirable outcomes irrespective of present position and one's personal ability to control those outcomes. The sense of optimism may be derived from multiple external and internal sources and assistance of others as well as personal strength (Marshall and Lang 1990) and benefits of situations that offer limited opportunity for perceived personal control. Optimism may be a more powerful determinant of psychological and behavioural adjustment. Scheier and Carver (1992) argued that optimism is associated with and leads to securing positive outcomes, whereas pessimism is associated with, and leads to negative outcomes. Optimistic people possess long-term vision being more realistic in nature, and are not demoralized by temporary petty failures, rather willing to see the big picture, and persevere at a task longer to fulfil their goals (Bandura 1986) to enjoy the fulfilment of purpose.

Researchers have found that optimism is an important causal determinant of both psychological (Scheier and Carver 1985) and physical adjustments (Chang 1998). Optimism, the inclination to expect favourable outcomes, is linked to both psychological (Carver and Gaines 1987; Scheier and Carver 1985) and physical well-being (Carver and Scheier 2001).

The findings suggest that dispositional optimism and anxiety have unique, albeit relatively similar effects on psychological and physical well-being. Similarly, optimism is associated with mood, coping and immune change in respect of stress (Scheier and Carver 1985; Forgeard and Seligman 2012; Nikolaou et al. 2007). Optimism and hope cause better resistance to depression when bad events strike in challenging jobs. Optimism is theoretically and empirically supported to be state like (Schneider et al. 2001; Seligman 2002). It is future focussed and provides buffering between the negative impact of unfavourable events and positive expectation for the future outcome and enhances the positive impact of favourable events (Peterson 2000; Forgeard and Seligman 2012).

Thus, optimism is a significant predictor of changes in perceived stress, depression and social support over time. It appears to be a mental attitude that interprets situations and events and helps to look forward to the future. It inculcates an attitude of hope and strength for future conditions. It appears to be very much future focused whereby optimist is more likely to anticipate that future event positively in nature. Together, the elements of optimism combine to impact upon performance (Judge et al. 1998). Nikolaou et al. (2007) stated that participants with an optimistic explanatory style improved in performance on a test after a failure feedback, while those with a pessimistic style did not. Evidence suggests that optimism can be developed within individuals (Seligman 1998). Several studies have found its relationship with performance and satisfaction (Luthans et al. 2006), job satisfaction and organizational commitment (Kluemper et al. 2009), and WB (Avey et al. 2010), PWB (Singh and Mansi 2009). Optimists expect better outcomes in all situations, and show higher commitments because of their positive thoughts and consequent feelings (Olason and Roger 2001). Researchers also found that optimism has considerable impact on job satisfaction, life satisfaction and PWB (Peterson et al. 1982).

Resilience

Resilience appears to be a class of phenomena resulting good outcomes in spite of serious threats to adaptation or development and results from the operation of basic human adaptive systems (Masten 2001). It is the capacity to bounce back from adversity, uncertainty and failure or even with positive and wonderful changes such as increased interest and responsibilities (Luthans and Youssef 2004). At the heart of resilience is the concept of adaptability, particularly when faced with adversity.

It is a positive way of coping with dangers or distress, ability to recuperate from stress, conflict, failure and change. Contu (2002) identified three characteristics of resilient people (and organizations) as a staunch acceptance of reality, a deep belief, often buttressed by strongly held values that life is meaningful, and an uncanny ability to improve. Lyubomorsky (2008) concluded happier and positive people are more resilient in the face of hardships.

The literature review suggests that it is past to present focused, and provides recovery from unfavourable events and maintains or extends the status quo. It can be developed through training based interventions. Resilient people can go through setbacks and burn-out situations reasonably well (Akgemci et al. 2013). They may even bounce back to higher levels of performance, finding new meaning of life and values (Luthans and Youssef 2004). It is chosen as an important determinant of PWB as psychological status and health of a person strongly depends on such an attribute.

The building of resilience call for the development of the adaptive systems (including cognitive and learning processes). Resilience has a clear impact on performance, and can be measured (Schwarzer and Knoll 2003), and developed at the individual level (Luthans and Youssef 2004). People with good emotional health possess the ability to bounce back from adversity, trauma and stress. One of the key factors in resilience is the ability to balance stress and emotions. The capacity to recognize one's emotions and express them appropriately helps them to avoid getting stuck in depression, anxiety and have persistence even to face the failures (McFarlin 1985). Contu (2002) indicated that resilience allows building bridges between present hardships to a better future. Researchers in occupational health and health psychology have demonstrated that PWB is influenced by resilience on challenged thriving and decent living (Keyes 2007; Ryff and Singer 2003).

5.3.3.2 Organizational Factors

PWB is determined not only by individual factors, but also by organizational factor. Some of the important and meaningful factors which were derived from the literature as having influence on PWB include organizational culture. A brief description of these variables is given below.

Organizational Culture

Organizational Culture (OC) is generally perceived as the people's behaviour in an organization and the meaning attached to it. It is stated as a summation of shared values, beliefs, assumptions and behavioural norms (Chang and Lu 2007; O'Reilly et al. 1991). Researchers indicated that OC may be useful in depicting the combined features of an organization's management practices, especially those, related to managing its human resources for individual and organizational prosperity

(Burke et al. 2006; Patterson 2001). OC reflects the shared behaviours, beliefs and values regarding goals and activities specially characterising an organization (Hofstede 1994; Wallace et al. 1999). OC shows the degree to which people are team oriented and encouraged to take risks, to be innovative, to exhibit the precision with attention to details, aggressive and competitive, rather than only being co-operative (Amar 2004; Anderson et al. 2002; Parish et al. 2008; Robins 1994). Denison (1984) organizational culture model identified the important factors involved in culture, which are important to employees and employers, wherein at the centre of the model were organization's basic beliefs and assumptions with four traits like involvement, consistency, mission and adaptability, each comprising three dimensions, e.g. involvement indicated developing employee capability, their empowerment and team orientation where value is given on working cooperatively (Bond et al. 2005; Ciulla 2000). The effect of OC is felt to have profound implications on employee psychological understanding and behaviour.

Cultures may support creativity, virtue and the highest qualities in life only when they are steady, prosperous and development oriented (Amar 2004; Denison 1984; Denison and Mishra 1995). Human strengths and virtues like courage, future mindedness, optimism, interpersonal skill, faith, work ethics, hope, honesty and perseverance help to prevent major emotional disorders, making people stronger, engaged and more productive (Bews and Rossouw 2002; Gonzalez et al. 2006; Michalos 1990). Organizations are supposed to develop such human strengths by adjoining global values to their local values (Sinha 2008).

Parasuraman et al. (1996) indicated that organizational culture on work family variables deserves greater attention along with structural reviews for effective leadership, administration and managerial effectiveness. Organizations should maintain a safe and healthy work environment and supporting climate that contributes to the well-being, satisfaction and motivation of employees (Bennett 2002; Clarke 1999; ILO 2005; McGuire and McLaren 2009). Dimensions of organizational culture indicate the constraints and the positive factors concerning the organization, how managers focus on outcomes rather than on how these outcomes are achieved, and work is organized around teams rather than individuals (Deery and Iversion 2005; Loscocco and Spitze 1990; Miyashiro 1996; Ilardi et al. 1993; Daus and Joplin 1999; Felfe and Schyns 2006). Management decisions should take into account the effects on people in the organization to have a consistent culture (Rice et al. 1985). The organization culture depicts what a group learns over time or the shared experiences (Schein 1990). It inspires loyalty in employees and motivates them to trust and to do the right things and the employee—organization fit leads to individual and organizational satisfaction and high performance (Singh and Srivastava 2009; O'Reily et al. 1991; Clark 2001). Out of the total cultural constituents, work family culture of the organization plays a crucial role in placing an effective impression in the minds of the employees which predominantly effect the mental health of employees and their behaviour on- the- job and off- the- job.

5.3.3.3 Impact of Psychological Well-Being on Mental Health and Employee Behaviour

In order to examine the impact of PWB and employee behaviour on some important work-related outcomes, this study has considered mental health in individual context which helps to improve behaviour and engagement level ensuring all round growth. Concerned details of these variables are described below.

Mental Health

Mental Health (MH) refers to the condition of psychological perception of one's health or emotional well-being. From the perspective of positive psychology, mental health may include an individual's ability to enjoy life amidst challenges and make a balance between life activities and efforts to gain psychological resilience. It includes not just the absence of mental health problems and other psychological issues, but the presence and nurturing of positive characteristics, showing the way people feel about themselves, the quality of their relationships, their ability to manage emotions, and deal with difficulties and showing enthusiasm for further personal development and welfare of others (Avison et al. 2007; Fredrickson 2004). So, it is the good effect of well-being and specially PWB.

PWB and MH are two stand alone individual concepts but are strongly related to each other. Higher PWB affect mental health condition and helps in exhibiting higher levels of happiness in employees, which may include their feeling about themselves and management, and their feelings and dealing with challenging situations, their quality of relationships and positive feeling about past life and present life. These are surfaced through their good physical health condition, less anger and anxiety level, degree of involvement in social functions and activities, level of prosperity and happiness. The shift in emphasis from disorder to WB and then to positive mental health is prominent in research studies (Ryff and Singer 1998; Seligman 2002).

The ability to be happy or relatively contended had been important criteria for mental health (MH) and WB is supported by many studies (Diener 1984). Jourard and Landsman (1980) identified few criteria for better MH like self-confidence, ability to care for others, openness to new ideas and people, creativity and the ability to do productive works. It can be explained by qualities like self-realization, self-reliance and self-actualization, honest and brave personality, autonomous thought and action, accurate perception of the world, environmental and social effectiveness, and absence of negative symptoms. Traditional views of mental health emphasized upon mastery of the environment, good family relationship, meaningful social relationships, positive self-image, satisfactory job and role adjustment. It can be improved by personal intervention by practicing self-discipline, limiting unhealthy habits like worrying, doing things that positively impact others, getting engaged in meaningful creative works and activities like enjoying the beauty of nature or art, exercising regularly to uplift the body and mind.

Mental health can be conceptualized as a state of PWB in which individual employee understands personal abilities and can cope with the normal stresses of life, can work productively while facing challenges, and is able to make valuable contribution to their physical and social well-being (Brief and Atieh 1987; Bromet et al. 1988; Faravelli and Pallanti 1989). MH promotion covers a variety of strategies aimed to have a positive influence on MH such as creating positive living conditions and environments to support it, and allow people to adopt and maintain healthy life styles, properly understanding the mind body relationship. This includes a range of actions that support chances of the betterment of health of individuals from different angles.

Socio-economic factors may also influence MH conditions. Greater vulnerability to MH disorders may be due to feeling of insecurity and hopelessness, rapid social change and inability to cope with the change, risk of violence and physical ill health. Organizational and social cultures that protect basic civil, political and socio-economic rights are important for mental health. This burning topic is given importance and taken up through National Mental Health Programme for India (Government of India, Ministry of Health and Family Welfare 1982).

Organizations, society and the government need to streamline the health promotion policy and programmes for a better environment, education, justice and welfare of employees. The efficacy of industry and business sector and the government should be judged by improvements in corporate social initiatives and activities, improvement in the quality of life (QoL). Measurement through proper survey and estimation of MH effects need to be done to properly understand the gravity of the situations to take up appropriate remedial actions. Cost effective interventions are required to promote MH by providing support for children's education, employing women, old age people and utilizing their experience for social development and stress control programme, properly realizing the causes and consequences of stress (Baker 1985).

Consequences of MH problems at work usually surface through absenteeism, work performance, staff behaviour and interpersonal relationships. Poor MH can cause low self-esteem, job satisfaction and job-related tension. Prolonged work stress can result in anxiety and depression (Blazer et al. 1991; Faravelli and Pallanti 1989; Kate et al. 2001; Kushnir and Melamed 1991), and thus contribute to relationship problems (Blazer and Hybels 2005; Daus and Joplin 1999). The risk of social exclusion due to poor MH greatly increases chances of loss of employment. There can be no health without mental health. The societal cost of poor MH is enormous. Even then, only about few employers express in writing useful MH policy. People who are mentally and emotionally healthy have a sense of contentment; a zest for living and the ability to laugh and have fun; the ability to deal with stress and bounce back from adversity (Goleman 1998; Slatten 2008). They possess a sense meaning and purpose, in both their activities and their relationships; the flexibility to learn new things and adapt to change; a balance between work and play, rest and activity; ability to build and maintain fulfilling relationships; self-confidence and high self-esteem. One needs to respect one's intelligence and pattern of positive thoughts and start feeling better with self-esteem and self-reliance, learning from failures and finding the recipes of success from the failures, to reach the destiny, instead of getting stressed and depressed on the failures. A healthy, happy and peaceful mind can transform nervousness into intelligence and help one to be strong with a positive belief system that one can win and remain satisfied even amidst challenges. Employee health is the best asset not only to the individual but also to organizations as well as to enhance social capital. So, employee mental health is taken as outcome variable to study effect of PWB on it for necessary improvement and hypothesis is formulated to test the relationship with the empirical data.

5.3.4 Gap Areas

(1) Benefits of PWB in individual, organizational and social level have drawn attention of researchers in India. The need for thorough and definite understanding of its broader impact, varied effects on emerging behavioural issues and its interaction with physical, social and organizational contexts deserves further exploration in Indian social cultural context, which is different from western/developed societies/cultures. The conceptualization of well-being is embedded in the social culture, including spiritual and religious thinking, and this calls for an examination of the concept of PWB and its antecedents and outcomes. The joint family system, religious attachment of people, enormous faith on the supreme power, following traditional rituals over generations, affect employee PWB and their performance in individual, organizational and social contexts.
(2) Earlier studies on PWB have provided limited explanations on the interactions of the determinants of PWB within themselves with overlapping of ideas arising out of all such variables. PWB has not been related to specific personality traits like agreeableness and conscientiousness, and important factors of positive psychological capital like optimism and resiliency.
(3) This study attempted to capture the dynamics and interplay of PWB in a more comprehensive approach including its determinants at the organizational and individual level, and their impact on employee behaviour.
(4) The literature also suggests that there is a need to examine the role of gender and job level in the organization, education and age of employees on PWB in Indian organizations. Studies are limited and inconclusive in their findings related to the impact of demographic and background variables like gender, age, education and job level on PWB.

5.3.5 Conceptual Framework

This study, while trying to address this gap, has been carried out in an exploratory framework using survey research and examined the relationship between the

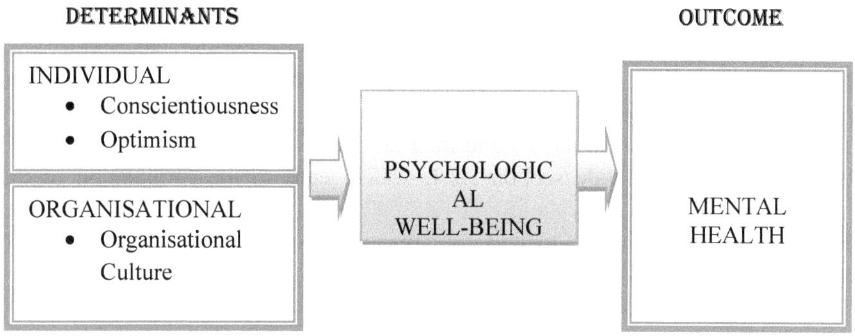

Fig. 5.1 Conceptual framework at the individual level study

antecedents of PWB and also the relationship of PWB with the outcome variables. In order to conceptualize this study, a framework for this study has been developed which shows the relationship amongst different variables and provides a basis for investigation (see Fig. 5.1).

5.3.6 *Objectives*

In order to address the gap in the literature, this study has proposed the following objectives.

(I) To examine the difference in the perceptions of PWB among employees with regard to demographic factors like gender, education, age and job level.
(II) To examine the relationship of individual and organizational with PWB.
(III) To explore the impact of PWB on mental health, and so to employee engagement.

5.3.7 *Hypotheses*

Based on the conceptual framework, a number of hypotheses have been formed to examine the relationships amongst the variables. The major objective of the study was to examine the strength of association of individual and organizational factors with PWB, and the effect of PWB on mental health. Accordingly, following hypotheses were formed.

H_1 The perception of PWB among employees would significantly differ across gender, job level, education and age.

Literature review, as stated under Section 1.1, supports such relationship and accordingly this hypothesis is formulated.

H_2 Individual factors, namely conscientiousness, optimism and resilience would be positively associated with PWB.

The details of individuals factors and their association with PWB are explained in the literature review, vide section 1.2.1, which leads to the formulation of this hypothesis.

H_3 Organizational factor, namely organizational culture would be positively associated with PWB.

This hypothesis is drawn based on the discussion in literature review under Section 1.2.2.

H_4 PWB would be positively associated with mental health.

This hypothesis is drawn in view of the detailed discussions in Section 1.3.1.

The literature review indicated the possibility of such relationships. The gaps found also prompted to draw the hypothesis accordingly to test this relationship with the empirical data.

5.4 Methods

This chapter deals with the description of sample, measures used, data collection procedures and data analysis techniques.

5.4.1 Sample

The data were collected from 350 respondents belonging to manufacturing and service sector. However, data pertaining to only 332 respondents were taken into consideration, rejecting some incomplete data using the criteria of having missing data >10%. All other missing values were replaced with appropriate mean values. This is done at the editing stage of the data processing step. The selection of the organization was based on convenience, while the selection of respondents was based on a random selection. Employees were selected on their own will, so that they remain enthusiastic and confident to provide right answers.

A glance at the respondents' profiles indicates that there were a lot of variations in terms of a number of demographic factors. Out of the total respondents, approximately 35% respondents were female, while 65% were male. 56% respondents were in junior management level. 44% of total respondents were from 26 to 35 years age group. Participants were from different organizations, working at different levels. 49% respondents were professional degree holders. Thus, the sample represented a very heterogeneous group, where employees vary on a number of criteria. Responses of qualified supervisory and managerial level

Table 5.1 A summary of sample characteristics

Profile		Govt.	Pvt.	Total
Age	<=25	0	128	128
	26–35	12	134	146
	36–45	7	38	45
	46–55	2	6	8
	>55	3	2	5
Gender	Male	15	201	216
	Female	9	107	116
Education	Below graduate	0	18	18
	General graduate	11	70	81
	Professional degree	7	157	164
	M.Tech, MBBS, MBA	4	62	66
	Ph.D., D.Sc.	2	1	3
Job level	Junior management	1	184	185
	Middle management	13	93	106
	Senior management	10	31	41

Source Primary data from Indian Industries

personnel were taken into account to get a considered view of the respondents. A summary of sample characteristics is given in Table 5.1

Out of 332 samples, 24 were from government and 308 were from private organizations. The self-selective sampling procedure is encouraged, which is now generally suggested by contemporary researchers. Employees were interviewed in their work places because of ease of availability. Based on the nature of the research, non-probability sampling design was chosen. Large scale manufacturing and service sector units were approached in government and private organizations across India for convenience sampling, as was proposed in sample design.

5.4.2 *Measures*

In this section, the scales measuring variables are described. In order to maintain uniformity five point, Likert scales were used for all the variables. Coding instructions were accordingly given from 1 to 5. The details of variables, source, number of items, reliability coefficient are given in Table 5.2, for ease of study at a glance.

The questions were structured and closed types, offering respondents a number of defined response choices. They were asked to mark their response using a tick or circle, making it more user-friendly. They were encouraged to answer all questions, preferably spontaneously at their own will and not by consulting others. Negatively worded items were included to reduce response bias. Response taking was not

Table 5.2 Characteristics of the scales

Variable	Source	No. of items	Reliability
Conscientiousness	Hofstee et al. (1992)	6	0.82
Optimism	Peterson and Seligman (2004)	5	0.79
Resilience	Wagnild and Young (1993)	14	0.75
Organizational culture	Patterson et al. (2005) OCM; Langford (2009) VCS	13	0.88
Psychological WELL-BEING	Ryff and Keyes (1995)	18	0.81
Mental health	Long (2004)	18	0.88

Source Literature review and reliability testing

outsourced. Questionnaire was not translated into many languages. Same response category was not used. A copy of the questionnaire is given in Appendix A.

Thus, planning for the study, selection of appropriate scales and questionnaire design were taken care. Few questions were changed to suit Indian requirements, proper understanding and correct response. Each variable was defined and marked. Each response was assigned a particular number and all this information is kept in a computer file for easy retrieval. Face validity was done by subjective judgement of expert. The reliability of data was tested using Cronbach's Coefficient Alpha (Cronbach 1951). The reliability of factors ranged from 0.75 to 0.88, indicating adequate internal consistency.

5.4.3 Data Collection Procedure

The initial design of the study and questionnaire construction was finalized with a lot of care, checking many alternatives, keeping in view the survey research design. First, it was checked with a pilot—test on some respondents randomly to ensure that they clearly understand the instructions, question and scale items. Accordingly, some modifications were made, and then it was administered. The self-report questionnaires were administered with instructions, describing the purpose of the study, emphasizing voluntariness and confidentiality. The organizations were approached first. After getting their consent the participants were selected randomly. Thus, organization selection was based on the convenience of the researcher as well as the organization and the participant's selection was based on their willingness to support the research keeping in view their spareable time. The participants were given full liberty to freely ask questions and were encouraged to respond to the items honestly and without taking any help from others. No separate record was kept for backtracking which was mostly uncommon.

5.4.4 *Data Analysis Techniques*

The data were analyzed using descriptive and inferential techniques to examine the difference amongst groups as well as the effects of independent variables on the dependent variable as and when required. The data were analyzed using the Statistical Package for Social Science version 15.0 (SPSS 15). The statistical analysis that was conducted included descriptive statistics, correlation, *t*-tests and Analysis of Variance (ANOVA) as well as Multiple Regression stepwise Analysis (MRA).

5.5 Results and Discussion

In this chapter, the results emerging from the analysis of the empirical data obtained have been discussed. For the purpose of data analysis, both differential and correlation analysis were used. The differential analysis was used to find out the differences across gender, job level, age and education. The correlation analysis was used to study the relationship between independent and dependent variable. The chapter begins with a description of correlation results, including independent and dependent variable. This is followed by regression analysis results to test the proposed hypotheses. It was proposed to undertake the results and discussion simultaneously for each of the hypotheses. All the variables in the analysis were treated as unidimensional in nature, as it is a composite measure of a specific concept and presents a better account for the pattern of relationship.

5.5.1 *Results of Correlation Analyses*

Preliminary analysis was performed to ensure no violation of the assumptions of normality, linearity and homoscedasticity was made. The results showed mostly significant and positive correlation amongst all the variables except in few cases where it was negative, vide Table 5.3. Mental health had a significant and positive relationship with conscientiousness ($r = 0.39$, $p < 0.01$), optimism ($r = 0.35$, $p < 0.01$) and resilience ($r = 0.16$, $p < 0.01$). Conscientiousness did not have a significant relationship with PWB ($r = 0.09$, $p > 0.05$). Optimism was positively and significantly related to PWB ($r = 0.28$, $p < 0.05$). Resilience was also positive and significantly related to PWB ($r = 0.21$, $p < 0.01$). Organizational culture ($r = 0.26$, $p < 0.01$) was positively and significantly related to PWB. All these information provides a good base to the conceptual model and hypothesis testing.

Table 5.3 Correlation amongst the variables

Sl	Variables	Mean (SD)	1	2	3	4	5	6
1	Conscientiousness	26.40 (3.256)	1					
2	Optimism	20.77 (6.605)	0.446**	1				
3	Resilience	56.57 (3.909)	0.428**	0.605**	1			
4	Organizational culture	55.66 (3.377)	0.422**	0.382**	0.282**	1		
5	Psychological well-being	61.97 (6.406)	0.098	0.283 *	0.209**	0.262**	1	
6	Mental health	82.61 (4.130)	0.396**	0.350**	0.159**	0.191**	0.231**	1

Note $*P < 0.05$, $**p < 0.01$

While examining the relationship amongst outcome variables and organizational factors, it was found that mental health was positively and significantly related to organizational culture ($r = 0.19$, $p < 0.01$).

Organizational culture was also positively and significantly related to all individual factors, namely, agreeableness ($r = 0.33$, $p < 0.01$), conscientiousness ($r = 0.42$, $p < 0.01$), optimism ($r = 0.38$, $p < 0.01$) and resilience ($r = 0.28$, $p < 0.01$).

Descriptive analysis was conducted to get an idea about the extent to which the variables were related to each other apart from the mean and standard deviations for all the variables. The overall results suggest that most of the variables had a significant relationship as expected. Multicollinearity amongst the variables was also not present, as none of the variables were highly correlated. This suggests that all the independent variables were related to PWB, and PWB was also related with most of the variables. The results also provided support to further examine the strength of association amongst the variables.

5.5.2 *The Analysis of Difference*

One of the objectives of the study was to examine the differences in the perceptions of PWB amongst employees with regard to demographic factors like gender, job level, education and age. Accordingly, the data were analyzed to test the differences in perception on PWB across all the demographic and background related factors. This was done to examine whether respondent's perception of PWB was affected by these variables. Independent samples t-tests were conducted and the results are presented in Table 5.3.

H1a: There would be difference in employee's perception of PWB across gender

In order to test this hypothesis, *t*-test was conducted for the following demographic and background variable. The *t*-test results regarding gender showed ($t = 2.19$, $p < 0.05$) significant differences in the perception of male and female as indicated in the mean score. A higher mean score from female suggests that female employees experienced higher levels of psychological well-being. Women scored significantly higher than that of men on positive relations with others and subsequent studies replicated the difference in male and female (Ryff 1995; Ghosh and Roy 1997). Females appear to be more committed to work and can maintain good work life balance. It is argued they show a positive attitude towards others and possess relatively more positive and trusting relationships compared to men in the workplace. They can better manage them, and exploit opportunities, are happier and more productive. Previous research work on family dynamics also indicated that females were more concerned related to time commitment to work and family (Frone et al. 1992; Gutek et al. 1991; Meyer and Daniel 1981), and that affects their PWB. Researchers have demonstrated factors influencing women's PWB within a positive functioning framework (Fujita et al. 1991). The results of t-tests are shown in Table 5.4.

H1b: There would be differences in employee's perception of PWB across education, age and job level.

In order to test the hypothesis, Analysis of Variance (ANOVA) was conducted and the results are stated in Table 5.5.

The results regarding education show that there is a significant difference on PWB level, ($F = 5.57$, $p < 0.01$). This suggests that education helps to fare better on PWB making them more optimistic and resilient compared to others due to better education, understanding and balanced work family life. They had greater control over their lives and better psychological health as they were not easily disturbed by petty failures, rather looked at the big picture. They were happier and engaged in their job and social activities and progressed well to fulfil the purpose of life. Thus, it appeared that higher education had a positive effect on life satisfaction and PWB.

The results across different age groups showed that there is a significant difference in their perception of a PWB ($F = 2.38$, $p < 0.01$). This indicates that employees between 46 and 55 years age group experienced higher PWB and better engaged compared to other age groups as reflected in their mean score. The reason behind it may be that people at a higher age group better enjoy the fulfilment of the

Table 5.4 A summary of the results of t-tests in differential analyses

Variables		Mean	SD	*t*-value	Significance level
Gender	Female	53.50	7.47	2.19	0.05
	Male	51.70	6.98		

Table 5.5 Summary of the results of differential analyses based on ANOVA

Variables		Mean	SD	*F*-value	Significance level
Education	Below graduate	57.17	7.98	5.57	0.01
	General graduate	51.83	5.54		
	Professional degree	51.30	7.26		
	M.Tech., MBA	53.67	7.69		
	Ph.D.	63.33	6.66		
Age (years)	<=25	50.96	6.97	2.38	0.05
	26–35	53.15	7.43		
	36–45	53.29	6.65		
	46–55	55.38	7.67		
	➢ 55	49.80	5.89		
Job level	Junior management	51.45	7.37	3.44	0.05
	Middle management	53.71	7.01		
	Senior management	52.73	6.39		

purpose of life, and remain more contended, having better environmental mastery. It might be that organizations have groomed them over the years, providing facilitative environment for long-term benefits.

The ANOVA results related to examining the difference in employee perception regarding PWB across different job levels showed that middle-level executives fared better on PWB and there was a statistically significant difference ($F = 3.44$, $p < 0.05$). The reason may be that middle-level executives might have contributed more towards business development, and in turn have enriched themselves and turned out to be more successful, happy and satisfied. Higher level of PWB in middle-level executives could be due to a positive adaptation to the service conditions in mid-career as compared to the junior level managers, who are new to the service and always look for better opportunities. Being in the growing learning curve middle level executives is more engaged and satisfied than the senior executives who normally lack role requirements at seniority level.

Means of Plots pertaining to education, age and job level which demonstrate the significant difference of PWB level are shown in Fig. 5.2.

Graphs above on mean of PWB are self-explanatory, outlining clearly the type of change, based on the empirical data and showing changes at different levels.

5.5.3 Results of Regression Analysis

Multiple Regression Analysis (MRA) was performed considering the independent variables as predictors and the dependent variable as the criterion variable. MRA was used to find out the strength of association between independent factors and PWB and then to observe the strength of association between PWB and outcome variable.

Fig. 5.2 Means of plots of education, age and job level with PWB

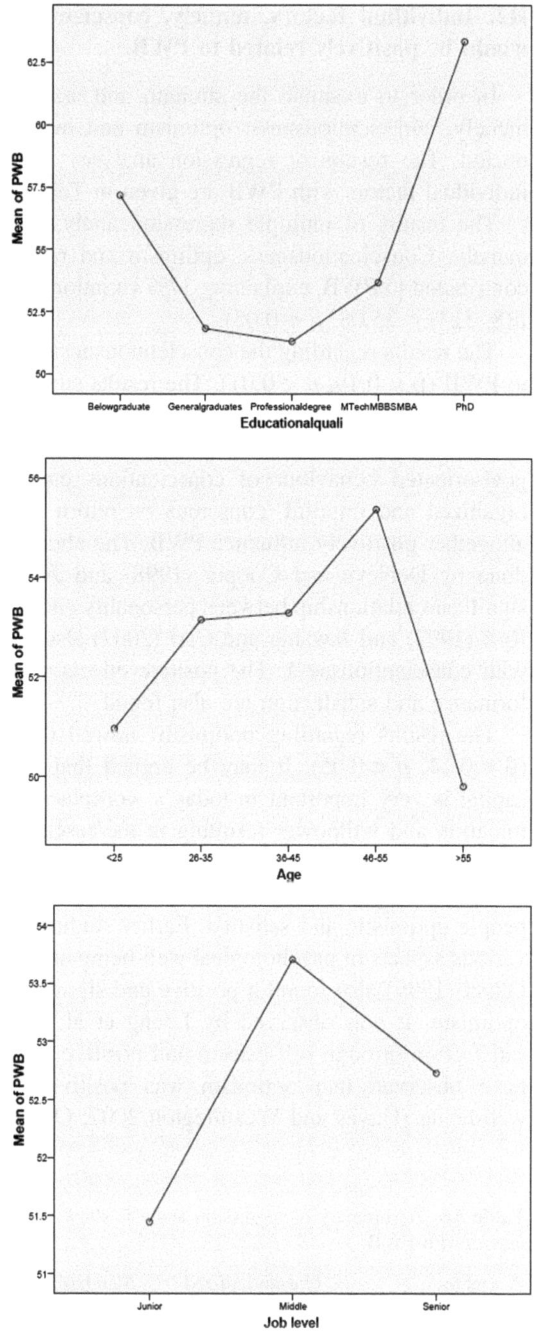

H2: Individual factors, namely, conscientiousness, optimism and resilience would be positively related to PWB.

In order to examine the strength and association between individual factors, namely, conscientiousness, optimism and resilience, and PWB, MRA was conducted. The results of regression analyses showing the strength of these three individual factors with PWB are given in Table 5.6.

The results of multiple regression analysis showed that all the three factors namely, Conscientiousness, optimism and resilience significantly and positively contributed to PWB, explaining 37% variation for the criterion measure ($R^2 = 0.37$, $F(8, 323) = 25.08$, $p < 0.05$).

The results regarding the conscientiousness showed that it was positively related to PWB ($\beta = 0.19$, $p < 0.01$). The results suggested that if we enhance the possibility of constructive encounters at the work place, then it would lead to enhanced PWB. It is argued that the high level of thoughtfulness and impulse control and goal-oriented behaviour of conscientious employees tend to make them more organized and mindful, conscious on return on time investment (ROTI), which altogether positively influence PWB. The above findings are supported by studies done by DeNeve and Cooper (1998) and Judge et al. (1998), in terms of the significant relationship between personality and PWB. The studies by Schmutte and Ryff (1997) and Jawahar and Carr (2007) also found PWB to be positively linked with conscientiousness. The positive effects with conscientiousness and job performance and satisfaction are also found.

The results regarding optimism showed that it is positively related to PWB ($\beta = 0.14$, $p < 0.05$). It may be argued that this type of positive psychological capital is very important in today's workplace, which allows rekindling of determination and willpower resulting in increased motivation to look for alternatives and new realities of the situation. It means people are optimistic and look at the future with a positive outlook, and long-term vision. This perspective makes such people optimistic and satisfied. Earlier studies also link optimism positively with various aspects of psychological well-being among adults (Li 1995). Magaletta and Oliver (1999) also found a positive and significant relationship of well-being with optimism. It was observed by Leung et al. (2005) that optimism predicted life satisfaction through self-esteem and positive relationship with others. Researchers have observed that optimism was positively related to life satisfaction and well-being (Hayes and Weathington 2007; Olason and Roger 2001). Optimism is

Table 5.6 A summary of regression analysis showing the strength of association of individual factors with PWB

Variables	Unstandardized coefficients	Standardized coefficients	t	Sig.	Adj-R^2	F
Conscientiousness	0.41	0.19	3.14	0.01	0.37	25.08
Optimism	0.33	0.14	2.04	0.05		
Resilience	0.15	0.14	2.30	0.02		

shown to have a significant relationship with performance, job satisfaction, happiness and organizational commitment (Luthans et al. 2007; Youssef and Luthans 2007).

Earlier research has also shown that optimism effects self-regulation of behaviour (Carver and Scheier 2001, 2002; Scheier and Carver 1992). Optimists seem to cope in ways that are generally beneficial to their health and they manage and reduce stressors and problems they face. Avey et al. (2010, 2011) also observed a positive effect of PPC on WB. The capacity of resilience helps individuals to take a balanced approach in the case of both positive and negative events; and when coupled with optimism, it helps them to recognize and acknowledge the impact of such events and allow people to recover rebound and return to a balanced state leading to higher levels of PWB.

The results related to resilience showed a positive and significant relationship with PWB ($\beta = 0.14$, $p < 0.05$). The results suggested that people high on resilience fared better on PWB. Resilient people have the capacity to better cope up with anxiety and conflict; and have better capabilities to change. Thus, such people do not lose their focus on the future and try to find out new meaning in life, which makes them happy and satisfied. Researchers (Luthans et al. 2007) also viewed it as a positive psychological capital construct affecting performance and life satisfaction. Resilience helps an individual to bounce back from adversity, failure and even positively, but seemingly overwhelming changes such as increased responsibility (Luthans and Youssef 2004; Masten 2001). Thus, it influences performance and increases psychological well-being (Luthans and Youssef 2004; Singh and Mansi 2009). Resilient people can maintain a pattern of low distress and adequate functioning while following stressful experiences. They possess a number of specific personal attributes that contribute to their ability to approach difficult situations in a way that also adds to their resilient nature and serves to continually expand their personal and psychological strength (Akgemci et al. 2013). They possess enough capacity to learn from the setbacks in life and to utilize that knowledge as a means of coping more effectively in future. Thus, the overall results showed that personality factors like conscientiousness, optimism and resilience were positively related, while agreeableness was negatively related and the hypothesis was partially accepted.

It can be argued that these individual factors significantly contribute to individual's PWB and management should consider as how to improve these factors to make employees more optimistic and resilient even in a fast changing environment, where organizations are uncertain about their system, structure and process, and are making constant efforts to bring home necessary changes to make them more profitable and growth oriented. This has significant implication for the people as organizations undergoing changes have significant influence on the people, as they are affected by these changes and people's qualities like optimism, conscientiousness and resilience can help them to better adapt to the changes taking place in the work life. The return on human capital investment needs to be checked to ascertain the higher returns and accordingly management must invest in people to develop such qualities through HRD intervention.

H3: Organizational factor, namely, organizational culture would be positively associated to PWB.

In order to examine the strength of association between the organizational level factor and PWB, MRA was conducted. A summary of MRA showing strength of association between organizational factor as independent variable and PWB as a criterion variable is stated in Table 5.7.

The results regarding organizational culture suggest that it has significantly contributed to PWB. It means that the culture of the organization has facilitated a better working environment for the employees, and imbibed norms and values in tune with the organizational goals and objectives. Organizational practices have also contributed to the development of a strong culture, which has helped employees to better adapt to the system and practices of the organization. A strong culture can help organizations to be more productive, and employees working in such organization feel more happy and satisfied, resulting in higher levels of well-being. This supports the long held view of previous researchers that employee satisfaction and well-being depends on a supportive culture. Researchers have also observed that organizational culture may be useful in developing organization's management practices concerning human resources to keep them fit for purpose and contended (Burke et al. 2006; Ouchi and Johnson 1978).

Thus, the overall result suggested that organizational factor, namely organizational culture is very important for employee well-being. The culture of an organization is very crucial to determine not only whether people use the family support, benefits that an organization provides, but also their general attitude towards the organization (Thompson et al. 1999) which ultimately affects their PWB. Culture inspires employees and motivates them to do the right things. Employee-organization fit leads to individual and organizational high performance (O'Reilly et al. 1991), and improves employee satisfaction and their mental well-being. The results of this research are conforming to this concept.

Organizations should provide benefits and facilities to employees and their family like scheduling work responsibilities, crèche facilities, medical and schooling facilities and other benefits to enable people not to bother too much about their family and focus on work to become productive. A better work–family integration can help a lot in this direction as it would result in balanced work–family life and would substantially increase the quality of life (QoL) including quality of work life (QWL). A supportive work–family culture is negatively related to work–family conflict (Anderson et al. 2002; Thompson et al. 1999), and positively related to employee PWB. The higher the supportive work–family culture, the higher will

Table 5.7 A summary of regression analysis results showing the strength and association of organizational factors with PWB

Variables	Unstandardized coefficients	Standardized coefficients	t	Sig.	Adj-R^2	F
Organizational culture	0.39	0.32	4.95	0.01	0.37	25.08

be the PWB score of employees. Employees in organizations that provide more work–family benefits reports less work–family conflict and more organizational engagement than those in organizations with fewer work family benefits (Thompson et al. 1999).

H4: PWB would be positively associated with mental health.

In order to examine the strength of association between PWB as a predictor and mental health and employee engagement, simple regression analysis was conducted. The results are given below.

The result of regression analysis showed that PWB significantly contributed to mental health ($\beta = 0.23, p < 0.01$) and explained five percent of the variance for the criterion variable ($R^2 = 0.05$, $F = 18.63$, $p < 0.01$). The results are presented in Table 5.8.

The results showed that people with better PWB would have better mental health. It means they would be worry free and happy in their life to go ahead to fulfil their purpose of life. People with better mental health seem to have balanced life, emotionally matured and manage their relationship very well. They would be having less anxiety, physically healthy and happy, go for better self-evaluation, take care of others, remain creative and productive. Mentally healthy individuals develop good family and societal relationship, which ultimately help to develop higher levels of PWB. A number of studies support this finding. There was a positive relationship between well-being and mental health (Diener 1984). There is clear evidence that people with higher levels of PWB are mentally and physically healthier and have happier lives, and live longer (Cartwright and Cooper 2009). Mentally healthy individuals have warm and trusting relationships, feel they are growing as a person, have a purpose in life, feel they can shape the world around them to fit their needs, and enable and direct their actions from internal standards (Ryff and Keyes 1995). Thus, PWB is positively associated with better mental health (Grzywacz and Bass 2003) and increasingly help to enhance mental capital. Work is a gateway to a civil and economic life of a community. Maintaining work can be critical for those who experience poor mental health (Fine-Davis et al. 2005).

5.6 Summary and Conclusion

This chapter provides a summary and conclusion based on the results. It also presents implications and contributions of the study. Limitations of the study are discussed, and finally future research scope is highlighted.

Table 5.8 A summary of regression analysis results showing the strength of association between PWB and mental health

Variables	Unstandardized coefficients	Standardized coefficients	t	Sig.	Adj-R^2	F
PWB	0.13	0.23	4.32	0.01	0.05	18.63

The major objective of this study was to explore the determinants of PWB in Indian social cultural context more specifically, to examine the relationship of independent variables with PWB and the impact of PWB on outcome variables. In addition to this, another objective was to explore the difference in employee perception of PWB with respect to demographic and background variables. In order to examine these objectives, extensive literature survey was carried out to identify the gap areas and hypotheses were formulated. The research hypothesis was subsequently tested by analyzing the data, applying various statistical tools and techniques. The summary of findings, their implications and contributions are discussed here.

5.6.1 Summary of Results

This study was conducted primarily to find out the employees' perception of PWB and the individual and organizational determinants and then the strength of association between PWB and outcome variable namely, mental health. The correlation analysis indicated both positive and negative correlations existing amongst the variables. Positive correlations were found between PWB and outcome variable.

The regression analyses also supported the hypotheses. It was found that employee perception on PWB differed across gender, age, education and job level. We need to further explore the life expectancies of the people, their social, cultural differences and how it contributes to PWB.

Next, the results regarding individual factor indicated that these factors significantly contributed. It is argued that in the light of changing global business scenario and VUCA (volatile, uncertain, complex and ambiguous) environment, it is required to develop these individual factors in the right direction to enhance PWB of employees. Organizations should now create favourable working conditions and conducive work environments that encourage developing employee personality traits/characteristics such as conscientiousness, and positive psychological capital (PPC) like optimism and resilience, through desired training interventions.

The hypothesis regarding organizational factors suggested that organizational culture was significantly related to PWB. Thus, if employee well-being is important to make them productive, organizations should facilitate a supportive work culture. Work family culture which includes managerial support for work–family balance, supportive work–family benefits like desirable time scheduling, not interfering with family responsibilities are well perceived by the employees. It can be concluded that organizations who provide a supportive work–family culture contribute to enhanced PWB of employees.

PWB was also positively related to outcome variable, namely mental health. Changes in employee behaviour due to improved eudaimonic well-being are demonstrated through possible mental health benefits of living a life rich in purpose, meaning and continual growth. Higher order PWB makes employees inspired, excited, enthusiastic, determined, alert, happy and engaged in work roles.

While it develops an engagement level at the organizational level and helps business to grow, it also ensures their prosperity and improves their stake in family life and social inclusion and involvement in social development and the whole gamut of individual, organizations and societies are altogether benefitted.

5.6.2 Implications

The study has certain implications for employers, employees and the academic fraternity. The information can be used by the organizational leaders to check and improve employee's PWB to ensure better engagement and growth with stability. Managers should provide a family supportive work culture so that they get enormous return on employee support and maintain a congenial and healthy work environment. Personality development, soft- skills development programmes may be initiated taking care of each employee, so that they can shoulder more responsibility and add to organizational growth while taking care to fulfil their purpose of life. The organizations need to be proactive and innovative in their business strategies and accordingly set the organizational culture so that employees are inspired to be involved with the organization and have a win situation. Improving employee engagement is a key factor for business development and a challenging activity and most of the industries are now severely lacking in this field. It is estimated approx. 20% of employees only are highly engaged in their works and 20% are actively disengaged (Attridge 2009), which indicates there is huge potential and need to develop in this field. Improved PWB and better MH care can considerably improve employee engagement level.

1. This study provides knowledge and incites interest amongst various stakeholders on measurement of PWB, leader behaviour, effect of supervisors on employees, employee personality traits, duty of care to employee quality of life, gender-role orientation, promotion of employee mental health and social capital.
2. Employee's social involvement due to their high-level PWB not only helps society to flourish, but also the employee, in turn, gets extremely benefitted. This study on PWB may show pathways not only to the individuals by strengthening their mental health but also to the organizations by creating a family supportive culture to ensure better employee engagement and productivity, which can help the society to enhance social capital getting benefits from the enriched organizations and inspired employees besides helping the researchers and opinion leaders for future planning.

5.6.3 Contributions

The study has contributed to the positive organizational behaviour literature through an examination of individual, organizational and social factors and their impact on PWB. It is a step towards better understanding how PWB helps in the pursuit of employee health and happiness and so to improve mental health and better organizational engagement. This will significantly contribute to the existing body of knowledge in this field.

This study gives a deeper insight in the domain of personality traits at the individual level. The controversy over the relationship and impact of personality traits on PWB has been supported. This study has made an effort to develop the CORE group (Conscientiousness, Optimism and Resilience), highlighting how these specific individual personality trait positively interfere with employee PWB.

This study explored a variety of practices in organizations in work and family domain across various strategic locations in India. It is an eye opener to organizations to realize how family supportive organizational culture can improve individual employee and their engagement level which is most coveted and a challenging task now even for the most upcoming organizations.

Mental health is increasingly being felt as a deep concern area all over the world, although it is much noted and seriously felt in developed countries, as the societal cost of opportunity loss due to poor mental health is enormous. It is also coming up as a great challenge in growing economies like India, where millions of people are engaged in manufacturing and services sectors and diagnosis and treatment of MH issues are typical concerns. This study offers useful information how developing PWB, employee's mental health can be taken care, which can be very useful not only for the employees and their families but also for the organizations and the society. Thus improvement in MH can be a win situation for the individual, organizations and societies.

Another contribution was showing the role of certain social-demographic variables which were not much focused on earlier studies. The study finds gender differences in PWB (females scored better) which is an important contribution in our cultural context. Again the level of education is important for higher PWB, which can instil a sense of self-esteem and competence among employees.

5.6.4 Limitations

Although the findings of this study provide some support regarding the linkages amongst independent variables, PWB and their consequences on employee behaviour, there are some acknowledged limitations of the present study that need to be addressed in future research.

1. The conclusion drawn using a convenient sampling process cannot be generalized as a diverse sample would have been better from a cross section of the industries. The convenient sample population was educated and better placed and their aggregate consent cannot be like that of all categories of less educated employees in other cultural settings. In absence of data for large number of workers of different trades and grades, it is difficult to establish any set pattern of their PWB.

2. All measures were self-report measures and it is difficult to avoid social desirability bias to improve the reliability of the data. It is advised to use mix methods of research to assess SWB to strengthen research in this area. Use of multiple measures can substantially improve the validity of conclusions and may lead to more insights. In-depth group interviews can be organized to have a variety of opinions on diversified topics.
3. The data were collected from only a few places in India and it cannot be representative of the population. Besides Indian social culture and work family enrichment varies due to diversity in racial cultural settings. The organizational culture is likely to vary and it becomes difficult to reach a consensus on the direct and mediation effect of PWB on the ultimate outcome variables. Future researchers may use multiple measures, multiple sources and methods, involving data collection in various states on varied geographical areas to have variety in information.
4. There is a need to use data as how perception changes over time and the relationships amongst variables may be difficult, keeping in view the dynamics of PWB.
5. The hypothesized model could have incorporated social and environmental factor as determinants of PWB. Change of governmental rules and regulations, globalization effect, VUCA effect and far reaching effects of natural and unnatural calamities, arson, safety and security threats through violence and terrorist activities also create considerable impact on employee PWB.
6. A major limitation of this research on PWB and employee behaviour is that it has focused almost exclusively on the experiences of individuals employed in large manufacturing and service sectors. No attention has been devoted to examining PWB and behaviour of men and women who are self-employed and in small scale sectors.
7. The data were analyzed using co-relational techniques which pose certain limitations. Structural Equation Modelling could have been used to examine the hypothesized relationships and the model fit.

References

Abbey, A., & Andrews, F. M. (1985). Modelling the psychological determinants of life quality. *Social Indicators Research, 16*(1), 1–34.

Abramson, L. Y., & Alloy, L. B. (1981). Depression, nondepression, and cognitive illusions: A reply to Schwartz. *Journal of Experimental Psychology: General, 110*(3), 436–447.

Akgemci, T., Demirsel, M. T., & Kara, O. (2013). The effect of psychological resilience on employees' burn out level. *Academic Journal of Interdisciplinary Studies, 2*(11), 122–128.

Alloy, L. B., & Ahrens, A. H. (1987). Depression and pessimism for the future: Biased use of statistically relevant information in predictions for self versus others. *Journal of Personality and Social Psychology, 52*(2), 366–378.

Amar, A. D. (2004). Motivating knowledge workers to innovate: a model integrating motivation dynamics and antecedents. *European Journal of Innovation Management, 7*(2), 89–101.

Anderson, S. E., Coffey, B. S., & Byerly, R. T. (2002). Formal organisational initiatives and informal workplace practices: Links to work-family conflict and job-related outcomes. *Journal of Management, 28*(6), 787–810.
Argyle, M. (1999). Causes and correlates of happiness. In D. Kanheman, E. Diener, & N. Schwarz (Eds.), *Well-being: The foundations of hedonic psychology* (pp. 353–373). New York: Russel Sage Foundation.
Ashmos, D. P., & Douchon, D. (2000). Spirituality at work. A conceptualisation and measure. *Journal of Management Inquiry, 9*(2), 134–144.
Ashrama, A. (2005). *Complete works of swami Vivekananda, Kolkata*. 12th impression, III, 4.
Aspinwall, L. G., & Taylor, S. E. (1993). Effects of social comparison, direction, threat, and self esteem on affect, self evaluation, and expected success. *Journal of Personality and Social Psychology, 64*(5), 708–722.
Attridge, M. (2009). Employee work engagement: Best practices for employers. *Research Works: Partnership for Workplace Mental Health, 1*(2), 1–12.
Avey, J. B., Luthans, F., Smith, R. M., & Palmer, N. F. (2010). Impact of positive psychological capital on employee well-being over time. *Journal of Occupational Health Psychology, 15*(1), 17–28.
Avey, J. B., Reichard, R. J., Luthans, F., & Mhatre, K. H. (2011). Meta-analysis of the impact of positive psychological capital on employee attitudes, behaviours, and performance. *Human Resource Development Quarterly, 22*(2), 127–152.
Avison, W. R., McLeod, & Pescosolido, B. A. (2007). *Mental health, social mirror*. New York: Springer.
Bakker, A. B., & Schaufeli, W. B. (2008). Positive organisational behaviour: Engaged employees in flourishing organizations. *Journal of Organisational Behaviour, 29,* 147–154.
Baker, D. B. (1985). The study of stress at work. *Annual Review of Public Health, 6,* 367–381.
Bandura, A. (1986). *Social foundations of thought and action: A social cognitive theory*. Englewood Cliffs, NJ: Prentice-Hall.
Barrick, M. R., & Mount, M. K. (1996). Effects of impression management and self deception on the predictive validity of personality constructs. *Journal of Applied Psychology, 81*(3), 261–272.
Belle, D., Doucet, J., Harris, J., Miller, J., & Tan, E. (2000). Who is rich? Who is happy? *American Psychologist, 55*(10), 1160–1161.
Bennett, D. (2002). Health and safety management systems: Liability or asset? *Journal of Public Health Policy, 23*(2), 153–171.
Bews, N. F., & Rossouw, G. J. (2002). A role for business ethics in facilitating trustworthiness. *Journal of Business Ethics, 39*(4), 377–390.
Blazer, D. G., Hughes, D., & George, L. K., et al., (1991). In L. N. Robins & D. A. Regier (Eds.), *Psychiatric disorders in America* (1st ed., pp. 181–203). New York. Free Press.
Blazer, D. G., & Hybels, C. F. (2005). Origins of depression in later life. *Psychological Medicine, 35,* 1–12.
Biswas, D. R., & Diener, E. (2001). Making the best of a bad situation: Satisfaction in the slums of Calcutta. *Social Indicators Research, 55,* 239–352.
Bond, J., Galinsky, E., Kim, S., & Brownfield, E. (2005). *National study of employers*. New York: Families and Work Institute.
Bozionelos, N. (2004). The big five of personality and work involvement. *Journal of Managerial Psychology, 19*(1), 69–81.
Bradburn, N. M. (1969). *The structure of psychological well-being*. Chicago: Aldine.
Brief, A. P., & Atieh, J. M. (1987). Studying job stress: Are we making mountains out of molehills? *Journal of Occupational Behaviour, 8*(2), 115–126.
Bromet, E. J., Dew, M. A., Parkinson, D. K., & Schulberg, H. C. (1988). Predictive effects of occupational and marital stress on the mental health of a male workforce. *Journal of Organisational Behaviour, 9*(1), 1–13.

Burke, R. J., Koyuncu, M., & Fiksenbaum, L. (2006). Organisational practices supporting women's career advancement and their satisfaction and well-being in Turkey. *Women in Management Review, 21*(8), 610–624.
Carmeli, A., Yitzhak-Halevy, M., & Weisberg, J. (2009). The relationship between emotional intelligence and psychological well-being. *The Journal of Managerial Psychology, 24*(1), 66–78.
Cartwright, S., & Cooper, C. L. (2009). *The Oxford handbook of organisational well-being*. Oxford: Oxford University Press.
Carver, C. S., & Gaines, J. G. (1987). Optimism, pessimism, and postpartum depression. *Cognitive Therapy and Research, 11,* 449–462.
Carver, C. S., & Scheier, M. F. (2001). Optimism, pessimism and self-regulation. *American Psychological Association, 399,* 31–51.
Chang, E. C. (1998). Dispositional optimism and primary and secondary appraisal of a stressor: Controlling for confounding influences and relations to coping and psychological and physical adjustment. *Journal of Personality and Social Psychology, 74,* 1109–1120.
Chang, K., & Lu, L. (2007). Characteristics of organizational culture, stressors and well-being. The case of Taiwanese organisations. *Journal of Managerial Psychology, 22*(6), 549–568.
Ciulla, J. B. (2000). On getting to the future first. *Business Ethics Quarterly, 10*(1), 53–61.
Clark, C. S. (2001). Work cultures and work/family balance. *Journal of Vocational Behaviour, 58*(3), 348–365.
Clarke, S. (1999). Perceptions of organizational safety: Implications for the development of safety culture. *Journal of Organizational Behaviour, 20*(2), 185–198.
Contu, D. L. (2002). How resilience works. *Harvard Business Review, 80*(3), 46–52.
Costa, P. T., Jr., & McCrae, R. R. (1990). Personality: Another hidden factor in stress research. *Psychological Inquiry, 1,* 22–24.
Costa, P. T., Jr., & McCrae, R. R. (1992). *Revised NEO personality inventory (NEO-PI-R) and NEO five factor inventory professional manual.* Odessa, FL: Psychological Assessment Resources.
Cronbach, L. J. (1951). Coefficient alpha and the internal structure of tests. *Psychometrika, 16,* 297–334.
Cropanzano, R., & Wright, T. A. (1999). A five-year study of change in the relationship between well-being and performance. *Consulting Psychology Journal: Practice and Research, 51*(4), 252–265.
Daus, C. A., & Joplin, J. R. W. (1999). Survival of the fittest: Implications of self reliance and coping for leaders and team performance. *Journal of Occupational Health Psychology, 4*(1), 15–28.
Deaton, A. (2008). Income, ageing, health and well-being around the world: Evidence from Gallup world poll. *Journal of Economic Perspectives, 22,* 53–57.
Deery, S. J., & Iverson, R. D. (2005). Labour-management cooperation: Antecedents and impact on organizational performance. *Industrial and Labour Relations Review, 58*(4), 588–609.
Deneve, K. M., & Cooper, H. (1998). The happy personality: a meta analysis of 137 personality traits and subjective well-being. *Psychological Bulletin, 124*(2), 197–229.
Denison, D. R. (1984). Bringing organizational culture to the bottom line. *Organizational Dynamics, 13*(2), 5–22.
Denison, D. R., & Mishra, A. K. (1995). Toward a theory of organisational culture and effectiveness. *Organisation Science, 6*(2), 204–223.
Diener, E. (1984). Subjective well-being. *Psychological Bulletin, 95*(3), 542–575.
Diener, E. (2000). Subjective well-being. The science of happiness and a proposal for national index. *American Psychologist, 55*(1), 34–43.
Diener, E., Emmons, R. A., Larsen, R. J., & Griffin, S. (2010). Satisfaction with life scale. *Journal of Personality Assessment, 49*(1), 71–75.
Diener, E., Oishi, S., & Lucas, R. E. (2003). Personality, culture, and subjective well-being: emotional and cognitive evaluations of life. *Annual Reviews of Psychology, 54*(1), 403–425.
Diener, E., Sapyta, J. J., & Suh, E. (1998). Subjective well-being is essential to well-being. *Psychological Inquiry, 9,* 33–37.

Diener, Ed., & Seligman, M. E. P. (2002). Very happy people. *Psychological Science. 13*(1), 81–84.
Diener, E., & Seligman, M. E. P. (2004). Beyond Monet: Toward an economy of well-being. *Psychological Science, 5*(1), 1–31.
Diener, E., & Suh, E. (2001). *Culture and subjective well-being*. Cambridge, Massachusetts: MIT Press.
Digman, J. M. (1990). Personality structure: Emergence of the five factor model. *Annual Review of Psychology, 41,* 417–440.
Donald, I., Taylor, P., Johnson, S., Cooper, C., Cartwright, S., & Robertson, S. (2005). Work environments, stress and productivity: An examination using ASSET. *International Journal of Stress Management, 12*, 409–423.
Edwards, J. R. (1992). A cybernetic theory of stress, coping and well-being in organizations. *The Academy of Management Review, 17*(2), 238–274.
Faravelli, C., & Pallanti, S. (1989). Recent life events and panic disorder. *American Journal of Psychiatry, 146,* 622–626.
Felfe, J., & Schyns, B. (2006). Personality and the perception of transformational leadership: The impact of extraversion, neuroticism, personal need for structure, and occupational self-efficacy. *Journal of Applied Social Psychology, 36*(3), 708–739.
Fierro, A. (2006). Emotional intelligence, does associate to happiness? A province outline. *Ansiedady Estress, 12*(23), 241–249.
Fine-Davis, M., McCarthy, M., O'Dwyer, C., Edge, G, & O'Sullivan, M. (2005). *The effects of flexible working on work life balance and social inclusion: An evaluation of a series of pilot projects.* Dublin: National Flexi-Work Partnership (Centre for Gender and Women Studies, Trinity, Dublin.
Forgeard, M. J. C., & Seligman, M. E. P. (2012). Seeing the glass half-full: A review of the causes and consequences of optimism. *Pratiques Psychologiques, 18*(2), 107–120.
Fredrickson, B. L. (2004). The broaden-and-build theory of positive emotions. *Philosophical Transactions, Biological Sciences, 359,* 1367–1377.
Freedman, J. (1978). *Happy people*. New York: Harcourt, Brace, Jovanovich.
Friedman, T. L. (2005). *The world is flat: A brief history of the 21st century*. United States: Farrar, Straus and Giroux.
Frone, M. R., Russel, M., & Cooper, M. L. (1992). Antecedents and outcomes of work-family conflict: Testing a model of the work-family interface. *Journal of Applied Psychology, 77*(1), 65–78.
Fujita, F., Diener, E., & Sandvik, E. (1991). Gender differences in negative affect and well-being: The case for emotional intensity. *Journal of Personality and Social Psychology, 61,* 427–434.
Ghosh, R. N., & Roy, K. C. (1997). The changing status of women in India: Impact of urbanisation and development. *International Journal of Social Economics, 24*(7/9), 902–917.
Goleman, D. (1998). What makes a leader? *Harvard Business Review, 76,* 93–104.
Gonzalez, J. V., & Garazo, T. G. (2006). Structural relationships between organisational service orientation, contact employee job satisfaction and citizenship behaviour. *International Journal of Service Industry Management, 17*(1), 23–50.
Government of India. (1982). *National mental health programme for India*. New Delhi: Ministry of Health and Family Welfare.
Graham, C., Eggers, A., & Sukhtankar, S. (2004). Does happiness pay? An exploration based on panel data from Russia. *Journal of Economic Behaviour and Organisation, 55*(3), 319–342.
Grzywacz, J. G., & Bass, B. L. (2003). Work, family, and mental health: testing different models of work-family fit. *Journal of Marriage and Family, 65*(1), 248–261.
Gutek, B. A., Searle, S., & Klepa, L. (1991). Rational versus gender role explanations for work-family conflict. *Journal of Applied Psychology, 76*(4), 560–568.
Harter, J. K., Schmidt, F. L., & Keyes, C. L. M. (2003). Well-being in the workplace and its relationship to business outcomes: A review of the Gallup studies. In C. L. M. Keyes & J. Haidt (Eds.), *Flourishing: Positive psychology and the life well-lived* (pp. 205–224). Washington, DC: American Psychological Association.

Hayes, C. T., & Weathington, B. L. (2007). Optimism, stress, life satisfaction, and job burnout in restaurant managers. *The Journal of Psychology, 141*(6), 565–579.

Helliwell, J., Layard, R., & Sachs, J. (Eds.). (2013). *World happiness report 2013*. New York: UN Sustainable Development Solutions Network.

Hofstee, W. K., De Raad, B., & Goldberg, L. R. (1992). Integration of the big five and circumplex approaches to trait structure. *Journal of Personality and Social Psychology, 63*(1), 146–163.

Hofstede, G. (1994). *Cultures and organisations: Intercultural co-operation and its importance for survival*. London: HarperCollins.

Huppert, F. A. (2009). Psychological well-being: Evidence regarding its causes and consequences. *Applied Psychology: Health and Well-Being, 1*(2), 137–164.

Ilardi, B. C., Leone, D., Kesser, T., & Ryan, M. (1993) Employee and supervisor's ratings for motivation: *Journal of Applied Social Psychology, 23*, 1789–1805.

ILO. (2005). *A global alliance against forced labour*. Global report under the follow-up to the ILO declaration on fundamental principles and rights at work. International Labour Office, Geneva.

Jacobson, N., & Greenley, D. (2001). What is recovery? A conceptual model and explication. *Psychiatric Services, 52*(4), 482–485.

Jawahar, I. M., & Carr, D. (2007). Conscientiousness and contextual performance. *Journal of Managerial Psychology, 22*(4), 330–349.

Jonker, C. S., & Scholtz, P. E. (2004). *Development of a work wellness programme: An emotional intelligence application*. Paper presented at the 2nd South African Work Wellness Conference. Potchefstroom, South Africa.

Jourard, S. M., & Landsman, T. (1980). *Healthy personality: An approach from the viewpoint of humanistic psychology* (4th ed.). New York: Macmillan.

Judge, T. A., Erez, A., & Bono, J. E. (1998). The power of being positive: The relationship between positive self-concept and job performance. *Human Performance, 11*(2/3), 167–187.

Kahn, W. A. (1990). Psychological conditions of personal engagement and disengagement at work. *Academy of Management Journal, 33*(4), 692–724.

Kate, S., Brian, F., & Carry, L. C. (2001). Well-being and occupational health in the 21st century workplace. *Journal of Occupational and Organizational Psychology, 74*(4), 489–509.

Keyes, C. L. M. (2007). Promoting and protecting mental health as flourishing: A complementary strategy for improving national mental health. *American Psychologist, 62*(2), 95–108.

Keyes, C. L. M., & Magyar-Moe, J. L. (2003). The measurement and utility of adult subjective well-being. In S. J. Lpoez & C. R. Synder (Eds.), *Positive psychological assessment: A handbook of models and measures* (pp. 411–425). Washington, DC: American Psychological Association.

Kluemper, D. H., Little, L. M., & DeGroot, T. (2009). State or trait: Effects of state optimism on job-related outcomes. *Journal of Organisational Behaviour, 30*(2), 209–231.

Kuiper, N. A. (1978). Depression and causal attributions for success and failure. *Journal of Personality and Social Psychology, 36*, 236–246.

Kushnir, T., & Melamed, S. (1991). Workload, perceived control and psychological distress in type A/B industrial workers. *Journal of Organisational Behaviour, 12*, 155–168.

Li, J. C. L. (1995). The moderating effect of optimism on the relation between hassles and somatic complaints. *Psychological Reports, 76*(3), 883–894.

Langford, P. H. (2009). Measuring organisational climate and employee engagement: Evidence for a 7 Ps model of work practices and outcomes. *Australian Journal of Psychology, 6*(4), 185–198.

Leung, B. W., Moneta, G. B., & McBridge-Chang, C. (2005). Think positively and feel positively: Optimism and life satisfaction in late life. *International Journal of Aging and Human Development, 61*(4), 335–365.

Lindfors, P., & Lundberg, U. (2002). Is low cortisol release an indicator of positive health? *Stress and Health, 18*(4), 153–160.

Long, P. W. (2004). *Mental health scale*.

Loscocco, K. A., & Spitze, G. (1990). Working conditions, social support and the well-being of female and male factory workers. *Journal of Health and Social Behaviour, 31*(4), 313–327.

Luthans, F. (2002). Positive organizational behaviour: Developing and managing psychological strengths. *Academy of Management Executives, 16*(1), 57–72.

Luthans, F., Avey, J. B., Avolio, B. J., Norman, S. M., & Combs, G. M. (2006). Psychological capital development: Towards a micro-intervention. *Journal of Organizational Behaviour, 27,* 387–393.

Luthans, F., Avolio, B. J., Avey, J. B., & Norman, S. M. (2007). Positive psychological capital: Measurement and relationship with performance and satisfaction. *Personnel Psychology, 60* (3), 541–572.

Luthans, F., & Youssef, C. M. (2004). Human, social, and now positive psychological capital management: Investing in people for competitive advantage. *Organisational Dynamics, 33*(2), 143–160.

Lyubomorsky, S. (2008). *The how of happiness: A scientific approach to getting the life you want.* New York: Penguin Press.

Lyubomorsky, S. (2013). *The myths of happiness: What should make you happy, but doesn't, what shouldn't make you happy, but does* (X, Trans.). Beijing, China: Cheers Books.

Lyubomorsky, S., King, J., & Diener, E. (2005). The benefit of frequent positive affect. Does happiness lead to success? *Psychological Bulletin, 131,* 803–855.

Magaletta, P., & Oliver, J. (1999). The hope construct, will, and ways: Their relations with self-efficacy, optimism and general well-being. *Journal of Clinical Psychology, 55,* 539–551.

Marks, N. F., Lambert, J. D., & Choi, H. (2002). Transitions to care giving, gender and psychological well-being. A prospective U.S. national study. *Journal of Marriage and the Family, 64*(3), 657–667.

Marshall, G. N., & Lang, E. L. (1990). Optimism, self-mastery, and symptoms of depression in women professionals. *Journal of Personality and Social Psychology, 59,* 132–139.

Marzuki, N. A. (2013). The impact of personality on employee well-being. *European Scientific Journal, 9*(20), 43–52.

Maslow, A. H. (1943). A theory of human motivation. *Psychological Review, 50,* 370–396.

Maslow, A. H. (1970). *Motivation and personality* (2nd ed.). New York: Harper & Row.

Masten, A. S. (2001). Ordinary magic: Resilience process in development. *American Psychologist, 56,* 227–239.

McFarlin, D. B. (1985). Persistence in the face of failure: The impact of self-esteem and contingency information. *Personality and Social Psychology Bulletin, 11,* 153–163.

McGuire, D., & McLaren, L. (2009). The impact of physical environment on employee commitment in call centres. The mediating role of employee well-being. *Team Performance Management, 15*(1/2), 35–48.

Meyer, G. F., & Daniel, D. P. (1981). Privacy, efficiency and the equality of men and women: A revisionist view of sex discrimination in employment. *American Bar Foundation Research Journal, 6*(3), 583–636.

Meyers, D. G., & Diener, E. (1995). Who is happy? *Psychological Science, 6,* 10–19.

Michalos, A. C. (1990). The impact of trust on business, international security and the quality of life. *Journal of Business Ethics, 9*(8), 619–638.

Miller, D. (1986). Communication key to success. *Fire Chief,* pp. 73–77.

Mishra, G. (2001). Culture and self: Implications for psychological inquiry. *Journal of Indian Psychology, 19,* 1–20.

Miyashiro, M. (1996). Exploring the many faces of leadership. *The TQM Magazine, 8*(2), 17–19.

Mroczek, D. K., & Spiro, A., III. (2005). Changes in life satisfaction during adulthood: Findings from the veterans affairs normative ageing study. *Journal of Personality and Social Psychology, 88*(1), 189–202.

Nahawat, S. S., & Rathore, S. (1996). Influence of hardiness & social support on well-being in elderly men & women. *Indian Journal of Clinical Psychology.*

Nikolaou, I., Tomprou, M., & Vakola, M. (2007). Individuals' inducements and the role of personality: Implications for psychological contracts. *Journal of Managerial Psychology, 22*(7), 649–663.

Olason, D. T., & Roger, D. (2001). Optimism, pessimism and fighting spirit: A new approach to assessing expectancy and adaptation. *Personality and Individual Differences, 31,* 755–768.

O'Reilly, C., Chatman, J., & Caldwell, D. (1991). People and organisational culture. A Q-sort approach to assessing fit. *Academy of Management Journal, 34*(3), 487–516.

Ouchi, W. G., & Johnson, J. B. (1978). Types of organisational control and their relationship to emotional well-being. *Administrative Science Quarterly, 23*(2), 293–317.

Parasuraman, S., Purohit, Y. S., Godshalk, V. M., & Beutell, N. J. (1996). Work and family variables, entrepreneurial career success, and psychological well-being. *Journal of Vocational Behaviour, 48,* 275–300.

Parish, J. T., Cadwallader, S., & Busch, P. (2008). Want to, need to, ought to: Employee commitment to organizational change. *Journal of Organizational Change Management, 21*(1), 32–52.

Patterson, F. (2001). Developments in work psychology. *Journal of Occupational and Organisational Psychology, 74,* 381–390.

Patterson, M. G., West, M. A., Shackleton, V. J., Dawson, J. F., Lawthom, R., Maitlis, S., et al. (2005). Validating the organizational climate measure: Links to managerial practices, productivity and innovation. *Journal of Organizational Behaviour, 26,* 379–408.

Pavot, W., & Diener, E. (1993). Review of the satisfaction with life scale. *Psychological Assessment, 5*(2), 164–172.

Petchsawang, P., & Duchon, D. (2009). Measuring workplace spirituality in an Asian context. *Human Resource Development International, 12*(4), 459–468.

Peterson, C. (2000). The future of optimism. *American Psychologist, 55*(1), 44–55.

Peterson, C. (2006). *A premier in positive psychology*. Oxford University Press.

Peterson, C., Semmel, A., von Baeyer, C., Abramson, L. Y., Metalsky, G. I., & Seligman, M. E. P. (1982). The attributional style questionnaire. *Cognitive Therapy and Research, 6*(3), 287–299.

Peterson, C., & Seligman, M. E. P. (2004). Character strengths and virtues: A handbook and classification. New York: Oxford University Press/Washington, DC: American Psychological Association.

Rafanelli, C., Park, S. K., Ruini, C., Ottolini, F., Cazzaro, M., & Fava, G. (2000). Rating well being and distress. *Stress Medicine, 16,* 55 61.

Rego, A., & Cunha, M. P. (2008). Workplace spirituality and organisational commitment: An empirical study. *Journal of Organisational Change Management, 21*(1), 53–75.

Rice, R. W., McFarlin, D. B., Hunt, R. G., & Near, J. P. (1985). Organizational work and the perceived quality of life towards a conceptual model. *The Academy of Management Review, 10* (2), 296–310.

Robertson, I. T., & Cooper, C. L. (2010). Full engagement: The integration of employee engagement and psychological well-being. *Leadership and Organization Development Journal, 31*(4), 324–336.

Robins, T. (1994). *Organisational behaviour*. Australian and New Zeeland, Australia: Prentice Hall.

Roysamb, E., Tawls, K., Reichborn-Kjenneruc, T., Neale, M. C., & Harris, J. R. (2003). Happiness and health. *Journal of Personality and Social Psychology, 85,* 1136–1146.

Ryan, R. M., & Deci, E. L. (2000). Self-determination theory and the facilitation of intrinsic motivation, social development and well-being. *American Psychologist, 55*(1), 68–78.

Ryan, R. M., & Deci, E. L. (2001). On happiness and human potentials: A review of research on hedonic and eudaimonic well-being. In S. Fiske (Ed.), *Annual review of psychology* (pp. 141–166). Palo Alto, CA: Annual Reviews Inc.

Ryff, C. D. (1989). Happiness is everything, or is it? Explorations on the meaning of psychological well-being. *Journal of Personality and Social Psychology, 57*(6), 1069–1081.

Ryff, C. D. (1995). Psychological well-being in adult life. *Current Directions in Psychological Science, 4,* 99–104.

Ryff, C. D. (2014). Psychological well-being revisited. Advances in the science and practice of eudaimonia. *Psychotherapy and Psychosomatics, 83*(1), 10–28.

Ryff, C. D., & Keyes, C. L. M. (1995). The structure of psychological well-being revisited. *Journal of Personality and Social Psychology, 69,* 719–727.

Ryff, C. D., & Singer, B. (1996). Psychological well-being: Meaning, measurement, and implications for psychotherapy research. *Psychotherapy and Psychosomatics, 65,* 14–23.

Ryff, C. D., & Singer, B. (1998). The contours of positive human health. *Psychological Inquiry, 9,* 1–28.

Ryff, C. D., & Singer, B. (2003). Flourishing under fire: Resilience as a prototype of challenged thriving. In C. Keyes & J. Haidt (Eds.), *Flourishing: Positive psychology and life well lived* (pp. 15–36). Washington, D.C.: American Psychological Association.

Ryff, C. D., & Singer, B. (2006). Know thyself, and become what you are: An eudaimonic approach to psychological well-being. *Journal of Happiness Studies, 9*(1), 13–39.

Ryff, C. D., Singer, B., & Love, G. D. (2004). Positive health: Connecting well-being with biology. *Philosophical Transaction: Biological Sciences, 359*(1449), 1383–1394.

Ryff, C. D., Singer, B., Love, G. D., & Essex, M. J. (1998). Resilience in adulthood and later life: Defining features and dynamic processes. In J. Lomranz (Ed.), *Handbook of aging and mental health.* New York: Plenum.

Scheier, M. F., & Carver, C. S. (1985). Optimism, coping and health: Assessment and implications of generalised outcome expectancies. *Health Psychology, 4,* 219–247.

Scheier, M. F., & Carver, C. S. (1992). Effects of optimism on psychological and physical well-being: Theoretical overview and empirical update. *Cognitive Therapy and Research, 16*(2), 201–228.

Schein, E. H. (1990). Organisational culture. *American Psychologist, 45,* 109–119.

Schimmack, U., Oishi, S., Furr, B. M., & Funder, D. C. (2004). Personality and life satisfaction: A facet level analysis. *Personality and Social Psychology Bulletin, 30*(8), 1062–1075.

Schmutte, P. S., & Ryff, C. D. (1997). Personality and well-being: Reexamining methods and meanings. *Journal of Personality and Social Psychology, 73*(3), 549–559.

Schneider, K. J., Bugental, J. F. T., & Pierson, J. F. (Eds.). (2001). *The handbook of humanistic psychology: Leading edges in theory, research, and practice.* Thousand Oaks, CA: Sage.

Schwarzer, R., & Knoll, N. (2003). Positive *coping: mastering demands and searching for meaning.* In S. J. Lopez, C. R. Snyder, (Ed.), *Positive psychological assessment: A handbook of models and measures* (pp. 393–409). Washington, DC.

Seligman, M. E. P. (1998). *Learned optimism.* New York. Pocket Books (Simon & Schuster).

Seligman, M. E. P. (2002b). *Authentic happiness.* New York: Free Press/Simon and Schuster.

Seligman, M., & Csikszentmihalyi, M. (2000). Positive psychology: An introduction. *American Psychologist, 55*(1), 5–14.

Seligman, M. E. P., Steen, T. A., Park, N., & Peterson, C. (2005). Positive psychology progress: Empirical validation of interventions. *American Psychologist, 60*(5), 410–425.

Sen, A. (2008). The economics of happiness and capability. In L. Bruni, F. Come-on, & M. Pugno (Eds.), *Capabilities and happiness.* Oxford: Oxford University Press.

Shamir, B. (1986). Self-esteem and the psychological impact of the unemployment. *Social Psychology Quarterly, 49*(1), 61–72.

Singh, S., & Mansi, (2009). Psychological capital as predictor of psychological well-being. *Journal of the Indian Academy of Applied Psychology, 35*(2), 233–238.

Singh, U., & Srivastava, K. B. L. (2009). Interpersonal trust and organisational citizenship behaviour. *Psychological Studies, 54*(1), 44–55.

Sinha, J. B. P. (1982). The Hindu (Indian) identity. *Dynamic Psychiatry, 15,* 148–160.

Sinha, J. B. P. (2008). *Culture and organisational behaviour.* Sage Publications.

Sinha, J. B. P., Sinha, T. N., Verma, J., & Sinha, R. B. N. (2001). Collectivism coexisting with individualism: An Indian scenario. *Asian Journal of Social Psychology, 4,* 133–145.

Slatten, T. (2008). Antecedents and effects of emotional satisfaction on employee-perceived service quality. *Managing Service Quality, 18*(4), 370–386.

Sousa, L., & Lyubomirsky, S. (2001). Life satisfaction. In J. Worell (Ed.), *Encyclopaedia of women and gender: sex similarities and differences and the impact of society on gender, 2* (pp. 667–676). San Diego, CA: Academic press.

Spector, P. E. (1997). *Job satisfaction: Application, assessment, causes, and consequences*. Thousand Oaks, CA, US: Sage Publications.
Strauser, D. R., & Lustig, D. C. (2008). Psychological well-being: Its relation to work personality, vocational identity and career thoughts. *The Journal of Psychology, 142*(1), 21–35.
Taylor, S. E., & Brown, J. D. (1988). Illusion and well-being: A social psychological perspective on mental health. *Psychological Bulletin, 103*(2), 193–210.
Tella, R. D., & MacCulloch, R. (2006). Some uses of happiness data, in economics. *The Journal of Economic Perspectives, 20*(1), 25–46.
Thompson, C. A., Beauvais, L. L., & Lyness, K. S. (1999). When work, family benefits are not enough: The influence of work, family climate on benefit utilization, organisational attachment, and work family conflict. *Journal of Vocational Behaviour, 54*(3), 392–415.
Vleioras, G., & Bosma, H. A. (2005). Are identity styles important for psychological well-being? *Journal of Adolescence, 28*(3), 397–409.
Wagnild, G. M., & Young, H. M. (1993). Development and psychometric evaluation of the resiliency scale. *Journal of Nursing Management, 1*(2), 165–178.
Wallace, J., Hunt, J., & Richards, C. (1999). The relationship between organisational culture, organisational climate and managerial values. *The International Journal of Public Sector Management, 12*(7), 548–564.
Warr, P. (1990). The measurement of well-being and other aspects of mental health. *Journal of Occupational Psychology, 63*(3), 193–210.
Wissing, M. P., & Temane, Q. M. (2008). The structure of psychological well-being in cultural context: Towards a hierarchical model of psychological health. *Journal of Psychology in Africa, 18*(1), 45–56.
World Health Organisation. (2001). *Mental health: New understanding, new hope*. Geneva: World Health Report, WHO.
Wright, T. A., & Cropanzano, R. (2000). Psychological well-being and job satisfaction as predictors of job performance. *Journal of Occupational Health Psychology, 5*(1), 84–94.
Wright, T. A., & Staw, B. M. (1999). Further thoughts on the happy-productive worker. *Journal of Organisational Behaviour, 20*(1), 31–34.
Youssef, C., & Luthans, F. (2007). Positive organizational behaviour in the workplace: The impact of hope, optimism, and resilience. *Journal of Management, 33*(5), 774–800.
Zwetsloot, G., & Pot, F. (2004). The business value of health management. *Journal of Business Ethics, 55*(2), 115–124.

Chapter 6
Maternal Anemia: A Village Level Empirical Observation in Assam

Pranti Dutta

6.1 Introduction

Globally, around 303,000 maternal deaths occurred and hundreds of thousands of women are still dying due to pregnancy related complication every year (WHO 2015). The International Safe Motherhood Initiative conference launched in 1987 at Nairobi, Kenya established the Safe Motherhood Initiative to address the issues of maternal health that had long been neglected. However, some issues of maternal health particularly maternal anemia have hitherto received very little attention and priority in these agendas. There are numbers of initiative from the Central Government to reduce maternal anemia through antenatal care, taking iron and folic acid supplements. Although such intervention has achieved some progress in targeting the pregnant women, maternal anemia is still a widespread public health challenge. This chapter focuses on prevention of maternal anemia at local context in order to enlighten the problems and challenges to various existing anemia prevention interventions.

6.2 Review of Literature

Maternal anemia is a nutritional deficiency disorder that largely preventable by taking care of dietary intake of iron, folic acid, and nutritional foodstuffs during and before pregnancy. However, it is directly and indirectly accountable for 40% of

P. Dutta (✉)
Department of Humanities and Social Sciences, IIT Guwahati,
Guwahati 781039, Assam, India
e-mail: pranti@iitg.ernet.in; prantidutta12@gmail.com

U.K. De et al. (eds.), *Issues on Health and Healthcare in India*, India Studies in Business and Economics, https://doi.org/10.1007/978-981-10-6104-2_6

maternal deaths in India (Kalaivani 2009). Occurrence of anemia among pregnant women varies according to socioeconomic conditions, lifestyles, and health-seeking behaviors across different cultures (Lone, Qureshi, and Emmanuel 2004). In many cases, anemia during pregnancy is due to low socioeconomic status, customs, and nutritional habits. There need more efforts to improve the quality of healthcare services including family planning programs, awareness about anemia, and utilization of healthcare services. Study also suggested to explore causes of failure to prevent anemia among women and redistribute the health services according to the needs of the population (Lone, Qureshi and Emmanuel 2004; Morsy and Alhady 2014).

Iron deficiency is the most common form of anemia due to poor eating habits, whereas other than nutritional deficiency, malaria, helminth and chronic infections play a major role in develop of all anemia cases (MacDonald, Mildon, Neequaye, Namarika, and Yiannakis 2007; Singh 2012). Indian diets are predominantly low in calories and ascorbic acid, rich in phytates and tannin, for which there is a significant deficit in bioavailability of dietary iron. It is argued that low intake or imbalanced consumption of hematopoietic nutrients contributes to nutritional anemia in pregnancy and it become more vulnerable during pregnancy as demand for iron is increased for expanding red cell and development of the fetus and placenta (Nair and Iyengar 2009; Hazra and Maitra 2001).

Assam is considered as India's one of the highest maternal deaths state with 300 per 100,000 live births (SRS 2013) and according to maternal death review, the highest maternal mortality occurred among the tea garden workers (Mahanta, Mahanta, Gogoi, Dixit, Joshi, and Ghosh 2014). Assam is also one of the largest tea producers of the state of India, accounts for 20% of tea garden labor community of the total the state population where around 50% of total tea plantation workforces are women (Saikia 2008). A number of studies have been addressing the health problems of tea garden laborers and it is found that there is a high prevalence of undernutrition and anemia among laborers of tea community of Assam. Medhi et al. (2006) carried out their study on some randomly selected gardens of Dibrugarh district of Assam and finding shows that high magnitude of nutritional problems like 60% of children were underweight and adults were seen with thinness (nearly 70%) as well. Apart from that, the problem of anemia also found widespread among females' tea laborers. The lack of education severally influences maternal health awareness and health-seeking behaviors among tea garden workers. A recent study conducted in tea gardens of Assam by Das, Sengupta, Chakrabarti, Rudra and Sengupta (2012) and Mahanta, Goswami, Trakroo, Mahanta and Gogoi (2013), identified anemia as a major problem among female tea garden workers and iron therapy found to be helpful in improving the hemoglobin level but for further improvement there need of other intervention like environmental modification and food supplementation by integrate approach of Integrated Child Development Services (ICDS) and Tea garden welfare system.

6.3 Objective

This chapter tries to examine the adverse factors for maternal anemia at the local context in order to improve the maternal health status of women particularly in Assam which is accounted for one of the states with the highest maternal mortality ratio in India. NFHS III report shows that anemia is a contributing factor to high maternal death rate in Assam that claims for prevalence of anemia among 72% of pregnant women within the reproductive age group.

Therefore to prevent maternal anemia, it is significant to identify the context-specific causes of maternal anemia that would help in taking appropriate preventive measures to combat anemia in a particular geographical arena rather than universal, "one-size-fits-all" type intervention. In other words, it will help in channelizing scarce resources according to the local needs.

6.4 Variable Selection

Based on the previous literature found that factors like women's education, nutrition, anemia, income, poverty, economic status, social status, cultural beliefs, and disadvantage group are largely associated with decision-making power to seeking maternal healthcare services (Culyer and Newhouse 2000; Ensor and Cooper 2004; Henderson 2005; Jack 1999; Grossman 1972; Kverndokk 2000; Goodman and Currie, 2010). Further, all these socioeconomic variables have a strong relationship with hemoglobin level because the concentration of better level of hemoglobin depends on the standard of living, social status, food habits, and utilization of healthcare services. Therefore, the following variables are considered in the regression model for examining the maternal anemia at local context.

6.4.1 Income

Income refers to money receipt by the individual from all sources including capital assets, labor, services, and property. Income is positively correlated with health outcomes (Case 2001; Engel et al. 2009). The lower levels of income may result in poor health indicators like higher mortality, morbidity, and less access to healthcare facilities due to lower social status, anemia, financial problem, early marriage, and lack of basic necessities like housing, nutritional foods, safe drinking water, sanitation, etc. In the context of maternal health, the low socioeconomic status of women has less access to nutritional foods during and before her pregnancy which results in lower concentration of iron and that leads to development of anemia among women of reproductive age.

6.4.2 Female Literacy

Previous literature has found female literacy as one of the significant determinants of reducing maternal deaths (Egmond 2004; Islam 2009; McCarthy and Maine 1992; McAlister and Baskett 2006). The changes in the rate of female literacy and rate maternal mortality are negatively related. In other words, increases in female literacy result in declining rate of maternal mortality (Pillai et al. 2013). The educated women more likely to have decision-making power over her marriage age, birth spacing, use of contraceptives, financial security, and seek proper healthcare before and during her pregnancy (McCarthy and Maine 1992). Additionally, female literacy makes women aware about nutritional requirement during pregnancy that helps preventing low birth weight, anemia, and hemorrhage (Jain 2012).

6.4.3 Age of Marriage

The age of marriage is largely influential on women health status and adolescent fertility in one hand. On the other hand, it results in the adverse and risky pregnancy, poor knowledge of nutritional diet, and use of family planning methods, birth order and lack of decision-making power for the well-being of her family, child, and herself as well. Previous studies done by Biswas and Baruah (2014), Morsy and Alhady (2014), and Singh (2012) have found age is one the contributing factors to anemia. Girls with early age of marriage are more likely to suffer from anemia due to lack of adequate nutrition as they require nutrition over and above the nutritional demand for their adolescent growth.

6.4.4 Land Ownership

Land ownership is an important factor from both as assets for a household and index for food availability at household level. Land ownership provides an opportunity for dietary diversifications with food fortification for home consumption and for market purpose as well. Household with land ownership can have homegrown foods to maintain a proper food habit during pregnancy as it gives balanced nutritional diet.

6.4.5 Food Expenditure

The 68th round of the Household Consumer Expenditure Survey conducted by National Sample Survey during 2012 accounted food expenditure nearly half of the total household expenditure, i.e., 52.9%, while medical expenses only 6.7%. Again, food expenditure also relates to consumption of heme and non-heme food products which are significant for dietary habit for women during her pregnancy.

6.5 Methods of Selection and Study Area

Estimated maternal mortality ratio for the year 2013–2014, Dibrugarh district is found to be one of the highest maternal mortality ratios among the districts of Upper Assam Administrative Divisions.[1] This study has been conducted in two villages, namely Lepetkatta Tea Estate and Janzimukh, a part of kalakhowa village under Barbaruah Block Primary Health Centre (BPHC) of Dibrugarh district which has recorded as the highest number of maternal deaths reporting BPHC.

The study has been carried out through a household survey with a structured questionnaire covering 15% of total household, i.e., total 35 respondents including pregnant women, mother with one-year old child and households with maternal death cases. The objective of the questionnaire is to get information on maternal health status and in-depth information on maternal deaths cases in order to investigate the different causes of maternal anemia at local context. Regression with robust standard error technique was used to examine the responsible factors on hemoglobin levels (as a proxy for anemia) among the sample population.

Janzimukh is located at the embankment of Dihing River, which is about 40 km away from Dibrugarh town with a total population of 654 as per 2011 census. On the other hand, Lepetkatta Tea Estate is located at nearby A T Road, Barbaruah, Dibrugarh with a total population of 1219 (Census 2011). The entire population of Janzimukh is Mishing Community belonging to the Scheduled Tribe (ST) and the population of Lepetkatta Tea Estate is Tea Tribes Community[2] (OBC). In both villages, a large section of population is illiterate (68.57%) and some of them went to school below tenth standards. The primary source of income of the villagers in Janzimukh is paddy cultivation and secondary source is daily wage laborer. The fertile soils allow the villagers to grow a number of green vegetables and paddy at homes. Fishery and poultry farms are common for every household. On the other hand, people of Lepetkatta Tea Estate are mostly engaged with tea garden seasonal works, factory and other allied activities at temporarily and permanent basis. For

[1]Upper Assam Division includes—Tinsukia, Dibrugarh, Sibsagar, Jorhat, Golaghat. Lower Assam Division includes—Kokrajhar, Dhubri, Goalpara, Darrang, Bongaigaon, Barpeta, Kamrup, Nalbari. North Assam Division includes—Marigaon, Nagaon, Sonitpur, Lakhimpur, Dhemaji. Hills and Barak Valley Divisions includes—Karbi Anglong, North Cachar Hills, Cachar, Karimganj, Hailakandi. *Source:* Annual Health Survey (AHS) 2010–11.

[2]Tea tribes originally brought from neighboring states of the present day Orissa, Madhya Pradesh, Bihar, Andhra Pradesh and West Bengal into Assam by British colonial planters about 150 years ago for engaging in tea gardens as labourers and subsequently settled in Assam permanently. They are recognized as Other Backward Classes by the Government (GOA).

their diet, they solely depend upon on daily market. The daily wage earner has to buy daily food-stuff on daily basis.

6.6 Results

After surveying in both villages and interviewing with pregnant women, mothers, family member of the deceased women, respective ANM and ASHA workers of the villages and hospital records, maternal anemia was found to be one of the major causes of maternal mortality and morbidities during and after the period of pregnancy. Apart from the three maternal death cases, a number of four high-risk pregnancies and three complicated pregnancy has been reported in Lepetkatta Tea Estate, whereas no maternal death case and any adverse pregnancy were found in Janzimukh during the year preceding the survey. The finding of the study shows that low age of marriage, land ownership and low bioavailability of iron intake in daily diet have a significant impact on high prevalence of maternal anemia among the tea laborers. The details have been discussed in the following heads.

6.6.1 Socioeconomic Causes of Maternal Anemia

From socioeconomic point of view, it is observed that age of marriage, literacy, birth order, hemoglobin level, and pregnancy complicacy in Lepetkatta T E are poor compared to Janzimukh. On the contrary, the level of yearly income is higher among tea garden laborers than that of Janzimukh. Summary of the table shows that women of tea laborers are more vulnerable from maternal health status point of view (Table 6.1).

6.6.2 Model Specification

In the following model, hemoglobin level as a proxy for anemia has been considered as dependent variable and variable such as literacy, income level, age of marriage, land ownership, and food expenditure are considered as an independent variable.

The functional relationship between the dependent and the independent variables as recommended by Henderson (2005) is used in the following estimation:

Hemoglobin Level = f (literacy, income level, age of marriage, land ownership, food expenditure)

Table 6.1 Some selected indicators of maternal health status of women

Background characteristic	Lepetkatta T E	Janzimukh
Average household income	47411.76	43823.52
Age of marriage		
<15	35.29	0
15–20	58.82	55.55
20>	5.88	44.44
Literacy		
Illiterate	82.35	55.55
literate	11.76	33.33
Only sign	5.88	16.66
Birth order		
1	23.52	27.77
2–3	52.94	61.11
4–5	17.64	11.11
6–7	5.88	0
Hemoglobin level		
<7	17.64	0
7–9	76.47	11.11
10–12	5.88	88.89
Pregnancy complicacy		
With complicacy	58.82	11.11
No complicacy	41.17	88.89

Source Survey data 2014–15

The Breusch Pagan test/Cook–Weisberg test and Cameron and Trivedi's decomposition have been carried out to detect heteroscedasticity in the data set and found hettest and IM-test are not significant ($p = 0.2801$). The VIF also shows no colinearity problem among the predictor variables. Therefore, the model is

$$Hb_i = \alpha + \beta_0 lit_i + \beta_1 Y_i + \beta_2 AgeM_i + \beta_3 landO_i + \beta_4 FdEx_i + \mu_i$$

where Hb = Hemoglobin Level, lit = Literature, Y = Income Level, AgeM = Age of Marriage, landO = Land ownership, FdEx = Food Expenditure, and μ = Error term.

Finally, robust standard errors have been applied to get reasonably an accurate *P* values and less bias in test statistics and confidence intervals as well. In addition, the data were analyzed using STATA, a statistical package, version 14.

The present study reveals the result of regression with robust standard errors where it is showed that better level of hemoglobin concentration is significantly associated with age of marriage ($p = 0.008$) and land ownership ($p = 0.007$) of the household rather than level of literacy, income, and food expenditure in studied villages (Table 6.2).

Table 6.2 Regression with robust standard errors result for associate variables on level of hemoglobin

Variables	Dependent Variable (MMR), $R^2 = 0.4963$, $F(5, 29) = 12.36$	
	Coefficient	t
Lit	−7203656 (0.9805152)	−0.73
InL	0.0000144 (0.0000137)	1.06
AgeM	0.2278308** (0.0799836)	2.85
landO	1.030845** (0.3515233)	2.93
FdEx	0.0000388 (0.0000378)	1.03
Constant	2.828356** (1.274435)	2.22

Source Survey data 2014–15
Note 1. $^{***}p < 0.001$, $^{**}p < 0.01$, $^{*}p < 0.05$
2. Figures in parentheses indicates standard errors of the coefficient

6.6.3 *Iron Bioavailability and Dietary Concern*

The significant fact is that the mothers and pregnant women under the study in Lepetkatta T E are suffering from anemia either severely or moderately (76.47%), while, except two, all respondents from Janzimukh are non-anemic (88.89%). Interviewed with ANM and ASHA workers, it is observed that apart from the awareness about family planning methods and distributing IFA tablets among pregnant women, without a proper diet, improvement of hemoglobin level is not possible. It is found that proper diet is not maintained among the tea labourers. For instance, consumption of heme product is less among tea laborers than that of people of Janzimukh (Table 6.3).

In response to proper nutrition during pregnancy, women from Janzimukh were quite aware of the nutritional food habits. Homegrown daily vegetables and green leafy vegetables, fishery, and poultry farms of their own found beneficial to follow the proper food habits. On the contrary, tea garden worker lives either in tea garden quarter provided by tea garden manager or temporary hut inside the tea garden and they do not possess land of their own. They do not have any homegrown food products and have limited access to daily intake of micronutrient for their ignorance and most of the time, do not have financial resources such that they can afford to maintain a nutritional diet. It is observed that protein intake is very low in their

Table 6.3 Average total food expenditure on heme and non-heme food product at monthly basis during 2013–14 (Rupees)

Villages	Non-Home product		Heme product		Others	Total food expenditure
	Cereals	Vegetables	Fish	Meat		
Janzimukh	1317.65	611.76	283.12	282.88	315.76	2855.29
Lepetkatta TE	905.88	519.41	174.71	161.76	270.59	2032.35

Source Survey data 2014–15

daily diet; typically they are based on staple foods which provide a low iron bioavailability.

6.7 Discussion

The first observation of the study age at marriage is similar with the finding of previous studies done by Morsy and Alhady (2014), Singh (2012), Biswas and Baruah (2014)—where they found the contributing factors to anemia are age, literacy, social beliefs and socioeconomic status of a woman. Girls with early age of marriage are more likely to suffer from anemia due to lack of adequate nutrition as they require nutrition over and above the nutritional demand for their adolescent growth which causes adverse and risky pregnancy during their reproductive age. Additionally, they are more responsible for high fertility without having decision-making power about the use of contraception within their family (Kavitha 2010). In studied villages, it is seen that women of Janzimukh are got married at the age of 20 and well informed as compared to women of Lepetkatta T E.

Again, land ownership has a significant impact on the concentration of hemoglobin level among women at reproductive age. Household with land of their own has opportunity to engage with economic activities such as agricultural works, home garden, livestock, and poultry farm of their own. An adequate amount of micronutrient food intake is necessary to ensure nutritional adequacy. Low-income households with land ownership can able to maintain their nutritional diet from their homegrown food product. On the other hand, those who have no access to land of their own have to rely on the market for their daily diet. Therefore, land ownership is one of the important factors to a household for self-sustain food product and income as well in other to maintain the hemoglobin level in the long run.

The second observation that relating to low bioavailability iron in the diet is also found significant in previous studies. It is observed that only iron supplementation does not help much in preventing anemia without an optimum diet maintained by the entire population. The amount of dietary iron absorption depends on the bioavailability of iron which is determined by amount of heme and non-heme iron in the meal. Low dietary intake and consumption of high non-heme product produce low bioavailability of iron. This results in low hemoglobin level and poor iron status in her body which becomes more vulnerable with the high birth order during her childbearing age (Nair and Iyengar 2009; Thompson 2013).

In Lepetkatta T E, population have no access to diversified diet due to lack of diversified food availability, resulting from scarcity of land and geographical bottlenecks, on the other hand, people of Janzimukh have diversified food availability at their own land as they live in the bank of Dihing river and every household of the village possess agricultural land and water bodies for doing farming.

Multiple nutritional benefits from food-based approach can be taken as preventive strategies of nutritional deficiency and malnutrition through promoting the availability of and accessing iron-rich foods which contain heme iron and non-animal food products that are good source of vitamin A and C, and folic acid. Considering the fact, promoting home gardens, small animal husbandry for maintaining a regional and local variation of diet, seasonal availability and increase the selection of iron containing foods is vital to enhance the bioavailability (Biswas and Baruah 2014). Alternatively, Nair and Iyengar (2009) have suggested for food fortification and food supplementation are the important component of food-based approach that can enhance the iron absorbability of the entire population. However, those households who have limited access to land encourages for small home gardening which requires minimal space, fast-growing example includes pumpkin, cucumber, and small animal husbandry for home consumption (Hillenbrand and Waid 2010; Ruel and Levin 2000; Waid 2011). It is therefore observed that context-specific preventive measures rather than universal, "one-size-fits-all" type intervention (in terms of distribution of IFA tablets) and government efforts to changes in the behavior of providers and consumers are very much needed for sustainable improvements in iron and nutritional level as well.

6.8 Conclusion

Maternal anemia is widespread public health problem which is largely preventable. The urgent requirement is to making villagers aware about the age of marriage and habitual nutritional diets which are significantly related to prevailing maternal anemia in the studied villages. Food-based approach is an alternative intervention of supplementation programs towards long term ensuring of adequate hemoglobin level before and after pregnancy particularly for the tea garden laborers. Assam is an agro-based state; there are numerous possibilities to develop the home garden, animal husbandry, and fishery for home consumption. However, there need to be cooperative efforts of government and non-governmental organization to support and promote food-based intervention along with iron supplementation programs in other to increase the efficacy to develop iron status among pregnant women. Therefore, it is an acute requirement of evaluation of anemia prevention intervention program at local context, in contrast with providing universal intervention to all anemia causes so that the actual cause of failure of such programs can be identified for better health outcome.

References

Biswas, M., & Baruah, R. (2014). Maternal anaemia associated with socio-demographic factors among pregnant women of Boko-Bongaon Block Kamrup, Assam. *Indian Journal of Basic and Applied Medical Research, 3*(2), 712–721.

Case, A. (2001). *Health, Income and Economic Development. Woodrow Wilson School of Public and International Affairs, Center for Health and Wellbeing,Princeton University,* Working paper 271, 1–40.

Census. (2011). *Census of India.* New Delhi: Office of the Registrar General & Census Commissioner, India, Goverenment of India.

Culyer, A. J., & Newhouse, J. (2000). The Human Capital Model. In A. J. Culyer & J. Newhouse (Eds.), *Handbook of Health Economics* 1, 347–408. Elsevier.

Das, B., Sengupta, B. S., Rudra, T., & Sengupta, S. (2012). Incidence of anemia among the female tea garden workers in a tea plantation in upper Assam, India. *Journal of Indian Medical Association, 110*(2), 84–87.

Egmond, V. K. (2004). Reproductive health in Afghanistan: Results of a knowledge, attitudes and practices survey among Afghan women in Kabul. *Disasters, 28*(3), 269–282.

Engel, J. P., Seligson, R. W., & Rope, W. L. (2009). *Socioeconomic Determinants of Health in Report of Prevention for the Health of North Carolina: Prevention Action Plan.* North Carolina: North Carolina Institute of Medicine.

Ensor, T., & Cooper, S. (2004). Overcoming barriers to health service access and fluctuating demand side through purchasing. *Health, Nutrition and Population Policy, Discussion Paper of World Bank.* pp. 1–78.

GOA. *Department of Tea Tribes.* Retrieved January 26, 2015, from http://online.assam.gov.in: http://online.assam.gov.in/web/tea-tribes/home.

Goodman, J., & Currie, J. (2010). Parental socioeconomic status, child health, and human capital. *International Encyclopedia of Education, 2,* 253–259.

Grossman, M. (1972). On the concept of health capital and the demand for health. *Journal of Political Economy, 80*(2), 223–255.

Hazra, M. N., & Maitra, N. (2001). Anemia in Pregnancy. In U. Krishna, D. Tank & S. Daftary (Eds.), *Pregnancy at risk: Current concepts* (pp. 229–232). New Delhi: Jaypee Brothers Medical Publishers (P) Ltd.

Henderson, J. (2005). Demand for health and medical care. In J. Henderson (Ed.), *Health economics and policy* (pp. 127–153). New Delhi: Cengage Learning.

Hillenbrand, E. P., & Waid, J. L. (2010). Adapting food-based strategies to improve the nutrition of the landless: A review of HKI's homestead food production programme in Bangladesh. *Food Based Approaches for Improving Diets and Raising Levels of Nutrition* (pp. 1–16). Rome: Food and Agriculture Organization of the United States.

Islam, M. (2009). Progress and challenges in making pregnancy safer: A global perspective. In J. Ehiri (Ed.), *Maternal and child health global challenges, programmes and policy* (pp. 399–417). New York: Springer.

Jack, W. (1999). The demand for health services. In W. Jack (Ed.), *Principles of health economics for developing countries* (pp. 55–87). Washington, D.C.: The International Bank for Reconstruction and Development/ The World Bank.

Jain, G. (2012). Female literacy and its relevance with maternal and infant mortality rates. *International Journal of Management, 3*(2), 65–79.

Kalaivani, K. (2009). Prevalence & consequences of anaemia in pregnancy. *Indian Journal of Medical Research,* 627–633.

Kavitha, N. (2010). Is young maternal age a risk factor for sexually transmitted diseases and anemia in India? An Examination in Urban and Rural Areas. *The Institute for Social and Economic Change, Bangalore; Working paper 245,* 1–16.

Kverndokk, S. (2000). Why Do People Demand for Health. *Health Economics Research programme, Oslo University, Working Paper 2000: 5,* 1–25.

Lone, F., Qureshi, R., & Emmanuel, F. (2004). Maternal anaemia and its impact on perinatal outcome in a tertiary care hospital in Pakistan. *Eastern Mediterranean Health Journal, 10*(6), 801–807.

MacDonald, C., Mildon, A., Neequaye, M., Namarika, R., & Yiannakis, M. (2007). Anemia—can its widespread prevalence among women in developing countries be impacted? A case study: Effectiveness of a large-scale, integrated, multiple-intervention nutrition program on decreasing anemia in Ghanaian and Malawian women. In L. E. Chamberlain (Ed.), *Women's Health in the Majority World: Issues and Initiatives* (pp. 65–108). New York: Nova Science Publications.

Mahanta, T. G., Mahanta, B. N., Gogoi, P., Dixit, P., Joshi, V., & Ghosh, S. (2014). Anaemia, its determinants and effect of different interventions amongst tea tribe adolescent girls living in Dibrugarh district of Assam. *Indian Journal of Community Health, 26*(2), 300–309.

Mahanta, T. G., Trakroo, A., Mahanta, B. N., & Gogoi, P. (2013). Prevalence of anaemia and associated factors amongst tea pluckers and the effect of directly observed iron therapy(DOIT) in Anaemia and Productivity in Dibrugarh District, Assam. *Medical Science, 3*(4), 22–25.

McAlister, C., & Baskett, T. F. (2006). Female education and maternal mortality: A worldwide survey. *Journal of Obstet Gynaecol Canada, 28*(11), 983–990.

McCarthy, J., & Maine, D. (1992). A framework for analyzing the determinants of maternal mortality. *Studies in Family Planning, 23*(1), 23–33.

Medhi, G. H., et al. (2006). Study of health problems and nutritional status of tea garden population of Assam. *Indian Journal of Medical Sciences, 60*(12), 496–506.

Morsy, N., & Alhady, S. (2014). Nutritional status and socio-economic conditions influencing prevalence of anaemia in pregnant women. *International Journal of Scientific & Technology Research, 3*(7), 54–60.

Nair, K. M., & Iyengar, V. (2009). Iron content, bioavailability & factors affecting iron status of Indians. *Indian Journal of Medical Research, 130,* 634–645.

Pillai, V. K., Maleku, A., & Wei, F. (2013). Maternal Mortality and Female Literacy Rates in Developing Countries during 1970–2000: A Latent Growth Curve Analysis. *International Journal of Population Research,* Article ID 163292, 1–11.

Ruel, M. T., & Levin, C. E. (2000). Assessing the potential for food-based strategies to reduce Vitamin A and iron deficiencies: A Review of Recent Evidence. *Food Consumption and Nutrition Division, Discussion paper No. 92,* 1–39.

Saikia, B. (2008). Development of tea garden community and adivasi identity politics in Assam. *The Indian Journal of Labour Economics, 51*(2), 307–322.

Singh, R. K. (2012). Life style behavior affecting prevalence of anemia among women in EAG states, India. *Population Association of America 2012 Annual Meeting Program,* (pp. 1–22). San Francisco, CA.

SRS. (2013). *India Sample Registration System Maternal Mortality Ratio Bulletin 2011-2013.* New Delhi: Office of the Registrar General and Census Commissioner (India).

Thompson, B. (2013). Food-based approaches for combating iron deficiency. *Food and Agriculture Organization,* 1–22.

Waid, J. (2011). *Adapting Food-based Strategies to Improve the Nutrition of the Landless.* Retrieved 2 7, 2015, from The Congressional Hunger Center: http://www.hungercenter.org/wp-content/uploads/2011/09/Adapting-Food-based-Strategies-Waid.pdf.

WHO. (2015). *Beyond the numbers: Reviewing maternal deaths and complications to make pregnancy safer.* Geneva: World Health Organization.

Chapter 7
Identification of the Factors Influencing Child Immunization in West Bengal: A Case Study of Darjeeling District

Maumita Ghosh and Shrabanti Maity

7.1 Introduction

Public health issues are of vital concern across the countries in the world (Tatlidil 1992). Measurement of health in terms of mortality, morbidity, and their consequences is essential to plan some effective ways to reduce the burden of illness and to frame health-related policies (WHO 1994). Construction of mothers' composite health index using the multiple correspondence analysis (MCA) to find out how children's health depends on the mother's health facilities during pregnancy and mothers' health status is an effort to add a dimension to the reproductive and child healthcare-related decision making for the policy makers. This article focuses on the health status of children in the form of childhood immunization which is very important for healthy development of a nation. At the same time, this study would help to find out whether mother's health facilities and health status determine her child's health status by constructing "mothers" health composite index. Darjeeling district in the Northern part of West Bengal having vast geographical diversity and remote hilly terrain has been chosen as a study area.

M. Ghosh
Department of Economics, Southfield College, Darjeeling, WB, India
e-mail: moum29@rediffmail.com

S. Maity (✉)
Assam University, Silchar, Assam, India
e-mail: sontoshe_sraban@yahoo.in

U.K. De et al. (eds.), *Issues on Health and Healthcare in India*, India Studies in Business and Economics, https://doi.org/10.1007/978-981-10-6104-2_7

7.1.1 Objectives of the Study

The main objective of the study is to identify the mothers' health status for those whose child's immunization is to be interrogated. Also, the socioeconomic factors influencing child's immunization are identified.

Related to the above-mentioned objectives the following research questions are investigated.

1. What is the status of mothers' health whose child's immunizations are interrogated?
2. What the sociocultural and socioeconomic variables influence child immunization?

The paper is organized as follows: After a short introduction and specification of the objectives in the first section, the existing literature is discussed in Sect. 7.2. Section 7.3 describes data related to the immunization status of 245 households and the methodology adopted to address the research questions. Section 7.4 incorporates the analysis of the results related to child's immunization and factors influencing child's immunization. Finally, Sect. 7.5 includes the policy conclusion.

7.2 Related Literature: A Bird's Eye View

Construction of a composite health index by Cayolla da Motta (1979) is an example of measurement of health-related issue. The statistical technique of principal component analysis (PCA), (see Anderson 1984), is useful for such index construction and this technique has been successfully applied in several studies (e.g., Kendall 1939; Pal 1963, 1971, and 1990; Mukhopadhyaya 1988; Pathak 1991 and 1995). As mentioned by Asselin (2002), if we have several categorical variables then the pattern of relationship can be analyzed better using MCA rather than PCA. Aselin, and Anh (2005); Asselin et al. (2005); Ki et al. (2005); Ningaye and Ndjanyou (2006); Njong (2007); Njong and Ningaye (2008); Hyder et al. (2012), applied MCA technique in their studies to compress several categorical variables into a single index.

After reviewing some earlier work in the next section, we presented the data and methodology related to this research work.

7.3 Data and Methodology

7.3.1 Data and Choice of the Study Area

The Human Development Report of West Bengal 2004 reveals that the ranking of Darjeeling in terms of health index, educational index, income index as well as human development index is much ahead of other North Bengal districts, namely, Jalpaiguri, Koch Bihar, Uttar and Dakshin Dinajpur, and Malda. In terms of health and educational index, it stands fifth and in Income Index it stands third just after Kolkata and Haora. Darjeeling ranks fourth in HDI in West Bengal and its educational index and health index separately are higher than other North Bengal districts. So it is expected that in this district, people's response toward some basic health-related issues would be positive. For the very purpose, a cross-sectional study was conducted in Naxalbari and Matigara blocks of Darjeeling district. These blocks have a mix of both plains and hilly terrain and most importantly most of the residents of these two regions are schedule caste. The data were mainly field-based, collected through personal interview. The sampled households were selected by random sampling technique using the random number table and the relevant information about scheduled caste households was collected from block development office.

7.3.2 Description of Data

The official age for vaccination is from birth to 1 -ear infants. Infants crossing this age are not refused for vaccination in a field situation. Information was collected from the field following the procedure of National Family Health Survey (NFHS) data on immunization. At the time of survey, mother's/family members were asked to show the vaccination card for each child born before 2 years of the survey to make sure that the child's age was 12 months to 2 years during the survey period or on mother's report in case of non-availability of the card. Totally, 400 households were interrogated from both the districts taking 200 from each district. We found totally 245 children from the households from Darjeeling district whose age come under the required age group (12 months to 2 years). In the process of interrogation, the parents were asked for the child immunization card to get the idea whether the child is fully vaccinated or not. We also tried to find out various factors related to mothers' health like age at the time of marriage, neonatal care received at the time of pregnancy, mothers knowledge about AIDS, whether the child had delivered in the presence of a trained person, whether the concerned mothers consulted doctors for their acute illness or whether they ignored their illness due to financial problems and observed whether their Body Mass Index (BMI) is appropriate according to age and weight. As already stated, we have collected the information to assess the immunization coverage with the evaluation of child immunization card and parents interview. At the same time, we also tried to find out the reasons for non-immunization, dropouts, disease susceptibility, and the mortality of children. To know the knowledge of parents about child immunization, we prepared the following score table (Table 7.1).

Here 0.25 Score has been allotted to know the Name of the Vaccine, 0.25 for Dose of the Vaccine, 0.25 for Time Schedule, i.e., in which age of the baby the dose should be given, 0.25 for Functions of the Vaccine. Therefore, score 1 would be

Table 7.1 Knowledge of vaccines of the parents on the basis of four point score

Scores	Father		Mother	
	Total number	Percentage	Total number	Percentage
0	85	42.5	76	38
0.25–1	59	29.5	65	32.5
1.25–2	35	17.5	25	12.5
2.25–3	14	7	26	13
3.25–4	7	3.5	8	4
Total	200		200	100

Source Authors' own calculation based on field survey

allotted to one vaccine. The maximum point would be four as there are four Vaccines. If somebody acquires 0.25 that means he knows the name of only one vaccine. In the interview, fathers and mothers were asked separately about the knowledge of the vaccines and we put the scores accordingly. In Darjeeling, 42.5% of fathers have acquired score 0 as they could not answer about the name, dose, time schedule, and function of all the four vaccines.

7.3.3 Methodology

Two models have been used for the analysis of data, one for the determinants of factors influencing child immunization and the other for the construction of composite mother's health index, who were interrogated for their children. Logistic regression (binary) analysis is used to examine the likelihood of the full immunization of children in terms of various factors, while Multiple Correspondence Analysis (MCA) is used to analyze the pattern of relationships among observations described taking a set of nominal variables. Along Yule's 'Q' Coefficient is computed to check the degree of associations between attributes.

7.3.3.1 MCA Model

MCA is nothing but a standard correspondence analysis of a matrix whose entries are 0 or 1. The MCA in this study is used to generate a mothers' composite health index (MCHI) for each sampled household. For the construction of a Mothers' Composite Health Index (MCHI) the monotonicity axiom is satisfied (Asselin 2002). The axiom implies that if a household i improves in terms of any health indicator, then the household's Composite Health Index value $MCHI_i$ increases and the households health status improves.

The *MCHI* constructed using MCA has a tendency of being negative in its lowest part and that makes interpretation difficult. Thus, in order to make the index value positive, a small absolute value of the average $C_{\min}$ is added to all *MCHI*. Asselin (2002) expressed this $C_{\min}$ as:

$$C_{\min} = \frac{\sum_{k=1}^{K} W_{\min}^{k}}{K} \tag{7.1}$$

The absolute value of $C_{\min}$ can then be added to the *MCHI* of each household to obtain the new positive *CHHI* scores.

For the purpose of comparison of the health status of different blocks, we have considered the UNDP recommended ranges and thus if the calculated $CMHI_i$ value falls below 0.050, it is called poor health status. If $CMHI_i$ takes values from 0.050 to 0.079, it indicates a medium health status and $CMHI_i$ value of 0.080 and above suggests high health status of the interrogated mother.

7.3.3.2 Yule's Coefficient

Yule's Coefficient is,also known as the coefficient of colligation. It is a measure of association between two binary variables. We have used Yule's '*Q*' coefficient of association to show the association or dissociation between child immunization and mothers' education, fathers' education, and fathers' occupation. With the help of Yule's coefficient, we explained the vulnerability by identifying the factor which made the group more vulnerable. As mentioned earlier, three attributes, viz, mother's educational status, father's educational status, and father's employment status with another attribute, the immunization status of the child are used to identify which attribute contributes more to the immunization status of the child. In this way, the group which has greater chance not to immunize children or stops the immunization process in the mid-way can be identified. It is to be noted here that all the variables are binary in nature; for example, if the sampled child is immunized, then we assign a value '1' and '0' otherwise. Similarly if the mother has completed 5 years of schooling, she would be considered as educated and thus assigned a value '1' and '0' otherwise and following the same methodology we assigned values to father's educational as well as employment status.

The Yule's coefficient of association is calculated using the following formula:

As a measure of the intensity of association between two attributes '*A*' and '*B*', following Yule (1911, 1912) the coefficient of association *Q*, can be defined as

$$Q = \frac{(AB) * (\alpha\beta) - (\beta A) * (\alpha B)}{(AB) * (\alpha\beta) + (\beta A) * (\alpha B)} = \frac{N\delta}{(\alpha B) * (\alpha\beta) + (\beta A) * (\alpha\beta)} \tag{7.2}$$

If '*A*' and '*B*' are independent, then $\delta = 0$ and thus $Q = 0$.

If '*A*' and '*B*' are completely associated, then either $(AB) = (A)$ and $(\beta A) = 0$, or $(AB) = (B)$ and $(\alpha B) = 0$

Thus in each case $Q = +1$, if 'A' and 'B' are in complete dissociation then either $(AB) = 0$ or $(\alpha\beta) = 0$ and we get $Q = -1$. Hence, 'Q' ranges from −1 to +1, that is, $-1 \leq Q \leq 1$.

7.3.3.3 Logit Model

In order to examine the factors influencing immunization status of the interrogated households, we consider the following variables:

1. Birth order of the child
2. Mother's age
3. Family income
4. Distance from the nearby health center
5. Sex of the baby
6. Religion of the interrogated household
7. Mother's level of education, measured by years of schooling
8. Composite Health Index of the mother.

The above-mentioned variables have been identified on the basis of field experience of the researchers (Kachari and Maity 2015; Maity and Kachari 2015) and these are the independent variables in the specified model. To form the model in the next step, the dependent variables need to be specified. Here we assigned value '1' for that child whose immunization at that particular age was complete and we assigned a value '0' for that child whose immunization status was either incomplete or not at all executed at that age. By this way, the relative immunization status of the interrogated children is explained by considering a binary system which is taken as dependent variable.

Using the above-mentioned eight variables, step-wise logistic regression model is used in our study. It is specified as follows:

$$p_i = \frac{1}{1 + e^{\alpha + \sum_{j=1}^{6} \beta_j x_j + u_i}} \quad \forall j = 1, 2, \ldots, 5 \text{ and } \forall i = 1, 2, \ldots, 245 \tag{7.3}$$

where

$p_i =$ immunization status of the child (if fully immunized at that age, then '1', otherwise '0')
$\alpha =$ coefficient of the constant term
$\beta_j =$ coefficient of the five independent variables
$x_j =$ Independent variables
$u_i =$ stochastic error

Here, $\alpha + \sum_{j=1}^{8} \beta_j x_j + u_i$ is not the response variable but a linear function of a set of independent or predictor variables. Adjusted values are calculated from Logit regressions incorporating all predictor variables simultaneously. At the time of calculating the adjusted values for a particular predictor variable, all other predictor variables are controlled by setting them to their mean values in the underlying regression.

7.4 Analysis of Research Results

At first, the results related to the mother's composite health index whose child's immunization pattern has been interrogated are discussed. After discussing these results, we discussed the results related to vulnerability; and finally, the results related to the factors influencing child's immunization are analyzed.

7.4.1 Analysis of the Results Related to Mother's Composite Health Index

In order to investigate the health status of the mothers for whom the information regarding child immunization were collected; we considered those indicators which gave us an overview of their knowledge of health. For the very reason, seven criteria of mothers' health have been assigned. The criterions include:

1. Age at the time of first child
2. Neonatal care taken during pregnancy
3. Postnatal care after delivery
4. Knowledge of the mothers about AIDS
5. Whether the child has delivered in the presence of a trained person
6. Whether the concerned mothers' consult doctors for their acute illness
7. Whether they ignored their illness due to financial problems
8. Whether their Body Mass Index (BMI) is appropriate according to age and weight.

All the answers furnished by the interviewed mothers are binary in character, and thus we applied MCA to obtain the weights for constructing the composite health index for the mothers. By nature, MCA always provides weights corresponding to all possibilities. Here the information are binary in nature, namely, Yes and No and thus by applying MCA we get two weights for each modality corresponding to two answers associated with each question. It is worth to mention here that, the answer which is considered to be desirable should achieve more weight relative to the other answer which is not thought to be desirable. For example, in case of the Neonatal Care, there are two options, namely, Yea and No. But from the point of view of health aspect the answer 'Yes' should be considered more desirable than the answer 'No' and the process of MCA should provide more weight to the answer 'Yes' than the answer 'No'. The weights related to all binary answers for all the criterions or modalities are presented in Table 7.2.

From Table 7.2, it is clear that the weights obtained using MCA are appropriate in the sense that all the desirable answers corresponding to all modalities received higher weight. For example in case of Neonatal care, the answer 'Yes' received weights 0.093 where as the answer 'No' received 0.030 only and it is true for all modalities.

After getting the weights corresponding to all modalities, we have constructed Composite Mothers' health Index. It is to be noted here that as mentioned earlier, we have interrogated the immunization status of 245 children and for them we considered 200 mothers. Thus, we have constructed Composite Mothers' Health Index for 200 interrogated mother and the results related to that is presented in Table 7.3a and 7.3b.

In the table, we presented the results related to 10 mother's composite health index for the Naxalbari block. The results related to 100 interrogated mothers' are presented in the appendix. Similarly in Table 7.3b, we presented the mother's composite health index for 10 mothers' taken from Matigara block and the mother's composite health index for all interrogated mothers are presented in the appendix.

For the purpose of comparison of health status of two blocks, namely, Naxalbari and Matigara, we presented the summary statistics of two blocks in Table 7.4.

Table 7.4 reveals that the mean value of MCHI for Naxalbari is 0.069 and according to the range it falls in the medium health standard. In case of Matigara,

Table 7.2 Variables included and weights obtained from multiple correspondence analyses for the calculation of mother's composite health index (MCHI)

Variable	Categories	Weights
Age at the time of first child	Below 18 or 18	0.014
	Above 18	0.111
Neonatal care	No	0.033
	Yes	0.093
Postnatal care	No	0.035
	Yes	0.090
Knowledge about AIDS	No	0.030
	Yes	0.090
Child delivery by trained person	No	0.030
	Yes	0.095
Consult doctor for acute disease	No	0.028
	Yes	0.098
Illness neglected due to financial problem	No	0.088
	Yes	0.038
BMI appropriate	No	0.024
	Yes	0.101

Source Authors' own calculation based on primary data survey

Table 7.3 **a** Mother's composite health index for Naxalbari block of Darjeeling District, **b** Mother's composite health index for Matigara block of Darjeeling District

Respondent	Mother's composite health index
a	
M–1	0.038
M–2	0.083
M–3	0.083
M–4	0.073
M–5	0.061
M–6	0.085
M–7	0.083
M–8	0.050
M–9	0.096
M–10	0.083
b	
M–101	0.096
M–102	0.096
M–103	0.071
M–104	0.096
M–105	0.083
M–106	0.083
M–107	0.084
M–108	0.096
M–109	0.096
M–110	0.085

Source Authors' own calculation based on primary data

Table 7.4 Summary results related to MCHI of Naxalbari and Matigara Blocks of Darjeeling District

Blocks	Mean	Std. Dev	CV	Max	Min	Mother's health status (in percentages)		
						Poor	Medium	Good
Naxalbari	0.069	0.023	32.550	0.096	0.013	21	35	44
Matigara	0.065	0.025	38.448	0.096	0.017	32	32	36
Total	0.067	0.024	35.527	0.096	0.013	40	33.5	26.5

Source Authors' own calculation based on primary data

the value is 0.065, also falls in medium standard category. The mean value of MCHI comes out 0.067 when we consider the case of all 200 mothers. The maximum and minimum values of the index become 0.096 and 0.013 in case of Naxalbari and the figures become 0.096 and 0.017 in case of matigara. It is to be noted here that Naxalbari lies in the Terai region at the base of the Himalayas while Matigara lies in the hilly region of the Himalayas. But in both case, the maximum value of the mother's composite health index is 0.096 while the lower value differs.

If we go by the figure then obviously, the performance of the Naxalbari block is slightly better than the Matigara block. The percentages of mother's poor health status are lower in Naxalbari (21%) than the Matigara block (32%). Considering the data as a whole, 40% of surveyed mothers' health status is revealed to be poor. In regard to good health status, 44% of the sampled mother in Naxalbari, 36% in Matigara and almost 27% in aggregate fall under good health status category. Although the table shows that the mother's health status is better in Naxalbari area rather than Matigara area but it is to be kept in mind that the Naxalbari is in Terai region while Matigara is in Hilly region. In that case, also the performance of the Matigara is impressive and the overall result supports the HDI (2004) report for Darjeeling in West Bengal.

7.4.2 Analysis of Results Related to Likelihood of Full Immunization of Children: Yule's 'Q' Coefficient

This section explains how well some of the very important determinants of child immunization are associated with immunization itself. As mentioned earlier for the very purpose the Yule's '*Q*' coefficient of the association have been calculated to show the association or dissociation between child immunization and mother's educational status, father's educational status and father's employment status. The result is presented in Table 7.5.

In the case of child immunization and various other immunization determining factors, the Yules' coefficients are calculated to find out the association between the two. The Yule's value corresponding to mother's educational status is 0.571. It reflects a moderately good degree of association. The Yule's value for father's educational status is 0.386. Although this is positive, mothers' educational status seems to have a better degree of association with child immunization scenario as compared to that of fathers. This result goes at par with the other studies that reveal that education of mothers is more intensely associated with child's vaccination coverage. For this reason, father's educational level is not considered as one of the determinants. The Yule's value for employment status of father is 0.0245 which shows very low association. So occupation may not be a good determinant for vaccination.

From the table, we can draw preliminary conclusion that for those children whose mothers did not complete minimum five years of schooling they were very

Table 7.5 Yule's '*Q*' coefficient

B → / *A* ↓	Mother's educational status	Father's educational status	Father's employment status
Child's immunization status	0.5713	0.3861	0.0245

Source Authors' own calculation based on primary data

vulnerable to immunization process. Thus, mother's level of education becomes an important determinant of child's immunization status.

7.4.3 Analysis of the Result Relating to the Factors Influencing Child's Immunization

Following the study Patra (2006), we have considered certain socioeconomic variables that influence the status of child immunization. It is already mentioned that there are two statuses of vaccination, viz, either fully vaccinated or partially vaccinated and in the survey, we found only two children who were not at all vaccinated. So we have two categories fully vaccinated and merging the two partially vaccinated and not at all vaccinated we got the other category of not vaccinated and accordingly we assigned values '1' and '0' to these two categories, respectively. The variables used for the regression as regressor are as follows:

1. Birth order,
2. Mothers' age,
3. Fathers' income,
4. Distance from the nearest health facility,
5. Gender of child, religion,
6. Mothers' education measured by complete years of schooling and
7. Composite health index of mother whose child is being interrogated

Among these variables before proceeding further, it is now imperative to describe the nature of the predictor variables.

7.4.3.1 Characteristics of the Predictor Variables

A strong association exists between children's immunization status and birth order; with children born into larger families and low vaccination uptake and the first child being more likely to be immunized on time than the second as well as the following children. Majority of first-order births occur to relatively younger women, who are more likely than older women to utilize maternal and child healthcare services. With the higher aged mother, probability of fully immunized child increases up to a level; but with the gradual increase in age, the probability decreases when a particular threshold level of age is crossed. Children of high-income group are more likely to be fully vaccinated than a poor household. Children from urban area are more likely to be vaccinated than their rural counterpart as the distance from a health facility is less in an urban area than that in the rural area and we can expect the existence of inverse relation. It has been found from many studies that there are, though not very severe, gender discrimination in child vaccination in mainly extreme rural areas of India. So we can hypothesize that a boy is more likely to be fully vaccinated than a girl. We assign the value '1' if the child is boy and '0' otherwise.

Hindu children are more likely to be fully immunized than those in other religion. We put the value '1' if child is Hindu and '0' otherwise. Higher the level of education of the mother higher will be the possibility of her child to be fully immunized, because of the awareness of the mother and thus mother's complete years of schooling is considered as one regressor for this regression. On the basis of the mother's performance about her knowledge of health, we constructed MCHI and we include that index value as one regressor.

Multicollinearity is checked by calculating partial correlation coefficient among the regressors and Pearson Correlation Matrix (not shown) shows the maximum correlation coefficient is 0.3, which is much less than the threshold magnitude. The regression result is presented in Table 7.6.

Regression analysis (Table 7.6) reveals that mother's age, family income, gender of the baby, religion, mother's level of education, and health status of the mother measured by calculated composite Health Index are significantly associated with the immunization status of the children and the sign of the associations are as expected. Distance from the nearest health center is as expected negatively influence the immunization status but the coefficient turns out statistically insignificant. One important observation is that influence of family income on immunization status is not much higher like mothers' education and health status as the value of the coefficient for family income is very meager.

Table 7.6 Factors influencing the child immunization in darjeeling district

Variables	Coefficient	z	*p*-value
Birth order of the child	−1.0425	−1.29	0.199
Mother's age	−0.279**	−2.42	0.015
Family income	0.0011*	3.18	0.001
Distance from the nearest health facility	−0.125	−1.29	0.196
Gender of the baby	2.854*	2.88	0.004
Religion	2.955**	2.27	0.023
Mother's level of education	6.244*	3.95	0.000
Composite health index of the mother	5.873*	−2.57	0.010
Constant (α)	−1.234	−0.44	0.659
Number of observations = 245 Log likelihood = −23.810893	LR chi2 = 269.94 Pseudo R2(5) = 0.8500 Prob > chi2 = 0.0000		

Source Authors' own calculation based on primary data
Note * and ** indicate that the coefficient is significant at 1 and 5% level of significance respectively

7.5 Conclusion and Policy Prescriptions

Our above discussion concludes that child's immunization is highly influenced by mother's health status, mother's level of education, mother's age, and gender of the baby, religion and on family income. The position of the health center also becomes an important factor to influence child's immunization. It has been found from the study that there is lack of access to health services both for the child and for its mother and low rates of participation in vaccination coverage among poor households, minorities, and people living in rural and remote areas. Distance from the health facility is very important for a district like Darjeeling where due to the ridge lines many rural areas are remote and accessibility is a real problem there. Sometimes bad weather condition, rain, land slip prevent the parents from remote areas to take their children to health centers for vaccination in a stipulated date.

One important finding is the need of good health status of mothers as a healthy mother has a strong inclination toward a healthy child and for healthy child vaccination is a prerequisite. From a policy perspective, emphasis should be given on serving the vulnerable groups as signified by religion, poor economic conditions, and accessibility. Improvements are also required in education among mothers which will bring exposure to the greater world that will again reflect in their decision-making behavior.

Appendix

See Table 7.7.

Table 7.7 **a** Mother's composite health index for Naxalbari Block of darjeeling district, **b** Mother's composite health index for Matigara Block of darjeeling district

Respondent	Mother's composite health index	Respondent	Mother's composite health index
a			
M–1	0.038	M–51	0.072
M–2	0.083	M–52	0.039
M–3	0.083	M–53	0.039
M–4	0.073	M–54	0.050
M–5	0.061	M–55	0.025
M–6	0.085	M–56	0.038
M–7	0.083	M–57	0.070
M–8	0.050	M–58	0.061
M–9	0.096	M–59	0.096
M–10	0.083	M–60	0.069

(continued)

Table 7.7 (continued)

Respondent	Mother's composite health index	Respondent	Mother's composite health index
a			
M–11	0.096	M–61	0.096
M–12	0.083	M–62	0.071
M–13	0.083	M–63	0.096
M–14	0.096	M–64	0.096
M–15	0.026	M–65	0.096
M–16	0.072	M–66	0.083
M–17	0.061	M–67	0.060
M–18	0.050	M–68	0.096
M–19	0.096	M–69	0.096
M–20	0.069	M–70	0.083
M–21	0.038	M–71	0.096
M–22	0.072	M–72	0.096
M–23	0.048	M–73	0.096
M–24	0.085	M–74	0.025
M–25	0.084	M–75	0.039
M–26	0.061	M–76	0.083
M–27	0.051	M–77	0.013
M–28	0.061	M–78	0.026
M–29	0.049	M–79	0.096
M–30	0.085	M–80	0.096
M–31	0.050	M–81	0.061
M–32	0.096	M–82	0.083
M–33	0.061	M–83	0.061
M–34	0.061	M–84	0.061
M–35	0.061	M–85	0.061
M–36	0.096	M–86	0.096
M–37	0.096	M–87	0.047
M–38	0.096	M–88	0.061
M–39	0.096	M–89	0.038
M–40	0.096	M–90	0.069
M–41	0.084	M–91	0.084
M–42	0.096	M–92	0.072
M–43	0.061	M–93	0.072
M–44	0.051	M–94	0.096
M–45	0.039	M–95	0.058
M–46	0.061	M–96	0.036
M–47	0.026	M–97	0.036
M–48	0.049	M–98	0.096

(continued)

Table 7.7 (continued)

Respondent	Mother's composite health index	Respondent	Mother's composite health index
a			
M–49	0.085	M–99	0.048
M–50	0.061	M–100	0.083
b			
M–101	0.096	M–151	0.021
M–102	0.096	M–152	0.039
M–103	0.071	M–153	0.029
M–104	0.096	M–154	0.055
M–105	0.083	M–155	0.075
M–106	0.083	M–156	0.021
M–107	0.084	M–157	0.063
M–108	0.096	M–158	0.039
M–109	0.096	M–159	0.055
M–110	0.085	M–160	0.039
M–111	0.084	M–161	0.029
M–112	0.096	M–162	0.075
M–113	0.082	M–163	0.039
M–114	0.083	M–164	0.075
M–115	0.061	M–165	0.047
M–116	0.072	M–166	0.059
M–117	0.096	M–167	0.064
M–118	0.096	M–168	0.058
M–119	0.096	M–169	0.017
M–120	0.096	M–170	0.075
M–121	0.036	M–171	0.039
M–122	0.096	M–172	0.075
M–123	0.096	M–173	0.067
M–124	0.096	M–174	0.075
M–125	0.069	M–175	0.039
M–126	0.083	M–176	0.056
M–127	0.096	M–177	0.026
M–128	0.096	M–178	0.032
M–129	0.096	M–179	0.028
M–130	0.072	M–180	0.058
M–131	0.096	M–181	0.022
M–132	0.083	M–182	0.050
M–133	0.061	M–183	0.046
M–134	0.084	M–184	0.058
M–135	0.096	M–185	0.065

(continued)

Table 7.7 (continued)

b			
M–136	0.083	M–186	0.059
M–137	0.049	M–187	0.038
M–138	0.083	M–188	0.020
M–139	0.096	M–189	0.058
M–140	0.096	M–190	0.045
M–141	0.096	M-191	0.063
M–142	0.061	M–192	0.031
M–143	0.049	M–193	0.038
M–144	0.070	M–194	0.022
M–145	0.070	M–195	0.036
M–146	0.025	M–196	0.064
M–147	0.037	M–197	0.030
M–148	0.084	M–198	0.058
M–149	0.096	M–199	0.048
M–150	0.096	M–200	0.042

References

Anderson, T. W. (1984). *An introduction to multivariate statistical analysis* (2nd ed.). USA: Wiley.

Asselin, L. M. (2002). Composite indicator of multidimensional poverty. CECI, June.

Asselin, L.-M., & Anh, V. T. (2005a). Multidimensional Poverty in Vietnam 1993–1998 according to CBMS indicators. *Vietnam Socio-Economic Development Review, 41*(Spring), 12–21.

Asselin, L-M., Gauss, C. F., & Anh, V. T. (2005). Multidimensional poverty and multiple correspondence analysis. Available via http://www.aed.auf.org/IMG/pdf/Louis-Marie_Asselin.pdf. Accessed September 7th, 2013.

Cayolla da Motta, L. (1979). A summary indicator of health status in the municipalities and districts of portugal for health planning purposes. In Walter W. Holland, Johannes Ipsen & Jan Kostrzewski (Eds.), *Measurement of Levels of Health*, WHO Regional Publications, European Series (7): 179–193.

Hyder, A., Puvanachandra, P., & Morrow, R. (2012). Measuring the health of population: explaining composite indicators. *Journal of Public Health Research., 1*(3), 10–18.

Kachari, S., & Maity, S. (2015). Socio-economic status of Bodo people: A case study of Udalguri district, Assam. *International Journal of Indian Culture and Business Management, 10*(3), 351–365.

Kendall, M. G. (1939). The Geographical Distribution of the Crop Productivity in England. *Journal of the Royal Statistical Society, 102,* 21–48.

Ki, J. B., Faye, S., & Faye, B. (2005). *Multidimensional poverty in senegal: A non-monetary basic needs approach.* Final Report, PMMA Working Paper-PEP.

Maity, S., & Kachari, S. (2015). Socioeconomic status and the factors influencing the socioeconomic status of Bodo Tribes: A case study of Udalguri District, Assam. *Socioeconomica—The Scientific Journal for Theory and Practice of Socio-economic Development, 4*(8), 1–23.

Mukhopadhyay, R. (1988). An analysis on spatial patterns and growth of indian agricultural activities: A study on the spatial variations in agricultural situation by district group, 1960–61 to 1980-81. Ph.D. Thesis submitted to Indian Statistical Institute, Calcutta, India.

Ningaye, P., & Ndjanyou, L. (2006). Multidimensional poverty in cameroon: Its determinants and spatial distribution. Final Report, AERC, Nairobi, Kenya.

Njong, M. A., (2007). *Multidimensional spatial Poverty comparisons in cameroon* (Vol. 46, pp. 33–58). Final Report submitted to AERC Research Workshop, Nairobi-Kenya, December and Wealth.

Njong, A. M., & Ningaye, P. (2008). Characterizing weights in the measurement of multidimensional poverty: An application of data-driven approaches to cameroonian data. OPHI Working Paper 21 August, 2008. Available via www.ophi.org.uk. Accessed March 6th, 2014.

Pal, M. N. (1963). A method of regional analysis of economic development with special reference to south india. *Journal of Regional Science, 5*(1), 41–58.

Pal, M. N. (1971). Quantitative techniques for regional planning. *Indian Journal of Regional Science, 3*(1), 1–33.

Pal, M. N. (1990). A generalised formulation of multi-collinear spatial indices for formal regional analysis. *Indian Journal of Regional Science, 22*(1), 11–33.

Pathak, P. (1991). Diagnostic regional analysis on the shortfalls in development and utilisation of human resources in india: A statistical study on the spatial variations by Districts of India., Ph. D. Thesis submitted to Indian Statistical Institute, Calcutta, India.

Pathak, P. (1995). A consistent phase-order preserving equispaced optimal index for regional analysis on non-development of basic skill among boys in India. In Essays on Regional Science: Regional Development and Planning, Vol. (Silver Jubilee Issue), ed. C.R. Pathak, Regional Science Association, India, I.I.T., Kharagpur: 41–56.

Patra, N. (2006). Universal immunization programme in India: The determinant of childhood immunization. Available at: http://ssrn.com/abstract=881224. Accessed June 27th, 2017.

Tatlidil, H. (1992). *A new approach for human development: Human development scores*. Sussex, Mimeo: IDS.

United Nations Development Programme (UNDP). (1993). Human Development Report 1993. Oxford University Press, Delhi.

World Health Organisation (WHO). (1994). Global Comparative Assessments in the Health Sector: Disease Burden, Expenditures and Intervention Packages. In C.J.L. Murray and A.D. Lopez (Eds.), Collected reprints from the Bulletin of the World Health Organization. Geneva, World Health Organization, 1994. viii, 196 p.

Yule, G. U. (1911). *An introduction to the theory of statistics*. London: Gri-n.

Yule, G. U. (1912). On the methods of measuring association between two attributes. *Journal of the Royal Statistical Society*, 75, 579–652.

Chapter 8
Health in North-Eastern States of India: An Analysis of Economic Vulnerabilities

Amrita Ghatak and N. Lalitha

8.1 Introduction

North-eastern states (NES henceforth) of India including Arunachal Pradesh, Meghalaya, Manipur, Mizoram, Tripura and Nagaland, and Assam show better life expectancy at birth and Infant Mortality Rates (IMRs) compared to rest of India. While the IMRs are 31.2 in 2006–2010 and 28.7 in 2011–2015 in the north-eastern states they are 54.3 and 49.2 during the same period in overall India (Ministry of Health and Family Welfare, Govt of India, 11,509). Despite having impressive statistical health indicators such as IMR and Life expectancy at birth the prevalence of communicable and non-communicable diseases along with the utilisation of healthcare services are yet major concern in the north-eastern region of India. Emergence of chronic non-communicable diseases (NCDs) is indicated to be one of the major health challenges in India and around the world by the National Health Policy (2015) and WHO (2014). However, both chronic non-communicable and infectious diseases seem to loom large in the north-eastern region of India. While communicable diseases are still accountable for 24.4% of the entire disease burden in India, NCDs are found to contribute 39.1% of the country's disease burden (DNHP 2015). Communicable diseases combined with increasing prevalence of chronic NCDs are expected to result in double burden of poor health in a country like India where health facilities are sparse in quantity and quality. Despite the adoption of Clinical Establishment Act by few of the north-eastern states the accessibility of quality and timely health facilities is still pertinent.

A. Ghatak (✉) · N. Lalitha
Gujarat Institute of Development Research, Gota, Ahmedabad 380060, Gujarat, India
e-mail: amrita@gidr.ac.in; amritaeconomics@gmail.com

N. Lalitha
e-mail: lalithanarayanan@gmail.com

U.K. De et al. (eds.), *Issues on Health and Healthcare in India*, India Studies in Business and Economics, https://doi.org/10.1007/978-981-10-6104-2_8

The burden of poor health is often understood by the number of deaths, health adjusted life years and/or disability adjusted life years. However, mortality and loss of life years or morbidity are not the only yardsticks to estimate the burden of illness. Lack of health, as a crucial element of labour productivity, also leads individual as well as a nation to suffer from economic burden of illness. NSSO 60th round unit level data (2004) provide with the information on health expenditure and loss of income due to illness at the household levels. While expenditure on health or medical treatments indicates the direct economic burden of health at the household level, the loss of household's income due to ailment indicates the indirect economic impact of health at the micro level. In a subsistence economy or in an economy where labour is mainly manual and informal in nature loss of income indicates loss of wages which in turn shows the loss of productivity of an individual worker due to ill-health (Ghatak and Madheswaran 2011). As a large proportion of population in north-eastern states are Scheduled Tribes or Scheduled Castes engaged in informal works the loss of their income due to illness is pertinent for policies that toward health and overall well-being of workers.

Given this context, this chapter presents the status of health of the population in north-eastern states including Assam, Tripura, Manipur, Meghalaya, Arunachal Pradesh, Nagaland and Mizoram. The chapter then looks into the economic vulnerabilities due to health ailments. In doing so, the paper relies entirely on the secondary data from different sources. The paper also provides a brief discussion on the adoption and advantages of the Clinical Establishment Act by a few of the north-eastern states.

Section 8.2 provides the status of critical health indicators of the north-eastern states. In Sect. 8.3, we discuss the status of health infrastructure in north-eastern states followed by the section on economic vulnerabilities suffered by the population of north-eastern states (Sect. 8.4). Section 8.5 highlights the features of the Clinical Establishment Act that would be implemented by Mizoram, Arunachal Pradesh and Tripura soon. Section 8.6 provides the conclusion.

8.2 Critical Health Indicators of North-Eastern States

Appendix Table 8.14 gives the critical health indicators for the NES. Assam and Meghalaya figure on the higher sides of the National average in the rural and urban combined birth rate, death rate and infant mortality rate, compared to the other NES. Except Sikkim and Mizoram (no data available for Nagaland), all other NES show a relatively less immunisation rate compared to the all India rate. Again all the NES, except Sikkim and Mizoram have a higher rate of children who have not been immunised at all.

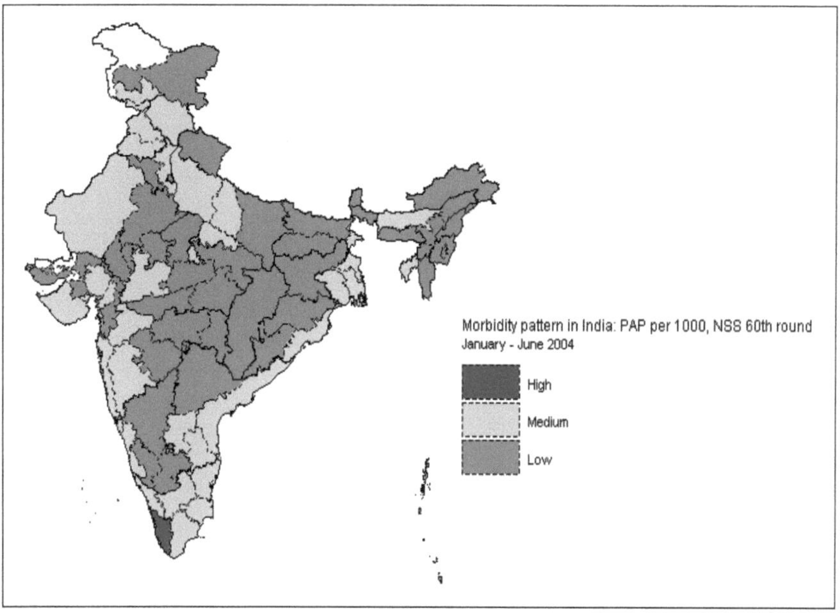

Map 8.1 Morbidity pattern across NSS regions in India. *Notes* Boundary shows the NSS regions. Levels of morbidity—low, medium and high are defined based on cumulative distribution of the concerned variable—PAP

It is found that in addition to a few northern States like Punjab, Haryana, Himachal Pradesh and part of Gujarat, Rajasthan, Uttar Pradesh and Uttarakhand, morbidity is reported to be high across the coastal belt of the country, being highest in the southern region of Kerala (Map 8.1). It indicates that the self-reported morbidity is higher in places with socio-economic, cultural and human development, as consciousness and positional objectivity play important role in explaining the variation in self-reported morbidity pattern. The morbidity data, based on the actual care of the ill, tend to provide the idea of availability of medical care. For instance, a village with a hospital may have more people treated, thereby, reporting more number of cases of illness compared to that of a village without a hospital. Hence we require corroborating the findings with the utilisation of public healthcare facilities.

Utilisation of public healthcare facilities across the NSS regions is found to form a contiguous belt that is congruous with the morbidity pattern (Map 8.2). It indicates that lack of awareness and proper perception about health is reflected in under-reporting of self-rated health status as well as under or low utilisation of public healthcare facilities forming the similar geographic contiguity (Table 8.1).

Overall, the data on morbidity by gender suggests that morbidity among women is higher than men in north-eastern states as well as in India. When we juxtapose

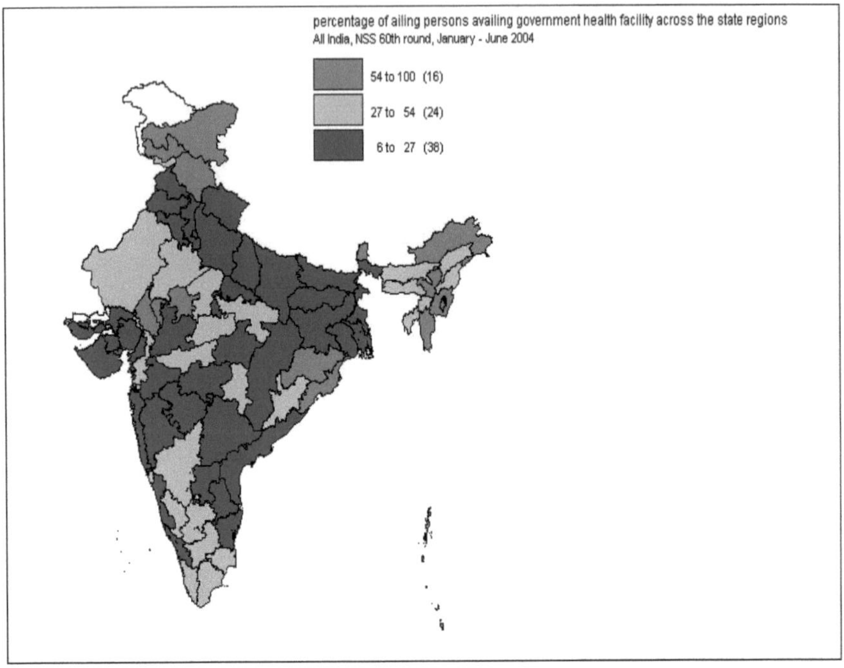

Map 8.2 Utilization of government health facilities across the NSS regions in India *Notes* Boundary shows the NSS regions. Figures for each category show the ranges of percentage of ailing persons availing public healthcare facilities. Figures in the *parenthesis* indicate the mean percentage value of each category

Table 8.1 Morbidity by gender

Area	Male	Female
NE states	7.48	8.15
All India	8.56	9.69

Note Morbidity is indicated by Proportion of Ailing Person in last 15 days period. Figures are percentages

Source Authors' calculation using unit level data on health and morbidity (NSS 2004). Figures are weighted according to NSS weights

Proportion of Ailing persons has been used as an indicator for morbidity

this with the data on body mass index, we get a clearer picture. Assam and Tripura have more number of men and women whose body mass index (BMI) is below normal. Also, these percentages are above the national average as well. Mizoram has the least percentage of men whose BMI is much below normal. Interestingly, Sikkim, which has the least number of females with below normal BMI, also has a relatively higher percentage of obese men and women compared to the other NE

Table 8.2 Body mass index by gender

	Women with BMI below normal (%)	Men with BMI below normal (%)	Women overweight or obese (%)	Men overweight or obese (%)
Arunachal Pradesh	16.4	15.2	8.8	7.1
Assam	36.5	35.6	7.8	5
Manipur	14.8	16.3	13.3	9.2
Meghalaya	14.6	14.1	5.3	5.9
Mizoram	14.4	9.2	10.6	11.4
Nagaland	17.4	14.2	6.4	5.7
Sikkim	11.2	12.2	15.4	11.9
Tripura	36.9	41.7	7.1	4.8
All India Total	35.6	34.2	12.6	9.3

Source DGHS (2013)

states as well as the national average, whereas women in Manipur are more obese than indicated by the national average, Meghalaya has the least number of women who are obese (Table 8.2).

8.3 Prevalence of Different Diseases and Variations Within NES

In the following section, we discuss the health status of the population in north-east, based on the available health data from the NSS 60th Round, for the year 2004–05 and the data from the Central bureau of health intelligence, Directorate general of health services, Ministry of Health and Family welfare, 2013, Government of India (referred as DGHS 2013). While the NSS data set here gives the aggregate figures of NE states, the DGHS data wherever relevant, provide the differences within the NES. The other advantage of using these two data are while the NSS relates to the year 2004–2005, the other pertains to 2013.

According to the NSS data, the health situation of the population in NE appears to be precarious (Table 8.3). NE states have a higher incidence of communicable enteric and febrile conditions which is way above the national average. In diseases concerning kidney/prostate, neurological, cancer, skin and disabilities issue, NE states have a sizeable share in all India. In the following paragraphs, we have given the situation prevailing in 2013.

Table 8.3 Prevalence of diseases in north-eastern States (in %)

Diseases	NE state	All India
	% of prevalence	
Enteric	24.5	10.4
Cardiovascular	14.1	20.26
Injuries/Bones	3.6	9.09
Kidney/Prostate	0.5	1.11
Metabolic disorders	3.1	5.05
Neurological	0.9	2.74
Skin/Gum/Gum	3.4	3.44
Febrile/Tetanus	36.4	25.81
Disabilities	3.5	3.67
Cancer	0.2	0.54
Others	9.9	17.88

Note Figures are weighted and are in percentages. Others include other diagnosed and undiagnosed diseases
Source Authors' calculation using data on health and morbidity (NSS 2004)

8.4 Communicable and Other Diseases

Appendix Table 8.15 provides the data on the prevalence and incidence of death in some of these diseases.

8.4.1 Typhoid

According to the DGHS data, while the NES account for 4% of the incidences of typhoid in 2013; these states account for 7% all deaths due to typhoid. These perhaps indicate the relatively less availability of timely healthcare in these States. Tripura, Nagaland and Manipur have the larger number of cases in that order and most deaths due to typhoid have occurred in Manipur. Chikungunya cases have been reported only in Meghalaya.

8.4.2 Pneumonia

At all India level, there were 703,532 cases and 2597 deaths due to pneumonia. The prevalence share of North-eastern states is 5.7 and 9.3%, respectively. Though in terms of number of cases, Assam and Meghalaya rank top two, however, the numbers of deaths are more in Mizoram followed by Assam. This perhaps indicates the relatively better healthcare in Assam compared to the other states.

The rate of non-polio acute flaccid paralysis per 100,000 people has declined both at all India level as well as for North-eastern states. Exception is Meghalaya, where the rate has actually increased.

In the case of hepatitis, north-eastern states account for 3% of the total incidences and 2% of deaths due to hepatitis at all India level. Sikkim and Arunachal Pradesh have more incidences compared to other states.

8.4.3 Acute Respiratory Infection

Compared to less than 3% of cases with acute respiratory infection, percentage of deaths at nearly 13% due to the infection is alarming in the case of north-eastern states. This indicates the lack of timely availability of healthcare for critical cases. Importantly, Assam and Tripura share a higher percentage of deaths due to respiratory infection compared to the percentage of instances reported in these two states. In contrast, though Meghalaya reports larger instances of infection, percentage share in deaths is relatively less. Deaths due to acute respiratory infection are higher in Assam (232) and Tripura (131) compared to other north-eastern states.

Nearly, 5% of all diarrhoea cases have occurred in north-eastern states with Meghalaya and Assam sharing as much as 56% of cases between them. Some of the reasons for the higher rate of diarrhoea prevalence could be due to the use of contaminated water and lack of sanitation facilities.

8.4.4 Death Due to TB

Totally, 3.6% of cases of death due to TB have occurred in north-eastern states. Among the north-eastern states, 69% of the TB deaths have occurred in Assam. TB shows an increase in Assam, Meghalaya, Mizoram and Nagaland. Sikkim has not recorded any cases.

8.4.5 Malaria

An interesting trend is noticed in the case of malaria instances and related deaths in the north-eastern states. Percentage of malaria instances have reduced from 14% in 2009 to 8% in 2013. Perhaps due to the availability of care, percentage of deaths has reduced from 42% in 2009 to 21% in 2012. We do find an increase to 30% in the number of deaths, which appears to be a sizeable percentage. Still, among the states, it is observed that Malaria is higher in Arunachal Pradesh and Assam. Mizoram shows an exceptionally higher number of cases of malaria. Considerable decline is reported in cases of malaria in 2009–2013. Importantly, the number of deaths is more in Meghalaya and Mizoram. An exceptional number of cases of death due to malaria has been registered in Arunachal Pradesh in 2010, but after that there is a steep reduction. Encephalitis is prevalent mainly in Assam compared to other NES (Table 8.4).

8.4.6 Measles, Chicken Pox and Whooping Cough

It is evident that 17% of total measles cases occur in north-eastern states. Here again a major number of occurrences has been in Assam, Manipur and Nagaland. north-eastern states account for 5.8% of all chicken pox cases in India. Within the north-eastern states, Meghalaya has a relatively higher prevalence followed by Mizoram. 8% of all India cases of a whooping cough are registered in the north-eastern states. Majority of the cases (74%) are found in Assam and the rest in Meghalaya.

Assam and Sikkim are part of the 21 states where the National Programme for prevention and control of Cancer, diabetes, cardiovascular diseases and strokes (NPCDS) is currently going on in 257 districts. These districts have been identified based on the backwardness, health indicators and poor accessibility (National Health Status Indicators 2013).

8.4.7 Proportion of Disabled Persons

North-eastern states account for a relatively lower 2.73% of the total disabled persons in India. This is also striking that of total disabled person in India 65% live in Assam.

8.4.8 Suicide Deaths

Though north-eastern states account for 3.53% of all the suicides in India, yet Assam followed by Tripura have higher incidences of suicide deaths compared to their counterparts.

8.4.9 Tobacco Use

It is observed that 48% of the total tobacco users in India live in the north-eastern states. Within the north-eastern states, Meghalaya and Mizoram have the largest number of male tobacco users. Seven out of eight north-eastern states rank above

Table 8.4 Prevalence of malaria cases and deaths due to malaria

Malaria	2009		2010		2011		2012			2013 (p)
State	Number fell sick	Number of death	Number fell sick	Number of death	Number fell sick	Number of death	Number fell sick	Number of death	Number fell sick	Number of death
Arunachal Pradesh	22,066	15	17,944	103	13,950	17	8368	15	5412	13
Assam	91,413	63	68,353	36	47,397	45	29,999	13	20,492	7
Manipur	1069	1	947	4	714	1	255	0	120	0
Meghalaya	76,759	192	41,642	87	25,143	53	20,834	52	23,860	62
Mizoram	9399	119	15,594	31	8861	30	9883	25	11,783	21
Nagaland	8489	35	4959	14	3363	4	2891	1	2286	1
Sikkim	42	1	49	0	51	0	77	0	41	0
Tripura	24,430	62	23,939	15	14,417	12	11,565	7	6227	6
NE states Total	233,667	488	173,427	290	113,896	162	83,872	113	70,221	110
All India Total	1,563,574	1144	1,599,986	1018	1,310,656	754	1,067,824	519	836,916	359
% share of NE in All India	14.94	42.7	10.8	28.5	8.7	21.5	7.9	21.8	8.4	30.6

Source DGHS (2013)

the national percentage in tobacco use. Tripura is the only exception which has the least percent of tobacco users. Mizoram, followed by Manipur, has 62% of female tobacco users above the age of 15 years.

8.4.10 Common Cancers

Incidence of cancer is collected through the population-based cancer registries set up in different states. Oesophagus, stomach, lung and nasopharynx are the four major types of cancer observed among the north-eastern men (Table 8.5). Among women, breast, oesophagus, lung and cervical cancers are more prevalent than other types. Prevalence of cancer in oesophagus is the most common among men in Assam. In Meghalaya, Oesophagus is prevalent among both men and women. In Mizoram, lung cancer is the most prevalent form among females which can be associated with the high tobacco consumption.

The crude mortality rate (CMR), age adjusted mortality rate (AAMR) and the truncated mortality rate (TMR) is higher among both men and women in the various PBCR of Mizoram, closely followed by Nagaland, compared to other north-eastern states (Table 8.6).

As the data reveal, the CMR is relatively lower compared to AAMR and the TMR. While the AAMR indicate that cancer is prevalent among the higher age groups, the higher rates of TMR indicate the wide prevalence of cancer among the age group of 35–64 in both men and women. While the exact cause of cancer may be hard to tell, high tobacco consumption, particularly above the age group of 15, could be associated with the TMR.

8.4.11 Prevalence of HIV and Other Sexually Transmitted Diseases

At all India level, HIV prevalence has reduced from 0.95% in 2004 to 0.35% in 2012–13. HIV AIDS is prevalence is higher in Manipur, Nagaland and Mizoram. Particularly in Nagaland, the prevalence rates have been consistently higher than other north-eastern states even after the reduction that has started occurring in 2010–2011. Assam has recorded the least prevalence rate (Table 8.7).

Prevalence of **gonococcal infection** is less than 1% in the north-eastern states (0.86%). Though there are no deaths reported, yet each of these states has reported incidence. However, among the north-eastern states, relatively higher prevalence is observed in Assam (42%), Meghalaya (25%) and in Manipur (16%).

Table 8.5 Type of cancers commonly found in NES

Common cancers in the various population-based cancer registries as per relative proportion between 2008 and 2011						
	Males			Females		
Districts	Most common	Moderately common	Least common	Most common	Moderately common	Least common
Areas						
Cachar (2009–10)	Oesophagus (8.7)	Lung (7 6)	Hypopharynx (7.6)	Breast (18.1)	Cervix Uteri (11.2)	Gallbladder (10.2)
Dibrugarh (2009–11)	Oesophagus (14.7)	Hypopharynx (11.9)	Mouth (9.0)	Breast (16.5)	Gallbladder (10.2)	Oesophagus (9.9)
Kamrup Urban (2009–11)	Oesophagus (14.5)	Hypopharynx (8.3)	Lung (7.3)	Breast (17.0)	Oesophagus (10.4)	Cervix Uteri (9.2)
Imphal West (2009–10)	Lung (14.9)	NHL (7.2)	Oesophagus (6.1)	Breast (16.3)	Lung (13.4)	Cervix Uteri (12.0)
Aizwal (2009–10)	Stomach (22.1)	Oesophagus (16.5)	Lung (15.1)	Lung (17.6)	Breast (13.7)	Cervix Uteri (12.9)
East Khasi Hills (2010–11)	Oesophagus (34.2)	Hypopharynx (10.6)	Stomach (5.6)	Oesophagus (24.9)	Breast (10.8)	Cervix Uteri (9.6)
States						
Mizoram excluding Aizwal (2009–10)	Stomach (25.0)	Lung (12.6)	Oesophagus (12.4)	Lung (16.1)	Stomach (15.5)	Cervix Uteri (13.5)
Manipur excluding IW (2009–10)	Lung (18.9)	Stomach (9.4)	Nasopharynx (6.9)	Lung (14.7)	Breast (11.6)	Cervix Uteri (10.5)
Mizoram (2009–10)	Stomach (23.5)	Oesophagus (14.5)	Lung (13.9)	Lung (16.9)	Stomach (13.7)	Cervix Uteri (13.2)
Manipur (2009–10)	Lung (17.8)	Stomach (8.2)	Nasopharynx (6.3)	Lung (14.3)	Breast (12.9)	Cervix Uteri (10.9)

(continued)

Table 8.5 (continued)

Common cancers in the various population-based cancer registries as per relative proportion between 2008 and 2011						
	Males			Females		
Districts	Most common	Moderately common	Least common	Most common	Moderately common	Least common
Sikkim (2009–11)	Stomach (15.9)	Liver (8.9)	Oesophagus (8.5)	Breast (10.3)	Cervix Uteri (8.0)	Lung (7.7)
Meghalaya (2010–11)	Oesophagus (29.8)	Hypopharynx (11.5)	Stomach (7.4)	Oesophagus (21.9)	Breast (11.2)	Cervix Uteri (10.4)
Tripura (2010)	Lung (18.8)	Oesophagus (8.9)	Hypopharynx (7.2)	Cervix Uteri (18.5)	Breast (13.8)	Gallbladder (9.6)
Nagaland (2010)	Nasopharynx (19.3)	Stomach (17.4)	Oesophagus (16.1)	Cervix Uteri (19.1)	Stomach (14.5)	Breast (11.8)

Source DGHS (2013)

Table 8.6 Crude mortality rate, age adjusted mortality rate and truncated mortality rate per 100,000 population in different PBCR

Areas	Males			Females		
	CMR	AAMR	TMR	CMR	AAMR	TMR
Cachar Dt (2009–10)	12.2	17.3	33.3	5.2	6.7	15.1
Dibrugarh Dt (2009–11)	21.8	31.2	54.5	11.8	16.8	33
Kamrup Urban Dt (2009–11)	37.2	57.3	79	20.9	32.6	53.9
Manipur state (2009–10)	10.2	14.6	24.8	7.6	10.6	21.5
Imphal West Dt (2009–10)	12.9	17.2	27.2	13.3	16	24.5
Manipur state excl IW (2009–10)	9.6	13.9	24.2	6.2	9	20.6
Mizoram state (2009–10)	69.9	110.3	187.9	49.2	76.5	134.2
Aizwal District (2009–10)	92.5	154.1	260.8	69	110.1	182.9
Mizoram state excl. Aizwal (2009–10)	57	87.7	150.2	37.6	57.8	108.2
Sikkim State (2009–11)	24.7	38.1	52.5	23.9	39.5	69.1
Meghalaya (2010–11)	25.1	51.5	105.7	13.4	25.6	52.2
East Khasi Hills (2010–11)	38.1	75.4	147.6	20	34.2	66
Tripura State (2010)	21.3	30.4	59.1	14.3	18.7	41.1
Nagaland (2010)	65.1	126.1	239.2	36	70.2	144.6

Source DGHS (2013)

Table 8.7 HIV prevalence levels

HIV prevalence levels	2004	2005	2006	2007	2008–09	2010–11	2012–13
Arunachal Pradesh	0.2	0.46	0.27	0	0.46	0.21	0.26
Assam	0.14	0	0.04	0.11	0.13	0.09	0.16
Manipur	1.66	1.3	1.39	1.31	0.54	0.78	0.6
Meghalaya	0	0	0.09	0	0.04	0.05	0.26
Mizoram	1.5	0.81	0.94	0.85	0.72	0.4	0.68
Nagaland	1.85	1.97	1.36	1.1	1.14	0.66	0.88
Sikkim	0	0.25	0.1	0.09	0	0.09	0.19
Tripura	0.25	0	0.42	0.25	0	0	0.19
All India Total	0.95	0.9	0.6	0.49	0.49	0.4	0.35

Source DGHS (2013)

8.4.12 *Syphilis*

According to the provisional figures available for the year 2013, at all India level 33,570 syphilis cases have been reported from different states. Of this, north-eastern states account for 1.5% of all India. Among the north-eastern states, Arunachal

Pradesh (37%), Meghalaya (34%) and Assam (11%) report a relatively higher prevalence rates compared to other states. However, no deaths have been reported.

8.5 Medical Infrastructure

The number cases and the deaths reported in the case of different diseases pose a query on whether the NES have adequate health infrastructure to cater to their population.

8.6 Medical Colleges

The seven states together have a total of 10 medical colleges in the government sector and none in the private sector. While Assam has four colleges, Arunachal Pradesh, Mizoram and Nagaland have none. These 10 colleges together produce an average of 110 doctors a year. The situation is still worse in the case Ayush institutes, as only Arunachal Pradesh and Assam have these colleges. In the all India provision of sub-centres, PHCs and CHCs, north-eastern states have 4.9% each of sub-centres and CHCs. These states have a share 6.3% in PHCs.

8.7 Hospitals and Beds

North-eastern states account for 7% share of hospitals and 4.6% share in hospital beds. Population served per hospital is the highest (83,533) in Manipur (which perhaps indicate the availability of a number of hospitals there) and relatively at a lower level of 18,950 in the case of Arunachal Pradesh. Sikkim serves 404 people per hospital bed and Assam serves 2341 people per hospital bed.

North-eastern states have 1.9 and 4.1% share in all India number of Ayush hospitals and dispensaries. Manipur and Meghalaya have relatively more number of AYUSH hospitals. However, Assam and Manipur have more number of dispensaries.

8.8 Doctors

Arunachal Pradesh, Assam and Sikkim are the three states which reported to have doctors with required qualification, which is 2.4% of all India total. Of these three states, Assam has the giant share of 94%. Between 2006 and 2012, a total of 1026 dental surgeons registered with Dental Council of India were available in Assam. Information for other states is not available.

Of all the government allopathic and dental surgeons in India, NES have 7.5 and 12.8%, respectively. In Assam, while on an average a government doctor serves 1.6 persons, in Nagaland government doctor serve on an average 21 persons. Perhaps because of the less number of dental surgeons in north-eastern states, average number of population served ranged from 3156 persons in Nagaland and 285 persons in Mizoram.

North-eastern states have less than 1% of Ayush doctors of all Ayush doctors in India. Interestingly, all the States except for Assam has majority number of Homoeopathy doctors (data not shown here). In Assam, 59% of doctors are Ayurvedic doctors.

Arunachal Pradesh, Manipur, Assam, Nagaland, Sikkim, Mizoram, Tripura and Meghalaya have serious shortages of staff, particularly regarding obstetricians, gynaecologists and paediatricians.

8.9 Availability of Paramedics

NES share 3.9, 1.7, 0.79 and 0.84% of ANMs, registered nurses and midwives, lady health workers and pharmacists, respectively, in all India. Among the NES, Assam has a large share of paramedical professionals in each of the category compared to other states. Assam, Tripura and Meghalaya are the only three states which have reported availability of lady health workers.

8.10 Availability of Human Resources in Rural Areas

Among all rural workers, 9.8% of all male health assistants in India and 7.3% of all doctors in India (PHCs) are available in the rural areas of the north-eastern states. The next highest human resource available is the number of ANMs in rural areas. We also notice that among the north-eastern states, Assam has a higher share of all the rural health human resources compared to other states. It should also be noted that the number of ANMs in all the north-eastern states is higher than the other types of human resources for healthcare available there. Mizoram, Sikkim and Tripura have no specialists at all in their PHCs and except for Assam which has 119 specialists in its CHCs, Arunachal Pradesh and Manipur have only one specialist in all their CHCs. One of the reasons for this could be the lack of super specialty courses available in most of these states except for a limited few in Assam.

There are lots of factors like the geographical location, spatial distribution of the population and resource constraints that explain the lack of availability of human resources for provision of appropriate medical care. When such is the kind of scenario regarding human resources in the north-eastern states, it will be natural that the existing facilities turn away the patients for want of healthcare professionals or due to the availability of physical infrastructure in these facilities. It is well known that the physical infrastructure in the public facilities leaves a lot to be desired, which has resulted in the increasing number of private healthcare facilities. The dependence on the private healthcare facilities results in the huge out of pocket expenditure (nearly 90% of the total expenditure) incurred by individuals towards healthcare. Several scholarly articles have been written in India on the economic vulnerabilities due to the burden of illness. This aspect of economic vulnerability in the context of NES is discussed in the following Sect. 8.5.

8.11 Economic Vulnerability Due to Illness

Using data on health and morbidity (NSSO 2004) the paper conceptualises economic vulnerability due to illness indicated by burden of healthcare expenditure and loss of income. The burden of health expenditure and loss of income due to illness are measured as their percentage share in total household income proxied by household expenditure. Descriptive statistical tables, maps and non-parametric regression techniques are used to ascertain the economic vulnerability of illness in India and particularly in NES parts of the country.

It is found that the health expenditure burden is the highest in few pockets of Bihar, Uttar Pradesh and Assam (Map 8.3), which forms further contiguity showing

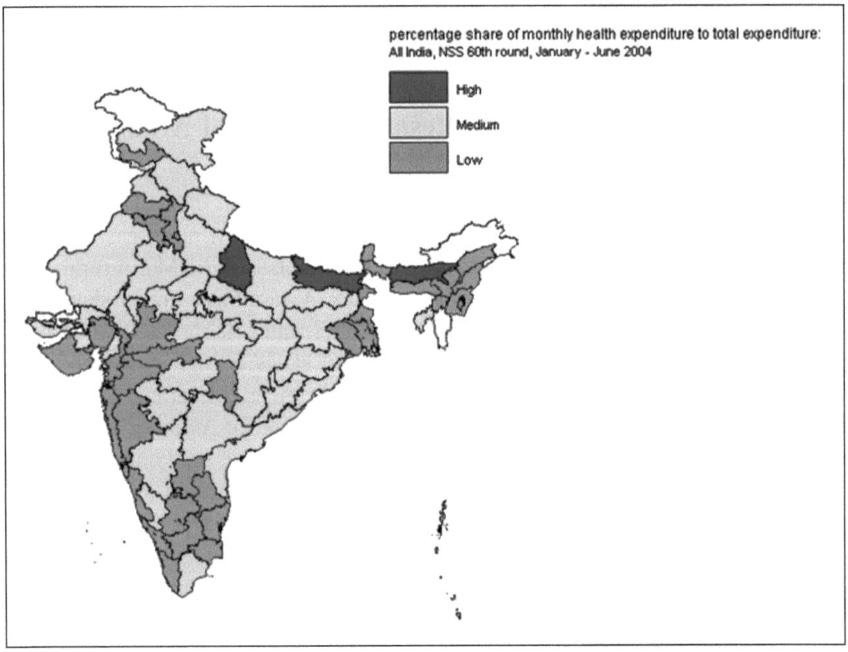

Map 8.3 Share of health expenditure to total expenditure at the household level: India. *Notes* Boundary shows the NSS regions. Low, medium and high are defined based on distribution of the concerned variable. *Source* Author's calculation NSS 60th round unit level data, schedule 25.0

moderately high burden in other areas such as parts of Bihar and Uttar Pradesh, Jharkhand, Chhattisgarh, Odisha, Rajasthan, Himachal Pradesh, major portions of Andhra Pradesh and Madhya Pradesh and some pockets in Karnataka. The geographic contiguity of relatively high health expenditure burden across the BIMARU States and their adjacent regions depict a different picture than the one found by Ghosh and Arokiasamy (2009). The burden of healthcare expenditure depending largely on individual's position varies across rural and urban areas and types of healthcare facilities (public or private) availed. In a nut shell, it differs depending on many formal and informal institutional factors.

Relatively low expenditure per treated ailments in the rural areas is reported in states including Tamil Nadu, Gujarat and West Bengal. Institutional factors such as the proportion of cases treated through government healthcare centres play an important role in determining the average expenditure per treated ailments. However, the data on expenditure were not collected for each spell of ailment or by the source of treatment. They were collected for a treated ailing person as a whole (NSS 2004). Therefore, one cannot conclude whether poor health status is the only driving factor towards the high health expenditure.

Ill-health forces a person to be away from work and even when a person is physically present despite the disability, reduces the productivity. The loss of income, interestingly, tells upon the economic well-being by affecting the productivity of labourers particularly for those who work manually and whose loss of a working day results in loss of a day's wages. Income and wages carry similar meaning for the individuals whose earning largely depends on the manual labour. In addition to the loss of labour productivity, loss of income due to illness also indicates individual's attribute towards health by deciding not to work for the particular day because of illness.

According to the nutrition-based efficiency wage hypothesis (Leibenstein 1957), it is argued that in subsistence economies, the amount of workers' effort would depend positively on their nutrition and health status and thus on wages. Health is found to be an important factor in determining individual's economic and non-economic well-being (Strauss 1986; Sahn and Alderman 1988), though the magnitude and process of health impacts on labour market and social welfare are not straight forward.

Some studies (Dohrenwend 1973; Pearlin 1989; House and Williams 2000) attempt to indicate that the individuals in the lower socio-economic status are subjected to suffer more from physical, psychological and social stresses than others. These stresses are often found to be linked with increased incidence of morbidity and mortality. A few studies (McIntyre et al. 2006; Ettner 1996) highlight the link between health and income at the household level. It has been observed that healthcare financing strategies that place considerable emphasis on out-of-pocket payments can impoverish households. However, in most of these studies the focus was on out-of-pocket expenditure. Evidently, poverty is reinforced when households face substantial medical expenses and loss of household income due to ill-health. However, India lacks in adequate empirical studies to examine whether ill-health actually makes the household lose appreciable amount of its income in ways affecting the well-being of household members. The NSS 60th round unit level information reveal that burden of income loss due to ailment forms a

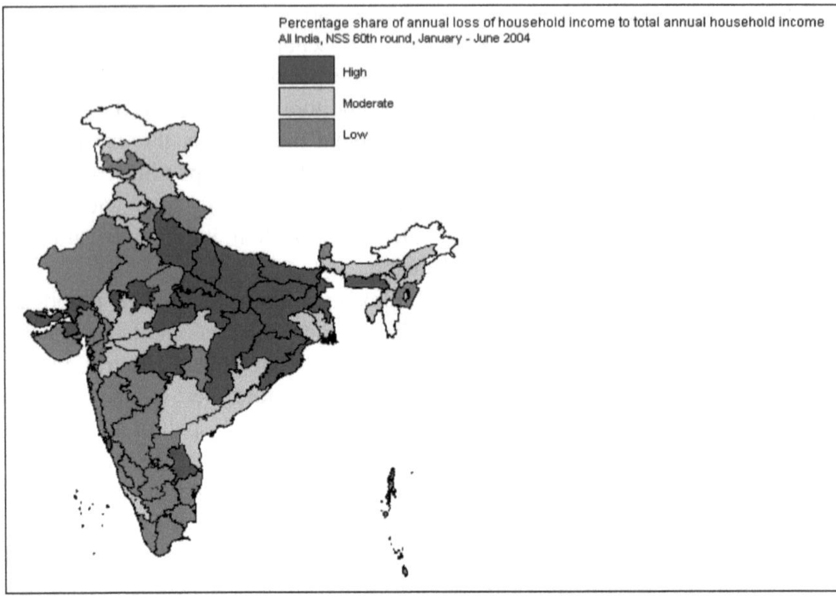

Map 8.4 Burden of income loss due to ailment across NSS regions. *Notes* Boundary shows the NSS regions. Levels of morbidity—low, medium and high are defined based on distribution of the concerned variable—the share of income loss due to ailment to the total household expenditure. The average burdens are 7, 15 and 28% for the low, medium and high burden groups, respectively

Table 8.8 Economic burden of illness at households and individual levels in north-eastern region and All India

Area	Burden of loss of income due to ailment at individual level	Burden of loss of income due to illness at household level	Burden of household's health expenditure
NE states	59.81	38.39	2.38
All India	49.92	11.76	2.90

Source Author's calculation based on data on health and morbidity (NSS 2004)
Figures are in percentages

geographic contiguity. North-eastern part of India along with eastern and central and part of northern and south-eastern India forms a belt of high to moderately high burden of households' income loss due to ailment (Map 8.4).

It is evident in Table 8.8 that both the per capita loss of income and the loss of household (HH) income are much higher in NES than the loss observed at all India level. Among all the MPCE quintile groups, the burden of income loss due to ailment is much higher particularly in the poorest of the poor (Table 8.9) group. This indicates that the NES, though has population belonging to the different percentiles, may suffer from ailments and lose their livelihoods, perhaps are not seeking healthcare. This could be due to two reasons. First is that they do not have

Table 8.9 Economic burden of illness across the income groups

MPCE quintiles	North-Eastern States		All India	
	Burden of income loss due to ailment	Burden of health expenditure	Burden of income loss due to ailment	Burden of health expenditure
Poorest	302.47	2.63	35.51	3.92
Poorer	10.29	1.84	9.95	3.63
Moderate	9.30	2.85	12.30	3.08
Richer	12.05	0.98	7.29	1.97
Richest	9.37	3.68	4.01	1.79

Source Author's calculation based on NSS 60th Round Unit level data. Figures are calculated in per capita percentages. Income is proxied by MPCE

Table 8.10 Economic burden of illness across MPCE and households amenities quintile groups in NES and India

Categories	North-Eastern States		All India	
	Per capita burden of loss of income due to ailment	Per capita burden of health expenditure	Per capita burden of loss of income due to ailment	Per capita burden of health expenditure
Poor MPCE with poor household amenities	14.98	3.31	24.94	3.51
Poor MPCE with good household amenities	12.40	3.25	20.22	3.65
Rich MPCE with poor household amenities	8.67	2.75	5.13	2.15
Rich MPCE with good household amenities	8.99	3.11	6.43	2.31

Source Author's calculation based on data on health and morbidity (NSS 2004). Figures are in percentages. Amenities index is constructed with the help of household level factors such as type of house structure, access to latrine, drainage facilities, quality of drinking water and fuel for cooking purpose

the economic resources to provide for health and or such healthcare is not available in their states and they have to travel elsewhere to access healthcare. Perhaps this is reflected among the richest group of individuals who might travel elsewhere outside NES to avail healthcare (Table 8.9).

Health of individuals depends on the household level amenities or household environmental factors such as house structure, latrine, drainage facility, safe drinking water, and clean fuel for cooking. Since these household level factors are correlated to each other, an amenities index has been constructed using principal component analysis. It has been found that the poorest of the poor income group with the poorest quality of household amenities suffer from the highest burden of income loss due to ailment (Table 8.10).

In order to identify the vulnerable group of individuals suffering from the burden of income loss due to illness to a large extent, we categorise individuals into two

Table 8.11 Average of burden of income loss due to ailment across income and household amenities quintiles among informal/casual workers and regular salaried/non-workers in India and NES

Categories	All India		North-Eastern States	
	Informal/Casual workers including self-employed	Non-workers and regular salaried	Informal/Casual workers including self-employed	Non-workers and regular salaried
Poorest with bad amenities	46.29191	10.82203	15.56781	14.57368
Poor MPCE with good household amenities	41.39379	7.66598	20.56735	7.89593
Rich MPCE with poor household amenities	10.31846	2.37922	14.97614	3.99138
Rich MPCE with good household amenities	14.30805	2.60646	19.2273	3.66691

Source Author's calculation based on NSS 60th round unit level data on health and morbidity
Note Figures are in percentages

groups one of which includes those who are in self-employment or in casual work or informal sector worked and the other one includes those who are regularly salaried or not in the workforce during the time of survey. Although the burden of income loss due to ailment is the highest in the poorest income group with worst household amenities, it is much higher among those who are self-employed or engages in informal or casual labour. The burden of income loss does not vary substantially across the income and household amenities quintiles indicating toward the dominance of informal sector works in NES (Table 8.11).

The variable namely burden of income loss due to illness takes the shape of a skewed distribution (Fig. 8.1). The sample shows that the data against burden of income loss due to illness are concentrated at zero with fewer observations at the higher values. Therefore, a non-parametric approach is followed. Background characteristics such as religion, social group and sector (rural/urban) are included as control variables in order to capture the unforeseen discrimination in the labour market that may influence the income loss. Relying upon data on usual activity status we have identified activities that are often informal and/or casual in nature. Therefore, one variable to capture the impact of participation in informal sector works or self-employment is included in the model. As explained earlier, the household amenities index, which is constructed using household level information such as house structure, latrine, drainage, safe drinking water and clean source of energy for cooking purpose, has been incorporated in the model. Health status is indicated by the number of sick days during which the respondent has been restricted from daily activities.

The regression results are reported in Tables 8.12 and 8.13. In the first model (Table 8.12), we have reported the case for all India controlling the impact of NES. However, in the second model (Table 8.13) an attempt has been made to examine the burden of income loss due to ailment within the NES. It is interesting to observe

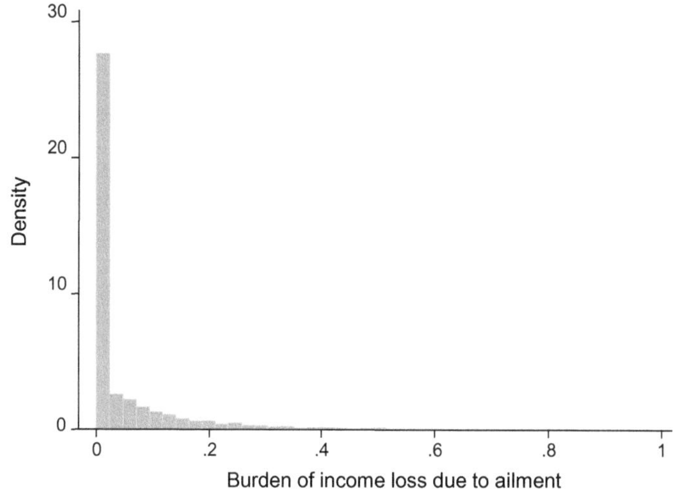

Fig. 8.1 Histogram of the burden of income loss due to illness. *Source* NSS data on health on morbidity (2004)

that number of restricted days due to sickness increases the burden of income loss due to ailments and the extent of its impact increases in the upper quantiles of the burden (Table 8.12). Similarly, household amenities reduce the burden of loss of income due to ailment and the magnitude of this reduction is higher in the upper quantile groups compared to the lower ones (Table 8.12). However, household amenities are not statistically significant determinant of the burden of loss of income due to ailment when we examine the case within NES (Table 8.13). Working in sectors that are largely casual and/or informal in nature leads to high burden of income loss due to ailment in both all India and NES (Table 8.13).

Further, the conditional impact analysis of burden of income loss due to ailment shows that the impact of illness on income loss is much higher in NES compared to that in all India (Fig. 8.2). Undoubtedly, income and health are causally related; however, the results indicate that impact of health on income is much relevant in the NES as the number of days spent in restricted mobility due to sickness leads to much higher burden of income loss in those seven States than that in all India. Those who remain absent from workplaces tend to suffer more from the loss of income in NES compared to all India. The informal and/or manual nature of work further reinforces the linkages between health and income to a large extent. It indicates that employment generation programmes and welfare schemes alone are not adequate to minimise the loss of income. Health is prerequisite for employment generation programmes. Having said this, we mean that the success of poverty eradication programmes relies heavily on health. Therefore, health development programmes should be strengthened for poverty eradication as well. The results also raise the need for understanding the supply and quality of healthcare facilities in NES.

Table 8.12 Quintile regression results for all India

For All India					
Dependent variable	Median regression	Quantile regression (60)	Quantile regression (70)	Quantile regression (80)	Quantile regression (90)
Burden of income loss due to ailment	Coefficient (Standard Err.)	Coefficient (Standard Err.)	Coefficient (Standard Err.)	Coefficient (Standard Err.)	Coefficient (Standard Err.)
Explanatory variables					
Whether resides in NES	0.037*** (0.006)	0.050*** (0.008)	0.052*** (0.010)	0.053*** (0.014)	0.068** (0.028)
Days on restricted mobility due to sickness	0.001*** (0.000)	0.004*** (0.000)	0.008*** (0.000)	0.013*** (0.001)	0.023*** (0.001)
Amenities index	-0.002^{W} (0.001)	−0.004** (0.001)	−0.004*** (0.002)	−0.006** (0.003)	−0.017** (0.005)
Rural	0.001 (0.003)	0.001 (0.004)	0.001 (0.006)	0.000 (0.008)	0.000 (0.015)
Muslim	0.001 (0.004)	0.001 (0.005)	0.000 (0.007)	0.000 (0.009)	0.000 (0.018)
Christian	0.001 (0.007)	0.002 (0.009)	−0.004 (0.012)	−0.003 (0.016)	−0.002 (0.032)
Others	−0.001 (0.007)	−0.004 (0.009)	−0.001 (0.012)	0.000 (0.016)	0.000 (0.032)
ST	0.003 (0.006)	0.011^{W} (0.007)	0.011 (0.010)	0.014 (0.014)	0.035^{W} (0.027)
SC	0.002 (0.004)	0.004 (0.005)	0.004 (0.007)	0.004 (0.009)	0.000 (0.018)
OBC	0.000 (0.003)	−0.001 (0.004)	−0.001 (0.005)	0.000 (0.007)	0.000 (0.014)
Age	0.000^{W} (0.000)	0.001** (0.000)	0.001^{W} (0.000)	0.000 (0.001)	0.000 (0.001)
Whether avails govt health facility	0.001 (0.003)	0.003 (0.003)	0.003 (0.005)	0.002 (0.007)	0.002 (0.013)
Casual/Informal worker according to usual activity status	0.061*** (0.003)	0.076*** (0.004)	0.095*** (0.005)	0.125*** (0.007)	0.178*** (0.013)
Constant	−0.002 (0.005)	−0.002 (0.006)	0.000 (0.008)	0.007 (0.011)	0.035 (0.022)
Number of observation	8369	8369	8369	8369	8369
Pseudo R^2	0.0056	0.0098	0.0117	0.0126	0.0111

Note Standard errors are in parentheses. ***, ** and * indicate levels of significance at less than 1%, less than 5% and less than 10% respectively. *W* indicates weakly significant at less than 20%
Source NSS data on health and morbidity (2004)

Table 8.13 Quantile regression results for NES

Dependent variable	Quantile regression (90)	Quantile regression (80)	Quantile regression (70)	Quantile regression (60)	Median regression (50)	Quantile regression (40)	Quantile regression (30)	Quantile regression (20)
Burden of income loss due to ailment	Coeff. (Std Err.)	Coeff. (Std Err.)	Coeff. (Std Err.)	Coeff. (Std Err.)	Coeff. (Std Err.)	Coeff. (Std Err.)	Coeff. (Std Err.)	Coeff. (Std Err.)
Explanatory variables								
Days on restricted mobility due to sickness	0.033*** (0.007)	0.022*** (0.003)	0.018*** (0.002)	0.012*** (0.002)	0.009*** (0.001)	0.006*** (0.001)	0.004*** (0.001)	0.001* (0.001)
Amenities index	−0.022 (0.032)	−0.006 (0.013)	−0.003 (0.010)	−0.004 (0.009)	−0.003 (0.006)	−0.002 (0.005)	−0.005 (0.005)	−0.003 (0.003)
Rural	0.007 (0.093)	0.029 (0.039)	0.018 (0.029)	0.003 (0.025)	0.013 (0.017)	0.005 (0.015)	−0.001 (0.013)	−0.001 (0.010)
Muslim	0.093 (0.132)	0.058[w] (0.055)	0.021 (0.041)	0.014 (0.035)	0.011 (0.024)	0.009 (0.021)	0.008 (0.019)	0.006 (0.014)
Christian	0.030 (0.114)	0.006 (0.048)	0.012 (0.036)	0.027 (0.031)	0.021 (0.021)	0.016 (0.019)	0.012 (0.016)	0.009 (0.012)
Others	0.167[w] (0.131)	0.160** (0.055)	0 086** (0.041)	0.044[w] (0.035)	0.031[w] (0.024)	0.015 (0.021)	0.022 (0.019)	0.013 (0.014)
ST	0.022 (0.119)	0.029 (0.050)	0.015 (0.037)	0.016 (0.032)	0.019 (0.021)	0.016 (0.019)	0.007 (0.017)	0.006 (0.013)
SC	0.147[w] (0.141)	0.005 (0.059)	0.011 (0.044)	0.035 (0.038)	0.033[w] (0.025)	0.030[w] (0.023)	0.022 (0.020)	0.011 (0.015)
OBC	-0.001 (0.103)	-0.013 (0.043)	-0.024 (0.032)	-0.016 (0.028)	-0.014 (0.018)	-0.015 (0.017)	-0.014 (0.015)	-0.002 (0.011)
Age	0.005 (0.006)	0.001 (0.002)	0.002 (0.002)	0.001 (0.002)	0.001 (0.001)	0.000 (0.001)	0.000 (0.001)	0.000 (0.001)
	0.049	0.017	0.015	0.015	0.016	0.006	0.001	-0.005

(continued)

Table 8.13 (continued)

Dependent variable	Quantile regression (90)	Quantile regression (80)	Quantile regression (70)	Quantile regression (60)	Median regression (50)	Quantile regression (40)	Quantile regression (30)	Quantile regression (20)
Burden of income loss due to ailment	Coeff. (Std Err.)	Coeff. (Std Err.)	Coeff. (Std Err.)	Coeff. (Std Err.)	Coeff. (Std Err.)	Coeff. (Std Err.)	Coeff. (Std Err.)	Coeff. (Std Err.)
Whether avails govt health facility	(0.074)	(0.031)	(0.023)	(0.020)	(0.013)	(0.012)	(0.011)	(0.008)
Casual/informal worker according to usual activity status	0.084[W] (0.080)	0.126*** (0.034)	0.104*** (0.025)	0.081*** (0.021)	0.085*** (0.014)	0.073*** (0.013)	0.062*** (0.011)	0.044*** (0.009)
Constant	−0.034 (0.131)	−0.028 (0.055)	−0.029 (0.041)	−0.015 (0.035)	−0.028 (0.024)	−0.009 (0.021)	0.002 (0.019)	0.003 (0.014)
Number of observation	476	476	476	476	476	476	476	476
Pseudo R^2	0.0009	0.0011	0.001	0.0009	0.001	0.0009	0.0007	0.0003

Note Standard errors are in parentheses. ***, ** and * indicate levels of significance at less than 1%, less than 5% and less than 10% respectively. *W* indicates weakly significant at less than 20%

Source NSS data on health and morbidity (2004)

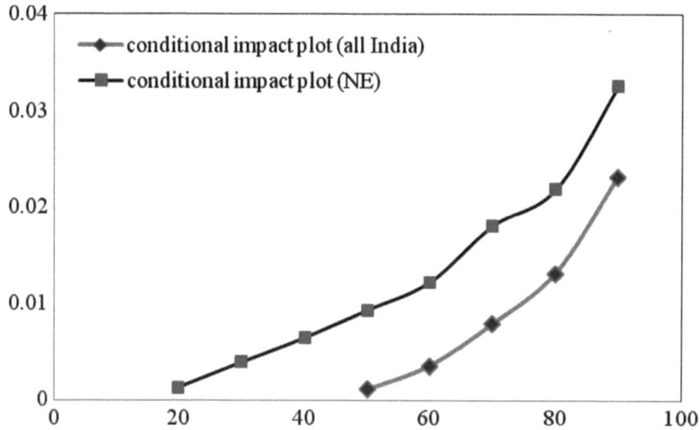

Fig. 8.2 Conditional impact analysis of burden of income loss due to ailment; NSS 60th round (2004), All India versus NES. *Source* NSS data on health and morbidity (2004)

8.12 Clinical Establishment Act

Two main points emerge from the foregoing sections are: (1) employment in informal sector and income loss is significantly associated and (2) dependency on the government healthcare is relatively high in the NES compared to the other parts of India, where the dependency on private healthcare providers is more. A point which cannot adequately be discussed in this paper is the extent to which the inadequacies in the health infrastructure can contribute to income loss for individuals dependent on government healthcare, particularly due to lack of facilities for appropriate diagnosis and treatment.

For instance, Mizoram Economic Survey of 2014–15[1] states that "State Plan outlay has been mostly spent for salary component and the Department is not able to take up other various health programmes within this meagre allocation of fund. The Department could not even provide the indispensable items such as Dict Supplies to patient in all CHC/PHC, supply of materials and equipments, maintenance of existing infrastructures and other development works for improving the existing 12 Community Health Centres (CHC), 57 Primary Health Centre (PHC) and 370 Sub-Centres (SC) as desired. Due to financial constraint, there is a ban on filling up of vacant post and creation of new post, thus the Department has insufficient staff to cater to the healthcare needs of the people which resulted in our high rate of Infant Mortality Rate (IMR) and Maternal Mortality Rate (MMR)" (p. 116). "Due to inadequate availability of state of the art equipments and shortage of man power, there are many instances when patients have to be referred outside the state for necessary investigation and treatment at the cost of the Government of

[1]Mizoram Economic Survey (2014–15)

Mizoram's exchequer.[2] Various measures have been made by the department to improve the treatment of facilities in the state so as to cut down Government spending as well as inconveniences to the patient. It is envisaged that the services and facilities of the District Hospitals be upgraded so that the people in the rural areas do not need to make long journey to the state capital to receive necessary treatment for their illness." (p. 122, Mizoram Economic Survey).

The report of the regional evaluation team of Arunachal Pradesh (RET 2011–12),[3] which visited the West Kameng district of Arunachal Pradesh for evaluation also observes an acute shortage of manpower in the case of specialists, medical officers, lab technicians, pharmacists. At district hospital of Bomadia, blood storage unit, X-ray unit, surgical and anaesthesia equipments were not available.

Similar report from Manipur (RET 2011–12) noted that the sub-centres visited at AimolThampak, KomlaThabi, Unopat and Saivom were not as per the IPHS. Two of these sub-centres did not have labour room facility. Though the PHC at Moreh had a good labour room, deliveries could not be conducted for want of equipments and instruments and the labour room was used for store. Similar inadequacies were also noted by the evaluation team in Mizoram, Meghalaya, Tripura and Nagaland.

It is in this context of different types of shortages in the government healthcare in NES that in this part of the paper, we briefly highlight the importance of the Clinical Establishment Act (CEA). CEA when implemented fully would serve both as a regulating as well as standards setting body in the healthcare for both public and private sector.

Under the Act, CEA provides certain minimum standards for human resources and physical infrastructure which are currently debated. Health facilities which adopt the standards will be subject to audits and will have to adhere to the specific rates prescribed for different services. Unlike several state Acts, this central Act applies to both public and private healthcare sectors and excludes only establishments under the armed forces and covers all streams of medicine. As this is a Central Act and health is a state subject, states will have to adapt the same through their legislative assemblies. For implementation at the central level, a National Council for Clinical Establishments would be established and that would be chaired by the Director General of Health Services (DGHS). At the state level, district registering authorities will be set up.

As of now, this Act is applicable in Mizoram, Arunachal Pradesh, Himachal Pradesh and Sikkim and all union territories. Already, 805 and 1157 CEs have been registered in the states of Himachal Pradesh and Jharkhand. The CEA provides standard treatment guidelines for a few diseases which if followed would be helpful in adopting rational use of drugs and prevent resistance to drugs.

---

[2]The Economic Survey of Mizoram states that due to inadequate health infrastructure, within the state, Mizoram govt has empanelled hospitals in Kolkota, Guwahati, Mumbai, Shillong, Hyderabad and Chennai.

[3]Report of the Regional Evaluation Team (2011–12).

As the CEA is applicable for the government sector as well, the hospitals have been categorised according to their types. Hospital level 1 includes PHC level services. The PHC level services provided by qualified doctors that include General Medicine, Paediatrics, First aid to an emergency patient and Out Patient Services, Obstetrics and Gynaecology Non-surgical and Minor Surgery and having a bed strength of not more than 30. The primary healthcare services can be provided through trained and qualified manpower; with support/supervision of registered medical practitioners with the required support systems for this level of care. Some of the primary requirement as per the CEA for PHCs are providing the name of the health provider, timing of the PHC, timing of the different facility provided at PHC, contact numbers of blood bank, police, safety signage like, electrical appliances, inflammable articles, radiation, etc., and providing appropriate access to physically challenged persons. Further, the CEA for the PHC specifies the area for hospital, wards, minor operation theatre/procedure room, labour room, size of the labour table, etc.

The furnitures and fixtures that a PHC is supposed to have include, wheel chair, medicine chest, examination lamp, washbasins fans, etc. Equipments specified include blood pressure apparatus, stethoscope, pulse oximeter, examination gloves and emergency equipments. Similar list is available for sub-centres also.

It is really a significant milestone for some of the NES like Sikkim, Arunachal Pradesh and Mizoram where CEA has already been adopted. If the implementation schedules are also planned soon, it could start with the government health sector, where the standards for the primary and preventive healthcare is already available. However, the success of implementation will be directly dependent on the resources for government healthcare. Appropriate provisioning for the essential infrastructure along with strict implementation of the CEA, would revitalise the healthcare and will have positive influence in reducing the health burden. Hence as a priority, the budget for the government healthcare in NES will have to be revisited and innovative ways of provisioning improved healthcare need to be planned.

8.13 Conclusion

The paper highlights three major concerns about health in north-eastern part of India—morbidity pattern and prevalence of diseases, economic burden of illness as indicated by burden of health expenditure and burden of loss of income due to illness and finally the Clinical Establishment Act (CEA) that aim to regulate the growth of the private sector healthcare institutions.

Although overall morbidity is less in NES, the prevalence of infectious diseases particularly febrile illnesses is much higher in NES compared to that in all India. Pattern of morbidity is found to be congruous with utilisation of public healthcare services. However, self-reported morbidity reflects the positional objectivity bias that is caused by general awareness and level of education.

As far as the economic burden of illness is concerned both expenditure burden and burden of loss of income due to health reasons are high in NES whereas the extent of burden of income loss is much higher in NES compared to that in all India. Further, the quantile regression analysis followed by a conditional impact analysis of burden of loss of income due to ailment indicates that health is pre-requisite for success over poverty that still prevails in the modern twenty-first century India and more so in the NES.

Government healthcare in NES suffers from various inadequacies which could contribute the health and economic vulnerabilities of individuals as the care and diagnosis may not be at the desired level. In this context, the paper also highlighted the importance of the Clinical Establishment Acts (CEA). With adequate resources and appropriate implementation of the CEA, health indicators will improve further but these can be achieved only when the government healthcare has adequate resources.

Appendix

See Tables 8.14 and 8.15.

Table 8.14 Health indicators in the NER vis-à-vis All India

States	Area	CBR 2010	CDR 2010	IMR 2010	Immunisation-1 2007–08	Immunisation-2 2007–08
Arunachal Pradesh	Rural	22.1	6.9	34	13.9	11.5
	Urban	14.6	2.3	12	12.5	13.7
	Combined	20.5	5.9	31	13.5	12.1
Assam	Rural	24.4	8.6	60	50.0	11.6
	Urban	15.8	5.8	36	55.3	7.1
	Combined	23.2	8.2	58	50.9	11.2
Manipur	Rural	14.8	4.3	15	44.1	11.6
	Urban	15.3	4.0	9	65.2	6.6
	Combined	14.9	4.2	14	48.5	10.6
Meghalaya	Rural	26.6	8.4	58	31.2	14.1
	Urban	14.8	5.6	37	55.1	12.9
	Combined	24.5	7.9	55	33.7	14.0
Mizoram	Rural	21.1	5.4	47	46.8	6.0
	Urban	13.0	3.7	21	68.4	1.2
	Combined	17.1	4.5	37	54.5	4.3
Nagaland	Rural	17.0	3.7	24	NA	NA
	Urban	16.0	3.3	20	NA	NA
	Combined	16.8	3.6	23	NA	NA

(continued)

Table 8.14 (continued)

States	Area	CBR 2010	CDR 2010	IMR 2010	Immunisation-1 2007–08	Immunisation-2 2007–08
Sikkim	Rural	18.1	5.9	31	77.1	0.5
	Urban	16.1	3.8	19	91.6	0.0
	Combined	17.8	5.6	30	77.8	0.5
Tripura	Rural	15.6	4.8	29	36.4	21.6
	Urban	11.5	5.7	19	63.4	5.7
	Combined	14.9	5.0	27	38.5	20.3
All India	Rural	23.7	7.7	51	50.6	5.2
	Urban	18.0	5.8	31	63.1	2.9
	Combined	22.1	7.2	47	54.1	4.5

CBR Crude birth rate, *CDR* Crude death rate, *IMR* Infant mortality rate, *Immunisation-1* Percentage of children aged 12–23 months fully immunised, *Immunisation-2* Percentage of children aged 12–23 months not received any vaccination, *NA* Data not available
Source Saikia and Das (2014)

Table 8.15 Prevalence of communicable and non-communicable diseases in north-eastern states of India

State	Cases	Death	Cases % to total NE	% deaths to total NE
Diarrhoea	**2013 (p)**			
Arunachal Pradesh	27,659	3	5.4	1.3
Assam	105,876	147	20.6	64.2
Manipur	25,333	37	4.9	16.2
Meghalaya	186,023	12	36.1	5.2
Mizoram	13,127	12	2.6	5.2
Nagaland	21,376	0	4.2	0.0
Sikkim	42,410	1	8.2	0.4
Tripura	92,826	17	18.0	7.4
Total of NE states	514,630	229	100	100
All India Total	10,762,500	1535		
% share of NE in All India	4.78	14.92		

(continued)

Table 8.15 (continued)

State	Cases	Death	Cases % to total NE	% deaths to total NE
Enteric fever (typhoid)	**2013 (p)**			
Arunachal Pradesh	6154	4	10.1	15.4
Assam	6521	0	10.7	0.0
Manipur	10,927	17	17.9	65.4
Meghalaya	9134	1	15.0	3.8
Mizoram	2766	3	4.5	11.5
Nagaland	12,520	0	20.5	0.0
Sikkim	186	0	0.3	0.0
Tripura	12,849	1	21.0	3.8
Total of NE states	61,057	26	100	100
All India Total	1,537,118	361		
% share of NE in All India	3.97	7.20		
Acute respiratory infection	**2013 (p)**			
Arunachal Pradesh	43,368	4	5.0	0.9
Assam	145,047	232	16.6	52.1
Manipur	31,648	36	3.6	8.1
Meghalaya	329,019	2	37.7	0.4
Mizoram	33,807	23	3.9	5.2
Nagaland	37,189	3	4.3	0.7
Sikkim	93,726	14	10.7	3.1
Tripura	158,988	131	18.2	29.4
Total of NE states	872,792	445	100	100
All India Total	31,738,762	3278		
% share of NE in All India	2.75	13.58		
Whooping Cough	**2013 (p)**			
	Cases		Cases % to total NE	
Arunachal Pradesh	0			
Assam	2324		74.94	
Manipur	13		0.42	
Meghalaya	684		22.06	
Mizoram	18		0.58	
Nagaland	0		0	
Sikkim	0		0	
Tripura	62		1.999	
Total of NE states	3101		100	
All India Total	36,621			
% share of NE in All India	8.47			

(continued)

Table 8.15 continued

Measles	**2013 (p)**		
	Cases	Death	Cases % to total NE
Arunachal Pradesh	44	0	1.6
Assam	1516	0	53.9
Manipur	429		15.3
Meghalaya	300		10.7
Mizoram	89		3.2
Nagaland	304		10.8
Sikkim	66		2.3
Tripura	65		2.3
Total of NE states	2813	0	100
All India Total	15,768	10	
% share of NE in All India	17.84		
Viral Hepatitis	**2013 (p)**		
	Cases	Death	Cases % to total NE
Arunachal Pradesh	525		16.7
Assam	426		13.5
Manipur	258		8.2
Meghalaya	518		16.4
Mizoram	419	10	13.3
Nagaland	110		3.5
Sikkim	692	1	21.9
Tripura	205	1	6.5
Total of NE states	3153	12	100
All India Total	104,145	512	
% share of NE in All India	3.03	2.34	

Rate of non-polio acute flaccid paralysis per 100,000 population		
	2012	2013
Arunachal Pradesh	6.47	3.46
Assam	4.73	4.05
Manipur	3.06	1.55
Meghalaya	3.47	4.41
Mizoram	3.69	2.48
Nagaland	4.07	1.39
Sikkim	3.26	0.46
Tripura	6.21	3.79
All India Total	13.94	11.81

Pneumonia 2013 (p)	Cases	Death	% Cases to total NE	% deaths to total NE
Arunachal Pradesh	274	5	0.7	2.1
Assam	19,022	67	47.4	27.6

(continued)

Table 8.15 (continued)

Pneumonia 2013 (p)	Cases	Death	% Cases to total NE	% deaths to total NE
Manipur	2414	0	6.0	0.0
Meghalaya	8896	46	22.2	18.9
Mizoram	1852	74	4.6	30.5
Nagaland	2520	2	6.3	0.8
Sikkim	784	6	2.0	2.5
Tripura	4377	43	10.9	17.7
Total of NE states	40,139	243	100	100
All India Total	703,532	2597		
% share of NE in All India	5.71	9.36		

Syphilis 2013 (p)	Cases	Death	% deaths to total NE
Arunachal Pradesh	194	0	37.0
Assam	62	0	11.8
Manipur	3	0	0.6
Meghalaya	182	0	34.7
Mizoram	12	0	2.3
Nagaland	47	0	9.0
Sikkim	9	0	1.7
Tripura	15	0	2.9
Total of NE states	524		100
All India Total	33,570	1	
% share of NE in All India	1.56		

Gonococcal 2013 (p)	Cases	Death	% deaths to total NE
Arunachal Pradesh	9	0	1.1
Assam	355	0	42.3
Manipur	139	0	16.6
Meghalaya	211	0	25.1
Mizoram	45	0	5.4
Nagaland	63	0	7.5
Sikkim	15	0	1.8
Tripura	2	0	0.2
Total of NE states	839	0	100
All India Total	97,180	0	
% share of NE in All India	0.86		

Death due to TB (2011)	Cases	% of NE
Arunachal Pradesh	71	3.1
Assam	1565	68.9
Manipur	90	4.0
Meghalaya	189	8.3
Mizoram	78	3.4
Nagaland	72	3.2
Sikkim	65	2.9

(continued)

Table 8.15 (continued)

Death due to TB (2011)	Cases	% of NE
Tripura	143	6.3
Total of NE states	2273	100
All India Total	63,261	
% share of NE in All India	3.59	

Chicken pox (2013)	Cases	Death	% of cases to total NE
Arunachal Pradesh	3	0	0.2
Assam	66	7	4.1
Manipur	200		12.3
Meghalaya	613		37.7
Mizoram	321		19.7
Nagaland	57		3.5
Sikkim	197		12.1
Tripura	171	2	10.5
Total of NE states	1628	9	100
All India Total	28,090	61	
% share of NE in All India	5.80	14.80	

Percentage of adults by status of tobacco use (above 15 years)	Male		Females		Total	
	Current tobacco user	Never a user	Current tobacco user	Never a user	Current tobacco user	Never a user
Arunachal Pradesh	64	33.9	31.7	65.1	47.7	49.6
Assam	52.6	44.8	25.3	73.8	39.3	58.9
Manipur	66.6	30.2	41.8	53.6	54.1	42
Meghalaya	73.2	23.2	36.7	61	55.2	41.9
Mizoram	72.5	24.1	61.6	37.7	67.2	30.7
Nagaland	69.2	26.6	43	51.5	56.8	38.4
Sikkim	48.7	47	33.2	64.6	41.6	55.1
Tripura	24	73.6	8.4	91.2	16.2	82.4
All India Total	47.9	48.2	20.3	77.6	34.6	62.4
% share of NE in All India						

Distribution of suicidal deaths categorised by gender 2012

	Male	Female	Total	% to total NE
Arunachal Pradesh	100	30	130	2.7
Assam	2392	872	3264	68.1
Manipur	23	18	41	0.9
Meghalaya	90	38	128	2.7
Mizoram	157	16	173	3.6
Nagaland	24	6	30	0.6
Sikkim	96	85	181	3.8

(continued)

Table 8.15 (continued)

Distribution of suicidal deaths categorised by gender 2012				
	Male	Female	Total	% to total NE
Tripura	560	284	844	17.6
Total of NE states	3442	1349	4791	100
All India Total	88,453	46,992	135,445	
% share of NE in All India	3.89	2.87	3.54	

Proportion of disabled population in India (2011)	Total No. of disabled persons	Total	% to total NE
Arunachal Pradesh		26,734	3.6
Assam		480,065	65.5
Manipur		54,110	7.4
Meghalaya		44,317	6.0
Mizoram		15,160	2.1
Nagaland		29,631	4.0
Sikkim		18,187	2.5
Tripura		64,346	8.8
Total of NE states		732,550	100
All India Total		26,810,557	
% share of NE in All India		2.732319	

Source DGHS (2013)
NE Indicates North-East India

References

Dohrenwend, B. S. (1973). Social status and stressful life events. *Journal of Personality and Social Psychology, 28*(2), 225–235.

Ettner, S. L. (1996). New evidence on the relationship between income and health. *Journal of Health Economics, 15*(1), 67–85.

Francis, P. A. (2015 April, 29) States and Clinical Establishments. *Editorial* www.pharmabiz.com.

Ghatak, A., & Madheswaran, S. (2011). Burden of income loss due to ailment in India evidence from NSS data, Working Paper No. 269. Institute for Social and Economic Change, Bangalore.

Ghosh, S., & Arokiasamy, P. (2009). Morbidity in India: Trends, patterns and differentials. *Journal of Health Studies, II,* 136–148.

House, J. S., & Williams, D. R. (2000). Understanding and reducing socioeconomic and Racial/Ethnic Disparities in Health. In D. S. Brian & S. L. Syme (Eds.), *Promoting health: Intervention strategies from social and behavioral research* (pp. 81–124). Washington, DC: 284 National Academy Press.

Leibenstein, H. (1957). The theory of underemployment in backward Economies. *The Journal of Political Economy, 65*(2), 91–103.

McIntyre, D., Thiede, M., Dahlgren, G., & Whitehead, M. (2006). What are the economic consequences for households of illness and of paying for health care in low- and middle-income country contexts? *Social Science & Medicine 62*, 858–865.

Mizoram Economic Survey. (2014–15). Government of Mizoram Planning & Programme Implementation Department (Research & Development Branch).

National Health Policy: Draft. (2015). Ministry of Health and Family Welfare, Government of India.

National Sample Survey. (2004). Health and morbidity round, schedule no. 25.0. MOSPI, Government of India.

National Sample Survey Organisation (NSSO). (2004). Health and Morbidity: Schedule No. 25.0. Ministry of Statistics and Programme Implementation, Government of India.

National Health Status Indicators. (2013). National Health Profile 2012, Central Bureau of Health Intelligence, Directorate General of Health Services, Government of India, New Delhi.

Pearlin, L. I. (1989). The sociological study of stress. *Journal of Health and Social Behavior, 30*(3), 241–256.

Report of the Regional Evaluation Team. (2011–12). Manipur and Arunachal Pradesh. https://nrhmmis.nic.in/Part%20B%20Demographic%20and%20Vital%20Indicators/Highlights%20on%20Evaluation%20Report%20of%20RETs/Highlights%20on%20Evaluation%20Report%20of%20RETs-2011-2012.pdf. Accessed October 3, 2015.

Report on Health Infrastructure. (2013). Directorate General of Health Services (DGHS), Government of India.

Sahn, D. E., & Alderman, H. (1988). The effect of human capital on wages, and the Determinants of Labour Supply in a Developing Country. *Journal of Development Econommics, 29*(2), 157–183.

Saikia, D., & Das, K. K. (2014). Access to public health care in North East India. *The NEHU Journal, 12*(2), 77–100.

Strauss, J. (1986). Does better nutrition raise farm productivity? *The Journal of Political Economy, 94*(2), 297–320.

World Health Organization. (2014). *Noncommunicable diseases country profile 2014*. Geneva, Switzerland: WHO.

Chapter 9
Association of Economic Inequality with Health Inequality: Women in Northeast India

Susmita Bharati

9.1 Introduction

Undernutrition or chronic energy deficiency (CED) is a poverty phenomenon. It is associated with the intake of inadequate food at the household as well as individual level. Undernutrition among women in India is highest in the world because 35.6% (15–49) years women in India suffer from chronic energy deficiency (CED). Now the question, why does still undernutrition among women is very high? The answer is that undernutrition is the combination of outcome and manifestation of poverty because it is going to happen that poor almost always means being deprived of full nutritional capabilities (Osmani 1992). It is seen that undernutrition among women in India from the poor and disadvantaged social groups remains very high (Jose and Navaneetham 2008). But it is also seen that rigidity in norm against women among the disadvantaged group in India is more flexible (Bardhan 1993; Drez and Sen 1995; Miller 1997) than rich or advantageous group. For example, it implies that in India, adult women and men are fare equally undernourished in poor and disadvantages social group of households. Another example can be cited that in 2005–2006 NFHS data, it is seen that 47% of women suffer from CED in poorest wealth index family and 24% CED is seen in richest wealth group. So only, economy can reduce 23% points or two times under this situation in India. Hence, it is proved that besides other factors, economic condition is one of the major controlling factors for promoting good health or accessories for uplifting good health. A regional coexistence of deprivation and poverty are responsible for undernutrition, association of rigid norms, and discrimination are also responsible for undernutrition among women. Here our focus of study is the condition of undernutrition among the women in northeast India and its assimilation with the economic condition. Northeast India refers to the easternmost region of India, consisting of eight dif-

S. Bharati (✉)
Sociological Research Unit, Indian Statistical Institute, Kolkata, India
e-mail: susmitabharati60@gmail.com

U.K. De et al. (eds.), *Issues on Health and Healthcare in India*, India Studies in Business and Economics, https://doi.org/10.1007/978-981-10-6104-2_9

ferent states. It is accounted for 7–9% of the total land space of the country. It is one of the backward country regions of India characterized by low per capita income, low capital formation, inadequate infrastructural facilities, geographic isolation, and communication bottleneck. The tribal people are more in numbers in the North Eastern Region (NER). It is thought that the status of women is comparatively better in tribal society (Handsdak 2012; Burman 2012). The Scheduled Tribe are 94.75% in Mizoram, 87.70% in Nagaland, 85.53% in Meghalaya, 63.66% in Arunachal Pradesh, 34.41% in Manipur, 30.95% in Tripura, and 12.82% in Assam (Zahol 2010). Besides this, excepting Assam, and Tripura, the rest six states are predominated by tribal population. In such a preface of northeastern region, the major objective of the present study are (i) to see the magnitude of difference of Chronic Energy Deficiency (CED) between poor and non-poor women; (ii) its variation across the states, and (iii) to see the probable reason of variation, if any.

9.2 Methodology

For this study, we have used the National Family Health Survey (NFHS—III) data conducted by the International Institute for Population Sciences (IIPS), Mumbai, in 2005–06. They collected data on reproductive aged women (15–49) years of 29 states in India and the population frame was based on 2001 census. The data is cross-sectional and unit-level data. As our focused area of study is Northeast India, so we have considered here only the data set of Northeast India. The sample sizes consist of 9402 women from eight states in Northeast India. Body mass Index (BMI) is considered as a measure of undernutrition. It is classified into following categories (WHO 2003) as follows:

Categories	Ranges of BMI (kg/m^2)
Chronic energy deficiency (CED)	<18.5
Normal	18.5–24.9
Overweight	25.0–29.9
Obese	≥ 30.0 only

The background explanatory variables are: (i) type of places, (ii) educational attainment of women and (iii) Age-groups of women (iv) religion, (v) occupational categories (vi) drinking water, and (vii) toilet facility of the family and wealth index of the family.

9.2.1 Methods

To make the differentiation of economic conditions, five categories of wealth index (Rutstein 1999) has been clubbed into two: (i) poor economic condition which includes poorest and poorer categories and (ii) non-poor economic condition which includes richest, richer, and middle. To see the relative and effective chronic energy deficiency among women of Northeast India, intervention was done about the actual conditions of the background variables through percentage distribution. To determine the differences of prevalence of CED between poor and non-poor group for each state, the percentage of CED of non-poor was subtracted from poor. Thus, a positive sign means the percentage has increased and a negative sign means just the opposite trend. Regression analysis was performed to establish the relationship between dependant (CED, overweight, and obesity) and independent (socioeconomic) variables.

Then relationship between CED with these background variables in total as well as in the context of two economic conditions was done. The risk of CED was regressed on various independent variables in total Northeast India and also on the context of economic conditions like poor and non-poor using categorical logistic regression analysis. Dependent variables are taken as binary. CED of women was considered as '1' and others are coded as '0'. An estimated odd ratio of '1' indicates that the nature of dependent variable is not different from the reference category. If the estimated odd ratio is >1, the probability of becoming affected is more in this category compared to the reference category and if it is <1, then it is just opposite to that of '>1' case.

9.3 Results

Table 9.1 describs the economic conditions of women in India, Northeast India, and different states of Northeast India on the basis of economic criteria of poor and non-poor (Fig. 9.1). It is also showing the percentages of chronic energy-deficient (CED) women according to the conditions of poor and non-poor in the same domain (Fig. 9.2). It is seen that in Northeast India, 34.8% women belong to poor economic condition and 65.2% women belong to non-poor condition while in India 36.6% women are poor and 63.4% women are non-poor. So the percentages are very close to all India level. But in different states of Northeast India, it varies in different degrees. Highest poor conditioned women are found in Assam (58.5%), followed by Arunachal Pradesh (52.8%). Lowest poor conditioned women are found in Sikkim (12.9%), followed by Mizoram (13.1%). On the other hand, the highest non-poor conditioned women are found in Sikkim (87.1%), followed by Mizoram (86.9%). And the lowest non-poor conditioned women are found in Assam (41.5%), followed by Arunachal Pradesh (47.2%). Percentages of CED women are found also on the basis of poor and non-poor conditions of the family. It is seen that that only in Assam and Tripura, 44.9 and 44.2% women are CED those who are belonging to the poor family. In non-poor family, highest percentage of CED is found in Tripura (36.1%), then it is followed by Assam (31.5%), respectively. It is obvious that CED is directly related to poor economic condition but the differences of CED between poor and non-poor family indirectly express the magnitude of other factors which are controlling the CED. If the differences are positive and magnitude is high; then it denotes that in general, the other factors which are regulating the health status are also poor. If the value of differences is negative, it means, besides economy, other factors are very sound which renders to keep health in well. Here, the differences of CED between poor and non-poor women in Northeast India is 8.7 but in India, it is 17.4. So in India, it proves that economy is the prime factor for controlling the health. But, in Northeast, as the differences is 8.7, so it denotes that besides economy, other factors for promoting health is much better than India. As the differences of variation is existing in all the states of Northeast region, on the basis of magnitude of differences from state to state, ranking of differences also denotes the position of CED variation between poor and non-poor women. It is seen though in Arunachal Pradesh and Assam, percentage of poor family are more or less fifty percent, but in Arunachal Pradesh, occurrences of total CED as well as percentage of CED in poor and non-poor family are very low and differences is very low also. It is also seen that in Mizoram and Sikkim, percentage of poor family are very low. The most noticeable thing is also seen that the ranking of differences of CED between poor and non-poor is (1) and negative, i.e., in poor conditioned women, CED is less than non-poor conditioned women. But in Assam followed by Tripura, the ranking is highest to next lowest as the value of differences in Assam is (13.4) then followed by Tripura (8.1). Here also, percentages of CED are very high compare to all states of northeastern region. Otherwise, in the rest of the states, the margin of differences is ranging from 4–5 unit.

Table 9.2 describes the percentages of chronic energy-deficient women as well as the socioeconomic condition of those women and also the relationship between poor and non-poor condition with CED among women. Normally in Northeast India, 32.6% women live in urban areas and 67.4% are in rural areas, but among poor economic group, 89.4% are rural and only 10.6% are urban. Among non-poor group, 55.7% are rural and 44.3% are urban. But in this situation, differences of CED between rural and urban are more or less same. Regarding education, among total and non-poor economic group, secondary educated women are highest within four educational categories of education and CED is also inversely related to educational condition. Among poor economic group, among higher educational categories, highest percentage of CED is also observed. It is seen that regarding working categories of women, it is unanimously seen that highest or near to highest percentage of CED are seen among the non-working and domestic or manual labored women in Northeast India as well as among poor and non-poor categories. It is also very interesting to say that among the women of service holder and those women who are belonging to non-poor economic categories, CED is low. In poor economic group, among service holder women, CED is very close to non-working

Table 9.1 Total and state wise percentages of poor and non-poor CED among women of Northeast India and their differences and ranking of differences between poor and non-poor

Zone and states	Economic conditions					Percentage of underweight			Poor and non-poor differences	Ranking of differences
	Poor		Non-poor		Total	Poor	Non-poor	Total		
	N	%	*N*	%	*N*	%				
Northeast	3269	34.8	6133	65.2	9402	26.6	17.9	20.9	8.7	
Arunachal Pradesh	456	52.8	407	47.2	863	18.6	14.3	16.6	4.3	6
Assam	860	58.5	610	41.5	1470	44.9	31.5	39.3	13.4	8
Manipur	414	22.4	1437	77.6	1851	16.9	13.1	13.9	3.8	5
Meghalaya	384	37.5	641	62.5	1025	14.6	13.1	13.7	1.5	3
Mizoram	111	13.1	734	86.9	845	13.5	18.0	17.4	−4.5	2
Nagaland	696	33.6	1374	66.4	2070	19.4	17.2	17.9	2.2	4
Sikkim	83	12.9	562	87.1	645	4.8	13.0	11.9	−8.2	1
Tripura	265	41.9	368	58.1	633	44.2	36.1	39.5	8.1	7
India	18,104	36.6	31,313	63.4	49,417	43.5	26.1	32.5	17.4	

Source Compiled from NFHS-3

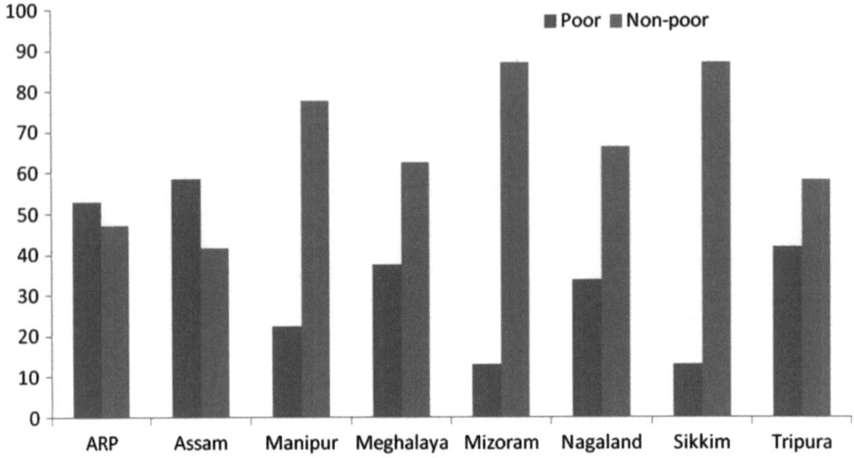

Fig. 9.1 Economic conditions in different states of Northeast India

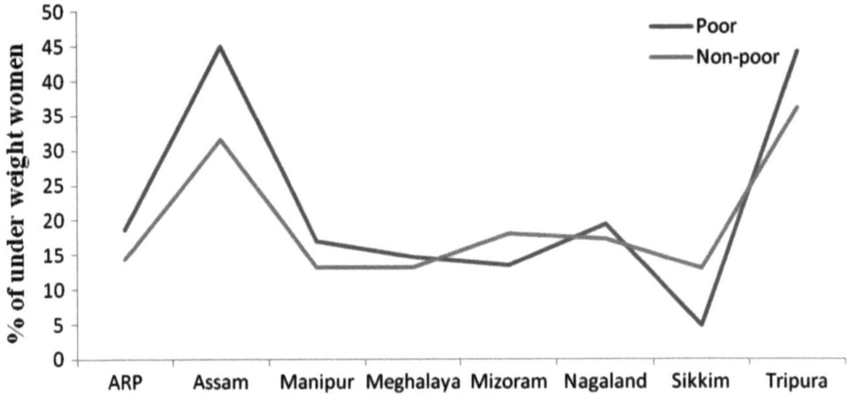

Fig. 9.2 Percentage of underweight women by economic conditions in different states of Northeast India

or domestic or manual worker women. It is also seen that safe drinking water and toilet facilities are directly related with the economic conditions of women but it is not much effective on CED.

Table 9.3 describs the sociodemographic conditions by the economy in different states of Northeast India. It is seen that in all the states of Northeast India, 85–96.4% women are rural who are belonging in poor economic condition but in non-poor economy, rural residence is mostly within the range of 50–60% except in Tripura, where it is 70.9%. It is also very interesting feature is that literacy varies on the basis of economic condition because among poorer women, illiteracy is always more than 50.0% excepting Tripura, where it is 45.7%. Besides illiteracy, always a

Table 9.2 Percentage of CED among northeast women in respect of different socioeconomic variables by economic differences

Socioeconomic variables	Total			Poor			Non-poor		
		Percentage			Percentage			Percentage	
Type of place	*N*	Conditions	CED	*N*	Conditions	CED	*N*	Conditions	CED
Rural	6336	67.4	22.8	2922	89.4	26.0	3414	55.7	20.0
Urban	3066	32.6	17.0	347	10.6	30.8	2719	44.3	15.2
Women's education									
Illiterate	2810	29.9	24.5	1792	54.8	26.4	1018	16.6	21.2
Primary	1869	19.9	22.6	794	24.3	24.3	1075	17.5	21.4
Secondary	4127	43.9	19.6	680	20.8	29.6	3447	56.2	17.6
Higher	595	6.3	7.4	3	0.1	33.3	592	9.7	7.3
Age-groups									
15–24	2851	30.3	25.8	1042	31.9	28.0	1809	29.5	24.5
25–34	4949	52.6	20.0	1581	48.4	28.8	3368	54.9	15.8
35–44	1488	15.8	14.6	589	18.0	18.3	899	14.7	12.1
45+	114	1.2	21.1	57	1.7	22.8	57	0.9	19.3
Smoking cigarette									
No	9036	96.2	20.8	3080	94.3	26.4	5956	97.1	17.9
Yes	361	3.8	21.9	186	5.7	27.4	175	2.9	16.0
Religion-caste									
Hindu	3234	34.4	25.0	977	30.0	35.8	2257	36.8	20.3
Muslim	1103	11.7	36.1	636	19.5	43.2	467	7.6	26.3
Christian	4176	44.5	15.4	1348	41.3	14.2	2828	46.2	15.9
Others	876	9.3	12.8	301	9.2	15.9	575	9.4	11.1
Occupation									
Not working	5533	58.3	23.3	1650	50.5	32.5	3883	63.3	19.4

(continued)

Table 9.2 (continued)

Socioeconomic variables	Total			Poor			Non-poor		
		Percentage			Percentage			Percentage	
Type of place	*N*	Conditions	CED	*N*	Conditions	CED	*N*	Conditions	CED
Professionals	348	3.7	8.0	20	0.6	15.0	328	5.3	7.6
Service/Sales	648	6.9	15.1	104	3.2	33.7	544	8.9	11.6
Agriculture	2164	23.1	16.3	1198	36.6	15.1	966	15.8	17.8
Domestic/Manual	694	7.4	27.5	292	8.9	38.4	402	6.6	19.7
Drinking water									
Unsafe	3152	33.5	20.8	1512	46.3	22.9	1640	26.7	18.9
Safe	6059	64.4	20.9	1712	52.4	29.9	4347	70.9	17.3
Toilet facilities									
Unsafe	5050	53.7	23.1	2773	84.8	26.5	2277	37.1	19.0
Safe	4156	44.2	18.1	448	13.7	27.2	3708	60.5	17.0

percentage of primary literate women is higher than the secondary literate percentage among poorer women and among non-poorer group, percentage of secondary educated women are highest than all other educational categories. Occupation-wise, percentage of non-working women is less among poor economic categories of women than non-poor economic categories in all states of Northeast India. Uses of safe drinking water by women among both poor and non-poor women are unanimously less (32.6:59.4) and (51.3:60.7) in Manipur and Nagaland, respectively. And it is also seen that in Arunachal Pradesh, very high percentages of women (79.1:94.6) are using safe drinking water of both poor and non-poor economic categories and then it is followed by Assam (62.0:84.1). Regarding using of toilet facilities, very low percentages are seen among poor economic categories in Arunachal Pradesh (10.4%) Assam (8.9%), Meghalaya (2.1%), and Sikkim (7.5%). But among the non-poor economic categories, percentages of safe toilet facility are also low because maximum states are belonging within the range of 50–60 %.

Table 9.4 expresses the logistic regression of different socioeconomic variables with CED of women in total Northeast India and among the poor and non-poor women of Northeast India. The result of total Northeast India is very indifferent from non-poor economic categories of women but it differs from poor economic categories in respect of most of the independent variables. It is seen that among total and non-poor group of women, education is inversely related to CED and the results are statistically significant but among poorer group, higher education is directly related with CED. Likewise, among professional and service-holder women, CED is inversely related in total Northeast women and non-poor group (results is statistically significant), but among poorer group of women, in case of service-holder women, it is directly related with CED. It is also seen that among the poorer group, CED is more among the women who use safe drinking water and safe toilet facility than unsafe users. But it is also seen in urban women that CED is less than rural women in all the groups and age is inversely related with the low CED excepting poorer women because among them, among poorer group, ages between 25 and 34, CED is directly related with CED and the result is statistically significant.

9.4 Discussion

Chronic energy deficiency (CED) is a poverty phenomenon because it reflects an inadequate access to food at the household level, individual level. It also reflects intra-household food distribution practices and impact of different disease. The present study deals with the condition of chronic energy deficiency among adult women in Northeast (NE) India on the basis of economic condition and its variation within different states of NE. The result also compared with total India. It is seen from our study that in Northeast India, 34.8% women are belonging in poor economic condition and in India 36.6% women are poor. So the percentages are very close to all India level. But in different states of Northeast India, it varies in different

Table 9.3 Socio-demographic conditions by economy in different states of north-east India

	Arunachal Pradesh		Assam		Manipur		Meghalaya		Mizoram		Nagaland		Sikkim		Tripura	
	Poor	Non-poor	Poor	Non-poor	Poor	Non-poor	Poor	Non-poor	Poor	Non-poor	Poor	Non-poor	Poor	Non-poor	Poor	Non-poor
Rural	84.8	54.8	91.3	63.0	85.3	55.8	93.8	58.8	92.8	50.0	87.9	45.6	96.4	66.4	91.3	70.9
Urban	15.1	45.2	8.7	37.0	14.7	44.2	6.3	41.2	7.2	50.0	12.1	54.4	7.6	33.6	8.7	29.1
Women's education																
Illiterate	72.4	30.7	48.8	17.9	51.7	15.7	59.1	25.4	53.2	1.9	53.7	15.6	56.6	23.7	45.7	9.0
Primary	14.7	21.1	26.4	15.3	20.5	11.3	25.0	22.3	29.7	22.6	23.1	14.9	32.5	23.1	37.0	24.5
Secondary	12.9	43.2	24.7	58.1	27.3	54.9	15.9	45.2	17.1	68.5	23.1	62.1	10.8	46.6	17.4	59.8
Higher	–	4.9	0.1	8.7	0.5	18.1	–	7.0	–	6.9	–	7.4	–	6.6	–	6.8
Religion-caste																
Hindu	29.5	30.0	48.7	74.4	21.0	57.0	7.3	7.2	–	1.6	8.5	11.0	61.4	60.5	76.0	86.3
Muslim	4.8	2.2	43.3	20.3	17.9	11.4	7.8	3.1	–	0.4	13.1	5.7	–	3.9	18.3	12.9
Christian	37.1	24.6	7.8	4.4	52.2	21.2	68.5	76.6	68.5	97.4	78.4	83.1	10.8	8.5	0.8	0.3
Others	28.6	43.2	–	0.8	8.9	10.4	16.4	13.1	31.5	–	–	0.2	27.7	27.0	5.0	0.5
Occupation																
Not working	20.6	51.5	76.7	80.5	31.2	47.0	46.9	68.2	69.4	61.9	41.1	65.4	59.0	73.5	66.7	84.4
Professionals	0.4	4.9	0.7	3.3	0.2	5.4	0.5	3.7	–	5.3	1.0	6.6	–	6.8	0.8	4.9
Service/Sales	4.0	13.8	1.6	3.4	9.2	11.9	3.1	9.8	4.5	10.1	1.0	8.0	–	6.9	3.8	2.7
Agriculture	69.0	24.6	5.5	2.3	51.7	20.5	34.4	13.4	24.3	21.0	54.5	17.9	38.6	9.1	20.8	6.0
Domestic/Manual	6.0	5.2	15.5	10.5	7.7	15.2	15.1	4.8	1.8	1.8	2.4	2.0	2.4	3.7	8.0	1.9
Drinking water																
Unsafe	20.9	5.4	38.0	15.9	67.4	40.6	66.9	21.1	58.6	18.1	48.7	39.3	45.0	16.7	50.4	19.1
Safe	79.1	94.6	62.0	84.1	32.6	59.4	33.1	78.9	41.4	81.9	51.3	60.7	55.0	83.3	49.6	80.9
Toilet facilities																
Unsafe	89.6	46.8	91.1	38.0	85.7	46.8	97.9	56.9	70.3	29.8	76.4	26.9	92.5	21.9	77.5	44.0
Safe	10.4	53.2	8.9	62.0	14.3	53.2	2.1	43.1	29.7	70.2	23.6	73.1	7.5	78.1	22.5	56.0

degrees. Highest non-poor conditioned women are found in Sikkim (87.1%), followed by Mizoram (86.9%). Latest data of Planning Commission revealed that in Sikkim, from comparison between 2004–05 and 2011–12, 22% declined poverty due to inclusive and equitable development of the entire state. And now, in Sikkim, only 8.19% lives below in poverty line and rural and urban differences, only 9.85% in rural and 3.11% in urban areas are below poverty line in comparison to national average 25.70% for rural and 13.70% for urban (Debroy 2012). Lowest non-poor conditioned women are found in Assam (41.5%), followed by Arunachal Pradesh (47.2%).

For inter-state variation, percentages of CED women are also found on the basis of poor and non-poor conditions of the family. It is seen that only in Assam and Tripura, 44.9 and 44.2% women are suffering from CED those who are belonging to the poor family and it denotes the maximum occurrences. In non-poor family, the highest percentage of CED is found in Tripura (36.1%), then it is followed by Assam (31.5%), respectively. So it is clear that very high percentage of CED is observed among the women of these two states rather than other states of NE. This situation supports the view of Tendulkar Committee from NSS 66th round of consumer expenditure that Manipur has the highest level of poverty followed by Assam where the highest number of persons below the poverty line and Tripura is in the lowest per capita consumption expenditure (Giribabu 2013).

It is obvious that CED is directly related to poor economic condition but the differences of CED between poor and non-poor family indirectly express the magnitude of other factors which are controlling the CED. If the differences are positive and magnitude is high, then it denotes that, in general, the other factors which are regulating the health status are also poor. If the value of differences is negative, it means, besides economy, other factors are very sound which renders to keep health in well. Here, the differences of CED between poor and non-poor women in Northeast India is 8.7 but in India, it is 17.4. So in India, it proves that economy is the prime factor for controlling the health. But, in the northeast, as the differences are 8.7, it denotes that besides economy, their factors for promoting health is much better than India. Regarding relationship between Chronic energy deficiency with socioeconomic variables, it is seen that rural–urban differences are not effective on CED. Through educational differentiation, it is seen that education is inversely related with CED but the most notable thing is that among the poorer but highly educated women, highest percentage of CED are observed in Northeast India. The probable reason is that among poorer group, 80–90% women are rural and mainly they are working as a cultivator, agriculture laborers, or low-paid service holder. As their overall economic conditions of their family are poor, they are suffering from CED. It is seen that among the non-working and domestic or manual labored women, the highest percentage of CED is seen among in general Northeast India as well as among poor and non-poor categories of women. It is also very interesting to say that among the service holder but belonging to non-poor economic categories, CED is low but among the poor economic group, among service-holder women, CED is very high. The probable reason is that though women are service holder what type of work the women are engaged is a big

Table 9.4 Results of categorical logistic regression of CED among women of Northeast India as a whole and their economic status

Sociodemographic variables	Total	Poor	Non-poor
Type of place			
Rural®	1.00	1.00	1.00
Urban	0.728	0.836	0.770**
Women's education			
Illiterate®	1.00	1.00	1.00
Primary	0.914	0.902	0.978
Secondary	0.810**	1.135	0.800*
Higher	0.353**	1.552	0.409**
Age-groups			
15–24®	1.00	1.00	1.00
25–34	0.834**	1.269*	0.650**
35–44	0.606**	0.811	0.514**
45+	0.899	1.124	0.778
Smoking cigarette			
No®	1.00	1.00	1.00
Yes	1.278*	1.321	1.077
Religion-caste			
Hindu®	1.00	1.00	1.00
Muslim	1.543**	1.433**	1.247*
Christian	0.576**	0.366**	0.749**
Others	0.433**	0.399**	0.464**
Occupation			
Not working®	1.00	1.00	1.00
Professionals	0.602*	0.359	0.643*
Service/Sales	0.823	1.363	0.697*
Agriculture	0.741**	0.594**	0.953
Domestic/Manual	1.287**	1.542**	1.044
Others			
Drinking water			
Unsafe®	1.00	1.00	1.00
Safe	1.109*	1.375**	0.958
Toilet facilities			
Unsafe®	1.00	1.00	1.00
Safe	0.900*	1.065	1.00

*Significant at 5% level
**Significant at 1% level
®Base category

question. It is also seen that safe drinking water and toilet facilities are directly related to the economic conditions of women but it is not much effective on CED. This is because, the percentage of safe toilet facilities are maximum 50–60% among the women of Northeast India.

From the above study, it is clear that CED has negative social and economic consequences. It is associated with social costs which in turn causing persisting CED in the society. Thus, it is necessary to improve the socioeconomic condition as a whole and especially to improve among women as a creator of present and future of the society.

References

Bardhan, K. (1993). Social class and gender in India: The structure of differences in the conditions of women. In A. W. Clark (Ed.), *Gender and political economy: Explorations of South Asian systems* (pp. 146–178). New Delhi: Oxford University Press.

Burman, J. J. R. (2012). Status of tribal women in India. *Mainstream*, *L*(12), March 10.

Debroy, B. (2012). Poverty in North East and Uts. *Economic Times*, April 6.

Drez, J., & Sen, A. (1995). *India: Economic development and social opportunity*. New Delhi: Oxford University Press.

Giribabu, M. (2013). Food and nutritional security in north-east India-some contemporary issues. *Internal Journal Development Research, 3*(05), 001–008.

Handsdak, E. V. (2012). The status of tribal women. In Fr. Agapit Turkey (Ed.), *Reporting to India's social challenges/-promoting Tribal Rights & culture* (on-line). Retrieved from http://www.Holycrossjustice.org/pdf/Asia/Indiassocialchallenges/promotingTribalRights/Thestatusoftribalwomen.pdf.

Jose, S., & Navaneetham, K. (2008). A fact sheet on women's malnutrition in India. *Economic and Political Weekly, 43*(33), 61–67.

Miller, B. D. (1997). Social class, gender and intra-household food allocations to children in South \Asia. *Social Science and Medicine, 44*(11), 1685–1695.

National family Health Survey. (2005–06). *Ministry of health and family welfare*. Government of India (NFHS-III).

Osmain, S. R. (1992). Introduction. In S. R. Osmain (Ed.), *Nutrition and poverty* (pp. 1–15). New Delhi: Oxford University Press.

Rutstein, S. (1999). *Wealth versus expenditure. Comparison between the DHS wealth index and household expenditures in your departments of Guatemala*. Calverton, Maryland: ORC Macro.

World Health Organization (WHO). (2003). *Diet, nutrition and the prevention of Chronic diseases*. Report of a joint WHO/FAO expert consultation. Technical Report Series No. 916. Geneva: WHO.

Zahol, L. V. (2010). *Status of tribal women (on line)*. Available: http://1/status.pdf. (October, 2012).

Part II
Methods and Modelling

Chapter 10
Prevalence of Malaria and Hb E in Northeast India: An Econo-genomics Study

R. Sarada, B.K. Misra and T. Vasulu

10.1 Introduction

Malaria is one of the pandemic diseases that afflict on an average of about 200–300 million people annually, resulting in 1–3 million deaths all over the globe (WHO 2001). This is one of the major global health and economic burdens of most of the tropical countries of the world (Detels et al. 2015). This is possibly the single largest endemic vector-borne disease draining the state exchequer for more than a century without any hope for remedies or cures. Of the various strategies adopted are related to curtail the disease or minimise the losses incurred in health and economic sectors. This is likely to continue unless we were able to find a cure and eradicate the disease. One possible promising investigation is to look at the genetics of pathogenesis of host–parasite interactions and the several genes that are involved in the pathways related to cell adhesion, immunity signal pathway, etc. This host–parasite interaction and the cascade of genes involved in the pathways (Kwaitkoski 2005) would help in developing genotype-based drug (pharmacokinetics) and even develop possible vaccine and other techniques for combating the disease. Such trials are already making headway and it is expected that in a decade or so we will be in a position to get an effective vaccine, panacea that will help to completely control the global epidemics and we will be in a position to be free from the economic and health burdens.

R. Sarada · B.K. Misra
RDAP, North-Eastern Hill University, Tura Campus, India
e-mail: saradapinky@gmail.com

B.K. Misra
e-mail: birendramishra14@gmail.com

T. Vasulu (✉)
BAU, Indian Statistical Institute, Kolkata, India
e-mail: vasulut@hotmail.com

U.K. De et al. (eds.), *Issues on Health and Healthcare in India*, India Studies in Business and Economics, https://doi.org/10.1007/978-981-10-6104-2_10

The studies related to welfare economics have helped us to understand the economic burden, health and policy implications of some of the endemic disease, poverty, natural calamities, etc. However, in the case of diseases which have underlying genetic causes, the economic burden and health, policy and management implications differ and studies concerning the economic aspects of genetic diseases require a separate area of investigation of a field of study. In general, such studies relating to the economic aspects of some traits which are primarily hereditary have been addressed, some decades ago. However, with the developments of genomics and knowledge of molecular genetics of several diseases, recently there have been attempts in the area what is now called as 'econo-genomics'. This is a recent development to the welfare economics—described under the preview of what is called as econo-genomics. In this regard, it interesting to state that there is another related area which can be described as geno-economics; in simple, the main premise is built around the fundamental concept that is related to understanding economic basis and principles of molecular genetic structure and genetic organisation and its function, whereas in case of econo-genomics, such efforts that have been initiated, more vigorously in recent times of a decade or so, give us more insights into our understanding of the economic implications of some of the genetic diseases. However, in the case of geno-economics, such initiative is yet to emerge and this could be an interesting area of fusion between molecular genetics and health economics. For the last decade, there have been impressive publications in the area of econo-genomics (e.g., Benjamin et al. 2007, 2012; Fredrickson et al. 2013; Rietveld et al. 2013). To be able to illustrate, we present here one simple example of health implications of malaria and Hb E disease in northeastern region, where both these are influenced by genetic factors.

10.2 Malaria Prevalence

10.2.1 Indian Scenario

Malaria is highly prevalent in most parts of the country, except perhaps at high altitudes and in some coastal areas. Health and hygiene, and living conditions promote the breeding of mosquitoes and the parasites, whose prevalence peaks during monsoon period and are more directly related to the wide spread of the disease. It is estimated that 12 states in India have more than 26% of the population below the poverty line and they contribute for 70% of total malarial cases. In most parts of the country, periodic epidemics of malaria occur every 5 to 7 years. About 65% of malaria infections in India are caused by *Plasmodium vivax* (*pv*) and 35% are caused by *Plasmodium falciparum* (*pf*) (Shiv lal et al. 1998).

There are several malaria-prone endemic zones in different parts of the country and also there are populations who are more severely affected than others, whereas some populations, especially in central regional tribal populations, are least affected possibly because of the prevalence of abnormal haemoglobin variants, e.g., sickle cell (or Hb S); others like Hb E are prevalent in northeastern parts (Bhasin and Walter 2001; Das et al. 1971; Deka et al. 1988; Dash et al. 2008; Bhaskar and Sengupta 2013). Though there have been studies reporting the prevalence of polymorphism and allelic variation of Hb, G6PD, etc., in regional castes and tribes and hospital-based studies (Balgir 2000, 2014; Bhasin and Walter 2001; Sarkar et al. 2010; Agarwal et al. 2011. Deb et al. 2015), but genetic studies dealing its association with malaria in Indian populations are hardly available. Recently, population genomic studies have reported variation in SNPs of some of the candidate genes of G6PD, TNF, CD36, etc. These studies have shown differences in some alleles among castes and tribes from endemic malarial regions, suggesting possible association of the observed polymorphism with malaria. However, genetic epidemiological studies dealing with the candidate genes and its association with malaria are hard to found, except one such study based on case–control comparison (Gaikwad et al. 2005), which has indicated the association of some specific alleles at two autosomal STRs with the malarial infection.

10.2.1.1 Northeast Region and Malaria

Northeastern parts of the country are populated (39 million—national 3.9%) primarily by Tibeto-Burman and Austro-Asiatic speaking tribal populations of East Asian (Mongoloid) ethnic origin (Das 1993). The favourable conditions of climate of NE region provide successful spread of about 27 mosquito species (Dutta et al. 2010). The virulent form of Malaria is caused by *P. falciparum* (*pf*) mostly transmitted by *Anopheles minimus*, *Anopheles fluviatilis* and *Anopheles dirus*. Of the total burden of malaria and its mortality in India, NE states contribute 10% malaria and 20% of deaths. There have been reports of chloroquine resistance in *P. falciparum* in different parts of the region. It is known that among endemic malarial region, the presence of Hb E among populations gives protection to malaria, known as balanced polymorphism; as a result, the Hb E is expected to maintain its frequency, despite its deleterious effect in the population (Chotivanich et al. 2010).

In Meghalaya, the number of deaths due to *pf* cases varied from 7 to 31. In the state 21,676 *pf* cases reported, there were 118 deaths (Directorate of Health Statistics). These deaths occur more in malaria-endemic regions of West Garo Hills, Ri Bhoi district. In 2010 (till November), the NVBD in Meghalaya reports a total of 40,180 recorded positive malaria cases and 38,042 of them being *pf* cases, there were 82 deaths. However, in 2010, there has been a decrease in the malarial cases which is attributed to health schemes; malaria control intervening methods (medicated mosquito nets), multiple drug usage, and surveillance by vector-borne disease officials. Northeast region is known as malarial-endemic parts of the country, and the incidence of malaria both from government records and other studies suggests the prevalence of malaria for decades, though recently, possibly with the effective intervention of preventive mechanisms, have shown a decreasing trend in the overall deaths due to malarial disease and its prevalence rates (Dhiman et al. 2011).

Populations of NE India harbour wide genetic diversity, and population genetic surveys show wide differences in allelic frequencies (e.g., serum proteins, enzymes, Mendelian characters) between populations within regions (Bhasin and Walter 2001; Singh et al. 2010). And they also show population-specific prevalence for some of the genetic traits, possibly, as a result of isolation and drift and other population structure factors. For example, the frequency of Hb E widely differs and is highly prevalent in some parts of the people of NE region; the frequency varies from less than 10% to more than 50% in different regional tribal populations (Das and Talukdar 2001). They also show a high prevalence of deficiency of G6PD in some populations (Bhasin and Walter 2001). Several enzymes, proteins such as G6PD, CD36 and Hb E, and an association of anaemia and expression levels of CD35, CD55 and CD59 are related to malarial infection (Luomi et al. 2002; Mahajan et al. 2011). It is known that Hb E-type (which is due to a mutation that had occurred at the 26th position of β-chain of the Hb molecule) gives less plasticity to the RBC for its free intracellular movement which inhibits the rapid spread of the parasite. It is also known that the G6PD deficiency gives protection against malarial infection. Of recent decades, the *P. falciparum* has developed resistance to antimalarial drugs, causing much public health concern and severe economic implications (Muller 2005; Mu et al. 2010).

Haemoglobin variants are composed of missense mutations that cause single amino acid substitutions in the globin protein, resulting in an abnormal or 'variant' Hb tetramer (Christopher et.al. 2013). Biochemical abnormalities due to Hb mutations are very common and show clinically significant symptoms. There are more than 1000 variants; a few are clinically significant but most of them are clinically insignificant, out of which few show clinical manifestations of varying severity. The most common and medically important Hb variants include Hb S, Hb C, Hb E, and various thalassemias all of which are under positive genetic selection because they confer survival advantages in areas where malaria is endemic (Weather all and Clegg 2001). The Hb variants that are clinically significant usually have altered O_2 affinity and so are relatively simple to diagnose through history (pedigree charts), physical examination and laboratory testing (Christopher et al. 2013; Saleh-Gohari et al. 2015).

In addition, recent molecular genetic studies in Southeast Asian populations have implicated some SNPs (Single Nucleotide Polymorphisms) and STR markers (e.g. Hb E gene) that play key role in causing malaria and variable expression in different populations. It is therefore expected that the polymorphism observed in the above genes is a result of malarial selection and/or due to other evolutionary forces and population structure variables in northeastern populations.

For several decades, there have been attempts to investigate the possible causes and methods to contain the wide spread of malarial infection and one promising area of much significance is to understand the molecular genetics mechanism. However, such studies are very few and Indian populations are expected to provide a wide platform to investigate a variety of candidate genes in malarial-endemic populations in different regions.

10.2.2 Haemoglobin E (Hb E)

Hb E is one of the world's most common abnormal haemoglobin mutations in Southeast Asians and among South Asian countries including India (Fucharoen and Winichagoon 2011). The occurrence of Hb E is most concentrated at the border of Thailand. It is estimated that 30 million Southeast Asians are heterozygous for Hb E and one million are homozygous (Badens et al. 2002; Weatherall et al. 2010; Chattopadhyay et al. 2012). It is one of the major health burdens of the world health economics primarily among the tropical and subtropical countries (Weatherall et al. 2010; Weatherall 2011). In 1954, Hb E became the fourth abnormal haemoglobin to be identified by electrophoresis, and a substitution of lysine for glutamic acid at position 26 of the β-globin chain was found in 1961. It results in a heterogeneous group of disorders whose phenotype ranges from asymptomatic to severe. As per Haldane's hypothesis the malarial-endemic regions provide an ecological advantage for the maintenance of the allele frequencies of some of the haemoglobinopathies, which in homozygous state is expected to be lethal and gets eliminated (selected out) in non-malarial environment (Haldane 1949), which has been validated by empirical studies in Africa and other Asian countries (e.g. Taylor et al. 2012). A case–control study in Thailand indicated the absence of association between Hb E prevalence and in vitro infectivity and neither proliferation of malaria parasite *P. falciparum* nor the production of hemozoin in northern region of the country (Lithanatudom et al. 2016).

10.2.2.1 Classification of Hb E Disorders

Asymptomatic forms: Haemoglobin E heterozygotes are clinically normal with minimal changes in blood counts and red blood cell indices. Red cell morphology is similar to that in thalassemia minor with normocytic or slightly microcytic red cells with MCH (mean corpuscular volume) 84 ± 5 fL. A few target cells may be present in the blood smear. Haemoglobin electrophoresis reveals both Hb A and Hb E. Haemoglobin E constitutes 25–30% of the hemolysate in Hb E trait. Homozygotes for Hb E usually have normal haemoglobin levels but some may be mildly anaemic. Clinical symptoms are rare. Few are jaundiced but most patients are not, and liver and spleen are usually not enlarged. Reticulocyte counts are consistently normal and nucleated red cells are not seen in the blood. Bone marrow examination shows a normal cellular pattern or minimal erythrocytic hyperplasia.

Haemoglobin levels are slightly reduced, red cells are microcytic and poorly haemoglobinized red cells with 20–80% target red cells. Haemoglobin analysis reveals 85–95% Hb E with reminder Hb F. There is defective β E-globin chain synthesis in all Hb E homozygote's which is due to decreased β E m RNA production, a result of abnormal RNA splicing caused by Hb E mutation (Galanello and Origa 2010; Khone 2011; Oliver et al. 2008, 2011).

Symptomatic forms: Haemoglobin E/βThal disease is a thalassemia syndrome of intermediate severity, although the clinical spectrum can be very heterogeneous (Sharma and Saxena 2009). Two types of Hb E/β thalassemia disease are there which depend on the presence of Hb A. Haemoglobin E levels of 30% or above suggest the interaction of Hb E with β-thalassemia. In Hb E-β thalassemia, the disease is characterised by Hb E and Hb F without detectable Hb A. Haemoglobin E constitutes between 40 and 60% of the hemolysate with the remainder Hb F. Different beta thalassemia genes result in a variable severity of disease because of different levels of Hb A. At birth infants with severe Hb E/βthal are asymptomatic because Hb F levels are high (Rees et al. 2010; Sanchaisuriya et al. 2007). As Hb F production wanes and is replaced by Hb E at 6–12 months of age, anaemia with splenomegaly develops. The genetic engineering and stem cell therapy appear to be one promising possible remedy for the haemoglobinopathies (Person 1998; Sherva et al. 2010).

10.2.3 Scope and Objectives of the Study

The people afflicted with Hb E trait (individuals who inherit a copy of the altered or mutated form of haemoglobin from their parents), often, may not have serious health issues or problems; however, they are responsible for transmitting the abnormal gene giving rise to various combinations of haemoglobinopathies and thalassemias in their progeny which is hazardous for the sustainability of the society. Therefore, this study might help people in understanding the consequences of the haemoglobinopathies and its related aspects with regard to health. It will pave a way for encouraging genetic counselling which is inseparable from genetic diagnosis. It will aim to provide a better insight about the causes of genetic disease with a better awareness of the problem, and expected to help in better family and individual health management. The study is expected to help them to get a better awareness of the resources available for diagnosis, treatment and prevention. The objectives of the study are as follows:

1. To study the prevalence of Hb E status among Garo population in Tura;
2. To inquire about the health implications, cultural and life style practices related to Hb E status, viz. Hb trait, Hb disease and Hb E with thalassemias.

10.3 Materials and Methods

10.3.1 Location of Study

The study has been conducted in Tura town, West Garo Hills of Meghalaya, India. It is located at 25.52°N and 90.22°E in the foot hills of the Tura hills and is the district capital of West Garo hills, with a total population of 78,858 (Source: census 2011). It has an average elevation of 349 m. It is the cultural and administrative centre of the Garo Tribes with a literacy rate of 7%, higher than the national average of 5%. Main residents of Tura are called Garo tribe.

10.3.2 Garo and Their Cultural and Primary Lifestyle

Garo are indigenous people of Meghalaya; they are one of the few matrilineal societies in the world. They are mostly influenced by Christianity and encourage tribe endogamy and consanguineous marriage in their society. There are a few studies on the prevalence of haemoglobin E among mongoloid tribes including Garo tribe. The Garo being East Asian ancestry, described earlier as mongoloid race (Das et al. 1971) also show high prevalence of Hb E trait in the world. They have been living in this region from times immemorial under similar habitat and environmental conditions maintaining their culture and biology.

The present study has been conducted in Tura town, district capital of West Garo Hills of Meghalaya, India. It is cultural and administrative centre for Garo tribes. The Garo have a matrilineal society where children adopt their mother's clan; the simplest family of Garo's consists of the husband, wife and children. The family increases with the marriage of the heiress, generally the youngest daughter, she is called *nokna* and her husband *nokrom*. The bulk of the property is bequeathed upon the heiress and other sisters receive fragments but are entitled to use plots of land for cultivation. The heiress is married to one of her father's nephews, but there are instances where the girl is married outside the family.

10.3.3 Sampling Method and Sample Size

The four major hospitals in the Tura town were covered as a part of survey regarding Hb E status among Garo in the Tura town. Doctors of the respective hospitals were approached to know the exact condition of Hb E in the Tura town and the researcher (RS) tried to look for people who have come for various checkups, to find, if any, Hb E-affected person approaching the doctor. But that did not help to find patients with Hb E; so the doctor was consulted to get the names of few people diagnosed with Hb E-type. Later by following snowball sampling method, it was possible to find people diagnosed with Hb E-type and fifty such people were approached with appropriate schedule containing relevant questions prepared by the researcher according to the objectives and variables drawn by reviewing various literatures. These fifty people (proband) were considered as the sample size in the study conducted.

10.3.4 Schedule Construction and Variables Used

To study Hb E, socio-psychological variables, clinical and haematological variables have been taken into account. Haemoglobin, red cell indices, includes MCV (average RBC size), MCH (Haemoglobin amount per RBC) and MCHC (the measure of concentration of haemoglobin in a volume of packed RBC) (Moiz et al. 2012); haemoglobin variants include Hb E+ HbA2, Hb F and Hb A (Moiz et al. 2012); and other haematological parameters like RDW (Khattak et al. 2013) are considered as quantitative variables for the study. Social variables such as gender, age, marital status and number of children (live and dead); psychological variables like tiredness, encouraging family members, quality of life, genetic awareness and social awareness; and clinical variables such as Hb E-type, symptoms and complications other than Hb E are considered as qualitative variables in the proposed study. A combination of open- and close-ended questionnaire was constructed by taking into account the objectives of the study and also based on findings in the literature. Expert opinion in the respective field has been taken in finalising the questionnaire besides verifying with the respondents per the nature of the objectives.

10.3.5 Data Collection

10.3.5.1 Primary and Secondary Data

The study was conducted for a period of 7 months from September 2014 to April 2015. The field work and data from hospitals and from families has been conducted by the first author (RS) in Tura town, West Garo Hills, Meghalaya (Fig. 10.1). Target people are the doctors from major hospitals and people diagnosed with Hb E from Garo hills. Probands are people from Garo tribe residing in Tura town identified with the help of snow ball sampling method. By using schedule questionnaire and interview method, primary data were collected from both male and female irrespective of Hb E-type (Hb AE, Hb EE, Hb E/βThal), age, economical background and occupation. Secondary data like medical reports mentioning the probands Hb E status were collected and different haematological parameters mentioned in the reports were taken into account for further statistical analysis to

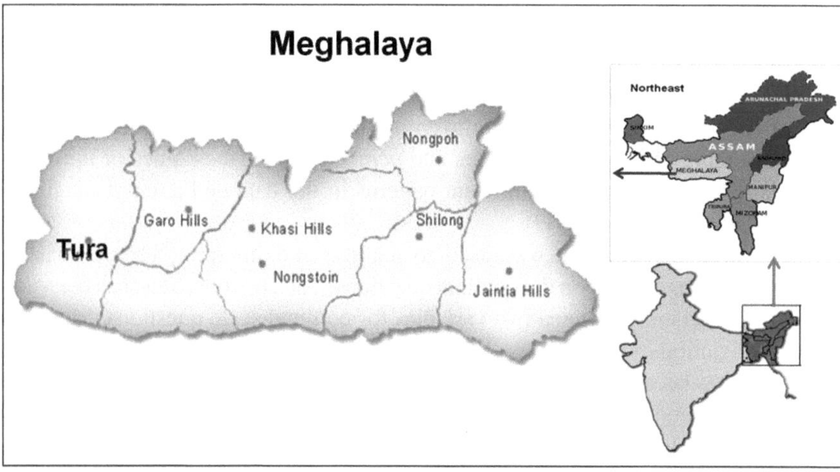

Fig. 10.1 Map showing the location of Tura Town where the field study was conducted

determine how each parameter differs across Hb E-type of the probands and from each other.

Doctors from major hospitals in the Tura town were consulted to understand the reasons for prevalence, frequency of Hb E-type in the tribe. The reasons mentioned by them were noted down for further study by the researcher (RS). Doctors were interviewed to know their observation, understanding of the haemoglobinopathies and the methods in the detection and characterization of abnormal haemoglobins (Wajcman et al. 2001, 2011).

10.3.5.2 Pedigree Chart

Along with probands, his/her family members were also consulted to find out the prevalence of Hb E in the family and also to find out the prevalence of malaria in the family. Pedigree chart was prepared as per the information shared by the probands and his/her family members. Actually, the purpose of drawing pedigree chart in the survey was to understand the pattern of inheritance of haemoglobinopathies in the family, but very few families consulted got their family members tested for Hb E, that too not all the individuals in three or four generations of a family were alive to get tested and other probands never got their family members tested for Hb E. The number who got tested was so negligible that the pattern of inheritance could not be determined (Khone 2011).

10.3.6 Statistical Tools Used for Data Analysis

The data were entered into SPSS version 17 to compute descriptive data. As a first step, a frequency analysis was undertaken on the primary data. Frequency analysis produces a table of frequencies counts and percentages for the values of individual variables to observe for any significant patterns in the data and attempt for further analysis (Gaur and Gaur 2009).

Cross-variable tabulation was used to analyse and interpret the relationships between variables applied on the nominal questions. The chi-square test has been used to test the association between two variables for nominal scale questions. Mean and standard deviations were also used to work out the average of the responses. The Cramer test has been used to find the effects of one variable (independent variable) on the other (dependent variable). Moreover, the one-way Analysis of Variance (ANOVA) and Levene "*t*" test has been used to compare the mean scores of haematological parameters for proband's Hb E-type and gender (Pallant 2011).

10.4 Results and Discussion

To find out the prevalence of Hb E status in Garo population of Tura town, West Garo Hills, Meghalaya, fifty probands were considered as the sample size for the analysis of genetic transmission of Hb E among Garo population. Analysis of socio-psychological and clinical parameters have been analysed and reported below.

10.4.1 Analysis of Socio-psychological and Clinical Parameters

Table 10.1 shows profile of the Hb E-affected respondents among the Garo population in Tura town. Probands profile was analysed between gender against age, marital status, Hb E-type spouse relationship as well as age against Hb E-type.

With regard to age of the probands, a majority (64%) of them belong to age group of 30 years and above, followed by age group of 16–20 and up to 15 years, whereas gender-wise analysis reveals that in case of male respondents with age group 30 years and above followed by 16–30 years age group. A similar pattern of age trend is observed among female respondents.

In the case of ratio of the gender-wise respondents in each age group, it is seen that majority of female respondents 81.8% belong to age group of 16–30, 65.6% belong to above 30 and 42.9% belong to age group up to 15. Majority (57%) of male respondents are seen in the age group of up to 15, followed by age group above 30 (34.4%) and 16–30 (18.2%). As regard with marital of the probands,

Table 10.1 Profile of Hb E probands

Profile			Gender		Total (%)
			Male	Female	
Age group	Up to 15 years	Count	4	3	7
		% within age group	57.1	42.9	100.0
		% Within gender	23.5	9.1	14.0
	16–30 years	Count	2	9	11
		% within age group	18.2	81.8	100.0
		% within gender	11.8	27.3	22.0
	30 above	Count	11	21	32
		% within age group	34.4	65.6	100.0
		% within gender	64.7	63.6	64.0
Total		Count	17	33	50
		% within age group	34.0	66.0	100.0
		% within gender	100.0	100.0	100.0
Marital status	Married	Count	11	20	31
		% within marital status	35.5	64.5	100.0
		% within gender	64.7	60.6	62.0
	Un married	Count	2	10	12
		% within marital status	16.7	83.3	100.0
		% within gender	11.8	30.3	24.0
	Children	Count	4	3	7
		% within marital status	57.1	42.9	100.0
		% within gender	23.5	9.1	14.0
Total		Count	17	33	50
		% within marital status	34.0	66.0	100.0
		% within gender	100.0	100.0	100.0
Hb E-type	Trait	Count	8	17	25
		% within Hb E-type	32.0	68.0	100.0
		% within gender	47.1	51.5	50.0
	Disease	Count	7	9	16
		% within Hb E-type	43.8	56.3	100.0
		% within gender	41.2	27.3	32.0
	Hb E/βThal	Count	2	7	9
		% within Hb E-type	22.2	77.8	100.0
		% within gender	11.8	21.2	18.0
Total		Count	17	33	50
		% within Hb E-type	34.0	66.0	100.0
		% within gender	100.0	100.0	100.0

(continued)

Table 10.1 (continued)

Profile			Gender		Total (%)
			Male	Female	
Spouse relation	Non-consanguineous	Count	11	24	35
		% within spouse relation	31.4	68.6	100.0
		% within gender	64.7	72.7	70.0
	NA	Count	6	9	15
		% within spouse relation	40.0	60.0	100.0
		% within gender	35.3	27.3	30.0
Total		Count	17	33	50
		% within spouse relation	34.0	66.0	100.0
		% within gender	100.0	100.0	100.0

Note Results are based on field survey (by RS) during September 2014–April 2015
Source Compiled from field survey by the author

irrespective of the gender, a majority (62%) of them were married, followed by 24% of them being unmarried. Gender-wise analysis reveals that 64.7% males and 60.6% females are married and 11.8% males and 30.3% females are unmarried.

In the case of ratio of gender-wise respondents, the unmarried (83.3%) and the married 64.5% are seen to be females followed by 35.5% married and 16.7% unmarried males. In children category 57.1% are seen to be males and 42.9% are seen to be females.

With respect to Hb E-type, irrespective of gender, 50% of them are reported to have Hb E trait, followed by Hb E disease (32%) which is further followed by Hb E/beta thalassemic probands (18%). Gender-wise analysis reveals that 47.1% of males and 51.5% females are Hb E trait people followed by 41.2% males and 27.3% females having its disease and 11.8% males and 21.2% females have been reported to being Hb E/beta thalassemia patients. In the case of ratio of gender-wise respondents, a majority of thalassemia (77.8%), trait (68%) and disease (56.3%) were female subjects followed by 22% thalassemia, 32% trait and 43.8% disease males (Fig. 10.2).

Relating to spouse relationship, since 70% of them are married, all of them informed that they had non-consanguineous marriages and in the remaining 40% unmarried probands including children, their parents relationship has been taken into account and they informed that they are of non-consanguineous marriages. In general, practice of consanguineous marriages is an important reason for the spread of genetic disorder in the population. However, among Garo population, since consanguineous marriage appears to be not the reason at least among the present generation, it is to be noted here that Garo tribe has the culture of consanguineous marriages in their community; usually the youngest girl who is considered as heiress to the property is usually married to one of her father's nephew (www.westgarohills.gov.in); therefore, it is likely that practice of consanguineous marriages among the forefathers (previous

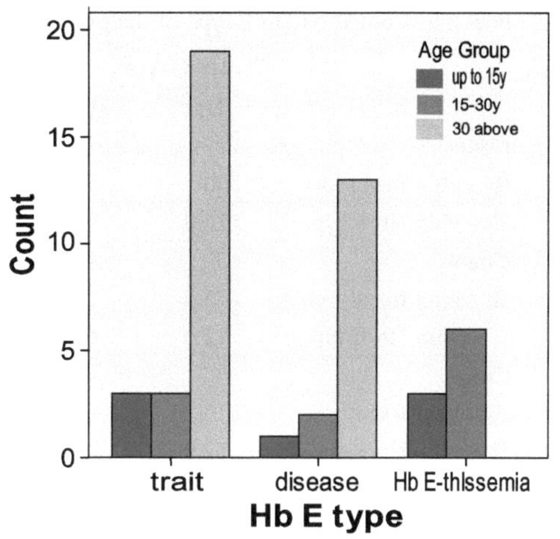

Fig. 10.2 Relation between Hb E-type and age group of the probands

generations) which is prime reason of high frequency of Hb E was observed among the Garo. There is a chance of increase in the frequency of (Hb E) trait and occurrence of (Hb E) disease among offspring of consanguineous parents. Studies among consanguineous parents do suggest increase of such rare recessive diseases (e.g. Brittle 2002; Teeuw et al. 2013). The results show that a majority of female probands are married and belong to age group of above 16 years, and report Hb E trait and disease. These all have reported non-consanguineous marriages.

With regard to the relationship between age of the probands and their respective Hb E-type, it is seen from the data that probands belonging to age group up to 15 have equal numbers (42.9%) of probands having Hb E trait and Hb E/βThal, and 14.3% of Hb E diseases have been reported. In the age group of 16–30 years, a simple majority (54.5%) record as having Hb E/βThal followed by Hb E trait (27.3%) and Hb E disease (18.2%). In the age group of 30 years and above, a majority (59.4%) were having Hb E trait followed by 40.6% being Hb E disease probands and there are no probands under Hb E/βThal.

Foetal loss has been taken into consideration as there were reports that Hb E/βThal or Hb E carrier mothers in their reproductive life either had spontaneous abortions and neonatal deaths (Balgir 2014). Table 10.2 explains foetal loss among married Hb E-type probands (Fig. 10.3). It is understood that a majority (86%) of them have not reported foetal mortality, whereas few of them (8%) have reported one foetal loss, followed by some (12%) of them reporting two foetal losses. Haemoglobin E-typewise analysis reveals that in case of trait equal number (12%) of foetal mortality, each in one foetal loss and two foetal loss category was reported followed by one foetal loss in case of Hb E disease respondents. It may be inferred that even though significant mortality was not reported among trait probands noticeable foetal loss was informed.

Table 10.2 Foetal loss-based on Hb E-type of the married probands

Foetal loss		Hb E-type			Total
		Trait	Disease	Hb E/βThal	
0.0	Count	12	12	0	24
	% within foetal loss	50	50	0.0	100.0
	% within Hb E-type	76.0	93.0	0.0	86.0
1.	Count	3	1	0	4
	% within foetal loss	75.0	25.0	0.0	100.0
	% within Hb E-type	12.0	6.3	0.0	8.0
2.	Count	3	0	0	3
	% within foetal loss	100.0	0.0	0.0	100.0
	% within Hb E-type	12.0	0.0	0.0	12.0
Total	Count	18	13	0	31
	% within foetal loss	50.0	32.0	18.0	100.0
	% within Hb E-type	100.0	100.0	100.0	100.0

Note Results are based on field survey (by RS) during September 2014–April 2015
Source Field survey

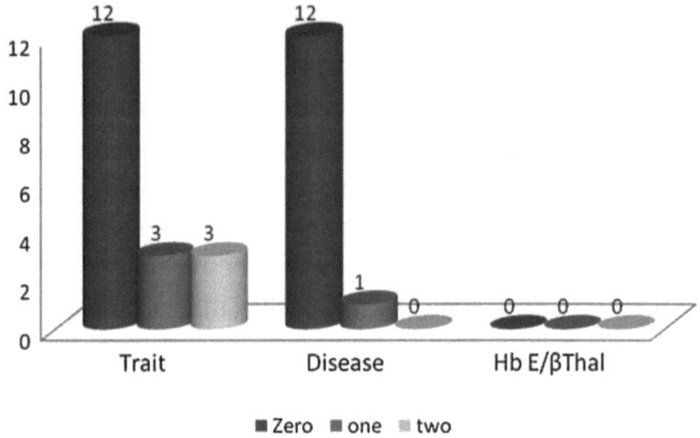

Fig. 10.3 Foetal loss-based on Hb E-type among the married probands

Table 10.3 reveals distribution Hb E-affected family members of the probands across Hb E-type (Fig. 10.4). Irrespective of the Hb E status and who the family member is, it is seen that 60% were diagnosed with any of the Hb E, whereas the rest 40% have never known about the importance of getting themselves diagnosed after the probands have been diagnosed. The reason, they stated, is that they never had any symptoms so as prompt them or felt the requirement of consulting a doctor for diagnoses nor they had any other major health problems in their lives.

When the data have been analysed with respect to Hb E-type of the probands, nearly one-third (34%) of the probands got their spouse and children diagnosed with Hb E-type, followed by other family members (16%) and parents (10%). Hb E-typewise analysis reveals that in case of Hb E/βThal, nearly 44.4% of their other

Table 10.3 Hb E-affected family members of probands across Hb E-type

Hb E effect on family members		Hb E-type			Total
		Trait	Disease	Hb E/βThal	
Parents	Count	3	1	1	5
	% within Hb E effect on family members	60.0	20.0	20.0	100.0
	% within Hb E-type	12.0	6.3	11.1	10.0
Spouse and children	Count	10	4	3	17
	% within Hb E affect on family members	58.8	23.5	17.6	100.0
	% within Hb E-type	40.0	25.0	33.3	34.0
Other family members	Count	1	3	4	8
	% within Hb E affect on family members	12.5	37.5	50.0	100.0
	% within Hb E-type	4.0	18.8	44.4	16.0
No idea	Count	11	8	1	20
	% within Hb E affect on family members	55.0	40.0	5.0	100.0
	% within Hb E-type	44.0	50.0	11.1	40.0
Total	Count	25	16	9	50
	% within Hb E affect on family members	50.0	32.0	18.0	100.0
	% within Hb E-type	100.0	100.0	100.0	100.0

Note Results are based on field survey (by RS) during September 2014–April 2015
Source Field survey

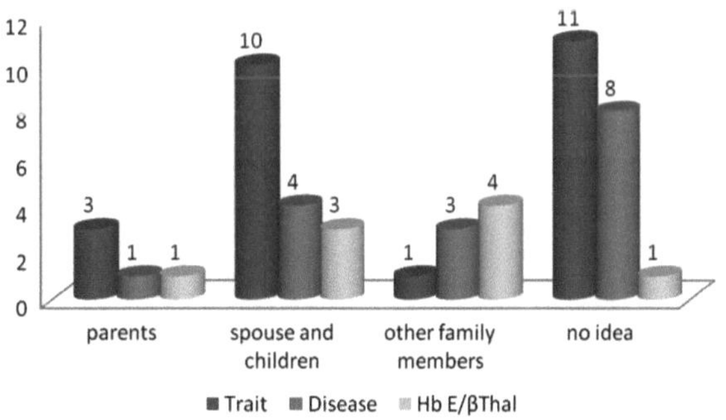

Fig. 10.4 Hb E-affected family members of probands across Hb E-type

family members were diagnosed followed by spouse and children (18.8%) and parents (11.1%). In the case of Hb E trait, in more than one-third (44%) of the probands, none of their family members were diagnosed for the Hb E status, whereas 40% of them got their spouse and children diagnosed, followed by parents

(14%) and other family members (4%). Among the probands, where none of the family members was taken for diagnosis and informed that they have no idea, in nearly 50% Hb E disease and 44% trait probands, none of their family members was diagnosed. It was also reported that in the case of probands diagnosed as trait, their parents (60%) and spouse and children (58.8%) were diagnosed, whereas in the case of disease (37.5%) and Hb E/β thalassemia, half (50%) of them got their other family members diagnosed. As a whole it may be concluded that relatively many of the probands having either of the Hb E-type kith or kin were diagnosed.

Clinical symptoms that prompted the probands to approach the doctor have been shown in Table 10.4 and Fig. 10.5, which were presented as per probands Hb E status. It is reported that nearly 32.0% of them had approached doctor due to symptoms related to severe headache, and symptoms of high fever and weakness followed by joint pains (28%) and routine health checkup (24%). It is further revealed that 10, 4, 2% approached doctor due to weakness, high fever and severe headache, respectively. Such symptoms have been reported in other populations associated with thalassemias (Vichinsky 2007; Trachtenberg et al. 2010).

Haemoglobin E-type analysis reveals more or less similar trend. It can be seen from the table that when subjects went for normal routine checkup got themselves diagnosed as Hb E trait and disease, respectively. It is significant to state that 88%

Table 10.4 Clinical symptoms that prompted probands to approach doctor—Hb E-typewise

Symptoms			Hb E-type			Total
			Trait	Disease	Hb E/βThal	
	Severe headache	Count	0	1	0	1
		% within symptoms	0.0	100.0	0.0	100.0
		% within Hb E-type	0.0	6.3	0.0	2.0
	High fever	Count	1	1	0	2
		% within symptoms	50.0	50.0	0.0	100.0
		% within Hb E-type	4.0	6.3	0.0	4.0
	Weakness	Count	4	1	0	5
		% within symptoms	80.0	20.0	0.0	100.0
		% within Hb E-type	16.0	6.3	0.0	10.0
	Severe headache, high fever, and weakness	Count	3	5	8	16
		% within symptoms	18.8	31.3	50.0	100.0
		% within Hb E-type	12.0	31.3	88.9	32.0
	Health checkup	Count	10	2	0	12
		% within symptoms	83.3	16.7	0.0	100.0
		% within Hb E-type	40.0	12.5	0.0	24.0
	Joint pains and others	Count	7	6	1	14
		% within symptoms	50.0	42.9	7.1	100.0
		% within Hb E-type	28.0	37.5	11.1	28.0
Total	Count		25	16	9	50
	% within symptoms		50.0	32.0	18.0	100.0
	% within Hb E-type		100.0	100.0	100.0	100.0

Results are based on field survey (by RS) during September 2014–April 2015
Source Field survey

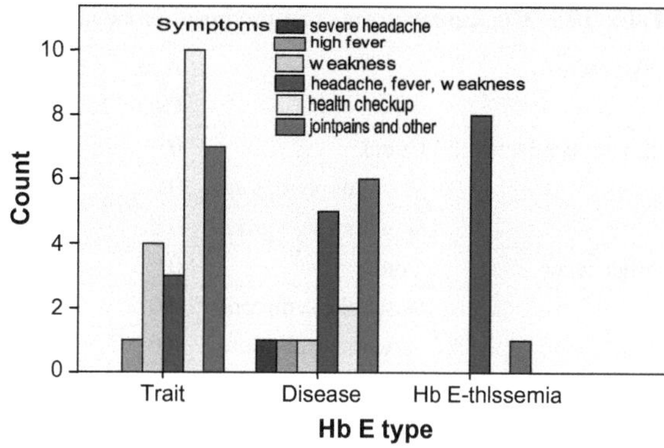

Fig. 10.5 Clinical symptoms that prompted probands to approach doctor—Hb E-typewise

of the probands having thalassemias had approached doctor when they suffered from severe headache, weakness and high fever. Symptom-wise analysis reflects, in general, the same trend, but severe headache, high fever and weakness cumulatively prompted mostly the Hb E/βThal probands to approach the doctor, followed by probands with disease and trait. Following those symptoms other symptoms like joint pains and routine health checkup are other major reasons for approaching doctor wherein they were diagnosed with their respective Hb E-type. From the above data it may be concluded that the major reason which prompted people to approach doctor for Hb AE, Hb EE and Hb E/ βThal disease diagnosis is when they have weakness, high fever and severe headache cumulatively. Many of the probands and their family members have reported of having suffered from jaundice at one point of their life and there are instances that they were diagnosed as malaria first which was later understood to be jaundice and in many literatures it was mentioned that jaundice is one of the symptoms of Hb E-type.

Table 10.5 presents clinical symptoms that have been responsible for prompting the probands to approach the doctor for diagnosis. Cross-variable analysis between age group and clinical symptoms is seen to follow an almost similar trend with more or less the same values like cross-variable analysis of clinical symptoms across Hb E-type (Fig. 10.6).

A slight change in trend can be observed in case of age group above 30 years where majority (37.5%) have approached doctor because of joint pains and others followed by routine checkup, whereas in case of 16 years and above 45.5% of severe headache, high fever and weakness cumulatively have played the major role for them to approach doctor followed by joint pains and others (18.2%). In case of up to 15 years age group, majority (57.1%) of severe headache, high fever and weakness cumulatively have played the major role for them to approach doctor followed by routine health checkup (42.9%).

It may be inferred from the table and the above discussion is that in case of higher age group, joint paints, routine health checkup and severe headache, high fever and weakness cumulatively are playing important role, whereas in other age groups, severe headache, high fever and weakness cumulatively have played a significant role.

Table 10.5 Clinical symptoms that prompted probands to approach doctor—age-wise

Symptoms		Age			Total
		Up to 15 years	15–30 years	30 above	
Severe headache	Count	0	1	0	1
	% within symptoms	0.0	100.0	0.0	100.0
	% within age group	0.0	9.1	0.0	2.0
High fever	Count	0	1	1	2
	% within symptoms	0.0	50.0	50.0	100.0
	% within age group	0.0	9.1	3.1	4.0
Weakness	Count	0	1	4	5
	% within symptoms	0.0	20.0	80.0	100.0
	% within age group	0.0	9.1	12.5	10.0
Severe headache, high fever, and weakness	Count	4	5	7	16
	% within symptoms	25.0	31.3	43.8	100.0
	% within age group	57.1	45.5	21.9	32.0
Health checkup	Count	3	1	8	12
	% within symptoms	25.0	8.3	66.7	100.0
	% within age group	42.9	9.1	25.0	24.0
Joint pains and other	Count	0	2	12	14
	% within symptoms	0.0	14.3	85.7	100.0
	% within age group	0.0	18.2	37.5	28.0
Total	Count	7	11	32	50
	% within symptoms	14.0	22.0	64.0	100.0
	% within age group	100.0	100.0	100.0	100.0

Note Results are based on field survey (by RS) during September 2014–April 2015
Source Field survey

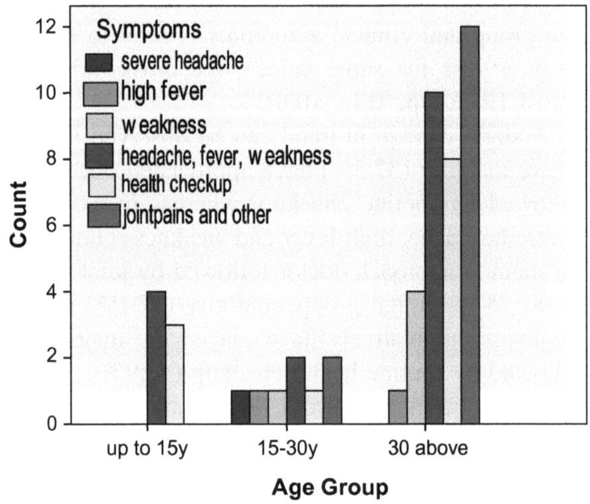

Fig. 10.6 Clinical symptoms that prompted probands to approach doctor—age-wise

Table 10.6 Complications experienced by the probands

Complications other than Hb E		Hb E-type			Total
		Trait	Disease	Hb E/βThal	
Yes	Count	7	7	9	23
	% within complications other than Hb E	30.4	30.4	39.1	100.0
	% within Hb E-type	28.0	43.8	100.0	46.0
No	Count	18	9	0	27
	% within complications other than Hb E	66.7	33.3	0.0	100.0
	% within Hb E-type	72.0	56.3	0.0	54.0
Total	Count	25	16	9	50
	% within complications other than Hb E	50.0	32.0	18.0	100.0
	% within Hb E-type	100.0	100.0	100.0	100.0

Note Results are based on field survey (by RS) during September 2014–April 2015
Source Field survey

Table 10.6 shows complications resulted as a part of Hb E-type and it is reported that relatively a majority (54%) of the probands did not have any complications, whereas few (46%) informed that they have complications other than Hb E. It was informed by the probands that wide range of complications was experienced by them but most of the complications differed from subject to subject. For example, a proband with Hb E trait suffers from psoriasis and irregular bowel moment; in another case, a proband with Hb E trait has congenital defect further more in two other cases, one proband with Hb E disease and other with Hb E/βThal have reported leukaemia; in few other cases especially people suffering from Hb E disease, few of them informed different forms of arthritis (poly-inflammatory arthritis, rheumatoid arthritis, seronegative arthritis and so on).

Haemoglobin E-typewise analysis reveals that in the case of disease and traits, 43.9 and 28.0% of them have informed that they have complications along with Hb E, but whereas in the case of Hb E/βThal, 100% of them have informed of having complications. Complication-wise analysis reveals that both Hb E disease and trait share same (30.1%) number of complications, whereas Hb E/βThal number is little higher (39.1%). As a whole it can be inferred that nearly half of the trait and the disease probands have complications, whereas all of the Hb E/βThal probands have complications.

The frequency and intensity of tiredness among Hb E-type are represented in Table 10.7. The table shows Hb E status and age group distribution in the case of probands who had reported for symptoms of tiredness while the probands are at work (Fig. 10.7). It was stated that irrespective of Hb E-type, 36% of them get tired, whereas 14% do not get tired while they are at work. Among the probands who reported of getting tired while at work, a simple majority (63.9%) of them belong to age group of 30 and above followed by 16–30 age group (22.2%) and up to 15 years (13.9%). In case of Hb E/βThal probands, there are no respondents at all in age group of 30 years and above, whereas in disease and trait, major number (84.6%) and (85.7%) of subjects belong to age group of above 30 years. In age

Table 10.7 Tiredness experienced by the probands

Tired of doing work				Hb E-type			Total
				Trait	Disease	Hb E/βThal	
Yes	Age group	Up to 15 years	Count	1	1	3	5
			% within age group	20.0	20.0	60.0	100.0
			% within Hb E-type	7.7	7.1	33.3	13.9
		15–30 years	Count	1	1	6	8
			% within age group	12.5	12.5	75.0	100.0
			% within Hb E-type	7.7	7.1	66.7	22.2
		30 above	Count	11	12	0	23
			% within age group	47.8	52.2	0.0	100.0
			% within Hb E-type	84.6	85.7	0.0	63.9
	Total		Count	13	14	9	36
			% within age group	36.1	38.9	25.0	100.0
			% within Hb E-type	100.0	100.0	100.0	100.0
No	Age Group	Up to 15 years	Count	2	0		2
			% within age group	100.0	0.0		100.0
			% within Hb E-type	16.7	0.0		14.3
		15–30 years	Count	2	1		3
			% within age group	66.7	33.3		100.0
			% within Hb E-type	16.7	50.0		21.4
		30 above	Count	8	1		9
			% within age group	88.9	11.1		100.0
			% within Hb E-type	66.7	50.0		64.3
	Total		Count	12	2		14
			% within age group	85.7	14.3		100.0
			% within Hb E-type	100.0	100.0		100.0

Note Results are based on field survey (by RS) during September 2014–April 2015
Source Field survey

group of 16–30 and up to 15 years subjects, they share equal percentages, 7.7 and 7.1, respectively in both disease and trait. Overall, it may be inferred that a greater majority of the probands were getting tired while performing work, irrespective of Hb E status; however, it is significantly higher in case of thalassemia patients.

In the present study, protective advantage of Hb E-type against malaria has been attempted. Table 10.8 discusses frequency of malaria affected by the Hb E-type probands. It is to state that there is positive sign of Hb E-type which was not affected by the malaria among a majority (68%) of the probands followed by 2–3 times (20%) and frequently (10%) and once in a while (2%) (Fig. 10.8).

Even cross-variable analysis reveals more or less the same with no significant difference in the case of probands identified as trait and disease, whereas in the case of probands identified as Hb E/βThal were never effected by malaria so far (Table 10.9). There are several studies on haemoglobinopathies being protective

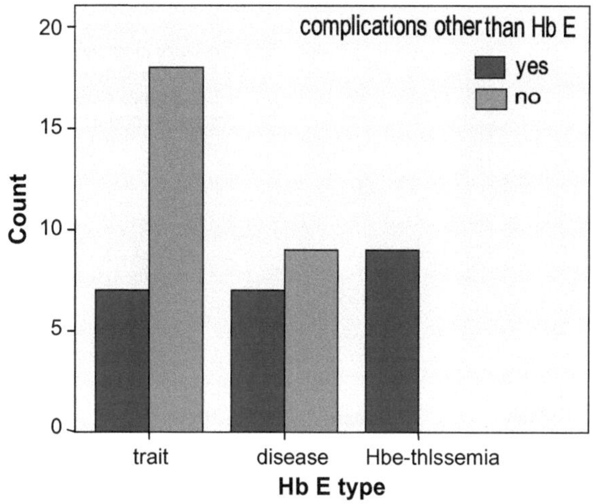

Fig. 10.7 Complications experienced by the probands

Table 10.8 Probands affected with malaria

Affected with malaria		Hb E-type			Total
		Trait	Disease	Hb E/β Thal	
Once in a while	Count	0	1	0	1
	% within malaria history no of times affected	0.0	100.0	0.0	100.0
	% within Hb E-type	0.0	6.3	0.0	2.0
Frequent	Count	2	3	0	5
	% within malaria history no of times affected	40.0	60.0	0.0	100.0
	% within Hb E-type	8.0	18.8	0.0	10.0
2–3 times	Count	5	5	0	10
	% within malaria history no of times affected	50.0	50.0	0.0	100.0
	% within Hb E-type	20.0	31.3	0.0	20.0
Never	Count	18	7	9	34
	% within malaria history no of times affected	52.9	20.6	26.5	100.0
	% within Hb E-type	72.0	43.8	100.0	68.0
Total	Count	25	16	9	50
	% within malaria history no of times affected	50.0	32.0	18.0	100.0
	% within Hb E-type	100.0	100.0	100.0	100.0

Note Results are based on field survey (by RS) during September 2014–April 2015
Source Field survey

against malaria and there is evidence that Hb E can also act as a protective mechanism against malaria (Sharma and Mahanta 2009). Similar to several such studies, the study also supports Haldane's hypothesis about the selective advantage of Hb E gene frequency in endemic malaria region in Garo hills. In the present

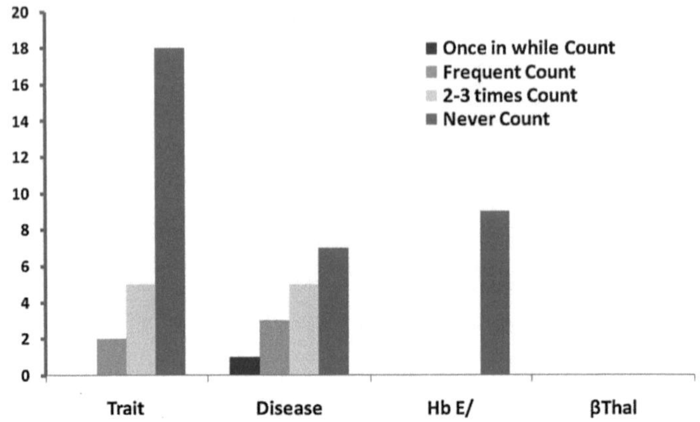

Fig. 10.8 Probands affected with malaria

Table 10.9 Effect of Hb E-type on quality of life

Hb E-type		Effect on quality of life		Total
		Yes	No	
Trait	Count	7	18	25
	Expected count	11.0	14.0	25.0
	H	28.0	72.0	100
	% of total	14.0	36.0	50.0
Disease	Count	8	8	16
	Expected count	7.0	9.0	16.0
	H	50.0	50.0	100.0
	% of total	16.0	16.0	32.0
Hb E/βThal	Count	9	0	9
	Expected count	9.0	0.0	9.0
	H	100.0	0.0	100.0
	% of total	18.0	0	18.0
Total	Count	22	28	50
	Expected count	22.0	28.0	50.0
	% of total	48.0	52.0	100.0

Chi-square and p value Yate's correction value = 7.23, $p = 0.027$, $df = 2$, Cramer's $V = 0.374$

Note Results are based on field survey (by RS) during September 2014–April 2015

Source Field survey

study, it may be understood that there is positive correlation between Hb E-type and incidence of malaria among Garo (Tibeto-Burman linguistic families) tribes in Tura town. From the above data, it may be concluded that the percentage of people with Hb E trait is more prone to malaria than Hb E disease people and people who are Hb E/beta thalassemia have never been affected (Fig. 10.9).

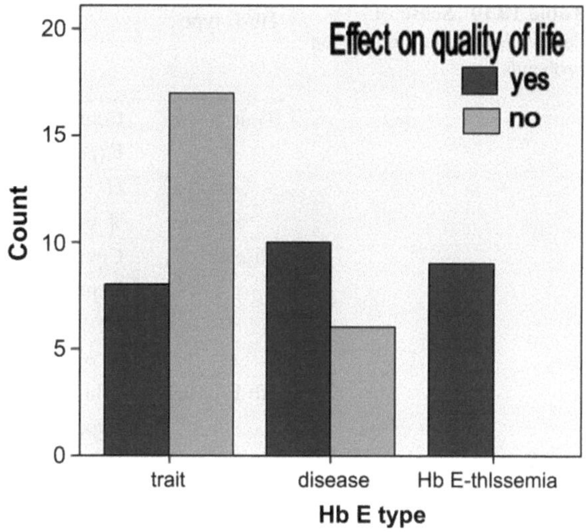

Fig. 10.9 Effect of Hb E-type on quality of life

In general, every individual quality of life is explained from both their personal and social life. In the context of Hb E-type proband, personal life is understood to be active to lead beyond minimal normal life. For example, if spouse proposes to go for shopping or to prepare some special food, he or she should be an active position to fulfil it. Similarly, social life is expected to be visiting friends and entertaining friends and relatives, participating various religious and social functions.

As regards the quality life is concerned among Hb E proband, it was reported that relatively a very simple majority (52%) expressed that their quality of life (as described above) was not very encouraging, whereas the remaining (48%) shared that they were attempting to have better quality of life to lead life like any other average being. Hb E-typewise analysis reflect that in case of Hb E disease probands equal number (50%) of them shared either of being positive or negative with regards to quality of life. In the case of trait-affected probands nearly three-fourth of them (72%) expressed their displeasure on their quality of life and 100% of Hb E/βThal probands were positive about their personal and social life. The chi-square test for independence was used to find the relationship between proband's Hb E-type and across effect on quality of life. The null hypothesis is 'there is no association between proband's Hb E-type and across effect on quality of life'.

In order to find whether there is any significant difference between Hb E-type and effect on quality of life, the chi-square was used to test the association between these two variables. The Pearson chi-square value (Yate's correction value) is 7.23 with an associated significance level of 0.027 ($p < 0.05$). This rejects the null hypothesis and the results suggest an association between proband's Hb E-type and effect on quality of life (χ^2 (2, $n = 50$) = 7.23, $p = 0.027$, Cramer's $V = 0.374$). The Cramer's V value is 0.374, and it indicates that the effect of Hb E-type on effect on quality of life is small.

Table 10.10 Sense of deprivation undergone by the probands

Hb E-type		Deprivation due to Hb E		Total
		Yes	No	
Trait	Count	3	22	25
	Expected count	9.0	16.0	25.0
	H	12.0	88.0	100.0
	% of total	6.0	44.0	50.0
Disease	Count	6	10	16
	Expected count	5.8	10.2	16.0
	H	37.5	62.5	100.0
	% of total	12.0	20.0	32.0
Hb E/βThal	Count	9	0	9
	Expected count	3.2	5.8	9.0
	H	100.0	0.0	100.0
	% of total	18.0	0.0	18.0
Total	Count	18	32	50
	% of total	36.0	64.0	100.0

Chi-square and p value Yate's correction value = 25.826, $p = 0.000$, $df = 2$. Cramer's $V = 0.667$

Note Results are based on field survey (by RS) during September 2014–April 2015

Source Field survey

Table 10.10 explains the sense of deprivation on expecting and achieving things in their career life. Sense of deprivation is understood to be either on their own as looking at others at times they feel they are not able to achieve as expected, or achieved like other counterparts. For example, one intends to start their own enterprise and promotion in a job, and facilitates their children and spouse to get the position. It is revealed that a majority (64%) shared their feelings that they are not deprived on some of their personal agenda, whereas a little more than one-third (36%) expressed that they were able to get whatever they are expecting in their career to a greater extent. Cross-variable analysis based on Hb E-type reveals that in case of trait respondents, majority of them were very positive about getting expected things followed by diseased probands, whereas none of the Hb E/βThal respondents was optimistic about realisation of their aspirations. As a whole it may be stated that a majority of them are optimistic about their life and aspiration (Fig. 10.10).

The chi-square test for independence was used to find the relationship between proband's Hb E-type and deprivation. The null hypothesis is 'there is no association between proband's Hb E-type and Deprivation'. The Pearson chi-square value (Yate's correction value) is 22.266 with an associated significance level of 0.000. This rejects the null hypothesis leading to the conclusion that there is an association between proband's Hb E-type and deprivation (χ^2 (2, n = 50) = 22.266, p = 0.000, Cramer's V = 0.667). The Cramer's V value is 0.667 and it indicates the effect of Hb E-type on deprivation is very strong.

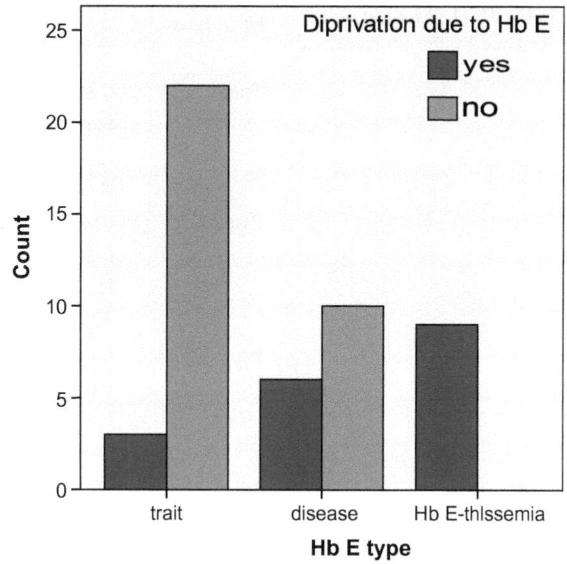

Fig. 10.10 Sense of deprivation undergone by the probands

The chi-square test for independence was used to find the relationship between proband's Hb E-type and across medication taken by them. The null hypothesis is 'there is no association between proband's Hb E-type and across medication'.

The results of cross tabulation (Table 10.11; Fig. 10.11) revealed that, as like any other chronic health problem, it is advised by medical practitioners that Hb E-type subjects are expected for medication for maintaining normal healthy life as like any healthy man. Accordingly, it was enquired whether medication prescribed by the respective doctors who treated them was followed or not was discussed in Table 10.11 and is shown in Fig. 10.11.

It is encouraging to state that relatively a majority of the probands were taking medication (folic acid supplements, foliate supplements), whereas it is dishcartening to state that nearly one-third of the respondents were not following any medication which is badly in need for maintaining and sustaining good health.

Haemoglobin E-based analysis presents that more or less positive trend of relatively a greater number of thalassemia patients were taking medicine as desired. It indicates that even though many were following medication, it is yet to encourage the remaining non-medicated people to approach appropriate government and social financial for support and assistance. In order to find whether there is any significant difference between Hb E-type and medications taken by the probands, the chi-square was used to test the association between these two variables. The Pearson chi-square value (Yate's correction value) is 1.043 with an associated significance level of 0.593 ($p > 0.05$). This accepts the null hypothesis and concludes that there is no association between proband's Hb E-type and medication taken by them (χ^2 (2, $n = 50$) = 1.043, $p = 0.593$, Cramer's $V = 0.142$). The

Table 10.11 Medication practised by the probands

Hb E-type		Medication		Total
		Yes	No	
Trait	Count	15	10	25
	Expected count	16.5	8.5	25.0
	H	60.0	40.0	100.0
	% of total	30.0	20.0	50.0
Disease	Count	11	5	16
	Expected count	10.6	5.4	16.0
	H	68.8	31.2	100.0
	% of total	22.0	10.0	32.0
Hb E/βThal	Count	7	2	9
	Expected count	5.9	3.1	9.0
	H	77.8	22.2	100.0
	% of total	14.0	4.0	18.0
Total	Count	33	17	50
	% of total	66.0	34.0	100.0

Chi-square and p value: Yate's correction value = 1.043, $p = 0.593$, $df = 2$, Cramer's $V = 0.142$

Note Results are based on field survey (by RS) during September 2014–April 2015

Source Field survey

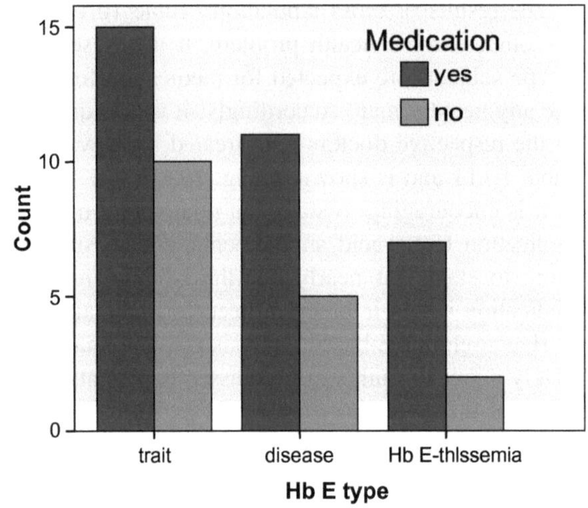

Fig. 10.11 Medication practised by the probands

Cramer's V value is 0.142 and it indicates that the effect of Hb E-type on precautions taken by the probands is small.

Regarding genetic awareness, it was enquired whether they were aware of that it is genetically inherited disease or not, and accordingly it is presented in Table 10.12 and Fig. 10.12.

Table 10.12 Probands knowledge about Hb E-type genetic inheritance

Genetic awareness on Hb E		Hb E-type			Total
		Trait	Disease	Hb E/βThal	
Yes	Count	16	10	3	29
	H	55.2	34.5	10.3	100.0
	V	64.0	62.5	33.3	58.0
No	Count	9	6	6	21
	H	42.9	28.6	28.6	100.0
	V	36.0	37.5	66.7	42.0
	Count	25	16	9	50
	Total	50.0	32.0	18.0	100.0
	% within Hb E-type	100.0	100.0	100.0	100.0

Note Results are based on field survey (by RS) during September 2014–April 2015
Source Field survey

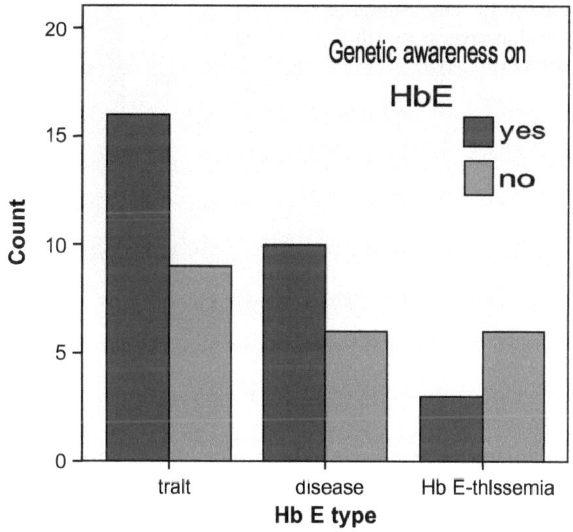

Fig. 10.12 Probands knowledge about Hb E-type genetic inheritance

There is a positive sign that at least a simple majority (58%) of the proband were aware that it is inherited from their ancestors, whereas remaining 42% were ignorant of its roots of getting affected in their health system.

Cross-variable analysis based on Hb E-type reveals that in the case of (64%) trait and 62% disease, probands stated that they were aware of its genetic roots, whereas a majority (66.7%) of Hb E/ βThal stated that they were not aware of it roots of inheritance.

It is to state that a simple majority of trait probands were aware of its roots that of other two types. As a whole it may be inferred that even though some awareness exists,

Table 10.13 Distribution of social awareness on Hb E across Hb E-type

Society awareness on Hb E		Hb E-type			Total
		Trait	Disease	Hb E/βThal	
Yes	Count	0	0	1	1
	H	0.0	0.0	100.0	100.0
	V	0.0	0.0	11.1	2.0
No	Count	25	16	8	49
	H	51.0	32.7	16.3	100.0
	V	100.0	100.0	88.9	98.0
	Count	25	16	9	50
	Total	50.0	32.0	18.0	100.0
	% within Hb E-type	100.0	100.0	100.0	100.0

Note (1) Results are based on field survey (by RS) during September 2014–April 2015, (2) *H* horizontal, *V* vertical. *Source* Field survey

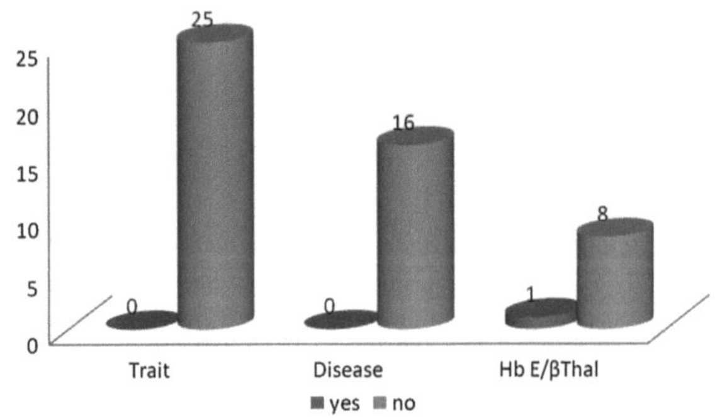

Fig. 10.13 Distribution of social awareness on Hb E across Hb E-type

still much more effort is to be initiated by the respective institutions to make them aware about the genetic inheritance of the disease and further to take preventive and corrective measures for defusing the Hb E from the society.

With regard to society awareness, on Hb E, societal awareness was inquired among the proband and accordingly, it is presented in Table 10.13 (Fig. 10.13). It is disheartening to state that a very greater majority (98%) expressed that societies at large were not aware of Hb E trait and its consequences, where only very insignificant (2%) stated that there is awareness among people with regard to Hb E. Hb E-type analysis reveals that in case of trait as well as disease proband expressed that there was no societal awareness, whereas a very insignificant (11%) of Hb E/βThal probands stated that there is awareness among tribe. As a whole societal awareness regarding Hb E-type, health problem is very insignificant which is to be promoted very genuinely and rationally (Table 10.14; Fig. 10.14).

With regard to encouraging the family members by the proband for going to get Hb E test done was inquired accordingly. It is presented in Table 10.15 and shown

Table 10.14 Probands attempt to encourage family members for Hb E diagnosis—age-wise

Encouraging family members for Hb E test			Age group			Total
			Up to 15 years	16–30 years	Above 30 years	
	Yes	Count	0	2	16	18
		H	0.0	27.8	72.2	100.0
		V	0.0	45.5	40.6	36.0
	No	Count	7	6	19	32
		H	21.9	18.8	59.4	
		V	100.0	54.5	59.4	64.0
Total		Count	7	8	35	50
		% of Total	14.0	16.0	70.0	100.0

Note Results are based on field survey (by RS) during September 2014–April 2015
H horizontal; *V* vertical; *Source* Field survey

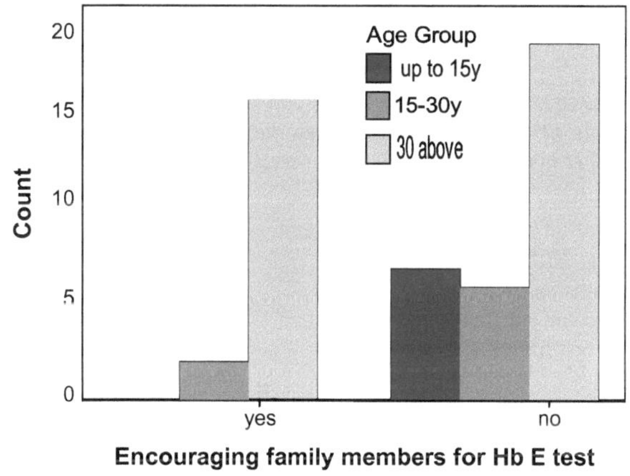

Fig. 10.14 Age-wise distribution of probands who encouraged family members to test for Hb E diagnosis

in Fig. 10.15. It is disheartening to state that 64% did not take any initiative to encourage their family members to undergo Hb E test, whereas as one-third were doing needed initiatives to send them to medical checkup. Age-wise cross-variable analysis reveals a simple majority. Among the subjects who belong to age group of 16–30 years, nearly little more than half (54.5%) were not encouraging their family members, whereas the remaining (45.5%) of the same age group attempted to advise them to go for the test. It is important to state here that respondents below the age group of up to 15 years, either due to ignorance (due to their age) or otherwise, were not able to advise their family members to go for the test.

Table 10.15 Probands attempt to encourage family members for Hb E diagnosis—Hb E wise

Hb E-type		Encouraging family members for Hb E test		Total
		Yes	No	
Trait	Count	8	17	25
	Expected count	9.0	16.0	25.0
	H	32.0	68.0	100.0
	% of total	16.0	34.0	50.0
Disease	Count	7	9	16
	Expected count	5.8	10.2	16.0
	H	43.8	56.2	100.0
	% of total	14.0	18.0	32.0
Hb E/βThal	Count	3	6	9
	Expected count	3.2	5.8	9.0
	H	33.3	66.7	100.0
	% of total	6.0	12.0	18.0
Total	Count	18	32	50
	% of total	36.0	64.0	100.0

Chi-square and p value: Yate's correction value = 0.611, $p = 0.737$, $df = 2$ Cramer's $V = 0.111$
Note (1) Results are based on field survey (by RS) during September 2014–April 2015, (2) *H* horizontal; *Source* Field survey

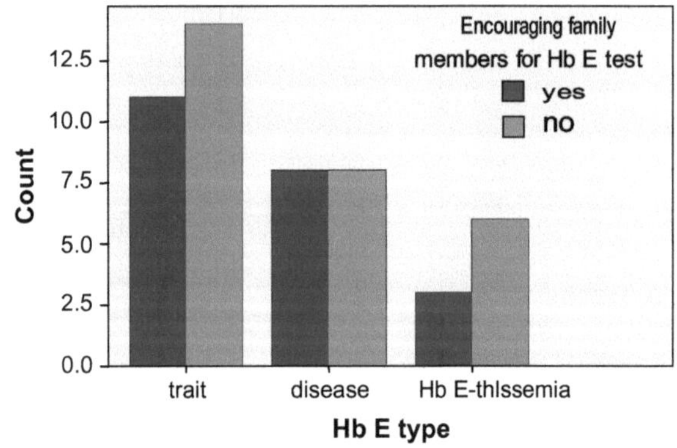

Fig. 10.15 Probands' Hb E status and who had encouraged family members to test for Hb E diagnosis test

The chi-square test for independence was used to find the relationship between probands Hb E-type and encouraging family members. The null hypothesis is 'there is no association between probands Hb E-type and encouraging family members'.

The results of cross tabulation (Table 10.15; Fig. 10.15) revealed that the majority of respondents do not encourage their family members 64% (32) even after they get tested positive for Hb E-type. It is seen from the table that majority of the probands under Hb E trait group, 34% (17) have no intention of taking their family for diagnosis even after it is mentioned in the reports that it is mandatory to bring their family for diagnosis (Doctors also have never focused on asking the 32 probands to bring his family members for checkup) and only 16% (8) of Hb E trait people have felt it necessary to get their family members diagnosed. In Hb E disease group, a total number of probands are 32% (16) of which 14% (7) of the respondents got their family diagnosed and 18% (9) of the respondents never took family members for diagnosis. In Hb E/βThal group, a total number of respondents are 18% (9) out of which only 6% took their family members for diagnosis and rest 18% (9) never took family members for checkup (few Hb E/βThal are children whose parents though are aware of its consequences never took other family members for checkup and have no plans too). In overall, the average numbers of probands who felt it necessary to get their family members diagnosed irrespective of Hb E-type they have, are 36% (18), and 64% (32) never took family members for diagnosis. In order to find whether there is any significant difference between Hb E-type and encouraging family members, the chi-square was used to test the association between these two variables.

The Pearson chi-square value (Yate's correction value) is 0.611 with an associated significance level of 0.737 ($p > 0.05$). This accepts the null hypothesis leading to the conclusion that there is no association between 36 probands's Hb E-type and encouraging family members for diagnosis (χ^2 (2, $n = 50$) = 0.611, $p = 0.734$, Cramer's $V = 0.111$). The Cramer's V value is 0.111 and it indicates that the effect of Hb E-type on encouraging family members is small.

References

Aggarwal, A., Saluja, S., Bhasin, S., Sharma, M., Gupta, D. K., Gupta, B., et al. (2011). Hb E variants—Retrospective analysis in a tertiary care centre. *Journal Indian Academy of Clinical Medicine, 12*(4), 263–265.

Badens, C., Mattei, M. G., Imbert, A. M., Lapouméroulie, C., Martini, N., Michel, G., et al. (2002). A Novel mechanism for thalassaemia intermedia. *The Lancet, 359,* 132–133.

Balgir, R. S. (2000). The burden of haemoglobinopathies in India and the challenges ahead. *Current Science, 79*(11), 1536–1547.

Balgir, R. S. (2014). Is hemoglobin E gene widely spread in the state of Madhya Pradesh in central India? Evidence from five typical families. *Page Press Italy, 6*(1), 1–7.

Benjamin, D. J., Cesarini, D., Matthijs, J. H. M., van der Loos, M. J., Dawes, C. T., Koellinger, P. D., et al. (2012). The genetic architecture of economic and political preferences. *Proceedings of National Academy of Sciences (PNAS), 109,* 8026–8031.

Benjamin, D. J., Chabris, F. C., Gleaser, E. L., Gudnason, V., Harris, T. B., Laibson, D. I., et al. (2007). Genoeconomics (Chapter 15). In M. Weinstein, J. W. Vaupel, & K. W. Wachter (Eds.), *Biosocial surveys* (428 pp). National Research Council. ISBN: 0-309-10868-3. http://www.nap.edu/catalog/11939.html.

Bhasin, M. K., & Walter, H. (2001). *Genetics of castes and tribes of India.* Delhi, India: KRE publishers.

Bhaskar, D., & Sengupta, R. (2013). Hemoglobin E genotype and fertility—A study among the Ahoms of Upper Assam, India. *International Journal of Research In Medical Sciences, 1*(4), 378.

Brittles, H. (2002). Endogamy, consanguinity and community genetics. *Indian Academy of Sciences, Journal of Genetics, 81*(3), 91–97.

Chattopadhyay, K., Biswas, R., Bhattacherjee, S., & Bandyopadhyay, R. (2012). An epidemiological study on the clinico-hematological profile of patients with congenital haemolytic anemia in a tertiary care hospital of Kolkata. *Indian Journal of Preventive and Social Medicine, 43*(4), 372–377.

Chotivanich, K., Udomsangpetch, R., Pattanapanyasat, K., Chierakul, W., Simpson, J., Looareesuwan, S., et al. (2010). Hemoglobin E: A balanced polymorphism protective against high parasitemias and thus severe *P. falciparum* malaria. *Blood, 100,* 1172–1176.

Christopher Thomas, S., Claire, Dikson F., & Weiss, Matchell J. (2013). Hemoglobin variants: Biochemical properties and clinical correlates. *Cold Spring Harbour Perspectives in Medicine, 3*(3), 1–8.

Das, B. M. (1993). *Physical anthropology of the tribes of northeast.* Kamala Raj Enterprises, Ed IV: 183.

Das, B. M., Chakravartti, M. R., Delbruk, H., & Flatz, G. (1971). High prevalence of Haemoglobin E, in two populations of Assam. *Human Genetics, 12,* 264–266.

Das, S. K., & Talukdar, G. (2001). A review on the origin and spread of deleterious mutations of the β-globin genes in Indian populations. *HOMO-Journal of Comparative Human Biology, 52* (2), 93–109.

Dash, A. P., Valecha, N., Anvikar, A. R., & Kumar, A. (2008). Malaria in India: Challenges and opportunities. *Journal of Bioscience, 33,* 583–592.

Deb, T., Deb, D., Kar, G., Pujar, R., & Bhattacherjee, R. K. (2015). Clinicohaematological spectum of haemoglobinopathies, a hospital based study. *Journal of Evolution of Medical and Dental Sciences, 4*(86), 14934–14941.

Deka, R., Reddy, A. P., Mukherjee, B. N., Das, B. M., Banerjee, S., Roy, M., et al. (1988). Haemoglobin distribution in ten endogamous population groups of Assam, India. *Human Heredity, 38*(5), 261–266.

Detels, R., Guilford, M., Abdul Karim, Q., & Tan, C. C. (2015). *Global public health* (6th ed.). China: Oxford University Press.

Dhiman, S., Gopalakrishnan, R., Goswami, D., Rabha, B., Baruah, I., & Singh, L. (2011). Malaria incidence among paramilitary personnel in an endemic area of Tripura. *Indian Journal of Medical Research, 133,* 665–669. (PMID: 21727668).

Dutta, P., Khan, S. A., Khan, A. M., Sharma, C. K., & Mahanta, J. (2010). Survey of mosquito species in Nagaland, a hilly state of north east region of India. *Journal of Environmental Biology, 31*(5), 781–785.

Fredrickson, B. L., Grewenb, K. M., Coffeya, K. A., Algoea, S. B., Firestinea, A. M., Arevaloc, J. M., et al. (2013). A functional genomics perspective on human well-being. *Proceedings of National American Academy of Sciences (PNAS), 110,* 13684–13689.

Fucharoen, S., & Winichagoon, P. (2011). Haemoglobinopathies in Southeast Asia. *The Indian Journal of Medical Research, 134,* 498–506 (PMID: 22089614).

Gaikwad, S., Ashma, R., Kumar, N., Trivedi, R., & Kashayap, K. (2005). Host microsatellite alleles in malaria predisposition. *Malaria Journal, 4,* 50. doi:10.1136/11475-2875-4-50.

Galanello, R., & Origa, R. (2010). Beta-Thalassemia. Bio-Med-Central Ltd. *Orphanet Journal of Rare Diseases, 5*(11), 1–15.

Garo's cultural and basic lifestyle. Retrieved From http://www.westgarohills.gov.in on 01.07. 2014.

Gaur, A. S., & Gaur, S. S. (2009). *Statistical methods for practice and research—A guide to data analysis using SPSS* (2nd ed.). Thousand Okas California: Sage. ISBN: 9788132101000.

Haldane, J. B. S. (1949). The rate of mutation of human genes. *Hereditas, 35,* 267–273.

Kohne, E. (2011). Hemoglobinopathies: Clinical manifestations, diagnosis, and treatment. *Deutscher Arzteblatt International, 108,* 532.

Kwaitkoski, D. P. (2005). How malaria has affected the human genome and what genetics can teach us about malaria? *American Journal of Human Genetics, 77,* 171–193.

Lithanatudom, P., Wipasa, J., Inti, P., Chawansuntati, K., Svasti, S., Fucharoen, S., et al. (2016). Haemoglobin E prevalence among ethnic groups residing in malarial-endemic areas of northern

Thailan and its lack of association with *Plasmodium falcipaurm* invasion *in vitro*. PLoS ONE, *11*(1), e0148079. doi:10.1371/journalpone.0148079.
Luomi, J., Ohashi, J., Naka, I., Patarapotikul, J., Hananantachal, H., Looareeswan, S., et al. (2002). Polymorphism of CD36 in Thai malaria patients. *Southeast Asian Journal of Tropical Medicine and Public Health, 33*(Supp. 3), 1–4.
Mahajan, R. C., Narian, K., & Mahanta, J. (2011). Anemia & expression levels of CD35, CD55 & CD59 on red blood cells in *Plasmodium falciparum* malaria patients from India. *Indian Journal of Medical Research, 132*, 662–664 (PMID: 21727667).
Moiz, B., Hashmini Mashhooda, R., Nasir, A., Rashid, A., & Moatter, T. (2012). Hemoglobin E syndromes in Pakistan population. *Bio-Med-Central Haematology, 12*(3), 1–6.
Mu, J., Myers, R. A., Jiang, H., Liu. S., Ricklefs, S., Waisberg, M., et al. (2010). *Plasmodium falciparum* genome-wide scans for positive selection, recombination hotspots and resistance to anti-malarial drugs. *Nature Genetics, 42*(3), 268–271.
Muller, I., Pioto, N., Julius, K., Rex, I., Tony, T., Steven, B., et al. (2005). Endemic malaria in the highlands of Papua New Guinea. *American Journal of Tropical Medicine and Hygiene, 72*(5), 554–560.
Olivieri, N. F., Muraca, G. M., O'Donnell, A., Premawardhena, A., Fisher, C., & Weatherall, D. J. (2008). Studies in haemoglobin E beta-thalassaemia. *Blackwell Publishing Ltd., British Journal of Hematology, 141*, 388–397.
OlivierNancy, F., Pakbaz, Z., & Vichinsky, E. (2011). Hb E/beta-thalassemia: A common & clinically diverse disorder. *Journal of Medical Research, 134*(4), 522–531.
Pallant, J. (2011). *SPSS survival manual—A step guide to data analysis using SPSS* (4th ed.). Australia: Allen and Unwin. ISBN: 9781742373928.
Persons, D. A. (1998). Hematopoietic stem cell gene transfer for the treatment of hemoglobin disorders. *American society of haematology, 2009*(1), 690–697.
Rees, D. C., Porter, J. B., Clegg, J. B., & Weatherall, D. J. (2010). Why are haemoglobin F levels increased in HbE/β-thalassemia? *Blood, 94*, 3199–3204.
Rietveld, C. A., Cesarini, D., Benjamin, D. J., Koellinger, P. D., De Neve, J. E., Tiemeier, H., et al. (2013). Molecular genetics and subjective well-being. *Proceedings of National Academy of Sciences (PNAS), 110*, 9692–9697.
Saleh-Gohari, N., Khademi Bami, M., Nikbakh, R., & Karimi-Maleh, N. (2015). Effects of α-thalassemia mutations on the haematological parameters of β-thalasemia carriers. *Journal of Clinical Pathology* (Online First). doi:10.1136/jclinpath-2014-202825.
Sanchaisuriya, K., Fuchareon, S., Ratanasiri, T., Sanchaisuriya, P., Fuchareon, G., Dietz, E., et al. (2007). Effect of the maternal β/E-globin gene on haematological responses to iron supplementation during pregnancy. *The American Journal of Clinical Nutrition, 85*(2), 474–479.
Sarkar, S., Biswas, N. K., Dey, B., Mukhopadhyay, D., & Majumder, P. P. (2010). A large systematic molecular-genetic study of G6PD in Indian populations indicates a new non-synonymous variant and supports recent positive selection. *Infection, Genetics and. Evolution, 10*(8), 1228–1236.
Sharma, S. K., & Mahanta, J. (2009). Prevalence of haemoglobin variants in malaria endemic in northeast India. *Journal of Biological Sciences, 9*(3), 288–291.
Sharma, V., & Saxena, R. (2009). Effect of α-gene numbers on phenotype of HbE/β thalassemia patients, *Springer, Annals of Haematology, 88*, 1035–1036.
Sherva, R., Sripichai, O., Abel, K., Ma Q., Whitacre J., Angkachatchai V., et al. (2010). Genetic modifiers of Hb E/β 0 thalassemia identified by two stage genome—Wide association study. *BMC Medical Genetics, 11*, 51.
Shiv Lal, G., Sonal, S., & Phukan, P. K. (1998). Status of malaria in India. *Journal of Indian Academy of Clinical Medicine, 5*(1), 19–23.
Singh, M. R., Choudhury, B., & Singh, T. S. (2010). Haemoglobin E distribution in four endogamous population of Manipur (India), Moment Publication. *Eurasian Journal of Anthropology, 1*(2), 109–117.

Taylor, S. M., Parobek, C. M., & Fairhurst, R. M. (2012). Haemoglobinopathies and the clinical epidemioilogy of malaria: A systematic review and meta-analysis. *The Lancet Infectious Diseases, 12,* 457–468.

Teeuw, M. E., Loukili, G., Bartels, E. A., Ten Kate, L. P., Cornel, M. C., & Henneman, L. (2013). Consanguineous marriage and reproductive risk: Attitudes and understanding of ethnic groups practicing consanguinity in western society. *European Journal of Human Genetics, 22,* 452–457.

Trachtenberg, F., Foote, D., Martin, M., Carson, S., Coates, T., Beams, O., et al. (2010). Pain as an emergent issue in thalassemia. *American society of hematology, 85*(5), 367–370.

Vichinsky, E. (2007). Haemoglobin E syndromes. *American Society of Hematology, 2007,* 79–83.

Wajcman, H., & Moradkhani, K. (2011). Abnormal hemoglobins: Detection and characterization. *Indian Journal of Medical Research, 1*(134), 538–546.

Wajcman, H., Prehu, C., Bardakdjian-Michau, J., Prome, D., Riou, J., Godart, C., et al. (2001). Abnormal hemoglobin: Laboratory methods. Hemoglobin. *Public Medicine, 25,* 169–181.

Weatherall, D. (2011). The inherited disorders of haemoglobin: An increasingly neglected global health burden. *Indian Journal of Medical Research, 134,* 493–497 (PMID: 22089613).

Weatherall, D. J., Allen, A., Fisher, C., Premawardhena, A., Peto, T., Allen, S., et al. (2010). Adaptation to anemia in hemoglobin E-β Thalassemia. *Blood, 116,* 5368–5370.

Weatherall, D. J., & Clegg, J. B. (2001). Inherited haemoglobin disorders: An increasing global health problem. *Bulletin of World Health Organisation, 79,* 704–712.

W.H.O. (2001). Severe falciparum malaria. *Transactions of Royal Society of Tropical Medicine and Hygine, 94,* S1/1–S/90.

Zarin Khattak, A., Sohail Taj, A., Ali Shah, S. M., & Farooq Khattak, M. (2013). Clinical and haematological presentations of Hb E disorders from northern Pakistan. *Journal of Medical Sciences, 21*(3), 134–136.

Chapter 11
Child Deprivation in Indian Context: Concern About Health- and Education-Related Issues

Soumyendra Kishore Datta and Krishna Singh

11.1 Introduction

Children in many societies are found vulnerable to adverse socio-economic and environmental conditions, which usually stunt their growth, deprive them of nutritious food and comfortable shelter, render them physically weak, expose them to high level of mortality, compel them to perform collection jobs like fuel, fodder or water and rob them of schooling opportunities. Poverty of the concerned households is supposed to be greatly instrumental in engendering such type of deprivation suffered by the children. Nutrition is the main driving force for a child's cognitive and physical development. Without the availability of proper nutritional diet, children suffer from stunted growth and underweight relative to their age. Apart from nutritional food, formative period of a child's health is also influenced by the measures of vaccination/immunisation administered at regular intervals and this serves as a proxy of health services. Unless the full course of immunisation measures are applied, children run the risk of being easily exposed to some dreaded diseases like polio, tetanus, pneumonia, diphtheria, etc. Poor sanitation can also lead to poor child health including diarrhoea and poor nutrition. Deprivation in sanitation is reflected in no access to improved sanitation facilities or having no toilet at all.

Children also have a right to enjoy adequate shelter for comfort, hygiene and dignity. Further availability of clean water near the site of the house serves as a basic necessity for ensuring sound child health since unsafe and dirty water causes diarrhoea. It has an adverse impact on the process of child nutrition. While drinking

S.K. Datta (✉)
University of Burdwan, Burdwan, West Bengal 713104, India
e-mail: soumyendra_d@rediffmail.com

K. Singh
Department of Economics, University of Gour Banga, Malda, West Bengal, India
e-mail: get84.krishna@gmail.com

U.K. De et al. (eds.), *Issues on Health and Healthcare in India*, India Studies in Business and Economics, https://doi.org/10.1007/978-981-10-6104-2_11

filthy water is a threat to children health, fetching safe water from distant sources also has an adverse impact on their physique; wastes time left for study and weakens their zeal to go to school. Access to a quality education is considered to be crucial factor in enabling a child to succeed in latter life in terms of social and economic accomplishment. Children whose growth is stunted or wasted at a young age may suffer a lifetime of consequences such as poorer schooling and lower earnings.

It is often said that child-bearing phase of mother and condition at birth are the first of several definitive life events that shape health outcomes within the course of an individual's lifetime. In this context, the impact of condition at pregnancy and subsequent child health needs to be placed in the right perspective when the lack in nutrition/medication support at the stage of a pregnant mother is likely to be reflected in multiple adverse exposures of children to diverse kind of health deformities and weak stature.

Since growth and faculty development of children during the period starting from birth to reaching the puberty stage, is usually greatly influenced by their maternal association, there is no denial to the fact that maternal health and outlook has a great bearing on their deprivation status. While maternal mortality reflects on the lacuna of provision of basic amenities during child-bearing phase, non-availability of skilled workers/personnel at the time of children's birth usually has an after-effect in terms of their poor physique and easy vulnerability to illness. The impact of poorer physical status of would-be mothers and lack of their proper nutrition during the child-bearing stage is often manifest in the form of underweight children at birth, stunting, wasting or higher infant mortality or chronic vulnerability to diseases.

Studies have consistently shown that birth weight decreases steadily with decreasing social status. In the UK Millennium Cohort Study based on 2000 enrolled babies, it was found that mothers living in the most privileged socio-economic group had an average birth weight 200 gm heavier than those living in the great disadvantageous condition. Since there exists a close association of birth weight with infant mortality, a reduction in mean birth weight of the magnitude of 200 gm is associated with higher rates of perinatal death (stillbirths and deaths in the first week of life).

The state of living under conditions of poverty also has a considerable weakening impact on physical and educational health and development of children. Persistent inability of poor parents to provide their children the basic needs for a healthy childhood and their chronic deprivation of the basic nutrients, essential food, water, sanitation and schooling facilities hamper their natural growth and accentuate a state of childhood in poverty.

The analysis is carried out in a number of interlinked sections. Section 11.2 deals with the objectives of the study. Section 11.3 presents survey of related literature, while Sect. 11.4 depicts data source and methodology of the study. The theoretical formulation of health deprivation index is represented in the Sect. 11.5. The Sect. 11.6 analyses the theoretical framework of educational deprivation of children. The analysis of recursive simultaneous equation system is represented in

Sect. 11.7. Finally Sect. 11.8 is devoted to concluding observations and policy prescriptions of the study.

11.2 Objectives of the Study

In this context it seems imperative

(i) To develop a health deprivation index of children based on some parameters and explain its variation by considering factors that reflect the deprivation status of mothers and poverty of the household.
(ii) To analyse the educational deprivation of children based on some well-conceived explanatory variables.
(iii) To focus on appropriate policy directives to reverse the processes of child deprivation.

11.3 Review of Related Literature

Swain (2008) carried out a study in Orissa and observed that the children here are exposed to deprivation, being stunted and wasted to some degree from early childhood. Most of the children work in fields or engage in forest collection activity. They are sacrificing their health and childhood as well as are nutritionally deprived. Most of the children suffer from persistent malnourishment as only one-fifth of the surveyed children are capable of obtaining the ideal calorie-intake. Asset poverty also accentuates their health deprivation. The outcome of the empirical analysis indicated a positive correlation between nutritional deprivation of children, and their weight deprivation.

In a study by UNICEF (2014) related to Uganda, child poverty is defined as children deprived in two or more of seven dimensions that include nutrition, health, water, sanitation, shelter, education and information. Under-nutrition is the most common form of deprivation of Ugandan children. Further it is most often children, especially girls, who have to bear the task-load of fetching water from a distance. Children's characteristics and socio-economic factors at the household level and beyond influence their experience of deprivation and poverty.

Mohanty (2010) using data from the National Family Health Survey-3, India developed a measure of multidimensional poverty and examined its linkages with child health in India. Poverty in multidimensional sense is measured in the sphere of education, health and living standard while state of child health is reflected in terms of infant mortality rate, the under-five mortality rate, immunisation of children and level of medical assistance at birth. According to his results, one-fifth of the households in India live in dire poverty and the poor have limited access to child care facilities.

On the basis of district level data Dreze and Khera (2012) examined the regional patterns of human and child deprivation in India. Together with HDI, they present a normalised variant of 'Achievements of Babies and Children' (ABC) index, to focus on the deprivation of children. To construct the (ABC) index, they used the same method as followed in the construction of HDI. It is based on consideration of four indicators of well-being of children: probability of surviving until age five; proportion of children fully immunised in the age group of 12–23 months; proportion of children aged 12–35 months who are not underweight; and female literacy rate in the 10–14 age group. The lower the value of the index, the higher is the inclination towards children deprivation. The composite indices help in highlighting broad regional patterns of human and child deprivation.

There are a number of studies (Bradshaw 2002; Duncan and Brooks-Gunn 2000) which state that children born into poverty are very likely to be born early with a low birth weight. These children are likely to be vulnerable to relatively higher infant mortality rate. Again this disparity is strongly associated with the larger proportion of low birth weight infants born to low-income parents. Huston (1991) also identifies a higher incidence of sudden infant death syndrome in low-income households and the shorter gestation periods seen among low-income women as the causal factors. These factors are, in turn, connected to low maternal weight gain, obstetrical complications, infections, and a lack of adequate antenatal care (ANC).

According to Larson (1980) poverty often acts as a driving force towards delayed cognitive development and poor school performance. This has been demonstrated to be largely influenced by the poverty and deficiency of the physical and social environment in which children live, maternal characteristics and the learning environment of the home. He further stresses that, a proportion of the observed cognitive delays can be attributed to exposure to lack of provision/support during pregnancy. Again, following delivery, poverty leads to decreased resources, which in turn gives rise to an adverse and intricate socio-cultural environment in the household that usually hampers the smooth process of child development.

Children health deprivation is often measured by deficiency in nutritional status in the family which is determined by his access to public goods, e.g. drinking water, toilet and sanitation facility etc. (Svedberg 2000; Monteiro et al. 2009; Onis et al. 2000; Taguri et al. 2008). Low-income status of the people also implies poor access to resource to combat health shock but also the economic impact of seeking treatment (Russell 2004). Maternal nutritional status also serves as a significant factor that accentuates children's growth retardation as reported in many studies (Morales et al. 2004; Mani 2007; Black et al. 2008). The event of low birth weight babies is likely to be greater in case of women who were themselves undernourished in their childhood (Setboonsarng 2005; Navaneetham and Jose 2005).

On the basis of a study across Indian states covering the period 1993–1994 to 2004–2005, Chaudhri and Jha (2012) observed that young children below 15 years of age and coming from poor and/or nutritionally deprived households were left vulnerable to multiple layers of deprivations which dissuade them from participating in elementary school education. Poor access to healthcare and schooling system facilities, opportunity cost of participation in education, etc. are some of stumbling blocks that hinder the growth of faculty of a child. Children from poor families are often compelled to spend shorter periods of time in pre-school education (Prentice 2007), due to difficulties of access and continuity, which results in early dropout. These lower participation rates adversely affect later academic attainments. Poverty, or low incomes, is often observed to be adversely affecting the quality and quantity of education at the macro, country level as well as the meso, region and school levels (Govinda 2002; Michaelowa 2001). Again some study (e.g., Dyer and Rose 2006) shows that education deprivation is caused not merely by poverty, but also by other related factors. In case of India, these factors are considered to be closely related to gender, caste, labour market opportunities, the quality of learning and facilities in schools.

In her study related to deprivation of school education in Calcutta, Nambissan (2003) focused on the proportion of out-of-school children and primary school completion rate/dropout rate as the major indicators of deprivation. From interaction with school providers it was revealed that, one most important factor that leads to non enrolment in education arises from the need of the labour of their children to support family income and stave off poverty. Further the cases of dropout and poor performance of students were revealed to be related to the household infrastructural environment and the level of literacy of parents, specially mothers.

In a study conducted on slum children in Delhi, Tsujita (2009) observed that the cost of schooling or the foregone child labour earnings was the most important reason for having never-attended and dropout children in slums.

However neither of these studies tries to develop separate composite index of child deprivation specially related to missed health opportunities or education deprivation, that might be explained by some pertinent variables identified from this literature survey. This analysis intends to cater to that unexplored area and bridge the gap.

11.4 Data Source and Methodology

This analysis is completely based on secondary data. To calculate the health deprivation index, we consider the variables like percentage distribution of children under 5 years classified as malnourished according to three anthropometric indices of nutritional status: stunting, wasting and underweight, percent of live births where the mothers did not receive medical attention of delivery, low body mass index of mother, unavailability of latrine facility within the premises, less than fully immunised children and infant mortality rate. To analyse the determinants of health deprivation index, we consider the variables like percentage of household below poverty line, female literacy rate, percentage of women who received full antenatal care, number of pregnant and lactating mother benefited from Integrated Child Development Scheme (ICDS) scheme and maternal mortality rate. Dropout rate of children (Class I–VIII) is analysed with the variables like percentage of household having no electricity or solar energy, household using firewood for cooking, source of drinking water facility away from home, female literacy rate, number of female-headed households, and percentage of BPL families and estimated value of health deprivation index. The data are taken from the website of planning commission and census of India, statistics on children in India (Hand Book 2012) and National Family Health Survey (2005–2006) covering all the major states in India. Most of data cover the year 2011, while data on some health related variables covers the year 2005–2006. Altogether 19 major states are considered for analysis.

There are great differences across state specific values of the different indicators of children health deprivation. In order to ensure better comparability of these data, each indicator has been 'normalised' using the UNDP goal-post method as used for measuring the initial international HDI. This is as follows:

$$\boldsymbol{W}_i = \frac{(\boldsymbol{w}_i - \boldsymbol{w}_{min})}{(\boldsymbol{w}_{max} - \boldsymbol{w}_{min})}$$

Where $\boldsymbol{W}_i$ is the normalised indicator for state i, $\boldsymbol{w}_i$ is the corresponding pre-normalisation figure, and $\boldsymbol{w}_{max}$ and $\boldsymbol{w}_{min}$ are the maximum and minimum values of the same indicator across all states. The normalised indicator takes value 0 for the state at the bottom of the scale of deprivation while, 1 indicates the state at the top of the degree of deprivation for all the individual categories of indicator, and it varies between 0 and 1 for all other states. Similar approach has also been followed to normalise the dropout rates (Class I–VIII).

Based on the aforesaid normalised figures, Principal Component Analysis (PCA) has been applied to calculate health-related deprivation index of children. A recursive simultaneous equation framework has been used to explain the variation of health deprivation of children as well as educational deprivation across the major Indian states, on the basis of some identified explanatory variables. While health deprivation index is considered to be influenced by some variables reflective of maternal mal-achievements and poverty status, education deprivation index based on dropout rates, is explained by considering poverty status as well as variables reflective of socio-physical barriers in the household together with the health deprivation index. Because of recursive nature of the relation, the individual regression is run with OLS technique with White's heteroscedasticity corrected standard errors (Robust Standard Errors).

11.5 Theoretical Frame of Health Deprivation of Children

Diverse individual categories of under-achievement are necessary to construct an overall health-related deprivation index of children by using the principal component method. The overall deprivation index is considered as a latent or unobserved variable. Here the problem is the weight assignment to the individual indicators which is critical to maximise the information from a data set included in an index.

A good composite index should comprise important information from all the indicators, but not strongly biased towards one or more of these indicators.

In this study, the health deprivation index is linearly determined by seven relevant indicators like less than full immunisation (X_1), no medical attention during birth (X_2), unavailability of sanitation facility in home (X_3), infant mortality rate (X_4), underweight (Weight-for-age) percentage below-2SD (X_5), stunting (Weight-for-age) percentage below-2SD (X_6) and wasting (Weight-for-age) percentage below-2SD (X_7). In latent form the health deprivation index $(\mathrm{HDPI})_i$ can be expressed as

$$(\mathrm{HDPI})_i = \gamma_1 X_{1i} + \gamma_2 X_{2i} + \gamma_3 X_{3i} + \gamma_4 X_{4i} + \gamma_5 X_{5i} + \gamma_6 X_{6i} + \gamma_7 X_{7i} + u_i$$

(Here i = 1–19)

We get the corresponding deprivation index according to the following weighted average:

$$(\mathrm{HDPI})_i = \frac{\sum_{j=1}^{7} \lambda_j P_j}{\sum_{j=1}^{7} \lambda_j}$$

Here λ_j (j = 1, 2, 3, 4, 5, 6, 7) denotes the jth Eigen value. Subscript j refers to the number of principal components that also coincides with the number of corresponding indicators. Noting that the values of λ_j gradually falls as the suffix increases, we denote P_j (j = 1, 2 … 7) as the jth principal component.

Although usually the whole set of causal variables is replaced by a few principal components, which account for a substantial percentage of the total variation in all the sample variables, here we consider as many components as the number of explanatory variables. This is due to our concern in order to avoid discarding information that could affect the estimates. Thus this procedure accounts for 100% of the total variation in the data.

Table 11.1 depicts the children health-deprivation index value of the different states and their respective ranks. The UNDP process of forming the respective indicator values of children deprivation is such that higher index values reflect higher level of children deprivation and so are the ranks assigned.

The results obtained from Table 11.1 reveal that Kerala, Punjab and Tamil Nadu occupy the first three ranks indicating lowest deprivation suffered by children in these states. The states like Bihar, Jharkhand and Madhya Pradesh represent the highest three ranks respectively reflecting gradually increasing degree of health related deprivation of children. Lower health facilities and provision for children in these states and lack of pure drinking water and sanitation facility within the periphery of home, drive the children here to extreme form of privation, abdominal diseases and poor physical development. Other states suffer from varied level of deprivation within these extreme ends.

It is often argued that the magnitude of the health related deprivation impact of children is largely determined by socio-economic disparities that occur during

Table 11.1 Health deprivation index values and corresponding rank of states

States	Index	Rank
Andhra Pradesh	0.651	6
Assam	0.914	11
Bihar	1.520	17
Chhattisgarh	1.270	15
Gujarat	0.954	12
Haryana	0.838	10
Himachal Pradesh	0.745	8
Jammu & Kashmir	0.646	5
Jharkhand	1.534	18
Karnataka	0.685	7
Kerala	0.096	1
Madhya Pradesh	1.615	19
Maharashtra	0.619	4
Odisha	1.160	14
Punjab	0.349	2
Rajasthan	1.057	13
Tamil Nadu	0.532	3
Uttar Pradesh	1.315	16
West Bengal	0.810	9

Source Authors calculation from secondary data

developmentally sensitive periods of maternal life, including the child-bearing phase. Extending this view, the deprivation index (HDPI) thus derived is explained by a number of variables that pertain to several birth-related conditions of maternal health, maternal awareness about care for children, and overall economic standing of children's family. These are captured by variables like low body mass index of mother, percentage of BPL family, female literacy rate, women getting full ante natal care (ANC), maternal mortality rate and maternal benefits from ICDS.

In this context, it may be said that the level of functioning of important Government schemes undertaking extension services has a tangible impact on female health during pregnancy, in the form of providing iron folic tablets, tetanus injections, and regular health check-ups etc. The impact of these schemes is reflected by considering variables like full ANC (Y_1) and benefit from ICDS (Y_2). Further better maternal awareness about the precautions and provisions about postnatal care for children and own health is also likely to influence mortality and well-being of children. Female literacy rate (Y_3) is supposed to represent this maternal awareness related factor that have a bearing on health related outcome of children. Deprivation of children experienced in diverse forms in the formative period of their life is also substantially shaped by the financial deprivation status of the families and this is represented by the variable 'percentage of BPL family' (Y_4). And variables like low body mass index of mother (Y_5), maternal mortality rate (Y_6), etc., indicating the birth time health indicators of maternal condition have a direct adverse impact on the post-birth physical and mental development process of children. It is expected that variables like full ANC and benefit from ICDS are negatively associated with deprivation status of children. As female literacy rate rises, increased maternal awareness is likely to result in full immunisation, better nutrition and improved hygienic condition in the lives of children and so child deprivation is likely to decline. As percentage of BPL families increase, lack of provision of the basic necessities and medication facilities for children may lead to higher deprivation status of children and so a positive relation may ensue. And low body mass index of mother and higher maternal mortality are likely to cause higher level of children deprivation in terms of greater infant mortality, increased number of underweight children as well as stunting and wasting phenomena. Thus while the first one is assumed to be inversely related, the second one is expected to be positively or directly associated with the incidence of children deprivation.

The corresponding regression equation takes the following form

$$(\mathrm{HDPI})_i = \alpha + \beta_1(Y_1)_i + \beta_2(Y_2)_i + \beta_3(Y_3)_i + \beta_4(Y_4)_i + \beta_5(Y_5)_i + \beta_6(Y_6)_i + u_{1i} \tag{11.1}$$

11.6 Theoretical Frame of Educational Deprivation of Children

Children in rural regions/poor families are known to assist their households in various ways. Sometimes they help their mothers in bringing water from great distances while fathers are away at work, take part in collecting fuel/fire wood from forest areas, and also have to cope with their study at night often in the absence of any provision electricity. This saps their energy and drive to continue study in higher classes when the scourge of poverty dissuades them from resorting to private coaching. This leads to early dropout from school education system because of sheerlack of family income, time and energy. Sometimes children of female-headed households have to bear the brunt of assisting their mother in earning or sharing the household work and in the process they act as substitute for their absent fathers. However, in case the females/mothers are literate, the dropout rate tends to decline, as with increased literacy mothers often are seen to encourage or continue children's education by motivating them or setting aside a part of family income for their education purposes though it might entail some degree of privation on their part. Dropout rate itself is considered reflective of children's educational deprivation (EDPI) as it implies low capability development, stifled growth of personality, sense of self-dignity, culture and lack of awareness of events around. This indicator variable is expressed in normalised sense and used as an index of education deprivation.

The following Table 11.2 depicts the children educational deprivation index value of the different states and their respective ranks.

Table 11.2 Educational deprivation index values and corresponding rank of states

States	Index	Rank
Andhra Pradesh	0.668	9
Assam	1.000	1
Bihar	0.999	2
Chhattisgarh	0.495	12
Gujarat	0.789	7
Haryana	0.210	18
Himachal Pradesh	0.221	17
Jammu & Kashmir	0.544	11
Jharkhand	0.785	8
Karnataka	0.576	10
Kerala	0.000	19
Madhya Pradesh	0.837	6
Maharashtra	0.493	13
Odisha	0.871	5
Punjab	0.491	14
Rajasthan	0.918	4
Tamil Nadu	0.404	15
Uttar Pradesh	0.264	16
West Bengal	0.921	3

Source Authors calculation from secondary data

The results obtained from Table 11.2 reveal that Kerala, Haryana and Himachal Pradesh occupies the first three ranks indicating lowest level of educational deprivation suffered by children in these states. The states like Assam, Bihar and West Bengal represent the highest three ranks respectively reflecting gradually increasing degree of education-related deprivation of children. The rest of the states suffer from varied level of deprivation within these extreme ends.

The variables considered for explaining the dropout index of children across the states are percentage of BPL families in the state (Y_4), percentage of household having no electricity or solar energy (Z_1), sources of drinking water away from home (Z_2), female literacy rate (Y_3), number of female-headed households in the state (Z_3), households using firewood for cooking (Z_4) as well as value of health deprivation index (HDPI).

The regression equation stands as

$$(\text{EDPI})_i = \theta + \delta_1(\text{HDPI})_i + \delta_2(Y_3)_i + \delta_1(Y_4)_i + \delta_1(Z_1)_i + \delta_1(Z_2)_i + \delta_1(Z_3)_i + \delta_1(Z_4)_i + u_{2i} \quad (11.2)$$

11.7 Analysis of Recursive Simultaneous Equation Model

Here the Eqs. (11.3) and (11.4) together form a recursive simultaneous equation system. In general form, the recursive simultaneous equation system may be rewritten as:

$$(\mathrm{HDPI})_i = \alpha + \beta_1(Y_1)_i + \beta_2(Y_2)_i + \beta_3(Y_3)_i + \beta_4(Y_4)_i + \beta_5(Y_5)_i + \beta_6(Y_6)_i + u_{1i} \tag{11.3}$$

$$\begin{aligned}(\mathrm{EDPI})_i = \theta + \delta_1(HDPI)_i + \delta_2(Y_3)_i + \delta_1(Y_4)_i + \delta_1(Z_1)_i \\ + \delta_1(Z_2)_i + \delta_1(Z_3)_i + \delta_1(Z_4)_i + u_{2i}\end{aligned} \tag{11.4}$$

The system comprises two endogenous variables (HDPI) and (EDPI) with 10 predetermined variables viz $Y_1, Y_2, Y_3, Y_4, Y_5, Y_6, Z_1, Z_2, Z_3$ and Z_4. And u's are stochastic variables statistically independent of the Y's and Z's. Moreover u_{2i} is assumed, to be statistically independent of (HDPI).

The model is complete and reduced form can be found. If we assume that G_1 indicates the number of included endogenous variables and G_2 stands for the number of excluded endogenous variables while K_1 stands for the number of included predetermined variables and K_2 indicates the number of excluded predetermined variables in the respective equations, then in Eq. (11.3) $G_1 = 1$, $G_2 = 1$, $K_1 = 6$, $K_2 = 4$; while in case of Eq. (11.4) $G_1 = 2$, $G_2 = 0$, $K_1 = 6$, $K_2 = 4$. The identification condition of the structural equations requires that $K_2 \geq G_1 - 1$. On this basis, both the structural equations are identified and it is possible to apply OLS method to derive consistent estimates of the structural parameters.

The regression results of first structural equation as disclosed in Table 11.3 were obtained using OLS regression model. It facilitates the testing of the hypothesised signs of the explanatory variables and their significance as well as overall significance of the model.

Table 11.3 Regression result of children's health deprivation index values

Variable	Coefficient	Std. error	t-Statistic	Prob.
ANC (Y_1)	−0.006772	0.004028	−1.681060	0.1086
ICDS (Y_2)	−5.55E−09	4.82E−08	−0.115123	0.9103
FEMALE LIT (Y_3)	−0.019045	0.006300	−3.023253	0.0106
BPL (Y_4)	0.026280	0.006248	4.206400	0.0012
LOW BMI (Y_5)	−0.009544	0.006124	−1.558480	0.1451
MMR (Y_6)	−0.006847	0.005557	−1.232205	0.2415
Constant	2.462838	0.620656	3.968121	0.0019
R^2	0.88			
F-Statistic	15.12047			0.0000

Source Authors calculation from secondary data

It is observed that variables like percentage of BPL and FEMALE LIT have the expected sign and highly significantly related with the extent of deprivation of children. With increase in the intensity of poverty in a state indicated by the percentage of BPL people, there is assumed to be enhanced likelihood of children deprivation in all dimensions. Similarly with rise in mothers' education and hence awareness, it is usually expected and children will be served with better care and protection thus leading to reduced deprivation. According to some studies, mother's education, standard of living, ethnicity, etc. are important factors of child nutrition and care (Mishra et al. 1999; Griffiths et al. 2002). Higher educated women owing to their exposure to the outside world are more aware of personal hygiene and issues on preventive, promotive and curative healthcare than uneducated or less educated women.

The results in the first equation have also some elements which are corroborated by the study undertaken by Das and Sahoo (2011). They used four indicators of child nutritional status, three of which are anthropometric in nature and the other is anaemia. The anthropometric measures of child malnutrition are based on weight-for-age, height-for-age, and weight-for-height. Four sets of logistic regression models for four dichotomous dependent variables (underweight, stunting, wasting and anaemia) are used by them. Among the predictor variables used by them, educational level of mother, wealth index of the household, body mass index (BMI) and haemoglobin level of the mother come closer to the predetermined variables used in the first structural equation.

Low BMI is as expected negatively related with the index of child deprivation at a level of significance less than 15% while the variable like full ANC is as expected negatively related with the deprivation index and significant at 10% level. This is because when mothers suffer from low body mass index due to malnutrition or do not get advantage of full ANC, it is likely that the infants may be exposed to higher mortality or underweight or wasting, etc. These results are similar to the findings of a number of studies (Morales et al. 2004; Chakrabarti 2012; Mani 2007; Black et al. 2008) who found maternal nutritional status as an important factor influencing child's growth retardation. As expected, maternal nutrition as measured by body mass index is observed to be strongly negatively associated with child nutrition. Intergenerational link of nutritional status is supported by this result. The implication is that under nourished mother usually faces stunted foetal growth that reduces birth weight of children leading to their greater deprivation in general. Similarly the result associated with the variable ANC is vindicated by the observation that preventive activities like antenatal visits, health worker's advice about mother reduce the probability of low birth weight babies (Wagstaff 2003). The regression is good fit as reflected by the very high value of R^2 which is significant at 1% level. Hence it is seen that the above regression result amply explains the health-related deprivation status of children and apart from poverty, maternal physical condition during child-bearing phase has a great relevance to it.

The following regression result in Table 11.4 explains the state-level variation in the dropout index value corresponding to second structural equation.

Table 11.4 Regression result of children's education deprivation index values

Variable	Coefficient	Std. error	t-Statistic	Prob.
Estimated (HDPI)	0.579167	0.302426	1.915070	0.0818
Female literacy (Y_3)	−0.021190	0.007250	−2.922707	0.0139
BPL (Y_4)	0.013530	0.006786	1.993811	0.0716
No electricity (Z_1)	0.006996	0.001897	3.687745	0.0036
Water source (Z_2)	0.004266	0.005015	0.850697	0.4131
Female headed (Z_3)	8.66E−08	3.70E−08	2.342643	0.0390
Fuel collected (Z_4)	0.000481	0.002164	0.222113	0.8283
Constant	0.406495	0.353318	1.150507	0.2743
R^2	0.85			
F-Statistic	9.158417			0.0007

Source Authors calculation from secondary data

With rise in the number of people in BPL category, children are often coerced to dropout at early stage of education as reflected in the positive and significant value of the coefficient. This is similar to the findings of Venkatanarayana (2009) who stated that educational deprivation of children is a consequence of multiple deprivations that could be summed up as the problem of insecurity. In a given socio-cultural setting, economic factors like levels of income below subsistence might lead to child deprivation.

It is observed that the coefficient of the variable availability of no electricity is positive and significant as expected implying higher dropout with lack of electricity in the house. As female-headed households rises in a state the dropout index also as assumed, increases in value in a significant manner. Female literacy is as expected inversely related to the dropout scenario and the coefficient is significant. The estimated value of health deprivation index has also positive significant impact on educational deprivation. Apart from this, the factors affecting child schooling is the cost of schooling that includes both direct and indirect (including opportunity) cost. Jodha and Singh (1991) write that in the context of an agrarian economy, the child labour is a peasant's adaptive strategy for survival, also taking part in diverse form of unpaid collection activities. The sign of the variables water-source and fuel collected in the second structural equation validates the assertion of Jodha et al. However they are not found to be significant. The entire regression is however found to be good fit as evident from high value of R^2 which is also significant.

11.8 Concluding Observations and Policy Prescriptions

The paper addresses the issue of child deprivation pertaining to aspects of health and elementary education. It is observed that, over the states there exist wide differences with respect to health deprivation of children. According to this study, children belonging to the states like Bihar, Madhya Pradesh, Chhattisgarh, Jharkhand, Odisha, Uttar Pradesh and Rajasthan, are deprived more in case of health aspect. Regarding determinants of health deprivation, the regression results suggest that factors like poverty, female literacy rate, low body mass index of mother and full antenatal care have significant association with the level of deprivation.

It is evident from the data that the achievement of the schooling system in India has remained far away from achieving universalisation of elementary education as per the constitutional dictum. This inefficacy is glaring when it is found that even after more than half a century of promise, around one-fourth of the children in the age group 5–14 still remain deprived of access to school. Household characteristics of the deprived children indicate that female literacy, poverty, availability of electricity, head of the household and health status play significant roles in the determination of their schooling status.

In order to redress the extent and intensity of health and education deprivation of children, there is no denial to the importance of introducing a host of policy measures that both directly and indirectly intervene in the system. Among the direct measures allusion may be made towards provisioning of delivery of nutrition through ration system, better monitoring of full immunisation programmes, full coverage of the child-bearing mothers in rural and poor families through extension of ICDS and basic health medicine through rural hospitals or primary healthcare units. Indirect measures cover huge investments in basic sanitation and water supply in the rural/semi-urban areas, promotion of schemes that ensure income security of parents, extension of basic education to the uneducated or low educated parents especially females. Further the provisions in NREGS scheme should be gradually extended towards engaging educated youth for mobilising them in creating social awareness about literacy, sanitation, healthcare, balanced nutritional diet, anti-liquor, family planning and even better child care.

Identification of deprived children is one of the important jobs of the concerned local/regional authority. For this purpose Panchayat/regional Governments may come forward to provide the necessary information and help in undertaking survey if required. The concerned authorities should acknowledge that social sector expenditures, particularly on health and education, are complementary in nature and if put together do produce large individual as well as social benefits. In order to prioritise the allocation of scarce resources, greater weight should be attached to intensively deprived regions and this would better address the aspect of redressing the deprivation of children.

References

Black, R. E., Allen, L. H., Bhutta, Z. A., et al. (2008). Maternal and child under-nutrition: global and regional exposures and health consequences. *Maternal and Child Under-nutrition Series 1, The Lancet, 371*(9608), 243–260.

Bradshaw, J. (2002). Child poverty and child outcomes. *Children and Society, 16*(2), 131–140.

Chakrabarti, A. (2012). Determinants of child morbidity and factors governing utilization of child health care: evidence from rural India. *Applied Economics, 44*(1), 27–37.

Chaudhri, D. P., & Jha, R. (2012). Child poverty and compulsory elementary education in India: Policy insights from household data analysis. *Indian Journal of Human Development, 6*(1), 5–30.

Das, S., & Sahoo, H. (2011). An investigation into factors affecting child under nutrition in Madhya Pradesh. *Anthropologist, 13*(3), 227–233.

Drèze, J., & Khera, R. (2012). Regional patterns of human and child deprivation in India. *Economic & Political Weekly, 47*(39), 42–49.

Duncan, G., & Brooks-Gunn, J. (2000). Family poverty, welfare reform, and child development. *Child Development, 71*(1), 188–196.

Dyer, C., & Rose, P. (2006). *Chronic poverty and education: A review of literature, revised draft*. Manchester: Chronic Poverty Research Centre.

Govinda, R. (Ed.). (2002). *India education report*. New Delhi: Oxford University Press.

Griffiths, P., Mathews, Z., & Hinde, A. (2002). Gender, family, and the nutritional status of children in three culturally contrasting states of India. *Social Science and Medicine, 55*(5), 775–790.

Huston, A. C. (Ed.). (1991). *Children in poverty: Child development and public policy*. Cambridge: Cambridge University Press.

Jodha, N. S., & Singh, R. P. (1991). Child labour in dry land agriculture in India. In R. Kanbargi (Ed.), *Child labour in the Indian subcontinent: Dimensions and implications*. New Delhi: Sage.

Larson, C. P. (1980). Efficacy of prenatal and postpartum home visits on child health and development. *Pediatrics, 66*(2), 191–197.

Mani, S. (2007). The Role of the household and community in determining child health. UNU-WIDER Research Paper No. 2007/78, University of Southern California, USA. https://ideas.repec.org/p/unu/wpaper/rp2007-78.html. Accessed on 23 Feb 2015.

Michaelowa, K. (2001). Primary education quality in francophone sub-Saharan Africa: Determinants of learning achievements and efficiency considerations. *World Development, 29*(10), 1699–1716.

Mishra, V. K., Lahiri, S.,& Luther, N. Y. (1999) Child nutrition in India, National Family Health Survey Subject Reports, No. 14. IIPS and East-West Center, Mumbai.

Mohanty, S. (2010). Multidimensional poverty and the state of child health in India. Asia Research Centre, Working Paper No. 30. https://papers.ssrn.com/sol3/papers.cfm?abstract_id=1833864. Accessed on 2nd Mar 2015.

Monteiro, C., Aquino Benicio, M. H., Conde, W. L., et al. (2009). Narrowing socioeconomic inequality in child stunting: The Brazilian experience (1974–2007). *Bulletin of the World Health Organization, 88*(4), 305–311.

Morales, R., Aguilar, A. M.,& Calzadill, A. (2004). The impact of mother's anthropometrics and geography on under nutrition in Bolivia. Prepared for presentation of the drafts on Child Health, Poverty and the Role of Social Policies papers, Res Networks, IADB: Washington, DC.

Nambissan, G. B. (2003). Educational deprivation and primary school provision: A study of providers in the city of Calcutta, IDS Working Paper 187. Brighton, England. http://www.ids.ac.uk/download.cfm?objectid=DE30DF3D-5056-8171-7BDBF9333B3D4154. Accessed on 23 Feb 2015.

Navaneetham, K.,& Jose, S. (2005). Poverty, malnutrition and mortality in South Asia: A review of issues and options, Paper presented at the CICRED Seminar on Mortality as Both a Determinant and a Consequence of Poverty and Hunger, Thiruvananthapuram, India.

Onis, M., Frongillo, E. A., & Blossner, M. (2000). Is malnutrition declining? An analysis of changes in levels of child malnutrition since 1980. *Bull World Health Organization, 78*(10), 1222–1233.

Prentice, S. (2007). Less access, worse quality: New evidence about poor children and regulated child care in Canada. *Journal of Children and Poverty, 13*(1), 57–73.

Russell, S. (2004). The economic burden of illness for households in developing countries: A review of studies focusing on malaria, tuberculosis, and human immunodeficiency virus/acquired immunodeficiency syndrome. *The American Journal of Tropical Medicine and Hygiene, 71*(2), 147–155.

Setboonsarng, S. (2005). Child malnutrition as a poverty indicator: An evaluation in the context of different development interventions in Indonesia, Asian Development Bank Institute Discussion Paper. No. 21. https://www.adb.org/sites/default/files/publication/156773/adbi-dp21.pdf. Accessed on 23 Feb 2015.

Svedberg, P. (2000). *Poverty and under-nutrition: Theory, measurement and policy*. Oxford: Oxford University Press.

Swain, S. C. (2008). Nutritional deprivation of children in Orissa. *Economic & Political Weekly, 43*(37), 49–56.

Taguri, A., Betilmal, I., Mahmud, S. M., et al. (2008). Risk factors for stunting among under-fives in Libya. *Public Health Nutrition, 12*(8), 1141–1190.

Tsujita, Y. (2009). Deprivation of education: A study of slum children in Delhi, India, Background paper prepared for the education for all global monitoring report 2010 reaching the marginalized, UNESCO. http://unesdoc.unesco.org/images/0018/001865/186592e.pdf. Accessed on 24 Feb 2015.

UNICEF. (2014). Report on situation analysis of child poverty and deprivation in Uganda. http://www.unicef.org/uganda/CPR_Summary.final.2014(1).pdf. Accessed on 24 Feb 2015.

Venkatanarayana, M. (2009). Schooling deprivation in India. *Economic & Political Weekly, 44*(32), 12–14.

Wagstaff, A. (2003). Child health on a dollar a day: Some tentative cross-country comparisons. *Social Science and Medicine, 57*(9), 1529–1538.

Chapter 12
Health Performance Index and Healthcare Expenditure in Assam: Are There any Structural Change?

Rimee Bhuyan, Nizara Kalita and Gayatri Goswami

12.1 Introduction

Any effort to develop human capital has a multiplier effect. Endogenous growth model of Lucas figured out that human capital accumulation by obtaining new skills and knowledge helps to achieve maximum productive capacity of workers which in turn increases the productivity of capital as well as other resources in the economy (Manash and Chakraborty 2006). Generation of human capital is possible through education and health. Stock of health determines the time a person can spend on market and non-market activities (Rao and Choudhury 2012). So along with education, skills, innovations and creativity, sound health is also imperative for building human capital (Hancock 1993). With good health, a country is able to produce more output with given combination of skills, physical capital, and technology and thus better health makes important contribution toward growth and development of a country (Howitt 2005). World Bank Report, 1991 also emphasizes that health and quality of life is an essential component of economic

R. Bhuyan (✉) · N. Kalita · G. Goswami
Department of Economics, Gauhati University, Gopinath Bardoloi Nagar,
Guwahati 781014, Assam, India
e-mail: rimeeb1@gmail.com

N. Kalita
e-mail: nizarakalita10@gmail.com

G. Goswami
e-mail: ggbezbarua@gmail.com

U.K. De et al. (eds.), *Issues on Health and Healthcare in India*, India Studies in Business and Economics, https://doi.org/10.1007/978-981-10-6104-2_12

development. Therefore, poor health is a constraint on development. For the achievement of economic growth and development, it is necessary to make improvement in the health indicators like life expectancy of people, reduction in IMR and MMR.

India has recorded an impressive economic growth, but this growth has failed to transmit into the healthy performance of Indian people (Chaurasia 2013). It is still lagging behind in achieving most of the health-related Millennium Development Goals.[1] However, according to UNESCAP, it has achieved some success in maternity health, child health, and on priority diseases with its effort through the National Rural Health Mission (NRHM), now expanded to both rural and urban areas as National Health Mission.[2] But the pace of improvement is substantially slower in comparison to the need for social and economic development of the country. In India, where the population is growing at a compound annual growth rate of 1.2% and currently ranked as the most populous country in the world with 26.1% people living below the poverty line, delivery of quality healthcare service is of utmost importance.

The picture is quite similar in Assam. It is one of the poorest states of India with an estimated Gross Domestic Product (GDP) Rs. 12,163 which is less than two-third of the national average and is facing a lot of challenges to fulfill the goals of improving its health outcomes (World Bank 2004). In terms of priority health indicators, Assam is still below the national level. As a result, NRHM has identified Assam one of the highly focused states on account of low-income and weak health indicators (Hooda 2013).[3] Indian Chambers of Commerce revealed that by April 2010, Assam was declared as a best-performing state in implementing NRHM among the north-eastern states.[4] In this context, the present study examines the performance of priority health indicators in Assam in pre-launch and post-launch of NRHM. And examine is there any structural change in the Performance Index of health indicators after the introduction of NRHM in 2005.

Further, it has been argued that countries which allocate highest level of public expenditure on health are able to achieve better health outcomes than the countries allocating low level of public expenditure (Berman and Ahuja 2008). Anand and Ravallion (1993) and Bhalotra (2007) have found statistical significant effect of public

---

[1]India's health outcomes like Infant Mortality Rate (IMR), Child Mortality Rate, and Maternal Mortality Rate (MMR) are one of the worse among the other developing countries of the world (Hooda 2013).

[2]United Nations Economic and Social Commission for Asia and the Pacific.

[3]NRHM (National Rural Health Mission) was implemented on April 12, 2005 on account of low public expenditure and uneven interstate distribution. It seeks to provide accessible, affordable, and effective healthcare to the people residing in rural areas with special focus on 18 states which have weak health indicators, including Assam where population health continues to be major concern (Chaurasia 2013). The mission aims to increase public health spending, to reduce infant mortality rate, maternal mortality rate, and total fertility rate. However, Assam's achievement in health is mostly below or at par at the all India level (Gupta and Choudhury 2013).

[4]"Healthcare Infrastructure and Services Financing in India, Operation and Challenges", Indian Chambers of Commerce.

health expenditure on health status of population. But public expenditure on medical, public health, and family welfare in India is low in comparison to the need of the people (Hooda 2013; Bhat and Jain 2004).[5] In case of Assam, per capita public spending on health was Rs. 162 in comparison to per capita private spending on health which was Rs. 612 in 2004–2005 (Joumard and Kumar 2015). But, at the same time, the share of SDP (State Domestic Product) spent on health is quite high and is more than the average of all other states (Dutta and Bawari 2007). Yet, Assam has been identified as the worst performer in selected health indicators (Gupta and Choudhury 2013). This may mean that increasing public spending on health in Assam has not been able to transform into good health indicators. In order to investigate this situation, we study the effect of public health expenditure by the state government on the performance index of health indicators in Assam.

So, based on these backgrounds, following are the main objectives of the study:

- To analyze the performance of health outcomes over the years in Assam.
- To identify the structural break in the performance index of selected health indicators of Assam over the years.
- To investigate the effect of public health expenditure on the performance index of health indicators in Assam.

12.2 Data Base and Methodology

The study is based on secondary data only. Data on the health performance indicators are collected from Ministry of Health and family Welfare Department and Planning Commission of India for the years 1995–2013.

Data on revenue expenditure as well as capital expenditure on medical and public health category are collected from the State Finance—A Study of Budget, Reserve bank of India for the years 2000–2013.

12.2.1 Line of Analysis

12.2.1.1 Performance of Health Indicators

Depending upon the annual availability of data for Assam, the present study has selected crude birth rate, crude death rate, infant mortality rate, and total fertility

[5]In this line, during the twelfth 5-year plan of India (2012–2017), an expert group constituted for the universal health coverage by Planning Commission recommended an increase in the public expenditure on health to a minimum of 3% of GDP from the 2.5% (Rao and Choudhury 2012). On an average, states spend just 0.6% of their State Gross Domestic product (SGDP) on health and family welfare (Gupta and Choudhury 2013).

rate as health status indicators to examine the performance of the health sector of Assam[6]:

1. Crude Birth Rate (CBR): It is the annual number of live births per 1000 population.
2. Crude Death Rate (CDR): It is the annual number of death per 1000 population.
3. Infant Mortality Rate (IMR): It is the number of death of babies under age one per 1000 live births per year.
4. Total Fertility Rate (TFR): It is the average number of children that would be born to a woman if she were to live from birth through the end of her reproductive life (15–49 years) and bear children in accordance with current age-specific fertility rates.

The performances of these indicators over the years 1995–2013 are presented with the help of trend line.

12.2.2 Structural Breaks

To investigate the structural change over time in the health indicators of Assam, we have first estimated the performance index. Performance index is estimated by finding the reciprocal of the average of the selected indicators, viz., CBR, CDR, IMR, and TFR for each year. Then, the association between the performance index and time is shown with the help of a line diagram.

Structural break in a series can be examined with a variety of techniques. Among those, Chow test is the most useful technique which has been developed by G.C Chow in the year 1987. However, in the recent years, this traditional method has been criticized mainly due to its method of identification of the break date. Chow test will be useless if we have doubt about the break dates in a given series of data and want to identify them endogenously. To deal with the presence or absence of structural break for unknown date we have to rely on Bai and Perron. Bai and Perron have developed an approach based on the least squares principle common to regression analysis for identifying breaks in a series. In order to determine is there any structural change in the performance index after the implementation of NRHM

[6]Health is defined in terms of various health indicators. Health status indicators are a set of data which help in supervising the assessment of the health of the population so that health priorities and necessary action can be properly identified. The World Health Organization identifies 750 indicators of public health under a broad range of key domains like life expectancy and mortality, cause specific mortality and morbidity, health service coverage, health workforce infrastructure, health expenditure, health inequalities, selected infectious diseases, etc. Increase or decrease in the value of health indicators would be the indicative of public health situation. For example, Kutty (2000) and Malik (2005) have examined health performance by infant mortality rate, life expectancy rate, crude death rate, per capital gross national income, etc.

in 2005, Bai and Perron structural break test is carried out with the help of the following model:

$$Y_t = \alpha + \beta X_t + \mu_t \quad t = 1995, 1996\ldots2013. \tag{12.1}$$

OLS regression estimation of Eq. (12.1) has been done to estimate the break dates as global minimisers of the sum of squared residuals using a dynamic programming algorithm (Bai and Perron 2002). For each partition $(T_1\ldots T_m)$ denoted by (T_p), given the number of breaks, by minimizing the sum of squared residuals, the associated least squares estimates $\mathrm{B}_p = (\alpha, X_t)_p$ are obtained:

$$\sum_{j=1}^{m+1} \sum_{t=T_{J-1}+1}^{Tj} [Y_t - \alpha - X_t]^2.$$

The sum of squared residuals denoted as $\mathrm{S}_T(T_1\ldots T_m)$ associated with the partition $\{T_p\}$ is computed by the resulting estimates $\wedge\beta_p$. Now the estimated breakpoints $(T_1\ldots T_m)$ are such that

$$(T_1\ldots T_m) = \mathrm{argmin}_{T_1\ldots\ldots T_m} \mathrm{S}_T(T_1\ldots T_m),$$

where the minimization is applied to all possible partitions $(T_1\ldots T_m)$ such that $T_i - T_{i-1} \geq h$ and it is here to be noted that h is the minimum length assigned to a segment and T_i is the ith breakpoint. After considering all possible combination of segments, the process selects that partition which minimizes the sum of squared residuals. Thus the least squares estimates of break dates are those that minimize the full-sample sum of squared residuals in (12.1).

For working with a trending series, the following points are to be noted. First, Bai has demonstrated that in the above-mentioned procedure, stationary of regressors or disturbances is not required for consistency of the breakpoints estimated. Second, we have derived the asymptotic distribution of the breakpoint estimator (needed for construction of the confidence interval) without assuming stationary of the disturbances. In order to estimate the optimal break point sequentially, the above procedure is used for the series starting from one to the maximum allowed by T and h. In the next step, i.e., to choose the number of break points in the time series, the Bayesian Information Criteria (BIC) which accommodates trending regressors is used. Here the number of breaks is selected in such a way for which BIC is at minimum. The number of breaks is selected starting from zero to the maximum. When multiple breaks are considered, this criterion is suitable as it introduces a penalty factor for additional break points which automatically reduces the sum of squared residuals as is apparent from below:

$$\mathrm{BIC}(m) = \ln \sigma^2(m) + p * \ln(T)/T$$
$$p* = (m+1)q + m + p$$
$$\wedge^{\sigma^2} = T^{-1} \sum_{t=1}^{T} u^2 t,$$

where m is the number of breaks, q is the number of explanatory variables, coefficients of whose are subjected to shift, and p is the number of explanatory variables coefficients whose are constant.

12.2.3 Regression Model

In this study, simple regression model has been used to examine the relative effect of public health expenditure on the health performance index. The model used in the present study involves the following type of specification:

$$Y_t = \alpha + \beta X_t + \mu_t \quad t = 2000, 2001\ldots 2013, \ldots \tag{12.2}$$

where Y is the average health performance index, α is the constant, β is the slope coefficient, and X is the log of health expenditure. The intercept term 'α' reflects the other factors which influence variations in explained variable Y_t, but not included in the model. The slope coefficient β shows the impact of marginal change in X_t on the dependent variable; and μ_t is the random disturbance term.

12.3 Results and Their Interpretation

This part of the study deals with the results from the study and the detailed interpretation of the study.

12.3.1 Performance of Selected Health Indicators in Assam

In order to analyze the performance of above-mentioned health indicators, trend line has been used over the years 1995–2012 as shown in Fig. 12.1.

It is observed from Fig. 12.1 that all the selected health indicators have been showing a declining trend over the years. Considerable improvement has been observed in case of IMR. Total numbers of infant death have declined from 77 per 1000 live births in 1995 to 54 in the year 2013. However, in the years 1997 and 2005, IMR has increased than the previous years. Assam is far away from reaching

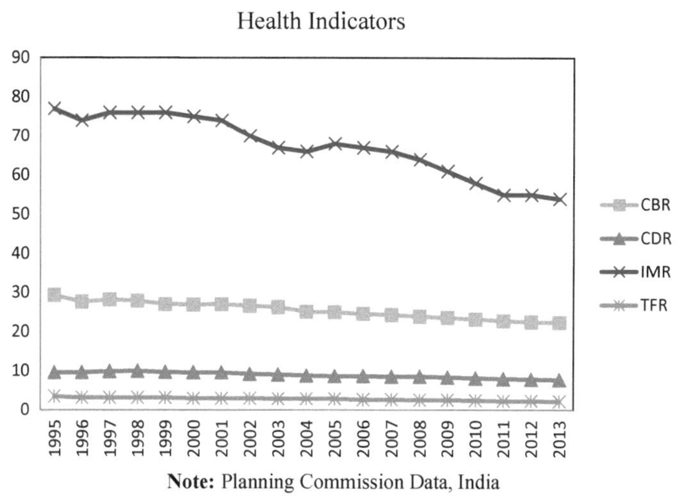

Fig. 12.1 Performance index of different health indicators of Assam. *Note* Planning Commission Data, India

the goal of reducing TFR to 28 per 1000 live births as provided by the eleventh 5-year plan. CBR has been declining from 29.3 live births per 1000 population (1995) to 22.4 lives births per 1000 population (2013) except for the years 1997 and 2001. Not much decline has observed for CDR and TFR. CDR was 9.6/1000 population in the year 1995 and it remains more or less stable up to the year 2003. It was after 2003, it has started showing declination and estimated to be 7.8 in the year 2013. TFR in Assam has achieved a perceptible decline over the years. It has declined from 3.5 (1995) children per woman to 2.3 (2013). However, Assam is yet to achieve the replacement level of 2.1 which is necessary to achieve the equal sharing of benefit of growth.

12.3.2 Structural Change After the Introduction of NRHM

The introduction of NRHM has been necessary on account of poor health indicators in Assam. For instance, in Assam IMR estimated to be 68 as comparison to all India level 58 in the year 2005. As shown in Fig. 12.1, all the selected health indicators have been showing declining trend over time, i.e., their performance has been improving. And it may possible that there is a structural change in the selected health performance indicators after the implementation of NRHM in Assam. So, a trend line has been constructed as shown in Fig. 12.2 to examine the fluctuation of performance index of the selected health indicators of Assam over time so that existence of structural change can be determined.

It is seen from Fig. 12.2 that performance index of different health indicators is positive though fluctuates overtime. From 1995 to 1997, it is increasing but from

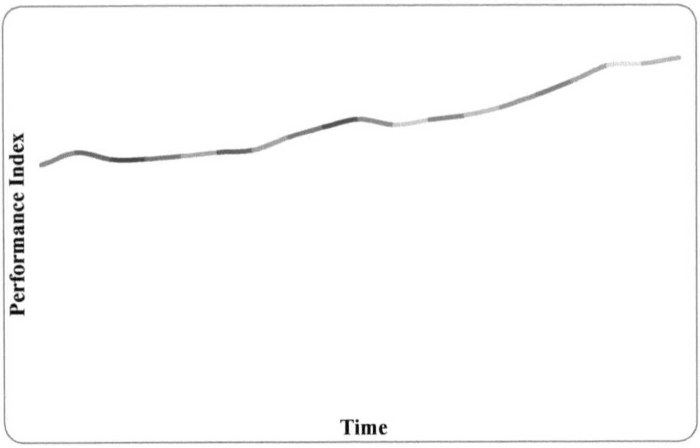

Fig. 12.2 Performance index of different health indicators of Assam

Table 12.1 Estimated trade break intensity

Break	Date	Schwarz criterion
First	2002	Min (−14.30)
Second	2005	
Third	2009	

1998 to 2002 it remained more or less stable thereafter performance index again increases marginally. However, after 2005 performance index of different health indicators is positive and it may be because of implementation of NRHM. But from the trend line, it is not possible to identify the structural break in the performance index. So, in the next unit, Bai–Perron test has been used to find out the break years in the performance index, i.e., find out the years in which performance of health indicators has faced a structural change.

12.3.2.1 Identifying Break Dates

To perform our second objective, it is necessary to estimate time variable and to identify the break year of health performance index if there any. The estimated break dates are presented in Table 12.1. It is clearly seen from table that there are three break points in the performance index namely first break in the year 2002, second break in the year 2005, and third break in the year 2009, respectively. Existence of structural break in 2005 implies that a positive structural change has taken place in the performance index of health indicators of Assam after the implementation of NRHM. We can justify the break in 2009 by the fact that Assam has again started to improve the performance of its health indicators in 2009 and by 2010 it has declared as best-performing north-eastern state in implementing NRHM.

Since the study period covers both post- and pre-implementations of NRHM and most of the structural changes occur in post-implementing period, therefore, lucidly we can conclude that NRHM made an environment for positive structural changes in different health indicators of Assam.

12.3.3 Relationship Between Health Assessment Index and Health Expenditure

In order to examine the direction of relationship between health assessment index and health expenditure, regression analysis has been used.

The estimated results of Eq. (12.2) by OLS, after examining the White correction for heteroscedasticity, are provided in Table 12.2. In the estimation, the estimated coefficients demonstrate their expected signs and are statistically significant at the one percent level. The adjusted coefficient of determination is 0.78; it implies that 78% of the variation in the health index is explained by the explanatory variable, i.e., public health expenditure. The F-statistic is significant at the one percent level, attesting to the overall strength of the model. Jarque–Bera statistic provided that the null hypothesis of normality of error term could not be rejected at any conventional level of significance which confirms the reliability of hypothesis testing.

The coefficient of public expenditure (X) is found to be positive and highly significant at 1% level of significance implying positive relationship between public expenditure on health and performance index. This implies that for one percent increase in the public expenditure on health, performance of selected health indicators has gone up by 0.005%, which indicates that increase in public expenditure on health by state government of Assam has improved the performance index of health indicators of Assam over the years.

Table 12.2 Health performance index and health expenditure

Variables	Coefficient
Constant	−0.002 (−0.0.27)
X_t	0.005 (6.62)***
Adj R square	0.78
F-stats	43.94***
Jarque–Bera = (p value)	0.71 (0.59)

Note 1. The asterisk *** indicates significant at 1% level
2. The heteroscedasticity bias of standard errors has been corrected by using the White's estimator

12.4 Conclusion

In this paper, it has been found that the selected health indicators of Assam, viz., CBR, CDR, IMR, and TFR, have been experiencing a declining trend over time although it is yet to achieve the replacement level. Again, by using Bai and Perron test we have found that there are three break points in the health performance index of health indicators of Assam over time and most of the structural changes occur after the implementation of NRHM in 2005. And, finally, from the regression analysis it has been comprehended that estimated coefficient of health expenditure positively influences the performance index of health indicators of Assam. Therefore, it can be implied that although health performance indicators of Assam are not at par the national level and below than most of the other states of India, yet in case of Assam in isolation, performance of health indicators is improving over time. And improvement has more pronounced after the implementation of NRHM as two of structural breaks have occurred after 2005. Improvement in the performance of health indicators may be because of increasing state expenditure in the public health by the government of Assam over time as the significant positive relation is observed over the years between the health performance index and public health expenditure. So, in Assam where poverty head count ratio is estimated to be around 36.1% compared to the national ratio of 26.1%, more public intervention is necessary in making healthcare service affordable by all so as to improve the health outcomes of Assam especially through the NRHM.

References

Anand, S., & Ravallion, M. (1993). Human development in poor countries: On the role of private incomes and public services. *The Journal of Economic Perspectives, 7*(1), 133–150.

Bai, J., & Perron, P. (2002). Computation and analysis of multiple structural change models. *Journal of Applied Econometrics, 18*(1), 1–22.

Berman, P., & Ahuja, R. (2008). Government health spending in India. *Economic and Political Weekly, 46*(26–27), 209–216.

Bhalotra, S. (2007). Spending to save? State health expenditure and infant mortality in India. *Health Economics, 16,* 911–928.

Bhat, R., & Jain, N. (2004). Analyzing of public expenditure on health using state level data. IIM Ahmedabad. Downloaded from http://www.iimahd.ernet.in/publications/data/2004-06-08rbhat.pdf, Accessed 10 April 2015.

Chaurasia, R. A. (2013). *India health sector performance assessment*. MLC Foundation, Shyam Institute, Bhopal, MP 462003. Accessed from http://www.shyaminstitute.in/hsperformance.pdf

Dutta, I., & Bawari, S. (2007). Health and health care in Assam—a status report. CEHAT and OKD, *Centre for Enquiry into Health and Allied Themes.* Downloaded from http://www.cehat.org/go/uploads/Hhr/assamreport1.pdf, Accessed 10 April 2015.

Gupta, I., & Choudhury, S. (2013). Scaling up health expenditure for universal health coverage: Prospects and challenges. India Infrastructure Report 2013/2014. Downloaded from http://www.idfc.com/pdf/report/2013-14/Chapter-04.pdf, Accessed 10 April 2015.

Hancock, T. (1993). Health, human development and the community eco-system: Three ecological models. *Health Promotion International,* Oxford Journals, *8*(1), 41–47. Downloaded from http://heapro.oxfordjournals.org/content/8/1/41.full.pdf+html, Accessed 10 April 2015.
Hooda, S. K. (2013). *Changing pattern of public expenditure on health in India, issues and challenges*. ISID-PHFI Research Collaboration Programme. working paper series 01. Downloaded from http://111.93.33.222/pdf/wp154.pdf, Accessed 10 April, 2015.
Howitt, P. (2005). *Health, human capital and economic growth: a Schumpeterian perspective*. Pan American Health Organisation. Downloaded from http://www.econ.brown.edu/fac/Peter_Howitt/publication/PAHO.pdf, Accessed 15 Mar 2015.
Joumard, I., & Kumar, A. (2015). *Improving health outcomes and health care in India*. OECD Economics Department. Working paper no. 1184. OECD Publishing. Downloaded from http://www.oecd.org/officialdocuments/publicdisplaydocumentpdf/?cote=ECO/WKP(2015)2&docLanguage=En, Accessed 15 Mar 2015.
Kutty, V. R. (2000). Historical analysis of the development of health care facilities in Kerala State, India. *Health Policy and Planning, 15*(1), 103–109.
Malik, G. (2005). *An examination of the relationship between health and economic growth*. ICRIER Working paper no. 185. Downloaded from http://icrier.org/pdf/Working_Paper_185.pdf, Accessed 15 Mar 2015.
Manash, R. G., & Chakraborty, B. (2006). Human capital accumulation and endogenous growth in a dual economy. *Hitotsubashi Journal of Economics, 47*(2), 169–195.
Rao, M. G., & Choudhury, M. (2012). *Health care financing reforms in India*. Working paper no.: 2012-100, National Institute of Public Finance and Policy. Downloaded from http://uhc-india.org/uploads/HealthcareFinancingreforms.pdf, Accessed 15 Mar 2015.
World Bank. (2004). *Assam health policy note*. Washington, DC: World Bank. Downloaded from http://documents.worldbank.org/curated/en/2004/06/5222995/assam-health-policy-note, Accessed 15 Mar 2015.
www.planningcommission.nic.in
www.rbi.org.in
www.mohfw.nic.in

Chapter 13
Assessing Burden of Infant Mortality on Socio-Economic Classes in North-Eastern India

Sanjeeva Kumar Jha and Ningthoukhongjam Vikimchandra Singh

13.1 Introduction

One of the most pressing issues in global agenda for health development is the pervasiveness of inequality (Oscar, Enrique, Elisabeth, Juan, Cortez-Escalante, Joaquin and Jorbas 2015). The World Economic Forum, recently identified, widening economic inequality as the second most important worldwide trend of global concern as it drives other social inequalities too (World Economic Forum 2014; Michael, Sharon, Ruth, Tanja and Sebastian 2013). Countries with high-income inequality have higher infant mortality than countries with similar level of income distribution (Flegg 1982). Infant mortality rate (IMR) in poor families in India has been observed to be twice as high as in better-off families (IIPS and ORC 2007). Recently released Indian Socio-Economic and Cast Census (SECC) survey 2011–2012 reports the economic status of India. In India, 69% of total population lives in rural India and out of these 92% households (HH) have a monthly income of less than Rs.10,000. In urban India, 3,500,000 HHs have no sources of income (Subodh 2015).

The Millennium Development Goal-4 (MDG-4), set by WHO, calls for reducing under 5 (U-5) mortality rate by two-third between 1990 and 2015 ("Levels & Trend" 2014). In 2013, the infant deaths globally were 4.6 million which constitutes 74% of all U-5 deaths (WHO). In case of India, the MDG-4 requires to bring IMR to less than 39 per 1000 live births by the end of 2015 ("India unlikely" 2015). However, the current IMR in India is 40, and hence it is feared that India may not achieve the goal set by MDG-4. In India, every year 1.34 million children die

S.K. Jha (✉) · N.V. Singh
Department of Statistics, North-Eastern Hill University, Shillong 793022, India
e-mail: skjha@nehu.ac.in

N.V. Singh
e-mail: n.vikim12@gmail.com

U.K. De et al. (eds.), *Issues on Health and Healthcare in India*, India Studies in Business and Economics, https://doi.org/10.1007/978-981-10-6104-2_13

before reaching their fifth birthday, of which 748,000 die within the first month of their life. It translates into nearly 2000 infant deaths every day and to a neonatal death in every 12 such deaths observed globally ("India unlikely" 2015; "Levels and Trend" 2014). Assam together with Madhya Pradesh tops the list with an IMR of 54 per 1000 live births and Meghalaya ranks third with 47 (Office of the Registrar General 2012). The Saiha district of Mizoram has an IMR of 93 per 1000 live births (MoHFW).

Infant mortality is a complex and multifaceted problem and it is associated with a variety of endogenous and exogenous factors such as premature age of mother, maternal health, quality and access to medical care, public health practices and socio-economic conditions. The socio-economic conditions controls most of the endogenous and exogenous factors and also identified as being the most serious cause for increased level of IMR globally. The present chapter tries to identify the type of relationship between the magnitude of IMR and the socio-economic classes and measure the effect of different socio-economic classes on IMR based on district-level data from the six north-eastern Indian states, namely Arunachal Pradesh, Assam, Manipur, Meghalaya, Mizoram and Tripura. The information for Nagaland was not available; therefore, Nagaland could not be considered for the analysis.

This chapter is divided into five sections. Section 13.1 is introductory in nature and Sect. 13.2 presents the literature review and the present data. Section 13.3 presents in brief the methodology of generalized linear mixed model (GzLMM) and conditional autoregressive (CAR) model used to analyse the data. The application of the models to the data is presented in Sect. 13.4, and Sect. 13.5 presents discussions on the findings.

13.2 Literature Review and Data

13.2.1 Literature Review

Ecological regression studies to identify the causal factors affecting IMR and measure the effects of various covariates on IMR have been performed by some of the researches in India. Dixit et al. used multiple regression modelling approached to examine socio-economic characteristics physical amenities and healthcare at district level and attempted to identify factors that influence infant mortality rates and life expectancy (LE) in the Indian Thar desert. They identified the number of health institution and percentage of households visited by health worker in the last 3 months as most important factors affecting IMR and LE (Dixit, Anand and Sharma 2006).

Kapoor used district-level data on IMR for 666 districts in India and applying Quantile regression approach identified the women literacy and women's labour force participation as influencing factors in reducing IMR (Kapoor 2010).

Singh et al. applied the geo-statistical techniques like Moran's I, univariate local indicators of spatial association (LISA), bivariate LISA, spatial error regression and spatiotemporal regression on National Family Household Survey (NFHS) 1992–1993, NFHS 1998–1999 and District Level Household Survey (DLHS) 2002–2004 data. Based on these, natural geographic regions as unit of observation obtained that regions which were underprivileged in terms of female literacy or child nutrition were also disadvantaged in terms of the two indicators of mortality during early childhood. Moreover, the effect of poverty on infant and under-five mortality reduced with time, whereas female literacy had a consistently increasing effect. Urbanization and coverage of safe delivery were not associated with either infant or under-five mortality (Singh, Pathak, Chauhan and Pan 2011).

Singatiya, based on state-level data, explored social and economic factors associated with IMR using regression analysis and principal component analysis. He concluded that women empowering indicators like percent female engaged in salaried works and female literacy rate had negative relationship but female work participation rate and percent female cultivator have positive association with IMR in India (Singatiya 2013).

Barma et al. had examined the trend of IMR in Assam between 1998 and 2012 and concluded that IMR in Assam is declining in both the rural and urban Assam. They also report that education among the female, gap between two births, vaccination of babies and hygienic conditions, reduces IMR, whereas absence of doctors and nurses, under-age and over-age marriage, and low-income group were observed to be positively associated with IMR (Barma and Talukdar 2014).

13.2.2 Data

The district-level infant mortality data as reported by the Ministry of Health & Family Welfare (MoHFW), Government of India, available at the URL: https://nrhm-mis.nic.in/hmisreports/frmstandard_reports.aspx, have been used for the analysis. The response variable constituted the sum of Infant deaths for the two consecutive years 2013–2014 and 2014–2015. The five socio-economic classes based upon wealth index as proposed by District Level Household and Facility Survey (DLHS-3) conducted by International Institute of Population Sciences (IIPS), Mumbai in collaboration with MoHFW, Government of India, were taken as regressors. IIPS has prepared a wealth index at national level by combining household amenities, assets and durable goods and has divided the HH into five groups on the basis of quintiles.

The present study considers the data for the seven north-eastern states of India, namely, Assam, Arunachal Pradesh, Manipur, Meghalaya, Mizoram, Nagaland and Tripura. However, Nagaland has to be excluded due to unavailability of data from the state in DLHS-3. There are 71 administrative districts in the remaining six north-eastern states. The data from these 71 districts were considered for the analysis.

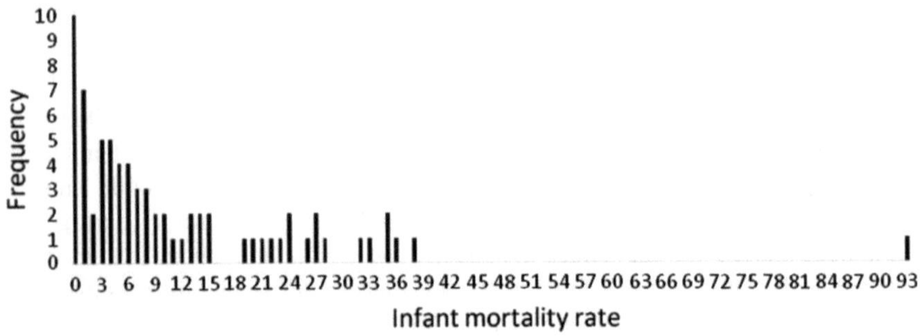

Fig. 13.1 District-wise infant mortality rate

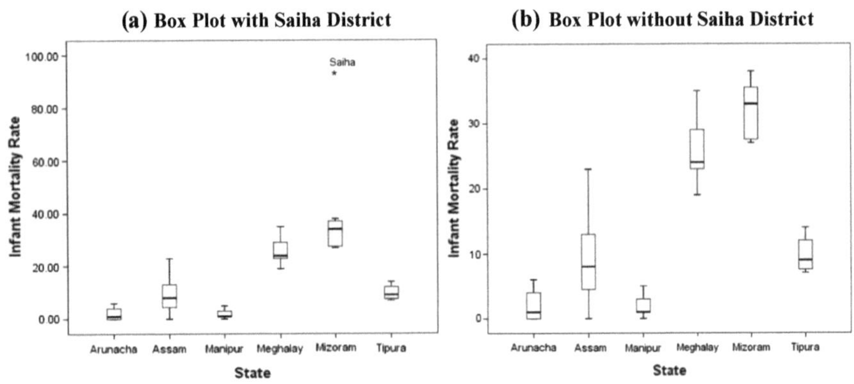

Fig. 13.2 Box plot for state-wise infant mortality rate

The district-wise pattern of IMR for the six north-eastern states is shown in Fig. 13.1. Altogether ten districts have IMR of zero of which seven districts are from Arunachal Pradesh, two are from Manipur and one is from Assam. The Saiha district of Mizoram has an IMR of 93. Except Saiha district all other districts have an IMR less than national average of 40. The IMR value for Saiha is cross checked from other reports and found to be correct.

The box plot of IMR for districts within a state is presented in Figs. 13.2. Figure 13.2 (a) presents box plots with the value from Saiha district and Fig. 13.2 (b) presents the same excluding value from Saiha district. The median IMRs in states in descending order are as Mizoram, Meghalaya, Tripura, Assam, Arunachal Pradesh and Manipur. The spread is highest in Assam followed by Meghalaya. Manipur has the best IMR scenario in respect to median as well as the spread.

Figure 13.3 presents the map of district-level IMR data. Most of the districts of Arunachal Pradesh and Manipur have an IMR between 0 and 5. The entire Mizoram and the six districts of Meghalaya have IMR of more than 22. All the districts of

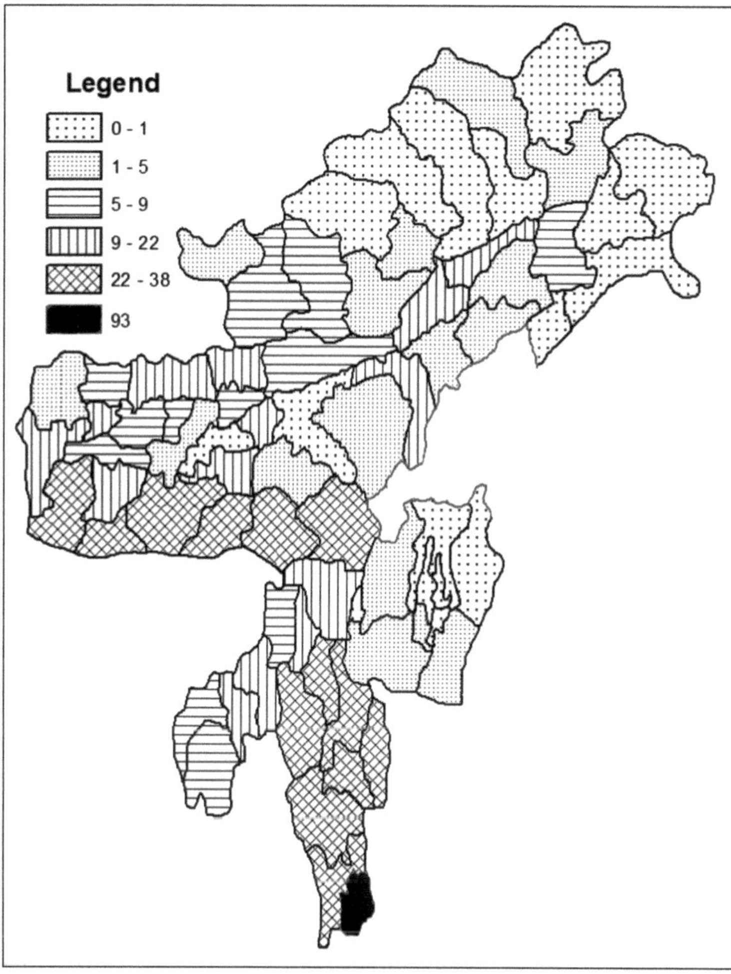

Fig. 13.3 Map of district-level raw IMR in six northeast Indian states

Assam and Tripura have IMR between 5 and 22. The Kamrup Metropolitan and Dima Hasao districts of Assam have an IMR of zero and 23, respectively.

The states form a natural grouping for the districts within it. Further, the spatial contiguity of districts is expected to introduce some spatial association between neighbouring districts. These considerations may lead to the district-level observations being dependent. To have an idea of the grouping effect due to states as well as the strength of spatial association, intra-class (state) correlation, and Moran's I, the measure of spatial correlation is computed together with their significance values and presented in Table 13.1.

The intra-class correlation obtained is 0.2854 and is significant for most of the α values. The spatial correlation computed is 0.3376 and is also highly significant.

Table 13.1 Correlations in district-level raw IMR data

	Parameter	Estimated value	p value
Spatial correlation	Moran's I	0.3376	0.0000
Intra-state correlation	ρ	0.2854	0.0000

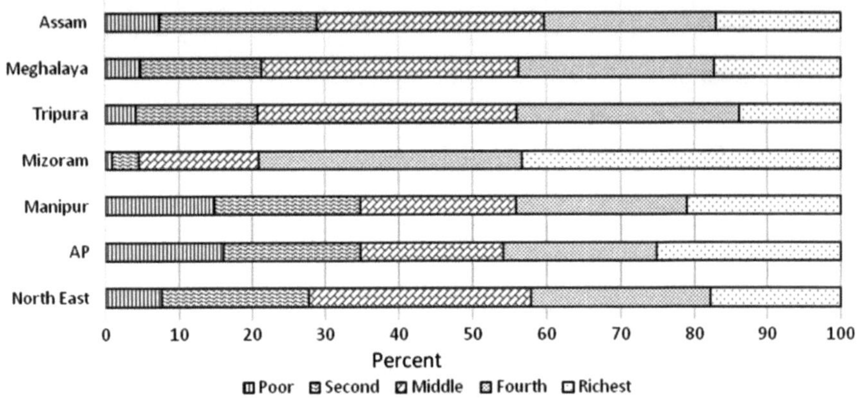

Fig. 13.4 Socioeconomic classes in northeast Indian states

These correlations make the multiple linear regression model inappropriate for analysing the present data. Two separate models, one capitalizing on the intra-class correlation and other capitalizing on spatial correlation, will be considered for analysing the data. The first goes in the name Generalized Linear Mixed Model (GzLMM) in the literature and the second is called conditional autoregressive (CAR) model. For these regression models, the response will be the observed IMRs at district level and the regressors will be the socio-economic classes of the corresponding districts. The distribution of state-wise population proportion together with the same for the whole study region is presented in Fig. 13.4. The percentage of 'poor' is nearly negligible in Mizoram, very small in Tripura, Meghalaya and Assam. The percentage of poor is less than 10% in the entire north-eastern region taken together. However, for the analysis district-level socio-economic classes will be used.

13.2.3 Modelling

As discussed earlier, the analyses of the data were performed using GzLMM, which capitalizes on the intra-class correlation and using CAR model, which capitalizes on spatial correlation which are given as follows.

13.2.4 Modelling Based on Group Structure

The study area is divided into q non-overlapping states and the ith state has $n_i(i = 1, 2, 3, \ldots, q)$ districts.

(Where, $\sum_i^q n_i = n$, i.e. total number of non-overlapping districts). y_{ij} and $\boldsymbol{x}'_{ij}$ are, respectively, the observed IMR and a vector of explanatory variables of jth district in ith state and $\boldsymbol{\beta}$ is a vector of regression coefficients. The response IMRs are small and positive integers. The Poisson distribution is suitable for modelling the response. In the presence of significant intra-class correlation coefficient, GzLMM approach can provide stable estimates of parameters. That is, IMR y_{ij} are conditionally independent and follow Poisson distribution with mean μ_{ij} where

$$\begin{aligned} y_{ij}|u_i &\sim \text{Poisson}\left(\mu_{ij}\right) \\ \log\left(\mu_{ij}\right) &= \text{offset} + x'_{ij}\boldsymbol{\beta} + u_i \; i = 1, 2, \ldots q; \quad j = 1, 2, \ldots, n_i; \\ u_i &\sim i.i.d\; N\left(0,\; \sigma_u^2\right) \end{aligned} \tag{13.1}$$

and the offset in this model is taken as total live births in the years 2013–2014 and 2014–2015, expressed in thousand.

13.2.5 Modelling Based on Spatial Neighbourhood Structure

As a second approach, the data are considered as the observations on a spatial lattice for the study area. Here, nearby observations are expected to be similar to the observations in their neighbourhood. This spatial dependence is expected to reduce for observations from two districts far apart. A Markovian approach will be followed where it is assumed that a district has a spatial association with its immediate neighbours and not with the districts which are not in its immediate neighbourhood. Clayton and Kaldor (1987) proposed a spatial regression approach, by considering a random effect for each district with a spatially structured prior distribution (Clayton and Kaldor 1987). It leads to empirical Bayes estimates wherein local estimates are a weighted average of the district-level data values and an average of observations in nearby or neighbouring districts. This model is called conditional autoregressive (CAR) model. Fully Bayesian formulation using Markov Chain Monte Carlo (MCMC) in Clayton and Kaldor approach was introduced by Besag et al. (1991) (Besag, York and Mollie 1991; Clayton and Kaldor 1987). The model is given as

$$\begin{aligned} y_i|u_i &\sim \text{Poisson}(\mu_i);\;\; i = 1, 2, \ldots n; \\ \log(\mu_i) &= x'_i\beta + u_i \\ u_i|u_{j\neq i} &\sim N\left(\frac{\sum_{j\neq i} c_{ij}u_j}{\sum_{j\neq i} c_{ij}}, \frac{1}{\tau_{CAR}\sum_{j\neq i} c_{ij}}\right), \end{aligned} \tag{13.2}$$

where y_i, μ_i and u_i are observed IMR, mean mortality rate and random effect, respectively, for the ith district. Also, x_i' is a vector of known explanatory variables for ith district, $\boldsymbol{\beta}$ is a vector of unknown regression coefficients, $c_{ij} = 1$, if ith district is in contiguity to jth district and $c_{ij} = 0$, otherwise. The parameter τ_{CAR} denotes a hyperparameter related to the conditional variance of u_i given the values of the other elements of **u**.

13.3 Result

The data were analysed by the above two models using R-software. Best results, in terms of deviance measures, are obtained on taking the regressors combination as 'poor & second', 'middle' and 'fourth & richest'. Therefore, these three regressors are considered for the analysis and the results are presented in Table 13.2. The 'A' part of Table 13.2 presents the results for the analysis based on group structure and part 'B' of Table 13.2 presents the results based on spatial structure. In both the models, the mean IMR is linked to the three regressors as follows:

Table 13.2 Parameter estimates and their confidence measures for models based on group structure and on spatial neighbourhood structure

A. Modelling based on group structure					
	Parameters	Estimated value	95% confidence interval		p value
			2.50%	97.50%	
Intercept	$\text{Exp}(\beta_0)$	11.2669	3.3860	37.1501	0.0000
Poor & second	$\text{Exp}(\beta_1)$	1.0380	0.9984	1.0781	0.0568
Middle	$\text{Exp}(\beta_2)$	0.9169	0.8639	0.9729	0.0041
Fourth & richest	$\text{Exp}(\beta_3)$	0.9673	0.9429	0.9909	0.0086
Spatial correlation in model residuals	Moran's I	−0.0501	–	–	0.6788
Intra-state correlation in model residuals	ρ	0	0	0.0042	0.9880
B. Modelling based on spatial neighbourhood structure					
Intercept	$\text{Exp}(\beta_0)$	7.3009	5.4617	9.2489	–
Poor & second	$\text{Exp}(\beta_1)$	1.0417	0.9307	1.1647	–
Middle	$\text{Exp}(\beta_2)$	0.9808	0.8443	1.1584	–
Fourth & richest	$\text{Exp}(\beta_3)$	0.9473	0.8894	1.0037	–
Spatial correlation in model residuals	Moran's I	−0.1327	–	–	0.9513
Intra-state correlation in model residuals	ρ	0.1476	0.0025	0.5953	0.0220
Hyperparameter related to the conditional variance of u_i	τ_{CAR}	2.0096	1.0364	3.6010	–

1. Modelling based on group structure.

$$\log(\mu_{ij}) = \beta_o + \beta_1(\text{poor \& second})_{ij} + \beta_2(\text{middle})_{ij} + \beta_3(\text{fourth \& richest})_{ij} + u_i.$$

2. Modelling based on spatial neighbourhood structure.

$$\log(\mu_i) = \beta_o + \beta_1(\text{poor \& second})_i + \beta_2(\text{middle})_i + \beta_3(\text{fourth \& richest})_i + u_i.$$

The results of the analyses based on the above two models are presented in Table 13.2. The estimated intercepts and slopes together with their 95% confidence interval are presented in the exponentiated forms. The estimated spatial and intra-class correlations in the residuals are also presented in the table. For both the models, the unit of the explanatory variable taken was 10,000 HH. Part 'A' of the table presents the results from GzLMM. Again, Part 'B' presents the results from CAR model.

In part A, the estimated overall mean IMR of the study region obtained on using GzLMM is 11.2669. The estimated exponentiated slope values for 'poor & second', 'middle' and 'fourth & richest' socio-economic classes have significant effects on the district-level IMRs of the study region. In increase of 10,000 HH in 'poor & second' socio-economic class increases the existing district-level IMR by 3.8%. This translates into increasing 1, and HH in 'poor & second' socio-economic class increases the existing district-level IMR by 0.00038%. Though the estimated value is significant at 10% level, it is not significant at 5% level of significance. Second, as the confidence interval for odds ratio contains 1, this effect cannot be taken as convincing, whereas the 'middle' and 'fourth & richest' socio-economic classes have negative effect on district-level IMR. With an increase of 10,000 HH in the 'middle' socio-economic class, the district-level IMR decreases by 8.3% of the existing value. And for an increase of 10,000 HH in the 'fourth & richest' socio-economic class, the district-level IMR decreases by 3.2% of the existing value. The estimated spatial and intra-class correlations in the model residuals are −0.0501 and 0 with p values 0.6788 and 0.9880, respectively, indicating the absence of significant correlations in residuals. The district-level estimated IMRs for study region are mapped and presented in Fig. 13.5.

In part 'B', the estimated overall average IMR using CAR model is obtained as 7.3009. The estimated 95% confidence intervals for odds of each of the model coefficients include 1. So, these explanatory variables cannot be taken to have a significant effect on IMR with confidence. Therefore, it may be concluded that these variables do not have any significant effect in explaining the district-level IMRs. The estimated spatial correlation in this model residual is −0.1327 with p value 0.9513, indicating the absence of significant correlation in residuals. Again, the intra-class correlation in the residuals is 0.1476 with p value 0.0220, indicating the

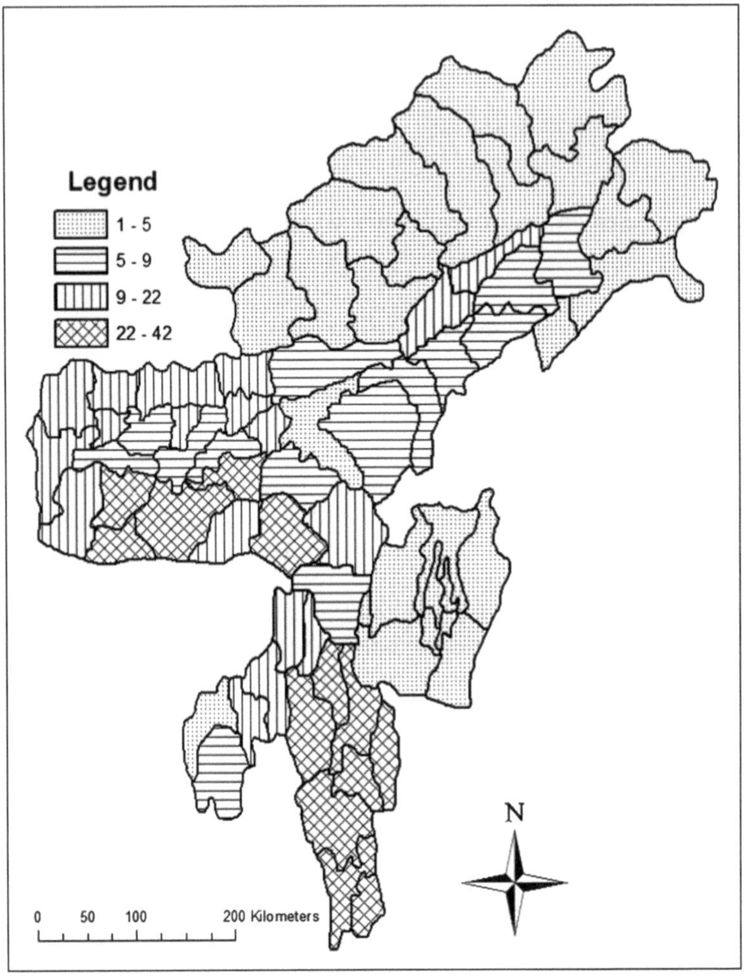

Fig. 13.5 Map showing district-level fitted IMR using Gzlmm for six northeast Indian states

presence of significant intra-class correlation in residuals. This suggests that the CAR model is not able to explain the variability in data.

13.4 IMR Surfaces

Figure 13.5 shows the estimated IMR from the GzLMM. It is to be noted that none of the districts has an estimated IMR of less than 1 and the maximum estimated IMR for a district, namely Saiha district of Mizoram, have a value of 42. Therefore, this modelling approach has smoothed the raw IMR data from 0 to 93 into 1 to 42.

The estimated IMR surface exhibits a relatively more similar pattern within states as compared to the raw IMR data surface presented in Fig. 13.3. All of the districts of Mizoram and five of the districts of Meghalaya, namely East Garo Hills, South Garo Hills, West Khasi Hills, Ri-Bhoi and Jainta Hills, fall in the category of highest IMR level districts having IMR between 22 and 42. All the districts of Arunachal Pradesh and Manipur fall in the lowest category IMR level.

13.5 Discussion

Infant mortality rate of Saiha district of Mizoram with an IMR value 93 was the most influential observation for the study region. Analyses using both the models were performed by including Saiha district value and excluding Saiha district value and for both the models the results obtained were quite similar. Therefore, the results presented here include the value from Saiha district also. Again, grouping of socio-economic classes into three groups, i.e. 'poor & second', 'middle' and "fourth & richest", were obtained from various combinations of socio-economic classes on the basis of measures like AIC, DIC and deviance.

In the presence of a high degree of intra-state correlation as well as high degree of inter-district, spatial correlation makes analysis such as multiple linear regression, unsuitable. Further, as discussed earlier, the CAR model is not suitable for modelling the present data set. Therefore, the results of GzLMM will only be discussed.

The overall mean IMR for the study region obtained using GzLMM is 11.2669 which is quite close to the overall mean of the raw data which is 11.55 and falls within the 95% confidence interval. The regression results indicate that an increase of 10,000 HH in the lowest two quintiles of socio-economic category of 'poor & second' in a district increases the mean IMR value of the district by 3.5%. However, the conclusion has a weak level of confidence. An increase of 10,000 HH in the 'middle' socio-economic category in a district decreases the IMR value of the district by 8.3%. Further, an increase of 10,000 HH in the 'fourth & richest' socio-economic category in a district decreases the IMR value of the district by 3.2%. The last two results are with a high level of confidence. The study region has 27.73% of population under 'poor & second' socio-economic class, 30.12% of population in 'middle' socio-economic class and 42.12% of population in 'fourth & richest' socio-economic class.

These results indicate upon the effects of the different socio-economic classes in a district in north-eastern India on the infant mortality. The 'poor & second' socio-economic group has a positive effect on district-level IMR, while the 'middle' and the combination of 'fourth & richest' socio-economic classes together have a negative effect with the same. The 'middle' socio-economic class of the society is the most effective class in reducing IMR. The socio-economic class of 'fourth & richest' has also an impact on reducing IMR though the effect is quite less as compared to the 'middle' socio-economic class.

The present overall results support the findings as reported in the literature that the IMR is relatively higher in the lower income group families. However, surprisingly the districts from the states of Arunachal Pradesh and Manipur have a relatively higher concentration of lower income group HHs, but the IMR is the lowest. Again, the districts of Meghalaya and Mizoram have relatively lower concentration in lower income group families but have the highest IMR levels within the study region. This issue needs further investigation.

Acknowledgements We would like to thank the R Core Team (2014). R: A language and environment for statistical computing, R Foundation for Statistical Computing, Vienna, Austria. The URL address is, http://www.R-project.org/. We extend our thanks to Duncan Lee (2013) and Bates D, Maechler M, Bolker B & Walker S (2014) for developing the useful R packages,'CARBayes' and 'lme4' respectively.

References

Baran, N., & Talukdar, D. (2014). Socio-economic factors affecting infant mortality rate in Assam. *International Journal of Science, Environment, 3,* 1893–1900.

Besag, J., York, J. C., & Mollie, A. (1991). Bayesian image restoration, with two applications in spatial statistics (with discussion). *Annals of the Institute of Statistical Mathematics, 43,* 1–59.

Clayton, D., & Kaldor, J. (1987). Empirical Bayes estimates of age-standardized relative risks for use in disease mapping. *Biometrics, 43,* 671–681.

Dixit, A. K., Anand, P. K., & Sharma, R. C. (2006). A study of district level development factors influencing infant mortality rate and life expectancy in the Indian Thar Desert. *Journal of Rural and Tropical Public Health, 5,* 42–45.

Flegg, A. (1982). Inequality of income, illiteracy, and medical care as determinants of infant mortality in underdeveloped countries. *Population Studies, 36,* 441–458.

India unlikely to meet infant mortality rate target of 2015 (2014, Dec 21). *The Economic Times.* Retrieved from the Business Standard website: http://www.business-standard.com/article/pti-stories/india-unlikely-to-meet-infant-mortality-rate-target-of-2015-114122100067_1.html.

International Institute for Population Sciences (IIPS), & ORC Macro. (2007). National Family Health Survey (NFHS-3), 2005–06: India (Vol. I). Mumbai.

Kapoor, Sh. (2010). Infant mortality rates in india: District level variation and correlation. Retrieved from the Indian Statistical Institute, Delhi Centre website: http://www.isid.ac.in/~pu/conference/dec_10_conf/Papers/ShrutiKapoor.pdf.

Levels & Trends in Child Mortality (2014). *Report 2014: Estimate Developed by the UN Inter-agency Group for Child Mortality Estimation.* Retrieved from the UNICEF website: http://www.unicef.org/media/files/Levels_and_Trends_in_Child_Mortality_2014.pdf.

Michael, M., Sharon, F., Ruth, B., Tanja, A. H., & Sebastian, T. (2013). Closing the gap in a generation: Health equity through action on the social determinants of health. Final Report. *Geneva: World Health Organization.* Retrieved from the website: http://whqlibdoc.who.int/publications/2008/9789241563703_eng.pdf.

Office of the Registrar General, India. (2012). *Vital Statistics of India based on the Civil Registration system 2012,* 43. Retrieved from the Census of India website: http://www.censusindia.gov.in/2011-Documents/CRS_Report/CRS_Report2012.pdf.

Oscar, J. M., Enrique, V., Elisabeth, C. D., Juan, J. Cortez-Escalante, D., Joaquin, M., & Jarbas, B. da Silva. (2015). *Socioeconomic inequalities and mortality trends in BRICS, 1990–2010.* Bulletin of World Health Organization. Retrieved from the World Health Organization website: http://www.who.int/bulletin/volumes/92/6/13-127977/en/.

Singatiya, M. R. (2013). Socioeconomic determinants of infant mortality rate in India. *The Journal of Public Health: Photon, 115,* 163–174.

Singh, A., Pathak, P. K., Chauhan, R. K., & Pan, W. (2011). Infant and child mortality in India in the last two decades: A geospatial analysis. *PLoS ONE, 6*(11), e26856. doi:10.1371/journal.pone.0026856.

Subodh, V. (2015, July 4). 92% rural homes run on less than Rs.10,000 per month. *The Times of India*. Retrieved from The Times of India website: http://timesofindia.indiatimes.com/india/92-rural-homes-run-on-less-than-Rs-10000-per-month/articleshow/47931716.cms.

World Economic Forum, (2014). *Outlook on the global agenda 2014.* Retrieved from the World Economic Forum website: http://www3.weforum.org/docs/WEF_GAC_GlobalAgendaOutlook_2014.pdf.

World Health Organization (WHO). *Global Health Observatory (GHO) data.* Retrieved from the World Health Organization website: http://www.who.int/gho/child_health/mortality/neonatal_infant_text/en/.

Chapter 14
Is India on the Path to Replacement Fertility Soon? Exploring the Role of Rural–Urban Differential Pace and Timing of Fertility Decline

Tapan Kumar Chakrabarty and Mallika Deb

14.1 Introduction

India, the second most populous country in the world after China, has crossed the 1210.2 million population mark according to the latest census, and will surpass China's, given that the current fertility policy of China does not change (Haub and Gribble 2011; Census of India 2011). During 2001 and 2011, the gap between India and China has been narrowed by about 55% bringing India on the track to become the most populous country in the world in about 15 years from now. According to United Nations estimates, during 2000–2010 (United Nations 2011), the world population grew at an annual rate of 1.23%. Annual growth rate of 0.53% during 2000–2010 has been registered by China, which is much lower, as compared to that of 1.64% in India during 2001–2011.

One of the most important features of the recently concluded census in India is that since independence, the percentage decadal growth showed the sharpest decline during 2001–2011. In India, the decadal growth percentage is reduced by 3.90% from 21.54% during 1991–2000 to 17.64% during 2001–2011. The rate of decline, however, has remained overshadowed by the wide regional and subregional variations with a growth of only 12.43% in the rural population as compared to the rate of 31.8% in the urban population during the last decade.

According to the Sample Registration System (SRS), which is the most reliable source of information in India on vital rates, total fertility rate (TFR) in India has fallen to 2.3 children per woman in 2013, which is less than half of its level of 5.2 in 1971. It is quite likely that true pace of decline might be even faster than it was

T.K. Chakrabarty (✉) · M. Deb
Department of Statistics, North-Eastern Hill University, Shillong, Meghalaya 793022, India
e-mail: tkchakrabarty@nehu.ac.in; tapankumarchakrabarty@gmail.com

M. Deb
e-mail: mallikadeb706@gmail.com

U.K. De et al. (eds.), *Issues on Health and Healthcare in India*, India Studies in Business and Economics, https://doi.org/10.1007/978-981-10-6104-2_14

reported in SRS, since an improvement in the birth registration system in India had taken place. The significant reduction in fertility rate during the recent past has necessarily brought the country like India on track to become the world's largest country to reach near the population-stabilizing 'replacement level' of 2.1 children per woman and sail through the third stage of demographic transition.

India is often noted as the first developing country to initiate a government policy of promoting a family planning programme in 1952, although the comprehensive policy documents were framed only during 2000. Nonetheless, operationally efficient measures were implemented in several states to reduce birth rate and to some extent, every state has witnessed a decline. United Nations Population Division estimated the TFR of India as 5.9 children per woman in the beginning of 1950s, which was observed to be substantially lower than many other developing nations having the average of seven children or more per woman.

The National Population Policy 2000 of India envisaged to achieve the long-term objective of a stable population by 2045, keeping the growth rate consistent with the necessities of socio-economic development and sustainable environmental protection. The instant objectives were to address the healthcare infrastructure, contraception needs and health personnel, and to provide basic reproductive and child healthcare services. Then, the medium-term objective was to reduce the TFR to replacement levels by 2010, through effective implementation and operational strategies. The decline of TFR to 2.3 children per woman by 2013 has masked the wide disparities in fertility by residence and state.

14.2 Pace of Fertility Decline in India

We begin with a close examination of India's fertility trajectory since 1950. According to the United Nations estimates 'World Population Prospects: The 2015 Revision' (United Nations 2015; World Bank 2011), the TFR remained constant at about 5.9 births per woman during the period 1950–1963. Thereafter, since 1965, fertility decline in India has been steady at a regular pace on the average. The previous literature identified the year 1965–1970 as the onset of fertility decline in India (Rele 1987; Arokiasamy and Goli 2012). TFR estimates at 5.7 births per woman during 1961–1971 and at 5.6 during 1970–1972 (Bhat et al. 1984) suggested by the Panel on India constituted by the Committee on Population and Demography of the U.S. National Research Council were found consistent with the United Nations estimates.

Since 1970, annual TFR estimates are available due to SRS in India (Registrar General of India 2014). When compared with the United Nations estimates provided in Fig. 14.1, the trend described by the SRS estimates is found to be overestimating the fertility decline that certainly needs explanation. While both the series are found to be almost identical for last 15 years, yet we can identify notable departures from the United Nations trend during 1971–1981. The gap between the two series during this decade may be attributed two major reasons. First, during this

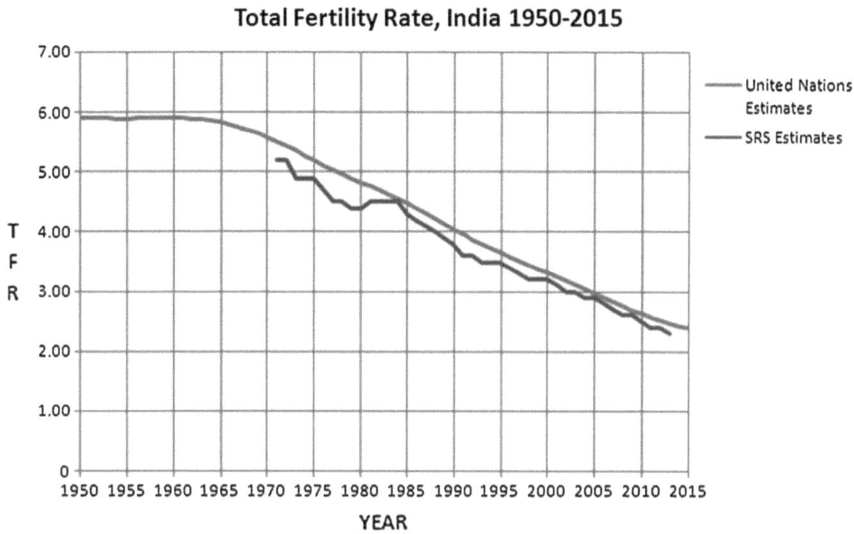

Fig. 14.1 Fertility in India according to SRS and United Nations, 1950–2015

period only India initiated the process of birth registration and completeness of birth reports was less than adequate. Second, the country has experienced emergency during this decade wherein the government introduced forceful family planning measures resulting in a sharp fall in TFR from 1975 to 1977 that is evident in the SRS estimates. The short-term impact of this period is obvious in Fig. 14.1. It was followed by an almost recovery of matching trend of United Nations estimates till 1990.

According to SRS, the TFR declined from 5.2 children per woman in 1971 to 2.4 children per woman in 2011, a record reduction of about 2.8 births per woman. Literatures suggest that the progress made in India in the reducing fertility rate is remarkable over the period 1971–2011 (Rele 1987; Arokiasamy and Goli 2012). In general, the dynamics in fertility change over the period 1971–2011 provides a strong ground for investigation and analysis for various reasons. First, the history of early family planning activities in India during the 1960s is quite unique. Second, its demographic transformations are likely to be greatly influenced by the recent economic expansions. Finally, unlike the countries like China, Brazil or Russia, India is a highly heterogeneous country characterized by complex sociocultural and religious subpopulations. The fact that fertility decline was almost linear over the past forty years in India could be due to its compositional effects. As a matter of fact, India's trends are nothing but the composite picture of different schedules of fertility decline observed across the nation. Urban areas or southern states have for instance experienced earlier changes in fertility behaviour than the rest of the country. Yet, the decomposition of fertility decline by rural and urban areas as shown in Fig. 14.2 conform to a similar trend pattern. Both in rural and urban areas, the overall downward trends remain linear and almost parallel across the

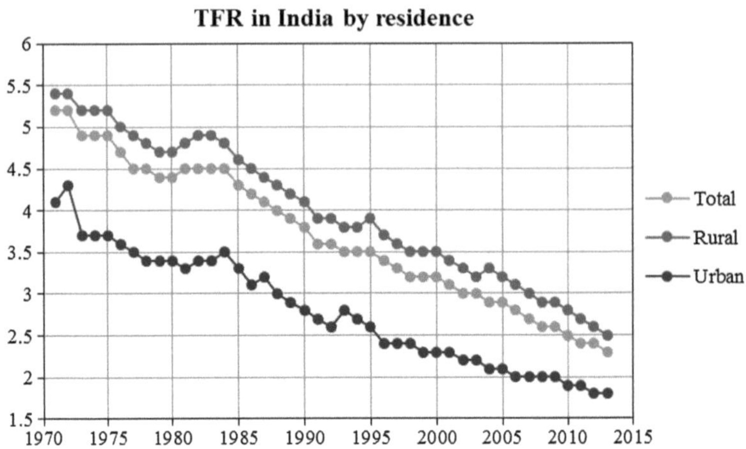

Fig. 14.2 Fertility in India by rural and urban compositions, SRS estimates, 1971–2013

Table 14.1 Rate of progress towards replacement level of TFR in India

India	Total fertility rate					Average annual rate of reduction				
	1971	1981	1991	2001	2011	1971–81	1981–91	1991–01	2001–11	1971–11
India	5.2	4.5	3.6	3.1	2.4	1.41	2.19	1.47	2.51	1.90
Rural	5.4	4.8	3.9	3.4	2.7	1.15	2.04	1.34	2.26	1.70
Urban	4.1	3.3	2.7	2.3	1.9	2.04	1.92	1.51	1.87	1.83

1971–2013 period. With a view to assess the differential pace of fertility decline in rural–urban fertility schedules over each of the last four decades, we adopt the following methodology (Chakrabarty 2014).

Let F_t denote the observed value of total fertility rate in the year t. The Annual Rate of Reduction (ARR) from year $t-1$ to year t is defined as,

$$\mathrm{ARR}_t = \frac{F_{t-1} - F_t}{F_{t-1}} * 100$$

So that average ARR (AARR) over a period can be obtained by taking just the arithmetic mean of these ARR_t's. For instance, AARR for the period 1971–81 can be obtained as

$$\mathrm{AARR}_{1971-81} = \frac{\sum_{t=1972}^{1981} \mathrm{ARR}_t}{10}$$

Table 14.1 calculates AARR for several periods in order to show the pace of decline in fertility in India including its rural and urban components. Accordingly, Fig. 14.3 displays the varying pattern of the pace of decline over the period 1971–2011. During the initial years of the onset of declining fertility 1971–1981, the extent of decline was highest in the urban area with 2.04% as compared to a figure of 1.15% in the rural area. Over the passage of time, the scenario has been reversed. During the decade 1981–1991, rural India has witnessed an unprecedented decline in fertility with a figure of AARR 2.04% against a figure of 1.92% of AARR for the urban. The most recent decade 2001–2011 has experienced the maximum decline of 2.26% of AARR in rural India as against of 1.87% of AARR in urban area.

14.3 Differential Timing in Fertility Decline: Change Point Analysis

We have seen in the preceding section that India has experienced a declining trend in fertility since 1971 and the pace of decline has accelerated since 1980. Consequently, the nation is currently passing through the third stage of demographic transition and moving forward to the next stage of population-stabilizing 'replacement level' of 2.1 children per woman. It is noticed that trends of fertility decline are not uniform in India across the rural–urban residences.

Previous studies attempted to examine the demographic transition process using trend analysis with the fitting and plotting of trend lines of fertility rates in order to differentiate the patterns. Such procedure does not capture the critical change points and the volume of change in fertility rates. Therefore, in this article, we have adopted non-parametric statistical method, abbreviated as Change Point Analysis (CPA) to identify the significant and multiple change points over the long-term fertility trends (Taylor 2000a, b, c). A significant change-point is defined as the point where a major shift in the trend of the process can be clearly isolated. The method helps in the assessment of variations in fertility transition across rural–urban residences by way of understanding the conditions of the steady-state differentials. A number of advantages the method enjoys. (i) CPA identifies the significant change points by statistically estimating the volume of changes in fertility. (ii) Using the confidence interval estimation method, the effectiveness of the change points is assessed. (iii) The method is robust against the presence of outliers and also is a powerful tool in terms of accuracy. (iv) It has the capability of detecting subtle changes in the time series data of TFR which are otherwise missed by the simple trend plots.

14.3.1 CPA Methodology

There are several approaches to performing a CPA. Herein, we have used the method proposed by Taylor (2000a, b, c) for performing CPA using cumulative sum (CUSUM) charts and a well-known resampling technique of bootstrapping to

Table 14.2 Significant change points of TFR trend in India by rural and urban residences

Table of Significant Changes for TFR (India)

Confidence Level = 90%, Confidence Interval = 95%, Bootstraps = 1000, Sampling Without Replacement

Year	Confidence interval	Conf.level (%)	From	To	Level
1976	(1976, 1976)	100	5.02	4.48	2
1986	(1986, 1986)	100	4.48	4	3
1991	(1991, 1991)	97	4	3.5167	1
1997	(1997, 1997)	98	3.5167	3.2	3
2002	(2002, 2002)	98	3.2	2.8833	2
2008	(2008, 2008)	99	2.8833	2.4667	3

Table of Significant Changes for TFR (Rural)

Confidence Level = 90%, Confidence Interval = 95%, Bootstraps = 1000, Sampling Without Replacement

Year	Confidence interval	Conf.level (%)	From	To	Level
1976	(1976, 1976)	100	5.28	4.81	3
1986	(1986, 1986)	100	4.81	4.3	2
1991	(1991, 1991)	98	4.3	3.8333	1
1997	(1997, 1997)	100	3.8333	3.5	3
2002	(2002, 2002)	98	3.5	3.1833	2
2008	(2008, 2008)	99	3.1833	2.7333	3

Table of Significant Changes for TFR (Urban)

Confidence Level = 90%, Confidence Interval = 95%, Bootstraps = 1000, Sampling Without Replacement

Year	Confidence interval	Conf.level (%)	From	To	Level
1973	(1973, 1973)	100	4.2	3.4846	2
1986	(1986, 1986)	99	3.4846	3.05	3
1990	(1990, 1990)	99	3.05	2.7	1
1996	(1996, 1996)	100	2.7	2.3125	3
2004	(2004, 2004)	100	2.3125	1.96	2

detect the critical changes. The construction of CUSUM charts is carried out by calculating and plotting cumulative sums based on the data. Let x_t be the observed values of TFR at time point $t(t = 1, 2, \ldots, n)$. The cumulative sums $S_0, S_1, S_2, \ldots, S_n$ are calculated as follows:

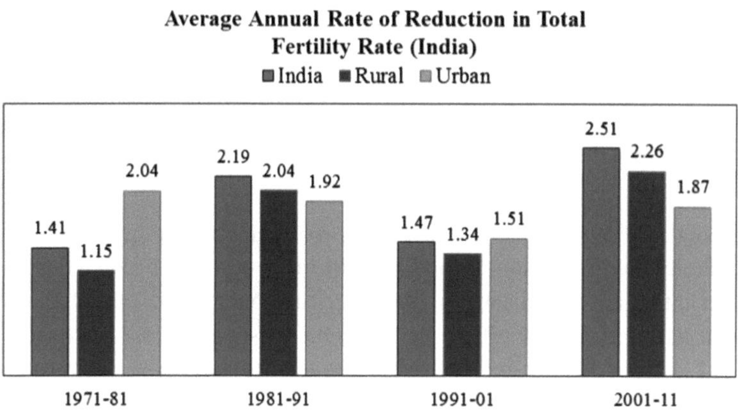

Fig. 14.3 Differential pace of fertility decline in India 1971–2013

1. Calculate the average $\overline{x} = \frac{1}{n}\sum_{t=1}^{n} x_t$.
2. Set $S_0 = 0$.
3. Calculate $S_t = S_{t-1} + (x_t - \overline{x})$.

It may be noted that the CUSUM is not the cumulative sums of the observed values of the variable. But these are the cumulative sums of differences between the values and the average. These differences sum to zero so that the cumulative sum also totals to zero. During a time period when the observed values are above the value of the average, CUSUM increases steadily. Thus, a CUSUM chart segment having upward slope is indicative of a period with higher observed values than the overall average. Similarly, we get the idea of lower observed values than the overall average from a segment with a downward slope. A change in its direction all of a sudden of the CUSUM indicates a sudden change or shift in the level of the process. It is clear that periods where the CUSUM chart follows more or less a smooth straight path, the overall process average did not change much.

Having identified the tentative change points, one has to affirm convincingly that these identified change points are statistically significant in terms of their volume of changes. For this, a confidence level for each of the tentative change points can be determined by performing a bootstrap analysis. It is necessary to obtain an estimator of the amount of change, before we carry out bootstrap resampling (Taylor 2000a, b, c). According to Taylor (2000a, b, c), an option which works well in any case of the distribution and regardless of the number of changes is S_{diff} defined as $S_{\text{diff}} = S_{\max} - S_{\min}$; where $S_{\max} = \max_{1 \le i \le n} S_i$ and $S_{\min} = \min_{1 \le i \le n} S_i$. Once the estimate of the magnitude of the change is available, one can perform the bootstrap analysis. According to Taylor (2000a, b, c), a single bootstrap (Hinkley and Schechtman 1987) is performed through the following steps,

1. Generate a bootstrap sample of n units, denoted as $x_1^0, x_2^0, \ldots, x_n^0$ by randomly reordering the original n observations.

2. Based on the bootstrap sample, calculate the bootstrap CUSUM, denoted as $S_1^0, S_2^0, \ldots, S_n^0$.
3. Calculate the maximum, minimum and difference of the bootstrap CUSUM, denoted as $S_{\text{max}}^0, S_{\text{min}}^0$, and S_{diff}^0.
4. Determine whether the bootstrap difference S_{diff}^0 is less than the original difference S_{diff}.

The bootstrap samples represent random reordering of the original data which would mimic the distribution of the CUSUM in the absence of any change. If the change point is not significant, in the long run, one would expect that S_{diff}^0 is consistent with the original difference S_{diff}. Otherwise, S_{diff}^0 would fall short of the value S_{diff} and the bootstrap CUSUM charts tend to stay closer to zero than the CUSUM of the data in its original order. This indicates that a change must have occurred. Further, a confidence interval of the estimate change point is calculated. Let N denote the number of samples generated by bootstrap and let D be the number of bootstraps for which $S_{\text{diff}}^0 < S_{\text{diff}}$. Then, the confidence level that a change has occurred as a percentage is calculated as,

$$\text{Confidence Level} = 100\frac{D}{N}\%$$

Typically, 90% or 95% confidence is desired to claim that a significant change has occurred. For instance, out of 1000 bootstraps, if 948 cases conform to $S_{\text{diff}}^0 < S_{\text{diff}}$, one gets a confidence level of 94.8% which provides a strong evidence that a change did occur.

14.3.2 Results of Change Point Analysis

Figure 14.4 depicts the 'Change-point analysis' trend line plots change points in total fertility rate trends in India by rural and urban residences using the methodology discussed in foregoing section. The plot reveals the changes by the shifts in the shaded background. The shaded background represents a region expected to contain all the values based on the current model. The control limits for the individual charts are also shown in each of the plots. These limits are indicative of the broader periods of changes. From Fig. 14.4, we see that there are about six change points for the entire country and the rural areas, while the urban India has experience only about five change points. Table 14.2 provides the additional information about each of these changes.

The assessment of the trend line plots and estimates of the change points indicates that India experienced six critical change points (1976, 1986, 1991, 1997, 2002 and 2008) during the period 1971–2013 and same is the scenario in respect of TFR in rural India. The urban India, on the other hand, experienced early critical change points (1973, 1986, 1990, 1996 and 2004) during the same period. The first

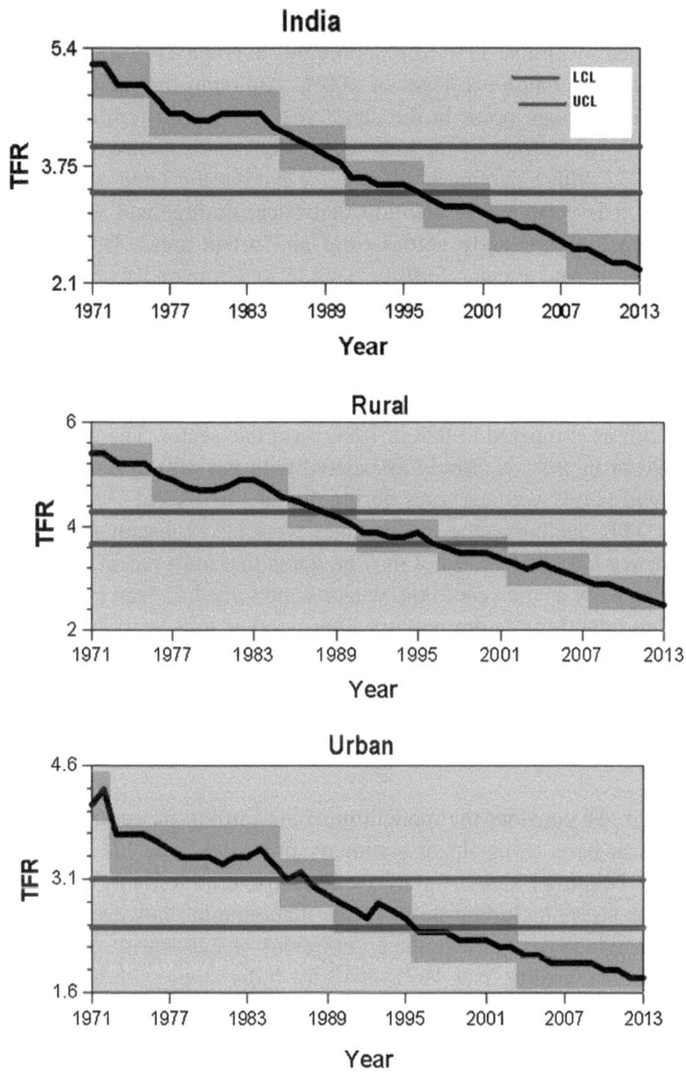

Fig. 14.4 Change point plots of TFR in India by rural and urban residences

Table 14.3 Augmented Dickey–Fuller test for unit root

Interpolated Dickey–Fuller test					
Place	Test Statistic $Z(t)$	1% critical value	5% critical value	10% critical value	MacKinnon approximate p-value for $Z(t)$
India	−0.654	−3.634	−2.952	−2.61	0.8584
Rural	0.031	−3.634	−2.952	−2.61	0.961
Urban	−1.272	−3.634	−2.952	−2.61	0.642

critical change in Indian fertility trend was observed in 1976; during this year, fertility declined by almost 11% from a previous average TFR of 5.02 to 4.48 births per woman with a confidence level of 100%. Although the rural India also experienced the first change point in the same year 1976 with fertility decline of 9% only, the urban counterpart of the nation experienced the first critical change point as early as 1973 with a decline of about 17% having the same confidence level of 100%. Thus, it is pertinent to mention that pace, timings and volume of fertility decline did vary significantly across rural and urban areas. Urban India indeed experienced early and greater fertility decline as compared to the decline of the entire nation which is mostly dominated by the fertility schedule of rural population.

The most notable change point in terms of greater volume of decline in TFR and directional change in the CUSUM chart were observed in 1991 for India as well as for rural sector as compared to that in 1990 for urban sector. The greatest decline of TFR in 1990 or in 1991 is closely associated with the shift in family planning and target-oriented family welfare goals during the late 1970s and 1980s. However, the volumes of TFR decline at the recent times were also substantial as measured by their confidence levels. Here too, it may be noted that most recent change point was found to be as early as the year 2004, whereas the same has been experienced by the rural population and the entire country after another four years in 2008.

14.4 Forecasting TFR Using Random Walk

In this section, we consider the modelling of the fertility processes in India and its rural and urban parts using linear stationary processes. The linear stationary processes are the building blocks of many econometric time series models. Many of the observed time series including those in the demography, however, have empirical features that are inconsistent with the assumptions of stationarity. We have analysed the three series of fertility over 1971–2013 for India along with its rural and urban series components as provided by SRS. Sample autocorrelation function (ACF) and sample partial autocorrelation function (PACF) were used to assess stationarity of all the three series. Persistent patterns of very slowly declining ACF for all the three series were evident and thus indicating lack of stationarity. For the sake of illustrations, we provide the plots of ACF and PACF of TFR (India) and its first difference series in Fig. 14.5.

The autocorrelations did not approach zero, as they should for a stationary linear process. A time variant mean is a common violation of stationarity. There are two popular models for non-stationary trending mean. The first one is trend stationary, in which the mean trend is deterministic. After estimating and removing the trend from the series, it results in a stationary stochastic process. The second one is difference stationary and the mean trend is stochastic. The d times differenced series yields a stationary stochastic process. We have used classical decomposition method to fit linear regression lines and examination of the model residuals did not

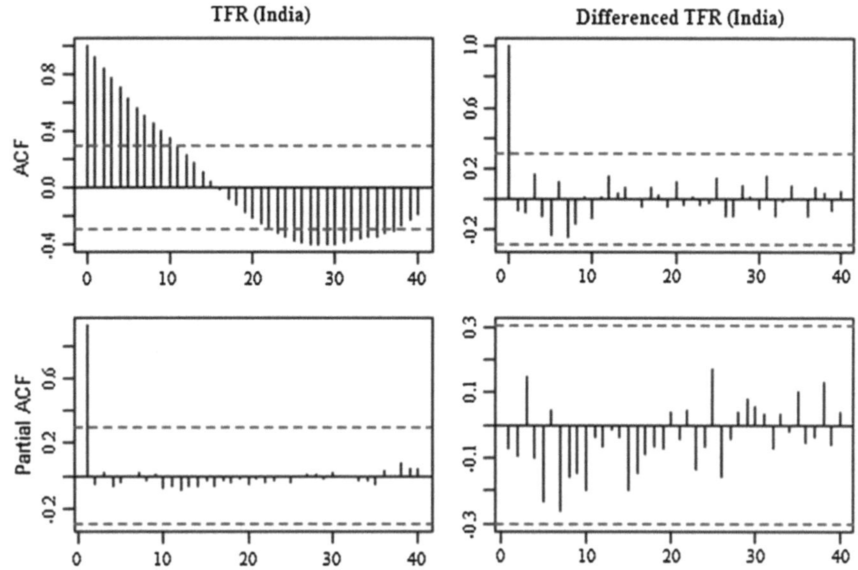

Fig. 14.5 ACF and PACF of observed TFR (India) and its first differenced series

yield stationarity. Thus, the possibility that the series consisting of deterministic trend components was ruled out. Unit root tests are the tools for assessing the presence of a stochastic trend in any observed series. Initial impressions were further confirmed using the augmented Dickey–Fuller Test of unit root (Dickey and Fuller 1979; MacKinnon 1991). The results presented in Table 14.3 confirm that all the three series are non-stationary at common significance levels.

Now, we have to search for the smallest d such that the dth differenced series will be stationary and ACF will be approach zero fairly quickly. In order to remove persistent pattern from the sample ACF of the TFR series, we had to take the first differences of the three observed time series. The first differences $y_t = f_t - f_{t-1}$ of all the series appear reasonably stationary which are verified using the ACF and PACF plots of the y_t values provided in the right panel of Fig. 14.5. The analysis indicates that there are opportunities for ARMA modelling of the first differences of these series; the representations may be approximate only.

The values of the first sample autocorrelations r_1 of the difference series y_t^{India} and y_t^{Rural} were −0.072 and 0.081 respectively; while the values of the second sample autocorrelations r_2 were found to be −0.089 and −0.082, respectively. It was found that all these sample autocorrelations were statistically insignificant indicating possibility of modelling TFR series of India as well as that of Rural using a Random Walk. The sample autocorrelations results for the TFR series of urban, on the other hand, show that the values of r_1 and r_2 are −0.346 and −0.052, respectively, of which the first one is statistically significant indicating the possibility of fitting of an integrated moving average process of order one.

14.4.1 Alternative Time Series Models of TFR

Various ARIMA$(p, 1, q)$ models of the following form $\phi_p(B)y_t = \delta + \theta_q(B)\varepsilon_t$ were fitted, where $y_t = (1 - B)^d f_t = f_t - f_{t-1}$ with $d = 1$, $\phi_p(B) = 1 - \phi_1 B - \phi_2 B^2 - \ldots - \phi_p B^p$ is the pth degree autoregressive lag operator polynomial, $\theta_q(B) = 1 - \theta_1 B - \theta_2 B^2 - \ldots - \theta_q B^q$ is the qth degree moving average lag operator polynomial and ε_t is an uncorrelated innovation process with zero mean and constant variance. The model random walk with drift written as $y_t = \delta + \varepsilon_t$ can be seen as a special case with $p = q = 0$ and denoted by ARIMA$(0, 1, 0)$.

We have used the 'forecast' package of statistical software '*R*' for the purpose of fitting different plausible models. We summarize the results of the fitted ARIMA$(p, 1, q)$ models for $(p, q \leq 2)$ in Table 14.4, to substantiate our findings. The summary provides the estimates of the coefficients along with their standard deviations and the AICc for selecting a model. Based on the values of AICc and the residual checks, we find that ARIMA$(1, 1, 2)$, ARIMA$(2, 1, 0)$, ARIMA$(2, 1, 1)$ and ARIMA$(1, 1, 1)$, etc., are not acceptable. A random walk model with drift, i.e. ARIMA$(0, 1, 0)$ fitted well to the series TFR (India) and TFR (rural). On the other hand, ARIMA$(0, 1, 1)$ is found to fit best for the series TFR (urban). However, we restricted our choice to ARIMA$(0, 1, 0)$ model for all the series as adding more parameters does not change the forecasts much.

14.4.2 Forecast and Their Accuracy

We use the estimated random walk with drift model to forecast total fertility rates of India and its rural and urban regions for the period 2014–2020. Random walk forecasts produced by using Box and Jenkins (1976) forecasting procedure are provided in Fig. 14.6 along with the 95% prediction bands. It may be noted that uncertainty increases and interval widens as we move forward into the future. The bottom left plot showing the forecast of the TFR for the urban India reveals widest prediction band for the forecasts implying the approximation of the model over ARIMA$(0, 1, 1)$. Forecasts of TFR for 2014–2020 resulting from all the fitted models have been provided in Table 14.5 for comparison. We find that the point forecasts from all the models do not have much difference for practical purposes. Our findings suggest that with the present rate of fertility decline, rural India will reach the target of replacement level of fertility in 2019, eventually taking the entire country to reach this important target in another 2 to 3 years of time.

Table 14.4 Estimated time series models for TFR

Model description		Coefficients estimates (standard error)					AICc
		ar1	ar2	ma1	ma2	drift	
ARIMA(0,1,0) with drift	Total					−0.069	−89.46
						(0.012)	
	Rural					−0.069	−86.3
						(0.0125)	
	Urban					−0.0548	−49.37
						(0.0196)	
ARIMA(1,1,0) with drift	Total	−0.0724				−0.0691	−87.35
		(0.1557)				(0.0112)	
	Rural	0.081				−0.069	−84.25
		(0.1554)				(0.0135)	
	Urban	−0.377				−0.0568	−52.79
		(0.1511)				(0.0134)	
ARIMA(0,1,1) with drift	Total			−0.0836		−0.0691	−87.39
				(0.1626)		(0.011)	
	Rural			0.0967		−0.0689	−84.3
				(0.1693)		(0.0136)	
	Urban			−0.4413		−0.0555	−53.94
				(0.1539)		(0.0103)	
ARIMA(1,1,1) with drift	Total	0.7173		−1		−0.0677	−89.25
		(0.118)		(0.0615)		(0.0027)	
	Rural	−0.6936		0.9011		−0.0687	−84.4
		(0.1645)		(0.0934)		(0.0135)	
	Urban	0.506		−1		−0.0539	−53.31
		(0.1467)		(0.0884)		(0.0026)	
ARIMA(2,1,1) with drift	Total	−0.4915	−0.1967	0.4316		−0.0688	−83.38
		(0.3848)	(0.1727)	(0.3628)		(0.0101)	
	Rural	−0.7243	−0.0694	0.8896		−0.0687	−81.99
		(0.1796)	(0.1624)	(0.098)		(0.0126)	
	Urban	−0.0966	−0.1063	−0.3258		−0.0554	−48.99
		(1.5296)	(0.6903)	(1.5503)		(0.0105)	
ARIMA(0,1,2) with drift	Total			−0.0414	−0.1377	−0.0687	−85.31
				(0.1631)	(0.2153)	(0.0099)	
	Rural			0.0929	−0.3333	−0.0681	−82.7
				(0.1805)	(0.4692)	(0.0096)	
	Urban			−0.4298	−0.111	−0.0546	−51.64
				(0.1578)	(0.3245)	(0.009)	

(continued)

Table 14.4 (continued)

Model description		Coefficients estimates (standard error)					AICc
		ar1	ar2	ma1	ma2	drift	
ARIMA(1,1,2) with drift	Total	−0.3472		0.2996	−0.1391	−0.0688	−82.97
		(0.571)		(0.5592)	(0.1538)	(0.0103)	
	Rural	−0.6259		0.792	−0.0883	−0.0687	−81.98
		(0.2521)		(0.2938)	(0.2217)	(0.0126)	
	Urban	0.7011		−1.2304	0.2304	−−0.0543	−51.18
		(0.2596)		(0.3017)	(0.2913)	(0.0031)	

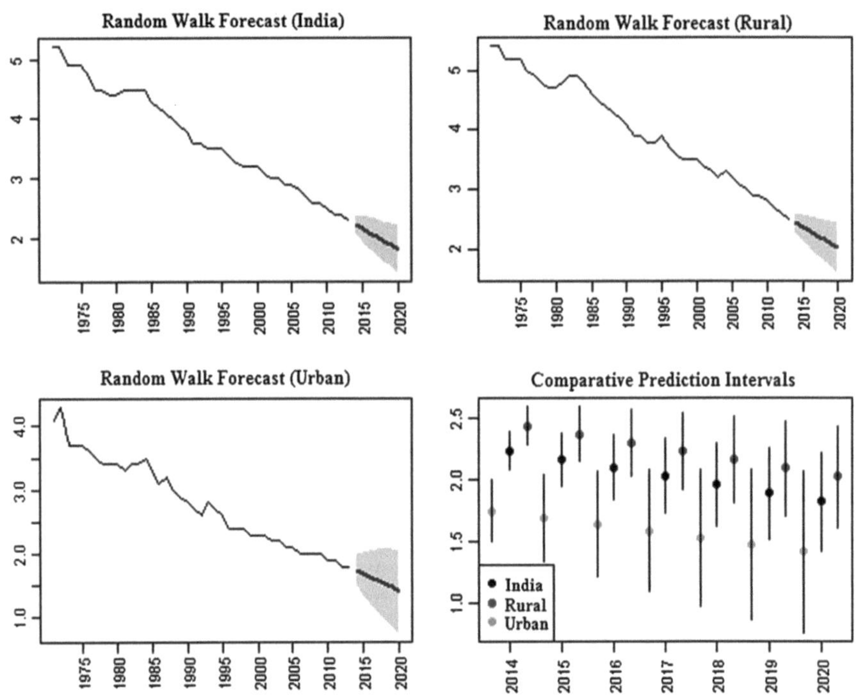

Fig. 14.6 TFR forecasts using random walk model with drift. *Bottom right panel* compares the region-wise forecasts of Indian fertility along with 95% P.I.s

14.5 Concluding Remarks

India is often noted as the first developing country to declare a policy to reduce fertility in 1952, at a time when it had an estimated TFR of about 5.9 children per woman by the United Nations Population Division. This figure was found to be not as high as in many other developing nations with an average of seven children per woman or more at that point of time. The country, which is home to 38% of the

Table 14.5 Comparative forecasts for TFR, 2014–2020

Year	Region	TFR forecast (India)						
		ARIMA						
		(0,1,0)	(1,1,0)	(0,1,1)	(1,1,1)	(2,1,1)	(0,1,2)	(1,1,2)
2014	India	2.23	2.23	2.23	2.23	2.22	2.22	2.23
	Rural	2.43	2.43	2.43	2.43	2.43	2.44	2.43
	Urban	1.75	1.72	1.72	1.68	1.73	1.72	1.69
2015	Total	2.16	2.16	2.16	2.16	2.16	2.16	2.16
	Rural	2.36	2.36	2.36	2.36	2.36	2.39	2.36
	Urban	1.69	1.67	1.67	1.60	1.67	1.66	1.61
2016	Total	2.09	2.09	2.09	2.09	2.09	2.09	2.09
	Rural	2.29	2.29	2.29	2.29	2.29	2.32	2.29
	Urban	1.64	1.61	1.61	1.53	1.62	1.61	1.54
2017	Total	2.02	2.03	2.03	2.02	2.02	2.02	2.02
	Rural	2.22	2.22	2.22	2.22	2.23	2.25	2.23
	Urban	1.58	1.56	1.56	1.46	1.56	1.55	1.48
2018	Total	1.95	1.96	1.96	1.95	1.95	1.95	1.95
	Rural	2.15	2.15	2.15	2.15	2.16	2.18	2.16
	Urban	1.53	1.50	1.50	1.40	1.50	1.50	1.42
2019	Total	1.89	1.89	1.89	1.88	1.89	1.89	1.89
	Rural	2.09	2.08	2.08	2.09	2.09	2.11	2.09
	Urban	1.47	1.44	1.45	1.35	1.45	1.45	1.36
2020	Total	1.82	1.82	1.82	1.81	1.82	1.82	1.82
	Rural	2.02	2.01	2.01	2.02	2.02	2.05	2.02
	Urban	1.42	1.39	1.39	1.29	1.39	1.39	1.30

world's seven billion population and is now in its third phase of demographic transition, although has taken effective measures to lower the birth rate in many of its states and its rural–urban parts, is yet to reach the population-stabilizing 're-placement level' of 2.1 children per woman.

The present article explores the role of rural–urban differentials in pace and timing of fertility decline in achieving this target of replacement. It has been observed that the national evolution pattern of the fertility process is dominated by the rural trend as India is essentially a nation with rural character. Urban places are generally defined as villages and towns consisting of 5000 or more people, many of such places lack adequate sanitation, safe drinking water and other basic amenities like roads and health services. Although the SRS figures suggest that urban India has already reached the target of replacement level of fertility as early as in 2004, the nation is yet to reach the target mainly due to a significant rural–urban gap in the pace and timing of fertility decline.

The article has explored that accelerated pace of fertility decline in urban India had started during 1971–1981 with the onset of fertility decline, but the same had been witnessed a decade later in the rural part of the nation. The change point analysis carried out here has clearly stated that urban India experienced critical change points much earlier to those of the rural and of the entire nation. Therefore, it is not denying that rural–urban differentials of pace and timing have certainly constrained the overall acceleration of fertility decline in India. However, the article has also underlined that in another couple of years, the nation will reach the replacement level and the rural India will witness it by 2020 assuming that the present rate of progress is continued.

Notwithstanding the facts stated above, this national fertility rate masks wide disparities by regions and states and much of the country's demographic future will depend on fertility trends of the northern and Empowered Action Group (EAG) States along with large populations have the highest levels of illiteracy and poverty. Bihar and Uttar Pradesh, the two states with highest TFRs had populations of 104 and 200 million, respectively in 2011. These two states along with the other EAG states Chhattisgarh, Jharkhand, Madhya Pradesh, Orissa, Rajasthan and Uttarakhand are all impoverished and are the focus of increased family planning efforts.

The size of India's future population will largely depend upon the course of fertility decline in the highly populous northern region and the rural part of the nation in general. While the country is clearly in the third phase of the demographic transition, how soon is it going to move to the fourth phase of replacement level of fertility? For the fourth phase to begin, fertility in the very large and poor states will have to decline to that of an industrialized country, around two or fewer children.

References

Arokiasamy, P., & Goli, S. (2012). Fertility convergence in the Indian states: An assessment of changes in averages and inequalities in fertility. *GENUS LXVII* (1), 65–88.

Bhat, P. N., Preston, S. H. T., & Dyson, T. (1984). *Vital rates in India, 1961–81. Committee on population and demography, Report No. 24*. Washington D.C.: National Academy Press.

Box, G. E. P., &Jenkins, G. M. (1976). *Time series analysis: Forecasting and control*. Holden-Day, Wiley Series in Probability and Statistics.

Chakrabarty, T. K. (2014). Forecasting rate of decline in infant mortality in South Asia using random walk approximation. *International Journal of Statistics in Medical Research, 3*(3), 282–290.

Dickey, D. A., & Fuller, W. A. (1979). Distribution of the estimators for autoregressive time series with a unit root. *Journal of the American Statistical Association, 74*(366), 427–431.

Haub, C., & Gribble, J. (2011). The world at 7 billion. *Population Bulletin 66*(2), Washington.

Hinkley, D., & Schechtman, E. (1987). Conditional bootstrap methods in the mean-shift model. *Biometrika, 74*(1), 85–93.

MacKinnon, J. G. (1991). Critical values for cointegration tests. In R. F. Engle, C. W. J. Granger (Eds.), *Long-run economic relationships: Reading in cointegration* (pp. 267–276). Oxford: Oxford University Press.

Office of the Registrar General and Census Commissioner, India. (2011). *Census of India, 2011, provisional population totals*. New Delhi: Ministry of Home Affairs, Government of India.

Rele, J. R. (1987). Fertility levels and trends in India, 1951–81. *Population and Development Review, 1393,* 513–530.

RGI (Registrar General of India). (2014). *Sample Registration System annual report 49, New Delhi*. Office of the Registrar General. http://censusindia.gov.in.

Taylor, W. (2000a). *Change-point analysis: A powerful new tool for detecting changes*. http://www.variation.com/cpa/tech/changepoint.html.

Taylor, W. (2000b). *Change-point analyzer 2.0 shareware program*. Illinois: Taylor Enterprises, Libertyville. http://www.variation.com/cpa.

Taylor, W. (2000c). A pattern test for distinguishing between autoregressive and mean-shift data. Submitted to *Journal of Quality Technologies*.

United Nations. (2011). *The Millennium development goals report 2011*. New York: The United Nations.

United Nations. Department of Economic and Social Affairs, Population Division. (2015). World Population Prospects: 2015 Revision, DVD Edition.

World Bank. (2011). *World development indicators 2011*, Washington, D.C., USA.

Chapter 15
Prevalence of Child Undernutrition in India: Estimating Extent of Deficits Using Distributions of Nutritional Outcomes

Tapan Kumar Chakrabarty

15.1 Introduction

Child undernutrition is recognized as an important public health indicator of a nation for its role in the development of future human resources. It has been increasingly recognized that undernutrition during childhood and adolescence may have severe consequences into adulthood, in terms of health and mortality and in terms of impeded cognitive development, involving reduced capacity of schooling and economic productivity (Schroeder and Brown 1994; Glewwe and Miguel 2007; Tarozzi 2008). Child nutritional status was measured by a large number of studies in the past few decades in developing countries since the introduction of 1978 WHO/NCHS (National Centre for Health Statistics) reference growth charts (WHO 1978) which was constructed using data on weight and height from a representative sample of children in the United States.

The appropriateness and use of this reference chart were being debated for children in developing countries, in particular, raising the concerns about the feeding practices related growth trajectories.

In order to assess nutritional status, progress of physical growth and well-being of children and adolescents, the use of growth standards and/or growth references is recommended (Wang and Chen 2012; WHO 1995; Dibley et al. 1987). When all the children have the ability to achieve the level of an optimal value, a growth standard is used while a growth reference is the distribution used for comparison (WHO 2006). Percentiles and *Z*-score transformations of anthropometric indicators are widely used to assess growth path and nutritional status of children. In 2006, WHO Multicentre Growth Reference Study (MGRS) has released new growth references for preschool age children having collected primary growth data and other salient information from approximately 8500 children from widely different

T.K. Chakrabarty (✉)
Department of Statistics, North-Eastern Hill University, Shillong, Meghalaya 793022, India
e-mail: tapankumarchakrabarty@gmail.com

U.K. De et al. (eds.), *Issues on Health and Healthcare in India*, India Studies in Business and Economics, https://doi.org/10.1007/978-981-10-6104-2_15

ethnic backgrounds and cultural settings (Brazil, Ghana, India, Norway, Oman, and the USA). The new growth curves are supposed to provide a single international standard that should represent the best description of physiological growth for all children from birth to 5 years of age and also to set up the normative model for growth and development for the breastfed infants.

The National Family Health Surveys (IIPS and Macro International 2007) in India has used this new international reference population (WHO 2006) to provide the estimates of stunting, underweight, and wasting prevalence.

For population-based nutritional assessments, the *Z*-score is widely recognized and recommended as the best system of analysis and presentation of anthropometric data for several reasons. First, *Z*-scores are calculated by standardizing the observed values with both the mean and the standard deviation of the reference distribution. Second, as standardized measures, *Z*-scores are comparable across the age and sex groups. Third, in nutrition surveys, subgroup level mean *Z*-scores and SD can be presented. In addition, *Z*-score values can quantify the growth status of children at both the extremes of the distribution (WHO 1994, 1995).

The present article formulates an alternative quantification of the prevalence of undernutrition in a population using the anthropometric *Z*-score measurements available from National Family Health Survey (IIPS and Macro International 2007). The paper is organized as follows. Section 15.2 describes the various anthropometric *Z*-scores, how are these computed, and WHO classification scheme for prevalence of malnutrition. Section 15.3 discusses certain methodological issues related to these classification schemes. We have carried out exploratory analysis of sample *Z*-scores in Sect. 15.4 for selected Indian states, where an attempt is made to show that the anthropometric data are substantially non-normal. Section 15.5 builds up a probability model for the *Z*-scores based on the empirical findings and finally, in Sect. 15.6, a model-based measure of nutritional deficit is obtained and empirical illustrations are provided.

15.2 Anthropometric *Z*-scores and WHO Classification Scheme

Basic information for nutritional assessment in children constitutes measurements of age, weight, and height along with the information on sex of the children. Survey data often contain measures of height, weight, sex, and age, particularly for the children. Malnutrition in children is affected by many intervening factors other than nutrient intake, in particular, genetic variation besides age and sex. It is possible to use physical measurements to assess the adequacy of diet and growth in infants and children by comparing indicators with the distribution of the same indicator for a “healthy” reference group and identifying “extreme” or “abnormal” departures from this distribution.

The three most widely used indicators of child nutritional status are weight for age (W/A), height for age (H/A), and weight for height (W/H) as mentioned above. In nutritional assessment research, it is a common practice to use the Z-scores as defined below.

Let g represent the group which a child under comparison belongs to, and let x_{ig} denote height/weight of a given child i in a group g. The group is specified by age and gender, when the indicator measures height. When the indicator measures weight, the reference group is identified by gender and either height (in the case of weight for height) or age (in the case of weight for age). In order to assess the nutritional status of a child, child's outcome is compared to the corresponding "normal/standard/ reference" outcome for a child belonging to the same group.

Definition 1 (*WHO/NCHS 1978*)

$$Z_{ig} = \frac{x_{ig} - \bar{x}_g}{s_g},$$

where $\bar{x}_g$ and s_g, respectively, denote the mean/median and the standard deviation of the corresponding indicator for children within the same group in the reference population. Under the assumption that the corresponding nutritional indicator in the reference population is approximately normally distributed, one can easily interpret the Z-scores. For example, if a child's height for age Z-score lies below −1.645 then his height is below that of 95% of the children in the reference population with the same age and same sex. A child is classified as stunted if her/his height for age Z-score is below −2, and severely stunted if the score is below −3. Similarly, a child is identified as underweight or wasted if the weight for age or weight for height Z-scores, respectively, are below −2. In India, Z-scores of the anthropometric indicators were calculated for the first two national family of health surveys using the WHO/NCHS 1978 charts (IIPS and ORC Macro 2002). We shall abbreviate as HAZ, WAZ, and WHZ, the three Z-scores corresponding to H/A, W/A, and W/H, respectively.

The concerns on the use and appropriateness of this WHO/NCHS 1978 reference chart were raised for children in developing countries, particularly in the context of feeding practices related growth path. Growing concerns over the use of this reference has led to the appearance of a new reference for the international comparisons (Waterlow et al. 1977; WHO Working Group 1986; WHO 2006). The new reference charts have been developed using an LMS model (Cole 1988; Cole and Green 1992) that appropriately adjusts the skewness and non-normality in the height and weight distributions in the reference population. Using this approach, for a given anthropometric measure x_{ig}, the Z-score is calculated by using the statistics like mean and standard deviation of the quantities obtained after applying Box–Cox transformation to the corresponding measures in the reference group. Thus, the Z-score is calculated for child i compared to a reference group g as follows:

Definition 2 (*WHO* 2006)

$$Z_{ig} = \frac{\left(x_{ig}/M_g\right)^{L_g} - 1}{L_g S_g},$$

where the power of the Box–Cox transformation is denoted by L_g, and M_g and S_g are the mean and the standard deviation, respectively, of the Box–Cox transformed variable in the reference population. In order to calculate the above expression, the values of the parameters L_g, M_g, and S_g are provided in this new chart. Such parameters are gender-height specific for the construction of weight-for-height scores, and gender-age specific for the height-for-age and weight-for-age Z-scores.

It is common to use a cutoff value of −2, that is, two standard deviations below the reference mean/median, to define abnormal anthropometry whatever be the specific indicator we use. For example, a child who's WAZ score is less than −2 is considered being underweight. Based on this principle, WHO (WHO 1995) has proposed a classification scheme to define prevalence of population-level malnutrition which is reproduced in Table 15.1.

15.3 Methodological Issues

At the most basic level, the anthropometric data analysis aims at quantifying the degree and level of undernourishment in a population or subpopulation. This is achieved by inspecting the distribution of the Z-scores of the indicator of interest in the population under study. A comparison of this distribution with the distribution of Z-scores in the reference population provides an idea of levels and dimensions of undernourishment in the population. However, it may be noted that a commonly used cutoff value of −2SD (i.e., two standard deviation below the reference median), to estimate the degree of prevalence of malnutrition in a particular subgroup, does not account for the distributional aspects of the Z-scores which may possibly differ markedly from those of the reference population. In fact, the measure "percentage of children below −2 Z-scores", reveals only a portion of the actual nutritional deficit that exists in a group or subgroup under question as it is explained in Fig. 15.1.

Thus, such a method suffers from a number of limitations. (i) Using a cutoff value of −2SD, about 2.3% of "healthy" children would be classified as having a

Table 15.1 WHO classification scheme for degree of population malnutrition

Prevalence of malnutrition (% of children <60 months, below −2 Z-scores)		
Degree of malnutrition	Weight for age/height for age	Weight for height
Low	<10	<5
Medium	10–19	5–9
High	20–29	10–14
Very high	≥ 30	≥ 15

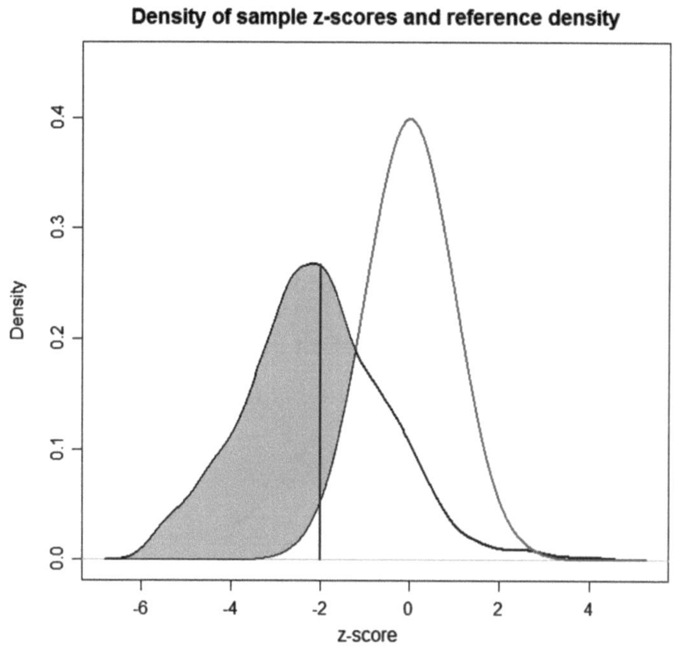

Fig. 15.1 Nutritional deficit: the shaded area under the kernel density estimate of the sample *Z*-scores (*black solid line*) not covered by the reference standard normal density (*red solid line*) (Color figure online)

particular deficit with respect to a given indicator. (ii) Two subgroups, having unimodal *Z*-score distributions with same degree of prevalence as per the Table 15.1 of Sect. 15.2, can have different levels of actual deficits (see Fig. 15.2). It is because of the fact that two distributions with same mean and same standard deviation can have different amount of skewness and thus can result in different values of nutritional deficits. (iii) Distributions characterized by heavy or thin tails may lead to different values of deficit when other features, e.g., mean, standard deviation, or skewness remain the same.

Consider a situation, in which the empirical distribution of the WAZ score has a probability density function (pdf) as plotted in Fig. 15.1. The empirical distribution has mean = −1.02, standard deviation = 1.21, and skewness = 0.03.

The reference population which is standard normal is plotted alongside this density. One can clearly visualize the nutritional deficit by way of WAZ score as prescribed by the World Bank Institute (O'Donnell et al. 2008; Chakrabarty 2011). An obvious way of estimating this deficit would be to estimate the shaded area between the two density curves. To calculate this, one requires a parametric form of distribution that approximately fits the sampled WAZ scores. Alternatively, one can obtain this estimate using appropriate nonparametric importance resampling procedure.

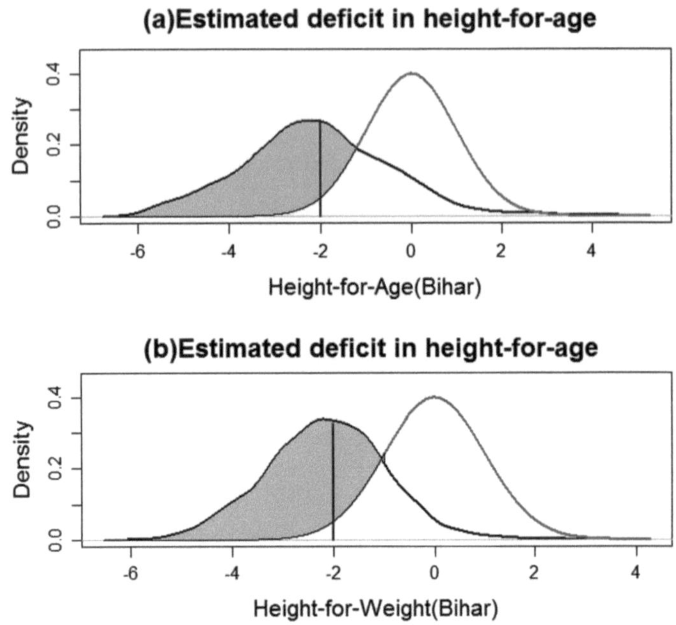

Fig. 15.2 Depicts actual deficits differ markedly even when % below −2SD Z-score remain same. **a** Estimated actual deficit is about 60.7% as against 55.6% below −2SD. **b** Estimated actual deficit is about 67.8% as against 55.9% below −2SD (Color figure online)

As we shall see in the following sections of this article, for most of the practical purposes, anthropometric Z-scores follow a skew normal distribution. As a result of which the estimates of nutritional deficits and the degree of undernourishment can be found with greater accuracy, if one uses this distribution.

15.4 Exploratory Analysis of Anthropometric Z-scores

We have calculated (Table 15.2) univariate descriptive and robust statistics in order to explore features of the empirical distribution of the Z-scores. The data on three anthropometric indices, height for age, weight for age, and weight for height were used for selected states of India (NFHS-3, 2005–06). First, three columns of each of these tables provide mean, 5% trimmed mean, and median of the empirical distribution of each of the Z-scores. Near equality of these values for a given score would mean a symmetric distribution and otherwise with a skewness. In most of the states, all the three scores display a higher value of mean than either the trimmed mean or median. It may be that the outliers or extreme values are responsible to pull it upwards. The skewness and kurtosis statistics also provide evidence of disproportionate values at the upper tails of the respective distributions. In few cases, such

Table 15.2 Descriptive and robust statistics for Z-scores

State	Mean	5% trimmed mean	Median	SD	Skewness	Kurtosis	% below −2SD	Number of children
HAZ								
Punjab	−1.49	−1.51	−1.47	1.55	0.181	0.24	36.7	1133
Uttar Pradesh	−2.18	−2.23	−2.26	1.68	0.46	0.68	56.8	5597
Bihar	−2.15	−2.18	−2.22	1.58	0.33	0.40	55.6	2,172
Mizoram	−1.56	−1.63	−1.71	1.63	0.73	1.37	39.8	732
Meghalaya	−2.05	−2.12	−2.24	1.84	0.67	1.00	55.1	739
Goa	−1.12	−1.12	−1.15	1.53	0.076	0.374	25.6	770
Kerala	−1.1	−1.14	−1.28	1.42	0.52	1.36	24.5	896
WAZ								
Punjab	−1.21	−1.20	−1.17	1.22	−0.06	0.15	24.9	1133
Uttar Pradesh	−1.83	−1.83	−1.80	1.19	−0.01	0.27	42.4	5597
Bihar	−2.20	−2.20	−2.20	1.16	0.04	0.16	55.9	2172
Mizoram	−1.08	−1.09	−1.05	1.17	0.14	0.78	19.9	732
Meghalaya	−2.05	−2.06	−1.97	1.44	0.11	−0.095	48.8	739
Goa	−1.11	−1.14	−1.18	1.29	0.32	0.27	25.0	770
Kerala	−1.22	−1.24	−1.23	1.08	0.21	0.35	22.9	896
WHZ								
Punjab	−0.51	−0.5	−0.51	1.13	−0.06	0.72	9.2	1133
Uttar Pradesh	−0.58	−0.55	−0.47	1.31	−0.34	0.88	14.8	5597
Bihar	−1.38	−1.36	−1.33	1.15	−0.18	0.48	27.1	2172
Mizoram	−0.28	−0.28	−0.27	1.37	0.00	1.4	9.0	732
Meghalaya	−1.24	−1.25	−0.97	1.83	−0.146	−0.35	30.7	739
Goa	−0.71	−0.74	−0.81	1.43	0.42	1.03	14.1	770
Kerala	−0.88	−0.88	−0.86	1.23	0.096	0.16	15.9	896

Source Author's own calculation

as, for Meghalaya and Uttar Pradesh, the WAZ and WHZ scores give evidence of a negative skewness. The so-called descriptive statistics are followed by a skewness–kurtosis plot that helped to select which distribution(s) to fit among the potential candidates. Figure 15.3 provides a skewness–kurtosis plot (Cullen and Frey 1999), in which values for common distributions are displayed so as to help the choice of suitable distributions. To take into account the sampling variability of the estimated values of kurtosis and skewness, the data set was bootstrapped 5000 times. The values of skewness and kurtosis are computed for each of the bootstrap samples and are reported in blue color on the skewness–kurtosis plot.

The literature on tests of normality and their statistical properties (Lilliefors 1967; Shapiro and Wilk 1965; Jarque and Bera 1980; D'Agostino and Stephens 1986) is very substantive. The omnibus test for normality that is most popular is the Shapiro–Wilk (SW). The Jarque–Bera (JB) test for normality is widely applied in economics, econometrics, and many other related fields. The omnibus test of normality based on empirical distribution function is the Lilliefors (Kolmogorov–Smirnov) (L(KS)) test. Being omnibus procedures, SW, JB, L(KS), and many others do not provide insight about the nature of deviations from normality, e.g., skewness, heavy tails or outliers. Therefore, specialized tests directed at particular alternatives are desired in many practical situations. In this article, tests of normality (Table 15.3) were carried out using various omnibus test procedures whenever possible. These omnibus tests are accompanied by various tests (Table 15.4 and 15.5) of symmetry and directed tests of normality against heavy-tailed alternatives and outliers (Gel et al. 2006).

Each of these tests is also followed by four goodness-of-fit plots (Fig. 15.3 lower panel). All of the results are not reproduced here to save the space. The tests of normality overlay a normal curve on actual data, to assess the fit. A significant test means the fit is poor. In majority of the cases, our analyses show that normality is an untenable assumption or it is reasonably poor. Results shown in Table 15.5 suggest that although the symmetry in many of the cases is evident, the empirical distributions are characterized by heavier tails or outliers and are substantially non-normal.

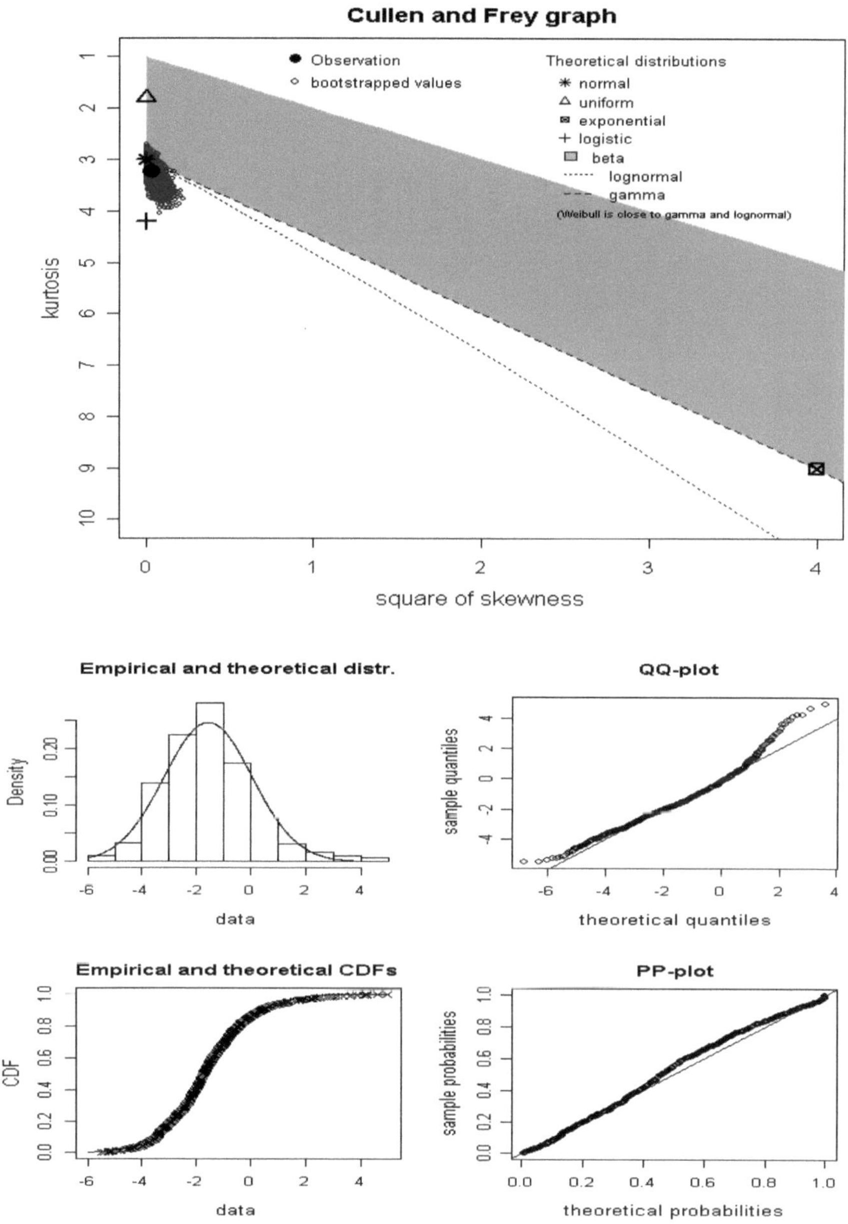

Fig. 15.3 Cullen and Frey plot (*upper panel*). Goodness-of-fit plots (*lower panel*)

Table 15.3 Omnibus tests of normality for height for age *Z*-scores

State	Shapiro–Wilk (*p*-value)	Anderson–Darling (*p*-value)	Cramer–von Mises (*p*-value)	Lilliefors (K-S) (*p*-value)	Pearson chi-square (*p*-value)	Classical Jarque–Bera (*p*-value)
Punjab	0.996 (0.007)	0.762 (0.048)	0.108 (0.087)	0.024 (0.131)	30.71 (0.481)	8.88 (0.012)
Uttar Pradesh	NA	9.234 (0.000)	1.410 (0.000)	0.031 (0.000)	217.43 (0.000)	283.0 (0.000)
Bihar	0.992 (0.000)	1.864 (0.000)	0.310 (0.000)	0.032 (0.000)	53.21 (0.064)	44.59 (0.000)
Mizoram	0.969 (0.000)	4.786 (0.000)	0.756 (0.000)	0.062 (0.000)	47.2 (0.007)	122.78 (0.000)
Meghalaya	0.975 (0.000)	3.236 (0.000)	0.581 (0.000)	0.066 (0.000)	39.70 (0.023)	77.4 (0.000)
Goa	0.993 (0.002)	1.434 (0.001)	0.234 (0.002)	0.040 (0.004)	32.34 (0.182)	15.26 (0.000)
Kerala	0.977 (0.000)	5.639 (0.000)	0.953 (0.000)	0.058 (0.000)	73.30 (0.000)	108.84 (0.000)

Source Author's own calculation

Table 15.4 Tests of symmetry for height for age Z-scores

State	MGG (*p*-value)	Mira (*p*-value)	Cabilio–Masaro (*p*-value)	D'Agostino (*p*-value)
Punjab	0.625 (0.532)	0.627 (0.531)	0.616 (0.538)	1.624 (0.104)
Uttar Pradesh	5.04 (0.000)	5.05 (0.000)	4.92 (0.000)	8.583 (0.000)
Bihar	1.385 (0.166)	1.383 (0.157)	1.357 (0.175)	3.619 (0.000)
Mizoram	3.683 (0.000)	3.574 (0.000)	3.449 (0.000)	4.879 (0.000)
Meghalaya	3.659 (0.000)	3.719 (0.000)	3.482 (0.000)	4.173 (0.000)
Goa	0.992 (0.32)	0.961 (0.337)	0.954 (0.339)	0.519 (0.604)
Kerala	5.119 (0.000)	4.814 (0.000)	4.841 (0.000)	3.995 (.000)

Source Author's own calculation

Table 15.5 Robust directed tests of normality against heavy-tailed alternatives for height for age *Z*-scores

State	Bonett–Seier (*p*-value)	SJ Test (*p*-value)	Robust Jarque–Bera (*p*-value)	Anscombe–Glynn (*p*-value)
Punjab	1.695 (0.09)	1.77 (0.047)	9.76 (0.007)	1.618 (0.106)
Uttar Pradesh	5.967 (0.000)	6.398 (0.000)	299.2 (0.000)	7.549 (0.000)
Bihar	3.33 (0.000)	3.473 (0.000)	50.02 (0.000)	3.157 (0.001)
Mizoram	6.028 (0.000)	6.892 (0.000)	178.02 (0.000)	4.88 (0.000)
Meghalaya	4.18 (0.000)	4.904 (0.000)	100.99 (0.000)	3.952 (0.023)
Goa	3.948 (0.000)	4.124 (0.000)	20.52 (0.000)	3.08 (0.002)
Kerala	5.418 (0.000)	6.447 (0.000)	138.98 (0.000)	5.314 (0.000)

Source Author's own calculation

15.5 Modeling *Z*-scores with Skew Normal Distribution

To model a skewed distribution having unimodal density function, we consider the skew normal distribution, proposed by Azzalini (1985). This distribution generalizes the standard normal distribution and the probability density function (pdf) is given by

$$f(z;\lambda) = 2\phi(z)\Phi(\lambda z), \quad -\infty < z < \infty, \tag{15.5.1}$$

where $\phi(x)$ and $\Phi(x)$ denote the $N(0,1)$ density and distribution function, respectively, and we write $Z \sim \mathrm{SN}(\lambda)$. The skewness is being regulated by the parameter λ and $\lambda = 0$ corresponds to the standard normal case. The distribution with pdf given by (15.5.1) has a number of properties akin to those of the normal distribution, for example, if X has the pdf, given by (15.5.1), then X^2 follows a chi-square distribution with one degree of freedom. Hence, all even moments of X and of standard normal distribution are exactly the same. For several other information, see Azzalini and Capitanio (1999) and Genton (2004). Arnold et al. (1993) have exhibited an elegant account of the skew normal distribution. In applications such as hidden function and/or selective reporting model, this distribution can arise very naturally as pointed out by Arnold and Beaver (2002).

A more flexible and suitable class of distributions (Pourahmadi 2007) incorporating the skewness factor, is a location and scale extension of the family defined in (15.5.1). Let us denote the location and scale parameters by ξ and ω, respectively, then for any $Z \sim \mathrm{SN}(\lambda)$, define a general SN random variable by

$$Y = \xi + \omega Z, \tag{15.5.2}$$

and write, $Y \sim$ SN(ξ, ω, λ) for this random variable. The pdf of Y can be shown as

$$f(y; \xi, \omega, \lambda) = \frac{2}{\omega}\phi\left(\frac{y-\xi}{\omega}\right)\Phi\left(\lambda\frac{y-\xi}{\omega}\right) \tag{15.5.3}$$

and the moment generating function of Y is given by

$$M_Y(t) = E\left(e^{tY}\right) = 2\exp\left(\xi t + \frac{\omega^2 t^2}{2}\right)\Phi(\delta\omega t), \tag{15.5.4}$$

where $\delta = \lambda/\sqrt{1+\lambda^2} \in (-1, 1)$. From (5.4), it follows that:

$$E(Y) = \xi + \omega\mu_z,\ \text{var}(Y) = \omega^2\left(1 - \mu_z^2\right)\ \gamma_1 = \frac{4-\pi}{2}\frac{\mu_z^3}{\left(1-\mu_z^2\right)^{3/2}},$$

and $\gamma_2 = 2(\pi - 3)\frac{\mu_z^4}{\left(1-\mu_z^2\right)^2}$, where $\mu_z = \delta\sqrt{2/\pi}$, γ_1 and γ_2 denote the standardized third- and fourth-order cumulants, respectively.

We have carried out the fitting of SN(ξ, ω, λ) using the software library 'sn' version 0.4–17 (Azzalini 2011). The function 'sn.em' is used for this purpose which is based on EM algorithm to locate the maximum likelihood estimates. The estimates obtained using this function are very robust, although it generally takes a longer computation time. Table 15.6 gives the maximum likelihood estimates of the parameters, the estimates of mean, standard deviation, and skewness. We also provide two values of log-likelihood at convergence; the first one corresponds to the default setting in which a global maximization is performed, and the second corresponds to the setting in which the shape parameter is fixed at 0. The maximum of the two leads to the choice of a SN distribution over a normal model.

15.6 Measurement and Estimation of Nutritional Deficit

We assume that the probability distribution of an anthropometric Z-score follows a location-scale skew normal distribution, i.e., $Y \sim$ SN(ξ, ω, λ) with pdf given by (15.5.2). The advantage of such an assumption is not only their close fit to the sampled data on Z-scores, but also that the reference population, with which it is usually compared to measure the degree of prevalence of malnutrition, belongs to the same family and thus facilitates the comparison.

In order to define a measure of deficit, let us consider the Fig. 15.1. Let τ be the cutoff point defined as the following

Table 15.6 Skew normal goodness-of-fit statistics for Z-scores

State	Parameter estimates			Estimates of			Log-likelihood	
	Location	Scale	Shape	Mean	SD	Skewness	SN	Normal
HAZ								
Punjab	−2.60	1.90	1.07	−1.49	1.55	0.16	−2099.4	−2102.1
Uttar Pradesh	−3.72	2.36	1.72	−2.09	1.71	0.37	−10223.4	−10297.8
Bihar	−3.43	2.09	1.37	−2.09	1.60	0.26	−3769.6	−3782.6
Mizoram	−3.23	2.32	2.10	−1.56	1.61	0.48	−1382.5	−1405.5
Meghalaya	−3.92	2.60	2.10	−2.04	1.81	0.48	−1306.8	−1324.4
Goa	−1.99	1.75	0.80	−1.12	1.52	0.08	−1416.5	−1417.1
Kerala	−2.43	1.94	1.70	−1.09	1.41	0.36	−1569.7	−1585.4
WAZ								
State	Parameter estimates			Estimates of			Log-likelihood	
	Location	Scale	Shape	Mean	SD	Skewness	SN	Normal
Punjab	−0.53	1.39	−0.77	−1.21	1.21	−0.07	−1827.22	−1827.74
Uttar Pradesh	−2.30	1.34	0.62	−1.73	1.22	0.04	−8509.84	−8510.99
Bihar	−2.84	1.37	0.81	−2.15	1.18	0.08	−3177.65	−3179.26
Mizoram	−1.87	1.40	0.96	−1.09	1.17	0.13	−1162.29	−1163.66
Meghalaya	−2.70	1.59	0.64	−2.02	1.43	0.05	−1168.71	−1168.71
Goa	−2.28	1.73	1.50	−1.14	1.29	0.30	−1286.51	−1292.83
Kerala	−2.04	1.35	1.18	−1.22	1.08	0.19	−1333.375	−1336.60
WHZ								
State	Parameter estimates			Estimates of			Log-likelihood	
	Location	Scale	Shape	Mean	SD	Skewness	SN	Normal
Punjab	0.12	1.30	−0.77	−0.51	1.13	−0.07	−1748.87	−1749.54
Uttar Pradesh	0.17	1.56	−1.10	−0.75	1.26	−0.17	−8669.44	−8686.59
Bihar	−0.62	1.37	−0.92	−1.36	1.16	−0.11	−3127.21	−3129.65
Mizoram	0.45	1.55	−0.74	−0.29	1.36	−0.07	−1275.26	−1275.61
Meghalaya	0.52	2.51	−1.64	−1.19	1.84	−0.35	−1326.90	−1330.42
Goa	−1.99	1.90	1.51	−0.73	1.42	0.30	−1357.14	−1366.93
Kerala	−1.59	1.42	0.82	−0.88	1.22	0.09	−1452.04	−1452.91

Source Author's own calculation

Table 15.7 Estimated nutritional deficit of various Z-scores and percentage below −2SD by selected states of India, 2005–06

State	HAZ		WAZ		WHZ	
	% of $\widehat{\nabla}$	% below −2SD (NFHS 3, 2005–06)	% of $\widehat{\nabla}$	% below −2SD (NFHS 3, 2005–06)	% of $\widehat{\nabla}$	% below −2SD (NFHS 3, 2005–06)
Punjab	47.5[a]	36.7	44.1[a]	24.9	14.2	9.2
Uttar Pradesh	60.2	56.8	56.8[a]	42.4	22.1	14.8
Bihar	60.7	55.6	67.8[a]	55.9	47.0[a]	27.1
Mizoram	50.8[a]	39.8	38.3[a]	19.9	11.4	9.0
Meghalaya	58.9	55.1	60.5[a]	48.8	35.9	30.7
Goa	37.5[a]	25.6	40.3[a]	25.0	27.4[a]	14.1
Kerala	38.9[a]	24.5	36.9[a]	22.9	29.9[a]	15.9

Source Author's own calculation
Note [a]Indicates more than 10% of shortfall

$$\tau = \min\left\{ y \middle| \frac{2}{\omega}\phi\left(\frac{y-\xi}{\omega}\right)\Phi\left(\lambda\frac{y-\xi}{\omega}\right) = \phi(y) \gg 0 \right\} \tag{15.6.1}$$

i.e., τ is the smallest value of the random variable Y at which the two curves intersect with a value of probability density greater than zero. Based on the value of τ, we can define a measure of deficit (Chakrabarty 2013) as

$$\nabla_{\text{def}}(\tau) = \int_{-\infty}^{\tau} f(y;\xi,\omega,\lambda)\mathrm{d}y - \int_{-\infty}^{\tau} \phi(t)\mathrm{d}t. \tag{15.6.2}$$

Clearly, $\nabla_{\text{def}}(\tau)$ measures the area of shortfall which lies below the ideal nutritional level. Let $\widehat{f} = f\left(y;\widehat{\xi},\widehat{\omega},\widehat{\lambda}\right)$ be the fitted distribution of the Z-score under consideration. Then, an estimate $\widehat{\nabla}_{\text{def}}(\tau)$ is obtained by using Eqs. (15.6.1) and (15.6.2). Table 15.7 provides the estimates of nutritional deficits in selected Indian states using the method described above.

The results obtained in Table 15.7 are indicative of the fact that there exist comprehensive gaps between the perceived level of undernutrition and the extent of actual nutritional deficit. The weight for age indicator, the only anthropometric index selected to assess progress towards Millennium Development Goals (United Nations 2011) of halving under-five undernutrition by 2015, is the worst victim. Noticeably, the progressive states like Kerala, Goa, Punjab accounts for 15–20% of shortfall with respect to height for age and weight for age, a result that could have been unidentified otherwise. Figure 15.4 depicts the estimated shortfall as observed in percentage covered by −2SD cutoff of estimated actual deficit. Noticeable extents

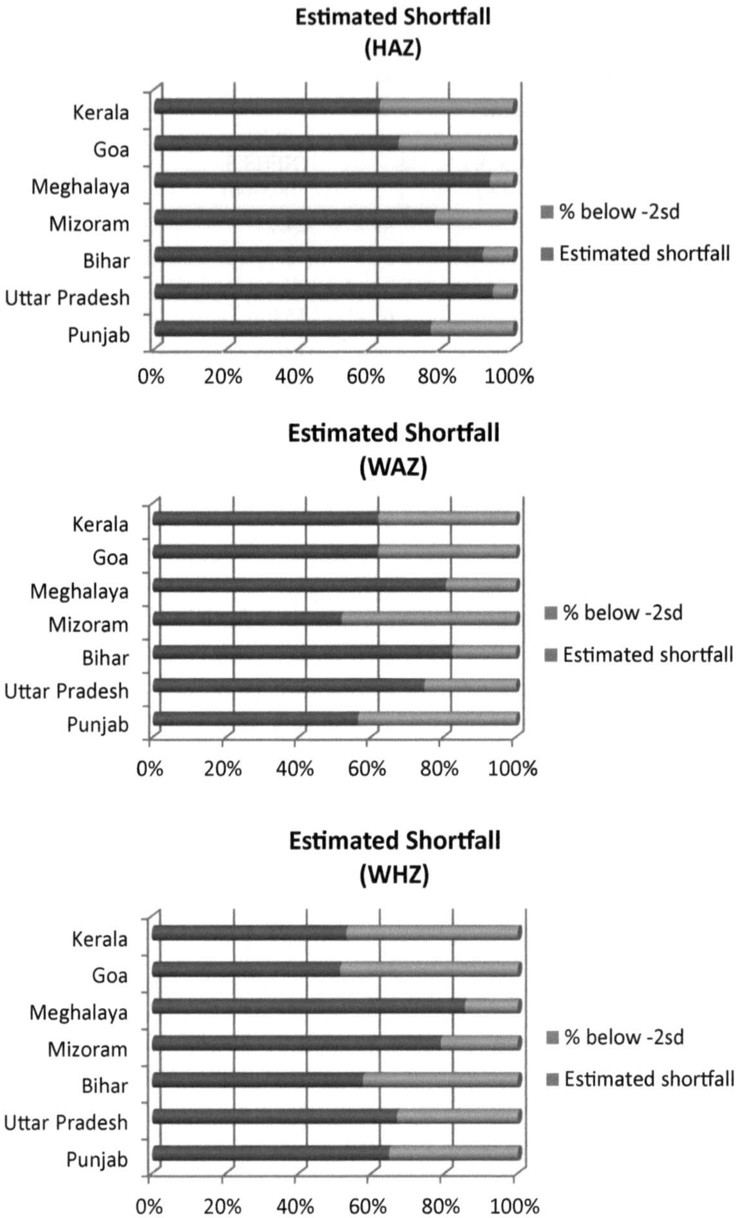

Fig. 15.4 Depicts percentage covered by −2SD cutoff of estimated actual deficit for various nutritional indicators

of shortfalls are seen with respect to weight for age and weight for height indices. Results are far below satisfactory in terms of the extent of coverage and, it reconfirms the observation of the report (NFHS-3, 2005–06) that a very slow pace of children's nutritional transition implying that undernutrition is an even more serious problem today than it was a decade ago.

15.7 Discussion and Concluding Remarks

The use of anthropometric indicators is the key to the measurement of nutritional status of children. While using the anthropometric Z-scores, lack of consensus on the cutoff points for prevalence estimates raises concerns on the use of such methods in population surveys. J. O. Mora (Mora 1989) proposed a simple method for estimating a standardized prevalence of child malnutrition from anthropometric indicators based on comparing the distribution of the indicator with that of the normalized NCHS reference population. It was assumed that both the underlying distributions are normal.

The present article finds that the probability distribution of sample Z-scores in the Indian context is substantially skewed and assumption of normality is frequently untenable. In the present work, we have moved another step forward from the Mora's method by introducing a location-scale family of skew normal distribution which includes normal distribution as a member of this class. In this sense, the method proposed here can be seen as a generalization of Mora's method and can suitably be applied to study undernutrition in the developing countries. We have applied the proposed method to the selected Indian states covering all the six regions accounting for the two extreme scenario of malnutrition. The results of our analysis suggest that in most of the cases, degree of prevalence as measured by the percentage of children below −2SD of reference population do not substantially differ with the values given in NFHS 3 report (IIPS and Macro International 2007), however, there are shortfalls of more than 10% as against their actual deficits. The shortfalls are found to be around 5% for the remaining. An interesting finding of the present study is that the states, in which the problem of undernutrition is less severe, are observed with relatively higher degrees of shortfall (10% or more). These findings are clearly indicative of the fact that there exist comprehensive gaps in the perceived level of malnutrition for Indian states. The task of combating the problem of nutrition with various intervention policy measures should necessarily be formulated by accounting for such gaps.

In conclusion, we observe that distributional lessons help visualizing the nutritional status at different extremes/tails in a quantifiable manner. While analyzing health inequality among children under age five, we should also examine the proximate and distant determinants of malnutrition and how do they vary over the entire support of the distribution. Policy intervention strategies should address the determinants depending on in which part of the distribution the children are located.

References

Arnold, B. C., & Beaver, R. J. (2002). Skewed multivariate models related to hidden truncation and/or selective reporting. *Test, 11,* 7–54.

Arnold, B. C., Beaver, R. J., Groeneveld, R. A., & Meeker, W. Q. (1993). The nontruncated marginal of a truncated bivariate normal distribution. *Psychometrika, 58,* 471–488.

Azzalini, A. (1985). A class of distributions which includes the normal ones. *Scandinavian Journal of Statistics, 12,* 171–178.

Azzalini, A., & Capitanio, A. (1999). Statistical applications of the multivariate skew-normal distribution. *Journal of the Royal Statistical Society: Series B, 61,* 579–602.

Azzalini, A. (2011). The skew normal and skew t distributions, package 'sn' for R. URL http://azzalini.stat.unipd.it/SN.

Chakrabarty, T. K. (2011). Under-nutrition among children in India: Evidences of gender inequality from North-East India. In De, U. K., & Ghosh, B. N. (Eds.), *Gender deprivation and empowerment of women*. Germany: Lambert Academic Publishing GmbH & Co.

Chakrabarty, T. K. (2013). Efficient estimation of tail probability for anthropometric Z-scores using parametric bootstrap: Measuring undernutrition prevalence among children under age five from North East India. *Assam Statistical Review, 27*(2), 96–115.

Cole, T. J. (1988). Fitting smoothed centile curves to reference data. *Journal of the Royal Statistical Society Series A., 151,* 385–418.

Cole, T. J., & Green, P. J. (1992). Smoothing reference centile curves: The LMS method and penalized likelihood. *Statistics in Medicine, 11,* 1305–1319.

Cullen, A. C., & Frey, H. C. (1999) *Probabilistic techniques in exposure assessment* (pp. 81–159). USA: Plenum Press. Evans, M., Hastings, N., & Peacock, B. (2000). *Statistical distributions*. New Jersey: Wiley.

D'Agostino, R., & Stephens, M. (1986). *Goodness-of-fit Techniques*. NewYork: Marcel Dekker.

Dibley, M. J., Goldsby, J. B., Staehling, N. W., & Trowbridge, F. L. (1987). Development of normalized curves for the international growth reference: Historical and technical considerations. *American Journal of Clinical Nutrition, 46,* 736–748.

Gel, Yulia R., Weiwen, Miao, & Gastwirth, Joseph L. (2006). Robust directed tests of normality against heavy-tailed alternatives. *Computational Statistics & Data Analysis, 51*(2007), 2734–2746.

Genton, M. G. (2004). *Skew-elliptical distributions and their applications: A journey beyond normality*. New York: Chapman and Hall.

Glewwe, P., & Miguel, E. A. (2007). The impact of child health and nutrition on education in less developed countries. In Schultz, T. P., Strauss, J. A. (Eds.), *Handbook of development economics* (pp. 3561–3606 Vol. 4). Amsterdam: Elsevier, (chapter 56).

International Institute for Population Sciences (IIPS) and ORC Macro. (2002). *National Family Health Survey (NFHS-2), India, 1998–99:* (Vol. I). Mumbai: IIPS.

International Institute for Population Sciences (IIPS) and Macro International. (2007). *National Family Health Survey (NFHS-3), 2005–06: India:* (Vol. I). Mumbai: IIPS.

Jarque, C., & Bera, A. (1980). Efficient tests for normality, homoscedasticity and serial independence of regression residuals. *Economics Letters, 6,* 255–259.

Lilliefors, H. (1967). On the Kolmogorov-Smirnov test for normality with mean and variance unknown. *Journal of the American Statistical Association, 62,* 399–402.

Mora, J. O. (1989). A new method for estimating a standardized prevalence of child malnutrition from anthropometric indicators. *Bulletin of the World Health Organization, 67*(2), 133–142.

O'Donnell, et al. (2008). *Analyzing health equity using household survey data: A guide to techniques and their implementation*. Washington DC: World Bank Institute.

Pourahmadi, M. (2007). Construction of skew-normal random variables: Are they linear combinations of normal and half-normal? *Journal of Statistical Theory and Application, 3,* 314–328.

Schroeder, D. G., & Brown, K. H. (1994). Nutritional status as a predictor of child survival: Summarizing the association and quantifying its global impact. *Bulletin of the World Health Organization, 72*(4), 569–579.

Shapiro, S., & Wilk, M. (1965). An analysis of variance test for normality (complete samples). *Biometrika, 52,* 591–611.

Tarozzi, A. (2008). Growth reference charts and the nutritional status of Indian children. *Economics and Human Biology, 6,* 455–468.

United Nations. (2011). The millennium development goals report 2011, New York.

Waterlow, J. C., Buzina, R., Keller, W., Lane, J. M., Nichaman, M. Z., & Tanner, J. M. (1977). The presentation and use of height and weight data for comparing the nutritional status of groups of children under the age of 10 years. *Bulletin of the World Health Organization, 55,* 489–498.

Wang, Y., & Chen, H. (2012). Use of percentiles and Z-scores in anthropometry, In Preedy, V. R. (Ed.), *Handbook of anthropometry: Physical measures of human form in health and disease* Springer Science+Buisness Media, LLC.

WHO Working Group. (1986). Use and interpretation of anthropometric indicators of nutritional status. *Bulletin of the World Health Organization, 64,* 929–941.

World Health Organization. (1978). A growth chart for international use in maternal and child health care. Geneva.

World Health Organization. (1994). *Working group on infant growth*. Geneva: An Evaluation of Infant Growth.

World Health Organization. (1995). Physical status: The use and interpretation of anthropometry. Report of a WHO expert committee. *World Health Organization Technical Report Series, 854,* 1–452.

World Health Organization. (2006). *WHO child growth standards: Length/height-for-age, weight-for-age, weight-for-length, weight-for-height, and body mass index-for-age: Methods and development*. Geneva, Switzerland: World Health Organization.

Chapter 16
Health Expenditures Across Major States of India: Issues of Convergence and Equality

Ramesh Chandra Das, Kamal Ray and Utpal Das

16.1 Introduction

Social sector's development is one of the key objectives of a government in any country, particularly of the countries of the less developed or emerging categories. India, as one of the most promising countries of the world, is not an exception in this regard. Out of the social sectors, the sector on which the central and state governments of India are deploying funds for improvement is the health sector. No governments till dates in either of the central or state levels have abstained themselves from this sector's development because it promotes good quality of physical health of the population in one side and capturing political power for governing the country or states on the other. The contributions or the funds allotted for improving health conditions of the Indian people are twofold. One is by the central government's financing to the states in the head of plan outlays and the other is by the state governments' own sources. But in case of India, the contribution by the central plan is more compared to that of the states. At the same time, as the population volumes of the states are not equal, the standardization of the total fund allocation to the health sector's development into per capita terms would further insist to examine whether there are growth and convergence relation in the sector. The convergence of the states in the per capita health expenditure would further lead to reduction of magnitudes of inequality or rising equality across the states which would be a great developmental objective of a nation or states.

R.C. Das (✉) · K. Ray · U. Das
Katwa College, Purba Bardhaman, West Bengal, India
e-mail: rameshdas22@yahoo.co.in

K. Ray
e-mail: kamal420ray@yahoo.co.in

U. Das
e-mail: utpal_312@yahoo.co.in

U.K. De et al. (eds.), *Issues on Health and Healthcare in India*, India Studies in Business and Economics, https://doi.org/10.1007/978-981-10-6104-2_16

The present chapter tries to examine whether the major states of India are converging in terms of per capita health expenditure out of the state-wise capital expenditure provided by the central government in the head of medical and public health for the period 1990–1991 to 2009–2010.

16.2 Review of Literature

The contribution of some of the existing literature on the issue of convergence in general and the convergence aspect of the health sector, in particular, cannot be denied so far as the development of the entire study is concerned. The earlier research works were mainly concentrated to the convergence or divergence analysis of the group of developed economies in reference to the per capita GDP of the economies (Barro and Sala-i-Martin 1992; Mankiw et al. 1992). Gaspar (2010) questioned the neoclassical concept of convergence or catching up in absolute sense. According to the idea of absolute convergence, the countries with lower GDP per capita will tend to grow faster than richer ones and do not necessarily ensure convergence. This means that economies are converging but the steady-state level is not always common, so countries may converge to different or own level of steady states. Nayyar (2008), in his work on economic growth and regional inequality in India, has pointed out that the concept of σ divergence is consistent with the concept of conditional β convergence and vice versa. In an another research effort, Domazet et al. (2012) tried to study the existence of convergence in consumption expenditure in the EU-27 countries, in the period 2000–2007 by using absolute β convergence method. They observed that the EU-27 countries reached a high level of convergence in consumer expenditure during the period 2000–2007 which provides a basis for developing a regional concept of the standardized international marketing for these countries' markets. In a different study, Kaitila (2004) has tried to examine the convergence of the EU-15 countries' in terms of the real GDP per capita levels adjusted for purchasing power and discussed the impact of EU membership, trade and investment upon two types of convergence results in line with both cross section and panel of the countries' data that reveals that the countries are converging with a high speed. In another study of convergence in the Indian states, the work of Das and Dinda (2014) explores how divergences in allocation of commercial bank credit over time may result in the growing disparities in growth of incomes in the states of India for the period 1972–2010. The study observed that there were diverging tendencies among the states during the post-reform period (from 1993–2010) with respect to per capita credit and aggregate credit.

Let us view the literatures related specifically to convergence aspects of health sector in the world economies. The study by Kerem et al. (2008) analyses the convergence in healthcare expenditure as share of GDP in EU countries for the period 1992–2004. The paper tested the β, σ and γ convergence of the healthcare expenditure. The study demonstrates that the countries in the zone converge in line of all three definitions. The work of Oyedele and Adebayo (2015) examined the convergence of health expenditures as well as health outcomes for a group of Economic Community of West African States (ECOWAS) between 1995 and 2011. The results showed that the variable that measures the speed of convergence in health expenditure among member of ECOWAS region is positive and significant for both absolute and conditional convergence which indicated that there is no convergence in health expenditure. However, the study found evidence of convergence in health outcomes. Odhiambo et al. (2015), in their work, tried to examine whether sub-Saharan Africa (SSA) countries are converging or diverging from the target in the post-Abuja declaration period and whether there is significant effect of the Abuja instrument on other health expenditure indicators. This study tested convergence of health expenditure in SSA by using the linear dynamic panel model on a panel of 41 SSA countries for the period 2000–2011. The empirical results show evidence of absolute and conditional convergence of health expenditure in SSA. Nixon (2000), on the other hand, has presented new evidence that confirms convergence in health outcomes, as represented by life expectancy and infant mortality rates. Using σ and *β-convergence* analysis, the study has revealed a common trend in that Southern Mediterranean countries have exhibited upward convergence towards the mean in health expenditure, and convergence towards the EU mean in improving directions for health outcomes. Contrary to this result, EU countries of the North, particularly those of Scandinavian zones, exhibited downward convergence towards the EU mean or below it in health expenditure. In another effort, Panopoulou and Pantelidis (2011) studied whether there is convergence in 19 OECD countries over the period 1972–2006 in per capita healthcare expenditures and health outcomes. The study reveals that there is convergence in healthcare expenditure in 17 countries, while the US and Norway follow a different path. A simple decomposition of per capita health expenditures reveals that the divergence of the US comes from the divergence of the 'healthcare expenditure over GDP' component, while Norway's divergence is mainly caused by the 'labour productivity' component. The results of the study also suggested that convergence in per capita health expenditures among the 17 OECD countries did not lead to convergence in health outcomes. In their discussion paper, Cherodian and Thirlwall (2013) tried to study the regional disparities in per capita state domestic products of Indian states for the period 1999–2000 to 2010–11 by applying unconditional and conditional Beta convergence and Sigma convergence. The study revealed that there was no evidence of unconditional convergence, but weak evidence of conditional convergence in respect of population growth, credit growth, male literacy, the share of agriculture in State GDP and State expenditure as a share of State GDP. Also, it observed that Sigma divergence had increased continuously, except among the poorest states.

There is a cluster of studies related to India in different aspects of healthcare expenditure including the aspect of convergence. According to Choudhury et al. (2011) on the state level distribution of health expenditure by the central government it was observed that there is no systematic difference in the level of per capita expenditure between states that are known to have a large gap in the level of health achievements and states that are known to have done relatively better in terms of health achievements. It is also observed that there is a bias in expenditure towards the north-eastern states. The share of expenditure in the north-eastern states is substantially higher than their share in the total population of the country. As a result, per capita expenditure in north-eastern states is on average, three to four times higher than the per capita expenditure in most other states. In a working paper, Bhat and Jain (2004) tried to analyse the magnitudes and dimensions of the allocations of public expenditure on the health sectors of the different states from their own exchequers. The basic point of discussion was whether the states were allocating the target (set by the central government) of 3% of their state GDPs upon the health sectors' developments. The findings suggested that the state governments achieved the goal of allocating only about 0.43% of state GDPs to health and medical care which was a great failure by the states. The analysis also suggested that elasticity of health expenditure when is only 0.68 which suggested that for every one percent increase in state per capita income the per capita public healthcare expenditure had increased by around 0.68%. The study by Prachitha and Shanmugam (2012) concentrated on measurement of the efficiency of Indian states in raising health outcomes using the stochastic frontier method for the period 2000–2009. The results showed average efficiency of 72.7%, implying that there was a scope for improving health performances, without additional resources. The results also pointed out that the states can improve their health performance by increasing their expenditure on health, providing all necessary facilities like medical doctors, educating people and create health awareness. In another working paper of the same institute, Purohit (2012) pointed out the main concern on both for the policy makers and people in terms of divergence or inequity of health outcomes across rich and poor and rural and urban states of the country. The paper tried to test the development paradigm that this inequity will converge and adjustment period will be lowered for equitable outcomes in health provided a fine tuning of health policy is carried out. The results of the study indicate an affirmative answer to the tested development paradigm. It further chalks out the possible central and state level policy strategy to shorten the duration of convergence. Bhalotra (2007) analysed the effects of state health expenditure on infant mortality in India using individual data on about 120,000 rural births that occurred during 1970–1998 across the 15 major Indian states. The main finding was that health expenditure had a significant effect upon reduction of mortality rates with a lag of 3 years. In the UNDP, India, project Kadekodi and Kulkarni (2006) reviewed different aspects of health sector's performance in India over the last two decades (from 1980–81 to 1998–99) at the macroeconomic level. The analysis of sectoral linkages between the health and medical sector with other sectors of the economy ascertains that the health and medical sector seems to have assumed its rightful place in India. The linkage analysis shows that the health sector's backward linkage has been declining and forward linkage increasing. This will mean that the development of this sector will be dependent on the advancement of technology, inflow of foreign capital, imports of drugs, etc.

The above-mentioned studies specific to Indian states did not emphasize on the issue of convergence of health expenditure with respect to the central government's capital expenditure for the states in the head of medical and public health. The present study has attempted to fill up this gap.

16.3 Data and Methodology

The entire work has been carried out by borrowing data from Planning Commission of India on state-wise capital expenditure by the central government on medical and public health for the period 1990–1991 to 2009–2010. The number of states that we have considered is 18 including Delhi. The data for Uttarakhand, Jharkhand and Chhattisgarh have been merged to their mother states from the year 2001, the year of birth.

We apply the Barro and Sala-i-Martin methodology of testing for convergence among which are absolute β convergence for homogeneous, conditional β convergence for heterogeneous groups of economies and the σ convergence. By the *absolute β convergence* approach, the states with low base level of per capita health expenditure will grow faster compared to the states with high base level of per capita health expenditure and ultimately in the long run, the poorer states will catch up the richer states and will meet the common steady-state level of per capita health expenditure. The magnitude of β also stands for the speed of convergence. The model of absolute β convergence can be presented by the following equation:

$$\log\left(h_{it}/h_{i,t-1}\right) = \alpha - \beta\log\left(h_{i,t-1}\right) + u_{it} \tag{16.1}$$

The speed of convergence can be estimated by Eq. (16.2) which is as follows:

$$1/T\left[\log\left(h_{it}/h_{i,t-1}\right)\right] = \alpha - \left[\left(1 - e^{-\lambda t}\right)/T\right].\log\left(h_{i,t-1}\right) + \varepsilon_{it}, \tag{16.2}$$

where h_{it} stands for the per capita health expenditure of ith state at period t and $h_{i,t\text{-}1}$ stands for the same in the previous period. β stands for the slope coefficient which should be positive and less than one, λ stands for speed of convergence. The above equations show that there will be an inverse relation between the average growth rate of per capita health expenditure (i.e. $\log(h_{it}/h_{i,t\text{-}1})$ and the health expenditure in the base or initial period (i.e. $\log(h_{i,t\text{-}1})$) to the happenings of absolute β convergence. If we allow the existence of heterogeneity among the states in terms of other structural variables then the absolute convergence is supplemented by the approach of conditional β convergence where the rate of convergence is estimated by Eq. (16.4) which is

$$\log(h_{it}) = \alpha + (1 - \beta)\log\left(h_{i,t-1}\right) + \delta Y_t + u_{it}, \tag{16.3}$$

where 'Y' is the vector of other variables (also known as conditional variables) that affect per capita health expenditure such as infrastructure development, population growth rates, degree of trade openness, etc.

The theory of β convergence is necessary but not sufficient in explaining reductions of inequality across the states. The sufficient approach of explaining convergence across the states is known as σ convergence which exists when the dispersion of the per capita health expenditure across states takes a downward trend over time (Friedman 1992; Quah 1993). This is done by estimating Eq. (16.4) which is

$$\text{CV} = \theta + \eta t + e_t, \tag{16.4}$$

where 'θ' is intercept constant, 'η' is the slope constant or rate of change of coefficient of variation (CV) over time and 'e' is the random disturbance term. If the sign of 'η' is found to be negative and significant then we say that there is convergence among the states by the criterion of σ convergence.

The existence of convergence (or divergence) in health expenditure among the states should lead to reductions (or rise) of inequality across the states. Hence, we have measured first the magnitudes of inequality by means of Gini coefficient and then by Theil index because the latter is unbiased with respect to population figure. The Gini coefficient is computed by

$$G = 1/n^2\mu \sum_{i=1}^{n} (2i - n - 1)x_i, \tag{16.5}$$

where n is the number of states and μ is mean values of all states' values of the per capita health expenditure, i is the rank of a state when arranged in ascending order, and x_i is the observed value of the variable at the corresponding ranks. If the computed value of $G = 1$ then it is said that there is extreme inequality or absolute inequality and if $G = 0$ then there is absolute equality among the states. On the other hand, Theil index (TI) (Theil 1967) with respect to distribution of health expenditure across the population size of the states computes inequality among the states by a simple ratio of the size of share of all India figure of health expenditure to share of total population of the state. It is, therefore, expressed by

$$\text{TI} = \sum_{i=1}^{n} \log(h_i/p_i), \tag{16.6}$$

where h_i is state ith share of health expenditure in all India level and p_i is the share of population of the ith state in all India level. If the trend of TI is decreasing (or increasing), then it is said that the states are converging (or diverging) from each other.

16.4 Empirical Investigations

Before to going in detail for examining the quantification of convergence parameters, we first look into the graphical views of the per capita health expenditures at base values for the period 1990–1991 and annual average growth rates of the same indicator across the states to have primary information on the inverse relation between the two. Figures 16.1 and 16.2 present them that show that the states with high base values of the per capita health expenditures are usually followed by low annual average values of the corresponding growth rates. So, there is the indication of convergence across the states in health expenditure. Jammu and Kashmir (J&K) (with Rs. 15) and Himachal Pradesh (HP) (with Rs. 12) stand in the first and second place, respectively, in the base values of the per capita health expenditures vis-à-vis maintain low annual average growth rates which are around 25% each and Andhra Pradesh (AP) (with Rs. 0.45) and Gujarat (with Rs. 0.39) like states with low base values maintain high annual average growth rates.

The states that start with the base values higher than All India value are J&K, HP, Assam, Delhi, West Bengal (WB), Uttar Pradesh (UP), Kerala and Haryana and the states that start with the base values lower than All India value are Gujarat, AP, Madhya Pradesh (MP), Bihar, Punjab, Rajasthan, Tamil Nadu (TN), Karnataka, Maharashtra and Orissa. So there is a disparity in the number of states in the upper panel and lower panel of the state with respect to the All India level. On the other hand, with respect to annual average growth rates of the states in per capita health expenditure, only Kerala stays below the All India growth rates and all remaining 17 states stay in the upper panel.

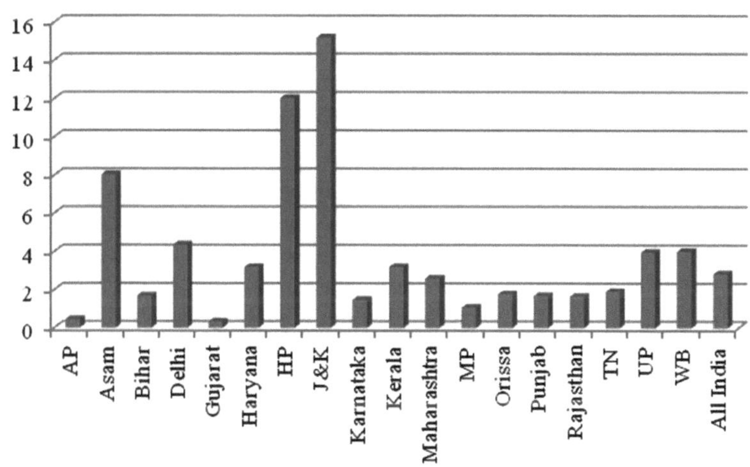

Fig. 16.1 Per capita base values (in 1990–1991) of per capita health expenditure of the states

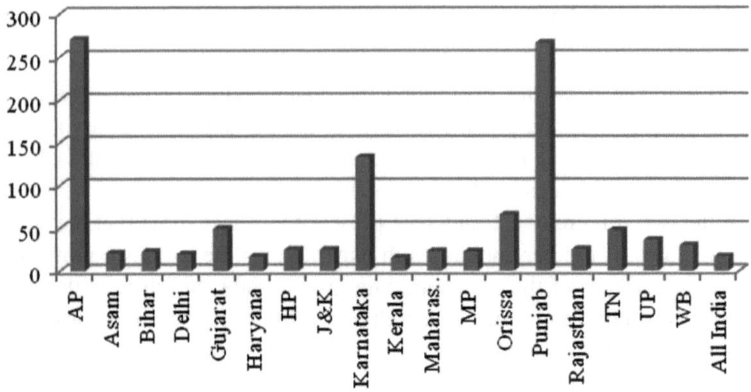

Fig. 16.2 Average annual growth rates of per capita health expenditure of the states

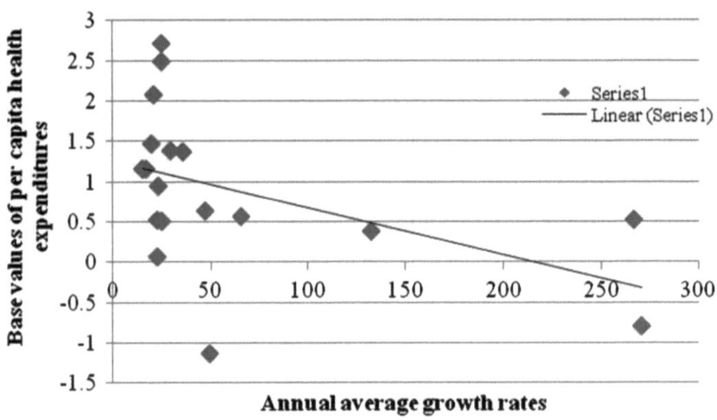

Fig. 16.3 Scatter diagram coordinating average growth rates and base values of per capita health expenditure

16.5 Absolute β and σ Convergence Analysis

Getting the view from the image of the distribution of per capita health expenditure and its annual average growth rates (refer to Figs. 16.1 and 16.2) indicating the possibility of having inverse relation between the two, we are here attempting to quantify whether the poorer states are trying to converge to the richer states in health expenditure out of the central plan outlays. We concentrate on examining whether there is absolute β convergence among the states in health expenditure. Primarily, we have plotted the annual average growth rates of the per capita health expenditure of all the 18 states vis-à-vis their per capita health expenditure in the initial period, 1990–1991, in a scatter diagram (Fig. 16.3) to see whether there is an inverse trend between them.

We observe from Fig. 16.3 that there is a clear indication of the poorer states with relatively lower base values to catch up with the richer states with higher base values of the per capita health expenditure. The linear correlation between the two is computed to be (−) 0.46 which is significant at 5% level of significance. Hence, we can conclude that there is absolute β convergence among the states so far as the distribution of per capita health expenditure is concerned.

Let us compute the value of β for calculating the speed of convergence by estimating Eq. (16.1). The estimated Barro growth equation is as follows:

$$\begin{aligned} &\log\left(h_{it}/\, h_{i,t-1}\right) = 95.5 - 37.6\log\left(h_{i,t-1}\right) \\ &p = 0.000 \text{ for - intercept} \\ &p = 0.05 \text{ for - slope} \\ &R^2 = 0.21 \end{aligned} \tag{16.7}$$

We observe that the estimated coefficient is of expected negative sign with a high value of 37.6. It shows that the states are converging at a very high speed. The existence of absolute β convergence does not necessarily imply that the interstate disparity will fall over time. This in other way implies that the concept of absolute β convergence does not cover all the concerned variables in discussing the issue in an inclusive manner. We could not test for conditional β convergence because of non-availability of the required data and time constraint.

The relatively general concept of measuring convergence is the σ convergence which can be justified by looking at the downward trend of the measure of dispersion which is usually considered to be the coefficient of variations. Figure 16.4 shows the upward trend of CV. This means the states are diverging so far as the methodology of σ convergence is concerned.

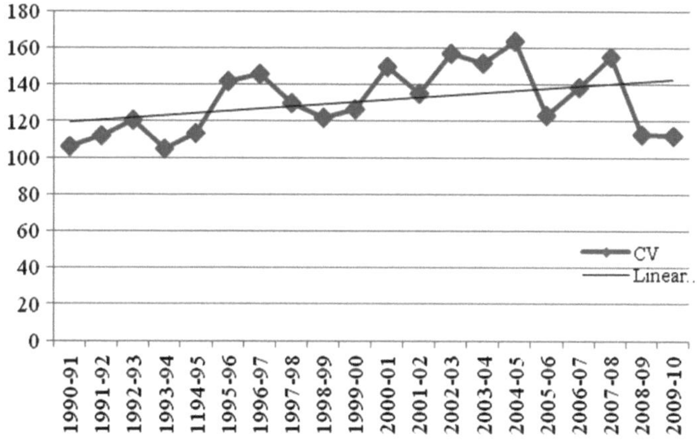

Fig. 16.4 Trend of CV

Hence, we arrive at the conclusion that the states are converging only if the catching up hypothesis by means of absolute β convergence is concerned but diverging if the overall dispersion of the variable is taken into account by means of σ convergence definition. This further reminds us that the concept of absolute β convergence is necessary but not sufficient in examining convergence across the states or regions of an economy. The factor that is responsible for this result is the variance of the disturbance term in the Eq. (16.1). It may happen under the condition that the initial value of dispersion of the error term begins below the steady-state value of the dispersion (Barro and Sala-i-Martin 2004).

16.6 Gini Values and Theil Indices for Measuring Interstate Concentration and Inequality

Let us concentrate our analysis upon computation of magnitudes of concentration and inequality by means of Gini values and Theil indices. The results are presented in Table 16.1 and in Figs. 16.5 and 16.6, respectively.

The results depicted in the table and the figures show that there is the sign of rising concentration and inequality in the distribution of per capita health expenditure across the states of India, although, there are some fluctuations in the trends

Table 16.1 Gini coefficients and Theil indices over time

Year	Gini coefficient	Theil index
1990–91	0.484917356	15.281611
1991–92	0.503922292	21.8282514
1992–93	0.547076872	27.3838668
1993–94	0.496	20.9780534
1194–95	0.532742106	37.131042
1995–96	0.605102539	50.6828873
1996–97	0.618996106	48.745144
1997–98	0.595436629	55.6994021
1998–99	0.57400489	56.0647246
1999–00	0.56688622	49.2035815
2000–01	0.602331051	65.2317338
2001–02	0.564041951	50.999802
2002–03	0.605676255	66.7188198
2003–04	0.626638924	55.4488178
2004–05	0.660150913	59.1586317
2005–06	0.584669949	41.1938851
2006–07	0.612544984	54.3070014
2007–08	0.617307879	40.9587363
2008–09	0.548099627	34.1792879
2009–10	0.522111881	29.1887853

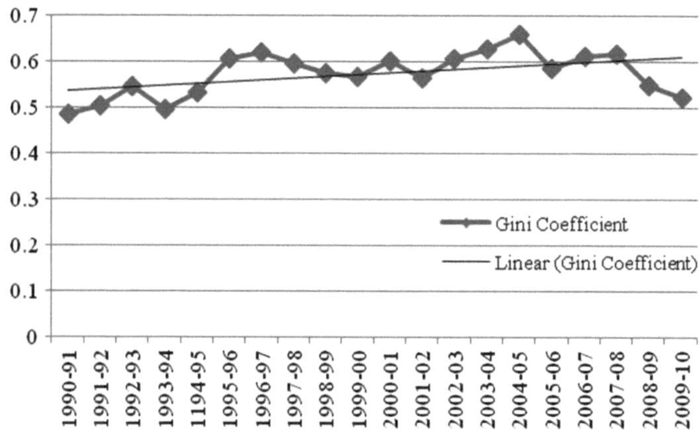

Fig. 16.5 Gini values

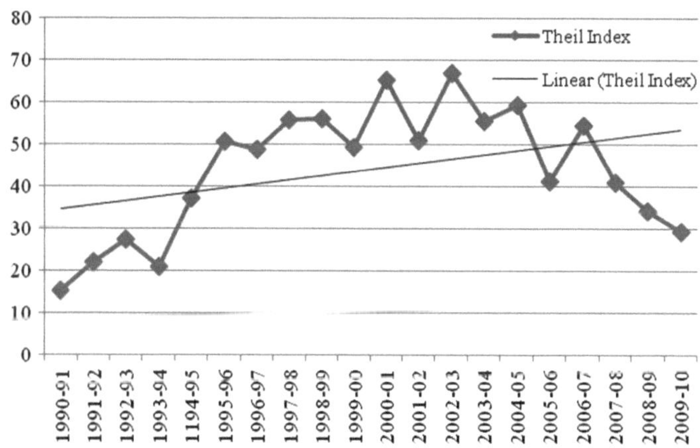

Fig. 16.6 Theil indices

of Gini values and Theil indices. The Gini value takes 0.485 in the initial period and ends in 0.522 after reaching 0.66 in the period 2004–05.

On the other hand, the Theil index takes the value 15.28 in the initial period and ends with 29.18 in the last period and taking highest value of 66.71 in the period 2002–03.

There may be some associations of the results of rising inequality and concentration with the regimes of the political parties that governed the country in the centre and the major policies taken in favour of economic progress.

The steep rising of the values of both the indices first appeared in the phase of 1993–94 to 1995–96 which may be attributable to the major reform that took place in the economy at that time (refer to Fig. 16.7). The states like Rajasthan and Delhi had got rising trends of the total grants allocated in the health sector from the centre

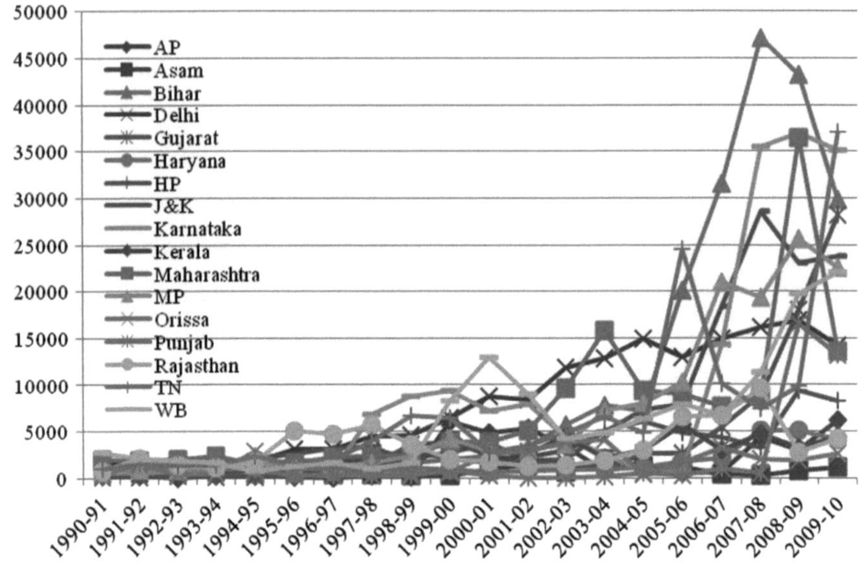

Fig. 16.7 Trends of allocations of health grants to the states by the centre (Rs. lakh)

and the states like Assam, WB, Punjab and Orissa faced falling trends of allocation of this grant. The period in which the values of concentration and inequality had taken highest values fell within the domain of the NDA Government in the centre where the source of inequality was the relatively large share of central grant in this head to the states like AP, Orissa, WB and MP, which probably might be due to the political supports by the regional parties governing in these states along with own government in the home state like MP in the later part of the regime of the NDA. In case of WB, although there was no support from the left front being in power of the state, the rising grant to the state was due to the support of Trinamool Congress to the NDA and some MPs of the party were in the post of cabinet ministers. After the end of NDA regime in 2004 and the onset of new innings of the UPA headed by Dr. Manmohan Singh, the interstate concentration and inequality in the allocation of health grants started falling because the states like UP, Bihar, TN, Karnataka, Maharashtra, MP started improving in the head. For example, UP started with Rs. 268 crore in the period 2004–2005 and ended up with Rs. 1297 crore in 2009–2010, Bihar with Rs. 72 to 297 crore, TN with Rs. 47 to 327 crore, etc. Hence, we can draw the inference that the sources of σ divergence and the associated increasing magnitudes of the interstate concentration and inequality in the allocation of health budget to the states are the pressure of sudden reforms in the entire economy and the governance of the NDA led by the Bharatiya Janta Party.

16.7 Conclusion

The study so far we have made can now be summarized. Starting with the hypothesis of testing whether there are convergence or divergence and the associated falling or rising concentration and inequality in the allocation of capital expenditure in medical and public health by the central governments to the states for the period 1990–1991 to 2009–2010, we observed that there is absolute β convergence but σ divergence among the states of India. Accordingly, we observed increasing trends of concentration and inequality among the states in the health sector's budget allocation. The study also drew inferences that the sources divergence and the associated increasing magnitudes concentration and inequality are the pressure of sudden and drastic reforms in the entire economy and the governance of the NDA led by the Bharatiya Janta Party.

References

Barro, R. J., & Sala-i-Martin, X. (1992). Convergence. *Journal of Political Economy, 110*(2), 223–252.

Barro, R. J, & Sala-i-Martin, X. (2004). *Economic growth*, published by Prentice-Hall of India Private Limited, New Delhi.

Bhalotra, S. (2007). Spending to save? State health expenditure and infant mortality in India. *Health Economics, 16,* 911–928.

Bhat, R., & Jain, N. (2004). *Analysis of public expenditure on health using state level data.* Indian Institute of Management, Ahmedabad, Working Paper, June.

Cherodian, R., & Thirlwall, A. P. (2013). *Regional disparities in per capita income in India: Convergence or divergence*? University of Kent, School of Economics Discussion Papers, 1313, August 5.

Choudhury, M., Amar Nath, H. K. & Datta, P. (2011). *Health expenditure by the central government in India: State level distribution.* National Institute of Public Finance and Policy, New Delhi, Working Paper, September.

Das, R. C., & Dinda, S. (2014). Convergence in bank credit: A study of the major Indian states over the period 1972–2010. In Dincer & Hacioglu (Eds.), *Global strategies in banking and finance* (Chapter. 7), Pennsylvania, USA: IGI Global.

Domazet, A., Sendic, R., & Alic, A. (2012). Convergence analysis of household expenditures using the absolute β-convergence method. *Business Systems Research, 3*(1), 23–29.

Friedman, M. J. (1992). Do old fallacies ever die? *Journal of Economic Literature, 30,* 2129–2132.

Gaspar, A. (2010). Economic growth and convergence in the world economies: An econometric analysis. In *Proceedings of the Challenges for Analysis of the Economy, the Businesses, and Social Progress, International Scientific Conference* (pp. 97–110).

Kadekodi, G., & Kulkarni, K. (2006). *Status of health and medical care in India: A macro perspective.* India: United Nations Development Programme.

Kaitila, V. (2004). *Convergence of real GDP per capita in the EU15-How do the accession countries fit in*? ENEPRI Working Paper No. 25, January.

Kerem, K., Puss, T., Viies, M., & Maldare, R. (2008). Health and convergence of health care expenditure in EU. *International Business & Economics Research Journal, 7*(3), 29–43.

Mankiw, G., Romer, P., & Weil, D. N. (1992). A contribution to the empirics of growth. *Quarterly Journal of Economics, 107,* 407–437.

Nayyar, G. (2008). Economic growth and regional inequality in India, *Economic and Political Weekly*, Feb 9–15, *43*(6), 58–67.

Nixon, J. (2000). *Convergence of health care spending and health outcomes in the European Union, 1960–95* (p. 183). Centre for Health Economics, Discussion Paper, No: The University of York.

Odhiambo, S. A., Wambugu, A., & Kiriti-Nganga, T. (2015). Convergence of health expenditure in Sub-Saharan Africa: Evidence from a dynamic panel. *Journal of Economics and Sustainable Development, 6*(6), 185–205.

Oyedele, O., & Adebayo, A. (2015). Convergence of health expenditure and health outcomes. *International Journal of Economics, Finance and Management, 4*(2), 46–53.

Panopoulou, E., & Pantelidis, T. (2011). Convergence in per capita health expenditures and health outcomes in OECD countries. *Applied Economics, 44*(30), 3909–3920.

Prachitha J., & Shanmugam, K. R. (2012). *Efficiency of raising health outcomes in the Indian States*, Madras School of Economics, Working Paper No. 70, May.

Purohit, B. C. (2012). *Health policy, inequity and convergence in India*, Madras School of Economics, Working Paper No. 74, September.

Quah, D. T. (1993). Galton's fallacy and tests of the convergence hypothesis. *The Scandinavian Journal of Economics, 95,* 427–443.

Theil, H. (1967). *Economics and information theory*. Amsterdam: North Holland.

Chapter 17
Health and Deprivation: A Suggested Application to the North-Eastern States of India

Atanu Sengupta and Parnasudha Karmodak

17.1 Introduction

The debate on growth and development has occupied an extensive place in the development discourse. The pro-growth school argues that high growth rate will bring automatic development. On the contrary, other school of thought disputing this argument, believe that without ensuring development of masses, high growth rate is useless and it will not sustain. However, researchers have found strong link between growth and development (Ramirez et al. 1998; Ranis and Stewart 2000, 2001; UNDP 1994). The objective of the chapter is not to study the link. The present study wishes to introduce an ethical dimension into the construction of Health Index keeping this link into consideration.

In the usual discourse of health, all focus seems to be on the achievements side. It reports on the improvement of life expectancy, of reduction of infant mortality, increase of public hygiene and so on and so forth. As such, they tell us half the story, leaving a large populace outside the ambit of analysis. Since development should be an inclusive phenomenon, the traditional measures do not provide any reliable snapshot of what is going on the reality.

To fix the idea, we take an example. Consider two families of same number of adult members who are completely illiterate (isolated illiterate as designated by Basu and Foster 1998). Now suppose a government drive makes two family member of one of the families literate untouching the other family. An alternative is where one member of each family is made literate. In the traditional HDI analysis, both these alternatives are same since they bring about a similar change in literacy

A. Sengupta (✉) · P. Karmodak
Economics Department, Burdwan University, Burdwan, India
e-mail: sengupta_atanu@yahoo.com

P. Karmodak
e-mail: parnasudha@gmail.com

U.K. De et al. (eds.), *Issues on Health and Healthcare in India*, India Studies in Business and Economics, https://doi.org/10.1007/978-981-10-6104-2_17

rate. However, Basu and Foster (1998) contrasted between these two situations. In the first case, the illiterates of one of the families now become proximate illiterate—they can share written information decoded by their literate relatives while the members of the other family are still steeped in darkness. The second situation is in this sense better. Thus, neglecting the negative side of human development might not tenable from the ethical point of view. A somewhat similar effect may be argued in the case of health. This chapter is a modest attempt in incorporating this negative aspect in constructing the health index.

The chapter is divided into four sections. In Sect. 17.2, the theoretical framework of the study is provided. In Sect. 17.3, the application of the suggested methodology is examined. Section 17.4 concludes the study.

17.2 Theoretical Framework

In our chapter, we have considered the twin aspects of preventive health—infrastructure of public hygiene and outcome. In order to make the analysis more sophisticated, we have coupled the achievement and deprivation within a single net index. Such netting captures the society's overall attitude to the winners and losers in the overall apsidal of preventive health and its impact. These two aspects of preventive health are more comprehensive than the normal attainment (GDP, HDI, Health Outcome, etc.) and deprivation (Head count poverty, HPI, Health poverty, etc.) indices. It is now possible to combine them in order to achieve a more generic picture that is a reflection of both level and distribution of preventive health facilities.

In order to do so, we have generalized a methodology used by some researchers (Thorat 2007). In this approach, the indices are put in a continuous scale of increasing attainment (or decreasing deprivation). The individual states are then placed in this scale pivoting them around the attainment for India as a whole. The states whose performances are better than the figure for India are regarded as "**Good**" performers. Similarly whose levels are below the figure for "**India**" is encapsulated as "**Bad**" performers. This scale is then varied for various attributes that the researchers dimmed as important.

The previous approach has two limitations. First, they segregate the achievement and failure separately without coupling them. This methodology denies the society's overall attitude in assessment of achievement and failure. In this context, Nayar (2007) referred two important works by Kosa (1969). He defined four possible approaches to poverty—(i) poverty is taken for granted and its existence is not perceived; (ii) poverty is taken for granted but its existence is perceived; (iii) poverty is not taken for granted and its existence is perceived and (iv) poverty is not taken for granted but its existence is not perceived. It is clear that all these approaches place different emphasis on the achievement and deprivation issue. In the effect of poverty is not perceived [(i) and (iv)], the standard measures are sufficient may be in the latter case there may be a slide correction for some possibilities of deprivation. However, for case poverty is perceived [(ii) and (iii)], the net indicator used by us is perhaps the sole measure that can capture the society's attitude. We can redesignate these four points as

Case (i) Pessimistic unawareness of poverty,
Case (ii) Pessimistic awareness of poverty,
Case (iii) Optimistic awareness of poverty,
Case (iv) Optimistic unawareness of poverty.

The traditional measure for health is appropriate with unawareness. The net measure of ours is appropriate for awareness.

Second—They present a uni-dimensional feature.

Since we use two-dimensional of preventive health—Hygiene and Outcome, our analysis will be two dimensional.

In Table 17.1, the first cell in the first row indicates virtuous situation. Both hygiene and outcome is good here. There is enough infrastructure and is properly used. In the second cell in the first row is the lop-sided public hygiene. Here, hygiene is bad but outcome is good. Probably private initiatives are more important here. These private initiatives may come from some NGO's or nonprofitable institutions. They may also come from private budget. The first cell in the second row represents lop-sided outcome. In this case, the hygienic facilities are not utilized. The last cell in the second row is the worst possible condition. There is neither infrastructure nor utilization.

There are various connotations of health structure and its use. The structure of health denotes the availability of the basic health infrastructure facilities such as drainage, sanitation, safe drinking water, etc. These facilities are often provided by the government to all its residents. Availability of these facilities is crucial for maintaining proper health. In India, there is serious asymmetry in the distribution of these available facilities across various states and/or economic or social categories. Our chapter concentrates on the first dimension of inequality.

The public hygiene variable chosen by us is a net indicator of these distributions of the facilities along with its inequality quotient. However, mere supply of these facilities is not enough. People must be given proper training and awareness of the good effect of a proper hygienic behaviour. In India, this factor is seriously lacking. People are observed not to use proper sanitation and defecate in open field. They do not wash their hand properly before eating. Even foods and water are not stored in a proper hygienic way in spite of they are available at zero cost. Some basic precautionary measures against disease prevention cause primary health aid that cut down mortality rate are seriously lacking. All these are reflected in the health outcome.

Our second variable captures the net outcome in a synthetic way. We hope that these two variables will go in a long way to capture the prospect of health in India. We now proposed to build an axiomatic structure to capture our insights into a neat mathematical framework.

Table 17.1 Definitional Matrix

Virtuous provinces (good outcome, good public hygiene)	Lop-sided public hygiene (good outcome, bad public hygiene)
Lop-sided outcome (bad outcome, good public hygiene)	Vicious provinces (bad outcome, bad public hygiene)

(i) **Positive Aspect of Health Index**

For the technical discussion of the aspect, we closely follow Chakravarty (2003). Suppose that the *i*th component of positive well-being is measurable and is quantified by a number x_i (where $i = 1, 2,\ldots,k$) that remains within the bounds $[m_i, M_i]$ that is defined on a real line R^1_+. For non-emptiness of the interval, we assume that $m_i < M_i$.

Let U associates a value $U(x_i, m_i, M_i)$ to each $x_i \in [m_i, M_i]$, where U is a real valued function and an indicator for i. It is assumed that U is twice differentiable and continuous. Further, it is assumed that U is independent.

We now suggest some properties for an arbitrary index U

Positive Normalization (PNOM): $U(x_i, m_i, M_i) \begin{matrix} = 0, \text{if} x_i = m_i, \\ = 1, \text{if} x_i = M_i \end{matrix}$

Normalization constraints the value of x_i between 0 and 1.

Positive Monotonicity (PMN): Monotonicity assures that for a give m_i and M_i, the index U increases with an increase in x_i.

Positive Translation Invariance (PTI): $U(x_i, m_i, M_i) = U(x_i + a, m_i + a, M_i + a)$, where a is any scalar such that $m_i + a \geq 0$. TI says that the index U is origin independent.

Positive Homogeneity (PHM): For any $a \geq 0$, $U(x_i, m_i, M_i) = U(ax_i, am_i, aM_i)$. HM posits that the index is scale independent.

Lower gain in indicator at higher level of attainment difference (LGI)[1]: Let $x_i \in [m_i, M_i]$ be any attainment level of attribute i. Then for any $\boldsymbol{\Delta} > 0$ such that $x_i + \boldsymbol{\Delta} \in [m_i, M_i]$, the magnitude of indicator gain $U(x_i, m_i, M_i) = U(x_i + \boldsymbol{\Delta}, m_i, M_i) - U(x_i, m_i, M_i)$ is a nonincreasing function of $\boldsymbol{\Delta}$. LGI indicates that gain in the indicator do not rise with an increase at the higher levels as compared to an equivalent increase at the lower level.

The property PNOM nearly constraints the health index between zero and unity. This is the standard unitary scale from which the indices are normally based. Monotonicity is simply a statement of derived nature of Health Index. It is PTI and PHM that are most important for defining the shape of Health Index. PTI makes the desired measure origin-free. In fact, the differencing from minimum is derived from PTI. PHM makes the measure scale-free. This gives the measure in the ratio form.

[1]This is less stringent than the LI of Chakravarty.

LGI is important in making the Health Index insensitive for further and further addition in one dimension.

Using these axioms the Positive Health Index (PHI) can be written as:

$$\mathrm{PHI} = \sum_{i=1}^{k} ((x_i - m_i)/(M_i - m_i))/k \tag{17.1}$$

In order to derive this result in the context of HDI, Chakravarty (2003) posited a number of theorems.[2]

(ii) **Negative aspect of Health Index**

Before proceeding further, let us provide the rationale behind the negative aspect of health. Any improvement in the component of the Health Index (HI) makes the society well-off. However, corresponding to each improvement there are vast "wastelands" that are untouched. Consider, for example, literacy rate—an important component of HDI. Overall illiteracy is clearly bad but for a group, the more important concern is the illiteracy of that group. Even if overall illiteracy falls, the group will feel deprived if its literacy rate remains constant (or worst still if it falls). The fact that overall literacy has improved is a little solace to it.

Similarly, if both per capita GDP and inequality index of a country rises, the gain in welfare due to an expansion of income is mitigated by the blow of inequality. Instances may be cited in favour of other dimensions of human development as well.

Following the above examples, we have to consider the negative aspect of Health Index (HI).[3] Let us consider y_i to be the quantified negative ith component of human well-being that lies within the interval $[N_{i,}, n_i]$ that is a subset of real line[4] R +. For existence of the bound, we assume that $N_i > n_i$. Hence we posit, as in the positive case a real valued function B that associates a value $B(y_i, N_i, n_i)$ to each $y_i \in [N_i, n_i]$. B is assumed to be twice differentiable and continuous. As in the positive case, function B is assumed in the same form for the entire negative attribute.

The arbitrary index B also possesses some properties as in positive case. These are:

Negative Normalization (NNM): $B(y_i, N_i, n_i) \begin{matrix} = 0 & \text{if}\, y_i = N_i \\ = 1 & \text{if}\, y_i = n_i \end{matrix}$

Negative Monotonicity (NMO): Given N_i and n_i, an increase in y decreases B.

[2]For the theorem and their proof see Chakravarty (2003).

[3]Since the positive and negative aspects comes in pair, the number of positive elements should be equal to the numbers of negative elements.

[4]In order to prevent unnecessary mathematical conundrums, we take the absolute value of the negative indicators. However, since these are negative indicators higher the value of negative attributes lower will be the social welfare.

Negative Translation Invariance (NTI): $B(y_i, N_i, n_i) = B(y_i - d, N_i - d, n_i - d)$, where d is any scalar such that $N_i - d \geq 0$.

Negative Homogeneity (NHM): For any $e > 0, B(y_i, N_i, n_i) = B(ey_i, eN_i, en_i)$.

Lower loss in Indicator at Higher level of attainment difference (LLI): Let $y_i \in [N_i, n_i]$ be any attainment level of attribute i. Then, for any $\alpha > 0$ such that $y_i + \alpha \in [N_i, n_i]$, the magnitude of indicator loss $B(y_i + \alpha, N_i + \alpha, n_i + \alpha) - B(y_i, N_i, n_i)$ is a nondecreasing function of α.

Using these axioms, Negative Health Index (NHI) can be written as:

$$\text{NHDI} = \sum_{i=1}^{k} [(y_i - n_i)/(N_i - n_i)]/k \quad (17.2)$$

(iii) **Effective (Net) Health Index (NHI)**

We have considered both the positive and negative sides of the various components of Health Index. It is now necessary to combine these two aspects into a single measure. The exercise involves number of interesting aspects. Consider, an index I defined over k dimensions, where I is a scalar index and all the components of I are lying between the same unit lengths.

In essence, I is a mapping from k unit lines to a scalar or mathematically, $I : [0, 1]^k \rightarrow k$

Let a_i be the positive component and b'_i be the negative components such that $b'_i = 1 - b_i$. We have taken b' instead of b in order to avoid inappropriate penalty. Suppose a country has a high per capita GDP attaining a high 'a' and a high degree of poverty attaining a low 'b'. It is clear that unless 'b' is corrected to take the impact of high poverty, this would give the country a higher net measure than a country with similar per capita GDP and a low level of poverty and hence a high 'b'. So, the achievement index

$$G\big((x_1, m_1, M_1), \ldots, (x_P, m_P, M_p), (y_1, N_1, n_1), \ldots (y_{k-p}, N_{k-p}, n_{k-p})\big)$$
$$\begin{bmatrix} \text{where}, k - p = p \\ k = 2p \end{bmatrix}$$

Can be written as

$$I(a_1, a_2 \ldots a_p, b'_1, b'_2, \ldots b'_{k-p}) \quad (17.3)$$

Assuming that there are p positive components and $(k - p)$ negative components. We impose certain properties on the lecture of I

Positive Normalization (PNOM): For any $z \in [0, 1], I(\underbrace{z, z \ldots, z}_{p},$

$\underbrace{0, 0 \ldots 0 \ldots 0}_{k-p}) = z$

Negative normalization (NNOM): For any $z \in [0,1], I(\underbrace{0,0\ldots,0}_{p}, \underbrace{z, z\ldots,z}_{k-p}) = -z$

Consistency in Aggregation (CIA): $a, b', c \in [0,1]^k$

$$I\left(a_1 + c_1, a_2 + c_2, \ldots, a_p + c_{p'} b'_1 + c_{p+1}, b'_2 + c_{p+2}, \ldots b'_{k-p} + c_k\right)$$
$$= I\left(a_1, a_2, \ldots, a_p, b'_1, b'_2, \ldots, b'_{k-p}\right) + I(c_1, c_2, \ldots, c_k)$$

Symmetry (SYM): For all $a \in [0,1]^k, b' \in [0,1]^k, I(a\,b') = I(a\,Pb'Q)$ where P and Q are any $k \times k$ permutation matrices.

Chakravarty (2003) have proved conclusively that if there is no negative component in the Human Development Index, the indicator function I takes the familiar additive form. Extending this we can easily show that the indicator function in our case in the context of Health Index will turn out to be

$$I\left(a_1, a_2, \ldots, a_p, b'_1, b'_2, \ldots, b'_{k-p}\right) = \frac{1}{p}\sum_{i-1}^{p} a_i - \frac{1}{k-p}\sum_{j=p+1}^{k} b'_j \tag{17.4}$$

However, in this simply netting procedure, we make no considerations for any weightage to the negative side. Such a weight structure can be introduced by tinkering with the NNOM preposition. Suppose we rewrite the NNOM in the following way

$$I\,(\underbrace{0,0\ldots,0}_{p}, \underbrace{b', b', \ldots, b'}_{k-p}) = -\theta b' \tag{17.5}$$

It is quite easy to show the Net Health Index (NHI) in the following way

$$I\left(a_1, a_2, \ldots, a_b, b'_1, b'_1, \ldots, b'_{k-p}\right) = \frac{1}{p}\sum_{i=1}^{p} a_i - \frac{1}{k-p}\theta\sum_{j=p+1}^{k} b'_j \tag{17.6}$$

Here, θ is the society's weight to the negative aspect of health Index. The weight attached to θ radically changes relative with rankings of the states in the context of Health Index.

A legitimate argument against the form (17.4) and (17.5) is that they may become negative.[5] We follow the cue from Lee (2007) to generate a Net (or

[5]This argument has been raised by a number of social thinkers in the case of effective literacy rate (Lee 2007).

Effective) Health Index that lies between zero and unity. To do this, we have to define the parameter θ in the following way:

$$\theta = -\sum_{i=1}^{p} a_i \tag{17.7}$$

By simple pairing and noting that $k - p = p$, we can write the equation as

$$I\left(a_1, a_2, a_p, b'_1, b'_2, \ldots b'_p\right) = \frac{1}{p}\sum \left\{a_i(1 - b'_i)\right\} \tag{17.8}$$

Or,

$$I\left(a_1, a_2, \ldots, a_p, b'_1, b'_2, \ldots b'_p\right) = \frac{1}{p}\sum_{i=1}^{p} (\Delta a_i), \tag{17.9}$$

where $\Delta a_i = \sum \left\{a_i(1 - b'_i)\right\}$

We cite a simple example to posit our logic. Consider a rise in Health infrastructure facilities. It raises human welfare. However, imagine a situation where the population is sharply divided between "health elites" and health deprived". The health deprived are seriously lacking in basic amenities of life. The elites, however, enjoy a very good health standard. Suppose improvement in health infrastructure implies a further rise in their amenities—for example having a fully air-conditioned hospital ward. Such improvement in health infrastructure will not add to the well-being of anybody. Hence, there is an "Efficiency Loss" of the rise in the "health infrastructure". The standard Health Index measure fails to address this problem. Our measure is more sensitive in this regard. Hence, it is admittedly better than the standard measure.

We are now equipped with a fully developed effective health index. In the following section, this index is applied to the data set of North-East India.

17.3 Empirical Analysis

In the empirical exercise, we now use the index developed by us in Sect. 17.2 to understand the ramification of preventive health in the context of north-eastern states of India. For this, we have to carefully choose positive and negative aspects of each factor that are deemed important to us.

The positive side of public hygiene is a combination of four indices—(i) Proportions of household having safe drinking water, (ii) Proportions of household having separate bathrooms, (iii) Proportions of household having hygienic latrine and (iv) Proportions of household having proper drainage facilities. The negative side of public hygiene is captured by other four indices—(i) Proportions of household not having safe drinking water, (ii) Proportions of household not having

Table 17.2 Effective (2001)

	Good public hygiene	Bad public hygiene
Good outcome		Arunachal Pradesh Manipur Mizoram Tripura Nagaland
Bad outcome	Sikkim	Assam Meghalaya

Source Authors' calculation
Note Detailed calculation of the table is presented in Appendix Table 17.4

Table 17.3 Effective (2011)

	Good public hygiene	Bad public hygiene
Good outcome	Sikkim	Arunachal Pradesh Manipur Tripura Nagaland
Bad outcome		Assam Meghalaya Mizoram

Source Authors' calculation
Note Detailed calculation of the table is presented in Appendix Table 17.5

separate bathrooms, (iii) Proportions of household not having hygienic latrine and (iv) Proportions of household not having proper drainage facilities.

For outcome, the positive side is captured by life expectancy at birth while negative side is infant mortality rate. Each of these variables is standardized by the standard goal post method used by UNDP.

$$\text{Positive Inde} = \frac{\text{Observation} - \text{Min value}}{\text{Max value} - \text{Min value}}, \text{Negative Index} = \frac{\text{Max value} - \text{Observation}}{\text{Max value} - \text{Min value}}$$
$$\text{Net Index} = \text{Positive Index} * (1 - \text{Nagative Index})$$

After this transformation, we have combined four positive indices of public hygiene into a single index using primary component analysis. Similar task has been performed for negative index of public hygiene. States with above India's average outcome and public hygiene are considered as good and states below India's average outcome and public hygiene are considered as bad (Table 17.2).

In the empirical exercise, we now use the index developed by us in Sect. 17.2 to understand the ramification of preventive health in the context of north-eastern states of India. For this, we have to carefully choose positive and negative aspects of each factor that deemed important to us (Table 17.3).

The positive side of public hygiene is a combination of four indices—(i) Proportions of household having safe drinking water, (ii) Proportions of household having separate bathrooms, (iii) Proportions of household having hygienic latrine and (iv) Proportions of household having proper drainage facilities. The negative side of public hygiene is captured by another four indices—(i) Proportions of household not having safe drinking water, (ii) Proportions of household not having separate bathrooms, (iii) Proportions of household not having hygienic latrine and (iv) Proportions of household not having proper drainage facilities.

For outcome, the positive side is captured by life expectancy at birth while negative side is Infant mortality rate. Each of these variables is standardized by the standard goal post method used by UNDP.

$$\text{Positive Index} = \frac{\text{Observation} - \text{Min value}}{\text{Max value} - \text{Min value}}, \text{Negative Index} = \frac{\text{Max value} - \text{Observation}}{\text{Max value} - \text{Min value}}$$

$$\text{Net Index} = \text{Positive Index}^{*}(1 - \text{Nagative Index})$$

After this transformation, we have combined four positive indices of public hygiene into a single index using primary component analysis. Similar task has been performed for negative index of public hygiene.

States with above India's average outcome and public hygiene are considered as good and states below India's average outcome and public hygiene are considered as bad.

We find that across the two census years (2001–2011), none of the north-eastern states remain virtuous. Thus, none of the states are richly endowed with all the health facilities

Similarly, the two states (Assam and Meghalaya) in the vicious category have remained there across the two time points. These states are traditionally poor states in all respects. The poorness is reflected in health also. They remain in eternal black hole with little light for exit. This verifies the element of structural poverty and pauperization in the Indian health scenario.

The only dynamics is in the intermediate groups. Mizoram is the only state which is bad in one dimension retained bad in both the dimensions. The condition of the state has deteriorated across the first decade of this new millennium making it a hapless state.

None of the states that are bad in both the dimensions become good in either of the dimensions. Sikkim is the only States that are good in one dimension became good in both dimensions. This state has gained from the development classes that India is ushering in her new health era. These may be regarded as the "**Poster Boys**" of development. Among the Lop-sided states, there is no movement. In no states, the failure in one dimension transmitted to other and vice versa.

17.4 Conclusion

Our chapter was a journey through the complex issues of health prevention and its utilization. The issue is complicated by the existence of achievement simultaneously failure. The traditional measure fails to capture the coupling of achievement and failure in the society's outlook as developed by Kosa (1969). The net measure developed by us is able to capture this more fruitfully. We have also considered the dimensions of hygiene infrastructure and outcome simultaneously.

However, the dimension of health could be fully understood if the healthcare is also considered using the same technique. The dimension of health could be fully understood if the healthcare is also considered using the same technique.

Appendix

See Tables 17.4, 17.5.

Table 17.4 Outcome and public hygiene (2000–01)

States	Positive		Negative		Effective(Net)	
	LEB	Positive public hygiene	IMR	Negative public hygiene	Net outcome	Net public hygiene
Assam	0.06	0.08	0.74	0.88	0.02	0.01
Arunachal Pradesh	0.66	0.48	0.32	0.50	0.45	0.24
Manipur	0.88	0.19	0.10	0.80	0.79	0.04
Meghalaya	0.34	0.32	0.64	0.63	0.12	0.12
Mizoram	0.94	0.38	0.04	0.63	0.90	0.14
Nagaland	0.99	0.38	0.01	0.60	0.99	0.15
Sikkim	0.58	0.58	0.41	0.40	0.34	0.35
Tripura	0.73	0.16	0.26	0.83	0.54	0.03

Source Compiled Data taken From SRS Abridge Life Tables 1998–2002 and 2006–10, SRS Bulletin, Volume 47 No. 1 (Sept., 2013); Vol. 48 (Sept., 2013) and census data 2000 and 2011 and author has done the calculation

Table 17.5 Outcome and public hygiene (2011)

States	Positive		Negative		Effective(Net)	
	LEB	Positive public hygiene	IMR	Negative public hygiene	Net outcome	Net public hygiene
Assam	0.00	0.10	0.90	0.86	0.00	0.01
Arunachal Pradesh	0.49	0.57	0.37	0.46	0.31	0.31
Manipur	0.67	0.38	0.07	0.62	0.63	0.14
Meghalaya	0.23	0.35	0.80	0.64	0.05	0.12
Mizoram	0.44	0.60	0.45	0.40	0.24	0.36
Nagaland	0.55	0.50	0.27	0.46	0.40	0.27
Sikkim	0.48	0.82	0.38	0.21	0.30	0.64
Tripura	0.47	0.27	0.40	0.76	0.28	0.06

Source Compiled Data taken From SRS Abridge Life Tables 1998–2002 and 2006–10, SRS Bulletin, Volume 47 No. 1 (Sept., 2013); Vol. 48 (Sept., 2013) and census data 2000 and 2011 and author has done the calculation

References

Basu, K., & Foster, J. E. (1998). On measuring literacy. *Economic Journal, 108*(451), 1733–1749.

Chakravarty, S. R. (2003). A generalized human development index. *Review of Development Economics, 7*(1), 99–114.

Kosa, J. (1969). *The nature of poverty.* In: Kosa J, Zola IK, (Eds.), *Poverty and health: A sociological analysis* (pp. 1–39). Massachusetts: Harvard University Press.

Lee, T. (2007). *Benchmarking the effective literacy rate.* CAE working paper 07-13.

Nayar, K. R. (2007). Social exclusion, caste and health: A review based on the social determinants framework. *Indian Journal of Medical Research, 126,* 355–363.

Ramirez, A., Ranis, G., & Stewart, F. (1998). *Economic growth and human development.* Working Paper 18, Queen Elizabeth House, Oxford.

Ranis, G., & Stewart, F. (2000). *Strategies for success in human development.* Working Paper 32, Queen Elizabeth House, Oxford.

Ranis, G., & Stewart, F. (2001). *Growth and human development: Comparative Latin American experience*. Discussion Paper No. 826, Economic Growth Centre, Yale University, New Haven.

Thorat, S. (2007). *Human poverty and socially disadvantaged groups in India.* Discussion Paper Series-18.

UNDP. (1994). *Human development report.* New York, NY: Oxford University Press.

Chapter 18
Inequalities in Child Survival in Eight Northeastern States of India

Partha De

18.1 Introduction

The demographic impact of child health programmes is generally expressed in terms of mortality change in the child population as a whole. But when the question of inequality arises with respect to utilization of certain social services then it leads to the examination and evaluation of different beneficiaries within the population. If certain socioeconomic sections of the population enjoy benefit more from healthcare programmes than others, then it creates disparities among the people. It indicates that the programme is not benefiting the desired section of the society those who need it most and thus definite action is needed to improve it. It has been observed that, when improvement in health services happened, instead of poor people the better off group get more access and advantage to the enhanced facilities. Thus, improvement in health services cannot guarantee the improvement of health condition of the vulnerable population (Gwatkin 2005). This argument also gives support to this point that inequalities in healthcare services are generally unfavorable to the underprivileged, changing largely across space and so, socioeconomic disparities in health appear to be increasing rather than reducing (Wagstaff 2002). Usually, the above-said disadvantaged group consists of people who belong to much lower socioeconomic status—indicating low levels of education along with poor standard of living, minimum access to health facility and therefore hardly any worries about healthcare. This results in under-utilization of medical amenities and unhealthy way of life, including nutritional deficiencies and very low standard of personal hygiene.

Now, this burden of socioeconomic inequality along with poverty falls overwhelmingly on children which resulted in a significant proportion of deaths occurring in childhood. These unwanted deaths may be attributed to insufficient

P. De (✉)
Population Studies Unit, Indian Statistical Institute, Kolkata, India
e-mail: partha@isical.ac.in; parthade@hotmail.com

U.K. De et al. (eds.), *Issues on Health and Healthcare in India*, India Studies in Business and Economics, https://doi.org/10.1007/978-981-10-6104-2_18

public health measures and poor access to available health facilities. Evidence from the past studies indicate that children born in families with poor socioeconomic status experience higher mortality rates (Claeson et al. 2003; Poerwanto et al. 2003; Goldani et al. 2001; Wagstaff 2000). Unfortunately, most of the death causes of children are preventable and therefore, these deaths are unnecessary and inequitable (WHO/World Bank 2002). India's National Health Policy (NHP) of 2002 observed wide disparities in public healthcare facilities and health standards in different parts of the country. So, it was a prime objective of NHP-2002 to develop a policy structure which helps to reduce the inequalities and also take care of the disadvantaged section of society for a fairer access to public health services (MOHFW 2002). Although in India, significant improvement happened in health facilities over time but still a significant portion of vulnerable mother and children from low socioeconomic status group are suffering and dying from various preventable infectious diseases, nutritional deficiencies, and from complicated pregnancy and delivery. Now, it is important to measure this inequality to know about its level and variability within different social groups. It is also interesting to note that, whether inequality in child mortality is changing over time and space. This may help us to find out the magnitude and extent of inequality in child death in different regions and states of India.

This inequality imposes big challenges in different layers of healthcare system in our nation. It becomes important to find out the health differentials to judge whether our country's national healthcare policies are really converging towards greater social justice in case of maternal and child healthcare or not. The maternal and child health programs are enormously important in a highly populous country like India, where we are still experiencing moderately high infant and child deaths within the underprivileged section of society. It is a social responsibility of researcher to measure socioeconomic disparity and also to monitor inequities in child health and survival. These measures will help us to understand the magnitude of inequalities which may be utilized for continuous monitoring and assessment of diverse policy measures in controlling infant and child death in Indian subcontinent.

Most of the past studies deal inequality considering different quintiles of people based on their socioeconomic well-being. Several past studies described inequality among different quintiles of population constructed on the basis of socioeconomic status. Generally, two types of approaches are available, one dealing with methodological aspect (Mackenboch et al. 1997; Kakwani et al. 1997; Wagstaff et al. 1991) and the other focused mainly on empirical perspective (Van Doorslaer et al. 1997; Mackenbach et al. 1997). The studies which concentrate on to find out correlation between inequalities and health outcomes mostly selected data from developing countries (Wagstaff et al. 2000; Gwatkin et al. 2000; Wagstaff 2000). Many determinants of socioeconomic inequality are identified by many scholars to describe their impacts on infant and child health in several countries of the world (Mosley and Chen 1984; Benefo and Schultz 1996; Wagstaff et al. 2001; Bhuiya et al. 2001; Szwarcwald et al. 2002; Hosseinpoor et al. 2006; Yazbeck 2009). Particularly in India, the available research work in this aspect mainly deals with inequality in children's nutrition along with inappropriate utilization of available health services. But unfortunately, very few attempts (Gwatkin et al. 2000; Filmer and Pritchett 2001; Deaton and Dreze 2002; Yazbeck 2009) have been made to find out the disparities in child health using important inequality measures across various regions and states in India.

The present study deals several aspects. It looks at different demographic and socioeconomic and healthcare characteristics of northeastern states of India. It is important to make an assessment about the accessibility and utilization of available reproductive and child healthcare facilities over there. This will help us to understand about the present status of health inequalities determining survival of children.

For the northeastern states of India, this study constructed concentration indices (which is a conventional measure of inequality) from different quintiles of wealth index (representing socioeconomic status of population) to assess state-wise variations of inequality in child mortality. The entire exercise was done utilizing infant and under-five mortality data available from the third National Family Health survey (NFHS-III) of 2005–07 for northeast states of India (IIPS and MACRO 2007). The wealth index variable has been constructed using household asset data and housing characteristics in NFHS-III.

18.2 Data and Methodology

The present study is performed by applying the data from the National Family Health Survey III (NFHS-III) in India. The birth history data is available for the children born during the last 5 years prior the survey (IIPS and MACRO 2007). In this study, only the northeast states of India are included to understand the real situation of inequality in child mortality in that part of India. According to Indian Census of 2011, northeastern states cover 1% of India's population (Census of India 2011).

The National Family Health Survey III reported that under-five mortality rate (U5MR) (usually express in per thousand live birth) has been reducing over the years. For example, it was 109 during NFHS-I (first phase of NFHS survey in 1992–93). It was 95 in NFHS-II (second phase of NFHS survey in 1998–99) and finally, it became 74 in NFHS-III (third phase of NFHS survey in 2005–06). But this decline over the years does not necessarily indicate decrease in inequality in child health and mortality for all sections of population. Evidences suggest that health inequalities for children are pervasive and may be observed in different dimensions. Different socioeconomic and demographic factors like, educational level of mother, caste–religion, sex of the child, residence (rural or urban), socioeconomic status, and many more are responsible for the inequality in child health. For example, according to NFHS-III, among illiterate mothers, the U5MR was 94.7, but among mothers with higher secondary (12 standards) level of education or more it was only 29.7. Considering child immunization for the age group 12–23 months, near about 71% children received full vaccination from household belonging to wealthiest quintile, but the figure is only 26% in case of poorest quintile. Again, children representing the household with low SLI (standard of living index) are twice as likely to be undernourished as children from the household with a high SLI (IIPS and MACRO 2007).

Now, to measure the health inequality between different socioeconomic class, and to find out the degree of inequality, a composite index has been prepared usually named as wealth index (WI). This type of index reveals the economic status of a household and normally utilized to find out the economic disparity in health outcome and utilization of healthcare services (Filmer et al. 2001). In the present study, this index is used to find out the inequality in health outcomes like infant and under-five mortalities evolving from socioeconomic disparities.

In NFHS-III report, the wealth index is calculated from a set of consumer durables like land size, housing quality and water, and sanitation facilities available to a household (IIPS and MACRO 2007). In this case, the entire sample population is segregated into five subgroups or quintiles. These groups of population are—lowest, second, middle, fourth, and highest.

As it is mentioned earlier that the health outcome indicator, utilized in this analysis, is the mortality of children or precisely the infant and under-five mortality. Unquestionably, these two child mortality rates are considered as vital health indicators and have an important role in calculating life expectancy at birth (Wagstaff 2000). It has already been mentioned that birth histories data are available in the NFHS study. So based on this information, different mortality rates for the children under different quintiles of wealth index are estimated utilizing the Kaplan–Meier method of survival analysis for all the northeastern states of India (Kaplan and Meier 1958; Hill and Yazbeck 1993). Then, using these data of infant and under-five mortalities, concentration curve (CC) has been plotted for each state and at the end concentration indices (CI) have been constructed. All these CC and CI are calculated from different quintiles of wealth index (WI) to understand inter-state variations of mortality among the children of different socioeconomic groups in the northeast of India.

In Fig. 18.1, mortality concentration curve has been drawn indicated by l(p), where p indicates the cumulative proportion of the study population. In y-axis, we measure the cumulative proportion of infant or under-five deaths and in x-axis, the

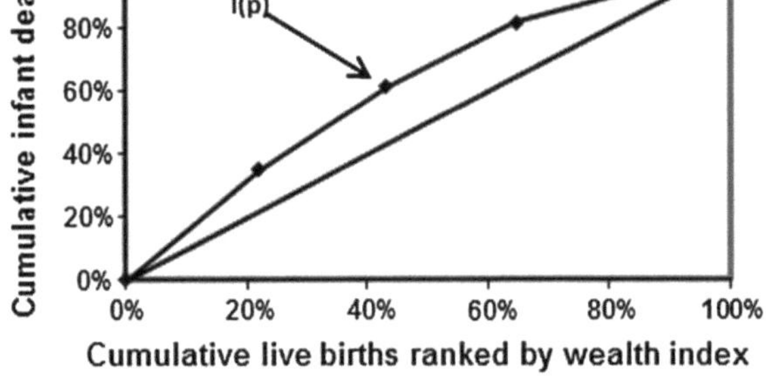

Fig. 18.1 Mortality concentration curve

cumulative proportion of live births of children at risk is ranked by the wealth index, where we start with the most disadvantaged child. In this diagram, we are interested to find out the distribution of infant or under-five mortality in different quintiles of socioeconomic status. When the curve l(p) overlaps with the diagonal, that means, all children have equal probability of death irrespective of their socioeconomic background. However, when the area within the curve and the diagonal increases that implies inequality simultaneously increases. Therefore, if the curve lies above the diagonal it indicates inequality in infant or under-five mortality favors the children of affluent class. So this kind of inequality may be labeled as "pro-rich". Again, if the curve lies below the diagonal then we may call the inequality as "pro-poor" (Wagstaff 2000). Now, when the curve l(p) lies above the 45° line, the magnitude of inequality increases along the wealth quintiles.

The socioeconomic inequality in health variable can be identified using the concentration curve (CC) and we also determine its variability over time and space utilizing this curve. However, it is not possible to find out the magnitude of inequality using this CC curve. So it will be difficult to compare inequality across several time periods or regions. The Nanak Chand Kakwani derived an index considering Gini framework to measure progressivity of social intervention (Kakwani 1977, 1980). This index is later used to measure the degree of health inequality and termed as concentration index (CI). The concentration index which can be derived using the concept of concentration curve has the power to quantify the degree of socioeconomic inequality for a healthcare variable (Kakwani et al. 1997; Wagstaff et al. 1989). In their study, Wagstaff et al. (1991) suggested about the use of related concepts of concentration curve and index. These concepts were utilized by them to find out the extent of inequalities in health status to different socioeconomic indicators similar to income or education. They claimed that CI is the most suitable measure of health inequality, which satisfies the three basic necessities of a health inequality index. First of all, it includes the entire situation experienced by the whole population under study. Another point is that it reflects the total scenario of health inequalities in different socioeconomic dimensions. Lastly, it is very much sensitive to reallocation of the population between different socioeconomic groups. The use of CI now becomes very popular in the health sector study. Few examples of its applications are presented below.

The concept of concentration index has been applied for measuring and comparing the socioeconomic allied inequality in infant and under-five mortalities (Wagstaff 2000). It also applied to observe the variability in child immunization (Gwatkin et al. 2003) and child malnutrition (Wagstaff et al. 2003). To understand the extent of inequality in adult health between different countries, the tool like concentration index has borrowed (van Doorslaer et al. 1997). Researcher also applied the concept of CI to quantify and differentiate health subsidies targeted towards the underprivileged in different countries under study (Castro-Leaf et al. 2000). Therefore, several applications are observed for CI.

However, CI has some limitations. First, concentration index needs at least one variable like socioeconomic status which has continuous ranking. This imposes limited applicability and use of this index. Second, CI denotes cumulative proportions of a health variable. So, when mean level of health changes then CI remains unchanged. This reflects the insensitivity of CI due to change in mean value of the variable. Then, for populations with diverse mean health levels we cannot compare the concentration index values; Third, CI is a measure of relative inequality and here we cannot merge efficiency with equity. Wagstaff (1991) recommended a way to determine equity-efficiency trade-off. He suggested an iso-elastic social welfare function which can be utilized to achieve a trade-off between efficiency in terms of health maximization and health equity.

Now let us define he concentration index (CI). Graphically, it can be defined as twice the area between the concentration curve [l(p)], and the line of equality indicated by the 45° line. The value of concentration index lies between −1 and +1. When the CC curve is above the diagonal line then values of CI are negative and when CC is below the diagonal the values are positive. When inequality is concentrated among disadvantaged people then we get the negative values of the variable. Similarly, just opposite happens for its positive values. Thus, the value of concentration index is zero when there is no inequality in wealth. If the child mortality is considered as a health variable, then negative value of CI indicates that mortality is higher among poor children.

For the measurement of health inequality, the concentration index (CI) may be computed using a formula described by Kakwani et al. (1997) and Wagstaff (2000). In the present study, inequality in health is investigated using group data and the groups comprising socioeconomic groups (based on wealth index). Let us denote the CI (Concentration Index) of a health variable with the letter 'C_h'. Here, we also define sample size as 'n'. Now, the number of existing socioeconomic groups defined by wealth index may be denoted as 'S'. If we consider that, tth group contains f_t proportion of the sample, then C_h can be derived as:

$$C_h = \frac{2}{\mu}\sum_{t=1}^{S} f_t \mu_t R_t - 1, \tag{18.1}$$

where μ is the total of mean mortality rate and μ_t (t = 1,…, S) the mean value of health variable (here, mortality rate) of the 't'th socioeconomic group. The term R_t be the relative rank of the 't'th socioeconomic group. So, the mathematical expressions for μ and R_t are presented below.

$$\mu = \sum_{t=1}^{S} f_t \mu_t \text{ and } R_t = \sum_{\eta=1}^{t-1} f_\eta + \frac{1}{2} f_t \tag{18.2}$$

The term R_t shows the cumulative proportion of the live births up to the midpoint of each socioeconomic group interval. The present study is using infant and under-five mortality data being derived from the National Family Heath Survey (NFHS) of India. So this data may be subject to sampling variation. It becomes important to calculate the standard error for the concentration index 'C_h'. The variance of the estimator of C_h is given by:

$$\mathrm{Var}\left(\hat{C}_h\right) = \frac{1}{n}\left[\sum_{t=1}^{S} f_t \alpha_t^2 - (1 + C_h)^2\right] + \frac{1}{n\,\mu^2}\sum_{t=1}^{S} f_t \sigma_t^2 (2\,R_t - 1 - C_h)^2 \quad (18.3)$$

Here, σ_t^2 is the variance of the mortality rate of the tth Socioeconomic group labeled by μ_t and,

$$\alpha_t = \frac{\mu_t}{\mu}(2\,R_t - 1 - C_h) + 2 - q_{t-1} - q_t \quad (18.4)$$

$$q_t = \frac{1}{\mu}\sum_{\eta=1}^{t} \mu_\eta f_\eta \quad (18.5)$$

being the ordinate of concentration curve l(p), $q_0 = 0$, and $p_t = \sum_{\eta=1}^{t} f_\eta R_\eta$, with $p_0 = 0$.

18.3 Findings

There is no doubt that India as a country has made considerable progress in healthcare facilities and infrastructure during past years. The National Rural Health Mission (NRHM) launched by the Government of India in 2005 accelerated the progress towards definite developmental goals related with the health sector in the country. However, the improvement in the health sector is quite uneven across the regions, particularly in the northeast, with limited accessibility in healthcare services in rural areas. According to Census 2011, about 81.6% of population of this region lives in rural area. We know that the northeast region includes eight states namely, Assam, Arunachal Pradesh, Manipur, Meghalaya, Mizoram, Nagaland, Sikkim, and Tripura. These states are quite different from the remaining states of the country. The reason is that the entire northeast region is physically isolated from rest of the country due to its topographical position. Various tribal and ethnic groups are inhabiting in this region and these people are characterized by their diverse social and cultural practices. It is a pity that we have very limited knowledge and understanding about them.

Table 18.1 shows the demographic features of the eight northeast states along with India as a whole. The women in the northeast, unexpectedly, are the least likely to have married early before the legal age of 18. In majority of the states, the percentage figures of early marriage are well below the national average. Similarly, women in the Northeast India attained basically the high level of education as those in the southern states of India. In majority of the states other than Arunachal

Pradesh, female literacy rates are very high, even higher than the national average (64.6%). The distribution of 0–6 year's children to state population (%) varies between 12.1 and 18.8%, where states like Sikkim, Tripura, and Manipur have lower percentage of child population than the national average (13.1%). The three northeastern states namely, Arunachal Pradesh, Meghalaya, and Nagaland are experiencing high level of fertility rate (TFR), whereas Assam, Tripura, and Sikkim have the fertility rate very much lower than the all India average. Among the states of this region, the states of Arunachal Pradesh (960), Meghalaya (970) and Mizoram (971) have recorded significantly higher sex ratio (0–6 yrs.) than that of national figure (914). On the other hand, Manipur has witnessed the lowest sex ratio (934) in the region. According to the UN study (UNFPA and UN Women 2014), northeast states like Manipur and Nagaland have shown a significant decline in the sex ratio of children between 2001 and 2011. The natural growth rate of other northeastern states is much lower than that of Meghalaya in the same decade. The growth rate of population in Meghalaya is highest due to the higher birth rates compared to other states like Tripura and Manipur. According to Sample Registration System Bulletin, 2011, the estimated birth rate of Meghalaya is 24.1 whereas estimated birth rates in respect of Manipur and Tripura are 14.8 and 14.3, respectively. It is well known that the birth interval has an important positive impact on the levels of fertility within the population. Particularly in Tripura, Assam, and Manipur, birth intervals are much higher than the remaining states and also to the national level.

From Table 18.1, we can also analyze the situation for neo-natal, infant and under-five mortalities for various northeastern states during NFHS-II and NFHS-III. Apart from Assam, Manipur, Mizoram, and Nagaland, all the other states have shown better improvement over the period with respect to neo-natal mortality (NMR). In case of infant mortality (IMR), Arunachal Pradesh, Assam, Mizoram, and Nagaland have improved unsatisfactorily and well below the improvement with respect to national average. The same thing also happened in case of under-five mortality (U5MR). However, Meghalaya is the only state which has shown a remarkable improvement from NFHS-II to NFHS-III in NMR, IMR, and U5MR. It would be interesting to know how this state has reduced all these child mortality rates drastically. The state Sikkim also has shown good improvement in mortality rates for the children over the period. States like Assam and Arunachal have higher mortality rates than the national figure in NFHS-III period. Although there has been some improvement in child death rates in the northeast region, the improvement is not at all uniform in all the states under the region. Particularly, states like Arunachal Pradesh, Assam, Mizoram, and Nagaland are far behind the improvement with respect to the national figures of NMR, IMR, and U5MR.

Table 18.2 represents utilization of different maternal and child health (MCH) care facilities in the northeast states of India. Getting the antenatal care (ANC) among the northeast states is lower than the national figure for the states like Arunachal Pradesh, Assam, and Nagaland. The ANC received at least three times in these regions is highest in Sikkim (70.1%) and Nagaland (32.7%) shows the lowest value. In case of receiving Tetanus Toxoid (TT) injection during pregnancy, except

Table 18.1 Demographic characteristics of all India and states in Northeast India

State	Marriage below 18 years (%)	% of child population (0–6) years	Female literacy rate (%)	Sex ratio (females per thousand males) (0–6) years	Natural growth rate (birth rate—death rate)	Total fertility rate	Birth interval (media no. of months since proceeding birth)	Neo-natal mortality rate (NMR)		Infant mortality rate (IMR)		Under-five mortality rate (U5MR)	
								NFHS-II	NFHS-III	NFHS-II	NFHS-III	NFHS-II	NFHS-III
Arunachal Pradesh	8.2	14.7	57.7	960	14.0	3.03	30.8	41.8	34.0	63.1	60.7	98.1	87.7
Assam	20.8	14.5	66.3	957	14.8	2.42	37.0	44.6	45.5	69.5	66.1	89.5	85.0
Manipur	6.3	13.0	72.4	934	10.3	2.83	35.4	18.6	18.7	37.0	29.7	56.1	41.9
Meghalaya	15.0	18.8	72.9	970	16.3	3.80	31.7	50.7	23.6	89.0	44.6	122.0	70.5
Mizoram	9.9	15.2	89.3	971	12.2	2.86	30.6	18.8	16.3	37.0	34.1	54.7	52.9
Nagaland	NA	14.4	76.1	944	12.8	3.74	28.6	20.1	19.8	42.1	38.3	63.8	64.7
Sikkim	16.0	10.1	75.6	944	12.0	2.09	34.5	26.3	19.4	43.9	33.7	71.0	40.1
Tripura	21.1	12.1	82.7	953	9.4	2.22	39.0	NA	33.1	NA	51.5	NA	59.2
All India	22.1	13.1	64.6	914	14.7	2.68	31.1	43.4	39.0	67.6	57.0	94.9	74.3

Sources NFHS-III (2005–06), Census—2011, Sample Registration System (SRS)—2011; *NA*—Not available

Sikkim and Manipur, all the percentage figures of remaining states are below the national figure (76.3). More severe situation is observed in receiving of IFA (iron and folic acid) during pregnancy of mothers in northeast region. Except Mizoram and Sikkim, the percentages of receiving IFA (at least 90 days during pregnancy) are very low compared to national figure (23.1). Particularly in Nagaland only 3.5% pregnant mothers receive IFA during pregnancy. It has been observed that women of lower socioeconomic status often do not avail the existing maternal healthcare services, particularly the services of delivery care. Institutional delivery is lowest in Nagaland (11.6%) and highest in Mizoram (59.8%). Particularly in the states like Nagaland, Arunachal Pradesh, Assam, and Meghalaya, institutional delivery is less than 30%. The assistance of the healthcare professionals is very important at the time of delivery because it is the most critical moment in the life of women. The percentage of deliveries with the assistance of health professional is highest in Manipur (59.0%) and lowest in Nagaland (24.7). In Manipur, Mizoram, and Sikkim, the percentages of deliveries with a post-natal checkup are comparatively high (more than 50%) than the all India figure (41.2).

There has been a vast difference across states in Northeast India on the parameter of child's health. In Table 18.2, the NFHS-III data shows the values of different child health parameters across northeast states in India. The full immunization coverage of vaccination is highest in Sikkim (69.9%) and lowest in Nagaland (21.0%). In Arunachal Pradesh, Assam, Meghalaya, and Nagaland immunization coverages are low compared to all India level of 43.5%. As we know that, child nutrition is the most important factor which helps in child development. It has been observed that inadequate nutritional intake, acute infections, and minimum access to healthcare facilities create a significant percentage of children to become moderate or severely malnourished.

The nutritional status of children in the northeast regional states is also shown in Table 18.2, according to the three anthropometric indices like: stunted, wasted, and underweight. All the northeast states except for Meghalaya are doing better compared to all India. The three states like, Manipur, Mizoram, and Sikkim are performing well compared with the remaining states in the northeast. Infant feeding practices have important effects on child health. The initiation of breast milk after birth and exclusive breast feeding up to 6 months of child's age are important for child growth and development. Table 18.2 shows that in almost all the northeast states there are very good practices of breastfeeding within the period of 1 hour of birth. The children who are breastfed within 1 hour of birth are highest in Mizoram and lowest in Tripura. But all the percentage of breast feeding practices in this region are still higher than the national average (24.5%). Young children suffering from anaemia is a serious concern. It results in developmental delay as well as resulted in increased morbidity or mortality from diseases arising from various infections. In all the NE states, except Assam are having lower percentage of anaemia compared to all India percentage of 69.5. However, in majority of the states except in Manipur, Mizoram, and Nagaland more than 50% of children are anaemic.

Table 18.2 Maternal and child health characteristics (in %) of all India and states in Northeast India

State name	ANC at least 3 times	TT at least 2 times during pregnancy	IFA (90 days during pregnancy)	Institutional delivery	Birth attended by health professional	Post-natal care (for last live births within 5 years)
Arunachal Pradesh	35.5	40.1	11.2	28.5	30.2	23.7
Assam	39.3	65.4	16.2	22.4	31.0	15.9
Manipur	68.6	79.2	13.1	45.9	59.0	50.1
Meghalaya	54.0	51.8	16.7	29.0	31.1	33.2
Mizoram	59.3	51.4	24.7	59.8	65.4	53.5
Nagaland	32.7	50.7	3.5	11.6	24.7	11.8
Sikkim	70.1	81.1	38.7	47.2	53.7	52.4
Tripura	60.0	74.9	18.0	46.9	48.8	33.7
All India	52.0	76.3	23.1	38.7	46.6	41.2

State name	Full immunization (children age 12–23 months)	No vaccination (children age 12–23 months)	Stunted (height for age) children <5 years	Wasted (weight for height) children <5 years	Under weight (weight for age) children <5 years	Breast feeding (within 1 h of birth)	Children with any anaemia (<11.0 g/dl)
Arunachal Pradesh	28.4	24.1	43.3	15.3	32.5	58.6	56.9
Assam	31.4	15.2	46.5	13.7	36.4	50.9	69.6
Manipur	46.8	6.5	35.6	9.0	22.1	57.8	41.1
Meghalaya	32.9	16.5	55.1	30.7	48.8	57.8	64.4
Mizoram	46.5	7.0	39.8	9.0	19.9	66.4	44.2
Nagaland	21.0	18.4	38.8	13.3	25.2	54.2	NA
Sikkim	69.6	3.2	38.3	9.7	19.7	42.9	59.2
Tripura	49.7	14.7	35.7	24.6	39.6	34.6	62.9
All India	43.5	5.1	48.0	19.8	42.5	24.5	69.5

Sources NFHS-III (2005–06)

To measure the socioeconomic disparity in childhood mortality, this study utilizes wealth index (WI). This WI truly reflects the socioeconomic status of the household under study because it is constructed mainly from housing characteristics and household asset data. On the other hand, the usefulness of concentration index which fulfills the necessary requirements as a measuring instrument of inequality has already described in the previous section. Thus, this study uses wealth index in constructing the concentration index, which helps us to determine magnitude and dimension of inequality in infant and under-five mortalities in northeast states of India.

Table 18.3 shows distribution of children along with infant and under-five mortalities based on wealth index (i.e., different quintiles of child population) utilizing NFHS-III data. This table describes the extent of inequalities exist in infant and under-five mortality experienced by the northeast states of India. From this table, it can be observed that distribution of child population within different wealth quintiles has large variation across the states. The children belong to lowest quintile are more concentrated (more than 14%) in the states of Arunachal Pradesh, Assam, Tripura, and Meghalaya. However, more than 24% belong to highest quintile in Mizoram and Sikkim. Particularly in the states of Assam, Meghalaya, Nagaland, and Tripura, less than 10% children belong to the highest quintile.

The extent of inequality in infant and under-five mortality under different wealth quintiles are shown in the table. In the lowest quintile of Sikkim state, the values of IMR and U5MR are equal to zero. This is due the fact that, in this quintile, the sample size is so small that it was difficult to calculate the mortality rates for this group. In all the states, except Mizoram, a wide gap has been observed for under-five mortality rates between the lowest and the highest quintile. The poorest quintile experienced the highest infant and under-five mortality rates in the states of Assam, Manipur, Meghalaya, Tripura, and Nagaland. One important observation for the Meghalaya state is that the infant and the under-five mortality rates are equal in magnitude in the highest quintiles. This implies for this state, the role of morality beyond 1 year of age and up to 5 years of age is negligible in the highest quintile. But for this state, first quintile (poorest) is contributing higher mortality rate in children relative to rest of the quintiles. Results indicate that both the infant and the under-five mortality data sharply decline from the poorest quintile to the richest quintile in majority of the northeast states. This tendency is much more noticeable for the under-five rates. Infant and under-five rates for the lowest quintile are the highest in Tripura (104.7) and Meghalaya (141.4) correspondingly. In Tripura, both the IMR and U5MR are same and lowest in the highest quintile compared to other states. From this evidence, it can be said that, in most of the NE states survival prospect for the children, born in underprivileged families, is inferior compared to survival prospect of those children born in prosperous families. As a conclusion, it can be argued that, if we move from the lower to the upper quintile along the scale of wealth index, then a steady decline has been observed in infant and the under-five mortality in the states under study.

However, from Table 18.3, we cannot specify which states have the maximum inequalities and which have the minimum. So we need comparison of concentration curves for all NE states, which are built utilizing mortality rates and wealth indices. To overcome the difficulties in presenting and comparing the concentration curves

Table 18.3 Percentage distribution of children (aged below 10 years), infant and under-five mortality rates, by quintile of wealth index in different states of Northeast India (NFHS-III, 2005–06)

States of India	Wealth index (percent)					Infant mortality (1q0)					Under-five mortality (5q0)					No. of children
	Quintiles					Quintiles					Quintiles					
	1	2	3	4	5	1	2	3	4	5	1	2	3	4	5	
Arunachal Pradesh	23.7	28.9	21.3	13.3	12.8	65.5	92.8	69.2	45.7	28.3	99.5	113.2	97.7	65.9	44.2	1873
Assam	27.8	34.9	19.4	11.1	6.8	95.0	70.6	65.9	52.6	15.5	122.1	98.2	77.2	52.6	23.3	3589
Manipur	3.8	20.7	36.1	28.1	11.3	97.5	48.0	39.4	19.3	20.9	119.6	63.5	55.6	25.0	23.0	3970
Meghalaya	14.7	26.8	30.3	19.4	8.8	80.3	53.7	35.3	41.6	26.3	141.4	87.2	47.0	50.1	26.3	2424
Mizoram	3.3	8.3	25.5	32.7	30.2	17.2	63.3	39.4	25.4	26.5	38.6	87.1	62.8	41.3	31.4	1675
Nagaland	10.9	28.2	29.4	22.4	9.1	58.4	59.1	49.4	36.3	22.3	109.5	87.3	73.0	42.7	26.0	4623
Sikkim	2.4	14.4	29.0	30.1	24.1	0.0	35.0	39.1	36.6	31.5	0.0	49.9	47.5	45.7	35.2	1599
Tripura	18.4	27.2	36.5	12.5	5.4	104.7	64.9	45.7	10.8	15.3	137.1	70.7	48.3	10.8	15.3	1344
All India	22.0	21.3	21.4	19.2	16.1	81.4	72.8	65.8	50.8	33.8	112.6	94.8	79.7	59.1	38.6	114,283

Sources Calculated from NFHS-III (2005–06) data

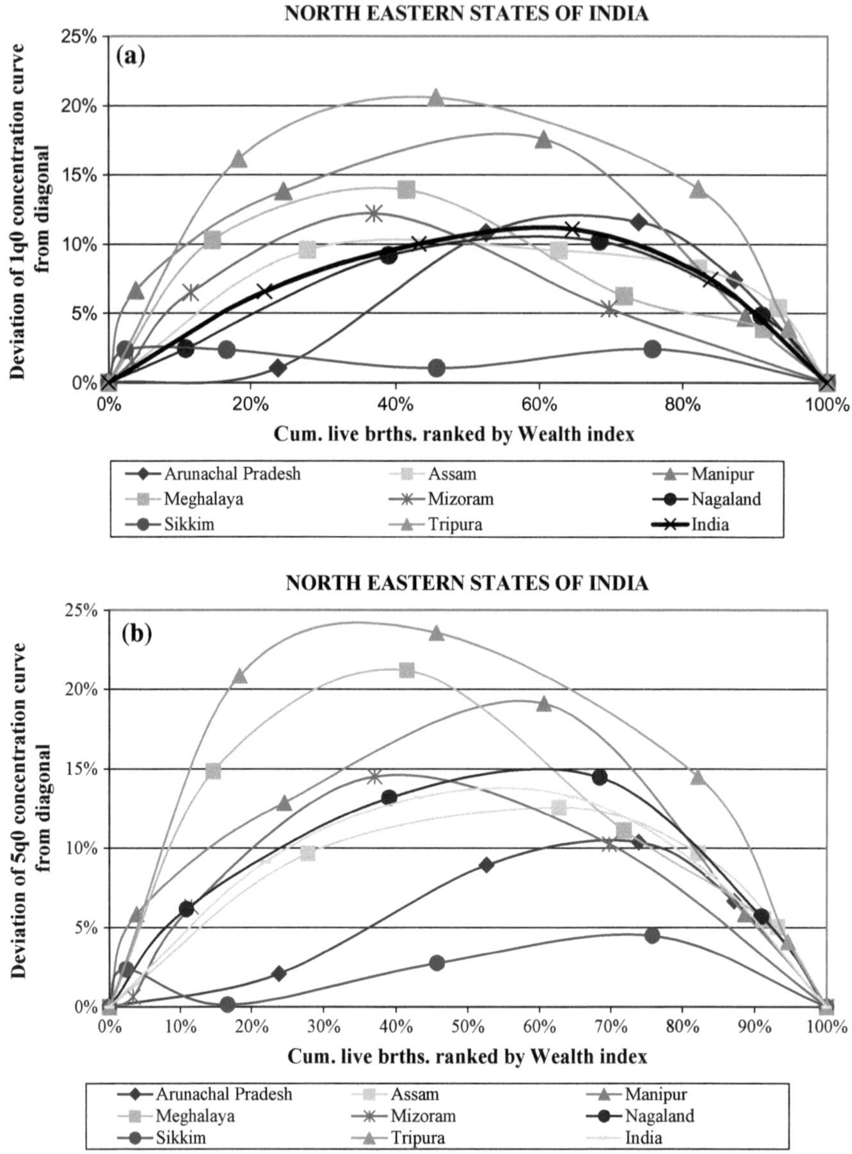

Fig. 18.2 **a** Concentration curve deviations for infant mortality in Indian Northeastern States (NFHS-III, 2005–06). *Sources* Graph derived from NFHS-III (2005–06) data. **b** Concentration curve deviations for under-five mortality in Indian Northeastern States (NFHS-III, 2005–06). *Sources* Graph derived from NFHS-III (2005–06) data

for all the states of Northeast India, we can find out just the deviations of the mortality concentration curves from the 45° line. This is presented in Figs. 18.2a, b, by northeast region of India.

Both the curves for infant and under-five mortalities are constructed. But the representation is clearer in case of U5MR than IMR. Along the horizontal axis, we measure the percentage of cumulative live births ranked by wealth index. Similarly, along the vertical axis, percentage deviation of mortality CC curve from diagonal (i.e., 45° line) is measured. Adam Wagstaff described this type of exercise as "dominance-checking exercise" (Wagstaff 2000). Thus, all concentration curves lie above the 45° line (in case of deviation it is above the horizontal axis), representing pro-rich inequality (Wagstaff 2000) in mortality exists in all the states. In the present study, the picture of inequality in mortality among the children is much more clear in case of under-five mortality.

Now the concentration curves of U5MR (Fig. 18.2b) for Tripura lie furthest from the horizontal axis and hence show highest inequality among all northeastern states. On the other hand, Sikkim has the lowest inequality as designated by the concentration curve. The curve for all India lies in the middle position of the figure. The curves for states like Sikkim and Arunachal Pradesh lie much below than the All India curve, representing less inequality in the under-five mortality over there. The state like Sikkim has the lowest inequality compared to the remaining states, although primarily it intersects with Arunachal Pradesh. Overall, Sikkim, Arunachal Pradesh, and Assam states have less inequality compared to all India. Nagaland and Manipur have comparatively higher inequality than Assam. It can be said that, in comparison inequalities are minimum in the states of Sikkim, Arunachal, and Assam. But, it is high in the states of Tripura, Meghalaya, and Manipur. Thus, remaining states like Nagaland and Mizoram are in intermediary position.

The concentration curves derived in this study actually give us a gross idea about inequality. With this, we can compare the inequality difference between two or more states. Table 18.4 displays the state wise estimates of the CIs discretely for infant and under-five mortality. Here, standard errors and corresponding t-statistics are calculated. It also provides ranking of different states with respect to the concentration index. These are calculated considering Eqs. 18.1–18.5 as described in the methodology section.

In this study, CI values for infant and under-five mortality for the NE states and at the all India level shows the negative values, indicating a heavy burden of childhood mortality among the deprived section in India. Now, according to their magnitude, the IMR and U5MR concentration indices for different states of NE India are ranked. It has been observed, in all the NE states, inequalities in under-five mortality are clearer than inequalities in infant mortality. In Mizoram and Arunachal Pradesh, the concentration indices for under-five mortality are statistically significant, but for infant mortality they are not. In all the states except in Sikkim, the inequalities in under-five mortality are statistically significant. The states on being organized according to the level of concentration index indicate considerable differences in levels of inequality.

Now, it can be argued that reduction in difference in absolute level of under-five mortality among different states cannot guarantee fall in intra-state inequality in under-five mortality. That is, state that has minimum burden of childhood mortality may not have lower child death burden shared by the underprivileged quintile of the population. Likewise, a clear evidence of inequality in under-five mortality is seen in the states where absolute level of under-five mortality is low.

Now the entire inequality situation with respect to U5MR for NE States may be compared with a standard state specific aggregate economic development indicator like Per capita Net State Domestic Product (PCNSDP) at constant prices (DES & CSO 2014). The All India per capita NNP (Net National Product) during the year 2004–2005 was 24143 (Rupee in Crores). The states behind the all India average were during the same period: Assam (16782), Manipur (18640), and Meghalaya (24086). The states which were above the All India level: Tripura (24394), Mizoram (24662), Sikkim (26690), Arunachal Pradesh (26721), and Nagaland (30441). Here, the states like Manipur and Meghalaya have low PCNSDP compared to All India figure, but higher inequality in U5MR for different socioeconomic groups based on WI of NFHS-III data. Similarly, Mizoram, Sikkim, and Arunachal Pradesh have comparatively high PCNSDP but lower inequality in U5MR. So it can be said that at least in the above five states socioeconomic development has positive impact on reduction in inequality in child mortality. On the other hand, in case of Tripura, Nagaland, and Assam, it can be argued that economic development cannot always be considered as the appropriate indicator for reducing disparity in child health situation among the different socioeconomic classes of population.

18.4 Summary and Conclusion

Utilizing the distribution of children according to wealth index, present study calculated different mortality rates for each quintile of wealth index and then magnitudes of inequality within different northeast states of India have been determined. Considering the values, states are classified into different groups according to the inequality levels. Highest inequality is observed in the states of Tripura, Manipur, and Meghalaya. On the other hand, Sikkim and Arunachal Pradesh experience minimum level of inequality in child mortality among different socioeconomic groups. The states like Mizoram, Nagaland, and Assam are in between the above two extreme categories of states. Thus, developmental progress in any region does not always ensure the improvement in child health for all categories of children enjoying different socioeconomic status. Inequality is the reflection of unequal distribution of resources among the people which adversely affects the health of underprivileged population (Wagstaff and Watanabe 2000; Van De Poel et al. 2008). The deprived sections are struggling with poor health and social injustice which directly affects their survival and livelihood. The poorer section of our society is unable to get access the available healthcare facilities due to disparities in geographical, socioeconomic, and political reasons. This is mirrored in the magnitude of under-five mortality.

India has already experienced with high level of economic growth and development. Although, it cannot ensure us about the equal distribution and accessibility

Table 18.4 Concentration indices, standard errors and *T*-values for infant and under-five mortality for different states of Northeast India (NFHS-III, 2004–05)

States	Infant mortality				Under-five mortality			
	CI	Rank	SE (CI)	*t* (CI)	CI	Rank	SE (CI)	*t* (CI)
Tripura	−0.280	1	0.099	−2.84	−0.324	1	0.100	−3.23
Manipur	−0.226	2	0.092	−2.45	−0.233	3	0.088	−2.65
Meghalaya	−0.164	3	0.059	−2.77	−0.253	2	0.065	−3.93
Assam	−0.147	4	0.079	−1.85	−0.167	6	0.076	−2.19
Nagaland	−0.130	5	0.054	−2.43	−0.193	4	0.069	−2.78
Mizoram	−0.125	6	0.086	−1.46	−0.169	5	0.059	−2.89
Arunachal Pradesh	−0.111	7	0.092	−1.21	−0.109	7	0.073	−1.50
Sikkim	−0.005	8	0.073	−0.07	−0.036	8	0.076	−0.47
All India	−0.142		0.051	−2.82	−0.179		0.054	−3.34

Sources Calculated from NFHS-III (2005–06) data

of helpful social services to all people. Thus, policies intend to minimize health inequalities should create the opportunity to all sections in our society. Along with this, necessary steps are also essential to minimize inequality in other aspects in the society. Health services to remote places and extensive transmission of health-related knowledge are prerequisite for spreading the benefits of development to common people. Future research may be directed to know specifically the reasons behind the failure of higher economic development in overall reduction of under-five mortality and failed to eliminate the inequality in child survival for different socioeconomic groups. The present study may be upgraded by considering different features of inequalities arising due to difference in literacy level, religion, and caste with respect to wealth status of population. The time-based inequality model may be developed by constructing composite index using time-dependent variable of inequality.

References

Benefo, K., & Schultz, T. (1996). Fertility and child mortality in Côte d'Ivoire and Ghana. *World Bank Economic Review, 10,* 123–158.

Bhuiya, A., Chowdhury, M., Ahmed, F., & Adams, A. (2001). Bangladesh: An intervention study of factors underlying increasing equity in child survival. In T. Evans, M. Whitehead, F. Diderichsen, A. Bhuiya, & M. Wirth (Eds.), *Challenging inequities in health: From ethics to action.* Oxford: Oxford University Press.

Castro-Leal, F., et al. (2000). Public spending on health care in Africa: Do the poor benefit? *Bulletin of the World Health Organization, 78*(1), 66–74.

Census of India. (2011). Puruliya (Purulia) District: Census 2011 data, Population Census 2011. Available at: http://www.census2011.co.in/census/district/14-puruliya.html, Last accessed on March 25, 2015.

Claeson, M., Gillespie, D., Mshinda, H., Troedsson, H., & Victoria, C. G. (2003). Knowledge into action for child survival. *The Lancet, 362,* 323–327.

Deaton, A., & Jean, D. (2002). Poverty and inequality in India: A re-examination. *Economic and Political Weekly, 37*(36), 3729–3748.

DES and CSO. (2014). Per-capita net state domestic product at constant prices, directorate of economics and statistics of respective State Governments, and for All-India—Central Statistics Office, released on 1st March, 2014.

Filmer, D., & Pritchett, L. (2001). Estimating wealth effect without expenditure data—Or tears: An application to educational enrollments in states of India. *Demography, 38,* 115–132.

Goldani, M. Z., Barbieri, M. A., Bettiol, H., Barbieri, M. R., & Tomkins, A. (2001). Infant mortality rates according to socioeconomic status in a Brazilian city. *Revista de Saude Publica, 35,* 256–261.

Gwatkin, D. (2005). How much would poor people gain from faster progress towards the Millennium Development Goals for health? *The Lancet, 365,* 813–817.

Gwatkin, D. R., Rustein, S., Johnson, K., Pande, R., & Wagstaff, A. (2000). *Socio-economic differences in health, nutrition and population.* Washington (DC): The World Bank, HNP/Poverty Thematic Group. Sources/URL: www.worldbank.org/poverty/health/data/index.htm. Accessed 15 Sept 2015.

Gwatkin, D. R., Rutstein, S., Johnson, K., Pande, R. B., & Wagstaff, A. (2003). *Initial country-level information about socio-economic differences in health, nutrition, and population* (vols. I and II). Washington, DC: World Bank. Sources/URL: http://devdata.worldbank.org/hnpstats/. Accessed 10 Sept 2015.

Hill, K., & Yazbeck, A. (1993) Trends in child mortality, 1960–90: estimates for 84 developing countries. In *World development report 1993: Investing in health.* New York: Oxford University Press for the World Bank.

Hosseinpoor, A. R., & Doorslaer, E. V. et al. (2006). Decomposing socioeconomic inequality in infant mortality in Iran. *Journal of Epidemiology, 35*, 1211–1219.

Kakwani, N. C. (1977). Measurement of tax progressivity: An international comparison. *Economic Journal, 87*(345), 71–80.

Kakwani, N. C. (1980). *Income inequality and poverty: Methods of estimation and policy applications.* New York: Oxford University Press. Sources/URL: http://documents.worldbank.org/curated/en/1980/01/439193/income-inequality-poverty-methods-estimation-policy-applications. Accessed 15 Dec 2014.

Kakwani, N. C., Wagstaff, A., & van Doorlsaer, E. (1997). Socioeconomic inequalities in health: Measurement, computation and statistical inference. *Journal of Econometrics, 77*(1), 87–104.

Kaplan, E. L., & Meier, P. (1958). Nonparametric estimation from incomplete observations. *Journal of American Statistical Association, 53,* 457–481.

Mackenbach, J. P., Kunst, A. E., Cavelaars, A. E. J. M., et al. (1997). Socioeconomic inequalities in morbidity and mortality in Western Europe. *The Lancet, 349,* 1655–1659.

Ministry of Health and Family Welfare (MOHFW). (2002). National Health Policy. *Government of India.* Sources/URL: http://www.mohfw.nic.in/np2002.htm. Accessed 22 Feb 2006.

Mosley, W. H., & Chen, L. C. (1984). An analytical framework for the study of child survival in developing countries. *Population and Development Review, 10,* 25–45.

IIPS and MACRO. (2007). *National Family Health Survey (NFHS-3), 2005–06: India International Institute for Population Sciences (IIPS) & ORC MACRO.* Mumbai: IIPS.

Poerwanto, S., Stevenson, M., & Klerk, N. (2003). Infant mortality and family welfare: Policy implications for Indonesia. *Journal of Epidemiology and Community Health, 57,* 493–498.

Szwarcwald, C. L., Tavares de Andrade, C. L., & Bastos, F. I. (2002). Income inequality, residential poverty clustering and infant mortality: A study in Rio de Janeiro, Brazil. *Social Science and Medicine, 55,* 2083–2092.

UNFPA and UN Women. (2014). Sex ratios and gender biased sex selection—History, debates and future directions. The United Nations Population Fund (UNFPA) and UN Women, Published by UN Women. Sources/URL: http://asiapacific.unwomen.org/en/digital-library/publications/2014/9/sex-ratios-and-gender-biased-sex-selection. Accessed 21 Mar 2015.

Van De Poel, E., Hosseinpoor, A. R., Speybroeck, N., Van Ourti, T., & Vega, J. (2008). Socioeconomic inequality in malnutrition in developing countries. *Bulletin of the World Health Organization, 86*, 282–291.

Van Doorslaer, E., Wagstaff, A., Bleichrodt, H., et al. (1997). Income-related inequalities in health: Some international comparisons. *Journal of Health Economics, 16*(1), 93–112.

Wagstaff, A. (1991). QALYs and the equity-efficiency trade-off. *Journal of Health Economics, 10,* 21–41.

Wagstaff, A. (2000). Socio-economic inequalities in child mortality: Comparison across nine developing countries. *Bulletin of the World Health Organization, 78*(1), 19–29.

Wagstaff, A. (2002). *Inequality aversion, health inequalities, and health achievement.* Policy, Research working paper series; no. WPS 2765. Washington, DC: World Bank Group. Sources/URL: http://documents.worldbank.org/curated/en/2002/01/1687158/inequality-aversion-health-inequalities-health-achievement.

Wagstaff, A., Paci, P., & van Doorslaer, E. (1991). On the measurement of inequalities in health. *Social Science and Medicine, 33,* 545–557.

Wagstaff, A., van Doorslaer, E., & Paci, P. (1989). Equity in the finance and delivery of health care: Some tentative cross-country comparisons. *Oxford Review of Economic Policy, 5*(1), 89–112.

Wagstaff, A., Van Doorslaer, E., Watanabe, N. (2001). *On decomposing the causes of health sector inequalities with an application to malnutrition inequalities in Vietnam.* Policy, Research working papers; no. WPS-2714. Washington, DC: World Bank Group. Sources/URL: http://documents.worldbank.org/curated/en/2001/11/1637744/decomposing-causes-health-sector-inequalities-application-malnutrition-inequalities-vietnam. Accessed 19 Jul 2004.

Wagstaff, A., & Watanabe, N. (2000). *Socioeconomic inequalities in child malnutrition in the developing world.* Washington (DC): World Bank; Policy Research Working Paper No. 2434. Sources/URL: http://www-wds.worldbank.org/servlet/WDSContentServer/WDSP/IB/2000/10/14/000094946_00100305302682/Rendered/PDF/multi_page.pdf. Accessed 29 May 2005.

Wagstaff, A., van Doorslaer, E., & Watanabe, N. (2003). On decomposing the causes of health sector inequalities, with an application to malnutrition inequalities in Vietnam. *Journal of Econometrics, 112*(1), 219–227.

WHO and World Bank. (2002). *Working group on child health and poverty. Better health for poor children.* Geneva: World Health Organization. Sources/URL: http://whqlibdoc.who.int/hq/2001a91061.pdf. Accessed 07 July 2004.

Yazbeck, A. S. (2009). Attacking inequality in the health sector—A synthesis of evidence and tools. *The World Bank.* Sources/URL: http://siteresources.worldbank.org/INTPAH/Resources/Publications/YazbeckAttackingInequality.pdf. Accessed 9 Aug 2010.

Chapter 19
The Determinants Out-of-Pocket Healthcare Expenditure in Bangladesh: Evidence from Household Income and Expenditure Survey-2010

Rashidul Alam Mahumud, Abdur Razzaque Sarker, Marufa Sultana, Nurnabi Sheikh, Md. Nurul Islam, Md. Ripter Hossain and Md. Golam Hossain

19.1 Introduction

Out-of-pocket (OOP) payment is the most common healthcare financing mechanism. OOP is the main healthcare financing system in Bangladesh (Majumder 2012), about 63% of health expenditure is made by individual or households (BNHA 2015). However, households who spend more than 50% of their non-food expenditure on healthcare are more likely to be impoverished and healthcare payments push large numbers of families into poverty (WHO 2009; Xu et al. 2006). Unpredictable health payments can expose households to substantial financial risk and, at their most extreme, can result in economic impoverishment. Conversely, healthcare expenditure that threatens a household's financial capability to preserve its subsistence needs is termed as catastrophic and comparatively small expenditures on health can be economically catastrophic for poor households. Consequently, demand for healthcare is a great challenge if the healthcare cost is unaffordable (WHO 2010) as a result, countless of the households are borrowing money, sell assets, or any divert resources from other needs to seek healthcare. However, high OOP payments, the absence of risk-pooling mechanisms, and high degree of poverty can result in shocking healthcare expenditure.

R.A. Mahumud (✉) · A.R. Sarker · M. Sultana
Health Economics and Financing Research, Health Systems and Population Studies Division, International Centre for Diarrhoeal Disease Research, Bangladesh (icddr,b), 68, Shahid Tajuddin Ahmed Sharani, Mohakhali, Dhaka 1212, Bangladesh
e-mail: rashidul.alam@icddrb.org

N. Sheikh · Md.N. Islam · Md.R. Hossain · Md.G. Hossain
Department of Statistics, Health Research Group, University of Rajshahi, Rajshahi 6205, Bangladesh

U.K. De et al. (eds.), *Issues on Health and Healthcare in India*, India Studies in Business and Economics, https://doi.org/10.1007/978-981-10-6104-2_19

The OOP payments increase when almost all the households meet their total health expenditure, then the range of catastrophic payments also increase. For this concern, one of the major objectives of national and international health policy is to replace OOP payments with more equitable modes of healthcare financing. In this situation, determinants of OOP payments can play important role for developing an effective health policy in developing countries. However, socioeconomic, geographic, and environmental factors are playing a significant role in determining health and health-seeking behavior. On the contrary, several numbers of factors such as availability of health services, financial resources, and community support perceived actual need for healthcare as well as patient satisfaction, i.e., multiple factors may contribute to health. Assured household characteristics, such as households headed by an elderly or disabled person and those who have a member suffering from any chronic diseases can influence the high out-of-pocket expenditure for healthcare (Waters et al. 2004). For this contest, out-of-pocket payment is considered as the most inequitable financing mechanism as well as strength of health services which can impose if regressive cost becomes burden on households or individuals. Therefore, policy-makers may need to recognize whether any characteristics make people more vulnerable to high out-of-pocket (OOP) payments in household's level. Special attention should be paid to developing countries like Bangladesh considering the healthcare expenditure influence on the family or individual life style among Bangladeshi people. Due to their main financial problem, it is important to investigate the relationship between the out-of-pocket payment for healthcare expenditure and important factors such as gender, age, marital status, education level, earner status, social financial safety, toilet facility, drinking water sources, first symptoms of illness, healthcare provider, residence and wealth quintile, in order to ensure corrective measures can be undertaken.

The aim of this study was to try to establish the effects of socioeconomic, demographic, and behavior factors on out-of-pocket health expenditure among people in Bangladesh.

19.2 Methods

Here, we intended to estimate the extent of OOP health expenditure of total health expenditure, change as a response to changes in multiple factors. Influencing factors for OOP spending on health was therefore estimated using multiple regression analyses.

19.2.1 Data and Variables

The sample of the current study consisted of 10,705 Bangladeshi who spent money for getting healthcare services. Cross-sectional data were derived from the Household Income and Expenditure Survey (HIES-2011). This is a national-level survey with the various districts of Bangladesh represented. The sampling technique, survey design, survey instruments, measuring system, and quality control have been described elsewhere (HIES 2011). OOP total healthcare expenditure was derived by summing up direct medical cost and direct non-medical cost. Direct medical costs included hospital outpatient fees, medicines, admission or registration fees, physician fees, diagnostic fees, and any other associated medical supplies (Sarker et al. 2014). The direct non-medical costs include transportation and conveyance, lodging, tips and other associated costs. Indirect costs like income or productivity losses were not captured in this study. However, like other study, intangible costs that is the costs related to suffering and grief, were also excluded from this analysis (Sarker et al. 2013).

In this study, OOP health expenditure was predicted by the explanatory variables like as demographic structure (gender, age), marital status, educational background, employment status (yes or no), social financial safety (yes or no), symptoms of illness (diarrhea, fever, dysentery, pain, injury, blood pressure, weakness, others), healthcare provider (public, private, pharmacy/dispensary, traditional and other) as well as economic status (lowest 20%, second 20%, middle 20%, fourth 20% and highest 20%). Age was considered into five groups as childhood (0–19), young adult (20–39), middle-aged adult (40–64), senior aged (65–84), and old senior aged (84 +). Marital status was categorized into three groups; unmarried, married, and others (widowed, divorced or separate). Educational level was considered as no education, primary education, secondary education, higher secondary, and higher education.

19.2.2 Econometric Estimation

OOP payment data are characterized by a large cluster of data at zero, and a right-skewed distribution of the remaining observations, but the values of zero were deleted in the current analysis. The natural logarithm of OOP healthcare expenditures was used to reduce the effects of the skewed nature of the expenditure variable. Multiple linear regression models were used to identify the influencing factors of the explanatory variables on OOP expenditures.

The multiple regression model considered is

$$y_i = \alpha + \sum_{i=1}^{n} \beta_i x_i + \varepsilon, \tag{19.1}$$

where y_i was the dependent variable (natural log of out-of-pocket healthcare expenditure), $x_i^{\prime}s$ were a number of control explanatory study variables. β was the coefficient for any independent variable, α represent unknown intercept term and ε was the error term.

19.3 Results and Discussion

A total of 10,705 sampled population reported illness and utilized healthcare during the last 30 days prior to the survey interview. Among the study samples, 53% were male and 47% were female. However, about 44.15% of those surveyed were aged of childhood (0–19 years) followed by 26.12% were young adult (20–39 years) and rest of around 7% were aged 65 years or older (Table 19.1). Approximately half of the household member's were illiterate compared to secondary education (24.21%). More than two-third of the household members were unemployed as well as only 25.12% of members were gainfully employed. The majority of the household's members (75%) had not have social financial security. About 81% of households had unhygienic toilet facilities, and 64.47% had used unsafe drinking water sources (Table 19.1). The higher percentage of household members received healthcare from private provider (37.18%) and local pharmacy (37.15%) and a few percentage (12%) was observed for receiving healthcare from public providers. More than 64% households were living in rural environment (Table 19.1).

Table 19.1 Background information for study population

Variables	n (%)	95% CI
Gender		
Male	5,668 (52.95)	52.00, 53.89
Female	5,037 (47.05)	46.11, 48.00
Age group		
0–19	4,726 (44.15)	43.21, 45.09
20–39	2,796 (26.12)	25.29, 26.96
40–64	2,453 (22.91)	22.13, 23.72
65–84	652 (6.09)	5.65, 6.56
85+	78 (0.73)	0.58, 0.91

(continued)

Table 19.1 (continued)

Variables	n (%)	95% CI
Marital status		
Unmarried	4,961 (46.34)	45.4, 47.29
Married	5,026 (46.95)	46.01, 47.9
Others	718 (6.71)	6.25, 7.20
Education level		
No education	5,377 (50.23)	49.28, 51.18
Primary education	2,134 (19.93)	19.19, 20.70
Secondary education	2,592 (24.21)	23.41, 25.03
Higher secondary	493 (4.61)	4.22, 5.02
Higher	109 (1.02)	0.84, 1.23
Earner status		
Yes	2,699 (25.21)	24.40, 26.04
No	8,006 (74.79)	73.96, 75.6
Social financial safety		
Yes	2,605 (24.33)	23.53, 25.16
No	8,100 (75.67)	74.84, 76.47
Toilet facility		
Hygienic	2,005 (18.73)	18.00, 19.48
Unhygienic	8,700 (81.27)	80.52, 82.00
Drinking water sources		
Safe drinking water	3,803 (35.53)	34.62, 36.44
Unsafe drinking water	6,902 (64.47)	63.56, 65.38
Healthcare provider		
Public	1,234 (11.53)	10.94, 12.15
Private	3,980 (37.18)	36.27, 38.10
Pharmacy/Dispensary	3,977 (37.15)	36.24, 38.07
Traditional	495 (4.62)	04.24, 05.04
Other	1,019 (9.52)	8.98, 10.09
Residence		
Rural	6,920 (64.64)	63.73, 65.54
Urban	3,785 (35.36)	34.46, 36.27
Wealth quintile		
Lowest 20%	2,232 (20.85)	20.09, 21.63
2nd	2,142 (20.01)	19.26, 20.78
3rd	2,126 (19.86)	19.11, 20.63
4th	2,069 (19.33)	18.59, 20.09
Upper 20%	2,136 (19.95)	19.21, 20.72

Note Figures in the parentheses represent percentage
Source Data extracted from HIES, 2011

Table 19.2 Distribution of self-reported illness in the past 30 days

Type of symptoms	Individual n (%)	Age groups				
		0–19	20–39	40–64	65–84	85+
Diarrhea	533 (4.98)	253 (5.35)	134 (4.79)	104 (4.24)	39 (5.98)	3 (4)
Fever	6148 (57.43)	3371 (71.33)	1424 (50.93)	1072 (44)	248 (38)	33 (42.31)
Dysentery	229 (2.14)	91 (1.93)	62 (2.22)	57 (2.32)	18 (2.76)	1 (1.28)
Pain	1090 (10.18)	173 (3.66)	375 (13.41)	418 (17.04)	109 (16.72)	15 (19.23)
Injury	178 (1.66)	53 (1.12)	56 (2)	57 (2.32)	12 (1.84)	–
Blood pressure	246 (2.3)	7 (0.15)	55 (1.97)	130 (5.3)	46 (7.06)	8 (10.26)
Weakness	267 (2.49)	41 (0.87)	89 (3.18)	99 (4.04)	30 (4.6)	8 (10.26)
Others	2014 (18.81)	737 (15.59)	601 (21.49)	516 (21.04)	150 (23.01)	10 (12.82)

Note Figures in the parentheses represent percentage
Source Data extracted from HIES, 2011

Table 19.2 represents the type of first symptoms of illness by age group. The overall high prevalence of fever (57.43%) among the self-reported suffering diseases was a common health problem and majority (71.33%) of them was children (aged between 0 to 19 years). However, the diseases pattern was increased with growing age (Table 19.2).

19.3.1 Distribution of Out-of-Pocket Healthcare Expenditure

The mean total out-of-pocket health expenditure in last 30 days was US Dollars ($11.22 ± 8.02). Medicine cost was the highest with US$ 6.95 ± 58.43, followed by diagnostic test $1.28 ± 7.49. Mean OOP payment for physician fee, hospital cost, conveyance cost, tips cost, other costs, maternity clinic cost, maternity midwife cost, and maternity others were $0.79 ± 2.44, $0.80 ± 17.49, $0.67 ± 4.09, $0.18 ± 12.7, $0.44 ± 6.63, $0.12 ± 3.96, $0.02 ± 0.47, $0.11 ± 5.81, respectively. However, the urban population had relatively higher OOP healthcare expenditure ($11.08 ± 52.33) than rural people ($11.49 ± 93.05). Regarding healthcare provider, the mean out-of-pocket expenditures per health service visit, who visited a particular health service: private physicians $25.13 ± 219.52, public physicians $17.58 ± 49.32, traditional healers $5.30 ± 15.30 as well as local pharmacy $3.49 ± 7.10. We found the poorest 20% of the population was higher average OOP healthcare expenditure $13.4 ± 157.91 followed by the rich 20% of the population $11.23 ± 56.41 (Table 19.3).

Table 19.3 Distribution of out-of-pocket healthcare expenditure in last 30 days (USD)

Items	Urban	Rural	Total
	Mean ± SD	Mean ± SD	Mean ± SD
Healthcare expenditure			
Physician fee	0.79 ± 2.46	0.79 ± 2.44	0.79 ± 2.44
Hospital cost	0.59 ± 10.76	0.91 ± 20.25	0.80 ± 17.49
Medicine cost	6.63 ± 20.25	7.12 ± 71.12	6.95 ± 58.43
Diagnostic test	1.33 ± 7.91	1.25 ± 7.26	1.28 ± 7.49
Conveyance cost	0.67 ± 5.22	0.67 ± 3.31	0.67 ± 4.09
Tips cost	0.36 ± 21.2	0.08 ± 1.87	0.18 ± 12.70
Other costs	0.42 ± 7.49	0.46 ± 6.11	0.44 ± 6.63
Maternity clinic cost	0.07 ± 2.73	0.15 ± 4.49	0.12 ± 3.96
Maternity midwife cost	0.01 ± 0.31	0.02 ± 0.54	0.02 ± 0.47
Maternity others	0.20 ± 9.43	0.06 ± 1.89	0.11 ± 5.81
Healthcare provider			
Public	17.52 ± 43.91	17.71 ± 58.07	17.58 ± 49.32
Private	27.15 ± 265.53	21.81 ± 107.03	25.13 ± 219.52
Pharmacy/Dispensary	3.53 ± 7.63	3.42 ± 6.02	3.49 ± 7.10
Traditional	5.00 ± 14.32	5.99 ± 17.38	5.30 ± 15.30
Other	3.94 ± 13.52	3.82 ± 8.65	3.90 ± 12.02
Wealth quintile			
Lowest 20%	14.27 ± 174.95	10.01 ± 55.00	13.40 ± 157.91
2nd	10.88 ± 30.63	9.19 ± 22.97	10.58 ± 29.39
3rd	9.54 ± 27.13	10.29 ± 26.48	9.77 ± 26.93
4th	11.46 ± 43.58	11.98 ± 49.94	11.68 ± 46.33
Upper 20%	10.17 ± 29.64	11.76 ± 65.96	11.23 ± 56.41
Total	11.35 ± 81.02	11.08 ± 52.33	11.22 ± 66.68

Source Data extracted from HIES, 2011

19.3.2 Influencing Factors on Out-of-Pocket Healthcare Expenditure

We considered all variables in the multiple linear regression models that were significant predictors of OOP payments in the univariate analysis (Table 19.4). The regression model explains 28.3% of total variations ($R^2 = 0.283$) by explanatory variables. The diagnostic tests were employed the regression model. The Breusch–Pagan/Cook-Weisberg test showed that heteroscedasticity was not present in the model ($p < 0.01$). Variance inflation factor (VIF) test with its mean (max) value of 2.15 ± 3.99 indicated that there was no evidence of multicollinearity problem in the regression model. Ramsey (RESET) test showed that there was sufficient evidence against the hypothesis of omitted variable bias in the model ($p < 0.01$).

The household member's of age groups ($p < 0.01$), female ($p < 0.01$), married ($p < 0.10$), urban households ($p < 0.05$), richest 20% of the population ($p < 0.01$),

Table 19.4 Effects of selected factors on OOP healthcare expenditure

Variables	Unadjusted Model		Adjusted Model	
	Co-efficient	95% CI	Co-efficient	95% CI
Constant	–	–	1.23**	1.06, 1.40
Gender				
Male (Ref)	0.00	–	0.00	–
Female	0.25**	0.06, 1.50	0.16**	0.10, 0.22
Age group				
0–19 (Ref)	0.00	–	0.00	–
20–39	0.45**	0.38, 0.52	0.23*	0.10, 0.35
40–64	0.61**	0.54, 0.68	0.35**	0.21, 0.49
65–84	0.65**	0.53, 0.77	0.30**	0.13, 0.46
85+	1.02**	0.70, 1.35	0.61**	0.30, 0.92
Marital status				
Unmarried (Ref)	0.00	–	0.00	–
Married	0.54**	0.48, 0.59	0.11*	−0.01, 0.24
Others	0.50**	0.38, 0.61	0.04	−0.13, 0.20
Education level				
No education (Ref)	0.00	–	0.00	–
Primary education	0.06**	0.01, 0.14	−0.02	−0.08, 0.05
Secondary education	0.03	0.01, 0.10	−0.05*	−0.11, −0.01
Higher secondary	−0.02	−0.16, 0.11	−0.14	−0.25, −0.02
Higher	0.12	0.030, 0.26	−0.23	−0.47, −0.10
Earner status				
Yes (Ref)	0.00	–	0.00	–
No	−0.12**	−0.19, −0.06	−0.23**	−0.30, −0.150
Social financial safety				
Yes (Ref)	0.00	–	0.00	–
No	−0.24**	–0.51 , –0.17	–0.13**	−0.20, −0.12
Toilet facility				
Hygienic (Ref)	0.00	–	0.00	–
Unhygienic	0.81**	0.48, 1.33	0.22**	0.13, 0.25
Drinking water sources				
Safe drinking water (Ref)	0.00	–	0.00	–
Unsafe drinking water	0.34**	0.04, 0.68	0.61**	0.13, 0.78
First symptoms of illness				
Diarrhea (Ref)	0.00	–	0.00	–
Fever	−0.49**	−0.62, −0.37	−0.38**	−0.49, −0.27
Dysentery	−0.47**	−0.68, −0.26	−0.39**	−0.58, −0.19
Pain	0.39**	0.25, 0.53	0.23**	0.10, 0.36
Injury	0.87**	0.64, 1.10	0.65**	0.44, 0.86

(continued)

Table 19.4 (continued)

Variables	Unadjusted Model		Adjusted Model	
	Co-efficient	95% CI	Co-efficient	95% CI
Blood pressure	0.43**	0.22, 0.64	0.19**	0.00, 0.38
Weakness	0.52**	0.32, 0.72	0.32**	0.13, 0.50
Others	0.69**	0.56, 0.83	0.53**	0.41, 0.65
Healthcare provider				
Public (Ref)	0.00	–	0.00	–
Private	0.12	0.08, 0.19	0.07*	0.01, 0.15
Pharmacy/Dispensary	−1.24**	−1.32, −1.15	−0.99**	−1.07, −0.90
Traditional	−1.17**	−1.30, −1.03	−1.10**	−1.23, −0.97
Other	−1.42	−1.53, −1.31	−1.28*	−1.39, −1.18
Residence				
Rural (Ref)	0.00	–	0.00	–
Urban	0.15*	0.05, 0.27	0.13**	0.08, 0.83
Wealth quintile				
Lowest 20% (Ref)	0.00	–	0.00	–
2nd	0.08*	0.01, 0.17	−0.15	−0.07, 0.08
3rd	0.05	0.01, 0.13	1.01	−0.09, 0.06
4th	0.06**	0.03, 0.15	1.21**	0.60, 1.91
Upper 20%	0.12	0.08, 0.21	2.53**	1.25, 3.52
Total observation (N)			10,705	
R-square (R^2)			0.28	
F-value (28, 10676) (Prob > F)			150.51 (0.001)	
Root MSE			1.25	
Mean VIF			2.15	
BP/Cook-Weisberg test (p > chi2)			279.51 (0.005)	
Ramsey RESET, F(p > F)			21.54 (0.01)	

Note **, 1% and * 5% level of significance
Source Data extracted from HIES, 2011

unsafe water source ($p < 0.01$), households with unhygienic toilets ($p < 0.01$), types of first symptoms of illness ($p < 0.01$), traditional healer ($p < 0.05$), local pharmacy ($p < 0.01$) were significantly associated with higher out-of-pocket health expenditures. On the other hand, working status ($p < 0.01$) and social financial safety ($p < 0.05$) were inversely associated with out-of-pocket healthcare expenditure.

Out-of-pocket health expenditures are more severe for poor households with any chronic conditions. However, policy-makers need to rely on precise and consistent OOP health expenditure estimates. Our study intends to find the determinants of out-of-pocket health expenditures among Bangladeshi people. This study found that different factors like socioeconomics, demographics, urban community, unsafe water source, and unhygienic toilets use were significantly associated with higher out-of-pocket health expenditures. Our results showed that age was significantly associated with OOP health expenditures. This effect was highest among people in age group of 65 years or above and consistent with some previous findings (Sarker et al. 2014). The lack of health sector resource allocation by management of specific chronic diseases in the elderly might be a possible explanation of the positive influence on OOP health expenditure. Existing health services should strive to minimize out-of-pocket to ensure equitable access to health services for all older people (Balarajan et al. 2011). Lack of hygienic toilets and safe drinking water increased the out-of-pocket expenditure significantly. Similar findings linked when parallel analyses were run in another data set. Although, investing sanitation, safe drinking water sources as well as improving living conditions may prevent infectious diseases such as fever, malaria, tuberculosis, gastrointestinal diseases, and so on. In turn, they may reduce healthcare treatments and the overall burden of out-of-pocket health expenditure. Study showed that OOP health expenditure was more significantly associated by the urban communities. Onwujekwe et al. (2010) found the consistent findings that the rural communities used more of reimbursement, installment payment, and in-kind payment mechanisms for healthcare due to ill. This may be because the urban dwellers are more educated and have more assets, economic power, individuals to either delay or not seek healthcare. Nevertheless, opportunities for healthcare payments are also more limited in the people of rural communities. Healthcare utilization from local pharmacy and traditional healers significantly increased the out-of-pocket health expenditure. However, people play significant role on the services of traditional healers in low-middle income countries (LMICs) (Stekelenburg et al. 2005; WHO 2008). Earlier study has also reported similar findings (Richard et al. 2009). As many people in LMICs hold multiple medical model for chronic diseases (Charles et al. 2007), their culturally rooted belief systems make them seek help from traditional and informal healers. On the other hand, household's socioeconomic status was also important predictors of determining OOP payments. Least poor household members have significant contribution to OOP payment. However, previous studies also found that rich households positively associated on OOP payment (Onwujekwe et al. 2010; Sanwald et al. 2014).

Our present study also found that unemployed peoples spent significantly less out-of-pocket health expenditure. Hence, less out-of-pocket health expenditures in such vulnerable people are better explained by poor financial resources than by reduced need for health services. Many unemployed people have limited access for healthcare and faces high out-of-pocket health expenditure. Since, they may lack of factors like health insurance as well as ability to access needed healthcare utilization, because they are unemployed and they may not afford it. This study also found that OOP spending on healthcare services remain a significant determinant of financial insecurity with inadequate healthcare services. Those most at risk include medicare beneficiaries, whose poor health and limited medicare benefits may impose financial burdens. Many rural people seek help from traditional healers. Improving the cultural competence of the primary care health professionals and integrating traditional healers with the existing health services may reduce their out-of-pocket health expenditure. Despite the concerns regarding such integration, appropriately trained traditional healers are helpful to promote health among the rural communities in LMIC.

19.4 Conclusion

This exercise would capture expenditure outflows from households to all healthcare platforms in the community, including hospitals, clinics, and pharmacies. The average out-of-pocket healthcare expenditure in the last 30 days among Bangladeshi population was US$ 11.22 ± 8.02, and the pattern of OPP expenditure for rural and urban population was almost same. The household member's of age groups, female, married, urban households, richest population, unsafe water source, households with unhygienic toilets, types of first symptoms of illness, traditional healer, local pharmacy were significantly associated with higher out-of-pocket health expenditures. On the other hand, working status and social financial safety were inversely associated with out-of-pocket healthcare expenditure.

This can help the decision-makers by stating OOPP determinants, discussing the mechanism causing them and thus making them into account to adapt OOP relevant regulations which highlights the emphasis to develop financial protection mechanisms in Bangladesh. Government should consider enhancing resources of healthcare policy. Parallel to government, spending other prudent and sustainable risk-pooling mechanism can help reducing intensity of OOP payments.

References

Balarajan, Y., & Selvaraj, S. S. (2011). Health care and equity in India. *The Lancet, 377*(9764), 505–515. doi:10.1016/S0140-6736(10)61894-6.

BNHA. (2015). *Bangladesh National Health Accounts 1997–2012. Research Paper No. 42a, Dhaka: Health Economics Unit, Ministry of Health and Family Welfare, Government of the People's Republic of Bangladesh* (pp. 1–198).

Charles, Helen; S.D. Manoranjitham, K. S. J. (2007). Stigma and Explanatory Models Among People With Schizophrenia and Their Relatives in Vellore, South India. *Int J Soc Psychiatry, 53*(4), 325–332.

HIES. (2011). *Household income & expenditure survey-2010.* In: BBS (ed.) HIES. Bangladesh bureau of statistic, Dhaka, Bangladesh.

Hossain, M., Saw, A., Alam, R., Ohtsuki, F., & Kamarul, T. (2013). Multiple regression analysis of anthropometric measurements influencing the cephalic index of male Japanese university students. *Singapore Medical Journal, 54*(9), 516–520.

Majumder, M. (2012). Economics of healthcare financing in WHO South East Asia Region. *South East Asia Journal Of Public Health,* 2(2), 3–4.

Richard, U., Christian, C. I., Modebe, A. I., Emeka, B., Ezeama N., Njelita I., Cleusa, P., Ferri, M. J. P. (2009). The epidemiology of dependence in older people in Nigeria: prevalence, determinants, informal care, and health service utilization. A 10/66 dementia research group cross-sectional survey. *Journal of the American Geriatrics Society, 57*(9), 1620–7. doi:10.1111/j.1532-5415.2009.02397 .

Onwujekwe, O. E., Uzochukwu, B. S. C., Obikeze, E. N., Okoronkwo, I., Ochonma, O. G., Onoka, C. a, Okoli, C. (2010). Investigating determinants of out-of-pocket spending and strategies for coping with payments for healthcare in southeast Nigeria. *BMC Health Services Research, 10,* 67. doi:10.1186/1472-6963-10-67.

Sanwald, A., & Theurl, E. (2014). What drives out-of pocket health expenditures of private households ? Empirical evidence from the Austrian household budget survey.

Sarker, A. R., Islam, Z., Khan, I. A., Saha, A., Chowdhury, F., Khan, A. I., … Khan, J. A. M. (2013). Cost of illness for cholera in a high risk urban area in Bangladesh: an analysis from household perspective. *BMC Infectious Diseases, 13*(1), 518. doi:10.1186/1471-2334-13-518.

Sarker, A. R., Mahumud, R. A., Sultana, M., Ahmed, S., Ahmed, W., & Khan, J. A. (2014). The impact of age and sex on healthcare expenditure of households in Bangladesh. *SpringerPlus, 3,* 435. doi:10.1186/2193-1801-3-435.

Stekelenburg, J., Jager, B. E., Kolk, P. R., Westen, E. H. M. N., van der Kwaak, A., & Wolffers, I. N. (2005). Health care seeking behaviour and utilisation of traditional healers in Kalabo, Zambia. *Health Policy (Amsterdam, Netherlands), 71*(1), 67–81. doi:10.1016/j.healthpol.2004.05.008.

Waters, H. R., Anderson, G. F., & Mays, J. (2004). Measuring financial protection in health in the United States. *Health Policy (Amsterdam, Netherlands), 69*(3), 339–49. doi:10.1016/j.healthpol.2004.01.003.

World Health Organization (WHO). (2008). Traditional Medicine [Online]. World Health Organization. Available from: http://www.who.int/mediacentre/factsheets/fs134/en/; last accessed 2015/6/25.

World Health Organization (WHO). (2009). *Health financing strategy for the Asia Pacific region (2010–2015).* Manila: World Health Organization, Regional Office for the Western Pacific.

World Health Organization (WHO). (2010). *The World Health Organization: The World Health Report – Health systems financing: The path to universal coverage 2010. Geneva: The World Health Organization.* Retrieved from http://www.who.int/whr/2010/en/index.html.

Xu, K., Evans, D. B., Kadama, P., Nabyonga, J., Ogwal, P. O., Nabukhonzo, P., & Aguilar, A. M. (2006). Understanding the impact of eliminating user fees: utilization and catastrophic health expenditures in Uganda. *Social Science & Medicine (1982), 62*(4), 866–76. doi:10.1016/j.socscimed.2005.07.004.

Part III
Facilities and Prevalence of Morbidity

Chapter 20
Access to Life-Saving Medicines and Healthcare: A Case Study of Aurangabad District of Bihar

Imteyaz Ahmad and Anita Rath

20.1 Introduction

The role of medicines in preventing deaths and reducing incidences of morbidity has been well recognised in modern health systems. There has been significant progress in medical sciences and pharmacology which can support production and delivery of essential medicines to meet the needs of everyone. However, lack of essential medicines for the poor and vulnerable has been a major concern. Lack of access to essential medicines has been recognised as a challenge in India's health and medicine policies consistently during last six decades.

Availability and accessibility of overall healthcare services have been a major concern in India. It is worthwhile to revisit the notion of medical care in this context. Medical care has certain distinct characteristics which do not permit its analysis in the standard framework adopted for other usual commodities (Arrow 1963). An individual's demand for medical services is unexpected and abrupt. It may not be regular. Its predictability is a concern. The value of medical services is recognised in case of health eventualities which affect normal health conditions. Medical service delivery system must address the health concerns satisfactorily and it should pay necessary attention to affordability issue. Financial burden of healthcare and their considerable impact on impoverishment of households is a serious concern in the Indian situation. The overall cost of illness goes much beyond the cost of medical treatment as illness has implications for complete loss or considerable fall in income due to lack of normal functioning of the affected individuals or families. The role of government in addressing healthcare needs

I. Ahmad (✉) · A. Rath
Tata Institute of Social Sciences, Mumbai, India
e-mail: imteyazahmad777@gmail.com

A. Rath
e-mail: anita@tiss.edu

U.K. De et al. (eds.), *Issues on Health and Healthcare in India*, India Studies in Business and Economics, https://doi.org/10.1007/978-981-10-6104-2_20

assumes significance under such circumstances. With some important policies for health sector, there is a stated commitment to address the healthcare needs of population at large. However, it is imperative to study the implications of such policies at the ground level.

It is in this context, a study was undertaken with the broad objective of assessing the availability and accessibility of medicines and healthcare by the poor at the level of PHCs in Aurangabad district of Bihar. This chapter reports the findings of the study.

Aurangabad district has 25,40,073 population as per 2011 Census. It has 11 PHCs and each PHC is assigned to a single block as their jurisdiction area. The study includes all PHCs of the district. The major difference in earlier studies and the present one is that, earlier studies were based on more than one city and even one state, while the present study is based on a district and restricted to PHCs in that district. Accessibility has been measured on three broad parameters—economic and financial condition of the patient, net availability of the medicines and status of healthcare services in all PHCs.

This chapter is structured in the following manner. There are five sections in this chapter including the introductory one. In the second section, an analysis of economic burden of healthcare and pattern of expenditure on medicines is provided. A review of regulations regarding essential medicines and drugs, in general, is given in the next section. The results of the primary study in Aurangabad are presented in the fourth section. Methodology of the study and major findings are outlined in this section. Finally, conclusions are made.

20.2 Economic Burden of Healthcare and Expenditure on Medicine

Epidemiological profile of India is quite bothersome. According to World Health Organisation, more than a quarter (2.8 million) of the world tuberculosis cases is found in India, which is the leading country in the world with maximum number of tuberculosis cases. The country is showing a rising trend in terms of new tuberculosis cases; i.e. 2.2 million in 2014 to 2.8 million in 2015 (Anand 2016). UNAID Report, 2016 revealed that the number of HIV/AIDS in India is 2.1 million in 2015 which places India in third rank across different countries (AVERT 2015). The prevalence of respiratory diseases in India varies between 2.05 and 3.5% of total population (Ghoshal et al. 2016). Child mortality due to diarrhoea is as high as 3 lakh every year, despite reduction in diarrheal deaths in recent years in India. Diarrhoea contributes 13% of under-5 years of age group deaths in India (Lakshminarayanan et al. 2015). The country has reported a considerable number of dengue and chikungunya cases; about 74,454 and 18,639 cases reported respectively in 2013 by National Vector Borne Disease Control Programme. Nearly 167 deaths happened due to dengue in 2013 (Cecilia 2014). There are 2.6 million cases of Malaria found in South-east Asia, among which India alone contributes 76% of total reported cases (NIMR, n.d.). According to NFHS-III, about 20–40% of maternal deaths are due to anaemia and one in every two women is anaemic in India (Kaur 2014). India's per lakh deaths due to cardiovascular diseases is higher than global average; nearly 235 people die every year globally while in India this rate is 272 per lakh of population (Prabhakaran et al. 2016). National Institute of Cancer Prevention and Research reveals that around 2.5 million cancer cases are reported in India with 7 lakh new cases every year on an average (Nandakumar 2009).

In this context access to medicine and affordable healthcare remains crucial in addressing the burden of disease. In this section, two major themes are discussed on the basis of available secondary information. These are pattern and trend of aggregate expenditure on healthcare and expenditure on medicines in India.

20.2.1 Expenditure on Healthcare in India

India has a wide gap in required health expenditure and what is actually being spent. Private spending dominates overall health expenditure; this is a reflection of inadequate public spending. The aggregate outpatient visits shows declining share of public sector; it declined from 25 to 20% and inpatient treatment have also declined from 60 to 40% during the decade of 1994–1995 to 2004–2005 (Selvaraj et al. 2009).

National Health Account of India illuminates the situation. India's health expenditure has been financed by three major sources; public, private and external sources. The burden of health expenditure is always catastrophic for the general population in India and it is evident from Fig. 20.1. Private expenditure is as high as 78.05% in total health expenditure and it has a share of 3.32% in GDP. Public expenditure remains as low as 19.67% with a meagre share of 0.84% in GDP. Despite the fact that external flow is a very small source of support to aggregate health expenditure but it makes a difference with 2.28% share in total health expenditure and constitutes a 0.10% share in GDP. However with a poor

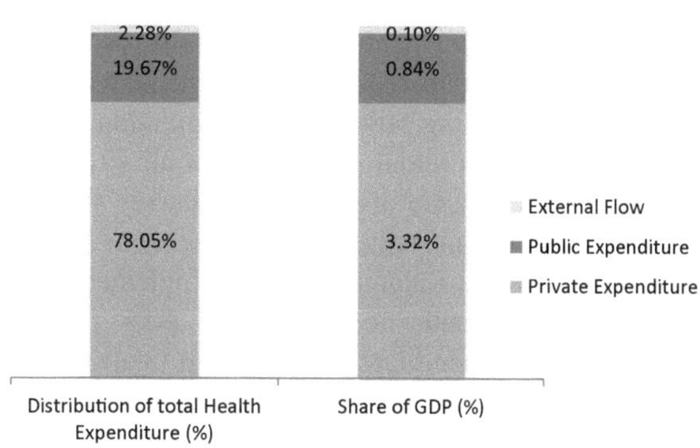

Fig. 20.1 Health expenditure in India 2004–05. *Source* National Health Accounts India 2004–05

contribution by public sector in health, total health expenditure constitutes 4.25% share in GDP (National Health Accounts: India 2004–05 2004).

India holds a very low rank and stands at 184th position in public health spending across 191 countries as revealed by World Health Statistics, 2007 (cited in Rao et al. 2012). In this group of 191 countries, India's per capita health spending is only $29 which is ranked at 164th position. India performs badly in terms of per capita public health spending in comparison to its neighbours—Sri Lanka and China. India's per capita public spending is just about one-third of that of Sri Lanka's spending. China's per capita public spending is higher than India by about 30 per cent (Rao et al. 2012). There is a situation of stagnation in public spending on health in last two decades—during the period 1990–1991 to 2009–2010. A nominal increase in public spending was recorded during this period and the share of health in total GDP increased marginally from 0.9 to 1.2% (Rao et al. 2012; National Health Accounts: India 2004–05 2009).

Financial duress is encountered by about 150 million people in the world in accessing healthcare. Many incur out-of-pocket (OOP) payments for healthcare. Some statistics indicate that around 100 million people are impoverished every year due to OOP payments on health. Expectedly, more than 90% of the mare the habitants of low income countries (Xu et al. 2007). India, Vietnam and Bangladesh top the list of OOP payments for health in whole Asia (van Doorsley et al. 2007). In India, 32–39 million people get impoverished due to high private health expenditure (van Doorsley et al. 2006; Bonu et al. 2007; Garg et al. 2009; Berman et al. 2010).

Low funding in public health system has affected both poor and non-poor adversely. There are various factors which intensify the situation such as very high payments to healthcare results in dissavings, selling of assets and significant borrowings from informal sources such as moneylenders.

Only about one-tenth of India's population is covered under some form of health insurance (Planning Commission 2008). Low insurance coverage coupled with high cost of treatment sought in private sector led to high spending out-of-pocket. Health expenditures have grown rapidly at 14% during the decade 1994–1995 to 2004–2005. The pace of growth of expenditure on inpatient care has been higher (Lal et al. 2005).

Recognising the need for risk pooling for health eventualities, Ministry of Labour and Employment launched Rashtriya Swasthya Beema Yojna (RSBY) in 2007. The initial intervention of the scheme was in 385 districts in 26 states. These districts were having 50% of BPL population. The coverage of BPL families was about 27% in this initial phase (Rao et al. 2012).

State governments also made initiatives in this regard. State government of Andhra Pradesh ran Rajiv Aarogyasri scheme, Vajpayee Aarogyasri was initiated in Karnataka and the Kalaignar scheme implemented in Tamil Nadu to make sure the reach of free healthcare services to poor people. There is evidence of high out-of-pocket expenditure on outpatient treatments. Outpatient low-cost treatments which go for a long period with high frequency of occurrence, costs households to fall under impoverishment. There are no current health schemes which provide protection from consistent costs of outpatients (Reddy et al. 2011).

20.2.2 Expenditure on Medicine

Over the years, India's drug policies have proven to be dualistic in nature. Generic and branded drugs are produced not only for domestic consumption but also for exports and the country is one of the leading producers of drugs. Therefore, India is also known as 'pharmacy of the global south' (Chaudhuri 2007; Lofgren 2012). It is worth mentioning that life-saving medicines are exported to developing countries and quality drugs are produced for rich and developed countries at affordable prices from India. The appreciable performance of India in the field of medicine production, however, does not reflect in accessibility of millions of Indian households to medicines (Chaudhuri 2007). This is the result of both financial as well as physical—lack of public health facilities. Since past two and a half decades, constraints in medicine accessibility have become worse.

According to National Sample Survey, a significant portion of health expenditure goes to medicines. In the 55th round of National Sample Survey, it has been found that about 77 and 70% of the health expenditure is on medicines in rural and urban households respectively. It is important to note that the share of expenditure on medicines in total health expenditure is higher in case of poorer households (Sengupta et al. 2008).

In Table 20.1, it has been shown that, in 1986–1987, for hospitalisation drugs prescribed for free had a share of 31.2% among three other categories (partly free, on payment and not received). The share of free drugs has fallen sharply in 2004 to

Table 20.1 Trends in access to medicines in India 1986–87 to 2004

	1986–87	1995–96	2004
Inpatient			
Free medicines	31.2	12.29	8.99
Partly free	15.0	13.15	16.38
On payment	40.95	67.75	71.79
Not received	12.85	6.8	2.84
Total (%)	100	100	100
Outpatient			
Free medicines	17.98	7.21	5.34
Partly free	4.36	2.71	3.38
On payment	65.55	79.32	65.27
Not received	12.11	10.76	26.01
Total (%)	100	100	100

Source Planning Commission (2011)

only 9%. For outpatient care share of free drugs has fallen, the margin of fall being 18–5% during 1986–1987 to 2004 (Planning Commission 2011).

It can be observed from Table 20.1 that out-of-pocket (OOP) payments for treatment of ailing population under inpatient care have increased from 41 % to about 72 %t. In case of outpatient care, out-of-pocket expenditure decreased from 80 % to 65% during mid-1990s to 2004. The data in the Table shows that since mid-1990s, when prices of medicines have started rising, there has been a decline in 'on payment' outpatient shares by almost one-fifth. It implies that patients did not receive medicines because of unaffordable prices of medicines.

In Table 20.2, it is clear that the lowest rung of population had higher share of medicine in total health expenditure compared to others. With a miniscule difference between rural and urban expenditure on share of medicine in total health expenditure, the lowest rung of population suffers the most. On the basis of Monthly Per capita Consumption, around 85% of health expenditure is made on medicines in both rural as well as urban areas. Table 20.2 also refers that with the increase in income, share of medicines comes down in total health expenditure. This is evident from the following Table which shows that the top 20% of the population had lower share of medicine (71.59% in rural areas and 62.3% in urban areas) against total health expenditure (Sengupta et al. 2008). National Sample Survey morbidity data strengthen this claim as it shows that expenditure on medicines constitute 81 and 75% share of medicine in total health expenditure in rural and urban areas, respectively (all-India 79%).

Medicine Price Inflation: The price movement of medicines have been steeper than other commodities. Critical and essential medicine prices have shown notable increase during past decades. In a study carried out by Rane (2003) it has been found that among 70 recognised brands that constitute nearly 20% of the pharmaceutical market, 67% were showing price increase, 19% were showing a fall in price whereas 14% had no change in price from 1999 to 2003.

Planning Commission (2011) analyzed the prices of medicines vis-a-vis other commodities. Figure 20.2 is showing the price index of all commodities and drugs from 1993–1994 to 2003–2004. It is clearly reflected from the figure that inflation

Table 20.2 Pattern of per capita monthly out-of-pocket expenses on medicine and healthcare in 1999–2000

	Region	Quintiles					
		First (Lowest)	Second	Third	Fourth	Fifth	Total
Health exp. (Rs)	Rural	7.72	13.79	19.61	29.98	77.47	29.58
	Urban	11.71	21.66	29.73	47	105.67	43.27
Exp. on medicine (Rs)	Rural	6.68	11.71	16.46	24.44	55.46	22.85
	Urban	9.91	17.79	22.72	34.34	65.9	30.14
Medicine % of health	Rural	86.47	84.89	83.94	81.53	71.59	77.24
	Urban	84.6	80.71	76.44	73.05	62.36	69.66

Source Sengupta et al. (2008)

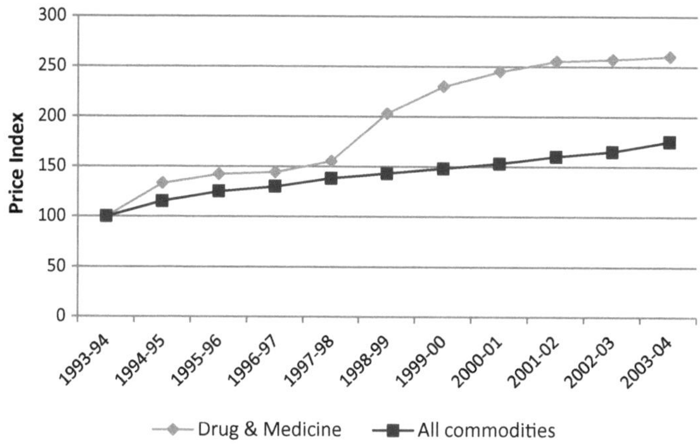

Fig. 20.2 Trends in pharmaceuticals and all commodity price index. *Source* Planning Commission (2011)

of drugs and medicines is higher than all commodities inflation. There is a sudden increase in rate of inflation of drugs in 1997–1998 to 1998–1999, while all commodities inflation is rising at normal and constant pace (Planning Commission 2011).

Insurance Regulatory and Development Authority (IRDA) conducted a study on medical insurance claims of two periods, 2007–2008 and 2009–2010, to estimate the inflation in medical sector. The insurance claims are subject to the limitations of sum insured, preexisting diseases, etc. Expenditure incurred by the insured reflects the actual amount claimed and hence paid, it is the base of medical cost for comparing the inflation over the years.

Table 20.3 is the base of discussion ahead. The claim severity has increased for 12 diseases. For remaining four diseases (Endocrine, Eye, Infection and Skin), claims are showing negative sign. The maximum claims are made for circulatory diseases, which is 56.99%. Average number of claims made has increased from 199,464 during 2007–2008 to 292,883 during 2009–2010. There is 27.09% increase in the claim severity and the average claim amount has increased from Rs. 98,101 to Rs. 134,550 over a period of 2007–2008 to 2009–2010 (Insurance Regulatory and Development Authority, n.d.).

There are some complications in these calculations. Same disease can be treated with many procedures and the medical cost for these procedures vary significantly based on the technology used, number of days of hospitalisation required and the type of medicines used. The disease-wise claims severity for various diseases are grouped according to the treatment procedure. This data is presented in Table 20.4. The percentage of all the diseases of claim severity is showing the increasing trend over the selected time period. Gall bladder stone has highest increase in claim severity (12.94). Senile cataract has the lowest increase in severities percentages (Insurance Regulatory and Development Authority, n.d.).

Table 20.3 Claim severity analysis of all major diseases

Disease name	2007–08			2009–10			Increase in average claimed amount for 2009–10 in comparison with 2007–08 (%)
	Number of claims	Average claimed amount	Proportion	Number of claims	Average claimed amount	Proportion	
Arthropathies	14,500	1,36,354	10.1	20,330	147,401	7.6	7.49
Blood Diseases	1435	95,992	0.7	1972	107,944	0.54	11.07
Circulatory	35,776	1,53,349	28.04	49,687	356,505	44.95	56.99
Digestive	25,881	75,694	10.01	36,420	79,564	7.35	4.86
Ear	1466	65,841	0.49	2371	68,066	0.41	3.27
Endocrine	5591	1,05,843	3.02	6426	103,402	1.69	−2.36
Eye	6298	60,137	1.94	12,623	57,168	1.83	−5.19
Infections	9759	88,200	4.4	12,969	83,301	2.74	−5.88
Injury	24,508	88,039	11.03	33,400	94,284	7.99	6.62
Neoplasm	21,999	96,287	10.83	31,475	103,566	8.27	7.03
Nervous	4152	1,10,135	2.34	6030	128,055	1.96	13.99
Pregnancy	15,391	56,148	4.42	28,539	57,820	4.19	2.89
Respiratory	8425	85,237	3.67	13,824	92,019	3.23	7.37
Skin	2255	78,747	0.91	3410	78,477	0.68	−0.34
Urology	22,028	72,023	8.11	33,407	77,455	6.57	7.01
Total	199,464	98,101	100	292,883	134,550	100	27.09

Source Insurance Regulatory and Development Authority

Table 20.4 Claim severity with specific diseases

Procedure	Disease name	2007–08			2009–10			Increase in severity for 2009–10 in comparison with 2007–08 (%)
		Number of claims	Claim severity	Proportions (%)	Number of claims	Claim severity	Proportions (%)	
Leiomyoma of uterus	Cancer	1819	66,049	9.54	2609	74,716	7.62	11.6
Senile cataract	Cataract	1667	52,577	8.74	4622	53,266	13.5	1.29
Senile cataract (other)	Cataract	739	53,240	3.88	1196	53,421	3.49	0.34
Acute appendicitis	Appendicitis	1513	60,355	7.94	2749	64,339	8.03	6.19
Inguinal hernia	Hernia	2032	64,417	10.66	3232	67,970	9.44	5.23
Cholelithiasis	Gall bladder stone	2154	63,664	11.3	3529	73,127	10.31	12.94
Calculus of kidney and ureter	Kidney stone	2209	60,701	11.59	4036	64,840	11.79	6.38
Calculus of kidney prostate	Prostate problem	1363	70,381	7.15	2118	75,338	6.19	6.58
Single spontaneous delivery	Pregnancy	1350	53,313	7.08	2025	53,776	5.92	0.86
Single Delivery by caesarean section	Pregnancy	4220	55,709	22.13	8113	56,891	23.7	2.08

Source Insurance Regulatory and Development Authority

Changes in drug policy in recent years have serious impact on drug prices. The implication of changing drug policies can be understood from the fact that 90% of the drugs were price-controlled in the late 1970s, while at the end of the last decade only 10% drugs were price-controlled (Pronab Sen Committee 2005). Pharmaceutical pricing policy has played a major role in the considerable and consistent increase of drug prices over the years (Selvaraj 2007).

20.3 Regulations for Essential Medicines and Drugs

A sizeable proportion of India's population is market-dependent and has to manage increasing health expenditures (particularly cost of medicines) from their own earnings. This makes price regulation of pharmaceutical products necessary (Srinivasan 2001). Steep growth in pharmaceutical industry appears in sharp contrast to high prices of medicines for the majority of Indians. Indian pharmaceutical industry has seen a tremendous growth of 14% since the beginning of 11th five year plan (2007–2012). The rise has been observed mainly from 2007 to 2009–2010; which in value terms implied an increase from Rs. 71,000 crores to more than Rs. 1 lakh crores. India produces 20% of global generics, 9% of the global bulk drugs and about 10% of total global production of medicines. The industry has prestigious ranks in the World—3rd in terms of volume and 14th in terms of value (Planning Commission 2012; National Pharmaceutical Pricing Policy 2012). The industry is highly fragmented; it contains 10,500 units and majority of them are working as unorganised units. Around 300–400 units are identified as organised and medium and small scale enterprises in nature. Of these, top 10 manufacturers have about 36.5% of the market share (Planning Commission 2012).

During the 11th five-year plan, India's pharmaceutical industry experienced a Compound Annual Growth Rate (CAGR) of about 19%, and India holds a position among top 20 pharmaceutical products exporting countries (Planning Commission 2012). Domestic competition, rapid growth of pharmaceuticals exports, contract manufacturing, contract research and development, outsourcing, bio pharmaceuticals, and clinical trials, are the major forces behind the growth of pharmaceutical industry (Dhopatkar 2012). This large-scale production and being a leading exporter of drugs has earned the name for Indian pharmaceutical industry as the 'pharmacy of the global south' (Chaudhuri 2007; Lofgren 2012). But this large production and relatively low prices have not brought the prosperity at home; the Indian health system still confronts the problem of access to essential medicines of good quality for all (Lofgren 2012).

There are regulations on drugs across the countries. Common policy tools applied to control the drug prices are mark-ups, controlled margins to wholesalers and pharmacists, price freezes, reference pricing, ceiling on promotional expenditure, differential value added tax on drugs, etc. (Selvaraj 2007). Apart from price control, there are issues of distribution, quality and patent having repercussions for affordability of healthcare. These issues are discussed here under two subsections: India's drug policy after independence and other issues.

20.3.1 India's Drug Policy After Independence

Regulations regarding essential medicines are important. WHO (1977) defines essential medicines as those medicines which meet the priority needs of healthcare of the population. Public health relevance, safety, efficacy and cost conditions are the guiding principles for defining the repertoire of essential medicines from time to time. The control regime for drugs in India after independence can be segregated into three phases: Pre-Patent Act Era (up to 1972), Post-Patent Act Era (1972–2005) and Full Trips Compliance (after 2005).

Pre-patent Act Era: Government of India, in 1948 appointed the Tek Chand committee to review the existing patent laws in India to ensure that the system was aligned with the national interest. The committee recommended that there was a need of efficient system to stop the abuse of patent rights and provision of compulsory licensing (Mueller 2007). In 1953, a patents bill based on the committee's report was introduced in Parliament but did not progress further. In 1957, another committee was appointed under Justice Rajagopala Ayyangar. Committee submitted its report in 1959 stating that most Indian patents were held by foreigners and system was being exploited by the foreign patent holders to achieve monopolistic control over the market (Adelman and Baldia 1996). After a long gap, these reports resulted in the formulation of Patent Act, 1970. The law was so constructed that older patent regime was completely disregarded, this was a deliberate step to encourage domestic manufacturing of low-cost generic drugs.

During this period, first statutory control on drugs was introduced in 1962 in the post-independence period in India. The government relented to the demands made by the pharmaceutical industry and agreed to certain changes in drug control policy. Therefore a list of 18 essential drugs was prepared and a tariff commission was setup to analyse the cost structure of these essential medicines. It was asked to suggest reasonable prices for the mentioned drugs. The commission emphasised the need for assessing the prices of drugs on occasions of phenomenal increases in prices. As a result, Drug Price Control Order (DPCO) was introduced by Government of India in 1970. The order provided an in-depth analysis of prices of life-saving drugs and came up with measures to keep the prices of essential enlisted drugs under control to ensure the affordability to consumers while considering required returns to the producers. There were 347 drugs incorporated into the essential medicine list of Drug Price Control Order (WHO 1977).

Drug Price Control Order took the form of Drug Price Control Policy 1979 with Hathi Committee recommendations. The policy came up with notable objectives such as to ensure adequate availability of drugs, to provide drugs at affordable prices, to ensure the quality of drugs and check medicines from being adulterated, to attain self-sufficiency in production and self-reliance in drug technology.

Post-patent Act Era (1972–2005): The Patent Act 1970, implemented in 1972, had indirectly built the base for self-reliant indigenous drug industry. Patents of pharmaceutical products were forbidden, only one production process is allowed to be patented and for the maximum of 7 years. Further, the Foreign Exchange Regulation Act (FERA) curtailed the foreign investments by regulating the companies to keep the foreign equity at 40% or less (Lofgren 2012).

The decade of 70 s has brought the prices of essential drugs to the reach of common people in India (WHO 1977). DPCO 1970 defined drugs under two categories; essential and non-essential. The prices of essential drugs were controlled and the permissible mark-up being not more than 75% of manufacturing costs. Non-essential category drugs were eligible to set mark-up prices up to 150% of manufacturing cost. The Drug Policy 1978 came up with new categorization of drugs. Four different categories were defined with different mark-ups: 40; 55; 100%; and fourth group completely exempted from price control (Selvaraj 2007).

In the 1990s and subsequent period, price control policy went through significant amendments. A reduction in number of drugs under price control was done in phases. In the first amendment in 1987, the list with 347 bulk drugs under purview of drug price control were reduced to 166 and further reduced to 142. Drug Price Control Order (DPCO) of 1995 further weakened the drug price control regime with only 76 drugs under controlled list (Selvaraj 2007).

The Drug Price Control Order (DPCO) vested the legal right to fix prices of medicines with the government (Anonymous 2005). In 1975, Hathi committee recommended the complete nationalisation of drug industry (Krishna 2002). But due to intense protests by the pharmaceutical firms, most of the committee's recommendations were not implemented.

Reverse engineering was another fascinating story of this period; domestic companies were free to produce patented drugs but with the process not patented. Indian government had only recognised one production process as patented; domestic companies used another processes or changed the formulation by adding or deducing any smaller molecule. Firms made new processes of medicines production at low cost. Consequently, this has resulted in the beginning affordable medicines (Reddy 2004).

Introduction of TRIPS compliance in the mid-1990s was an important turning point in the politics of pharmaceuticals. The coalition of public health advocates and domestic firms was weakened over product patents as major domestic firms embarked on discovery research activities. The opposition of product patents was slacked from the domestic firms' side; as opportunity of their financial growth is more attractive by opening for their own patenting and the collaboration with MNCs.

At the same time, process of liberalisation was on high, which paved the way for changes in 'Patent Act 1970' possible. The pharmaceutical sector was opened up for Foreign Direct Investments (FDI) and the drug price control policy was weakened (Lofgren 2012). The DPCO has been revised in several years for example in 1979, 1987, 1995 and 2002; the number of drugs under DPCO have fallen sharply from 347 in 1979 to 142 in 1987 and then to just 76 in 1995. The drug policy of 2002 has further reduced it to 35 only, but due to civil society agitations the 2002 policy was stayed by the Karnataka High Court in 2003 (Selvaraj and Farooqui 2012).

The need of National List of Essential Medicines (NLEM) was recognised in 1996, which paved the way for such listing of medicines. The revised list was released in 2003 by the Ministry of Health. A Task Force was constituted under the chairmanship of Principal Advisor, Planning Commission, Dr. Pronab Sen to consider the issue of price control, options other than price control, and to make recommendations for ensuring availability of life-saving drugs at reasonable prices (National Pharmaceutical Pricing Policy 2011, 2012).

After 2005—Full TRIPS Compliance: In 2005, TRIPS as legislation has been passed in India. It has resulted in re-introduction of the policy similar to prior 'Patent Act 1970'. The patents for pharmaceutical products, foods and chemicals again started taking place. The achievements and benefits from business model of reverse engineering became irrelevant; Indian companies were debarred from reverse engineering practices and they have to get a license to manufacture patented drugs from patent holder (Lofgren 2012).

In National Pharmaceutical Pricing Policy draft, the prices of medicines would be determined by the Market-Based Pricing (MBP) principles and not by the Cost-Based Pricing (CBP) principles which was adopted in the 1994 drug policy (National Pharmaceutical Pricing Policy 2011, 2012).

20.3.2 Other Issues

In India, drug prices were considerably high and regarded as one of the highest in the world (Hathi Committee Report on Drugs and Pharmaceuticals 1975). Access to medicines is significantly determined by drug prices. Private sector takes pivotal role in health service provision and financing in the absence of comprehensive public health insurance systems. The Indian drug companies have developed their capability to indigenously produce both bulk and formulation drugs. India has advantage in drug production costs which translates in lowest drug prices among major drug producing countries at present. However, changes in the 1990s policy have meant that the coverage of drug price control is only applicable to 10% of the market in 1995 (Lofgren 2012).

There are considerable price variations among different variants of the same formulation of drug. It has been experienced that pharmaceutical industry uses the loopholes of lax regulations to set the prices of medicine by complex price setting activities. It is striking that the price variation can be to the tune of 1000% in certain cases of therapeutically similar drugs (Sengupta et al. 2008).

A 40% increase in all drug prices has been reported by Sengupta and others (2008) between 1996 and 2006. Inactivity of drug price control can be realised when prices of drugs in essential medicine list increased by 15%, while the price of controlled drugs rose only by 0.02% for the above mentioned period. It is worthwhile to note that the prices of drugs neither under price control nor under essential drug list increased by 137%. Liberal policies of 1990s gave sudden rise to drug prices which were never seen in the last 15 years (Sengupta 2008).

There are many instances of companies indulging in unethical practices such as promotion of medicine which are close substitute of price controlled essential medicine; they are often found taking advantage of such loop holes in drug price control regime. GlaxoSmithKline (GSK), a well-known pharmaceutical MNC, sales 'Actifed', a drug prescribed for cold and cough. The ingredient used in this is pseudoephedrine. But, the Company uses Phenylpropanolamine (PPA) in India as the ingredient, which is notable for increased risk of cerebro-vascular accidents and has been banned in several countries. It is due to the fact that pseudoephedrine is under price control in India (Sengupta 2008).

Procurement and Distribution Systems: Reliable and efficient public procurement systems are crucial for drug availability. It necessitates use of funds in a proper and adequate manner. It is also important to take care of the phenomena of drug shortages. There are different kinds of procurement mechanisms adopted in India in different states: pooled or centralised procurement at the state level which is in vogue in Tamil Nadu and Kerala, decentralised procurement as in Chhattisgarh and some combination of the above two as in Bihar. TNMSC of Tamil Nadu is considered as an ideal model. Kerala has adopted this model and other states are planning to adopt this model.

The mix approach of two models has been proven to be an efficient procurement system. This fragmented nature of drugs purchase is non-competitive, therefore value money is less emphasised.

If the essential drug lists are not followed in the drug procurement processes by the states, it may result in an environment where physicians prescribe and use irrational drugs in the public health system. Cost-effectiveness of the drugs also gets compromised in the process. To cite an example, 239 medicines were procured by the state of Bihar during 2008–2009, with only 82 drugs (34.89%) from in EDL list (Selvaraj et al. 2010). Approximately 71% of state's drug budget was used for these drugs. This episode could have been an outcome of decentralised procurement and distribution system of drugs (Selvaraj et al. 2010).

Regulation of Drugs Quality: Health policy should be designed to optimise the use value of medicines. With this view, government agencies monitor and regulate the manufacturing, marketing and distribution of medicines. They must ensure that drugs made available to patients should meet necessary safety, quality and efficacy standards (Lofgren 2012).

Safety, quality and efficacy regulation cannot ensure the access to essential drugs for all and hence, cannot optimise the use value of medicines and also rational or 'quality use' of medicines. Improvement in health outcomes requires measures to ensure the quality use of medicines, including appropriate regulation and monitoring of service providers and prescribers (Srinivasan 2006).

In India, universal access to essential medicines and policy for quality use of medicines is at its vestigial stage, it has yet to achieve safety and efficacy regulations (Planning Commission 2011; Parliamentary Standing Committee on Health and Welfare 2012).

Drugs and Cosmetics Act of 1940 was far from being effective. This necessitated an effective drug regulatory system to control prices, quality and availability of drugs. The Central Drugs Standard Control (CDSCO) was set up to approve and qualify new drugs and clinical trials, defining standards, set control over drug imports, coordinate state drug control authorities. Further, State Drug control authorities were also set up with the express mandate of managing and regulating the manufacturing, sale and distribution of drugs.

Regulatory mechanisms are essential for addressing the case of spurious and substandard drugs in the market. The public consciousness regarding the quality issue—sub-standardisation, inefficacious or unsafe quality of drugs—develops over time. The issue of drugs quality regulation was realised an unfortunate incident when a women in Jodhpur, Rajasthan died due to contaminated drug. While violation of quality norms can be done by any producer, small-scale producers often face allegations of ineffective and standard violations in drug production.

Drugs Patent and its implications: With the affirmation to full TRIPs compliance, a large section of Indian population has been deprived of accessing new medicines. Newly invented drug are now protected under monopoly rights. It is unfortunate as many of these newly invented medicines address important contemporary health concerns, such as, oncology, certain mental conditions and HIV/AIDS. Adoption of such patent regime has its impact on prices of new medicines affecting the access to new life-saving drugs by masses (Planning Commission 2011).

Indian generic drugs have facilitated availability of cheaper drugs to patients across the globe with the large-scale low-cost production of ARVs in 2001. Earlier, the ARV vaccine was monopolised by US due to patents and the price was US $10,439 per annum per patient for AIDS treatment. Indian generic drug industry ensured its availability at only US$350 per annum per patient in 2005 (Menghaney 2009). Now, the cost of the drug is less than US$70 per patient. The irony is that patents prevent the availability of life-saving drugs to the needy and many curable diseases or avoidable deaths cannot be prevented. To cite an example, pegylated interferon alfa-2a, which is used for treatment of Hepatitis C, costs US$390 per 180 mg Pre-Filled Syringe (PFS). This is unaffordable by many middle-class patients (Menghaney 2009).

20.4 Primary Study in Aurangabad

Primary study is discussed under two subsections. The first subsection outlines the methodology adopted for the study. Major findings of the study are presented in the second subsection.

20.4.1 Methodology

Focus Area: Aurangabad is one of the 38 districts of Bihar, situated at the southern part of the state. The major city nearby Aurangabad is Gaya. The district of Aurangabad is administered with two subdivisions namely; Aurangabad and Daudnagar. The district is comprised of 11 blocks namely; Aurangabad, Daudnagar, Rafiganj, Nabinagar, Barun, Haspura, Madanpur, Dev, Obra, Goh and Kutumba (District Health Society, n.d., *b*). The district has been selected as the study area because it is located in rural surroundings and has sufficient reason for a researcher to consider it as a point of study on health at micro-level.

The district has one PHC in each block but population load on each PHC area is excessive. Indian Public Health Standards proposed a PHC with four–six indoor beds for 30,000 rural populations. But in Aurangabad, each PHC is serving a population of approximately 2 lakhs and more. Information provided in District Health Action Plan of 2011–2012 of Aurangabad regarding number of existing PHCs and PHCs required is furnished in Table 20.5.

Collection of Data: Data for this study has been collected in two different phases in 2012—May–June and October–November. The first process was a pilot study. Subsequently, final data collection was done. Two structured interview schedules were prepared to record the responses and information; one for the PHCs and the other for the households.

Block Health Managers were contacted for assessment of services and availability of essential medicines at PHCs. The researcher attained the approval from district Civil Surgeon to get the necessary information from PHCs. All 11 PHCs were covered for assessment of availability of services and medicines.

Table 20.5 Population and number of PHCs in Aurangabad

Block	Population	PHCs/referral at present	PHCs required (after including referral/DH)
Aurangabad	29,006	1	2
Obra	235,222	1	2
Daudnagar	219,785	1	2
Haspura	165,339	1	1
Goh	242,874	1	2
Rafiganj	315,732	1	3
Madanpur	218,147	1	2
Deo	180,895	1	1
Kutumba	240,630	1	2
Nabinagar	320,027	1	3
Barun	212,033	1	2
Total	2,642,689	12	22

Source District Health Society (n.d., *a*)

Table 20.6 Occupational distribution of sample households

Occupation	Persons employed (numbers)	Persons employed (%)
Labour	83	69.2
Vendor/small business/self-employed	9	7.5
Agriculture Labour/share cropper/self cultivator	24	20
Govt./Private employed	4	3.3

Source Field Survey 2012

A total of 86 households were interviewed. Households were selected both at PHC outpatient sections and in villages. Purposively six OPD patients were interviewed from six selected PHCs. The responsible person with patient or patient himself was interviewed in the PHCs. Their responses as immediate users were recorded. Apart from that, 50 households from four villages from different blocks were selected for data collection. All households selected were BPL card holders. There were in total 495 members in these 86 households. Thus, the average household size was 5.76.

Occupational Profile of Respondent Households: There were 120 working members in these 86 households. The worker–population ratio is less than 1:4. The categorization of occupation and corresponding number of employed persons is presented in Table 20.6.

There are four occupation categories mentioned in the table. First category is Labourer, second is Vendor/Small Business holders/Self-Employed, third is Agriculture Labour/Share Cropper/Self Cultivator, fourth is Government/private employee. Data reflects that a large portion of PHC users are labourers by their occupation; about 69.2%. People involved in agricultural activity in various forms constitute 20% and remaining employed are self-employed (7.5%) or government/private employed (3.3%).

20.4.2 Findings

Analysis of Healthcare Services: According to Indian Public Health Standards, PHCs are classified into two types depending on institutional delivery case load and services provided in PHCs. First, 'Type A PHC', has the case load of institutional delivery less than 20 in a month. Second, 'Type B PHC', has the case load of 20 or more institutional deliveries in month. By this criteria all PHC in the district are 'Type B PHCs'.

The number of outdoor patients attended and number of institutional deliveries conducted in the last three months prior to data collection, that is July, August and September, 2012 was analyzed. On an average each PHC has treated 11,168 outdoor patients in a month. If we exclude PHC 1—because it was not fully functional —then each functional PHC has treated 12,085 outdoor patients in a month.

Institutional deliveries that took place during these 3 months on an average in these PHCs are 250 in a month. After excluding PHC 1, average institutional deliveries in each fully functional PHC are 274 in a month. Hence, PHCs are overburdened with large number of outpatients and large number of institutional deliveries.

Table 20.7 shows availability of Reproductive and Child Health (RCH) services in select PHCs. The list includes 19 services, these services are expected to be there as mentioned in the India Public Health Standards guidelines for PHCs. Female gynaecologist or Lady Health Visitor (LHV) was not available in almost all PHCs. Medical Termination of Pregnancy (MTP) is also not available anywhere except one PHC. Tubectomy and Vasectomy service should be available on priority basis as these are necessary services for successful implementation of family planning. There are few PHCs with fixed days of services for adolescent health and immunisation. Availability of other services is satisfactory.

There have been incidences of outbreak of diseases in most of the PHC areas. The respondents mentioned that in all the PHCs, doctors were available to meet the eventualities of such outbreaks. Adequate care and drugs for chronic illness is

Table 20.7 Availability of reproductive and child health services

RCH services	Available in total number of PHCs	Percent of total ($n = 11$)
Ante-natal clinics	11	100
Normal delivery facility 24 h	11	100
Deliveries monitored through partograph	5	45.5
Tubectomy Services	9	81.8
Vasectomy Services	7	63.6
Female gynaecologist	1	9.1
Examination for gynaecological conditions	6	54.5
Treatment for gynaecological disorders	10	90.9
Fixed day health services for adolescent health	3	27.3
Fixed day health services for family planning	8	72.7
Family planning counselling during MCH services	11	100
Facility for Medical Termination of Pregnancy	1	9.1
Anaemia treatment	11	100
Low birth weight babies managed	9	81.8
Fixed immunisation day	4	36.4
BCG vaccines	11	100
Measles Vaccine	11	100
Treatment for children suffering from pneumonia	9	81.8
Management of children suffering from diarrhoea with dehydration	10	90.9

Source Field Survey 2012

available in eight PHCs. Public display mechanism for complaints and grievances is non-existent in five PHCs.

Medicine Availability: In the context of functioning health systems, essential medicines are expected to be available at all times in certain amount and dosage forms to fulfil the needs of people adequately. At the same time, the systems must facilitate information regarding essential medicines to achieve the goal of efficacy and ensure availability of medicines at reasonable price so that individual and the community can afford (WHO 1977).

Indian Public Health Standards' essential medicines list for PHCs was taken into consideration in this study. There are total of 165 medicines including their different formulations. In Table 20.8 information on availability of medicines is presented. Availability of medicines is distributed in quartile range in order to locate their status of availability. Around 90 medicines are in first quartile of lowest availability; notably among them 52 medicines are not available at all. About 36 medicines are in fourth quartile of maximum availability and remaining 19 and 20 medicines falls in second and third quartile, respectively. Maximum number of medicines prevails in the two extremes of quartile range; mainly in first quartile. More than 50 % of medicines are poorly available and more than half of them are not available. In the other extreme of high availability, it is showing very less number of medicines; only 36 out of 165.

Table 20.9 represents the medicines which are not available in any PHC, and their nature of essentiality. There are 32 names in the first column of medicines; these medicines have various formulations of same molecule, hence there are total 52 medicines with different formulations. The essentiality of medicines varies from vitamins and minerals to cardiovascular, anti-asthmatic medicines. The absence of these medicines has serious implications for public health. The implications include dependence on market, out-of-pocket payments, travelling and travelling cost, unregulated market price and quality of medicines consumed.

A quick review of Table 20.10 shows that almost all the PHCs (except PHC 5) are with less than 40% of essential medicines. The PHC 5 is just above the 40% (40.6%). The average availability of medicine in the whole district at PHC level is only 34.5%.

Treatment, Financing Pattern of Treatment and Perspectives of Users of PHC Services: In this important section, the responses of users are discussed. As mentioned earlier, households were selected purposively to understand the situation of access to essential medicines. As the concern of this study was to record the

Table 20.8 Number of essential medicines available in percent range

Quartile (%)	Number of medicines
<25	90
25–50	19
50–75	20
75–100	36
Total	165

Source Field Survey 2012

Table 20.9 Medicines not available in any PHC and their nature of essentiality

Medicines with various formulations	Nature of essentiality
Acetyl Salicylic Acid 300, 75, 50 mg tab	Cardiovascular—Antianginal medicine
Promethazine 10 mg, 25 mg tab and 500 mg cap	Anti-allergic medicine used in Anaphylaxis
Carbamazepine 200 mg tab and 20 mg syrup	Anticonvulsant/Antiepileptics
Mebendazole 100 mg suspension	Anti-worm
GlyserylTrinitrate 5 mg injection and 0.5 mg sublingual tab	Treatment for Angina and Heart failure
Propranolol 10 mg, 40 mg tab	Antimigraine medicine
Enalapril Maleate 2.5 mg, 5 mg, 10 mg tab and 1.25 mg injection	Cardiovascular—Antihypertensive medicine
Tab. Metoprolol 25, 50, 100 mg tab	Cardiovascular—Antianginal medicine
Hydrochlorthiazide 12.5 mg, 25 mg tab	Cardiovascular—Antihypertensive medicine
Tab. Captopril 25 mg	Antihypertensive and treatment of congestive heart failure
Nalidixic Acid 250 mg, 500 mg tab	Treatment of bacterial infections of the urinary tract
Nitrofurantoin 100 mg tab	Anti-infective—Antibacterial
Griseofulvin 125 mg, 250 mg cap or tab	Anti-infective—Antifungal medicine
Nystatin 500,000 IU tab	Anti-infective—Antifungal medicine
Metronidazole Pessaries 100,000 IU	Treatment for gynaecological disorder
Dipropionate Calamine lotion	Anti-inflammatory and antipruritic medicine
Benzoin Compound tincture	Antiseptic
Formaldehyde IP solution	Disinfectant
Potassium Permanganate crystals for solution	Disinfectant
Aluminium Hydroxide + Magnesium Hydroxide suspension and tab	Gastrointestinal—Antacid and antiulcer medicine
Domeridone 1 mg/ml syrup	Gastrointestinal—Antiemetics
Hyoscine Butyl Bromide 10 mg tab	Gastrointestinal—Antispasmodic medicine
Bisacodyl tab/suppository 5 mg	Gastrointestinal—Laxative
Isphagula Granules	Gastrointestinal—Laxative
Sulphacetamide Sodium 10%, 20%, 30% eye drops	Opthalmological Preparations—Anti-infective agent
Tetracycline Hydrochloride eye 1% ointment	Opthalmological Preparations—Local Anaesthetics
Prednisolone Sodium Phosphate 1% eye drops	Opthalmological Preparations—Anti-inflammatory agent
Beclomethasone Dipropionate 50 mg, 250 mg/dose inhalation	Anti-asthmatic medicine
Salbutamol Sulphate 2 mg/5 ml syrup	Anti-asthmatic medicine
Dextromethorphan 30 mg tab	Antitussive
Ascorbic Acid 100 mg, 500 mg tab	Vitamin and Mineral
Clofazimine 100 mg tab	Anti-leprosy medicine

Source Field Survey 2012

Table 20.10 Availability of all essential medicines PHC-wise

	Number of available medicines	Percent of total prescribed medicines*
PHC 1	23	13.9
PHC 2	60	36.4
PHC 3	52	31.5
PHC 4	65	39.4
PHC 5	67	40.6
PHC 6	58	35.2
PHC 7	63	38.2
PHC 8	50	30.3
PHC 9	64	38.8
PHC 10	62	37.6
PHC 11	63	38.2
Mean	57	34.5

Note *Percent out of 165 medicines in essential category at the time of survey
Source Field Survey 2012

situation of poor families, therefore, purposively only BPL families were selected in the PHCs and the villages.

A total of 86 households were interviewed, while total number of individuals in those households was 495. Individuals identified as patients were cumulatively 171 (34.5%). Table 20.11 is showing treatment order of households. There are three orders in the list representing the number of persons under treatment, number of persons treated in the last 6 months of data collection and number of persons who did not seek treatment or discontinued treatment. All the orders include both minor as well as major nature of illness.

The data is showing that among identified 171 patients, 105 were under treatment. In the last 6 months, 37 patients were treated; there are 29 patients who either did not get any treatment or those who discontinued their treatment. The reasons for not seeking or discontinuation of treatment were many. Lack of money for treatment or loss of livelihood and assets due to treatment, prolonged period of treatment, etc. were the most common reasons. It is important to note that perceptions such as, treatment not available in PHC or lack of faith in public health system widely exists. People still believe that public hospitals (PHCs) do not provide quality treatment. They believe that corruption in public health centres causes extraction of money from patients.

Some respondents said that they have no time for treatment. In other words, they do not want to wait in queue for a minor treatment wasting their whole day. Either they could afford to let those illnesses as they are or managed to visit any private medical outlet and buy a tablet for Rs. 1 or 2. In case of emergency treatment, they choose to go to a private hospital in nearby place instead of going to a PHC or District Hospital.

Most patients visited PHCs for treatment of minor illnesses such as fever, cough, cold, various types of body pain and others (see Table 20.12). This is followed by

Table 20.11 Access to treatment (including all the family members) (n = 171)

Treatment	Patients (in number)	Patients (in %)
Ongoing treatment	105	61.4
Treated in last six months	37	21.6
No treatment/treatment discontinued	29	17.0

Source Field Survey 2012

Table 20.12 Nature of illness/treatment (n = 171)

Nature of illness	Patients	Percentage
Child birth/Reproductive health problem	37	21.6
Heart/Diabetics/Respiratory/BP Patients	20	11.7
Apendice/Jaundice/Piles	9	5.3
Tuberculosis	4	2.3
Injury/Accident	7	4.1
Disability treatment	18	10.5
Leprosy	3	1.7
Mental illness/Epilepsy	8	4.7
Minor illness/Fever/Cough/Cold	65	38.0

Source Field Survey 2012

Table 20.13 Financing of treatment (n 83; No response: 3)

	Number of households	Households (in %)
Money borrowed on interest	58	69.8
Borrowed without interest	5	6.0
Self-financed	83	100
RSBY smart card	0	0.0
Health insurance	13	15.6

Source Field Survey 2012

child births/reproductive health problem and illnesses related to heart/diabetics/respiratory/blood pressure problem. Data in percentage signifies the share of minor illness in the next column.

Table 20.13 is showing the financing pattern of treatment by the households in terms of five major sources. The first source of financing of treatment is self-finance, so it is represented as 100% by all responded households.

After self-financing, if expenses of health are not met then households borrow money mainly on interest; about 70% households are in debt. Only 6% of households borrowed money which is interest-free. About 15.6% households have health insurance coverage. There are 12.8% of households having RSBY Smart Card but none of them have used this card for treatment. This was due lack awareness. When enquired about the use of this card, most of them thought of it as another kind of identity proof just like voter ID card.

20.5 Conclusions

Low level of drugs availability has many implications. First, it may lead to a serious loss of patient's life, if necessary medicines are not available at the time of need. This kind of experiences may change the belief of general people towards public health system. This assumed situation is not very far away from the reality. In case of emergency, people rarely think of going to public hospital; instead they rush directly to any private hospital. The importance of life for them is such that for obvious reasons, they are ready to spend more than their income and whole savings. Second, there may be some private medical supplier nearby PHC and is patronised by patients in the hospital in need of essential medicines that are not available in the PHC. Again this is also not an assumption, there are number of private medical outlets around all the PHCs of Aurangabad, flourishing on the missing contents of the PHCs. Patients have no option other than purchasing the medicines from these private outlets with no financial support such as reimbursement from health centre. Third, the qualities of medicines are always compromised by the private retailers to achieve greater margins on prices of medicines. In other words, there is no quality check of the drugs provided by petty sellers near PHCs. They are most unregulated and settled around the PHCs on temporary basis because whenever drug administrator (Drug Inspector) gets tough on them they disappear from the sight. Fourth, many treatments are of prolonged nature and regular dependency on private medicines can push the households into severe poverty and make them liable for large debts. This statement is again based on field experiences, which is showing that 17% of identified patients either have no treatment or treatment discontinued due to lack of money. The relationship between households and public health services needs to be improved by addressing the issues such as low awareness about public health programmes and schemes, developing a more user-friendly environment in the PHCs, improving the availability of essential drugs and services, ensuring that no private costs are incurred on health inside the PHC as well as outside the PHC by ensuring proper coverage of state-provided insurance.

References

Adelman, M. J., & Baldia, S. (1996). Prospects and limits of the patent provision in the TRIPS agreement: The case of India. *Vanderbilt Journal of Transnational Law, 29,* 507.

Anand, G. (2016). *'True scale' of India's tuberculosis problem: 2.8 million new cases, The New York Times*. https://www.nytimes.com/2016/10/14/world/asia/true-scale-of-indias-tuberculosis-problem-2-8-million-new-cases.html. Accessed June 28, 2017.

Anonymous. (2005). Drug prices: Requiem for DPCO? *Economic and Political Weekly, 40*(33), 3620.

Arrow, K. J. (1963). Uncertainty and the welfare economics of medical care. *The American Economic Review, American Economic Association, 53*(5), 941–973. http://www.jstor.org/stable/1812044. Accessed February 2, 2013.

AVERT. (2015). *HIV and AIDS in India*. https://www.avert.org/professionals/hiv-around-world/asia-pacific/india. Accessed June 28, 2017.

Berman, P., Ahuja, R., & Bhandari, L. (2010). The impoverishing effect of healthcare payments in India: New methodology and findings. *Economic & Political Weekly, 45*(16), 65–71.

Bonu, S., Bhusan, I., & Peters, D. H. (2007). Incidence, intensity and correlates of catastrophic out of pocket health payments in India. ERD Working Paper No 102, Asian Development Bank.

Cecilia, D. (2014). Current status of dengue and chikungunya in India. *WHO South-East Asia Journal of Public Health, 3*(1), 22–27. www.searo.who.int/publications/journals/seajph. Accessed June 28, 2017.

Chaudhuri, S. (2007). The gap between successful innovation and access to its benefits: Indian pharmaceuticals. *The European Journal of Development Research., 19,* 49–65.

Dhopatkar, V. (2012). Indian Pharmaceutical Industry. *Maharashtra Economic Development Council Monthly Economic Digest, 41*(03), 37–39.

District Health Society. (n.d., *a*). *District health action plan 2011–12*. Bihar: Aurangabad.

District Health Society. (n.d., *b*). *District health action plan: 2012–13*. Bihar: Aurangabad.

Garg, C. C., & Karan, A. K. (2009). Reducing out-of-pocket expenditures to reduce poverty: A disaggregated analysis at rural-urban and state level in India. *Health Policy and Planning, 24* (2), 116–128.

Ghoshal, A. G., Ravindran, G. D., et al. (2016). The burden of segregated respiratory diseases in India and the quality of care in these patients: Results from the Asia-Pacific burden of respiratory diseases study. *Lung India, 33*(6), 611–619. https://www.ncbi.nlm.nih.gov/pmc/articles/PMC5112817/. Accessed June 28, 2017.

Hathi Committee Report on Drugs and Pharmaceuticals. (1975). *Department of chemical and fertilizers*. New Delhi: Government of India.

Insurance Regulatory and Development Authority. (n.d.). *Report on medical inflation over the years*. New Delhi: Insurance Information Bureau, Government of India.

Kaur, K. (2014). Anaemia 'a silent killer' among women in India: Present scenario. *European Journal of Zoological Research, 3*(1), 32–36. http://www.scholarsresearchlibrary.com/articles/anaemia-a-silent-killer-among-women-in-india-present-scenario.pdf. Accessed June 28, 2017.

Krishna, I. V. R. (2002, March 16–29). *Patent Issues: The Doha-Delhi Odyssey. Frontline*. http://www.frontline.in/navigation/?type=static&page=archive. Accessed June 14, 2017.

Lakshminarayanan, S., & Jayalakshmy, R. (2015). Diarrheal diseases among children in India: Current scenario and future perspectives. *Journal of Natural Science, Biology and Medicine, 6* (1), 24–28. https://www.ncbi.nlm.nih.gov/pmc/articles/PMC4367049/. Accessed June 28, 2017.

Lal, P. G., & Sinha, D. (2005). *The Commission report: Building on values*. New Delhi: National Commission on Macroeconomics and Health, Ministry of Health and Family Welfare.

Lofgren, H. (2012). The pharmaceutical industry and access to medicines in India. In Hans Lofgren (Ed.), *The politics of the pharmaceutical industry and access to medicines: World pharmacy and India* (pp. 1–23). New Delhi: Social Science Press.

Menghaney, L. (2009). Without Compulsory Licensing-Patients the World Over Will Pay the Price. Centre for Trade and Development, Policy Brief Series No 9, New Delhi.

Mueller, J. M. (2007). The Tiger Awakens: The Tumultuous Transformation of India's Patent System and the Rise of Indian Pharmaceutical Innovation. *University of Pittsburgh Law Review, 68*(3), 491–641.

Nandakumar, A. (2009). *National Cancer Registry Programme. Indian Council for Medical Research, Consolidated report of the population based cancer registries 1990–96*. http://www.icmr.nic.in/ncrp/ncrp_p/cancer_reg.pdf. Accessed June 28, 2017.

National Health Accounts: India 2004–05. (2009). *National Health Accounts Cell, Ministry of Health and Family Welfare, Government of India, New Delhi*. http://planningcommission.nic.in/reports/genrep/health/National_Health_Account_04_05.pdf.

National Pharmaceutical Pricing Policy. (2011). Department of Pharmaceuticals, Ministry of Chemicals and Fertilizers, Government of India, New Delhi.

National Pharmaceutical Pricing Policy. (2012). Department of Pharmaceuticals, Ministry of Chemicals and Fertilizers, Government of India, New Delhi.

NIMR. (n.d.). *Estimation of true malaria burden in India*. http://www.mrcindia.org/MRC_profile/profile2/Estimation%20of%20true%20malaria%20burden%20in%20India.pdf. Accessed June 28, 2017.

Parliamentary Standing Committee on Health and Welfare. (2012). *The Function of the Central Drugs Standard Control Organisation (CDSCO)*. New Delhi: Government of India.

Planning Commission. (2008). *Eleventh Five Year Plan: 2007–12 Volume II: Social Sector*. New Delhi: Oxford University Press, Government of India.

Planning Commission. (2011). *High level expert group report on Universal health coverage for India. Planning commission of India. New Delhi*. http://planningcommission.nic.in/reports/genrep/rep_uhc0812.pdf. Accessed June 22, 2017.

Planning Commission. (2012). Drugs and Pharmaceuticals: Report. Working Groups/Steering Committees for the Twelfth Five Year Plan 2012–2017, Government of India, New Delhi.

Prabhakaran, D., Jeemon, P., et al. (2016). Cardiovascular Diseases in India: Current Epidemiology and Future Directions. *American Heart Association 133*(16), 1605–1620. http://circ.ahajournals.org/content/133/16/1605. Accessed June 28, 2017.

Pronab Sen Committee. (2005). *Report: Task force to explore options other than price control for achieving the objective of making available life-saving drugs at reasonable prices*. Ministry of Chemicals and Petrochemicals, Government of India, New Delhi. http://pharmaceuticals.gov.in/sites/default/files/Dr.%20Pronab%20Sen%20Committee%20Report1_0.pdf. Accessed June 23, 2017.

Rane, W. (2003). Have drug prices fallen? *Economic and Political Weekly, 38*(44), 4640–4642.

Rao, M. G., & Choudhury, M. (2012). Health care financing reforms in India. National Institute of Public Finance and Policy, Working Paper No: 2012-100.

Reddy, A. K. (2004). Innovating drugs: Emerging perspectives. In Pharmacophore 2004: International Symposium, Hyderabad.

Reddy, K. S., Selvaraj, S., Rao, K. D., et al. (2011). *A critical assessment of the existing health insurance models in India*. New Delhi: Public Health Foundation of India.

Report on Medical Inflation over the years. (n.d.). Insurance Regulatory and Development Authority, Insurance Information Bureau, Government of India, New Delhi.

Selvaraj, S. (2007). *How effective is India's drug price control regime?* Boston, MA: Harvard School of Public Health.

Selvaraj, S., Chokshi, M., Hasan, H., & Kumar, P. (2010). *Improving Governance and accountability in India's medicine supply system*. New Delhi: Public Health Foundation of India.

Selvaraj, S., & Farooqui, H. H. (2012). Draft drug price policy 2011: Legitimising unaffordable medicine prices? *Economic and Political Weekly, 47*(46), 13–17.

Selvaraj, S., & Karan, A. K. (2009). Deepening health insecurity in India: Evidence from national sample surveys since 1980s. *Economic & Political Weekly, 44*(40), 55–60.

Sengupta, A., Joseph, R. K., Modi, S., Syam, N. (2008). *Economic constraints to access to essential medicines in India*. New Delhi: Society for Economic & Social Studies and Centre for Trade & Development.

Srinivasan, S. (2001). Drug price control: Who is in charge? *Economic and Political Weekly, 36* (12), 997–998.

Srinivasan, S. (2006). *Lay person's guide to medicines*. Baroda: LOCOST.

Van Doorslaer, E., O'Donnell, O., Rannan-Eliya, R. P., et al. (2006). Effect of payments for health care on poverty estimates in 11 countries in Asia: An analysis of household survey data. *The Lancet, 368*(9544), 1357–1364.

Van Doorslaer, E., O'Donnell, O., Rannan-Eliya, R. P., et al. (2007). Catastrophic payments for health care in Asia. *Health Economics, 16*(11), 1159–1184.
World Health Organisation. (1977). *Health topics: Essential medicines*. Geneva. http://www.who.int/topics/essential_medicines/en/. Accessed June 23, 2017.
Xu, K., Evans, D. B., Carrin, G., et al. (2007). Protecting households from catastrophic health spending. *Health Affairs, 26,* 972–983. doi:10.1377/hlthaff.26.4.97.

Chapter 21
Meteorological Conditions and Malaria Cases—Study in the Context of Meghalaya

Strong P. Marbaniang and Laishram Ladusingh

Malaria defeated the international community many years ago. We cannot allow this to happen again. A single global action plan for malaria control, that enjoys Partnership-wide support, is a strong factor for success.

Margaret Chan, WHO Director-General

21.1 Introduction

Malaria is caused by parasites belonging to the genus Plasmodium, which is transmitted through the bite of the infected female Anopheles mosquitoes. The parasites multiply in the liver and then start infecting the red blood cells. Symptoms of malaria include fever, headache, and vomiting. If not treated within 24 h, malaria becomes life threatening because it affects the blood supply to the vital organs of the body. In many parts of the world, the parasites have developed resistance to a number of antimalarial medicines. The four types of parasite species that cause malaria in a human being are Plasmodium falciparum (P.f), Plasmodium vivax (P.v), Plasmodium malariae, and Plasmodium ovale (Malaria, n.d.). Malaria transmission depends on climatic conditions, such as rainfall, temperature, and humidity, which may affect the number and survival of mosquitoes. In many places, transmission is seasonal, with the peak happening during and just after the rainy season. Epidemics of malaria can occur when climatic and other environmental conditions suddenly change in places where people have either little immunity or no immunity at all to malaria. People living in stable malaria endemic and high malaria transmission region like the sub-Saharan Africa and the forest area in the Indian states like Jharkhand, Odisha, Chattisgarh, Madhya Pradesh and Northeast India, develop immunity against malaria at the early age, but

S.P. Marbaniang (✉)
International Institute for Population Sciences (IIPS), Mumbai 400088, India
e-mail: marbaniangstrong@gmail.com

L. Ladusingh
Head, Department of Mathematical Demography and Statistics, (IIPS), Mumbai 400088, India

U.K. De et al. (eds.), *Issues on Health and Healthcare in India*, India Studies in Business and Economics, https://doi.org/10.1007/978-981-10-6104-2_21

people living in unstable endemic areas tend to have low immunity against malaria (Immunity n.d.). This can also occur when people with low immunity migrate into the region where there is high incidence and continuous transmission of malaria. Exposure over a number of years helps develop partial immunity, which, though does not provide complete protection, does reduce the risk of contracting severe disease (Malaria fever, n.d.). Malaria is a disease that can be prevented and treated if clean and hygienic living environment are maintained by the people. In 2012, approximately 207 million cases of malaria occurred worldwide. In the 11 countries of the South East Asian Region of WHO, 1.2 billion people are exposed to the risk of malaria, most of them live in India (Kondrachine 1992).

The National Vector Borne Disease Control Programme (NVBDCP) is an umbrella program in India for prevention and control of vector-borne diseases (VBDS), including Japanese Encephalitis, Malaria, Kala-Azar, Dengue, Filariasis, and Chikungunya; it is an integral part of the country's National Rural Health Mission (NRHM). The Directorate of the NVBDCP has framed technical guidelines/policies and provides most of the resources for the program. Indicators for the monitoring of the program have been developed at the national level and there is uniformity in collection, compilation, and onward submissions of data. Community Health Centers, Public Health Centers, Malaria Clinics, and other health institutions carry out passive surveillance of malaria. Accredited Social Health Activist (ASHA)—a village volunteer is also involved in the program to provide diagnostic and treatment services such as Rapid Diagnostic Tests and the Artemisinin Combination Therapy (ACT) for the treatment of P. f. malaria cases.

21.2 Background History of Meghalaya

Meghalaya is one of the seven northeastern states—situated in the eastern sub-Himalayas—and also one of the most beautiful states in the country. About 300 km in length and 100 km in breadth, Meghalaya is surrounded in the north by the Goalpara, Kamrup, and Nowgong districts of the state of Assam, in the east by the Karbi Anglong and North Cachar Hills districts also of Assam, and on the south and west by Bangladesh. The state enjoys abundant rainfall, sunshine, unspoiled forests, plateaus, waterfalls, and clear rivers and is home to sturdy, intelligent, and friendly people. Meghalaya became an autonomous state on April 2, 1970 and gained full statehood on January 21, 1972, marking the beginning of an era of mutual understanding and peace in the region. The total land area of Meghalaya is 22,429 km^2 and 15,675 km^2 are under the forest area (Meghalaya, n.d.). Forest in Meghalaya are not categories as very dense forest, the region of the states mostly covered by forest are Ri Bhoi, southern part of Jaintia Hills, southeastern part of West Garo Hills and southern part of East Garo and South Garo Hills district, geographically Meghalaya varies in altitude from 200 m above sea level (ASL) in the west and northwestern part to 1960 m ASL in the state capital (Dikshit 2014). Shillong, the capital of Meghalaya, is located at an altitude of 1496 meters above sea level. The capital city derives its name from the manifestation of the creator called Shyllong. The climate of Meghalaya varies with altitude. The climate of the Khasi and Jaintia Hills is uniquely pleasant—neither too warm in summers nor too cold in winters. In the plains of the Garo Hills, the climate is warm and humid, except during the winter. The sky is mostly overcast in Meghalaya, with the average annual rainfall over western Meghalaya being about 2600 mm, over northern Meghalaya between 2500 and 3000 mm, and over south-eastern Meghalaya about 4000 mm. There is a great variation in the rainfall received in central and southern Meghalaya. At Sohra (earlier known as Cherrapunjee), the average annual rainfall is as high as 12,000 mm. By contrast, Shillong, which is no more than 50 kilometers away from Sohra, receives an average of only 2200 mm of rainfall annually (Meghalaya, n.d.).

21.3 Review of Literature

Many studies on malaria cases and its association with meteorological factors have been conducted in the different region of the world. In a study done in Zimbabwe in 1988–1999, inter-annual variations in average temperature, rainfall, and vapor pressure were found to have a strong positive association with the incidence of malaria, while maximum and minimum temperature were found to have no such association (Mabaso et al. 2006). In East African Highland, climate variability was found to be the main causes leading to the increase in the number of malaria outpatients (Zhou et al. 2004). A study in Tanzania found that the incidence of malaria during the month of October to March are due to the increased in rainfall, while during the month of April to September are due to high rainfall together with high maximum temperature (Jones et al. 2007). In a study done in Motuo County found that temperature, rainfall, and relative humidity are the favorable conditions for the transmission of malaria with relative humidity being the main factor that contributes to the survival of mosquito (Huang et al. 2011, Al-Mansoob et al. 2005). A study about the malaria incidence among the forest and non-forest area in Kokrajhar district found that relative humidity is positively correlated with malaria incidence in forest area while the temperature was negatively correlated with malaria incidence in the non-forest area (Nath and Mwchahary 2012).

21.4 Need for the Study

The sixth goal of the United Nations' Millennium Development Goals (MDG) was to halt and begin to reverse the incidence of malaria by 2015, achieving which was a challenge for countries like India with a high prevalence of malaria cases. The NVBDCP is the governing body In India, responsible for policy making, monitoring, and giving technical help to the states so as to halt and reverse the incidence of malaria. Meghalaya is one of the high malaria endemic states in India among the seven northeastern states. The main goal of the Global Fund to Fight AIDS, Tuberculosis and Malaria Round 9 was to reduce malaria-related mortality and morbidity in the seven northeastern states by at least 30% by 2015 as compared to 2008. The impact indicators of the program were the Annual Parasite Index and the Number of deaths with Malaria Confirmation. According to the NVBDCP classification based on the Annual Parasite Index (API), malaria is endemic in almost all the districts of Meghalaya. Three districts Eastgaro, Westgaro, and Southgaro have API > 10, Ribhoi has an API ranging between 5 and 10, the West Khasi Hills and Jaintia Hills have an API of 2–5, and the East Khasi Hills have an API of 0.1–1 (NVBDCP, n.d.). A number of studies related to meteorological variables and malaria cases have been done before and the findings are different from one study to another. There have been few studies studying the association between malaria cases and meteorological cases in Meghalaya. This study aims to help understand in what way the meteorological conditions in Meghalaya are related with malaria cases. It has been noted from earlier studies conducted in different geographical regions having different meteorological conditions that there are variations pertaining to the association between malaria cases and temperature and rainfall. This means that one region differs from another in how malaria cases are related to temperature and rainfall, necessitating an in-depth study to get broad insights on the nature of this relationship in the specific context of Meghalaya. This study also aims to gain an understanding of the prevalence of malaria cases in the different districts of the state and an age and sex-wise distribution of malaria and deaths resulting from it so as to help the Malaria State Control Programme in framing a plan and designing activities to tackle malaria and achieve the desired goal.

21.5 Objectives of the Study

The three specific objectives of this study are

1. To study the district-wise prevalence of malaria cases.
2. To assess district-wise age and sex distribution of death cases.
3. To study the relationship between malaria cases and the meteorological conditions in the state of Meghalaya.

21.6 Materials and Methods

The data on malaria for this study were collected from the Department of Health Services (Malaria), Government of Meghalaya. The data on temperature and rainfall were collected from the Directorate of Agriculture, Government of Meghalaya. For this study, we have taken into consideration only 3 years (2011–13) of malaria data and meteorological data on temperature and rainfall, recorded on a monthly basis for all the seven districts of Meghalaya. Rainfall is measured in millimeter (mm) and temperature in degree Celsius (°C).

For the first objective, we took the sum of the monthly malaria cases for the years 2011, 2012 and 2013, and then the total of all the 3 yearly malaria cases so as to get the district total malaria cases from the year 2011 to 2013. This method was repeated for all the seven districts. To obtain the district total fever cases from 2011 to 2013, a similar method, as in the case of malaria cases, was applied. After obtaining the 3-year total malaria cases and fever cases for each district, we obtained the district-wise prevalence of malaria cases by using the following formula:

$$\text{District Malaria Prevalence Rate} = \frac{\text{District total malaria cases from the year 2011 to 2013}}{\text{District total fever cases from the year 2011 to 2013}} \times 1000$$

For the second objective, we took the sum of malaria death cases for all the 3 years and the malaria cases for each district for the different age groups and sex. Then we calculated the malaria death cases per 1000 malaria cases for each district for the different age groups and sex.

$$\text{Malaria Death Rate (Male)} = \frac{\text{Total malaria death in male age group } x \text{ to } x+n}{\text{Total malaria Cases in male at the corresponding age group } x \text{ to } x+n} \times 1000$$

$$\text{Malaria Death Rate (Female)} = \frac{\text{Total malaria death in female age group } x \text{ to } x+n}{\text{Total malaria Cases in female at the corresponding age group } x \text{ to } x+n} \times 1000$$

$$\text{Annual Blood Examination Rate (ABER)} = \frac{\text{Total blood smear collected during the year}}{\text{Total population under surveillance}} \times 100$$

$$\text{Annual Parasitic Indices (API)} = \frac{\text{Total number of blood smears positive for malaria during the year}}{\text{Total population}} \times 1000$$

For the third objective, we used multiple linear regressions to test the association between the dependent variables and the independent variables. Here the dependent variable is the monthly Malaria Incidence Rate (MIR), and the independent variables are the monthly average temperature and the monthly rainfall. SPSS 12 was used to calculate the multiple linear regressions.

$$\text{Malaria Incidence Rate (MIR)} = \frac{\text{Total malaria cases during the month}}{\text{Total population during the month}} \times 100,000$$

21.7 Results and Discussion

Figure 21.2 shows the district-wise percentage distribution of malaria cases. West Garo Hills and East Garo Hills were the highest contributors of malaria cases with 33% each in the whole state during 2011–2013. South Garo Hills, with 15%, comes next. The West Khasi Hills (8%), Ri Bhoi (6%), the East Khasi Hills (3%), and the Jaintia Hills (2%) made the lowest contribution of malaria cases. Figure 21.1 shows the district-wise percentage distribution of fever cases. From this figure, we see that the West Garo Hills had the highest percentage of fever cases with 43% of the total cases. The East Garo Hills, with a 13% contribution, come next. This is followed by the Jaintia Hills (11%), Ri Bhoi (10%), the South Garo Hills (8%), and the East Khasi Hills (8%). At 7%, the West Khasi Hills had the lowest percentage of fever cases.

Figure 21.3 shows the district-wise prevalence of malaria cases per 1000 fever cases. We observe that the East Garo Hills had the highest malaria prevalence rate of 164 malaria cases per 1000 fever cases. Next come the South Garo Hills with a malaria prevalence rate of 109 malaria cases per 1000 fever cases. This is followed by the West Khasi Hills with a malaria prevalence rate of 73 malaria cases per 1000 fever cases. The West Garo Hills had a malaria prevalence rate of 47 malaria cases per 1000 fever cases. Ri Bhoi had 36 malaria cases per 1000 fever cases. The East

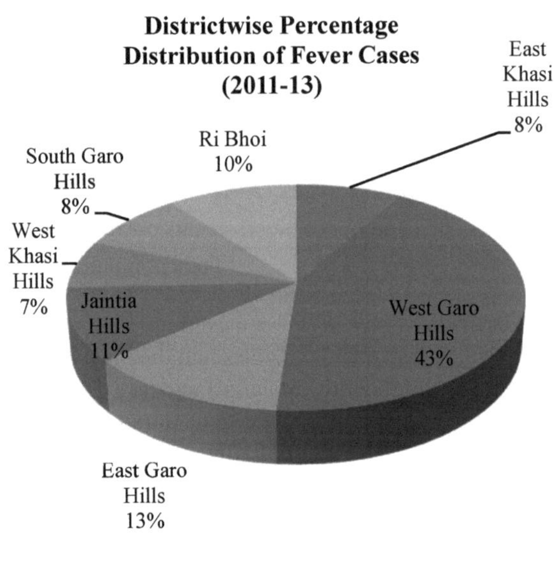

Fig. 21.1 District-wise prevalence of fever cases

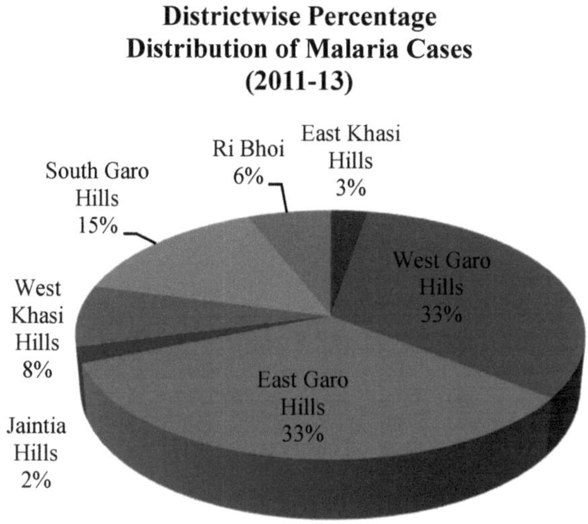

Fig. 21.2 District-wise prevalence of malaria cases

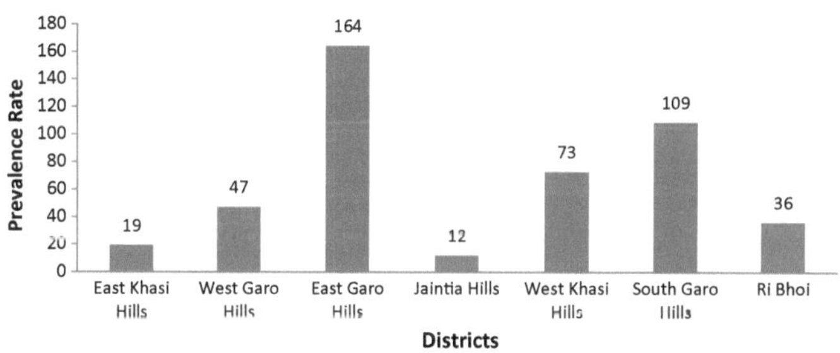

Fig. 21.3 District-wise prevalence of malaria cases per 1000 fever cases

Khasi Hills had a malaria prevalence rate of 19 malaria cases per 1000 fever cases, and the Jaintia Hills showed the lowest malaria prevalence rate of 12 malaria cases per 1000 fever cases.

From Fig. 21.4, we observe that the West Khasi Hills recorded the highest number of deaths per 1000 malaria cases, followed by the Jaintia Hills, East Khasi Hills. The West Garo Hills recorded the lowest deaths per 1000 malaria cases. From Fig. 21.5, we observe that the Jaintia hills recorded the highest death cases per 1000 malaria cases, whereas the East Garo Hills and the West Khasi hills recorded the lowest death cases per 1000 malaria cases. Figure 21.6 shows that the East Khasi Hills had the highest number of deaths per 1000 malaria cases, whereas the other districts were well below it. From Fig. 21.7, we observe that the Jaintia Hills had the highest death cases per 1000 malaria cases, followed by the East Khasi Hills. The East Garo Hills recorded the lowest figure. Figure 21.8 tells us that the East

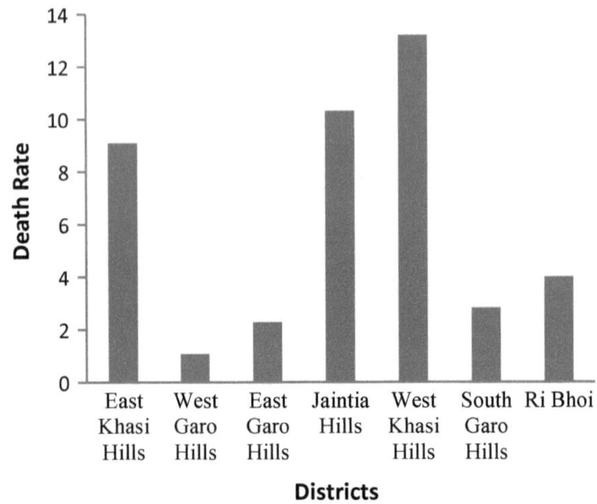

Fig. 21.4 Death cases per 1000 malaria cases in male 0–4 age group

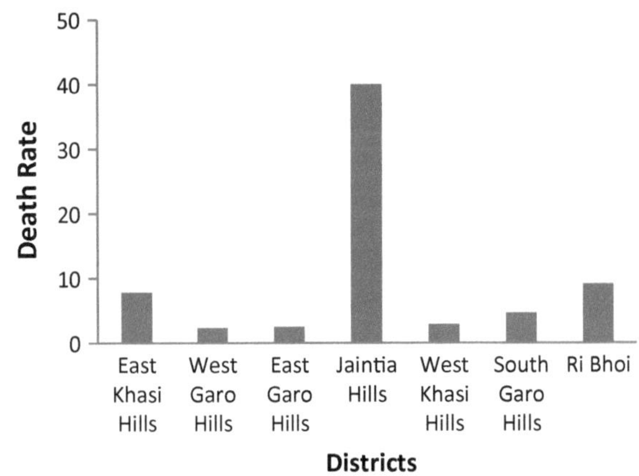

Fig. 21.5 Death cases per 1000 malaria cases in female 0–4 age group

Khasi Hills had the highest death cases, followed by the Jaintia Hills. The lowest deaths were recorded in the West Garo Hills. Figure 21.9 shows that the Jaintia Hills had the highest deaths per 1000 malaria cases, followed by the West Khasi Hills. The East Khasi Hills recorded no death per 1000 malaria cases. Figure 21.10 shows the surveillance of the different district blocks in Meghalaya in terms of ABER (2013). ABER denotes the total number of slides collected per 100 population under surveillance. Most parts of the Garo Hills and Ri Bhoi districts had an ABER of greater than 10, whereas some areas of the West Khasi Hills and the East Khasi Hills, which had a low surveillance, had an ABER of less than 5. On the

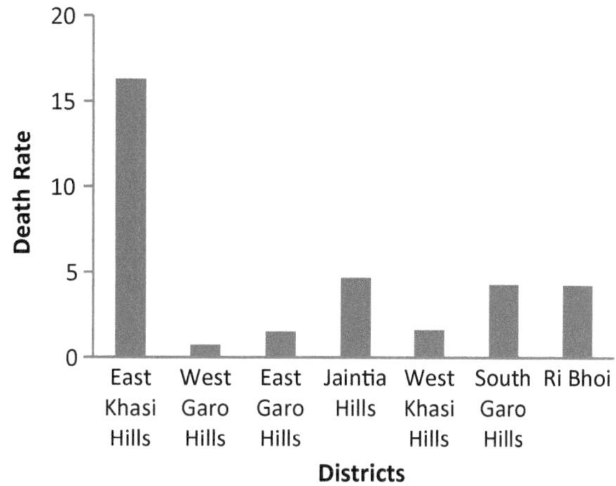

Fig. 21.6 Death cases per 1000 malaria cases in male 5–14 age group

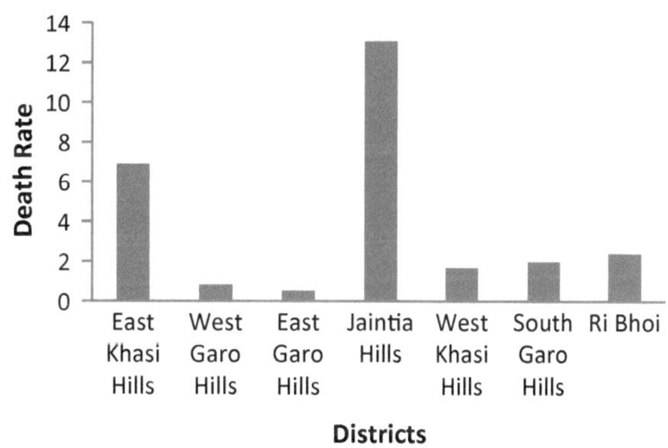

Fig. 21.7 Death cases per 1000 malaria cases in female 5–14 age group

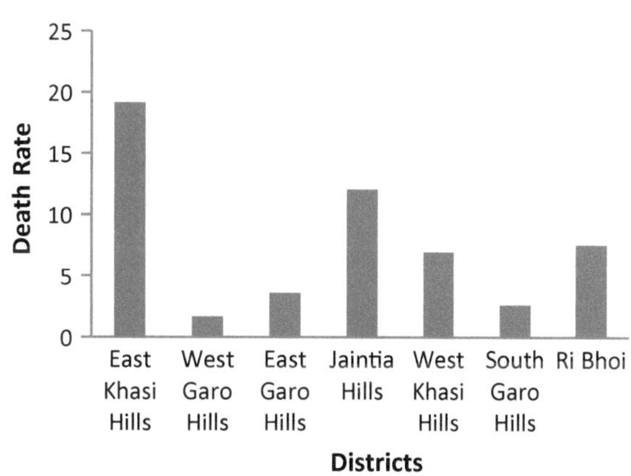

Fig. 21.8 Death cases per 1000 malaria cases in male 15 + age group

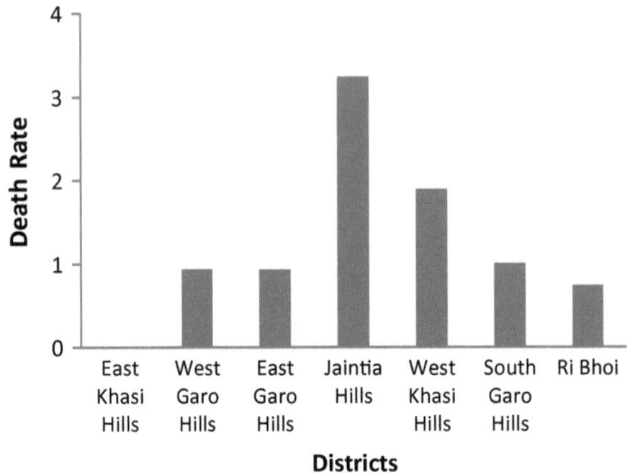

Fig. 21.9 Death cases per 1000 malaria cases in female 15+ age group

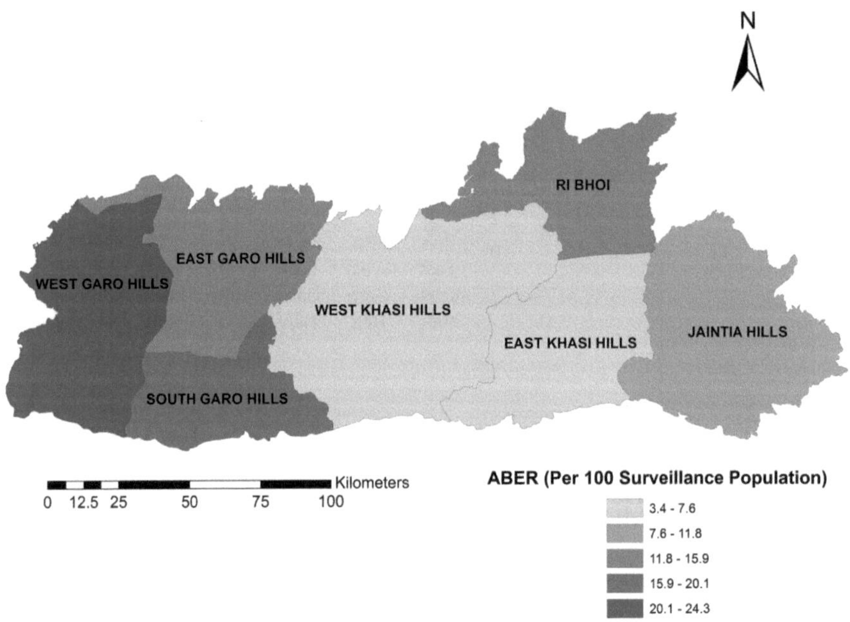

Fig. 21.10 District-wise distribution of average annual blood examination rate (ABER), (2011–2013)

other hand, some parts of the Jaintia Hills had an ABER which was a little higher compared to the East Khasi Hills and the West Khasi Hills. In Fig. 21.11 most of the areas in the Garo Hills, where the ABER was high, the API was high too. But in the East Khasi Hills and the West Khasi Hills, where the ABER was low, the API was also low. So Figs. 21.10 and 21.11 give us an idea as to why the East Khasi

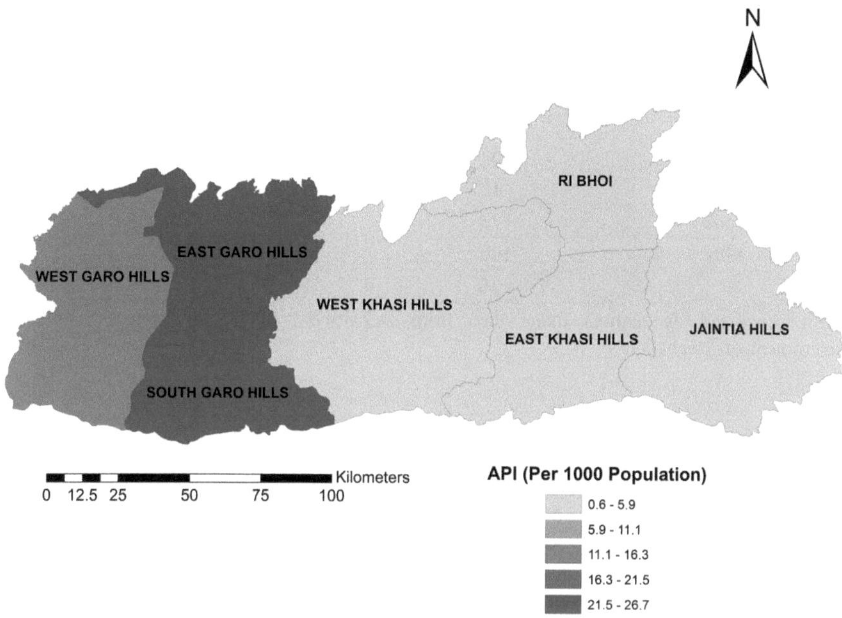

Fig. 21.11 District-wise distribution of average annual parasitic incidences (API), (2011–2013)

Table 21.1 Percentage of malaria cases and fever cases during the year 2011–2013

Districts	Malaria		Fever	
	n	%	*n*	%
East Khasi hills	1863	3	96,101	9
West Garo hills	22,775	33	483,523	43
East Garo hills	23,328	34	142,183	13
Jaintia hills	1415	2	118,994	11
West Khasi hills	5602	8	77,120	7
South Garo hills	10,349	15	95,366	8
Ri Bhoi	4253	6	117,097	10

n: Number of cases

Source Analyzed by authors using data from Department of Health Services (Malaria), Government of Meghalaya

Hills, the Jaintia Hills, and the West Khasi Hills are statistically higher in death cases per 1000 malaria cases as compared to the districts of the Garo Hills and Ri Bhoi. And the reason may be the low surveillance in these areas (Tables 21.1, 21.2 and 21.3).

Table 21.2 District-wise prevalence of malaria per 1000 fever cases

Districts	Prevalence rate	%
East Khasi hills	19	4
West Garo hills	47	10
East Garo hills	164	36
Jaintia hills	12	3
West Khasi hills	73	16
South Garo hills	109	24
Ri Bhoi	36	8

Source Analyzed by authors using data from Department of Health Services (Malaria), Government of Meghalaya

Table 21.3 District-wise death cases per 1000 fever cases (2011–2013)

District	Male			Female		
	0–4 year	5–14 year	15+ year	0–4 year	5–14 year	15+ year
East Khasi hills	9	16	19	8	7	0
West Garo hills	1	1	2	2	1	1
East Garo hills	2	2	4	3	1	1
Jaintia hills	10	5	12	40	13	3
West Khasi hills	13	2	7	3	2	2
South Garo hills	3	4	3	5	2	1
Ri Bhoi	4	4	8	9	2	1

Source Author's calculation using the data from Department of Health Services (Malaria), Government of Meghalaya

Table 21.4 Multiple linear regression analysis

Predictors	Coefficient	95% confidence interval	
Average temperature	0.20983***	0.1955	0.224
Rainfall	−0.0006***	−0.00081	−0.00043
Constant	1.57118***	1.25982	1.88254

Dependent Malaria Incidence Rate, $p < 0.01$:***
Source Author's calculation using the data from Department of Health Services (Malaria) and Directorate of Agriculture, Government of Meghalaya

21.7.1 Relationship Between Malaria Cases and the Meteorological Condition

Table 21.4 depicts the multiple linear regression analysis. The results from the data demonstrate that average temperature has a significant positive association (coeff. 0.2, $p < 0.01$) with the incidence rate of malaria cases in Meghalaya, whereas rainfall indicates a significant negative association. However, there is a relatively small negative effect that rainfall has on the rise in malaria cases (coeff. −0.0006, $p < 0.01$).

21.7.2 Discussion

The high cases of malaria in East Garo Hills, South Garo Hills, West Khasi Hills and West Garo Hills may be due to the lack of proper healthcare facilities in these districts, the lack of health facilities and private hospital makes the people in these areas to depend only on the government health center, transportation is another problem which affects the supply of medical resources to these areas. The whole part of Garo Hills district lies in low altitude area and mostly covered with forest area as compared with the Khasi and Jaintia Hills. Garo Hills district has tropical climate characterized by high rainfall and humidity generally warm summer and moderately cold winter. Khasi and Jaintia Hills have high rainfall, moderately warm summer and severe winter with periodic depression below freezing point marked by the appearance of ground frost at night and morning over higher elevated areas. This geographical and climatic condition of Garo Hills makes the environment conducive for the breeding and survival of mosquitoes. The prevalence of malaria cases in West Khasi Hills is high in those areas which are bordering with East Garo Hills and South Garo Hills. Another finding in this study is that the district of East Garo Hills, South Garo Hills and West Khasi Hills with high prevalence of malaria cases shows a low prevalence in the death cases, but the district of Jaintia Hills, East Khasi Hills and Ri Bhoi district which have less prevalence of malaria cases shows a high prevalence of death cases. The reason for this may be that people from the districts having a high prevalence of malaria cases developed immunity against severe malarial infections which prevent them from malaria death, whereas those people from districts with a low prevalence of malaria lack in the immunity against severe malarial infections which result in the increase of malaria death. People living in high endemic areas also known as stable malaria zone usually exhibit a high level of immunity. This immunity against malaria is developed by people with repeated episodes of malaria, whereas people living in low endemic areas also known as unstable malaria zone have weak immunity to the disease and they are vulnerable to malaria (Communicable, n.d.). A study done in East Africa highland found that people living in the region, where they are regularly exposed to malarial infection, develop immunity against severe malarial infection, whereas people living in the region not exposed to malarial infection regularly lack immunity against severe malarial infections (Zhou et al. 2004).

Weather conditions like temperature play a major role which leads to the rise in the malaria cases in the state of Meghalaya but the rainfall shows a negative effect on the malaria cases. A study in Madhya Pradesh found no association between the rainfall and malaria incidence (Singh and Sharma 2002). Cases of Malaria usually rise after the rainfall period, but if there is continuous excess heavy rainfall, this may result in flushing away the mosquito larvae from the breeding places (Gonzalez et al. 1997).

The limitations of the study include lack of information on malaria cases in age group classification and also for pregnant women, because it will help in understanding the prevalence of malaria cases among children under 5 and pregnant women. Humidity, which is the important factor that influences the breeding of the malaria parasite, is not considered in the study due lacking information.

21.8 Conclusion

According to this study, weather conditions like temperature play a major role in the rise in the malaria cases in the state of Meghalaya. However, rainfall shows a very small negative effect in increasing the malaria cases. This leads to the idea that with an increase in temperature, which is conducive for the malaria parasites, there is a chance that malaria cases may rise in the region. This finding may help the malaria control program in eradicating the disease. We also observed here that there are districts where the prevalence of malaria cases is low but the death rate in terms of per 1000 malaria cases is high. This regional difference in the prevalence of malaria cases and death cases may help the policy makers of the malaria eradication program make a region-wise plan and policy so that malaria can be eradicated.

Acknowledgements The authors are very thankful to the administrative personal of the Department of Health Services (Malaria) and Directorate of Agriculture, Meghalaya for providing the information on monthly malaria cases and monthly temperature, rainfall for the study.

References

Al-Mansoob, M. A. K., & Al-Mazzah, M. M. (2005). The role of climate on malaria incidence rate in four governorates of Yemen. *Medical Journal of Malaysia, 60*(3), 349.

Communicable Diseases Module: 5. Malaria Epidemiology and Transmission. (n.d.). Retrieved June 29, 2017 from http://www.open.edu/openlearncreate/mod/oucontent/view.php?id=88&printable=1.

Dikshit, K. R., & Dikshit, J. K. (2014). *North-east India: Land, people and economy*. Dordrecht: Springer.

Gonzalez, J. M., Olano, V., Vergara, J., Arévalo-Herrera, M., Carrasquilla, G., Herrera, S., et al. (1997). Unstable, low-level transmission of malaria on the Colombian Pacific Coast. *Annals of Tropical Medicine and Parasitology, 91*(4), 349–358.

Huang, F., Zhou, S., Zhang, S., Wang, H., & Tang, L. (2011). Temporal correlation analysis between malaria and meteorological factors in Motuo County, Tibet. *Malaria Journal, 10,* 54.

Immunity. (n.d). Retrieved August 14, 2017 from http://www.malariasite.com/immunity/.

Jones, A. E., Wort, U. U., Morse, A. P., Hastings, I. M., & Gagnon, A. S. (2007). Climate prediction of El Niño malaria epidemics in north-west Tanzania. *Malaria Journal, 6*(1), 162.

Kondrachine, A. V. (1992). Malaria in WHO Southeast Asia Region. *Indian Journal of Malariology, 29,* 129–160.

Mabaso, M. L., Vounatsou, P., Midzi, S., Da Silva, J., & Smith, T. (2006). Spatio-temporal analysis of the role of climate in an inter-annual variation of malaria incidence in Zimbabwe. *International Journal of Health Geographics, 5*(1), 20.

Malaria. (n.d.). Retrieved June 29, 2017 from http://www.who.int/ith/diseases/malaria/en/.

Meghalaya State Portal. (n.d.). Retrieved June 28, 2017 from http://meghalaya.gov.in/.

Malaria fever. (n.d.). Retrieved June 29, 2017 from http://medifitbiologicals.com/malaria-fever/ .

Nath, D. C., & Mwchahary, D. D. (2012). Association between climatic variables and malaria incidence: A study in Kokrajhar district of Assam, India. *Global Journal of Health Science, 5* (1), p 90.

NVBDCP. (n.d.). Retrieved January 7, 2016 from http://nvbdcp.gov.in/Round-9/IMCP-II-Round-9-proposal.pdf..

Singh, N., & Sharma, V. P. (2002). Patterns of rainfall and malaria in Madhya Pradesh, central India. *Annals of Tropical Medicine and Parasitology, 96*(4), 349–359.

Zhou, G., Minakawa, N., Githeko, A. K., & Yan, G. (2004). Association between climate variability and malaria epidemics in the East African highlands. *Proceedings of the National Academy of Sciences of the United States of America, 101*(8), 2375–2380.

Chapter 22
Comparative Study of Health-Related Physical Fitness Among Children Attending Municipal and International Schools in Nasik City

Manjusha Bhakay and Sabiha Vali

22.1 Introduction

India is one of the rapidly developing countries in terms of population and economy, with a population of 1.21 billion (Census of India 2011) and increasing at the rate of 10–14% annually. Rapid demographic, nutritional, and epidemiological transition has led to changes in lifestyles and dietary behaviors. The environment has gradually changed to one which requires less and less physical activity and promotes an ever-increasing sedentary lifestyle. Paradoxically, as this trend continues, the overall importance of physical activity in promoting and maintaining adequate health is only now being realized.

Physical fitness is a complex phenomenon with several dimensions, related to health and well-being and influenced by many dimensions of life. Nature can explain some aspects of physical activity and physical fitness like age, sex, or heredity, whereas nurture and culture can explain others like socioeconomic factors, diet, environment, or leisure habits (Van Der Horst K et al. 2007, p 1250). Furthermore, these factors are often associated, with one another and habitual physical activity and then health-related fitness could be mediated by all the variables. Adult health appears to be related with childhood physical activity and physical fitness (Kemper et al 2001; Twisk et al 1997, p 888) and there is a great deal of evidence of the close relationship between health status and childhood physical fitness. Physical activity and physical fitness are important in public health primarily as they affect health outcomes.

M. Bhakay (✉)
Food Science and Nutrition, S.M.R.K.B.K.A.K.Mahila Mahavidyalaya, Nasik, India
e-mail: manjushabhakay@gmail.com

S. Vali
Home Science (Retired), RSTM Nagpur University, Nagpur, India
e-mail: sabihavali@hotmail.com

U.K. De et al. (eds.), *Issues on Health and Healthcare in India*, India Studies in Business and Economics, https://doi.org/10.1007/978-981-10-6104-2_22

Socioeconomic status (SES) is an important determinant of health and well-being because it influences people's attitudes, experiences, and exposure to several health risk factors. The health-related physical fitness components are concerned with the development of qualities necessary to function efficiently and maintain a healthy lifestyle. These components include muscular strength, muscular endurance, cardiorespiratory endurance, flexibility, and body composition. The physical fitness tests for these components aim to look at anatomical and physiological components which determine a person's physical performance capacity (Power and Dodd 1996).

This study is aimed at comparing the health-related fitness components of children who attended International English medium schools and Municipal Marathi medium schools in the city of Nasik (Maharashtra state).

22.2 Methodology

236 children from three different International schools and 234 children from three different municipal schools of Nasik city, aged between 7 and 9 years who were studying in standard 2nd, 3rd and 4th were selected by purposive sampling.

The following health-related physical fitness components were assessed

- Muscular strength and endurance—bent knee sit ups/min test.
- Cardiorespiratory endurance—one-mile run/walk test.
- Body composition:

  a. Body weight—nearest to 0.1 kg was taken using a certified electronic scale.
  b. Height—nearest to 0.01 m was measured by Standard stadiometer.
  c. BMI—Calculated as Weight (kg)/Height (m^2)
  d. Waist measurement—Standard measuring tape
  e. Waist-to-Height Ratio—Calculated as Waist/Height

- Flexibility—sit and reach test.
- A questionnaire was given to the students to elicit information regarding their physical activity and dietary patterns.

22.3 Statistical Analysis

Statistical analysis was done using SPSS software (version 16.0). The data obtained on the above parameters was coded and entered in the SPSS sheet for further analysis. Pearson and Spearman correlations were applied to the data for finding associations. A priori, an alpha value of <0.05 was considered to be significant.

22.4 Results and Discussion

The field of anthropometry encompasses a wide variety of human body measurements, such as height and body size, weight, skin-fold thickness, circumferences. Anthropometry is a key component of nutritional status assessment in children. Anthropometric data for children reflects general health status, dietary adequacy, and growth and development over time. A child's growth can be compared with that of his or her peers, by referring to norms on an appropriate growth chart. More important, the indicators of a child's growth were a dynamic statement of his or her general health condition. In this study, WHO standards of 2007 had been used to compare the anthropometric parameters of the children who were distributed according to the school they attended.

The mean age of IS children was 8.00 years, while the mean age of MS children was 9.00 years. The reported ages of few of them were also above 9.00 years, yet these children were studying in 3rd or 4th standard. Ignorance was the main reason why parents of the MS children did not admit their wards at the appropriate age and time in schools (Table 22.1).

The mean height of IS children (1.30 mts) was more than MS children (1.21 mts). The range of height of IS and MS was similar (1.03–1.51). The mean weight of children also showed the same trend, that IS children weighed more (28.96 kg) than the MS children (21.07 kg). The IS children were heavier in weight, while the MS children were lean and thin. The IS children had a higher BMI (16.81) when compared to MS children (14.25). That was not surprising taking into account their mean height and mean weight.

Table 22.1 Mean anthropometric measurements of children distributed school wise

Parameter	Mean, std deviation, range	Type of school	
		IS[a] (n = 236)	MS[b] (n = 234)
Age (Years)	M	8.00	9.00
	SD	0.81	1.21
	R	7.00–9.00	7.00–12.00
Height (M)	M	1.30	1.21
	SD	0.07	0.07
	R	1.03–1.51	1.03–1.51
Weight (Kg)	M	28.96	21.07
	SD	7.68	3.88
	R	15.20–58.40	12.90–41.00
BMI	M	16.81	14.25
	SD	3.32	1.36
	R	11.09–28.59	10.80–21.22

Source Field survey conducted on children of International and Municipal school as part of the research study. SPSS (version 16) was used as the tool of analysis
Note [a]indicates International School, and [b]indicates Municipal School

Table 22.2 Results of '*t*' test for anthropometric measurements—IS versus MS

Parameters	Schools	*t*-test for equality of means		
		t	df	Sig. (two-tailed)
Height (M)	IS versus MS	12.862	468	[b]0.000
Weight (Kg)	IS versus MS	14.030	468	[b]0.000
BMI	IS versus MS	10.883	468	[a]0.049

Source Field survey conducted on children of International and Municipal school as part of the research study. SPSS version 16 was used as the tool of analysis
Note [a]significant, [b]highly significant

The result of '*t*' test (Table 22.2) indicated that there was a significant difference between the International school and Municipal school children with respect to the anthropometric measurements. The children from MS reflect a lower mean height and weight and hence a lower BMI, whereas the IS children were taller, weighed more and hence had a higher BMI. This was a reflection of the type of diet consumed by the children attending international and municipal schools.

22.4.1 Fitness Component Measurements of Children

Muscular strength refers to the maximal force that can be generated by a specific muscle or muscle group, while muscular endurance was the ability of a muscle group to execute repeated contraction over a period of time sufficient to cause muscular fatigue or to maintain a specific percentage of the maximum voluntary contraction for a prolonged period of time. Muscular strength and endurance can be combined into one component of health-related physical fitness titled muscular fitness to better describe their integrated status. Cardiorespiratory fitness was related to the ability to perform large muscle, dynamic, moderate to high intensity exercise for prolonged periods.

Flexibility is the ability to move a joint through its complete range of movement. Flexibility is dependent upon which muscle and joint was being evaluated, therefore it was joint specific. Body composition refers to the relative percentage of body weight that was fat and fat-free tissue. The demand on the cardiorespiratory system was greater when the percentage of body fat was high. Body composition was a major area of concern in physical fitness.

Muscular strength and endurance was tested by the Bent knee sit ups/min. It was observed that the MS children had higher mean muscular strength and endurance (21.52 sit ups) followed by the IS children (19.38 sit ups). The one-mile run test was conducted for cardiorespiratory fitness. Not all children could complete the one-mile run test. It was observed from the above table that maximum number of children from IS (1.86) could finish the one-mile run test, than the MS children (1.85). The range for this test was coded as follows: (1) meaning that the children could not complete the run, and (2) meaning that the children could finish the one-mile run test. With regard to the time of completion of the one-mile run test (which was performed to test the cardiorespiratory fitness), the MS children again registered the lowest time (10.66 min) followed by the IS children (11.09 min). The flexibility test was conducted by the sit and reach test and measured in inches. The data revealed that the MS children were more flexible (13.37 inch), than the IS children (12.97 inch). Table 22.3 indicates that the MS children had the least waist-to-height ratio (WHtR) (0.40), the normal being 0.5. The IS children had more WHtR as compared to MS children (0.46).

The overall observations tested statistically, surprisingly indicate that MS children were better than IS children in nearly all the fitness components. The result of '*t*' test for measurement of fitness components, IS versus MS as presented in Table 22.4 showed significant difference in muscular strength and endurance ($P = 0.008$), cardiorespiratory fitness—time of completion of test ($P = 0.023$) and highly significant for waist-to-height ratio ($P = 0.000$). It was insignificant for flexibility ($P = 0.084$) and cardiorespiratory—completion of test ($P = 0.571$).

From Table 22.5 it was observed that, 0.6% children from MS could perform at the 90th percentile, while only 0.4% children from IS were at the 90th percentile. Majority of the MS children were at the 50th percentile indicating that their performance was average. A large number of the IS (35%) children performed poorly in the sit up test as compared to the MS children (20.5%). The MS children played a

Table 22.3 Mean fitness components of children according to school

Sl. No	Fitness components	Mean, std deviation, range	Type of school	
			IS ($n = 236$)	MS ($n = 234$)
1	Muscular strength and endurance (Bent knee sit ups/min)	M	19.38	21.52
		SD	8.91	8.55
		R	0.00–40.00	0.00–38.00
2	Cardiorespiratory fitness—completion of test [a]	M	1.86	1.85
		SD	0.33	0.35
		R	1.00–2.00	1.00–2.00
3	Cardiorespiratory time (completion of test in min)	M	11.09	10.66
		SD	1.95	1.70
		R	6.00–18.29	7.12–16.39
4	Flexibility (Sit and reach in inches)	M	12.97	13.37
		SD	3.04	2.98
		R	7.50–19.00	7.00–19.00
5	Waist-to-height ratio	M	0.46	0.40
		SD	0.05	0.03
		R	0.24–0.66	0.29–0.53

Source Field survey conducted on children of International and Municipal school as part of the research study. SPSS version 16 was used as the tool of analysis

Note [a]1 = could not complete the test, 2 = could complete the test

Table 22.4 Results of '*t*' test for fitness components—IS versus MS

Fitness components	Schools	*t*-test for equality of means		
		t	df	Significance
Muscular strength and endurance	IS versus MS	−2.65	46	[a]0.008
Cardiorespiratory fitness—completion of test	IS versus MS	0.56	46	0.571
Cardiorespiratory fitness—time of completion of test	IS versus MS	2.27	46	[a]0.023
Flexibility	IS versus MS	−1.73	46	0.084
Waist-to-height ratio	IS versus MS	11.43	46	[b]0.000

Source Field survey conducted on children of International and Municipal school as part of the research study. SPSS version 16 was used as the tool of analysis
Note [a]significant, [b]highly significant

Table 22.5 Muscular strength and endurance of children distributed according to type of school (percentile)

Sl. No	Type of school	Muscular strength and endurance fitness category						Total
		90th percentile (%)	75th percentile (%)	50th percentile (%)	25th percentile (%)	10th percentile (%)	Poor performance (%)	
1	International school	0.4	14	28.6	14	8	35	100
2	Municipal schools	0.6	17	36	8.4	17.5	20.5	100

Source Field survey conducted on children of International and Municipal school as part of the research study

Table 22.6 Cardiorespiratory fitness—completion of test by the children distributed according to type of school

Sl.No	Type of school	Cardio fitness category		Total
		Could not finish the test	Could finish the test	
1.	International school	13.1%	86.9%	100
2.	Municipal school	15%	85%	100

Source Field survey conducted on children of International and Municipal school as part of the research study

lot of outdoor games, they walked to school, were more involved in strenuous activities as compared to IS children and hence, their muscular fitness was good.

Table 22.6 reveals that nearly equal number of children from both the schools (IS = 13.1%, MS = 15%) could not finish the one-mile run test, however majority of the children from both types of schools could finish the one-mile run test.

Table 22.7 shows that all children had a wide range of variation in performance with 2% IS children were on the 90th percentile and 9% children with poor performance. Among MS children, on the other hand, 4% were on the 90th percentile while only 3% children had performed poorly. Again, the majority of the children

Table 22.7 Cardiorespiratory fitness—(time of completion of test) by the children distributed according to type of school (percentile)

Sl. No	Type of school	Cardiorespiratory fitness—time							Total
		0 (%)	90th percentile (%)	75th percentile (%)	50th percentile (%)	25th percentile (%)	10th percentile (%)	Poor performance (%)	
1.	International school	13	2	8	34	17	17	9	100
2.	Municipal schools	15	4	10	41	9	18	3	100

Source Field survey conducted on children of International and Municipal school as part of the research study

Table 22.8 BMI according to type of school (percentile)

Sl. No	Type of school	BMI category				Total
		High risk $\geq$ 18.3 (%)	Some risk $\geq$ 17.6 (%)	HFZ 17.5–13.5 (%)	Very lean $\leq$ 13.4 (%)	
1.	International school	22	5	61	12	100
2.	Municipal schools	1	1	58	40	100

Source Field survey conducted on children of International and Municipal school as part of the research study

from both the schools were on the 50th percentile, indicating average performance. The performance of the MS children surprisingly was better when compared to IS children. This can again be attributed to their being more active, playing outdoor games. MS children played free outdoor games for more than one hour per day. Similar results were also seen by Ulf Ekelund et al. (2004, p 590).

The BMI category of the children is shown in Table 22.8. The table reveals that maximum number of children from IS (22% children) are in the high risk category (BMI $\geq$ 18.3), compared to only 1% of the children from MS. On the other hand, maximum number of lean children (BMI $\leq$ 13.4) is from MS (40% children). However, majority of the children irrespective of the type of school were in the healthy fitness region with BMI between 17.5 and 13.5. Children attending International School consumed more, oily deep-fried foods, sweet preparations, more often and hence their weight was more as compared to children attending Municipal schools whose lean diet comprised of chapatti bhaji, chutney, and dal.

The result of flexibility fitness category as seen in Table 22.9 indicated that the children from both the schools had done well in the test. 13% children from MS, and 11% from IS were at the 90th percentile. The MS had fewer poor performers (17%) as compared to IS (23%). Quite a few of the children from both schools were also at the 75th percentile (MS−23%, IS−20%,). The increased flexibility of MS children could be because of their lower BMI.

Table 22.9 Flexibility according to type of school (percentile)

Sl. No	Type of school	Flexibility fitness category						Total
		90th percentile	75th percentile	50th percentile	25th percentile	10th percentile	Poor performance	
1.	International school	11	20	22	10	14	23	100
2.	Municipal schools	13	23	19	13	15	17	100

Source Field survey conducted on children of International and Municipal school as part of the research study

Table 22.10 Waist-to-height ratio (WHtR) according to type of school (percentile)

Sl.No	Type of school	WHTR category		Total
		High	Normal	
1.	International school	22.0	78.0	100
2.	Municipal schools	0.4	99.6	100

Source Field survey conducted on children of International and Municipal school as part of the research study

From Table 22.10, it was observed that a greater number of IS children (22%) had a higher WHtR. Only 0.4% children from MS had a high WHtR. Majority of the children from both the types of schools had normal WHtR. Kuriyan et al (2011) in their study linked lifestyle, eating, and sedentary behavior to waist circumference among urban South Indian children aged 3–16 years. This study also showed similar results. These results also were observed by Esmaeilzadeh (2012, p 105), Lumeng et al (2006, p 422).

In spite of all the luxuries of life enjoyed by the International School children, the Municipal School children showed better physical fitness. Health-related physical fitness; the mode of commuting to school, frequency and duration of indoor and outdoor games played by the children, consumption of fried foods and sweets was also studied. The findings were as follows:

Figure 22.1 revealed that 119 IS children (50.5%) came by school bus, 68 children (28.8%) traveled by rickshaw, 1 child (0.4%) came cycling, 22 children (8.9%) were dropped at the school by parents. 26 children (11.4%) came walking (they stayed in hostels inside the school campus, a distance of less than a km). Of the MS children on the other hand, showed that 1 child (0.4%) came by city transport service, 4 children (1.78%) came by a shared rickshaw, 2 children (0.85%) came by cycle, 32 children (13.67%) children were brought to the school by the parents (on a cycle or two wheeler) and 196 children (83.3%) came to school walking, from the nearby slums (maximum distance of 2 km).

It was observed from Fig. 22.2 that the mean duration of indoor play for IS children (0.49) was less than 30 min of play per day. The MS children show a mean duration slightly higher (0.55) than IS. They played indoor games once or twice a week. The mean frequency of indoor games for IS children was somewhat higher (1.42) than MS children.

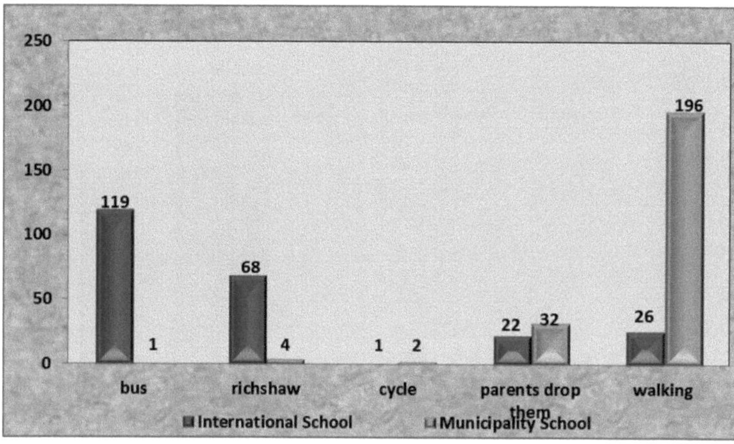

Fig. 22.1 Mode of commuting to school by children from different schools (frequency)

Figure 22.3 indicated that mean duration of outdoor play of IS children was 1.28, that meant that these children played for approximately 30 min per day. While the MS children played for a longer period of time (more than 30 min but less than one hour). The mean frequency of outdoor games played per week showed that IS children played for approximately three times/week (mean IS−3.31), whereas MS children played for more days per week (mean 4.41) as compared to IS children.

The MS children had fried food, once in 15 days (mean 4.29), while the IS children had fried food once a week (mean 3.39). The higher frequency of fried food was reflected in the higher BMI of IS children, as compared to MS children (Fig. 22.4).

All children like sweet preparations. The mean of frequency of consumption of sweets is shown in Fig. 22.5. From the figure, it is observed that the frequency of sweet consumption among IS children is 2.44, that is, they have sweet preparations nearly twice a week. The MS children had sweet preparations nearly once in a week.

The data was further analyzed by linear regression for health-related physical fitness components and activity of the children (indoor and outdoor games—frequency and duration), consumption of fried foods and frequency of consumption of sweet preparations.

When health-related fitness parameters of Municipal school children (muscular strength and endurance, cardiorespiratory fitness, body composition and flexibility) were controlled for, duration and frequency of outdoor games was significantly ($p = 0.000$) associated with physical fitness. The frequency of consumption of sweet preparation showed significant co-relation ($p = 0.000$) to BMI. In International School children, the frequency of outdoor games was significantly co-related to all the fitness parameters. The frequency of consumption of sweet preparation also showed significant co-relation ($p = 0.000$) to BMI and waist-to-height ratio (WHtR).

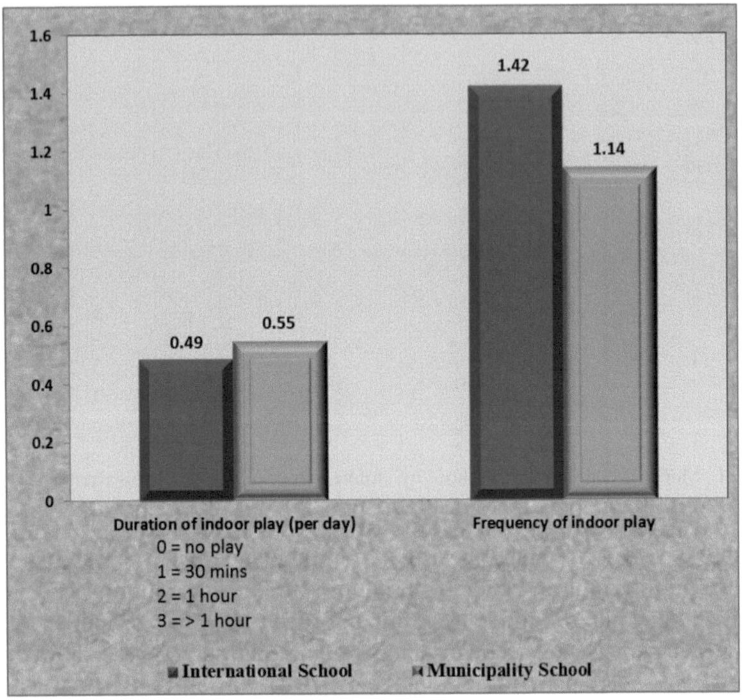

Fig. 22.2 Mean duration and frequency of indoor play

Health-related physical fitness is dependent on both, lifestyle-related factors, such as daily physical activity levels and nutritional habits and genetic factors and is an important indicator of health status (Takken et al 2003, p 885).

Adult health appears to be related to childhood physical activity and physical fitness and there is a great deal of evidence of the close relationship between health status and childhood physical fitness. The amount of physical activity during childhood is the determining factor that would prevent the prevalence of sedentary-related diseases such as obesity, cardio vascular diseases, diabetes, and some types of cancers in adults (Pino-Ortega et al. 2010).

Tharkar and Viswanathan (2009) in a cross-sectional study determined the impact of socioeconomic status on prevalence of overweight and obesity among children and adolescents in urban India. There were highly significant differences in the prevalence of overweight and obesity between LSES and USES ($P < 0.05$). The result also showed widespread prevalence of unhealthy lifestyle habits.

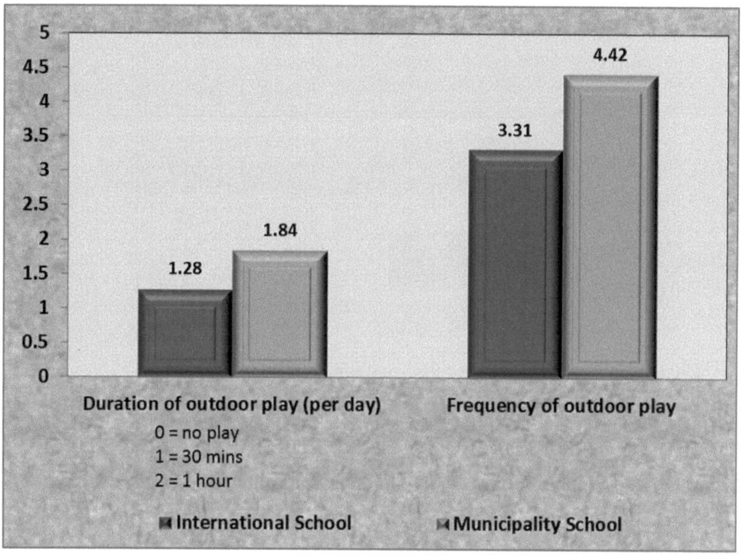

Fig. 22.3 Mean duration and frequency of outdoor play

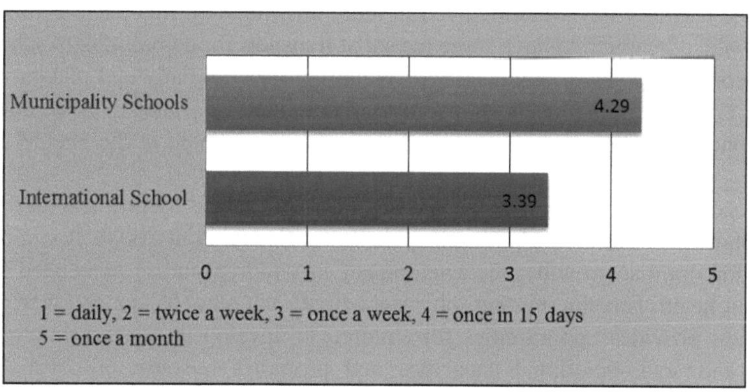

Fig. 22.4 Mean consumption of fried food by children from different schools

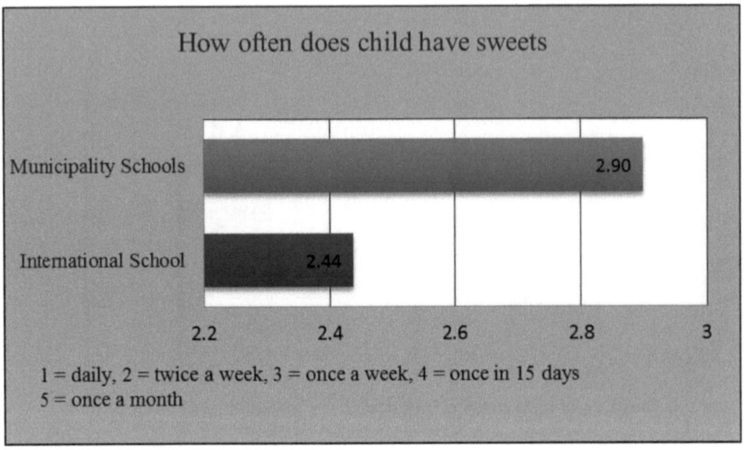

Fig. 22.5 Mean consumption of sweets by children from different schools

22.5 Conclusion

The MS children had better physical fitness as compared to children at IS. This could be because they were involved in more unstructured, free play, as they were not privileged enough to have some means of transport for commuting to school, no membership of clubs or any coaching. Walking to school daily and playing on the streets was the only means of exercise. Their diet was also a basic one with occasional sweet preparations, which helped them to remain in the healthy fitness zone.

Physical activity is considered as a key factor for a healthy physical and mental development of children (Andersen et al. 2008; Ortega et al 2008). It is a prerequisite for optimal growth and development in children and is associated with a range of health benefits. Further, physical activity via play, leisure and recreational activities, provides opportunities for children to develop their sensorimotor, cognitive and socio-emotional capacities and promotes a sense of psychological well-being. Excessive sedentariness among children potentially leads to the development of chronic health problems during adolescence and adulthood including obesity, osteoporosis, diabetes, and cardiovascular diseases (Dwyer et al 2008).

References

Andersen, L. B., Sardinha, L. B., Froberg, K., Riddoch, C. J., Page, A. S., & Anderssen, S. A. (2008). Fitness, fatness and clustering of cardiovascular risk factors in children from Denmark, Estonia and Portugal: The European Youth Heart Study. *International Journal of Pediatric Obesity, 3*(1), 58–66.

Dwyer, G. M., Higgs, J., Hardy, L. L., & Baur, L. A. (2008). What do parents and preschool staff tell us about young children's physical activity?: A qualitative study. *International Journal of Behavioral Nutrition and Physical activity, 5,* 66. doi:10.1186/1479-5868-566.

Ekelund, Ulf., Sardinha, L. B., Anderssen, S. A., Harro, M., Franks, P. W., Brage, S. et al. (2004). Association between objectively assessed physical activity and indicators of body fatness in 9–10 years old European Children: A population based study from 4 distinct regions in Europe. (The European Youth Heart Study). *American Journal of Clinical Nutrition, 80*(5), 584–590.

Esmaeilzadeh, S., & Ebadollahzadeh, K. (2012). Physical fitness, physical activity and sedentary activities of 7 to 11 year old boys with different body mass indexes. *Asian Journal of Sports Medicine, 3*(2), 105–112.

Kemper, H. C. G., De Vente, W., Van Mechelen, W., & Twisk, J. W. R. (2001). Adolescent motor skill and performance: is physical activity in adolescents related to adult physical fitness? *American Journal of Human Biology, 13*(2), 180–189.

Kuriyan, R., Thomas, T., Lokesh, D., Aheth, N., Mahendra, A., Joy, R., Sumitra, S., Bhatt, S., & Kurpad, A. (2011). Potential factors related to waist circumference in urban South Indian Children. Indian Pediatrics, PII: S 097475591NPE 10000225-1.

Lumeng, J. C., Rahnama, S., Appugliese, D., Kaciroti, N., & Bradley, R. H. (2006). Television exposure and overweight risk in preschoolers. *Archives of Pediatrics and Adolescent Medicine, 160*(4), 417–422.

Ortega, F. B., Ruiz, J. R., Castillo, M. J., & Sjostrom, M. (2008). Physical fitness in childhood and adolescence: A powerful marker of health. *International Journal of Obesity, 32,* 1–11.

Pino-Ortega, J., De la Cruz-Sánchez, E., & Martínez-Santos, R. (2010). Health—related fitness in school children: Compliance with physical activity recommendations and its relationship with body mass index and diet quality. *Archieves Latino America Nos De Nution, 60*(4), 1.

Powers, S. K., & Dodd, S. L. (1996). Total fitness—Exercise, nutrition and wellness. Boston: Allyn and Bacon.

Takken, T., Van Der Net, J., Kuis, W., & Helders, P. J. M. (2003). *Annals of the Rheumatic Diseases, 62,* 885–889.

Tharkar, S., & Viswanathan, V. (2009). Impact of socioeconomic status on prevalence of overweight and obesity among children and adolescents in urban India. *The open obesity Journal, 1,* 9–14.

Twisk, J. W. R., Kemper, H. C. G., Van Mechelen, W., & Post, G. B. (1997). Tracking of risk factors for coronary heart disease over a 14 year period: A comparison between lifestyle and biologic risk factors with data from Amsterdam growth and health study. *American Journal of Epidemiology, 145,* 888–898.

Van der Horst, K., Paw, M., Twisk, J. W. R., & Van Mechelen, W. (2007). A brief review on correlations of physical activity and sedentariness in youth. *Medicine and Science in Sports and Exercise, 38*(8), 1241–1250.

Chapter 23
Faces of Primary Health Centres (PHC) of Bengal Dooars: A Review in Terms of Potential Service Delivery Space Index (PSDSI) and Physical Accessibility Index (PAI)

Subhasis Bhattacharya

23.1 Introduction

Healthcare is fundamentally different from usual commodities like food, clothing and shelter. Health goods are not homogeneous in nature; as a result, the market-clearing situation at some part does not imply that absence of imperfection in others. Under a proper healthcare system, alternative providers are available and we have to choose among them depending upon the improvements on expected outcome (Arrow 1963). Considering this, a rational consumer tries to choose the alternative which yields the highest utility (Dreze and Sen 1995). The literature on healthcare is not only confined to the qualities of healthcare use but also extends to the quality of service provided by them (Farrell 1957). The performance of the health sector is a very important indicator of human development index of a society (Grossman 1972). Productivity factor of a society is severely affected by the poor health condition. The publicly provided health facilities have some common features like higher tier hospitals or health units overloaded with patients, whereas the basic levels are underutilized (Gertler and Van der Gaag 1988). Hence, it is an important and significant task for the stakeholders to consider the efficient side as well as the inefficient side of the health support function of the publicly provided institution (Banker et al. 1984).

In this study, we try to capture the scenario of healthcare delivery system of Primary Healthcare Centres (PHCs) in Bengal Dooars. More generally, it attempts

S. Bhattacharya (✉)
Department of Economics, Sidho-Kanho-Birsha University, Purulia, India
e-mail: suva69eco@gmail.com

U.K. De et al. (eds.), *Issues on Health and Healthcare in India*, India Studies in Business and Economics, https://doi.org/10.1007/978-981-10-6104-2_23

to assess the impending room for service release of the PHCs (Bloom et al. 2008; Alderman and Gertler 1989). The room for service release means that to what extent government and its associates allow the resources (existing and additional) for the improvement of service delivery (Evans et al. 2000) of the PHCs and to achieve specific objectives of health outcomes in the Bengal Dooars. The present study considers basically, two issues regarding healthcare need. One is how much the need is satisfied by the existing system and the other is how much remain unmet in the Bengal Dooars area. The study considers a simple supply demand frame to observe this. Two main research questions are fitted in the study are (1) Services rendered by PHCs in terms of service grouping and (2) Service rendered by PHCs in specific geographical areas. The first one identifies that what amount of additional competencies are to be allowed to the PHCs of Bengal Dooars to face the extra (uncertain/certain) burdens of future, which may generate from inpatient care, outpatient care, maternal and child healthcare, etc. The second one recognizes the most vulnerable blocks in terms of inefficiencies of PHCs. These areas require investment that is more intensive or allocation of resources, and here the maximum gap is between technically efficient and inefficient PHCs.

Kaplan et al. (1982) defines the health output in terms of a number of years with no ailments at all. The study tries to find out good standard measures of health status which helps in health decision-making, planning and evaluation. In this study, various results from psychology are taken for the explanation of the study. The study by Bothwell and Cooley (1982) defines output as an improvement of health statuses like encounters with doctors, encounters with health personal and hospital discharge. The inputs are defined as organizational services, services provide by the hospital services, services provided by the medical professional staff and health centre services. A study by Wouters (1993) observes that service deliveries basically to poor people are not offered in low-cost level. The behaviour of the healthcare cost shows that for inpatient level, increasing return to scale in short run and for outpatient level, it follows constant return to scale. To exemplify the performance trend of technical efficiency, the parametric and non-parametric efficiency measurement techniques are used by Hollingsworth and Wildman (2003). In case of Data Envelopment Analysis (DEA)-based analysis of panel data, they used Malmquist Indices to explain the productivity of health behaviour. Purohit (2008) tries to analyze the health efficiency system of state West Bengal, India using stochastic frontier analysis and evaluate its performance. Ensor and Witter (2001) have studied that the lack of regulation and under-funding influenced the motives of practitioners in developing countries and resulted as unofficial activities. The study observed that in low-income countries individuals suffer by dual attack of diminishing share of health expenditure of the government and increasing cost of medical care. As a result, the household health expenditure in low-income countries increased rapidly.

23.2 Data and Methods

The service delivery space of PHCs in the case of inpatient care, outpatient care, institutional deliveries, immunizations are variable in nature. As for example, the PHCs are mainly deal with outpatient services rather than inpatient care. Thus, to allocate resources for the PHCs, the government has to make a priority-based list which may be termed as enormity of space. Thus, to consider such issues, the study considers two scenarios, one is base or foundation or existing scenario and the other is the desirable scenario. The base scenario is estimated from the household survey, patients' survey and administrative facility survey of the PHCs. The desirable scenario can be derived on the basis of a certain set of assumptions. Then we can assess the service delivery space by comparing these two scenarios.

Western Dooars, a cluster of biosphere reserves and home about 2.5 million people, is a part of Jalpaiguri district of West Bengal state and it is the agglomeration of 13 blocks (Bhattacharya 2007). The nature of the study is both the primary and secondary type. For the purpose of the study, detailed visits were made in all the 38 Primary Health Centres (PHCs) under structured questionnaire. The infrastructure, manpower, medicines, inpatients admission and outpatients visits were observed very carefully for each PHC under structured questionnaire. For some yearly results in case of patient's admissions and outpatient's visits were collected from the district Chief Medical Officer of Health (CMOH) office at Jalpaiguri. During the visits of PHCs, another parallel survey has been conducted on the inpatients and outpatients visited at that time of that concerned PHCs. In case of outpatient department (OPD), every second patient in the speciality queue was approached and briefed about the study by the investigator. If he or she agreed, they were asked about their socio economic conditions at that time. As they finished their visits in the PHCs completing all types of services like doctor's advice, medicines allocation, diagnostic tests, etc. they again approached at the gateway of PHCs regarding the experiences they gathered from such facilities. By this way, a total of 919 patients has been surveyed from OPD facilities of the existing PHCS. In case of inpatient department (IPD) visits the study first consider that bed size of the all 38 PHCs of Jalpaiguri district varies from 0 to 10, and there are total 256 beds providing IPD services for the 3.1 million people at the primary level healthcare. Here the study meets with the two third patients of the IPD in each PHC. The selection of the patients has been made on the basis of every first and second patient from the three patients admitted in the respective PHCs. Thus, out of 256 beds, 171 patients have been interrogated regarding their perception of service quality rendered by the PHCs of the study area.

Here, the base scenario conditions are already known to us for the following inputs and what level of output produced by them is also in our knowledge. Among these outputs, one major output is number of child birth taking place in the institution like PHCs. One may consider this as a proxy for the very significant health indicator like institutional delivery. Table 23.1 explains such space of service delivery situation for institutional birth.

Table 23.1 Estimation of gap in institutional delivery of PHCs, Western Dooars, 2014

	Estimated birth in 2014	Estimated institution delivery in 2014	Estimated deliveries in PHCs, 2014	Total birth delivered at PHCs	Additional load on PHCs
Assumptions	Population 3.5 million, birth rate 2.2% p.a	60% of population as per district health information	10% of the estimated institutional delivery	From HMIS data, 2014	If institutional delivery increase by 10%
Western Dooars	77000	46200	4620	4353	1037

Source Assumptions and data of Jalpaiguri district health office, 2011

The estimation of Table 23.1 points out that if, institutional delivery increases by 10%, the PHCs of Bengal Dooars delivered extra 1037 births (considering other facts remain same). Now if we assume that average length of stay for a birth delivery is 3 days, then the number of inpatient days translated to 3100 (roughly) days. Now in the study area, there are 256 bed performing for the year, i.e. there will be 93,440 bed days. If the average length of stay is 3 days, then this will generate 31,147 bed days per patient. Now due to 10% increase in institutional delivery 3100 inpatient days further generated which is 9.95% of the present capacity. However, our survey study on PHCs indicates that they (PHCs) are already close to the saturation level, though there are some gaps in the manpower and infrastructural facilities. Now the additional burden of 9.95% in inpatient capacity will make the conditions of PHCs more critical, and this has happened due to increase in institutional delivery by 10%. Thus additional support for the PHCs become an urgent need, otherwise, we will observe a huge referral tendency and bypass inclination to the higher tier hospitals.

The inputs of the specified health system used by the PHCs are defined as bed, equipment, doctor, nurse, health assistant, group-D staff and medicines. All these inputs are used to produce four qualified output like Quality-adjusted inpatient output (QAIPD), Quality-adjusted outpatient output (QAOPD), Number of child birth, and Number of health education sessions.

The inputs and outputs are exposed in Table 23.2. Before going to the analysis, the study tries to illustrate the output specifications of this analysis. The true fact is that state has not supplied the full component of staff including doctors, required to all the PHCs of our country. Health managers know that more or less homogeneous inputs need not always lead to same outputs. Thus, it is an important task from their end also to mark the critical performers regarding the production of health outputs. This will help them to identify the areas which need to be strengthened and the investment that needs to be carried out for removing the weakness of those health units.

Table 23.2 Input and output list of the DEA analysis

List of inputs	List of outputs
Bed	Quality-adjusted outpatient per day (QAOPD)
Equipment	
Doctor	Quality-adjusted inpatient per day (QAIPD)
Nursing staff	
Health support staff	Number of child deliveries (NCD)
Group-D staff	
Medicine	No of health education sessions (HES)

Source Model formulated in the study, 2014

The first output (QAOPD) significantly determines the care of quality of doctors and nursing staff for outdoor patients per day. To determine the study we construct an index known as Doctors Involvement Index (DII). This can be calculated as

$$\mathrm{DII} = \frac{\text{Actual OPD hours Per} - \text{week day}}{\text{Normal OPD hours Per} - \text{week day}}$$

Since data on numbers of doctors in position in PHCs are already collected, from that we calculate the total number of OPD doctors' hours for each PHC considering to actual norms (a total 28 OPD hours per week, i.e. 5 h norms from Monday to Friday and 3 h for Saturday).

To consider the issues of doctor service quality render for outpatient services, the study rationally adopts QAOPD as a specified output. The QAOPD can be worked out by the multiplication of a number of outpatients per day by DII of the specific PHC. The study considers QAOPD index because the main research question is, if the doctors have given the full standard hour (according to service condition) in PHCs OPD, then how many patients can be served with time and quality. However, the reality is something different.

This can be explained with the help of an example. Suppose the number of patients visiting OPD = N. If they are serving according to PHCs standard, then doctors have to allotted 'x' hours for them. In reality, doctors offer 'y' hours (where $y/x \leq 1$) for the OPD patients. Then the doctors can able to serve only $\{N(y/x)\}$ number of OPD patients with quality. So obviously, a much lower number of patients receive OPD services.

Table 23.3 shows the average value of DII in each block which is calculated on the basis of collected data from the PHC administration visits and PHC patient visits. Here, during this survey on PHCs, each and every PHC were visited three days of a week to collect the information related to IPD and OPD patients and to understand the uses of equipments and manpower. On each day the presence of the doctor for that day was observed and by this way considering for three days, the study prepare the DII value for that PHC by averaging the doctor attendance of those days. The calculated value of DII shows that for the district the average doctor involvement is near about 62%. This means that doctors are contributing about two third of their involvement what is actually due from their end. The disaggregated data (Fig. 23.1) from the districts show that in some blocks like Falakata, Madarihat, Nagrakata and Kalchini the value of DII is low though there is high demand for health staff. This is important to note that when the poor villagers have not found proper healthcare in the PHCs then they have two options, either they visit the upper tier facilities or they remain absent from taking any type of care.

The second output, i.e. the quality-adjusted inpatient admitted less referred (QAIPD) can be calculated on the basis of perception of the inpatient about the PHC services. In this regard, the quality index can be constructed in terms of perception (sensitivity) index (PI) of the inpatient department (IPD) patients about the PHC services. The PI is generated only from the perception of quality by the inpatients because they only have perception about the services of the PHC in terms of cleanliness, manpower efficiency, behaviour, diet, etc. The PI is calculated on the same pattern like DII. Here, we consider the factors like cleanliness, manpower efficiency, behaviour, and diet offered in PHC in terms of four point scale like *A*, *B*, *C*, and *D*, where *A* means 'excellent', *B* means 'fair', *C* means 'moderate', and *D* means 'not satisfactory'. The weight on the basis of such grading can be marked as $A = 1.0, B = 0.5, C = 0.25,$ and $D = 0$. During inpatient survey, another question is also asked: whether they come back to that PHC in future if they will have some ailments. This is also an influencing factor of PI. If the answer is yes, it takes value '1' and if the answer is no, the value obtains '0'. Whatever may be the

Table 23.3 Doctors involvement index in PHCs of different blocks

Block	PHC	Manpower	DII	PI
Jalpaiguri	5	17	0.75	1.33
Maynaguri	6	21	0.67	1.83
Dhupguri	3	7	0.72	0.25
Rajganj	3	10	0.61	0.92
Mal	3	9	0.597	0.66
Meteli	2	6	0.59	0.83
Nagrakata	2	6	0.46	0.49
Kumargram	2	6	0.67	0.75
Falakata	2	4	0.41	0.17
Madarihat	3	8	0.45	0.75
Kalchini	2	5	0.495	0.155
Alipurduar-I	2	7	0.895	1.215
Alipurduar-II	3	11	0.796	1.32
Average DII and PI			0.6241	0.821
Max value			0.895	1.83
Min value			0.41	0.155
Correlation coefficient between DII and PI			0.614999076	

Source Patient survey during PHC visits, 2014

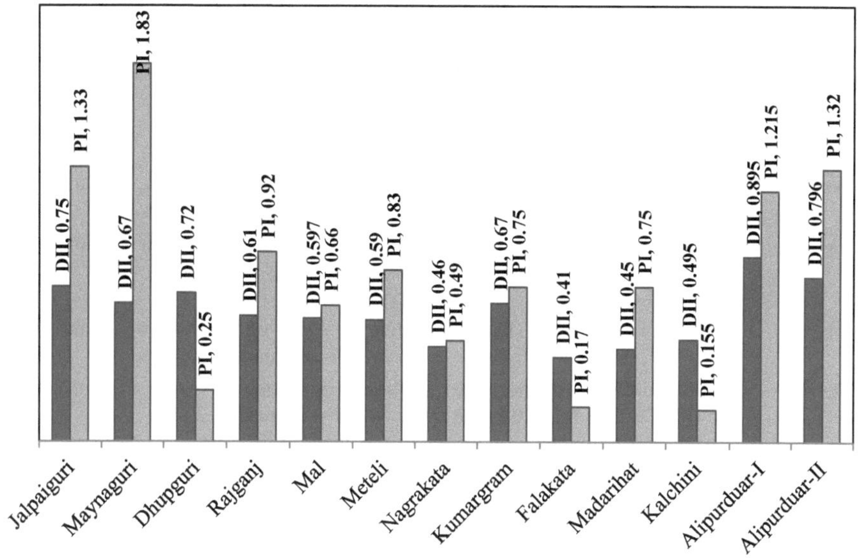

Fig. 23.1 DII & PI value for the blocks PHCs in the study area. *Source* Patient survey data, 2014

fact the PI can be calculated for each PHC and aggregated for each block. The PI can be calculated from the following formula:

$$PI = \frac{[\text{Actual Perception value}]}{1} + \frac{[\text{Value fixed for future come back}]}{1}$$

Here, the highest value of PI for any PHC can be '2', and that can be judged as the best functioning PHC according to inpatient perception, and the minimum value of PI can be '0', which can be identified as worst performing PHC in the view of inpatient services. Now, in each block we take the average value of PI for PHCs are shown in Table 23.3. The significant factor from Table 23.3 shows that the value of PI can be higher for those blocks where the bed number is more frequent than the PHCs where it is low, and also for blocks like Nagrakata and Kalchini the values of PI are the lowest like DII. It is very much rational for the patients that if they are well informed regarding the availability of doctors or nurses in particular PHCs, and then it becomes easier for them to decide to go or bypass that health unit during their ailing periods. This may be the reason behind the positive correlation between DII and PI. The value of correlation coefficient between DII and PI is 0.615. This means that doctor's involvement index is quite highly correlated with the patient perception index which is also quite expected in such health staff arid region.

Accessibility in a block is classified in three categories—good, moderate and poor. Blocks with good, poor and moderate physical accessibility index are identified by the following criterion as shown in Table 23.4.

Table 23.4 Physical accessibility index

Indicators	Block category		
	Good	Poor	Moderate
1st	More than 50% of the village have bus services within 5 km	Less than 50% of the village have bus services within 5 km	Otherwise
2nd	More than 10% of the villages have railway line within 5 km	Less than 35% of the villages have railway line within 5 km	Otherwise
3rd	Less than 10% of the villages have river bodies on their approach roads	More than 50% of the villages have river bodies on their approach roads	Otherwise
4th	Less than 10% of the villages have 10% area under forest	More than 10% of the villages have 10% area under forest	Otherwise
5th	Distance of farthest sub-centre to BPHC is less than 20 km or less than 2 h journey	Distance of farthest sub-centre to BPHC is more than 20 km or less than 2 h journey	Otherwise

Source Methodology of the research

23.3 Results

The study used output-oriented DEA model in the analysis because inputs of the PHCs are not controlled by themselves, it has to depend on others. For example, the deployment of human resources in the PHCs is not in the management part of the PHCs. It is difficult as well as unethical up to some point to reduce inputs, which are already in short supply position. Therefore, we have made an attempt to look at the possibility of maximizing the output with the given level of inputs. The output-oriented approaches of DEA identify how much output units can be increased with the same use of inputs. Again, DEA stipulated that input-oriented approach and output-oriented approach leads to the same frontier. Thus, the study can identify the PHCs as the best efficient performer according to output-frontier and input-frontier is same. However, the measures change for the inefficient PHCs. Thus, it is expected that the choice of the process will not affect the results significantly.

Table 23.5 presents the descriptive statistics for outputs and inputs of 38 PHCs in Western Dooars. The general findings of the DEA analysis presented in Table 23.6 indicate high inefficiency among the PHCs and wide dispersions of efficiency score across PHCs. The measurement of QAOPD and QAIPD output shows the per day basis value according to the definition of these outputs constructed as per our purpose.

The technical efficiency (TE) and scale efficiency (SE) scores for the PHCs are given in Table 23.5. Out of the 38 PHCs, 39.5% (15) are established to be relatively technically efficient with a TE score of 100% and they should be considered as the peer group among the lot. The remaining 60.5% (23) are technically inefficient since they had a TE score of a lesser amount than 100%. These 23 PHCs are situated below the efficiency frontier with a mean score of 65.48% on a scale of

Table 23.5 Mean and SD for PHCs inputs and outputs

Variables	Total	Mean	SD	Maximum	Minimum	CV
Outputs						
QAOPD	121.262	3.191	2.315	9.156	0.301	72.547
QAIPD	10.243	0.27	0.189	0.629	0	69.97
Number of deliveries covered (NCD)	4353	114.553	51.384	227	0	44.856
Health education sessions (HES)	301	7.921	3.802	18	3	47.999
Inputs						
Bed	256	6.737	2.767	10	0	41.072
Equipment	335	8.816	2.779	16	5	31.522
Doctors	27	0.711	0.46	1	0	64.697
Nursing staff	21	0.553	0.504	1	0	91.139
Health support staff	36	0.947	0.226	1	0	23.865
Group-D staff	33	0.868	0.343	1	0	39.516
Medicine	462	12.158	4.051	21	6	33.32

Source DEA analysis results of selected inputs and outputs, 2014

0–100. The 10.53% (4) of the inefficient PHUs have a TE score of less than 50%. The overall sample average TE score is 79.11% [standard deviation (SD) = 21.23%]. This implies that if the inefficient PHCs are to work as efficiently as their 15 peers on the efficient frontier, outputs can be increased by about 20.89% without changing the point of inputs used. The mean TE score among the inefficient (23) PHCs is 65.48% (SD = 16.31%). This means that their output can be expanded by 34.52% without altering their input combinations. The study shows a high degree of variation across different PHCs. In the study, 15 PHCs are found efficient. This means that further increase in output is not feasible in the current structure. Some PHCs are found with such a low efficiency score that 60% expansion of their output can be possible by more efficient utilisation of resources. The maximum degree of such increase can be possible for Satali PHC of Kalchini block and Jhar Altagram PHC of Dhupguri block.

In case of scale efficiency scores, the study identifies that 31.58% (12) PHCs have a scale efficiency (SE) score of 100%. This means that these PHCs would significantly improve their efficiency and reduce their unit cost by increasing scale of operation and they have the most productive size for the particular input–output combinations. Thus, the other 68.42% (26) PHCs are performing as scale inefficient with a scale efficiency counting less than 100%. The average scale efficiency score of all the PHCs is 79.32% with SD equal to 20.48. This implies that usually, the scale inefficient PHCs can decrease their size by 20.68% without affecting their current output status. The average scale efficiency score for all 26-scale inefficient PHCs is 73.8% with SD equals to 19.64. Thus, for these 26 scale inefficient PHCs,

Table 23.6 Technical and scale efficiency scores for PHCs

Sl No	Block	PHC (DNUs)	TE score	SE score	The minimum extent to which all the outputs can be expanded (in %)	The extent to which scale of operation needed to be changed (in %)
1	Alipurduar-I	Munshipara	100	100	0	0
2	Alipurduar-I	Silbari Hat	81	75	19	25
3	Alipurduar-II	Samuktola	100	100	0	0
4	Alipurduar-II	Jasodanga	83	58	17	42
5	Alipurduar-II	Turturi	52	66	48	34
6	Dhupguri	Duramari (Salbari)	59	57	41	43
7	Dhupguri	Shakarjhora	44	53	56	47
8	Dhupguri	Jhar Altagram	37	71	63	29
9	Falakata	Jateswar	75	100	25	0
10	Falakata	Chhoto Salkumar	41	100	59	0
11	Jalpaiguri	Rangdhamali	100	100	0	0
12	Jalpaiguri	Kharija Berubari	100	88	0	12
13	Jalpaiguri	South Berubari	82	93	18	7
14	Jalpaiguri	Bahadur	77	84	23	16
15	Jalpaiguri	Nandanpur Boalmari	63	100	37	0
16	Jalpaiguri	Joygaon	73	96	27	4
17	Kalchini	Satali	36	42	64	58
18	Kumargram	Kumargram	100	100	0	0
19	Kumargram	Barabisha	100	100	0	0
20	Madarihat	Totapara	100	86	0	14
21	Madarihat	Madhyarangali Bazar	100	68	0	32
22	Madarihat	Sishujhora (Sishubarihat)	78	39	22	61
23	Mal	Chak Moulani (lataguri)	100	100	0	0
24	Mal	Dakshin Hanskhali	100	48	0	52
25	Mal	Uttar Saripukhri	54	91	46	9
26	Maynaguri	Barnies	100	100	0	0
27	Maynaguri	Singimari (Domohoni)	100	73	0	27
28	Maynaguri	Bhurangabari	72	62	28	38
29	Maynaguri	Churabhandar	69	64	31	36

(continued)

Table 23.6 (continued)

Sl No	Block	PHC (DNUs)	TE score	SE score	The minimum extent to which all the outputs can be expanded (in %)	The extent to which scale of operation needed to be changed (in %)
30	Maynaguri	Ramsi	62	81	38	19
31	Maynaguri	Saptibari	53	100	47	0
32	Meteli	Indong	100	97	0	3
33	Meteli	Mathachulka	66	46	34	54
34	Nagrakata	Looksan	100	85	0	15
35	Nagrakata	Dhumppara	68	55	32	45
36	Rajganj	Kalinagar	100	100	0	0
37	Rajganj	Sikarpur	93	87	7	13
38	Rajganj	Kakurjan (Sukbari)	88	49	12	51

Source Calculation from the DEA results, 2014

scope of size reduction is 26.2 on an average basis. In case of scale efficiency (SE), we observe that among 38 PHCs 31.58% (12) show constant return to scale, which means that these PHCs are operating at their most productive scale sizes. The number of PHCs operating under decreasing returns to scale is 55.26% (21), implying that scale of operation of these PHCs should be contracted for achieving efficiency and reduction of unit costs, and 5 (13.15%) PHCs are functioning at increasing returns to scale position. The most of the PHCs are functioning under decreasing returns to scale implying that they are going beyond their capacity and hence need reduction of their scale operation. Highest reduction in scale is required for the Sishujhora PHC of Madarihat block (61%).

The findings of this study disclose that more than half of the PHCs are functioning at less than optimal levels of purely technical and scale efficiency. The recital of some of the PHCs in the sample is actually scrutinized to be very low and lifts much anxiety for planners and policymakers. Table 23.7 gives us the concrete result derived from Table 23.6.

Now from Table 23.7, we can derive the efficiency status of the PHCs in all blocks of the district, and that is described in Table 23.8. The block wise efficiency character of the PHCs is shown in Table 23.8 in terms of a number of efficient PHCs, the percentage of efficient PHCs out of total number of PHCs in the block, average technical efficiency scores, and scale efficiency scores. The block wise picture paints that Kumargram, one of the extreme east side block of the Western Dooars, has performed as the best performer in the area followed by Alipurduar-II, Madarihat and Mal blocks of Jalpaiguri district. In terms of average technical efficiency score, the block Kumargram again is the peer and situated on the extreme boundary of the health production possibility frontier. Figure 23.2 shows the average technical and scale efficiency scores of the blocks. Considering both the

Table 23.7 Summary results of DEA for 38 PHCs

Item	TE score	SE score
Number of efficient PHCs	15	12
Number of inefficient PHCs	23	26
Mean score of efficient PHCs	100	100
Mean score of all PHCs	79.11	79.32
Mean score of inefficient PHCs	74.74	73.8
Median score of all PHCs	81.5	60.66
Standard deviation	21.23	20.48
Minimum score	36	39

Source Calculation from the DEA results, 2014

Table 23.8 Efficiency status of PHCs in different blocks

Block	Number of efficient PHCs	% of number of efficient PHCs	Av. TE score	Av. SE score
Jalpaiguri	7	40	84.4	93
Maynaguri	2	33.33	76	80
Dhupguri	0	0	46.67	60.33
Rajganj	1	33.33	93.67	78.67
Mal	2	66.67	84.67	79.67
Meteli	1	50	83	71.5
Nagrakata	1	50	84	70
Kumargram	2	100	100	100
Falakata	2	0	58	100
Madarihat	2	66.67	92.67	64.33
Kalchini	0	0	54.5	69
Alipurduar-I	1	50	90.5	87.5
Alipurduar-II	1	66.67	78.33	74.67

Source Calculation from the DEA results, 2014

scores the Kumargram block is the most superior compared to other blocks. Figure 23.2 shows that the efficient blocks (both with TE and SE scores) in terms of the functioning of PHCs are Jalpaiguri Sadar, Mal, Kumargram and Alipurduar-I blocks of the district.

Now in Table 23.6, we have already measured the minimum extent to which all the output can be expanded by TE score deficiency from the frontier and also the extent to which the scale of operation needed to be changed by scale efficiency deficiency. Here, the study can easily identify the best performer and worst performer PHCs in terms of both output expansion and scale expansion possibility. The PHCs which have the minimum possibility of expanding output according to its technical efficiency scores, as well as the least value of the scale expansion possibilities, should be identified as the best performer and vice versa for the worst

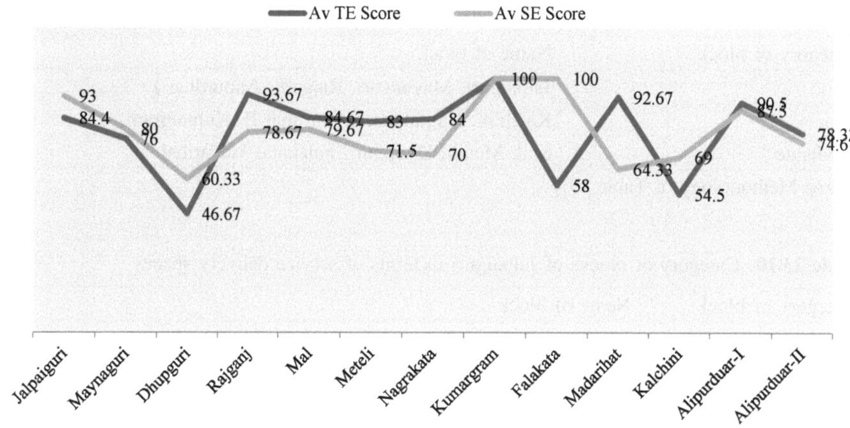

Fig. 23.2 Block wise average technical and scale efficiency scores of PHCs. *Source* Calculation from the DEA results, 2014

performer. Now the scopes of expansion of outputs have two possibilities, one is 'radial expansion' and the other is 'slack movement'. By radial expansion, we mean that all the outputs can be expanded by minimum percentage, and by slack movement, we mean the amount by which further expansion of at least one output is possible in addition to the radial expansion. In this study, the positive slack movement means that, in addition to radial expansion which is measured by technical efficiency scores, further expansion in output is possible. All the technically inefficient PHCs have the scope of radial expansion, i.e. expansion of all of the outputs.

On the basis of criterion fitted in Table 23.4, the study categorizes the accessibility of all 13 blocks of the district Jalpaiguri which is shown in Table 23.9. Table 23.9 shows that out of 13 blocks, four blocks have good physical accessibility, four have poor accessibility and five have moderate accessibility. All the blocks with poor accessibility show that they have some larger part under the national protected forest area. The geographical distribution of the blocks over the district represents the physical accessibility criteria according to this study. All the 13 blocks of the district are analysed in terms of secondary data collected from the district administration and district forest office. On the basis of such data level, a rough categorization has been made and the results in this respect indicate that blocks like Kalchini, Nagrakata, Alipurduar-II and Kumargram have poor physical accessibility compared to others. As there is no alternative regarding the opening to take advantage of the technology based on Geographic Information System (GIS) to plan out the physical accessibility to healthcare, it is always better to approximate the geographic coverage in terms of accessibility and availability of the existing PHCs setup in each block of the Bengal Dooars. Anyone can able to use "*AccessMode*" software developed by World Health Organization (WHO) for

Table 23.9 Category of blocks of Jalpaiguri in terms of physical accessibility

Category of block	Name of block
Good	Jalpaiguri, Maynaguri, Rajganj, Alipurduar-I
Poor	Kalchini, Nagrakata, Alipurduar-II, Kumargram
Moderate	Mal, Meteli, Dhupguri, Falakata, Madarihat

Source Methodology of Table 23.4

Table 23.10 Category of blocks of Jalpaiguri in terms of service delivery spaces

Category of block	Name of block
Good	Kumargram, Alipurduar-I, Jalpaiguri, Rajganj, Mal
Poor	Dhupguri, Kalchini
Moderate	Falakata, Madarihat, Maynaguri, Meteli, Nagrakata, Alipurduar-II

Source Methodology of Table 23.8

modelling physical accessibility to healthcare. However, in this study, such type of application is not possible due to data unavailability and time.

The service delivery space index is measured by the study in terms of both the technical efficiency and scale efficiency scores. If the PHC is performing with scores equal or very close to 100, it means it is the efficient one. Table 23.8 shows the technical and scale efficiency scores of the PHCs for each block. On the basis of such demarcation, Table 23.10 shows the category of blocks in terms of service delivery space.

Table 23.11 agglomerates the cases of Tables 23.9 and 23.10 in a single Table both in terms of physical accessibility and service delivery spaces. Practically Table 23.11 shows a matrix where the physical accessibility and service delivery spaces are described in terms of good, moderate and poor categories. The study shows that Jalpaiguri, Alipurduar-I and Rajganj blocks are in better position with the identification that all of these blocks have better accessibility and better service delivery spaces. These blocks are in a much superior spot and need less resource since they are more reachable and have got their service space more utilized. The significant identification shows that Mal and Kumargram blocks have good service delivery spaces but they are in the position with poor physical accessibilities. The worst conditions in terms of both the physical accessibility and service delivery spaces are found specially in case Kalchini block and for Dhupguri block where the service delivery spaces are poor but the physical accessibility is moderate. The study found no one blocks with 'good' ranking in terms of physical accessibility and poor in terms of service delivery spaces. Such informations may bring some kind of relief for the health managers.

Table 23.11 Category of blocks in terms of both service delivery spaces and physical accessibility

		Physical accessibility		
		Good	Moderate	Poor
Spaces for service delivery	Good	Jalpaiguri, Alipurduar-I, Rajganj	Mal	Kumargram
	Moderate	Maynaguri	Falakata, Madarihat, Meteli	Nagrakata, Alipurduar-II
	Poor		Dhupguri	Kalchini

Source Methodology of Tables 23.9 and 23.10

23.4 Conclusions

The study observes that service delivery spaces for the existing PHCs are limited by various factors. The physical accessibility of the blocks is derived on the basis of the infrastructure available within the blocks. The secondary-level data were collected from the district administration to construct such index in terms of approach bus road distance from the existing villages. The approach rail road distance from the same villages, numbers of river bodies on these approach roads, percentage of villages where more than 10% of the area is covered by forest area, and the distance factor from the farthest sub-centre to performing BPHC of that particular block. The service delivery spaces are defined in terms of technical efficiencies and scale efficiencies derived for all 38 PHCs of the Jalpaiguri district. By considering both the physical accessibility and service delivery spaces for all the blocks in macro terms, the study can identify the strongest and weakest blocks performing in terms of both service delivery spaces and physical accessibility index. Next, considering the technical and scale efficiency scores of each PHCs the study tries to identify the PHCs at a micro or individual level which offers health support at primary level. Here, the study tries to identify the best practicing PHCs and the PHCs need special attention. Regarding the best practicing PHCs, the study tries to identify the PHCs with full capacities of inputs, like 10 beds, and then from that level of selection, the study tries to identify the PHCs with doctors involvement index (DII) and Perception index (PI) above the average, and from that the study filtres the PHCs with all values of output above the average level. Then for the PHCs needed special attention shows that selected PHCs among the peer group performing with low inputs, and from those select those PHCs whose quality indexes are above average level.

References

Arrow, K. J. (1963). Uncertainty and the welfare economics for medical care. *American Economic Review, 53*(5), 921–969.

Alderman H., & Gertler, P. (1989). *The substitutability of public and private healthcare for the treatment of children in Pakistan*. LSMS Working paper 57.

Banker, R. D., Charnes, A., & Cooper, W. W. (1984). Some models for estimating technical and scale efficiencies in data envelopment analysis. *Management Science, 9,* 1078–1092.

Bhattacharya, K. (2007). *Book, silent departure* (pp. 263–271). Kolkata: Papyras Publication.

Bloom, G., Kanjilal, B., & Peters, D. H. (2008). Regulating health care markets in China and India. *Health Affairs, 27*(4), 952–963.

Bothwell, J. L., & Cooley, T. F. (1982). Efficiency in the provision of healthcare: An analysis of health maintenance organisations. *Southern Economic Journal, 48*(4), 970–984.

Dreze, J., & Sen, A. (1995). *India: Economic development and social opportunity* (pp. 68–77). Oxford: Clarendon Press.

Ensor, T., & Witter, S. (2001). Health economics in low income countries: Adapting to the reality of the unofficial economy. *Health Policy, 57,* 1–13.

Evans D. B., Tandon, A., Murray, J. L., & Lauer J. (2000). *The comparative efficiency of national health systems in producing health: An analysis of 191 countries*. GPE Discussion Paper series. 29.

Farrell, M. J. (1957). The measurement of productive efficiency. *Journal of the Royal Statistical Society Series, 120,* 253–281.

Grossman, M. (1972). On the concept of health capital and demand for health. *Journal of Political Economy, 80*(2), 223–255.

Gertler, P., & Van der Gaag, J. (1988). *Meaning of willingness to pay for social services in developing countries*. LSMS Working paper No. 45.

Hollingsworth, B., & Wildman, J. (2003). The efficiency of health production: Re-estimating the WHO panel data using parametric and non-parametric approaches to provide additional information. *Health Economics, 12*(6), 493–504.

Kaplan, R. M., & Bush, J. W. (1982). Health-related quality of life measurement for evaluation research and policy analysis. *Health Psychology, 1*(1), 61–80.

Purohit, B. C. (2008). Efficiency of healthcare system: A sub-state level analysis for West Bengal (India). *Review of Urban Regional Development Studies., 20*(3), 212–225.

Wouters, A. (1993). The cost and efficiency of public and private health care facilities in Ogun state, Nigeria. *Health Economics, 2*(1), 31–42.

Chapter 24
Factors Affecting Morbidity and Utilization of Healthcare Services: A Case Study of Nagaon District of Assam

Nirmala Devi and Rajshree Bedamatta

24.1 Introduction

Morbidity is a condition of being in ill health or perpetual suffering from sickness or disease of any kind adversely affecting bodily functioning. The 52nd round of National Sample Survey Organization (NSSO) defines morbidity in terms of ailments, illnesses or any kind of injury.[1] Morbidity conditions thus reflect the health status of population. It is not only helpful in providing information about various diseases prevalent in the community but also in formulating policies and programmes meant at targeting (Duraisamy 1998; Gumber and Barman 1997). Morbidity measurements are mainly of two types—self-perceived morbidity and clinical or observed morbidity. Self-perceived morbidity measures morbidity based on various illnesses as perceived by an individual herself. Clinical or observed morbidity employs scientific methods by the interviewer to check the presence of illnesses. In most Indian surveys, the method of self-perceived morbidity has been used as it is less costly than the use of clinical method (Belcher et al. 1976).

The databases on morbidity provided by the Ministry of Healthcare are based on data collected from different public health institutions. This has resulted in underestimation of morbidity because in rural areas there is heavy dependence on pharmacists and traditional healers for minor illnesses, which are not recorded in government heath institutions or hospitals. Similarly, many do not even seek any

[1]The report has defined ailment or illness as 'any deviation from the state of physical or mental well-being' (NSSO 1998).

N. Devi (✉) · R. Bedamatta
Department of Humanities and Social Sciences, Indian Institute of Technology (IIT), Guwahati, Assam, India
e-mail: d.nirmala@iitg.ernet.in

R. Bedamatta
e-mail: rajshree@iitg.ernet.in

U.K. De et al. (eds.), *Issues on Health and Healthcare in India*, India Studies in Business and Economics, https://doi.org/10.1007/978-981-10-6104-2_24

kind of treatment. Therefore, survey-based methods of collecting data on morbidity provide better datasets.

Morbidity prevalence has also been linked to the stage of health transition in a country. In the later stage of demographic transition, mortality and fertility rates are seen to have declined as also various kinds of childhood diseases. Regions in the early phases of transition therefore experience relatively higher morbid conditions. Among the Indian states Kerala is said to be facing less morbid conditions being in the late transition phase while Tamil Nadu, Punjab, Maharashtra, Karnataka, West Bengal, Andhra Pradesh, Haryana and Gujarat are in the mid transition phase. States, which are in the early transition phase, are Assam, Bihar, Jharkhand, Orissa, Rajasthan, Uttar Pradesh, Madhya Pradesh and Chhattisgarh (Peter et al. 2003). Risks of morbidity are also determined by socio-economic factors such as age, education, social groups and incomes. Gender differentials in terms of morbidity prevalence rate have been widely studied (NCAER 1995; Sekhar 1997; Duraisamy 1998; Sundar and Sharma 2002; Dilip 2002; Krishnaswami 2004; Navaneetham et al. 2009; Gosh and Arokiasamy 2009). The prevalence rate of any kind of morbidity whether acute or chronic also largely depends on the extent of utilization and access to institutional healthcare facilities. Utilization and access includes among other things, the cost of healthcare and physical availability of healthcare facilities (Getler and Van der Gag 1990).

This paper examines the extent of morbidity, factors affecting morbidity as well as utilization of healthcare services in one of the villages of Nagaon district of Assam. Section 24.2 discusses the level and pattern of morbidity across various states of India and the relative position of Assam. Section 24.3 discusses the sample design and methodology of the field survey. Section 24.4 discusses the state of morbidity in the study village and the differentials in utilization of healthcare services by place of treatment. Some of the important factors affecting morbidity are also discussed in this section. Section 24.5 concludes and summarizes the paper.

24.2 Levels and Pattern of Morbidity in India and Assam: An Overview

The National Sample Survey Organization (NSSO) and National Council of Applied Economic Research (NCAER) have been conducting surveys on morbidity from time to time. The first report of NCAER on *Household Survey of Medical Care* was published in 1992. This report provided data on nature of illnesses suffered, source of medical treatment and costs borne by the patient during the period of treatment. In 1993, another survey on *Household Survey of Healthcare Utilization and Expenditure* was carried out and published in 1995.[2] The former survey conducted by NCAER referred only to treated illnesses while the latter

[2]Referred to as NCAER (1995) in this paper.

collected information on both treated and untreated ailments. It collected information on prevalence rate of morbidity by gender, hospitalized and non-hospitalized cases, utilization of healthcare services by type of provider, use of various systems of medicine, and expenditure on hospitalized and non-hospitalized treatment.

Likewise the NSSO has been publishing reports on morbidity and healthcare since 1953–54 (7th round). Since then there have been a number of surveys by the NSSO: 1961–62 (17th round), 1973–1974 (28th round), 1986–87 (42nd round), and 1995–96 (52nd round). The main objective of the 52nd round survey was to study the pattern of utilization of public and private healthcare services together with creating a morbidity profile of the population. Another round of survey on morbidity was conducted from January to June, 2004 (60th round). The report was entitled *Morbidity and Condition of the Aged*. This report collected information on general healthcare system, utilization of healthcare services provided by the public and private sector and expenditure incurred on medical treatment by the households. Information on conditions of health of the aged was also collected in this round.

The 71st round of the NSSO released a report entitled *Key Indicators of the Social Consumption in India: Health*. The main focus of this round is to understand the trends and patterns in morbidity rates, to study the role of public sector in providing access to various public healthcare services and to study the cost of healthcare in both public and private healthcare sector. In the earlier rounds only those individuals were considered to be sought treatment who received some kind of medical treatment, but in the 71st round, those who were self-medicated were also considered as being treated (Sundararaman and Muraleedharan 2015).

For an overview of morbidity status in India and Assam the data from NCAER (1995), NSSO (1998, 2004) has been used. Table 24.1 provides the information on morbidity prevalence rate among different states of India. NCAER (1995) estimates show that the morbidity prevalence rate (based on treated and untreated) was higher than the Indian average in the states of Andhra Pradesh, Karnataka, Madhya Pradesh, Orissa, Punjab, Uttar Pradesh and Kerala. In this report, Assam is seen to have relatively lower levels of morbidity prevalence. The prevalence rate of morbidity in India was 105 per one thousands population while the morbidity prevalence rate in Assam was only 86 per one thousand population. In 1995–96, Assam is seen to have a very high increase in the rate of morbidity. Other states that showed higher rates than the Indian average were Haryana, Maharashtra, Orissa, Punjab, Tamil Nadu, Uttar Pradesh, West Bengal and Kerala. In 2004 while all other states showed a morbidity prevalence rate of below or at least close to the Indian average, Assam is seen to be experiencing morbidity at a very high level (at least 1.5 times higher than the Indian average) along with Kerala. However, Kerala may be considered to be an outlier in all the years, showing a morbidity prevalence rate much higher than the Indian average. For example, the morbidity estimate in 1995–96 is seen to be almost three times higher than the Indian average. However since Kerala is in the last stage of demographic transition it is expected to be experiencing lower levels of morbidity prevalence. One of the explanations of

Table 24.1 Prevalence rate of morbidity (per thousand population) for the major states of India during the 52nd, 60th Round of National Sample Survey Organization

Major states	NCAER (1995)	52nd round (1995–96)	60th round (2004)
Andhra Pradesh	126	126	99
Assam	*86*	*140*	*132*
Bihar	98	84	54
Gujarat	76	98	73
Haryana	75	143	95
Karnataka	117	96	69
Madhya Pradesh	115	93	67
Maharashtra	67	137	81
Orissa	191	126	105
Punjab	132	197	109
Rajasthan	114	80	43
Tamil Nadu	78	149	83
Uttar Pradesh	110	155	94
West Bengal	82	170	103
India average	105	128	86
Kerala (outlier)	**195**	**358**	**178**

The value of Kerala has been depicted in bold because among all the states of the country Kerala is an outlier. The morbidity levels in Kerala is extremely high with respect to the other states of the country. Assam has been indicated in italics to specifically focus on the morbidity trend of the state with respect to other states of the country as the study is based on two districts of Assam
Source NSSO, 52nd and 60th round (1998, 2004), NCAER (1995)

Kerala's high morbidity estimate is that reporting is very high in this case as the population in general is highly literate. Secondly the nature of disease prevalence, unlike in the case of other states, is mostly related to lifestyle diseases. In other states the incidence of communicable diseases are relatively high.

24.3 Sample Design and Methodology of the Study

This study is based on a household survey conducted in Nagaon district of Assam. A ranking of districts was carried out based on selected socio-economic indicators with emphasis on primary and secondary indicators of health.[3] Based on the ranking of districts Nagaon was selected for the morbidity study. A further survey literature was done to identify the block in which the sample survey can be carried out. Kaliabor Development Block was selected from which a list of revenue villages

[3]See Appendix for the indicators used and the ranking of districts based on the composite index. The methodology of calculation of the composite index was adapted from Ram and Shekhar (2006).

was created. Bamunipathar revenue village was randomly selected for the study.[4] A census enumeration of the village showed a total of 247 households, out of which 99 (40%) of the households were selected randomly for a sample survey. The information on morbidity was gathered from the individual residents of these 99 households constituting 485 individuals.

Information on both acute and chronic morbidity has been collected from the usual residents of the households. Acute morbidities here refer to those illnesses which are of short duration, i.e. a period of less than 30 days. Chronic illnesses are of long duration continuing for a period of more than one month (based on NSSO 1998).

Morbidity is generally measured in terms of morbidity prevalence rate, which is the ratio of estimated proportion of persons reporting ailments during a particular reference period and the total number of persons exposed to the risk of some illness. However, the World Health Organization Expert Committee on Health Statistics (1959) had defined morbidity prevalence rate as the ratio between the number of spells of ailments suffered during a particular reference period and the total population exposed to the risk.[5] The results of the two measures differ only marginally (NSSO 1998). For this paper, we have followed the measure used by the NSSO. A logistic regression model has been used to determine the factors affecting morbidity in this paper.

24.4 Levels and Pattern of Morbidity in the Study Village of Nagaon District of Assam

In order to understand the morbidity pattern of the sample population in the study village, the prevalence rate of morbidity is calculated by various background characteristics of the respondents. Table 24.2 shows the pattern of prevalence rate of morbidity by various background characteristics. Prevalence rate of acute morbidity is higher among infants comprising age group 0–5 years (21%), while the percentage of chronic morbidity is higher among the elders, above 60 years of age (3%). It implies that the young are susceptible to acute morbidity and adults are susceptible to chronic morbidity or illnesses.[6] It was also observed that the percentage of untreated acute illnesses is higher among the age group 6–14 years (6%) and 15–59 years (6%). Untreated morbidity comprises those cases in which the respondent does not visit a health facility or health personnel for treatment instead; they rely on other sources like traditional healers, home remedial measures or purchase of medicines directly from the pharmacy. The percentage of untreated illnesses is comparatively lower among infants aged 0–5 years (1%). This is

---

[4]The backward block has been selected on the basis of the available literature on *Identification of Backward Blocks* by Barua (2012).

[5]Spell of ailment refers to a continuous period of sickness with respect to a particular ailment (NSSO 1998).

[6]Evidences based on other studies have also shown that children and elders are susceptible to more illnesses than the other age groups (Krishnaswami 2004; NSSO 1998).

Table 24.2 Prevalence rate of acute morbidity, chronic morbidity and untreated morbidity by background characteristics, Bamunipathar village, Nagaon (%)

Background characteristics	Acute morbidity	Untreated acute morbidity	Chronic morbidity	Untreated chronic morbidity	Total morbidity
Age					
0–5	20.9	1.5	0.8	0	23.1
6–14	18.8	5.8	0.6	0	25.3
15–59	17.2	6.4	1.7	0.1	25.3
60 and above	16.7	2.8	3.0	0	22.5
Gender					
Male	21.3	2.4	1.7	0.1	25.4
Female	14.0	8.4	1.2	0	23.6
Religion					
Hindu	20.5	3.6	1.4	0.1	25.5
Muslims and others	19.5	1.6	1.6	0	22.8
Caste					
Upper caste	13.3	2.5	1.5	0	22.3
SC	14.8	5.2	1.4	0	21.4
ST	24.4	9.0	1.5	0.1	35.0
Others	17.9	3.0	1.3	0.1	16.3
Education					
Illiterates	19.5	2.7	1.1	0	23.2
Below primary	24.0	2.7	1.5	0	28.1
Above primary	16.8	12.2	1.2	0	30.2
Above secondary	13.7	3.0	2.1	0.2	18.9

Source Survey data, Bamunipathar, Nagaon, 2014

probably because of fear of early death of the child which forces them for treatment of the infants at the earliest.

Gender-wise categorization of the sample population indicates that the proportion of population suffering from both acute and chronic illnesses is higher among males. The proportion of male population suffering from acute illnesses is 21% and from chronic illnesses 2%. Females suffering from acute and chronic illnesses are 14 and 1%, respectively. Although the proportion of acute and chronic morbidity is high among the males, the proportion of untreated illnesses is higher among females (8%) than among the males (2%). From observations based on personal interviews, we conclude that the illnesses among female members are neglected by other members of the households. In many cases, the respondents observed that the male members are busy with their daily activities and do not find time to go to health institutions for the female counterparts. In many cases, the females themselves also hesitate to go to health institutions because of engagement in daily household activities and shyness. They prefer to go to a health institution only if it is of utmost necessity. Some of the health problems of women are also hidden by the women themselves and the information had to be collected after probing again and again. The women members therefore resort to self-medication, home remedial measures or temporary treatment of the illnesses by purchasing medicines from the pharmacy. However, in case of males it has been observed that as they are the main earning agents of the households and other family members are dependent on them, they get preferential health treatment.

There appears no difference in morbidity prevalence when matched by religion. Percentage of population suffering from acute morbidity is almost same for both the groups (Hindus and Muslims in this case). It is 21% among Hindus and 20% among Muslims. There is not much variation even in case of chronic morbidity between the two groups. It is 1% among Hindus and 2% among Muslims. The percentage of Hindus suffering from untreated illnesses is 4% and Muslims 2%.

Percentage of population suffering from acute morbidity is higher among the Scheduled tribes (24%) and other backward classes (18%). However, the percentage of chronic morbidity is almost similar among all caste groups. The percentage of untreated illnesses is, however, higher among the ST's (9%). It was observed that the ST households were located remotely within the village, far away from the other households and had less physical access to institutional healthcare. Therefore, their preference towards self-medication and other ways of treatment was higher. Probing further on this, the ST households reasoned that treatment other than institutional healthcare would save both money and time which can be utilized for other activities. They are prone to more illnesses because of residing in unhygienic conditions, with unsafe drinking water, non-availability of toilet facility, absence of proper drainage system and use of firewood for cooking purposes. The data shows that only 36% of ST households use safe drinking water, 40% has toilet facility, 88% use firewood for cooking purposes and only 6% have drainage facility. A very high proportion suffers from chronic diseases such as malaria, diarrhoea, typhoid, tuberculosis and asthma.

In terms of educational level the prevalence rate of acute morbidity is highest among the below primary level category (29%) while chronic morbidity is high among the illiterate (2%). The overall prevalence rate of morbidity is lower among those who have education above secondary level (17%). The percentage of population with untreated ailments is higher for the below poverty line category (12%).

24.4.1 Disease Specific Prevalence Rate of Morbidity in the Study Area

To assess the overall morbidity condition of the study village we studied disease specific morbidity among households. Among the incidence of acute illnesses, 41% of the population is estimated to be suffering from fevers of short duration. The second most common disease is diarrhoea and gastroenteritis dysentery (26%). The

Table 24.3 Respondents suffering from disease specific acute morbidity and share of untreated cases by disease, Bamunipathar village, Nagaon

Type of disease	Percentage of people suffering from the specific disease	Percentage of population untreated, by disease
Diarrhoea and gastroenteritis dysentery	26	24
Whooping cough	12	15
Fevers of short duration	41	17
Chicken pox	3	67
Heart failure	2	0
Acute respiratory infection	1	0
Diarrhoea and whooping cough	3	0
Ear problem	1	0
Joint pains	1	0
Malaria	1	0
Headache	2	50
Accident	1	0
Allergy problem	1	40
Asthma	1	0
Hypertension	1	0
Skin problem	3	0

Source Survey data, Bamunipathar, Nagaon, 2014

percentage of people suffering from whooping cough is 12%, chicken pox 3%, and diarrhoea and whooping cough together 3% (Table 24.3).

Among the various acute illnesses, the most untreated cases are for chicken pox (67%). The popular belief among households is that chicken pox is incurable by doctors and therefore they prefer to go to traditional healers of the village for treatment. In case of diarrhoea and gastroenteritis, untreated illnesses accounted for 24% of total acute morbidity. In cases of minor illnesses like headache, whooping cough, fever of short duration and allergy complains, 50, 15, 17 and 40%, respectively, were not treated. Thus, in case of minor illnesses a major proportion of the population remained untreated, as they preferred self-medication. Minor illnesses are generally ignored as they are not considered to have serious implications. Moreover, financial hardship was also mentioned as one of the reasons behind untreated illnesses.

In terms of chronic illnesses, the highest share of disease comprises joint pains (17%). Moreover, fever of unknown origin accounted for 11% of the total chronic illnesses. The other diseases which are prevalent in the study area are diabetes (9%), hypertension (9%), malaria (11%), tuberculosis (5%), typhoid (5%) and asthma (6%). Malaria was an epidemic in the region during last few years but the frequency has declined recently. The proportion of untreated morbidity is less in case of chronic morbidities. The share of untreated illnesses among the population is 10%

Table 24.4 Respondents suffering from disease specific chronic morbidity and share of untreated cases by disease, Bamunipathar village, Nagaon

Specific chronic diseases in the study area	Percentage of respondents suffering from disease specific chronic morbidities	Most untreated chronic illnesses
Diabetes	9	0
Hypertension	9	0
Joint pain	17	0
Asthma	6	0
Kidney	2	0
Liver	3	0
Fever of unknown origin	11	10
Ear problem	5	0
Accident	1	0
Stomach trouble	7	17
Dog biting	1	0
Vision problem	2	0
High pressure	2	0
Malaria	11	0
Paralysis	1	0
Tuberculosis	5	0
Typhoid	5	0
Lump on the head	1	0
Heart problem	1	0
Uric acid	1	0

Source Survey data, Bamunipathar, Nagaon, 2014

for fever of unknown origin while the proportion of untreated ailments is observed for stomach problem (17%). See Table 24.4.

24.4.2 Differentials in Utilization of Healthcare Services by Place of Treatment

Households in Bamunipathar village are mainly dependent on three sources for treatment of illnesses. They are government health services, private healthcare services and other sources. Government health services here include primary health centre (PHC) and sub-centre located within the village. The first referral unit (FRU) for the village is located at the nearest town Jakhalabandha, 13 km away from the revenue village. The nearest civil hospital is located in Tezpur town which is 35 km away from the revenue village. Private healthcare includes private clinics and nursing homes located in Jakhalabandha and Tezpur. Other sources include treatment through self-medication, traditional healers (*Ojhas*) and home remedial measures.

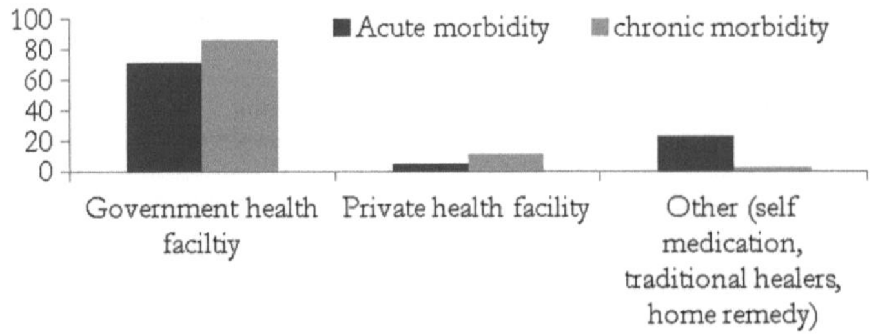

Fig. 24.1 Utilization of health facilities for acute and chronic morbidity by source of treatment (in %)

24.4.2.1 Utilization of Healthcare Services for Acute and Chronic Morbidity

In terms of individuals seeking treatment, whether chronic or acute, use of government health facilities is very high in Bamunipathar. The percentage of individuals seeking treatment at chronic morbidity at government health institutions is 86% and acute morbidity 72%. However, the dependence on private health facilities is higher for chronic morbidity (11%) in contrast to acute morbidity (5%) (see Fig. 24.1). Due to lack of proper equipments, medicines and health specialist, most of the patients move to the FRU at Jakhalabandha. The FRU is mostly overcrowded and due to shortage of beds in the FRU, people have to go to the nearby private clinics or hospitals. Since the Civil hospital is physically very distant, in case of chronic morbidities, people prefer to go to nearby private clinics and hospitals. This leads to an adverse impact especially on the poorer sections of the village in terms of heavy expenses on chronic diseases. Although the dependence on government health institutions is high among the study population, due to deteriorating or low quality of care and other loopholes, people move towards private healthcare. In cases of acute morbidity, 23% took recourse to home remedial measures or direct purchase of medicines without consulting health professionals. However, people did not seem to take chances in cases of chronic morbidity and dependence on other sources in this case was found to be only 2%.

Thus, dependence on government health facilities is high in cases of both acute and chronic morbidity in the study village. Cases of untreated acute morbidity are higher than chronic morbidity. NCAER (1995) and NSSO (1998) had found higher dependence on private health facilities for acute morbidity and higher dependence on government health facilities for chronic morbidity.[7]

[7]See Appendix for estimates of utilization of healthcare services by place of treatment and other background characteristics.

24.4.2.2 Utilization of Healthcare Facilities for Acute and Chronic Morbidity by Gender

In Bamunipathar village, 88% of male patients suffering from acute morbidity were treated in government health facility while the proportion of females was only 52%. The reason behind low utilization of government health facility in case of females is that their preference for other sources for treatment (39%). Only 10% of the males depended on other sources. However, there is not much gender variation in treatment of morbidity in the private health institutions. The dependence on private health facility is 5% among males and 9% among females (see Fig. 24.2). Figure 24.3 indicates utilization pattern of health services in case of chronic morbidity by gender. As in the case of acute morbidity, in cases of chronic morbidities as well, utilization of government health facilities is higher among males (90%) than females (78%). However, the utilization of private health facility is higher among females (19%) than males (8%). Higher dependence on private health facilities among the females is probably because of negligence of diseases at the initial stages. Negligence at the initial stages of the disease leads to complications requiring referral to private hospitals having better facilities than the PHC or sub-centre. The utilization of other sources of treatment is same for both the males (3%) and the females (3%) in case of chronic morbidity. While dependence on other

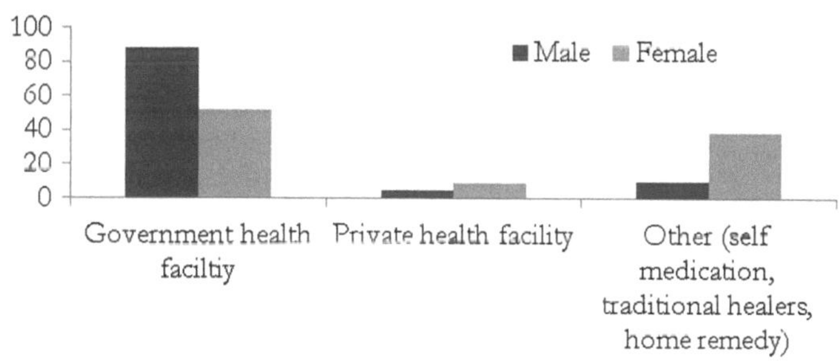

Fig. 24.2 Utilization of health facilities for acute morbidity (in %)

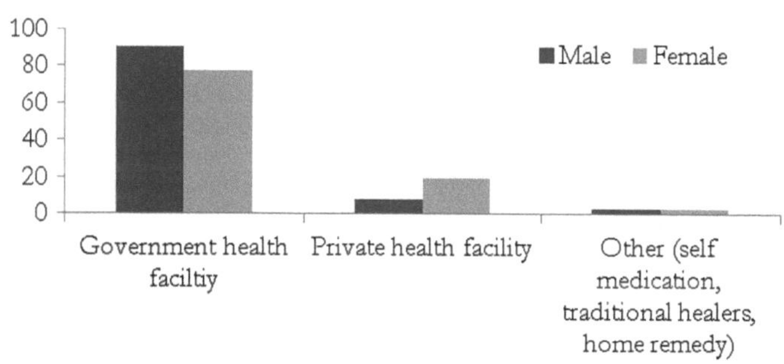

Fig. 24.3 Utilization of health facilities for chronic morbidity (in %)

sources is very low, that chronic morbidity is also being treated without help of health professionals is a matter of concern.

24.4.3 *Factors Influencing Morbidity*

A logistic regression model has been used to identify causal relationship between morbidity conditions and factors affecting morbidity.[8] The dependent variable used in the model is 'whether an individual is suffering from any kind of illness or not' if 'yes' the variable takes the value 1, or 0 otherwise. The functional form of the logistic regression model is[9]:

$$\begin{aligned} Z_i = {} & \alpha + \beta_1(\text{SEX}) + \beta_2(\text{RL}) + \beta_3(\text{CS}) + \beta_4(\log \text{ of AGE}) \\ & + \beta_5(\text{MOCC}) + \beta_6(\text{EDU}) + \beta_7(\text{HSS}) + \beta_8(\text{OH}) \\ & + \beta_9(\log \text{ of MI}) + \beta_{10}(\text{SOH}) + \beta_{11}(\text{SDW}) + \beta_{12}(\text{ATF}) + \beta_{13}(\text{RSBY}) + \mu_i \end{aligned}$$

The explanatory variables are defined in Table 24.5. For the model fit, we have considered 13 explanatory variables keeping in mind the composition of households and the data collected from the household survey. Coefficient β_1 explains sex of the individual taking value 1 if male or 0 otherwise. Likewise, the other β coefficients are also explained. However, β_3 (CS1, CS2 and CS3), β_6 (EDU1, EDU2 and EDU3) and β_7 (HSS1, HSS2, HSS3) contains three dummies, respectively. Further in case of each of the dummies one is taken as the reference variable. For example, in the case of β_3 which is the caste variable, while there are three dummies (CS1, CS2 and CS3), CS3 referring to OBCs is taken as the reference category. The other caste dummies are explained with reference to CS3. Likewise, with β_6 and β_7, that considers education by different levels and household size consisting of different size categories, respectively.

---

[8]The logistic regression estimation has been used because the dependent variable is dichotomous in nature. In a number of empirical studies related to morbidity this model has been used (Navaneetham et al. 2009; Dilip 2002; Mukherjee et al. 2001). However, some studies have also used probit regression model to identify the factors influencing morbidity (Ghosh 2009; Duraisamy 1998). In the present study, the logistic regression model has been used as there is little justification on whether to use either probit or logit model in case of dichotomous dependent variables. More or less both the models give almost the same results (Gujarati 1998; Maddala 2007).

[9]In order to test multicollinearity among the variables the Variance Inflation Factor Test has been conducted which shows that there is absence of multicollinearity among the variables. See Table 24.9 in Appendix.

Table 24.5 Definition of the explanatory variables used in the study

Sl. No.	Variable	Description
1.	SEX	Sex of the respondent (1 = Male, 0, otherwise)
2.	RL	Religion of the respondent (1 = Hindu; 0, otherwise)
3a.	CS1	Caste of the respondent (1 = SC; 0, otherwise)
3b.	CS2	Caste of the respondent (1 = ST; 0, otherwise)
3c.	CS3 (R)	Caste of the respondent (1 = others, 0, otherwise)
4.	LN_AGE	Log of age of the respondent (in years)
5.	MOCC	Main occupation of the household (1 = Daily wage labour, 0, otherwise)
6a.	EDU1	Education of the respondent (1 = above primary; 0, otherwise)
6b.	EDU2	Education of the respondent (1 = above secondary, 0, otherwise)
6c.	EDU 3 (R)	Education of the respondents (1 = illiterates, 0, otherwise)
7a.	HSS 1	Household size (1 = greater than 5, 0, otherwise)
7b.	HSS 2	Household size (1 = greater than 7, 0, otherwise)
7c.	HSS 3 (R)	Household size (1 = less than 5, 0, otherwise)
8.	OH	Operational holding of land (in acres)
9.	LN_MI	Log of monthly income (in Rs.)
10.	SOH	Structure of the house (1 = Kutcha, and Semi Pucca; 0 otherwise)
11.	SDW	Availability of safe drinking water (1 = Yes; 0, otherwise)
12.	ATF	Availability of toilet facility (1 = Yes; 0, otherwise)
13.	RSBY	Possession of Rashtriya Swasthya Bima Yojana Card (1 = Yes; 0, otherwise)

Note (R) refers to reference category

24.5 Results and Discussion

The logistic model is statistically significant with a significant Likelihood Ratio Test (L-R Ch2) of p value less than 0.05. The independent variables that were found to have a significant causal relationship with morbidity conditions are sex of the individual, age, levels of education, operational holdings of land, and availability of toilet facility. The β_1 coefficient (Sex) is found to have positive and significant correlation with the dependent variable implying males have higher probability of being ill. The higher probability of illnesses among males is probably because a major proportion of them (50%) are working as daily wage labour or construction workers. In many cases, the workspaces are unhygienic. The ST population which constitutes 26% of all households is also found to be high consumer of intoxicants such as tobacco and alcohol. Since the female counterparts are mostly engaged in household activities, their exposure to workplace risks such as unhygienic conditions is less. The partial probability of β_1 coefficient is estimated at 0.0830. This implies that if the respondent is male, the probability of being ill increases by 0.0830 points, other things remaining the same. The β_2 coefficient (Age) indicates that there is a positive and significant relationship between morbidity and age. It implies that as the age of an individual increases the probability of being ill also increase. The partial probability of age is estimated to be 0.0446. This implies that with an increase in age of the respondent, the probability of being ill increases by 0.0446 points.

Similarly, β_6 coefficient (education level) was found to have negative and significant relationship with the dependent variable. Respondents having some level of education were found to face low levels of morbidity than the illiterate. The partial probability of dummy EDU1 explaining education above primary is estimated to be −0.0919 while that of dummy EDU2 explaining education above secondary level is estimated to be −0.1308. This implies that the probability of being ill is decreased by −0.0919 and −0.1308 points if the respondent is literate above primary and above secondary level, respectively. Thus, education level has a significant impact on probability of being ill. Higher the level of education lower is the chances of being in a state of morbidity.

The negative causal relationship with availability of toilet facility can likewise be explained (Table 24.6).

Table 24.6 Results of logistic regression on factors determining morbidity in the study village of Nagaon district of Assam, 2014

Explanatory variable	Maximum likelihood estimates (MLE)		Marginal effects (MFX)	
	Coefficient	Standard error	dydx	Standard error
SEX	0.3440***	0.2021	0.0830	0.0485
RELIGION	−0.0116	0.2667	−0.0028	0.0645
CASTE 1	−0.1817	0.2717	−0.0435	0.0642
CASTE 2	0.3324	0.2585	0.0812	0.0636
LN_AGE	0.1845***	0.1046	0.0446	0.0253
M OCC	0.0235	0.0458	0.0056	0.0110
EDU 1	−0.3825***	0.5631	−0.0919	0.0523
EDU 2	−0.5631**	0.2753	−0.1308	0.0606
HSS 1	−0.3311	0.2525	−0.0812	0.0624
HSS 2	−0.3085	0.2998	−0.0729	0.0689
OH	0.0959**	0.0462	0.0232	0.0111
LN_MI	−0.2189	0.1799	−0.0529	0.0435
SOH	0.0483	0.3738	0.0117	0.0910
SDW	−0.2973	0.2124	−0.0722	0.0517
ATF	−0.5092**	0.2097	−0.1231	0.0503
RSBY	0.01882	0.2148	0.0045	0.0519

Log likelihood: −312.83
L-R ch2 (16): 33.08
Prob > chi2: 0.0072
Pseudo R2: 0.050
Number of observations: 485
Degrees of freedom: 16

Note * Implies significant at 1% level ** implies significance at 5% level; *** implies significance at 10% level. For a dummy variable, dy/d*x* is the discrete change of dummy from 0 to 1

Source Calculation based on survey data

The coefficient of the variable operational holding (OH) is also found to be positive and significant. This implies that those who have higher operational holdings have higher probability of being ill. Generally, higher operational holdings imply higher levels of income. However, in case of the study village, it has been observed that those who have operational holdings are mainly engaged in agricultural activities for half of the year and are engaged as daily wage labourers for another part of the year. Moreover, due to financial hardship, they are not able to cultivate their land with proper facilities which resulted in low yield and thus low income. Thus, even if the households have higher operational holding they have low income indicating a lower living standard and prone to more diseases. The partial probability of operational holding is estimated to be 0.0232. This implies that other things remaining the same, the probability of being ill increases by 0.0232 point with an increase in the amount of operational holding among the respondents.

24.6 Summary and Conclusion

The study indicates that the morbidity prevalence rate varies with individual and socio-economic characteristics of the respondents. The proportion of morbidity is higher among males than females. However, the proportion of untreated morbidity among females is much higher in comparison to their male counterparts. Based on a social group classification, it was found that acute morbidity is much higher among the scheduled tribes. A significantly high ST population was also found dependent on self-medication and traditional healers. Unhealthy living conditions, including unsafe water and no toilet facility are major contributors to morbidity conditions. Morbidity also depends on the age of the individuals; it increases with the age of an individual. Acute morbidity is highest among the infants while chronic morbidity is highest among the elder above 60 years of age.

The disease profile of the village indicates that most of the people are suffering from non-specific fever and communicable diseases like malaria, tuberculosis, typhoid and asthma. However, the dependence on government health facilities is more among the sample population. Since a large proportion of households are living below the poverty line (38%) and a high level of illiteracy (37%), accessibility to private healthcare facility is low among households. However, in cases of chronic morbidity, large proportion of population were found dependent on private health facilities for treatment because proper treatment is not available at nearby public health facilities.

The study also indicates some of the factors which are significantly affecting morbidity in the study area. The significant factors are sex of the respondent, age of the respondent, operational holding, educational level of the respondent and availability of a toilet facility. Moreover, negative relationship has been found between safe drinking water and morbidity, structure of house and morbidity. The role of RSBY is negligible in the study area. Almost 30% of the population possesses RSBY card, but practically they are not benefitted by the scheme. The concept of health insurance is vague among the study population.

Appendix

See Tables 24.7, 24.8, 24.9 and 24.10.

Table 24.7 List of indicators used for ranking of the districts

Mortality indicators	Health coverage indicators	Risk factors	Demographic and socio-economic characteristics
1. Infant mortality rate	1. Provision of full antenatal care to pregnant women	1. Low Birth Weight of new born infants	1. Crude birth rate
2. Under five mortality rate	2. Post natal care to women within 48 h of delivery	2. Source of drinking water	2. Natural growth rate
	3. Contraceptive prevalence rate	3. Household access to toilet facility	3. Female literacy rate
	4. Full immunization of children of 12–23 months of age	4. Household access to electricity facility	4. Women with birth order 3 and above
	5. Financial assistance from Janani Suraksha Yojana for institutional delivery		
	6. Delivery at government health institutions		

Sources of information

Categorization of health indicators adapted from WHO (2011) *Global Health Indicators*

Ram and Shekhar (2006) for the methodology

Index value = $\frac{\text{Max}(X_{1d}) - X_{1d}}{\{\text{Max}(X_{1d}) - \text{Min}(X_{1d})\}}$

Composite index = $1/16 \sum_{i=1}^{16} X_{id}$

Government of India (2011a) and Government of India (2011b) for district level data

Table 24.8 Ranking of the districts based on composite index

District	Rank
Sibsagar	1
Nalbari	2
Jorhat	3
Lakhimpur	4
Dibrugarh	5
Kamrup	6
Tinsukia	7
Dhemaji	8
Golaghat	9
Marigoan	10
Barpeta	11
Darrang	12
Goalpara	13
Bongaigoan	14
Karbi-Anglong	15
Sonitpur	16
Dhubri	17
Kokrajhar	18
Karimganj	19
North Cachar Hills	20
Hailakandi	21
Nagaon	22
Cacher	23

Table 24.9 Percentage distribution of acute and chronic illnesses by source of treatment and household characteristics (%)

	Acute morbidity			Chronic morbidity		
Household characteristics	Government	Private	Others	Government	Private	Others
Age						
0–5	80	13	7	83	17	0
6–14	71	5	24	83	17	0
15–59	67	6	27	87	13	2
59 and above	71	14	14	100	0	0

(continued)

Table 24.9 (continued)

	Acute morbidity			Chronic morbidity		
Household characteristics	Government	Private	Others	Government	Private	Others
Educational level						
Illiterate	80	5	15	90	3	7
Below primary	70	15	10	90	10	0
Above primary	55	3	42	79	21	0
Above secondary	71	18	9	73	27	0
Caste						
Upper caste	79	11	11	75	25	0
SC	70	4	26	96	4	4
ST	72	8	30	87	13	0
Others	73	7	20	88	12	6
Religion						
Hindu	66	6	28	89	8	3
Muslim	88	4	8	83	17	0

Source Survey data, Bamunipathar, Nagaon, 2014

Table 24.10 Multicollinearity diagnostic for the independent variables influencing morbidity for the study village of Nagaon district of Assam

Variable	VIF	1/VIF (tolerance)
SEX	1.13	0.89
RL	1.46	0.69
CS1	1.29	0.77
CS2	1.43	0.70
LN_AGE	1.21	0.82
MOCC	1.24	0.81
EDU1	1.32	0.76
EDU2	1.35	0.74
HSS1	1.13	0.88
HSS2	1.28	0.78
LN_MI	1.25	0.80
OH	1.13	0.88
SOH2	1.29	0.78
SDW	1.18	0.85
ATF	1.22	0.82
RSBY	1.20	0.84
Mean VIF	1.26	

Note There are many acceptable values for VIF. In this paper the most commonly used VIF (10) has been used to detect the presence of multicollinearity among the variables

Source Calculation based on survey data

References

Barua, J. (2012). *On Identification of Backward Blocks*. Research Paper Series, 4, Omeo Kumar Institute of Social Change and Development (OKDISCD), Guwahati.

Belcher, D. W., Newman, A. K., Wurapa, F. K., & Lourie, I. M. (1976). Comparison of morbidity interviews with a health examination survey in Rural Africa. *American Journal of Tropical Medicine and Hygiene, 25*(5), 751–758.

Dilip, T. R. (2002). Understanding levels of morbidity and hospitalization in Kerala, India. *Bulletin of the World Health Organization, 80*(9), 746–751.

Duraisamy, P. (1998). Morbidity in Tamil Nadu-levels, differentials and determinants. *Economic and Political Weekly, 33*(17), 982–990.

Ghosh, S. (2009). *The utilization of Healthcare Services in India: Do Education and income Matter?* A paper presented in the conference of Indian Association for Social Sciences and Health.

Getler, P., & van der Gaag, Jaques. (1990). *The willingness to pay for medical care: Evidence from two developing countries*. Baltimore, MD: Johns Hopkins University Press.

Gosh, S., & Arokiasamy, P. (2009). Morbidity in India-trends, patterns and differentials. *Journal of Health Studies, 2,* 136–148.

Government of India. (2011a). *Annual Health Survey*, Office of the Registrar General and Census Commissioner of India, Ministry of Home Affairs, Vital Statistics Division, 2/A, Mansingh Road, New Delhi. Available at censusindia.gov.in.

Government of India. (2011b). *Census of India*, Office of the Register General and Census Commissioner, Ministry of Home Affairs.

Gujarati, D. N. (1998). *Basic econometrics*. Singapore: McGraw-Hill Inc.

Gumber, A., & Berman, P. (1997). Measurement and pattern of morbidity and the utilization of health services: Some emerging issues from recent health interview surveys in India. *Journal of Health and Population in Developing Countries, 1*(1), 16–43.

Krishnaswami, P. (2004). *Morbidity study-incidence, prevalence, consequences and associates*. Discussion Paper No. 63, Kerala Research Programme on Local Level Development, Centre for Development Studies. Available at http://www.cds.ac.in/krpcds/publication/downloads/63.pdf.

Maddala, G. S. (2007). *Introduction to econometrics*. Singapore: Willy India.

Mukherjee, S., & Levesque, J. F. (2012). Morbidity and outpatient care for the elderly in Kerala, South India: Evidence from a National Population based Survey. *Population Ageing, 5,* 177–192.

National Council of Applied Economic Research (NCAER). (1995). *Household Survey of Health Care Utilization and Expenditure*, New Delhi.

National Sample Survey Organization (NSSO). (1998). *Morbidity and Treatment of Ailments*, Ministry of Statistics and Programme Implementation, New Delhi, Government of India. 52nd Round, July 1995–June 1996.

National Sample Survey Organization (NSSO). (2004). *Morbidity Health Care and Condition of the Aged*, Ministry of Statistics and Programme Implementation, New Delhi, Government of India. Report No 507(60/25/0/1), 60th Round.

Navaneetham, K., Kabir, M., & Krishnakumar, C. S. (2009). *Morbidity Patterns in Kerala: Levels and Determinants*. Working Paper series, 411, International Institute of Population Sciences. Available at SSRN: http://ssrn.com/abstract=1629544.

Peter, D. H., Sujatha, K. R., & Fryatt, R. (2003). Lumping and splitting: The health policy agenda in India. *Health Policy Plan, 18*(3), 249–260.

Ram, F., & Shekhar, C. (2006). Ranking and mapping of districts based on socio-economic and demographic indicators. *International Institute of Population Sciences*, Ministry of Health and Family Welfare, Government of India. Available at http://www.iipsindia.org/publications05_b_13a.htm.

Sekhar, P. S. (1997). Levels of morbidity in Andhra Pradesh. *Economic and Political Weekly, 32* (13), 17–21.

Sundar, R., & Sharma, A. (2002). Morbidity and utilization of health care services—A survey of urban poor in Delhi and Chennai. *Economic and Political Weekly, 37*(47), 4729–4740.
Sundararaman, T., & Muraleedharan, V. R. (2015). Falling sick, paying price, NSS 71st round on morbidity and costs of healthcare. *Economic and Political Weekly, 12*(33), 17–20.
Vadiyanathan, A. (1995). *An assessment of nutritional and health status*. Discussion Paper No. 3, UNDP Research Project, CDS. Available at http://203.200.22.249:8080/jspui/bitstream/2014/8539/1/ISEC%3DRR-GD15064.pdf.

Chapter 25
Morbidity Pattern of Elderly in India

Poulomi Chowdhury, Mausam Kumar Garg and Laishram Ladusingh

25.1 Introduction

Epidemiological transition goes hand in hand, as the country undergoes the process of modernization from developing to developed nation status. Presently India is facing double burden of diseases—the burden of communicable diseases as well as non-communicable diseases. It has been recognized that as the societies modernize, they experience significant changes in their pattern of health and disease. The World Health Organization (WHO) reports NCDs to be by far the leading cause of death in the world, representing over 60% of all deaths. Out of the 36 million people who died from NCDs in 2005, half were under age 70 and half were women. Of the 57 million global deaths in 2008, 36 million were due to NCDs which is approximately 63% of total deaths worldwide. Risk factors such as a person's age, sex, residence, lifestyle and environment are known to increase the likelihood of certain NCDs. According to GBD Report (2004), the burden of non-communicable disease now accounts for nearly half of the global burden of disease. Population ageing and changes in the distribution of risk factors have accelerated the non-communicable disease share of the total disease burden in many developing countries. Global cancer deaths are projected to increase from 7.4 million in 2004

P. Chowdhury (✉) · M.K. Garg
International Institute for Population Sciences, Mumbai, India
e-mail: poulomi378@gmail.com

M.K. Garg
e-mail: mausamkumar39@gmail.com

L. Ladusingh
Department of Mathematical Demography and Statistics,
International Institute for Population Sciences, Mumbai, India
e-mail: lslaishram@iips.net

U.K. De et al. (eds.), *Issues on Health and Healthcare in India*, India Studies in Business and Economics, https://doi.org/10.1007/978-981-10-6104-2_25

to 11.8 million in 2030, and global cardiovascular deaths from 17.1 million in 2004 to 23.4 million in 2030. Overall, non-communicable conditions are projected to account for just over three quarters of all deaths in 2030.

Historically, many NCDs were associated with economic development and were so-called a ‘diseases of the rich’. The burden of non-communicable diseases in developing countries has increased however, with an estimated 80% of the four main types of NCDs—cardiovascular diseases, cancers, chronic respiratory diseases and diabetes—now occurring in low and middle-income countries. If present growth trends are maintained, by 2020, NCDs will attribute to seven out of every 10 deaths in developing countries, killing 52 million people annually worldwide by 2030. In recent decades, a growing volume of literature has documented that India is also facing a rapid pace of health-epidemiological transition with a swift increase in the prevalence of chronic illness. In developed and developing countries women’s biological, psychological and social development across life span is compromised by cultural, political and economic factors. The remarkable thing about older women in our culture is that they still survive against all odds against them. Long experience of discrimination, deprivation and neglect reflects in their last years. There is no retirement for an elderly woman until either death or dementia or disability occurs. Poverty, malnutrition, poor healthcare and depression are also the major problems faced by elderly women. The growing proportion and size of older women thus poses critical challenges to tackle multiple problems of their health and well-being in India (Gulati and Rajan 1999; Ghosh and Arokiasamy 2010). Women are at greater risk of suffering with poorer health conditions than men, in terms of self-rated health, functional status, physical functioning and greater immobility (Dhak 2009; Pandey et al. 2002; Park et al. 2010). According to the study of Murray and Chen (1992), a larger proportion of deaths will result from the chronic diseases of old age, such as, cardiovascular diseases and neoplasms. Stein et al. (1996) found that prevalence of coronary heart disease is positively correlated with age. Dilip (2002) mentioned that the prevalence rate for chronic ailments is higher among older adults than that of prevalence rate for acute ailments. Agarwal and Keshri (2014), pattern of morbidity indicate that older women were reporting significantly greater prevalence of major chronic diseases such as diabetes, heart diseases, diarrhea, mental illnesses, hypertension and other non-communicable diseases. Pattern of morbidity seen within the country are rather complicated, because they include a mixture of diseases of poverty and diseases of affluence (Panikar and Soman 1984). This can create greater burden of morbidity in the country simply because it is difficult to monitor. As a result, it can be attributed to the real burden of morbidity within the population of the country concerned. The strategies taken by the Government had demonstrably improved health, yet the double burden of communicable and non-communicable diseases will continue to be a global health challenge if it accounts negative change in its pattern, which may led to drastic increase in hospitalization rate and health expenditure for the future decades.

25.2 Need for the Study

Morbidity represents illness-any departure from normal well-being (Weeks 2004). According to Ingle and Nath (2008), the elderly people in India suffer from dual health problems, i.e. both communicable as well as non-communicable diseases. From a study by Reddy (1996), it was found that the aged population had not only risen but also 10% out of them suffer from impaired physical mobility and it is rising with increasing age and more than 50% of the 70+ aged population suffer from one or more chronic conditions. In India, the aged population accounts around 8% out of the total population which might increase in the future, this may led to changes in the disease pattern and more over in India due to high longevity female constitute higher proportion among elderly population. Most of these female are less educated and economically dependent to support themselves in later part of their life. Thus, it becomes important to study how trend and pattern of chronic morbidity among elderly changing over time, along with the change in trend of gender gap in the prevalence of morbidity.

In view of the previously mentioned, it is important to study the change in pattern of chronic diseases among the elderly. It can not only enrich literature in understanding the burden of NCD among the elderly but also will be instrumental in monitoring and strengthening public health programs to meet the impending escalation in NCD among the most vulnerable segment of the population.

25.3 Data Sources

For the propose objective of this study, data from the following sources were utilized.

1. **NSSO 60th round (2004)**: The National Sample Survey Organization (NSSO) was set up in 1950 as a permanent survey organization to collect data on various facets of the Indian economy through nation-wide sample surveys in order to assist in socio-economic planning and policy-making. In the Sixtieth round of NSS, data was collected through a survey on the subject of 'Morbidity and Healthcare'. The following main aspects were covered:

    I. Morbidity and utilization of healthcare services including immunization and maternity care,
    II. Problems of aged persons, and
    III. Expenditure of the households for availing the healthcare services.
    (Note: The total number of sample for 60+ population =34,831)

2. **SAGE (2007)**: Study on Global Ageing and Adult Health (SAGE) India, 2006 is being initiated by the World Health Organization as a part of multi-country in six of the seventy countries that participated in the World Health survey, 2003. The goals of SAGE are to promote a better understanding of the effects of

ageing on well-being, to examine the health status of individuals aged 50+ years and changes, trends and patterns that occur over time, and to improve the capacity of researchers to analyze the effects of social, economic, healthcare and policy changes on current and future health.
(Note: The total number of sample for 60+ population =3971)

3. **LASI** (2011): Although adult health and ageing is a subject that is increasingly being investigated, there are currently no comprehensive and internationally comparable survey data in India that cover and connect the full range of topics necessary to understand the economic, social, psychological, and health aspects of adults and the ageing process. Longitudinal Ageing Study in India (LASI) is designed to fill this gap. LASI focuses on the health, economic, and social well-being of India's elderly population.
(Note: The total number of sample for 60+ population =614)

25.4 Methodology

Based on the International Classification of Diseases (ICD), the diseases were classified into three categories:

1. **Communicable Diseases**: An illness caused by an infectious agent or its toxins that occurs through the direct or indirect transmission of the infectious agent or its products from an infected individual or via an animal, vector or the inanimate environment to a susceptible animal or human host.
2. **Non-communicable Diseases**: Is a medical condition or disease that is by definition non-infectious and non-transmissible among people.
3. **Other Diseases and Disabilities**: Other diseases refer to other diagnosed diseases and disability refers to the consequence of an impairment that may be physical, cognitive, mental, sensory, emotional, developmental, or some combination of these. A disability may be present from birth, or occur during a person's lifetime.

The following table shows the several type of diseases whose information is collected in NSSO, SAGE, LASI and which was included in Communicable, Non-Communicable and Other Diseases and Disabilities using International Classification of Diseases (ICD—10) (Table 25.1).

The prevalence rate of the diseases among elderly was calculated by the following formula:

$$\text{Morbidity} = \frac{\text{Number of elderly person affected by the disease} * 1000}{\text{Total elderly population}}$$

Table 25.1 Disease classification by different data sources

Disease	NSSO 60th round	WHO-SAGE	LASI
Non-communicable	Cardiovascular diseases	Hypertension	Hypertension
	Bronchial Asthma	Diabetes	Diabetes
	Diseases of Kidney/Urinary system	Chronic lung disease	Chronic lung disease
	Neurological disorders	Angina	Heart problem
	Diabetes mellitus	Arthritis	Arthritis
	Accidents/Injuries/Burns/Fractures/Poisoning	Asthma	Other NCDs
	Other NCDs	Other NCDs	
Communicable	Gastro-intestinal diseases	NA	Jaundice
	Febrile illnesses	NA	Tuberculosis
	Tuberculosis	NA	Malaria
	Other CDs	NA	
Other diseases and disabilities	Locomotor	Cataracts	Eyesight (including blind)
	Visual including blindness (excluding cataract)	Oral health	Oral health
	Speech	Disability	Hearing
	Hearing		
	Diseases of Mouth/Teeth/Gum		
	Other diagnosed ailments		

The above calculation of prevalence rate was based on the no. of days prior to the survey like in NSSO it was 15 days while in SAGE, it was for last 12 months and for LASI it was last days 30 prior to the survey.

Then this prevalence was used to apply decomposition method (Sharma et al. 2010) for gender gap and this analysis was focused on following three factors:

1. Calculation of Gender gaps for NSSO 60th round, SAGE and LASI.
2. Calculation of difference in the gender gaps for NSSO & SAGE, SAGE & LASI and NSSO and LASI.
3. Testing the significance of the differences in gender gaps.

These are explained as follows:

The gender gap in the prevalence of morbidity was calculated as the difference in the prevalence of morbidity among males and females.

The parameter of interest was:

$$\begin{aligned}\text{Delta}(\Delta) &= \text{Difference in gender gaps in two surveys}\\ &= (\text{Gender Gap})_{\text{Data 1}} - (\text{Gender Gap})_{\text{Data 2}}\\ &= \ (\text{Prevalence of morbidity among Males}\\ &\quad - \text{Prevalence of morbidity among Females})_{\text{Data 1}}\\ &\quad - (\text{Prevalence of morbidity among Males}\\ &\quad - \text{Prevalence of morbidity among Females})_{\text{Data 2}}\end{aligned}$$

Calculation of Standard error of Delta:

Let

P_{M} Prevalence of morbidity among Males
P_{F} Prevalence of morbidity among Females

Then;

$$\begin{aligned}\text{Delta}(\Delta) &= (P_{\mathrm{M}} - P_{\mathrm{F}})_{\text{Data 1}} - (P_{\mathrm{M}} - P_{\mathrm{F}})_{\text{Data 2}}\\ \text{Var}(\Delta) &= \text{Var}\left[(P_{\mathrm{M}} - P_{\mathrm{F}})_{\text{Data 1}} - (P_{\mathrm{M}} - P_{\mathrm{F}})_{\text{Data 2}}\right]\\ &= \text{Var}(P_{\mathrm{M}} - P_{\mathrm{F}})_{\text{Data 1}} - \text{Var}(P_{\mathrm{M}} - P_{\mathrm{F}})_{\text{Data 2}}\\ &= \text{Var}(P_{\mathrm{M}})_{\text{Data 1}} + \text{Var}(P_{\mathrm{F}})_{\text{Data 1}} + \text{Var}(P_{\mathrm{M}})_{\text{Data 2}} + \text{Var}(P_{\mathrm{M}})_{\text{Data 2}}\\ &= \frac{(P_{\mathrm{M}})_{\text{Data 1}}(Q_{\mathrm{M}})_{\text{Data 1}}}{n_{\mathrm{M\ Data\ 1}}} + \frac{(P_{\mathrm{F}})_{\text{Data 1}}(Q_{\mathrm{F}})_{\text{Data 1}}}{n_{\mathrm{F\ Data\ 1}}}\\ &\quad + \frac{(P_{\mathrm{M}})_{\text{Data 2}}(Q_{\mathrm{M}})_{\text{Data 2}}}{n_{\mathrm{M\ Data\ 2}}} + \frac{(P_{\mathrm{F}})_{\text{Data 2}}(Q_{\mathrm{F}})_{\text{Data 2}}}{n_{\mathrm{F\ Data\ 2}}}\end{aligned}$$

$$\text{SE}(\Delta) = \text{SQRT}[\text{Var}(\Delta)]$$

Test of significance for delta (Δ) was done by Z-score as follows:

$$Z = ((\Delta)/\text{SE}(\Delta))$$

The analysis has been carried out by using software like SPSS and MS-Office.

25.5 Result and Discussion

25.5.1 Prevalence Rate of Morbidity Among Elderly Population

The morbidity scenario in India has been estimated by calculating the prevalence rate of the diseases. The prevalence of chronic morbidity among older adults within different time periods is being presented in Table 25.2 by the help of common demographic characteristics from each data source. This provides a foundation for comprehensive understanding of the current chronic morbidity trend and pattern of older adults in India.

25.5.2 Status of Morbidity in 2004

It has been observed that in 2004 (NSSO), the prevalence rate among elderly accounted for 558 per 1000 for NCDs, followed by 173 per 1000 for CDs and 194 per 1000 for other diseases and disabilities not included under NCDs and CDs. Among males the prevalence rate accounted for NCDs is 560 per 1000 whereas among females it was 557 per 1000, followed by 170 per 1000 among males and 178 per 1000 among females for CDs and 190 per 1000, 201 per 1000, respectively, among males and females for other diseases and disabilities. The rates of CDs and other diseases and disabilities were higher among females but the burden of NCDs was higher among males in 2004. The older adults in old-old age cohort (70–79 years) suffer more from CDs, i.e. 158 per 1000, while the corresponding figures for young old (60–69 years) and older old age cohort (80 and above) were 155 per 1000 and 17 per 1000, respectively. Similarly, the prevalence rate for NCDs was higher among old-old age cohort, i.e. 652 per 1000 whereas for young old and older old age cohort it is 438 per 1000 and 57 per 1000, respectively. Again, the old-old age cohort accounted higher for other diseases and disabilities, i.e. 212 per 1000, followed by 151 per 1000 and 25 per 1000 among young old and older old age cohort. The burden of diseases was found to be higher among old-old age cohort than that of other two cohorts. The rate of illness in rural India were higher for CDs and other diseases and disabilities, i.e. 210 per 1000 and 218 per 1000, respectively, while the corresponding figures were 83 per 1000 and 137 per 1000 for the urban sector. The rate of prevalence was higher for NCDs in urban sector, i.e. 709 per 1000,

Table 25.2 Prevalence rate of morbidity among elderly population in India

Demographic factors	NSSO (2004)			WHO-SAGE (2006)		LASI (2011)		
	Communicable diseases	Non-communicable diseases	Other diseases and disabilities	Non-communicable diseases	Other diseases & disabilities	Communicable diseases	Non-communicable diseases	Other diseases & disabilities
Sex								
Male	170	560	190	424	326	37	399	452
Female	178	557	201	403	391	51	483	483
Age groups								
60–69 years	155	438	151	396	287	29	407	427
70–79 years	158	652	212	460	468	61	492	497
80 and above	17	57	25	369	457	70	465	577
Sector								
Urban	83	709	137	481	369	38	500	576
Rural	210	494	218	385	355	46	419	430
Total	173	558	194	413	359	44	440	467

Source NSSO 60th round, WHO-SAGE and LASI

Note Rates are in per thousand. In case of NSSO.60th round West Bengal, Assam, Karnataka, Kerala, Punjab, Maharashtra, Uttar Pradesh and Rajasthan were included

followed by 494 per 1000 in rural sector. The rates of NCDs were higher for urban sector in 2004.

25.5.3 Status of Morbidity in 2007

The pattern of chronic morbidity prevalence shows a marginal decline for NCDs and a significant increase for other diseases and disabilities in accordance with SAGE data 2007. The rate of prevalence has been decreased by 0.74 times for NCDs, i.e. from 558 to 413 per 1000 and a negative change has also taken place in case of other diseases and disabilities, it has been increased by 1.85 times, i.e. from 194 to 359 per 1000. In case of both the male and female the changes have taken place positively for NCDs, i.e. from 560 to 424 per 1000 and 557 to 403 per 1000, respectively. Noteworthy difference was that the rates for NCDs were still higher among males in 2007. The prevalence of other diseases and disabilities among older adults, i.e. male and female have also increased negatively from 190 to 326per 1000 and 201 to 391 per 1000. The rates for other diseases and disabilities shown a contrasting picture, it was found to be higher among females. The older adults in old-old age cohort had the higher rate of prevalence for NCDs than young old and older old age cohort. The prevalence for NCDs has positively changed among young old and old-old age cohort, i.e. from 438 to 396 per 1000 and 652 to 460 per 1000, respectively, in 2007. However, the calculated figures for older old age cohort showed a negative change in 2007, i.e. from 57 to 369 per 1000. The old-old age cohort suffers more from other diseases and disabilities than young old and older old age cohorts and has shown negative increase in their rates, i.e. from 212 to 468 per 1000, 151 to 287 per 1000 and 25 to 457 per 1000, respectively. The rate of illness for NCDs is higher in urban sector but has shown positive decrease in its rate, i.e. from 709 to 481 per 1000, same picture was seen in the rural sector also it has positively declined, i.e. from 494 per 1000 it has reduced up to 385 per 1000, respectively. The rates for other diseases and disabilities have negatively increased for rural as well as urban sector, i.e. from 218 to 355 per 1000 and 137 to 369 per 1000. The prevalence for NCDs and other diseases and disabilities were higher in urban sector than that of rural sector in 2007.

25.5.4 Status of Morbidity in 2010

However this pattern suffers many exceptions. The 2010 LASI data assessed the present chronic morbidity pattern of elderly persons and shown a negative increase in its rates. The rate of prevalence has been increased by 1.06 times for NCDs, i.e. from 413 to 440 per 1000, followed by CDs which has also been decreased by 0.25 times, i.e. from 173 to 44 per 1000 and in case of other diseases and disabilities again a negative increase has been observed, it has risen by 1.30 times, i.e. from

359 to 467 per 1000, respectively. Among males the prevalence rate accounted for NCDs has shown a positive decrease from 424 to 399 per 1000, whereas for females the negative increase has been observed, i.e. from 403 to 483 per 1000. The prevalence for NCDs was found to be higher among females than that of males in 2010. The rate of illness for CDs among males and females were 170 per 1000 and 178 per 1000 which has been decreased from 37 per 1000 and 51 per 1000, respectively, in 2010. In case of both male and female the negative changes have been observed, the rate increases for other diseases and disabilities from 326 to 452 per 1000 and 391 to 483 per 1000, respectively. The estimated figures showed a higher prevalence among females than that of males in 2010. The NCDs were found to be high in the old-old age cohort, i.e. 492 per 1000, followed by young old and older old age cohorts which were 407 per 1000 and 465 per 1000, respectively, in 2010. The prevalence of NCDs follows an increasing trend and pattern among the old age cohorts in 2010, the calculated figures had increased from 396 to 407 per 1000, 460 to 492 per 1000 and 369 to 465 per 1000. The burden of CDs among young old, old-old and older old age cohort came to be 29 per 1000, 61 per 1000 and 70 per 1000 compared 155 per 1000, 158 per 1000 and 17 per 1000 in 2004. The rates of CDs were found to be higher among older old age cohort in 2010. The prevalence of other diseases and disabilities was higher for older old age cohort being 577 per 1000 against 427 per 1000 and 497 per 1000 among young old and old-old age cohort. It has shown a sharp increase in its trend and pattern against 287 per 1000 (60–69 years), 468 per 1000 (70–79 years) and 457 per 1000 (80+ and above) among old age cohorts in 2007. It possessed rather a negative increase in 2010. The prevalence of NCDs was higher for urban sector being 500 per 1000 against 419 per 1000 in rural sector. It was found to be less prevalent in 2007 which was 481 per 1000 for urban sector and 385 per 1000 for rural sector. CDs are more prevalent in rural sector, i.e. 46 per 1000 compared 38 per 1000 in urban sector. It has been seen to reduce in 2010 against 210 per 1000 for rural sector and 83 per 1000 for urban sector in 2004. The prevalence of other diseases and disabilities was marginally higher for urban sector being 576 per 1000 against 430 per 1000 for rural sector. The rates were subsequently less for both urban and rural sector (369 per 1000 and 355 per 1000) in 2007 against the calculated figures of 2010.

The Result of Z-test (Decomposition Method):

The results of Z-test have been noted down in Tables 25.3, 25.4 and 25.5. The main results are listed below.

25.5.5 Communicable Diseases

In both the surveys LASI-NSSO, the prevalence of communicable diseases among females is found to be higher than the males. The gender gap being eight per 1000 in NSSO has increased to 14 per 1000 in LASI, the difference being statistically insignificant ($Z = 0.33$, $p > 0.10$).

Table 25.3 Overall difference in gender gap in NSSO-SAGE

	Prevalence (NSSO 60th)	Prevalence (SAGE)	Δ	*Z*-Test
Communicable				
Male	0.170	NA		
Female	0.178	NA		
Non-Communicable				
Male	0.560	0.424	0.065	181.62***
Female	0.557	0.403		
Other diseases and disabilities				
Male	0.190	0.325	0.057	192.27***
Female	0.201	0.391		

Table 25.4 Overall difference in gender gap in NSSO and LASI

	Prevalence (NSSO 60th)	Prevalence (LASI)	Δ	*Z*-Test
Communicable				
Male	0.170	0.037	0.0056	0.33
Female	0.178	0.051		
Non-communicable				
Male	0.560	0.399	0.085	2.11*
Female	0.557	0.483		
Other diseases and disabilities				
Male	0.190	0.452	0.020	0.49
Female	0.201	0.483		

Table 25.5 Overall difference in gender gap in SAGE and LASI

	Prevalence (SAGE)	Prevalence (LASI)	Δ	*Z*-Test
Communicable				
Male	NA	0.037		
Female	NA	0.051		
Non-communicable				
Male	0.424	0.399	0.152	3.76***
Female	0.403	0.483		
Other diseases and disabilities				
Male	0.190	0.452	0.0372	0.91
Female	0.201	0.483		

Note ***($p < 0.001$), **($p < 0.05$), *($p < 0.10$)

25.5.6 Non-communicable Diseases

In both the surveys SAGE-NSSO, the prevalence of non-communicable diseases among males is found to be higher than the females. The gender gap being three per

1000 in NSSO has increased to 21 per 1000 in SAGE, the difference being statistically significant (Z = 181.62, $p < 0.001$).

Similarly, in both the surveys LASI-NSSO, the prevalence of non-communicable diseases among females is found to be higher than the males. The gender gap being three per 1000 in NSSO has increased to 84 per 1000 in LASI, the difference being statistically significant (Z = 2.11, p < 0.0.10).

Again, in both the surveys LASI-SAGE, the prevalence of non-communicable diseases among females is found to be higher than the males. The gender gap being 21 per 1000 in SAGE has increased to 84 per 1000 in LASI, the difference being statistically significant (Z = 3.76, $p < 0.001$).

25.5.7 *Other Diseases and Disabilities*

In both the surveys SAGE-NSSO, the prevalence of other diseases and disabilities among females is found to be higher than the males. The gender gap being 11 per 1000 in NSSO has increased to 65 per 1000 in SAGE, the difference being statistically significant (Z = 192.27, $p < 0.001$).

Similarly, in both the surveys LASI-NSSO, the prevalence of other diseases and disabilities among females is found to be higher than the males. The gender gap being 11 per 1000 in NSSO has increased to 31 per 1000 in LASI, the difference being statistically insignificant (Z = 0.49, $p > 0.10$).

Again, in both the surveys LASI-SAGE, the prevalence of other diseases and disabilities among females is found to be higher than the males. The gender gap being 65 per 1000 in SAGE has decreased to 31 per 1000 in LASI, the difference being statistically insignificant (Z = 0.91, $p > 0.10$).

25.6 Summary Findings and Conclusion

This study has illustrated the complex task of determining the trend and pattern of morbidity among elderly population in India. However the pattern suffers many exceptions. There is a tendency to conclude that the trend and pattern for non-communicable diseases as well as other diseases and disabilities is been increasing whereas for communicable diseases it is being decreasing. The prevalence rate for chronic ailments is higher among older adults than that of prevalence rate for acute ailments (Dilip 2002). The non-communicable diseases are found to be more prevalent among old-old age cohort whereas among older old age cohort the prevalence is found to be more for communicable diseases and other diseases and disabilities. The chronic morbidities are more prone with an increasing age among elderly (Lubitz et al. 2001).

The present study also examines the increasing trend in gender gaps over three different time periods. Although overall prevalence of communicable diseases

(CDs) has remained the same in two survey periods (LASI, NSSO), the gender gap in the prevalence of CDs has widened. Particularly, the prevalence of CDs among females has shown a significant decline. Studying the delta (Δ) in the gender gap, it is noted that the increase in gender gap is more for non-communicable diseases. The prevalence of non-communicable diseases (NCDs) has not remained the same in two survey periods (SAGE, NSSO), the gender gap in the prevalence of NCDs has widened. Particularly, the prevalence of NCDs among females has shown a significant decline. Similarly, the prevalence of NCDs has not remained the same in two survey periods (LASI, NSSO), the gender gap in the prevalence of NCDs has widened because of the significant decline in the prevalence of NCDs among females. Again, the prevalence of NCDs has not remained the same in two survey periods (LASI, SAGE), the gender gap in the prevalence of NCDs has widened because of the significant increase in the prevalence of NCDs among females. Lastly, the prevalence of other diseases and disabilities has not remained the same in two survey periods (SAGE, NSSO), the gender gap in the prevalence of other diseases and disabilities has widened. Particularly, the prevalence of other diseases and disabilities among females has shown a significant increase. Then, the prevalence of other diseases and disabilities has remained the same in two survey periods (LASI, NSSO), the gender gap in the prevalence of other diseases and disabilities has widened. The prevalence of other diseases and disabilities among females has shown a significant increase. Again, in case of two survey periods (LASI, SAGE), the gender gap in the prevalence of other diseases and disabilities has narrowed. Particularly, the prevalence of other diseases and disabilities among females has shown a significant increase. From the above results and discussion we may say that the prevalence of chronic morbidities is found to be significantly increasing among females. This is in context to health inequality by sex in India due to discriminatory practices in healthcare.

The medical facilities should be more female oriented because in India female constitute higher proportion among elderly population out of which most of them are widowed and neglected. This has led to increase in prevalence among them compared to males. Overall, the scenario shows an increasing pattern of chronic morbidities within different time periods which may generate health problems among older adults (Swami et al. 2002). To reduce the loss of healthy life, the Govt. should initiate appropriate intervention strategies and fix priorities for planning healthcare services against the elderly.

Appendix

See Tables 25.2, 25.3, 25.4 and 25.5.

References

Agrawal, G., & Keshri, K. (2014). Morbidity patterns and health care seeking behavior among older widows in India. *PloS one, 9*(4), e94295.

Dhak, B. (2009). Gender difference in health and its determinants in the old-aged population in India. *Journal of Biosocial Science, 41*(5), 625.

Dilip, T. R. (2002). Understanding levels of morbidity and hospitalization in Kerala, India. *Bulletin of the World Health Organization, 80*(9), 746–751.

Ghosh, S., & Arokiasamy, P. (2010). Emerging patterns of reported morbidity and hospitalisation in West Bengal, India. *Global public health, 5*(4), 427–440.

Gulati, L., & Rajan, S. I. (1999). The added years: Elderly in India and Kerala. *Economic and political weekly,* WS46-WS51.

Ingle, G. K., & Nath, A. (2008). Geriatric health in India: Concerns and solutions. *Indian Journal of Community Medicine: Official Publication of Indian Association of Preventive & Social Medicine, 33*(4), 214.

Lubitz, J., Greenberg, L. G., Gorina, Y., Wartzman, L., & Gibson, D. (2001). Three decades of health care use by the elderly, 1965–1998. *Health Affairs, 20*(2), 19–32.

Longitudinal Aging Study in India. (2011). Pilot Wave. Harvard School of Public Health, International Institute of Population Sciences, Mumbai, India, and RAND Corporation. Available: https://mmicdata.rand.org/megametadata/?section=study&studyid=36.

Murray, C. J., & Chen, L. C. (1992). Understanding morbidity change. *The Population and Development Review, 18*(3), 481–503.

National Sample Survey Organisation. (2004). *Morbidity, healthcare and the condition of the aged.* Report no. 507, Department of Statistics, Government of India, New Delhi.

Online statistics for the Global Burden of Disease [Update 2004. Database on the Internet]. World Health Organization, 2008. Available from: http://www.who.int/healthinfo/global_burden_disease/2004_report_update/en/index.html. Accessed on June 29, 2009.

Pandey, A., Sengupta, P. G., Mondal, S. K., Gupta, D. N., Manna, B., Ghosh, S., ... & Bhattacharya, S. K. (2002). Gender differences in healthcare-seeking during common illnesses in a rural community of West Bengal, India. *Journal of Health, Population and Nutrition,* 306–311.

Panikar, P. G. K., & Soman, C. R. (1984). Health Status of Kerala: the paradox of economic backwardness and health development. *In Health Status of Kerala: the paradox of economic backwardness and health development.* Centre for Development Studies.

Park, S. M., Jang, S. N., & Kim, D. H. (2010). Gender differences as factors in successful ageing: a focus on socioeconomic status. *Journal of biosocial science, 42*(1), 99–111.

Reddy, P. H. (1996). The health of the aged in India. *Health Transition Review, 6*(3), 233–244.

Sharma, P. P., Kumar, A., & Singh, P. (2010). A study of gender differentials in the prevalence of tuberculosis based on NFHS-2 and NFHS-3 data. *Indian journal of community medicine: official publication of Indian Association of Preventive & Social Medicine, 35*(2), 230.

Swami, H. M., Bhatia, V., Dutt, R., & Bhatia, S. P. S. (2002). A community based study of the morbidity profile among the elderly in Chandigarh, India. *Bahrain Medical Bulletin, 24*(1), 16–20.

Stein, C. E., Fall, C. H. D., Kumaran, K., Osmond, C., Barker, D. J. P., & Cox, V. (1996). Fetal growth and coronary heart disease in South India. *The Lancet, 348*(9037), 1269–1273.

Weeks, J. R. (2004). Morbidity. *In Encyclopedia of Women's Health* (pp. 847–849). US: Springer.

World Health Organization. (2006). *WHO SAGE Survey Manual: The WHO Study on Global AGEing and Adult Health (SAGE).* Geneva, World Health Organization.

Chapter 26
Association of Nutritional Status and Drinking Water Among the Children of North East India

Madhuparna Srivastava, Papiya Roy, Susmita Bharati, Manoranjan Pal and Premananda Bharati

26.1 Introduction

Poverty and hunger has been a curse to humanity since ages. Thus, elimination of poverty and hunger is not only a humanitarian issue but also more of a human rights issue. Perhaps so 'eradication of extreme poverty and hunger' finds foremost priority as the first goal among the eight Millennium Development Goals. However, for the purpose of the present study we concentrate mainly on target 1.C (of the first goal), i.e. 'to halve, between 1990 and 2015 the proportion of people who suffer from hunger'.[1]

Now the term hunger can be seen in different ways, as Dreze and Sen (1989) points out that while in its narrow sense hunger implies to the 'discomfort or painful sensation caused by want of food', in its broader sense it implies towards 'food

[1]The Millennium Declaration, made during the UN Millennium Summit on September 2000, was signed by 189 countries and included eight goals called the Millennium Development Goals (MDGs). Targets were set as quantitative benchmarks for attaining the MDGs. The United Nations Development Group (UNDG) provided a framework of indicators which are categorized according to targets, for measuring the progress towards individual targets. While MDG goals are general in nature, the targets under MDGs are more specific and the indicator(s) for measuring the progress of these targets are defined in concrete terms.

M. Srivastava · M. Pal (✉)
Economic Research Unit, Indian Statistical Institute, 203, B.T. Road, Kolkata 700108, India
e-mail: manoranjan.pal@gmail.com

P. Roy · P. Bharati
Biological Anthropology Unit, Indian Statistical Institute, 203, B.T. Road, Kolkata 700108, India
e-mail: pbharati@gmail.com

S. Bharati
Sociological Research Unit, Indian Statistical Institute, 203, B.T. Road, Kolkata 700108, India

U.K. De et al. (eds.), *Issues on Health and Healthcare in India*, India Studies in Business and Economics, https://doi.org/10.1007/978-981-10-6104-2_26

deprivation in general—seen in terms of its manifold consequences which includes undernourishment, debilitation, fatigue, morbidity and possibly mortality with obvious effects on human well-being and productivity'.

Undoubtedly, to combat hunger in both its narrow and the broader sense food security is of utmost importance. The definition of food security[2] identifies four main dimensions, i.e. food availability, food access, utilization and stability (Burchi and Muro 2012) and embraces hunger in both its sense.

However, even with these concentrated efforts, the worldwide scenario has not been pleasant. While hunger continued to decline, progress in reducing undernutrition has been uneven across regions and countries (The Millennium Development Goals Report 2014).

Similar was the situation at the national front where India ranked 63rd in the Global Hunger Index 2013 and was home to the largest number of undernourished people in the world: 217 million as of 2012 (The State of Food Insecurity in the World 2012).

Although India is said to have achieved self-sufficiency and has surplus food production it is still facing food insecurity problem at micro level (household) and the nutritional status of its citizens is also grave. Now in the context where food availability and access (Geneva Office of the United Nations High Commissioner for Human Rights 1999) is said to have been primarily achieved, the prevalence of undernutrition indicates towards the nutritional or utilization dimension of food security. The utilization dimension of food security includes adequate diet, clean water, sanitation and healthcare to reach a state of nutritional well-being where all physiological needs are met. This brings out the importance of non-food inputs in food security. For the purpose of this chapter we have focused on only one such input, i.e. drinking water keeping in mind that safe drinking water is an essential requisition for well-being of an individual and also that water-borne diseases are claiming lives of about millions around the world (Ramachandraiah 2004).

26.2 Materials and Methods

The prevalence of underweight and stunted children, under-five years of age is considered as an indicator to measure undernutrition situation (The Millennium Development Goals Report 2014). Thus, information on the nutritional status of children is assessed, through the data of the latest round of National Family Health Survey-III (2005–2006). The survey was conducted by the International Institute for Population Sciences (IIPS) designated as the nodal agency for the survey by the Ministry of Health and Family Welfare, Government of India.

[2]General Comment 12: Right to Adequate Food, states that 'the right to adequate food is realized when every man, woman and child, alone or in community with others, has physical and economic access at all times to adequate food or means for its procurement'.

All the sampled children of age 0–59 months of the states of North East India namely, Arunachal Pradesh, Assam, Manipur, Meghalaya, Mizoram, Nagaland, Sikkim and Tripura is taken for the analysis. The sample size is 43,737.

For assessing the nutritional status of children, the height, weight and age data are taken to compute the health parameters, namely Weight-for-age (underweight) and Height-for-age (stunted). The standard reference levels of weight and height for each age have been taken as prescribed by WHO. Then '*z*' scores of the health parameters have been computed. '*z*' score is defined as the deviation of the value observed for an individual from the median of the reference population, divided by the standard deviation of the reference population. '*z*' score value '−2' is used as a cut-off point for the estimation of prevalence of undernutrition, based on the classification of '*z*' score (followed by NCHS/WHO) which is as follows: 'below normal' (<-2), 'normal' (-2 to $<+2$) and 'above average' ($\geq +2$).

For assessing the association between drinking water and nutritional status, drinking water has been categorized into 'Piped Water', 'Tube Well and Others', 'Protected Water', 'Unprotected Water', 'Rain Water', 'Tanker Water', 'Bottled Water' and 'Others'.

26.3 Result and Discussion

The nutritional status of the study population is presented in Table 26.1 through the two parameters, i.e. Weight for age and Height for age. The prevalence of underweight is 35.1% at the national level and 22.7% for the eight northeastern states. While Tripura shows the highest incidence (36.6%), Sikkim shows the lowest incidence (17.5%) of underweight children among the northeastern states. As for the second parameter, the percentage of stunted children is 41.2% at the national level and 31.9% for the northeastern states in which Assam shows the highest percentage (42.8%) and Sikkim shows the lowest (31.8%) of stunted children.

Table 26.2 presents the different type of source of drinking water of the study population. While piped water, tube well and protected water categories have been considered safe for consumption, Arunachal Pradesh (69%), Assam (59%) and Sikkim (40.8%) tops the list for the above categories, respectively. However, the picture seems gory to consider that a sizeable section of the population from the northeastern states still obtains drinking water from 'unprotected' sources with Manipur (45.1%) topping the list, followed by Nagaland (40.6%), Meghalaya (37.5%), Tripura (31.3%) and Assam (28.5%). Rainwater, which is considered as the purest form of water seems to be consumed by a small section of the population only in the state of Mizoram (6.3%) and Nagaland (1.2%).

Table 26.1 State-wise analysis of nutritional status among the under-five children of North East India

State	Weight for age			Height for age		
	Underweight (%)	Normal (%)	Above average (%)	Stunted (%)	Normal (%)	Above average (%)
Sikkim	17.5	67.2	15.4	31.8	50.4	17.8
Arunachal Pradesh	29.0	62.5	8.6	39.4	50.3	10.4
Nagaland	21.6	67.3	11.1	33.3	52.5	14.2
Manipur	21.3	76.3	2.5	33.9	61.4	4.7
Mizoram	19.2	74.7	6.2	38.2	53.6	8.2
Tripura	36.6	57.2	6.2	33.7	58.6	7.7
Meghalaya	35.9	38.5	25.6	41.2	31.6	27.2
Assam	33.7	61.3	5.0	42.8	51.3	5.9
North East	22.7	56.4	8.0	31.9	45.4	9.8
India	35.1	58.9	6.0	41.2	51.1	7.6

Source National Family Health Survey-III (2005–06)

Table 26.3 tries to explore the relation between source of drinking water and the nutritional status of the study population. Incidence of underweight is shown to be the highest (33.0%) in the case where the population draws its drinking water from tube well. Similarly, a higher percentage (29%) of underweight children falls in the section where the source of drinking water is from unprotected sources. A similar result is seen in the case of stunted children. Where the percentage of stunted children is 38.8 and 38.3% in the case where the source of drinking water is tube well and unprotected sources, respectively. However, a lower percentage of underweight (11.7%) and stunted (28.6%) children can be observed in the case where rainwater is the source of drinking water.

The above mentioned findings have also found support from other studies which states that although India has progressed in having access to safe drinking water in the household from 38% in 1981 to 85.5% in 2011 and have also reduced the gap in terms of level of rural-urban differential in access to safe drinking water in the households, regional differential (state-wise) in access to safe drinking water in household still exists. Nine states namely Odisha, Assam, Tripura, Mizoram, Jharkhand, Nagaland, Manipur, Meghalaya and Kerala have more than 25% households without access to safe drinking water (Kumar and Das 2014).

A very similar view is echoed by Saikia and Das (2014), where reports of DLHS-3, 2007–08 states that all the northeastern states except Arunachal Pradesh and Sikkim are below the national level in terms of households having access to improved sources of drinking water.

Table 26.2 State-wise analysis of source of drinking water among the under-five children of North East India

State	Source of drinking water							
	Piped water (%)	Tube well and others (%)	Protected water (%)	Unprotected water (%)	Rainwater (%)	Tanker water (%)	Bottled water (%)	Others (%)
Sikkim	39.2	0.0	40.8	19.7	0.0	0.0	0.0	0.3
Arunachal Pradesh	69.0	15.1	2.0	13.4	0.0	0.2	0.0	0.2
Nagaland	36.5	7.7	12.8	40.6	1.2	0.9	0.0	0.3
Manipur	28.9	8.2	11.0	45.1	0.1	5.0	0.1	1.7
Mizoram	54.4	0.1	20.8	17.1	6.3	1.3	0.0	0.0
Tripura	27.3	37.0	2.8	31.3	0.0	0.2	0.0	1.3
Meghalaya	40.1	3.3	18.5	37.5	0.0	0.5	0.0	0.0
Assam	9.4	59.0	3.0	28.5	0.0	0.0	0.0	0.0
North East	34.6	16.3	12.3	32.0	0.8	1.4	0.0	0.5
India	41.6	36.1	4.5	15.9	0.2	1.1	0.2	0.3

Source National Family Health Survey-III (2005–06)

Table 26.3 Relationship between source of drinking water and nutritional status among the under-five children of North East India

Source of drinking water	Weight for age			Height for age		
	Underweight (%)	Normal (%)	Above average (%)	Stunted (%)	Normal (%)	Above average (%)
Piped water	22.0	67.7	10.3	33.7	54.0	12.3
Tube well and others	33.0	60.9	6.1	38.8	53.5	7.7
Protected water	23.9	64.2	11.9	40.0	46.1	13.9
Unprotected water	29.0	61.9	9.1	38.3	50.2	11.4
Rainwater	11.7	85.7	2.6	28.6	67.5	3.9
Tanker water	16.1	78.6	5.4	28.6	52.5	8.9
Bottled water	0.0	100.0	0.0	66.7	33.3	0.0
Others	23.9	69.6	6.5	30.4	58.7	10.9
Total	26.2	64.6	9.2	36.8	51.9	11.3

Source National Family Health Survey-III (2005–06)

26.4 Conclusion

It can be stated that the quantity and quality of water are of fundamental importance to life and health and access to water is not a matter of choice but an essential need to all human being. Problems of inadequate access to water, increasing privatization of water along with growing awareness of the social and economic rights of citizens due to civil society actions has brought 'right to water' to the centre stage. From the human rights perspective, the state is duty bound to protect and enable the citizens to enjoy their rights and India is no exception. While the end of this year sees closure to the MDGs it also calls for a rigorous promotion of the right to water so that it finds utmost priority in the Post-MDG frameworks.

References

Burchi, F., & Muro, P. D. (2012). A human development and capability approach to food security: Conceptual framework and informational basis. United Nations Development Programme Regional Bureau for Africa (WP 2012-009).

Dreze, J., & Sen, A. K. (1989). *Hunger and public action*. Oxford: Clarendon Press.

Food Insecurity in the World. http://www.fao.org/docrep/016/i3027e/i3027e.pdf, (p. 48).

Geneva Office of the United Nations High Commissioner for Human Rights. (1999). *CESCR general comment No. 12: The right to adequate food (Art. 11)* (Contained in document E/C.12/1999/5).

Kumar, A., & Das, K. C. (2014). Drinking water and sanitation facility in india and its linkages with diarrhoea among children under five: Evidences from recent data. *International Journal of Humanities and Social Science Invention, 3*(4).

Ramachandraiah, C. (2004). *Right to drinking water in India.* Working Paper No. 56. Hyderabad: Centre for Economic and Social Studies.

Saikia, D., & Das, K. K. (2014). Access to public health-care in the rural Northeast India. *The NEHU Journal, XII*(2).

The Millennium Development Goals Report 2014. http://www.un.org/millenniumgoals/2014%20MDG%20report/MDG%202014%20English%20web.pdf (p. 12).

MIX
Papier aus verantwortungsvollen Quellen
Paper from responsible sources
FSC® C105338

If you have any concerns about our products,
you can contact us on
ProductSafety@springernature.com

In case Publisher is established outside the EU,
the EU authorized representative is:
Springer Nature Customer Service Center GmbH
Europaplatz 3, 69115 Heidelberg, Germany

Printed by Libri Plureos GmbH
in Hamburg, Germany